Digital bus handbook

DIGITAL BUS HANDBOOK

Other McGraw-Hill Reference Books of Interest

Avallone and Baumeister • MARKS' STANDARD HANDBOOK FOR MECHANICAL ENGINEERS
Benson • AUDIO ENGINEERING HANDBOOK
Benson • TELEVISION ENGINEERING HANDBOOK
Coombs • BASIC ELECTRONIC INSTRUMENT HANDBOOK
Coombs • PRINTED CIRCUITS HANDBOOK
Croft and Summers • AMERICAN ELECTRICIANS' HANDBOOK
Di Giacomo • VLSI HANDBOOK
Fink and Beaty • STANDARD HANDBOOK FOR ELECTRICAL ENGINEERS
Fink and Christiansen • ELECTRONIC ENGINEERS' HANDBOOK
Harper • HANDBOOK OF ELECTRONIC SYSTEMS DESIGN
Harper • HANDBOOK OF THICK FILM HYBRID MICROELECTRONICS
Harper • HANDBOOK OF WIRING, CABLING, AND INTERCONNECTING FOR ELECTRONICS
Hicks • STANDARD HANDBOOK OF ENGINEERING CALCULATIONS
Inglis • ELECTRONIC COMMUNICATIONS HANDBOOK
Juran and Gryna • QUALITY CONTROL HANDBOOK
Kaufman and Seidman • HANDBOOK OF ELECTRONICS CALCULATIONS
Kurtz • HANDBOOK OF ENGINEERING ECONOMICS
Stout • MICROPROCESSOR APPLICATIONS HANDBOOK
Stout and Kaufman • HANDBOOK OF MICROCIRCUIT DESIGN AND APPLICATION
Stout and Kaufman • HANDBOOK OF OPERATIONAL AMPLIFIER CIRCUIT DESIGN
Tuma • ENGINEERING MATHEMATICS HANDBOOK
Williams • DESIGNER'S HANDBOOK OF INTEGRATED CIRCUITS
Williams and Taylor • ELECTRONIC FILTER DESIGN HANDBOOK

Other

Antognetti • POWER INTEGRATED CIRCUITS
Antognetti and Massobrio • SEMICONDUCTOR DEVICE MODELING WITH SPICE
Elliott • INTEGRATED CIRCUITS FABRICATION TECHNOLOGY
Hecht • THE LASER GUIDEBOOK
Mun • GaAs INTEGRATED CIRCUITS
Siliconix • DESIGNING WITH FIELD-EFFECT TRANSISTORS
Sze • VLSI TECHNOLOGY
Tsui • LSI/VLSI TESTABILITY DESIGN

DIGITAL BUS HANDBOOK

JOSEPH DI GIACOMO Editor in Chief
Department of Electrical Engineering
Villanova University

MCGRAW-HILL PUBLISHING COMPANY

New York St. Louis San Francisco Auckland Bogotá
Caracas Hamburg Lisbon London Madrid Mexico
Milan Montreal New Delhi Oklahoma City
Paris San Juan São Paulo Singapore
Sydney Tokyo Toronto

Library of Congress Cataloging-in-Publication Data

Digital bus handbook / Joseph Di Giacomo, editor-in-chief.
p. cm.
ISBN 0-07-016923-3
1. Microcomputers—Buses. 2. Computer architecture. I. Di Giacomo, Joseph.
TK7895.B87D54 1990
621.39′81—dc20 89-37272

1234567890 DOC/DOC 895432109

ISBN 0-07-016923-3

The editors for this book were Daniel A. Gonneau and Stephen M. Smith, the designer was Naomi Auerbach, and the production supervisor was Richard A. Ausburn. It was set in Times Roman by University Graphics, Inc.

Printed and bound by R. R. Donnelley & Sons Company.

CONTENTS

CONTRIBUTORS

R. V. Balakrishnan *National Semiconductor Corporation, Santa Clara, California (CHAP. 14)*

Matt Biewer *STD Bus Manufacturers Group, Pro-Log Corporation, Monterey, California (CHAP. 8)*

Clyde R. Camp *Texas Instruments, Inc., Dallas, Texas (CHAP. 15)*

W. K. Dawson *TRIUMF, Vancouver, British Columbia, Canada (CHAP. 6)*

Samuel Gazit *Rogers Corporation, Rogers, Connecticut (CHAP. 10)*

David B. Gustavson *Computation Research Group, Stanford Linear Accelerator Center, Stanford, California (CHAP. 16)*

David Hawley *National Semiconductor Corporation, Santa Clara, California (CHAP. 7)*

John Hyde *Intel Corporation, Hillsboro, Oregon (CHAP. 9)*

Gerry Laws *Texas Instruments, Austin, Texas (CHAP. 3)*

Stacey G. Lloyd *BiiN, Hillsboro, Oregon (CHAP. 11)*

Leslie F. McDermott *IBM Corporation, Boca Raton, Florida (CHAP. 5)*

J. F. McDonald *Center for Integrated Electronics and Department of Electrical, Computer and Systems Engineering, Rensselaer Polytechnic Institute, Troy, New York (CHAP. 12)*

Shlomo Pri-Tal *Motorola Microcomputer Division, Tempe, Arizona (CHAP. 1)*

Mike Pritchard *Oregon Systems Division, Intel Corporation, Portland, Oregon (CHAP. 2)*

Atlant G. Schmidt *Digital Equipment Corporation, Tewksbury, Massachusetts (CHAP. 4)*

Scott S. Simpson *Rogers Corporation, Rogers, Connecticut (CHAP. 13)*

Gurbir Singh *BiiN, Hillsboro, Oregon (CHAP. 17)*

Robert G. Skegg *TRIUMF, Vancouver, British Columbia, Canada (CHAP. 6)*

Michael Smolin *Smolin & Associates, Palo Alto, California (CHAP. 15)*

Paul Sweazey *Apple Computer, Inc., Cupertino, California (CHAP. 18)*

PREFACE

Today, the emphasis in computer systems is on networking logic/memory modules so that data and instructions can be shared. This process of transmitting information is called busing. Busing requires both a physical medium and an information protocol.

Since there are many different computer applications, there are also many different bus structures. Attempts have been made to standardize bus structures in order to simplify the process of selection for computer engineers. However, this is difficult because no single bus system can fit all applications. Some bus structures may become more standard than others, but users will always need to know the total bus choices that are available to them.

The purpose of the *Digital Bus Handbook* is to help the many people associated with digital design to understand the full concept and use of digital bus networks. The Handbook outlines and discusses the various bus schemes that are available for the design of new products. It clearly illustrates the relationships that exist between the protocol, interconnection, performance, and standards areas, and gives the user an understanding of bus schemes, bus protocols, and bus interconnect techniques. The tasks involved in digital bus design cover many disciplines. This Handbook describes these relationships in great detail and presents these methods for easy understanding by both technical and nontechnical personnel.

Each chapter of Part 1 discusses a particular bus technique, and in doing so discusses bus lines, electrical specifications including pin identifications, and bus protocol. The buses that have been selected are generally believed to have the most usage and the broadest possible coverage of application areas. Those buses not discussed because of space limitations are listed in Chap. 15 of Part 3, Bus Standards.

The chapters of Part 2 are important from a practical standpoint. They discuss fundamental problems, such as those of speed, noise, power, interconnect, connector, and interface, that bus designs have to account for; these problems limit the performance of various bus protocols.

Each chapter of Part 3 covers an important topic in digital buses. Chapter 15 describes the organizational relationships of standards, the classification of documents, and the bus standard development cycle. Chapter 16 gives some practical guidelines to use in the selection of a bus. Chapter 17 discusses the performance problem of relating memory speed to processor cycle time. Chapter 18 details the limits of performance of digital buses in a backplane environment.

The material presented in this Handbook is intended to serve as a solid foundation for users of digital buses. It is a practical manual that provides both a specific, in-depth understanding of bus concepts and a broad coverage of bus systems. The references listed at the end of most chapters can supply more information.

I would like to express my grateful appreciation to the contributing authors of the *Digital Bus Handbook.* They have given graciously of their time and talent to provide very useful and readable information on this important topic.

Joseph Di Giacomo

DIGITAL BUS HANDBOOK

P • A • R • T • 1

DIGITAL BUS CONFIGURATIONS

CHAPTER 1
VMEbus

Shlomo Pri-Tal*
Motorola Microcomputer Division
Tempe, Arizona

1.1 INTRODUCTION

The VMEbus is a standard backplane interface that simplifies integration of data processing, data storage, and peripheral control devices in a tightly coupled hardware configuration.

It evolved from Motorola's VERSAbus, a bus structure designed originally to allow the interconnection of the various printed-circuit-board modules that made up Motorola's line of VERSAmodules, products designed to take full advantage of the capabilities of the 16- and 32-bit MC68000 family of microprocessors. A more compact version of the boards, called VERSAmodule Eurocards (VMEmodules), was developed in Motorola's Munich facility and quickly became a standard in Europe. In 1981, Motorola, in collaboration with Mostek, Signetics/Philips, and Thompson CSF of France, announced the VMEbus as a nonproprietary standard in the public domain.

The VMEbus interfacing system is defined by the VMEbus specification. This system has been designed to do the following:

1. Allow communication between devices without disturbing the internal activities of other devices interfaced to the VMEbus.
2. Specify the electrical and mechanical system characteristics required to design devices that will reliably and unambiguously communicate with other devices interfaced to the VMEbus.
3. Specify protocols that precisely define the interaction between devices.
4. Provide terminology and definitions that describe system protocol.
5. Allow a broad range of design latitude so that the designer can optimize cost and/or performance without affecting system compatibility.
6. Provide a system where performance is primarily device limited, rather than system interface limited.

*With the assistance of Lois Hunt.

The structure of the system can be described from two points of view: its mechanical structure and its functional structure. The mechanical specification describes the physical dimensions of subracks, backplanes, plug-in boards, etc. The functional specification describes how the bus works, what functional modules are involved in each transaction, and the rules that govern their behavior. In addition to these two points of view, the VMEbus includes specifications that define the electrical requirements that components must meet to ensure compatibility and performance.

1.2 MECHANICAL STRUCTURE

The mechanical structure of the VMEbus is composed of subracks, backplanes, and plug-in boards. The VMEbus specification provides information to ensure that all these components fit together properly. The dimensions conform to relevant International Electrotechnical Commission (IEC) Eurocard specifications. The VMEbus was the first 32-bit bus to make use of the Eurocard standard. In the wake of its success, this mechanically superior format has been adopted by virtually all second-generation buses.

Figure 1.1 is a front view of a 19-in.-wide subrack which shows how single-height and double-height boards can be mixed in a single subrack. Boards are

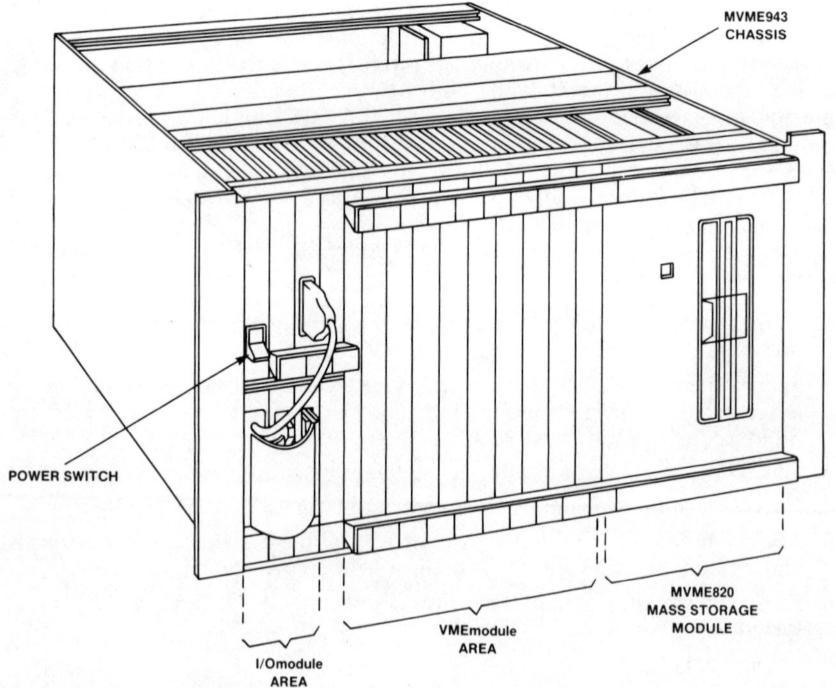

FIGURE 1.1 The VMEbus 19-in-wide subrack.

inserted into the subrack from the front, in a vertical plane with the component face of the board on the right. The subrack's dimensions ensure that each board's connectors mate properly and that adjacent boards do not touch each other. It also guides the cooling airflow through the system and ensures that inserted boards do not disengage themselves from the backplane during vibration.

Backplanes may have up to 21 slots. Where backplanes with fewer slots are used, the subrack can be narrower than the standard 19 in. Each backplane includes several 96-pin connectors and signal paths that bus their pins. All VMEbus systems have a J1 backplane that provides all of the signal paths needed for 24-bit addressing and 16-bit transfers. It is mounted in the upper portion of the subrack.

In systems that utilize the full 32-bit address and data paths, a J1/J2 backplane is provided. This backplane provides additional 96-pin connectors and signal paths needed for 32-bit addressing and 32-bit data transfers. (Only the center row of this additional connector is used.)

VMEbus boards may be either single or double height (see Fig. 1.1). A single-height board is 100 mm (3.937 in) high and 160 mm (6.299 in) deep with an area of 160 cm^2 (24.8 in^2). It has only one connector on its back edge, called the P1 connector. A double-height board is 233.35 mm (9.187 in) high and 160 mm (6.299 in) deep with an area of about 373 cm^2 (57.9 in^2). It has either one connector (P1) or two connectors (P1 and P2) on its back edge.

1.3 FUNCTIONAL STRUCTURE

The VMEbus functional structure consists of backplane interface logic, four groups of signal lines called *buses,* and a collection of *functional modules.* The four buses and the functional modules associated with them (see Fig. 1.2) work together to perform specific duties.

As shown in Fig. 1.2, there are two layers of VMEbus protocol. The lowest layer, called the backplane access layer, is composed of the backplane interface logic, the utility bus modules, and the arbitration bus modules. The VMEbus' data transfer layer is composed of the data transfer bus and priority interrupt bus modules.

1.3.1 Data Transfer Bus

This is one of the four buses provided by the VMEbus backplane. It allows bus masters to direct the transfer of binary data between themselves and slaves. In addition to the master and slave, the data transfer bus' collection of functional modules also includes the location monitor and the bus timer. The data transfer bus consists of 32 data lines, 32 address lines, 6 address modifier lines, and 5 control lines.

The master initiates data transfer bus cycles in order to transfer data between itself and a slave module. A data transfer bus cycle is a sequence of level transitions on the signal lines of the data transfer bus that result in the transfer of an address and data between a master and a slave. There are nine basic types of data transfer bus cycles: read, write, unaligned read, unaligned write, block read, block write, read-modify-write, address-only, and interrupt acknowledge cycle.

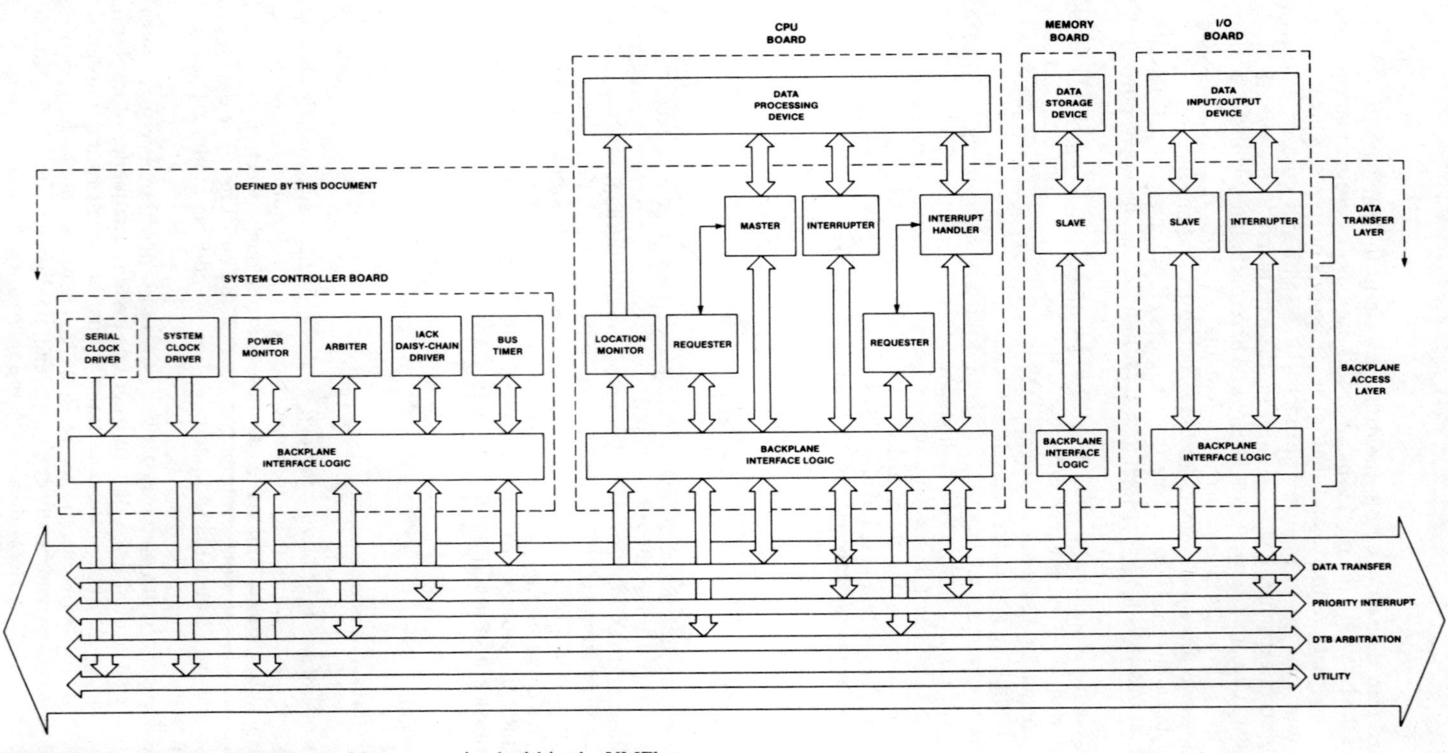

FIGURE 1.2 Functional modules and buses contained within the VMEbus.

The slave detects data transfer bus cycles initiated by a master, and when those cycles specify its participation, transfers data between itself and the master.

The location monitor monitors data transfers over the data transfer bus in order to detect accesses to the locations it has been assigned to watch. When an access occurs to one of these assigned locations, the location monitor alerts its on-board logic. For example, it might signal its on-board processor by means of an interrupt. In such a configuration, if processor board A writes into a location of the global VMEbus memory monitored by processor B's location monitor, processor B will be interrupted.

The bus timer measures how long each data transfer takes and terminates the data transfer bus cycle if it takes too long. A bus timer is useful when a master tries to transfer data to or from a nonexistent slave location. Since the master waits for a slave to respond, it might wait forever. The bus timer prevents this by terminating the cycle.

To provide for newer technologies while maintaining compatibility with the old, the protocols of the VMEbus are totally asynchronous. The *n*-channel metal-oxide semiconductor (NMOS) technology used in first-generation microprocessors is limited, because of heat dissipation problems, to about 10 MHz. Several new 16- and 32-bit microprocessors make use of complementary metal-oxide semiconductor (CMOS) technology to reduce power dissipation and run at clock rates from 10 to 16 MHz. Further development will likely lead to 20-MHz clock rates. During the transition period, most systems will contain both the old and new technology chips. The asynchronous protocols of the VMEbus make this possible.

The data transfer bus features nonmultiplexed address and data lines to maximize system performance for all applications. The bulk of bus traffic in most system applications is generated by the processor fetching instructions from memory. It does this by executing single-transfer read cycles, where it outputs an address first and then reads the data. Unlike multiplexed buses, the nonmultiplexed VMEbus does not impose a speed penalty when executing single-transfer cycles.

1.3.2 Priority Interrupt Bus

This is the second bus defined by the VMEbus specification. It allows interrupter modules to request interrupts from interrupt handler modules. The priority interrupt bus consists of seven interrupt request lines, one interrupt acknowledge line, and an interrupt acknowledge daisy chain.

The interrupter generates an interrupt request by driving one of the seven interrupt request lines. When its request is acknowledged by an interrupt handler, the interrupter provides 1, 2, or 4 bytes of status or identification to the interrupt handler. This allows the interrupt handler to service the interrupt.

The interrupt handler detects interrupt requests generated by interrupters and responds by asking for status or identification information. This information is received from the interrupter during a special kind of data transfer bus cycle—the interrupt acknowledge cycle. After reading the status or identification information from the interrupter, the interrupt handler initiates the appropriate interrupt servicing sequence.

The interrupt acknowledge daisy-chain driver is the third functional module defined for use on the priority interrupt bus. Its function is to activate the interrupt acknowledge daisy chain whenever an interrupt handler acknowledges an interrupt request. This daisy chain ensures that only one interrupter responds with its status or identification when more than one has generated an interrupt request.

1.3.3 Arbitration Bus

The VMEbus is designed to support multiprocessor systems where several masters and interrupt handlers may need to use the data transfer bus at the same time. However, before taking control and transferring any data over the data transfer bus, they must get permission to use the bus. The process that selects the one master or interrupt handler that is granted use of the data transfer bus is called *arbitration.* The arbitration bus allows an arbiter module and several requester modules to coordinate use of the data transfer bus. It consists of four bus request lines, four daisy-chained bus grant lines, and two other lines called *bus clear* and *bus busy.*

The requester resides on the same board as a master or interrupt handler. It requests use of the data transfer bus whenever its master or interrupt handler needs it. The requester then waits for the arbiter to acknowledge this request, granting it exclusive use of the data transfer bus. When granted the bus, it takes control of it by driving the bus busy line and then signals its on-board master or interrupt handler that the bus is available.

The arbiter accepts bus requests from requester modules and grants control of the data transfer bus to only one requester at a time. Some arbiters have a built-in time-out feature that causes them to withdraw a bus grant if the requesting board does not start using the bus within a prescribed time. This ensures that the bus is not locked up as a result of a transient edge on a request line. Other arbiters drive the bus clear line when they detect a request for the bus from a requester whose priority is higher than the one that is currently using the bus. This ensures that the response time to urgent events is bounded.

1.3.4 Utility Bus

This bus includes signals that provide periodic timing and coordinate the power-up and power-down sequences of the VMEbus system. Three modules are defined by the utility bus: the system clock driver, the serial clock driver, and the power monitor. It consists of two clock lines, a system reset line, an ac fail line, a system fail line, and a serial data line.

The system clock driver provides a fixed-frequency 16-MHz signal. It is located on the system controller board in slot 1. It provides a clock signal that is useful for the various system functions that require a fixed time reference. Note, however, that the system clock does not have any fixed phase relationships with other VMEbus signals.

The serial clock driver provides a periodic timing signal that synchronizes operation of the VMSbus. The VMSbus is part of the VMEsystem architecture and provides an interprocessor serial communication path. Although the VMEbus specification reserves two backplane signal lines for use by the VMSbus, its protocols are completely independent of the VMEbus.

The power monitor module monitors the status of the primary power source to the VMEbus system. When power strays outside the limits required for reliable system operation, it uses the ac fail line to broadcast a warning to all boards on the VMEbus system in time to effect graceful shutdown.

Since most systems are powered by an ac source, the power monitor is typically designed to detect drop-out or brownout conditions on the ac line. When power is then restored to the system the power monitor broadcasts a reset signal to ensure that all VMEbus modules are initialized. The power monitor also monitors a manually operated push button, initializing the system whenever that button is depressed by the operator. Since the power monitor is an optional module, other VMEbus boards may include a push button, so that manual system initialization may be achieved.

In addition to these functional modules, the utility bus includes a system fail line. It allows VMEbus boards to broadcast to the system that their status has changed. The action taken by the system in response to the system fail line is out of the scope of the VMEbus specification.

1.3.5 System Controller Board

This board resides in slot 1 of the VMEbus backplane and includes all the one-of-a-kind functions that have been defined by the VMEbus. These functions include the system clock driver, the arbiter, the interrupt acknowledge daisy-chain driver, and the bus timer. Some system controller boards also include an optional serial clock driver and a power monitor. The system controller board might also include other functions that users find useful in their VMEbus systems, e.g., a global interrupter, a time-of-day clock, additional serial ports, a printer port, diagnostic programmable read-only memories (PROMs), etc.

1.3.6 Signaling Protocols

Two signaling protocols are used on the VMEbus: closed-loop protocols and open-loop protocols. Closed-loop protocols use interlocked bus signals while open-loop protocols use broadcast bus signals.

Interlocked bus signals coordinate internal functions of the VMEbus system, as opposed to interacting with external stimuli. Each interlocked signal has a source module and destination module, both of which are defined within the VMEbus specification. Since an interlocked signal must be acknowledged by the receiving module, an interlocked relationship exists between the two modules until it is acknowledged. For example, an interrupter can send an interrupt request that is answered later by an interrupt handler with an interrupt acknowledge signal. (No time limit is prescribed by the VMEbus specification.) The interrupter does not remove the interrupt request until the interrupt handler acknowledges it.

The address strobe and data strobes are interlocked signals that are especially important. They are interlocked with the data acknowledge or bus error signals and coordinate the transfer of addresses and data, which are the basis for all information flow between modules in the data transfer layer.

Broadcast bus signals are generated by modules in response to an event. There is no protocol for acknowledging a broadcast signal; instead, the broadcast is maintained long enough to ensure that all appropriate modules detect the signal. Broadcast signals might be activated at any time, irrespective of any other activity taking place on the bus. They are each sent over a dedicated signal line. Some examples are the system reset and ac failure lines. These signal lines are not sent to any specific module, but rather announce to all modules the occurrence of a special event.

Other broadcast signals are sometimes also monitored from outside the system to gain information about system status. For example, the system fail line is a broadcast signal which is defined by the VMEbus specification, but the action taken in response to it is not. This broadcast line is monitored outside the system and may be used to turn on a red light-emitting diode (LED), initiate software diagnostics, etc.

1.4 ELECTRICAL SPECIFICATIONS

The electrical specifications of the VMEbus describe the signal line drivers, backplane termination, power distribution, and pin assignments with which VMEbus products must comply.

1.4.1 VMEbus Signal Line Drivers

Some bus specifications prescribe maximum or minimum rise and fall times for the signal lines. This creates a dilemma for board designers, since they have very little control over these times. If the backplane is heavily loaded, the rise and fall times will be very long. If it is lightly loaded, these times may be very short. Even if designers know what the maximum and minimum loading will be, they must spend time in the lab, experimenting to find out which drivers will provide the needed rise and fall times.

In fact, rise and fall times are the result of a complex set of interactions involving the impedance of the signal line, its terminations, its capacitive and resistive loading, and the source impedance of the driver. In order to take into account all of these factors, the board designer would have to study transmission line theory, as well as certain specific parameters of drivers and receivers that are not normally found in most manufacturers' data sheets.

In keeping with its "designer-friendly" philosophy, the VMEbus specification does not specify rise and fall times. Instead, it specifies the required parameters for the drivers and receivers. These specifications take into account the characteristics of the backplane: the maximum length of its signal lines, the maximum number of slots, its signal line impedance, propagation time, termination values, etc. To help the designer find components that meet these requirements, some widely available parts are also suggested.

In order to ensure that a board meets the timing specifications, designers must take into account the propagation of the signal line drivers on this board. Since these propagation delays depend on how heavily the signal lines are loaded, the VMEbus specification also tells designers how to estimate the propagation delay of their drivers, based on the worst-case loading of the bus. These guidelines assure designers that their boards will exhibit the correct bus timing without the need for empirical work in the lab.

1.4.2 Backplane Terminations

Because the VMEbus system is intended to deliver high performance, its design takes into account the transmission line effects of the backplane. In order to control ringing on the signal lines, terminators are specified at each end of the VMEbus signal lines except the daisy-chain lines. These terminations serve four purposes:

1. They reduce reflections from the ends of the backplanes.
2. They provide a high-state pull-up resistance for open-collector drivers.
3. They restore the signal lines to the high level when three-state devices are disabled.
4. They provide a standing current for the driver sink transistor to switch off, causing the signal line to rise more swiftly on positive transitions.

1.4.3 Power Distribution

In a VMEbus system, power is distributed on the backplane(s) as regulated +5 V dc, ±12 V dc, and +5 V dc standby voltages. The +5 V dc voltage is the main power source for VMEbus systems. The ±12 V dc voltage is often used for powering RS232-C drivers, metal-oxide semiconductors (MOS), and analog devices.

TABLE 1.1 J1/P1 Pin Assignments

Pin number	Signal mnemonics		
	Row a	Row b	Row c
1	D00	BBSY*	D08
2	D01	BCLR*	D09
3	D02	ACFAIL*	D10
4	D03	BG0IN*	D11
5	D04	BG0OUT*	D12
6	D05	BG1IN*	D13
7	D06	BG1OUT*	D14
8	D07	BG2IN*	D15
9	GND	BG2OUT*	GND
10	SYSCLK	BG3IN*	SYSFAIL*
11	GND	BG3OUT*	BERR*
12	DS1*	BR0*	SYSRESET*
13	DS0*	BR1*	LWORD*
14	WRITE*	BR2*	AM5
15	GND	BR3*	A23
16	DTACK*	AM0	A22
17	GND	AM1	A21
18	AS*	AM2	A20
19	GND	AM3	A19
20	IACK*	GND	A18
21	IACKIN*	SERCLK	A17
22	IACKOUT*	SERDAT*	A16
23	AM4	GND	A15
24	A07	IRQ7*	A14
25	A06	IRQ6*	A13
26	A05	IRQ5*	A12
27	A04	IRQ4*	A11
28	A03	IRQ3*	A10
29	A02	IRQ2*	A09
30	A01	IRQ1*	A08
31	−12 V	+5 V STDBY	+12 V
32	+5 V	+5 V	+5 V

In some cases −5 V dc voltage, using on-board regulators, bias voltage, or −5.2 V dc emitter-coupled logic (ECL) voltages, is also derived from the −12 V dc source. The +5 V dc standby voltage is used to sustain memory, time-of-day clocks, etc., when the +5 V dc power is lost.

1.4.4 P1 and P2 Connector Pin Assignments

The VMEbus specification defines the use of two IEC 603-2 connectors called P1 and P2. Each has three rows of 32 pins, for a total of 96 pins per connector. While the VMEbus specifies the use of all three rows on P1 and the center row of P2, it does not define the use of the two outside rows of the P2 connector. These 64 pins may be used to provide signal paths for the VMEsystem's local subsystem bus—the VMXbus—or to provide user-defined input/output (I/O) connections to 64-

TABLE 1.2 J2/P2 Pin Assignments

Pin	Signal mnemonics		
number	Row a	Row b	Row c
1	User defined	+5 V	User defined
2	User defined	GND	User defined
3	User defined	Reserved	User defined
4	User defined	A24	User defined
5	User defined	A25	User defined
6	User defined	A26	User defined
7	User defined	A27	User defined
8	User defined	A28	User defined
9	User defined	A29	User defined
10	User defined	A30	User defined
11	User defined	A31	User defined
12	User defined	GND	User defined
13	User defined	+5 V	User defined
14	User defined	D16	User defined
15	User defined	D17	User defined
16	User defined	D18	User defined
17	User defined	D19	User defined
18	User defined	D20	User defined
19	User defined	D21	User defined
20	User defined	D22	User defined
21	User defined	D23	User defined
22	User defined	GND	User defined
23	User defined	D24	User defined
24	User defined	D25	User defined
25	User defined	D26	User defined
26	User defined	D27	User defined
27	User defined	D28	User defined
28	User defined	D29	User defined
29	User defined	D30	User defined
30	User defined	D31	User defined
31	User defined	GND	User defined
32	User defined	+5 V	User defined

pin ribbon cables. Tables 1.1 and 1.2 show the pin assignments for the P1 and the P2 connectors.

1.5 VMEbus SPECIFICATION FORMAT

The format of the VMEbus specification was explicitly designed to help board designers develop VMEbus products and promote compatibility among products designed by different vendors. To achieve these goals, the protocols of the VMEbus are defined with the aid of the five types of keywords, a method for the specification of timing requirements, sequence diagrams, flow diagrams, and a special notation for the requirements of signal interconnection.

1.5.1 VMEbus Keywords

The creators of the VMEbus specification recognized that engineers using it to design complex multiprocessing systems might find themselves venturing into unfamiliar territory. Until these engineers gained some experience with VMEbus, they might have difficulty making best use of its features. To help them, the specification offers practical advice which is based on experience.

However, while this advice is useful, it is also confusing. Where the specification says DO THIS, engineers might be left wondering whether they are reading advice that can be disregarded or a requirement that must be followed.

To solve this problem five *keywords* were used to label the pertinent paragraphs within the specification. These five keywords are as follows:

RULE
RECOMMENDATION
SUGGESTION
PERMISSION
OBSERVATION

Any text not labeled with one of these keywords describes the VMEbus structure or operation. It is easily recognized by its narrative style and exclusive use of the present tense.

Rules. The keyword RULE is used to label rules that must be followed to ensure an acceptable level of compatibility between VMEbus designs. These rules are sometimes expressed in the form of text and sometimes in the form of figures, tables, or drawings. Rules are written in a distinctly imperative style, using the uppercase words MUST and MUST NOT. An example of a rule is given below:

RULE 7.3: VMEbus backplanes MUST NOT have more than 21 slots.

Recommendations. The keyword RECOMMENDATION is used to label advice which, if followed, will allow an engineer to avoid some awkward problems or poor performance. While the VMEbus is designed to support high-performance systems, it is possible to design a VMEbus system that complies with all the rules but does not perform well. In many cases designers need experience with VMEbus in order to design boards that deliver top performance. Recommendations are based on this kind of experience, and are provided to engineers to speed their traversal of the learning curve. An example of a recommendation is given below:

> RECOMMENDATION 6.1: Design and connect backplanes so that the power supply sense point is located somewhere near the center of the backplane and as close as possible to the point where power is introduced into the backplane.

Suggestions. The keyword SUGGESTION is used to label advice which is helpful but not vital. When encountering a suggestion, board designers should weigh its merits against other concerns and then decide either to accept it or reject it. Some suggestions have to do with designing boards that can be easily reconfigured, while others describe design techniques that simplify the job of debugging. An example of a suggestion is given below:

> SUGGESTION 7.2: Where possible, avoid the use of cable connections to the front edge of VMEbus boards. This makes it much easier to install and remove boards from the subrack during maintenance.

Permissions. The keyword PERMISSION labels text that clarifies the limits of a rule. For example, a rule might not specifically prohibit a certain design approach, but the reader might be left wondering whether that approach might violate the spirit of a rule, or whether it might lead to some subtle problem. Permissions reassure the reader that a certain approach is acceptable and will cause no problems. The uppercase word MAY is reserved for stating permissions. An example of a permission is given below:

> PERMISSION 7.18: The termination circuitry MAY either be built onto the ends of the backplane or it MAY be provided by separate modules that plug onto either the front or the back of the backplane at the two end slots.

Observations. The keyword OBSERVATION is used to label sections of text that offer no specific advice, but simply enlarge upon what has just been discussed. For example, an observation might spell out the implications of a rule or bring attention to things that might otherwise be overlooked. In some cases observations give the rationale behind a rule, so that the reader understands why the rule must be followed. An example of an observation is given below:

> OBSERVATION 4.6: RULE 4.8 prevents the interrupt handler from misinterpreting the low level on the interrupt request line as a new interrupt request.

1.5.2 Timing Requirements

In keeping with the designer-friendly philosophy, the VMEbus specification provides many examples of typical system operation. These examples make use of three special types of diagrams: timing diagrams, sequence diagrams, and flow diagrams.

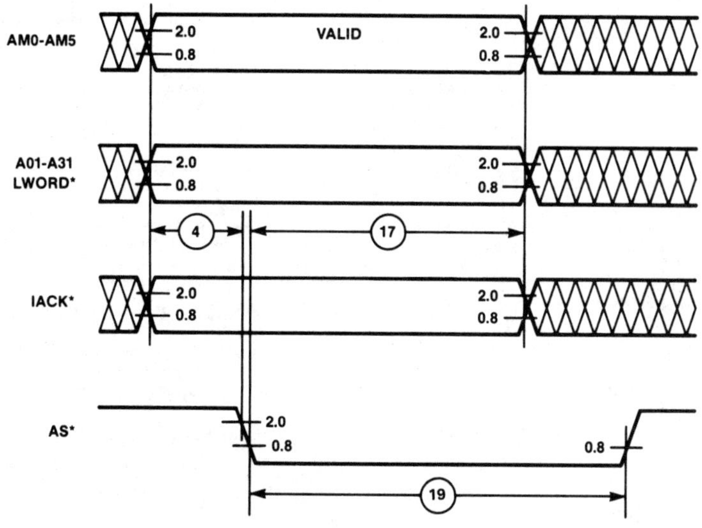

Parameter number	Master Minimum	Master Maximum	Slave Minimum	Slave Maximum	Location monitor Minimum	Location monitor Maximum
4	35		10		10	
17	40		10		10	
19	40		30		30	

FIGURE 1.3 Example of timing diagram. All times are in nanoseconds.

Timing diagrams show the timing relationships between signal transitions. The times involved have minimum and/or maximum limits associated with them. These limits are defined in special tables. Each timing parameter has a number associated with it that is consistently used in all timing diagrams. In addition to the timing parameter table and the timing diagrams, the timing requirements are defined in timing rules for each type of functional module. Some of the timing parameters specify the behavior of the backplane interface logic, while others specify the interlocked behavior of the functional modules. Figure 1.3 is an example of a timing diagram.

1.5.3 Sequence Diagrams

Sequence diagrams are similar to timing diagrams but show only the interlocked relationship of the functional modules. They specify the sequence of events rather than the times involved. For example, a sequence diagram might indicate that a module cannot generate signal transition A until it detects that some other module has generated a transition on signal B. Figure 1.4 is an example of a sequence diagram.

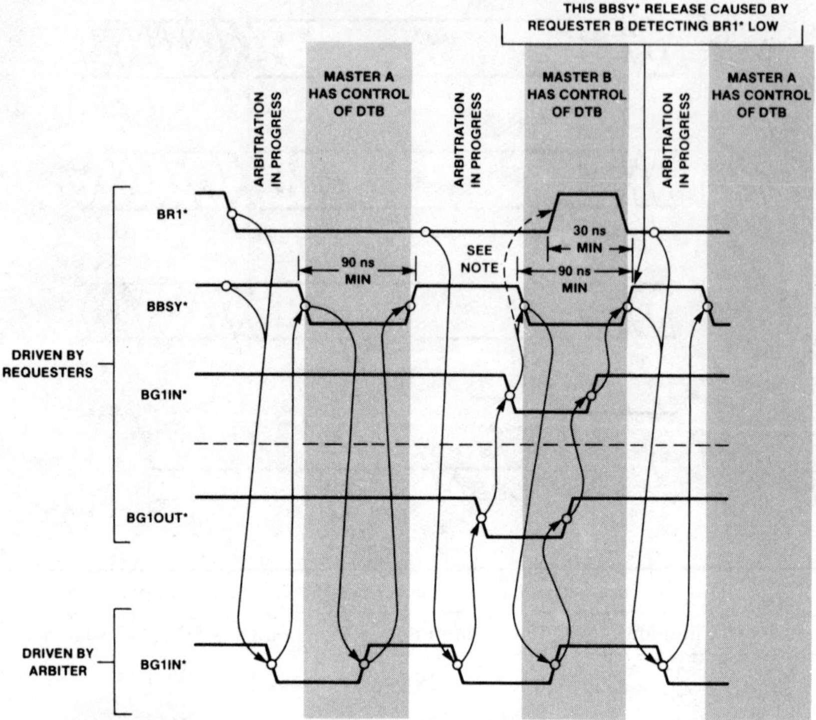

FIGURE 1.4 Example of sequence diagram. (*Note:* In this example, each requester maintains its bus request line low until it is granted the DTB. In some cases a requester might release its bus request line without receiving a bus grant.)

1.5.4 Flow Diagrams

Flow diagrams show the stream of events as they would occur during a VMEbus operation. The events are stated in words and result from the interaction between two or more functional modules. Flow diagrams describe VMEbus operations in a sequential manner and, at the same time, show the interaction between functional modules. Figure 1.5 is an example of a flow diagram.

1.5.5 Special Notation for Signal Interconnection

To allow the optimization of a system designer's designs to the requirements of the application, the VMEbus offers a range of choices. For example, the designer may choose to implement a 16-bit capability if the application does not require the full 32-bit capability defined by the VMEbus. This would require that only a subset of the data and the address lines must be driven and monitored by the functional modules. Special mnemonics have thus been developed to allow the

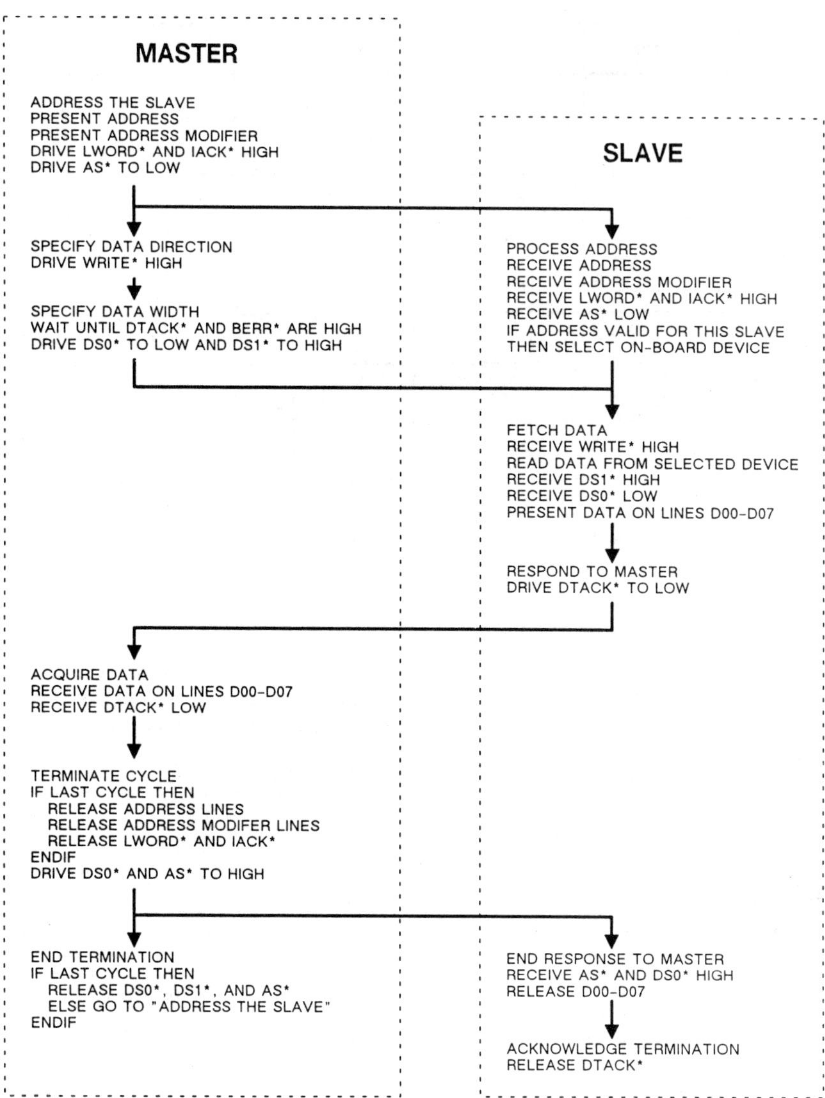

FIGURE 1.5 Example of flow diagram.

definition of the supported options in a clear and concise manner. Defining these special mnemonics makes it possible to specify the interconnect requirements concisely in the form of tables, rather than in lengthy, often ambiguous text. Figure 1.6 is an example of the use of this special notation. After a mnemonic has been defined and its relevance specified, it is used to define signal interconnect requirements in subsequent tables.

MNEMONIC	DESCRIPTION	COMMENTS
DVBM	DRIVEN VALID BY MASTER	RULE #2.21: MASTER MUST DRIVE DVBM LINES TO A VALID LEVEL
DVBS	DRIVEN VALID BY SLAVE	RULE #2.25: SLAVE MUST DRIVE DVBS LINES TO A VALID LEVEL

MNEMONIC	TYPE OF CYCLE	D24–D31	D16–D23	D08–D15	D00–D07
D32:BLT	QUAD BYTE BLOCK TRANSFERS QUAD BYTE BLOCK READ QUAD BYTE BLOCK WRITE	 DVBS DVBM	 DVBS DVBM	 DVBS DVBM	 DVBS DVBM

FIGURE 1.6 Use of mnemonics to specify signal interconnect requirements.

1.6 CAPABILITIES OF THE VMEbus

The wide acceptance that the VMEbus has enjoyed is largely due to its great versatility. Designers are permitted to choose from a long list of optional capabilities which have been carefully defined to avoid introducing incompatibility. These optional capabilities are discussed below.

1.6.1 Addressing Capabilities

The smallest addressable unit of storage on the VMEbus is the byte. Table 1.3 shows how bytes are organized in VMEbus memory. A set of byte locations whose addresses differ only in the two least significant bits is called a 4-byte group or a BYTE(0–3) group. Masters can access some or all of the bytes in a 4-byte group simultaneously using a single data transfer bus cycle.

TABLE 1.3 Four Categories of Byte Locations

Category	Byte address
BYTE(0)	XXXXXX· · ·XXXXXX00
BYTE(1)	XXXXXX· · ·XXXXXX01
BYTE(2)	XXXXXX· · ·XXXXXX10
BYTE(3)	XXXXXX· · ·XXXXXX11

Masters broadcast the address over the data transfer bus at the beginning of each cycle. These addresses might consist of 16, 24, or 32 bits. The 16-bit addresses are called *short addresses,* the 24-bit addresses are called *standard addresses,* and the 32-bit addresses are called *extended addresses.* The master broadcasts a 6-bit address modifier (AM) code along with each address to tell slaves whether the address is short, standard, or extended.

Short addressing is intended primarily for addressing I/O. It allows I/O slaves to be designed with less logic, since they do not have to decode as many address lines. While I/O boards can be designed to decode standard addresses and extended addresses, short addressing usually makes this unnecessary.

Standard and extended addressing modes are intended primarily for addressing memory, although there is no rule against designing I/O boards that also respond to these addressing modes. Standard and extended addressing modes allow much larger addressing ranges.

1.6.2 Basic Data Transfer Capabilities

There are four basic data transfer capabilities associated with the data transfer bus: D08(EO) (even and odd byte), D08(O) (odd byte only), D16, and D32. These capabilities allow flexibility when interfacing different types of processors and peripherals to the bus. Eight-bit processors can be interfaced to the bus as D08(EO) masters. Sixteen-bit processors can be interfaced to the bus as D16 masters. Sixteen-bit memory devices or 16-bit I/O slaves can be interfaced to the bus as D16 slaves. The VMEbus protocols define an environment where the number of bytes to be transferred is defined dynamically, on a cycle-by-cycle basis. This allows 8-, 16-, and 32-bit devices to coexist in the same system. Table 1.4 shows how the size of the data transfer and the byte locations that are accessed are selected.

Many existing peripheral chips have registers that are only 8 bits wide. While these chips often have several of these registers, they cannot provide the contents of two registers simultaneously when a D16 master attempts to access two adjacent locations with a double-byte read cycle. These 8-bit peripheral integrated circuits (ICs) can be interfaced to the data transfer bus as D08(O) slaves. D08(O) slaves provide only BYTE(1) or BYTE(3) locations and respond only to single-byte accesses. Since single-byte accesses to these odd-byte locations always take place over data lines D00–D07, D08(O) slaves do not need interface logic to transfer data over any other data lines. As D08(O) slaves cannot respond properly to quadruple-byte data transfers that simultaneously select both BYTE(1) and BYTE(3), they ignore them.

Since most 32-bit microprocessors can also access memory 8 or 32 bits at a time, most 32-bit central processing unit (CPU) boards are designed to behave as D08(EO) and D16, as well as D32, masters. This not only allows them to do 8- and 16-bit data transfers to and from memory but also to access D08(O) slaves. Since D08(O) slaves respond only to odd-byte addresses, they cannot provide

TABLE 1.4 Selecting the Size and Byte Locations of a Data Transfer

Byte locations accessed	Size of data transfer	DS1*	DS0*	A01
BYTE(0)	8 bits	Low	High	Low
BYTE(1)	8 bits	High	Low	Low
BYTE(2)	8 bits	Low	High	High
BYTE(3)	8 bits	High	Low	High
BYTE(0–1)	16 bits	Low	Low	Low
BYTE(1–2)	16 bits	Low	Low	High
BYTE(2–3)	16 bits	Low	Low	High
BYTE(0–2)	24 bits	Low	High	Low
BYTE(1–3)	24 bits	High	Low	Low
BYTE(0–3)	32 bits	Low	Low	Low

contiguous memory. D08(O) slaves are typically I/O, status, or control registers, while D08(EO), D16, and D32 slaves might also be memory.

1.6.3 Types of Cycles

Five basic types of data transfer cycles are defined by the VMEbus specification. These cycle types include the read cycle, the write cycle, the block read cycle, the block write cycle, and the read-modify-write cycle. Two more types of cycles are defined: the address-only cycle and the interrupt acknowledge cycle. With the exception of the address-only cycle, which does not transfer data, all these cycles can be used to transfer 8, 16, or 32 bits of data.

Read and write cycles can be used to read or write 1, 2, 3, or 4 bytes of data. The cycle begins when the master broadcasts an address and an address modifier code. Each slave captures this addressing information and checks to see if it is to respond to the cycle. If it is, then it retrieves or stores the data and then acknowledges the transfer. The master then terminates the cycle.

Block transfer cycles are used to read or write a block of 1 to 256 bytes of data. Masters often access several memory locations in ascending order. When this is the case, block transfer cycles are very useful. They allow the master to address a single location and then access that location, as well as those with higher addresses, without providing additional addressing information.

When a master initiates a block transfer cycle, the responding slave latches the address into an on-board address counter. The master then repeatedly accesses the slave, while the slave increments its on-board address counter and uses the counter to provide the addresses needed to execute the subsequent data transfers.

Block transfer cycles of indefinite length are not allowed, because this complicates the design of memory boards. Specifically, all block transfer slaves, the one that responds as well as those that do not, would need to latch the initial address and then increment the address counter on each bus cycle. All slaves would then have to decode the incremented address to see if the block transfer has crossed a board boundary into their own address range. While this is certainly possible, the extra address decoding time increases the access time of the slave.

The VMEbus specification limits the maximum length of block transfers to 256 bytes. However, the fact that only the lower seven address lines can change during a block transfer makes it easier to design block transfer slaves. If a memory board has an array size of at least 256 bytes, and the first access falls within the board's boundaries, so will all of the rest. The upper address lines only have to be decoded once, at the beginning of the block transfer cycle, allowing much faster access times on all subsequent data transfers. If a master needs to transfer more than 256 contiguous bytes of data, it can do so by doing several block transfer cycles.

Read-modify-write cycles are used both to read from and write to a slave location in an indivisible manner, without permitting any other master to access that location. This cycle is most useful in multiprocessing systems where certain memory locations are used to provide semaphore functions.

In multiprocessor systems that share resources such as memory and I/O, a method is needed to allocate these resources. One very important goal of this allocation algorithm is to ensure that a resource being used by one task cannot be used by another at the same time. The problem is best described by the following example.

Two processors in a distributed processing system share a common resource (e.g., a printer). Only one processor may use the resource at a time. The resource is allocated by a bit in memory—i.e., if the bit is set, the resource is busy; if it is cleared, the resource is available. To gain use of the resource, processor A reads the bit and tests it to determine whether it is cleared. If the bit is cleared, processor A sets the bit to lock out processor B. This operation takes two bus cycles: a read cycle to test the bit and a write cycle to set it. However, a difficulty may arise if the bus is given to processor B between these two bus cycles. Processor B may then also find the bit cleared and assume that the resource is available. Both processors will then set the bit in the next available cycle and attempt to use the resource.

This conflict is avoided in VMEbus systems through the use of a read-modify-write cycle. This cycle is very similar to a read cycle, followed by a write cycle, except that it does not permit control of the data transfer bus to be exchanged between the read and write.

Address-only cycles consist of an address broadcast, but no data transfer. Slaves do not acknowledge address-only cycles and masters terminate the cycle without waiting for an acknowledgment. Address-only cycles allow a processor board to begin a bus cycle before it has had time to decode the address to determine whether it will select a local or a global memory location. If the address decode later reveals that the location is on-board, then the processor board terminates the bus cycle without waiting for a slave to respond.

Interrupt acknowledge cycles are initiated by interrupt handlers and are used to read status or identification information from an interrupter. An interrupt handler generates this cycle when it detects an interrupt request from an interrupter and has been granted control of the data transfer bus. The interrupter may request the transfer of 8, 16, or 32 bits of status or identification information from the interrupter.

1.6.4 Unaligned Transfer Capability

Some 32-bit microprocessors store and retrieve data in an unaligned fashion. For example, a 32-bit value might be stored in four different ways, as shown in Fig. 1.7. The master can transfer the 32 bits of data using several different sequences

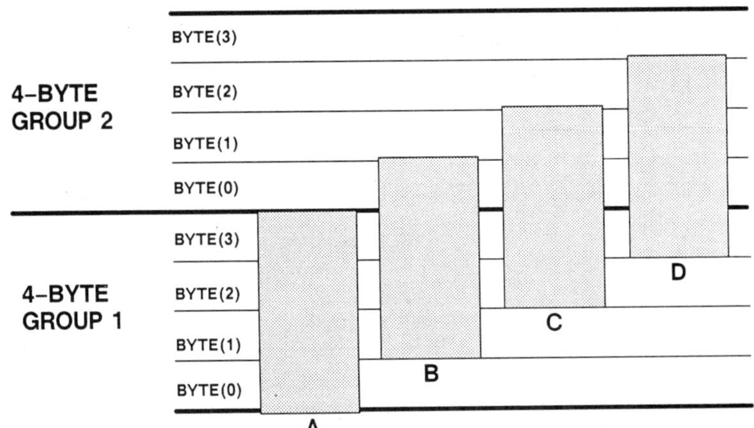

FIGURE 1.7 The four possible types of quadruple-byte transfers.

TABLE 1.5 How Quadruple-Byte Transfers Are Accomplished on the VMEbus

Example	Cycle sequence used to accomplish the transfer	Data bus lines used	Byte location accesses
A	Quadruple-byte transfer	D00–D31	GRP 1, BYTE(0–3)
B	Single-byte transfer	D00–D07	GRP 1, BYTE(1)
	Double-byte transfer	D00–D15	GRP 1, BYTE(2–3)
	Single-byte transfer	D08–D15	GRP 2, BYTE(0)
	or		
	Triple-byte transfer	D00–D23	GRP 1, BYTE(1–3)
	Single-byte transfer	D08–D15	GRP 2, BYTE(0)
C	Double-byte transfer	D00–D15	GRP 1, BYTE(2–3)
	Double-byte transfer	D00–D15	GRP 2, BYTE(0–1)
D	Single-byte transfer	D00–D07	GRP 1, BYTE(3)
	Double-byte transfer	D00–D15	GRP 2, BYTE(0–1)
	Single-byte transfer	D08–D15	GRP 2, BYTE(2)
	or		
	Single-byte transfer	D00–D07	GRP1, BYTE(3)
	Triple-byte transfer	D08–D31	GRP2, BYTE(0–2)

of data transfer bus cycles. For example, it can transfer the data one byte at a time, using four single-byte data transfers. However, a master can accomplish the transfer much more quickly by using one of the cycle sequences shown in Table 1.5. As shown, each of these 32-bit transfers can be accomplished with a combination of single- and double-byte transfers. However, when done in this manner, examples B and D require three bus cycles. Because of this, the VMEbus data transfer bus protocol also includes two triple-byte transfer cycles. When used in combination with a single-byte cycle, these triple-byte cycles allow data to be stored as shown in examples B and D, while using only two bus cycles.

Some 32-bit microprocessors also store and retrieve data 16 bits at a time in

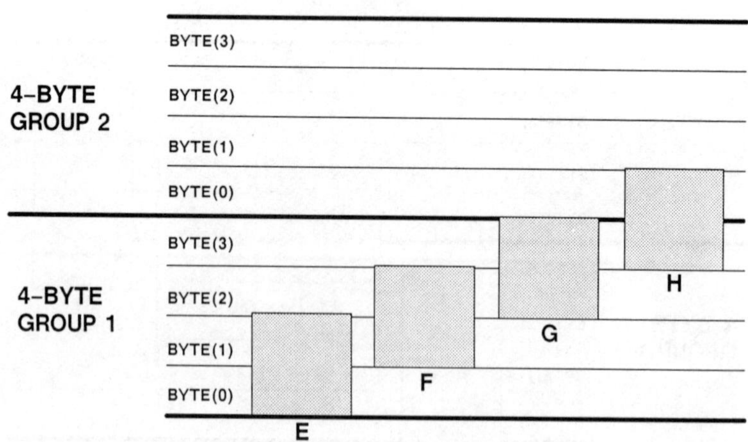

FIGURE 1.8 The four possible types of double-byte transfers.

TABLE 1.6 How Double-Byte Transfers Are Accomplished on the VMEbus

Example	Cycle sequence used to accomplish the transfer	Data bus lines used	Byte location accesses
E	Double-byte transfer	D00–D15	GRP 1, BYTE(0–1)
F	Single-byte transfer	D00–D07	GRP 1, BYTE(1)
	Single-byte transfer	D08–D15	GRP 1, BYTE(2)
	or		
	Double-byte transfer	D08–D23	GRP 1, BYTE(1–2)
G	Double-byte transfer	D00–D15	GRP 1, BYTE(2–3)
H	Single-byte transfer	D00–D07	GRP 1, BYTE(3)
	Single-byte transfer	D08–D15	GRP 2, BYTE(0)

an unaligned fashion, as shown in Fig. 1.8. The master can transfer the 16 bits of data using several different sequences of data transfer bus cycles. As shown in Table 1.6, the 16-bit transfer in example F can be accomplished by executing the two single-byte transfers. This, however, requires two bus cycles. Therefore, the VMEbus data transfer bus protocol also includes a double-byte transfer cycle that allows data to be stored as shown in example F using only one bus cycle.

1.6.5 Address Pipelining Capability

The VMEbus protocol allows a master to broadcast the address for the next cycle, while the data transfer for the previous cycle is still in progress. This in effect allows "overlapping" of one cycle with the next. This *address pipelining* allows memory boards on the VMEbus to begin providing the necessary access time to their on-board memory ICs without having to wait until the last data transfer finishes on the VMEbus.

1.6.6 Types of Requesters

Two types of requesters are described in the VMEbus specification: a *release when done* (RWD) requester and a *release on request* (ROR) requester. The RWD requester signals the arbiter that it has finished using the bus as soon as its on-board master or interrupt handler indicates that it no longer needs the bus. The ROR requester does not signal the arbiter unless some other requester on the bus drives one of the bus request lines low. To do this it must monitor the levels of all of the bus request lines (see Fig. 1.9). ROR requesters reduce the number of requests and of bus arbitrations in systems where one master is generating most of the bus traffic.

1.6.7 Types of Arbiters

When several boards request use of the data transfer bus simultaneously, the arbiter uses some algorithm to decide who gets to use the bus first. Out of the many algorithms that are possible, the VMEbus describes three: prioritized, round robin, and single level.

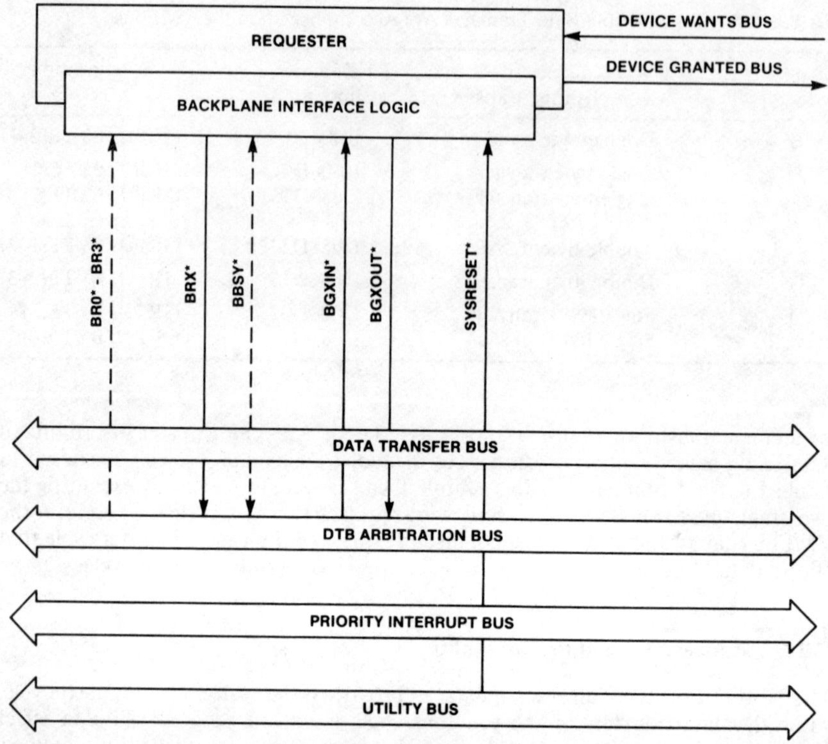

FIGURE 1.9 Block diagram of the ROR requester.

Priority arbitration assigns the bus according to a fixed priority scheme, where each of the four bus request lines is assigned a priority.

Round robin arbitration assigns the bus on a rotating priority basis. If the bus is granted to the requester on bus request line *n,* then the highest priority is assigned to bus request line $n - 1$.

Single-level arbitration only accepts requests on bus request line 3, and relies on that level's daisy chain to ensure that only one requester uses the bus.

Although not described by the VMEbus specification, other scheduling algorithms may be used. For example, an arbiter's algorithm might give highest priority to bus request 3, but use the other levels to grant the bus in a round-robin fashion.

1.6.8 Releasing the Data Transfer Bus

The bus arbitration protocol determines how and when the data transfer bus is granted to the various types of masters and interrupt handlers in the system. It does not, however, dictate when masters and interrupt handlers must release the data transfer bus. Masters and interrupt handlers use several criteria in deciding when to release the data transfer bus. Interrupt handlers give up the bus after their interrupt acknowledge cycle. Masters give up the bus when they finish their data transfers.

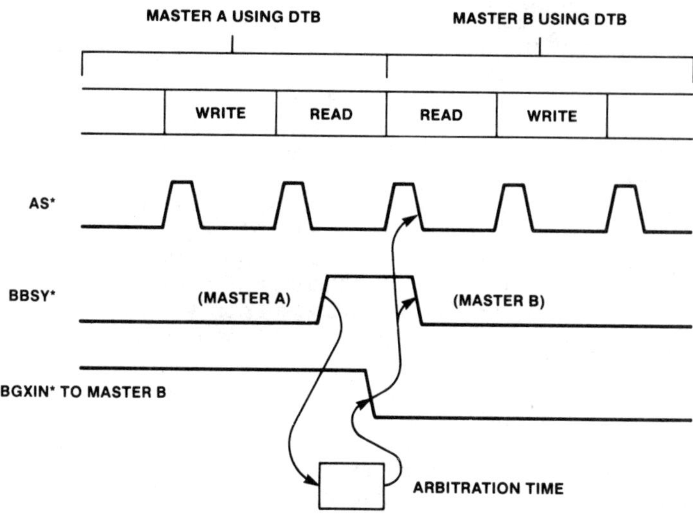

FIGURE 1.10 Master exchange sequence: Arbitration during last data transfer.

Masters and interrupt handlers may release the data transfer bus either during or after their last data transfer. If a requester releases the bus busy line during the last transfer, arbitration takes place during the last transfer. If the requester releases it after the last data transfer, however, then the data transfer bus remains idle while the arbitration is done. Figures 1.10 and 1.11 provide two examples that show possible sequences when a master finishes using the data transfer bus and allows arbitration to take place.

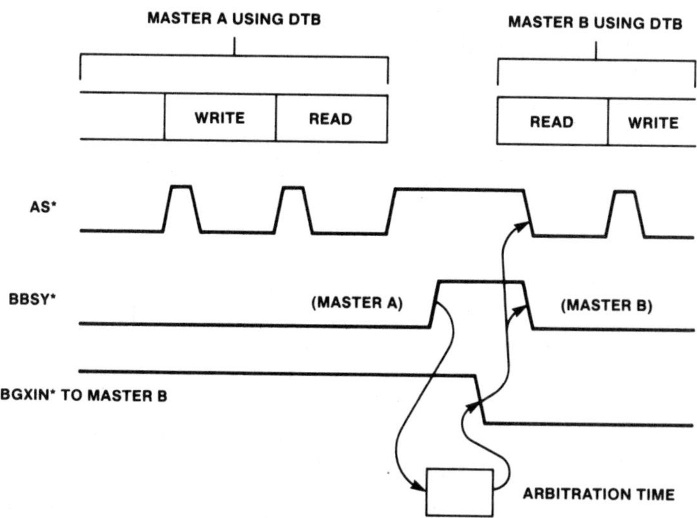

FIGURE 1.11 Master exchange sequence: Arbitration after last data transfer.

Master A, partway into its last cycle, indicates that it is getting ready to relinquish use of the data transfer bus. It does so by allowing its requester to release the BBSY* line to high. Since master A gives this early notice that the data transfer bus will soon be available, the arbitration process is done concurrently with its last data transfer; thus the arbitration is completed and master B is granted permission to use the data transfer bus before master A has actually finished its cycle. However, master B waits until master A finishes using the bus before actively using it. This is accomplished by monitoring the AS* line which, when high, signals that mastership of the bus may be exchanged.

In this sequence, master A waits until after its last cycle before allowing its requester to release the bus busy line. In this example the data transfer bus is idle while the arbitration process is taking place. Master B is then granted the data transfer bus, and because the AS* line is high, begins using it immediately.

1.6.9 Interrupt Methods

The VMEbus provides two ways that processors in a multiprocessing system can communicate with each other: by using interrupt request lines or by using location monitors (Sec. 1.6.10).

Any system that has interrupt capability includes software routines that are invoked by the interrupts and are thus called interrupt service routines. Each of these routines may be thought of as a task that is activated by an interrupt. The VMEbus specification does not dictate what will happen when these interrupt service routines are activated.

Using Interrupt Request Lines. When interrupts are generated with the VMEbus' interrupt request lines, the following sequence occurs (see Fig. 1.12):

Phase 1: The interrupt request phase starts when an interrupter drives an interrupt request line low, and ends when the interrupt handler gains control of the data transfer bus.

Phase 2: The interrupt-acknowledge phase, during which the interrupt handler uses the data transfer bus to read the interrupter's status or identification.

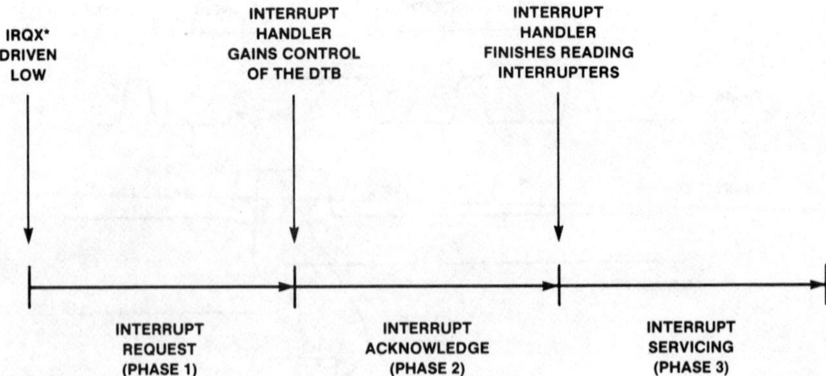

FIGURE 1.12 The three phases of an interrupt sequence.

Phase 3: The interrupt servicing phase, during which a prescribed interrupt service routine is executed. The protocol for the interrupt subsystem in the VMEbus describes the interaction between modules during phase 1 and phase 2 only. Phase 3 is not specified, and any data transfers that take place during phase 3 will follow the data transfer bus protocol.

Selection of the Responding Interrupter. Each interrupter with an active interrupt request waits until it sees a falling edge on its interrupt acknowledge daisy-chain input before responding with status or identification information. However, since some other interrupter might have a request on a different line, it must also check a 3-bit interrupt acknowledge code on the address lines (see Table 1.7). If the code on these three address lines does not correspond to its interrupt line number, it passes the daisy chain's falling edge to the next board. Therefore, before responding, the interrupter verifies that the followig conditions are met:

1. It has an interrupt request pending.
2. Its interrupt request line number matches the code indicated on the three lower address lines (see Table 1.7).
3. It has received an incoming falling edge on the interrupt acknowledge daisy-chain.

If any of these three conditions is not met, the interrupter does not respond with status or identification information. If condition 3 is met, but either 1 or 2 is not, then it passes the falling edge down the interrupt acknowledge daisy chain to the next interrupter.

Releasing Interrupt Request Lines. Many widely used peripheral ICs generate interrupt requests. Unfortunately, there is no standard method for indicating to these ICs when it is time for them to remove their interrupt request from the bus. Three methods are used:

1. When the relevant processor senses an interrupt request from a peripheral device, it enters an interrupt service routine, and reads a status register in the device. The peripheral device interprets this read cycle on its status register as a signal to remove its interrupt request.

TABLE 1.7 The 3-Bit Interrupt Acknowledge Code

Interrupt level being acknowledged	Interrupt acknowledge code on address bus		
	A03	A02	A01
1	Low	Low	High
2	Low	High	Low
3	Low	High	High
4	High	Low	Low
5	High	Low	High
6	High	High	Low
7	High	High	High

2. When the relevant processor senses an interrupt request from a peripheral device, it enters an interrupt service routine and writes to a control register in the device. The peripheral device interprets this write cycle on its status register as a signal to remove its interrupt request.

3. When the relevant processor senses an interrupt request from a peripheral device, it reads a status or identification from the device. The peripheral device interprets this read cycle as a signal to remove its interrupt request.

The VMEbus specification calls interrupters that use methods 1 and 2 *release on register access* (RORA) interrupters and those that use method 3 *release on acknowledge* (ROAK) interrupters.

Types of Interrupt Subsystems. Interrupt subsystems may be classified into two groups:

1. Single-handler systems, which have only one interrupt handler that receives and services all bus interrupts.
2. Distributed systems, which have two or more interrupt handlers that receive and service bus interrupts.

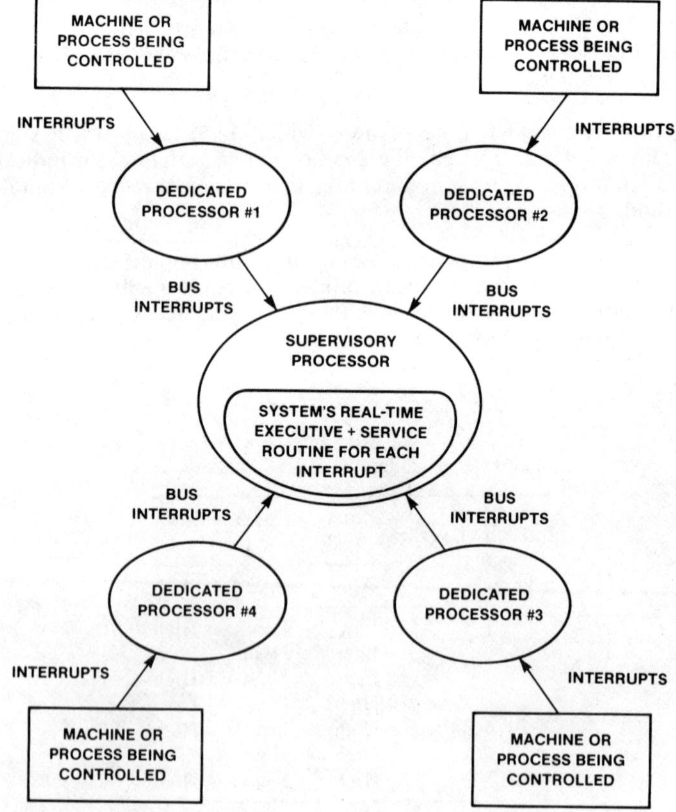

FIGURE 1.13 Interrupt subsystem structure: Single-handler system.

In single-handler systems all interrupts are received by one interrupt handler, and all interrupt service routines executed by one processor. Figure 1.13 shows the interrupt structure of a single-handler system. This type of architecture is well suited to machine or process control applications, where a supervisory processor coordinates the activities of dedicated processors. The dedicated processors are typically interfaced to the machine or the process being controlled.

The supervisory processor is the destination for all bus interrupts, servicing them in a prioritized manner. The dedicated processors are not required to service interrupts from the bus and can give primary attention to controlling the machine or the process that they are assigned.

In single-handler interrupt systems, the seven interrupt request lines are all monitored by a single interrupt handler. The interrupt request lines are prioritized such that level seven has the highest priority, and level one has the lowest priority. When the interrupt handler detects simultaneous requests on two interrupt request lines, it first services the interrupter that has a pending request on the higher-priority request line.

As shown in Fig. 1.14, distributed interrupt systems include from two to seven interrupt handlers, each servicing only a subset of the bus interrupts. In a typical implementation, each of the interrupt handlers resides on a different processor board. This type of architecture is well suited to distributed computing applications, where multiple, coequal processors execute the application software. As each of the coequal processors executes part of the system software, it may need

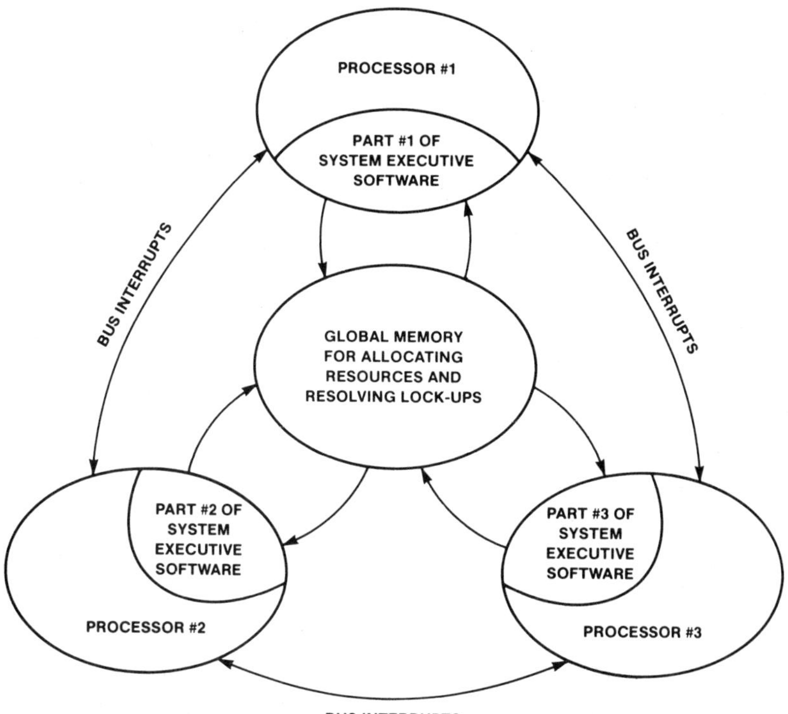

FIGURE 1.14 Interrupt subsystem structure: Distributed system.

to communicate with the other processors. In the distributed system, each processor services only those interrupts directed to it.

1.6.10 Establishing Virtual Communication Paths

The location monitor functional module is intended for use in multiple-processor systems. It monitors all data transfer cycles over the VMEbus and activates an on-board signal whenever an access is done to any of the locations that it is assigned to watch.

In multiple-processor systems, events that have global importance need to be broadcasted to some or all of the processors. This can be accomplished if each processor board includes a location monitor. To configure the system for broadcast operation, all of these location monitors are configured to watch a common location in global VMEbus memory. The occurrence of an event can then be broadcasted by accessing this location. The location monitors on the various processor boards sense the access to this location and alert their local processors.

1.7 APPLYING THE VMEbus CAPABILITIES

In the following paragraphs are a few examples of how system applications can benefit from some of the capabilities that are provided by the VMEbus.

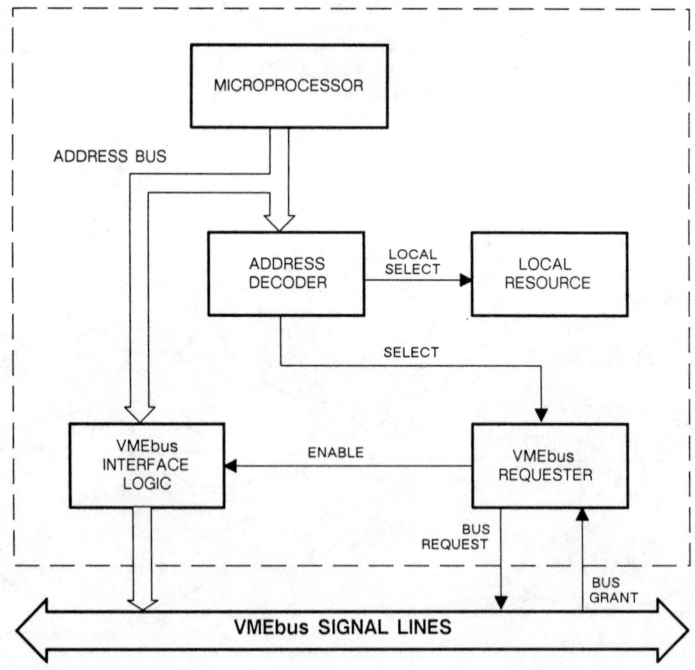

FIGURE 1.15 Simplified block diagram of a typical VMEbus CPU board.

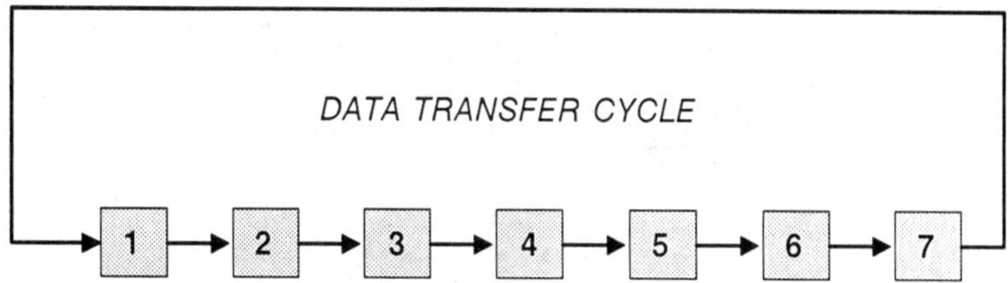

FIGURE 1.16 Normal operational sequence.

1.7.1 Improving CPU Performance

Figure 1.15 is a simplified block diagram of a typical VMEbus processor board. It includes a microprocessor, an address decoder, a VMEbus requester, and VMEbus interface logic.

During normal operation the following sequence, shown in Fig. 1.16, is repeated over and over:

Step 1: The microprocessor outputs an address.

Step 2: The address decoder determines whether the address is for an on-board resource or for a VMEbus resource. If the VMEbus is required, it selects the requester.

Step 3: The VMEbus requester requests the bus.

Step 4: The VMEbus requester is granted the bus.

Step 5: The VMEbus requester enables the VMEbus interface logic, allowing the microprocessor to broadcast the address of the VMEbus resource.

Step 6: The microprocessor accesses the VMEbus resource.

Step 7: The VMEbus requester releases control of the bus.

Steps 2, 3, and 4 determine how quickly the microprocessor can access the resource.

If any of these steps can be shortened or eliminated, then the processor can access bus resources more quickly. The VMEbus specification defines a *release on request* (ROR) requester. It maintains control of the bus even after the on-board processor completes its current data transfer. Since the requester does not relinquish the bus, it need not repeat steps 3 and 4 when its microprocessor needs to use the VMEbus again. This speeds up any subsequent data transfers (see Fig. 1.17).

While an ROR requester might maintain control of the bus from a previous

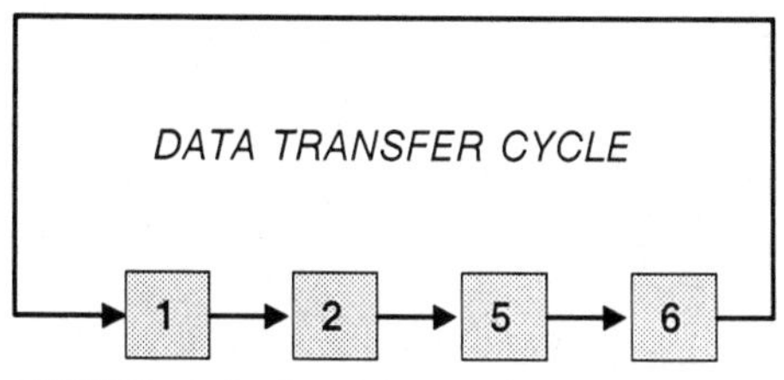

FIGURE 1.17 Operational sequence with an ROR requester.

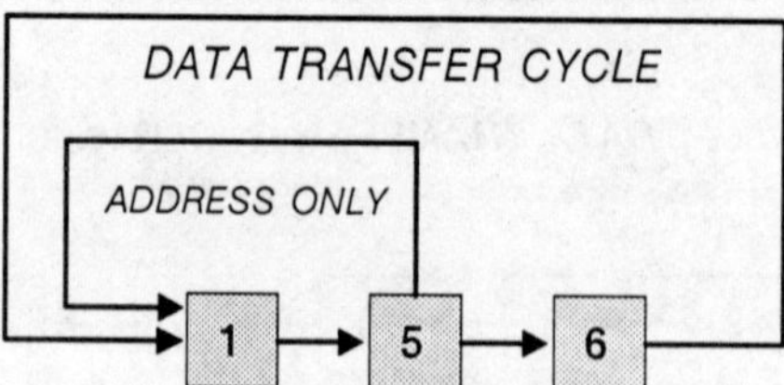

FIGURE 1.18 Operational sequence with an ROR requester and address-only cycle.

cycle, the processor board must still decode the address to determine whether the addressed resource is on VMEbus before starting a bus cycle. This means that the processor cannot broadcast the address until its address decoder determines that a VMEbus cycle is required.

The address-only cycle permits a processor board to broadcast an address over the VMEbus and then terminate the cycle without ever doing a data transfer. Thus a processor board can start a VMEbus cycle before its address decoder determines whether the address is for a VMEbus resource or not. Performing steps 2 and 5 concurrently eliminates the delay associated with step 2, as shown in Fig. 1.18.

1.7.2 Timely Response to Critical Events

Some real-time system applications require that the response to external events be done in a timely fashion and as quickly as possible. As most of these external events will involve the transfer of data, the master who is currently using the bus must first give it up.

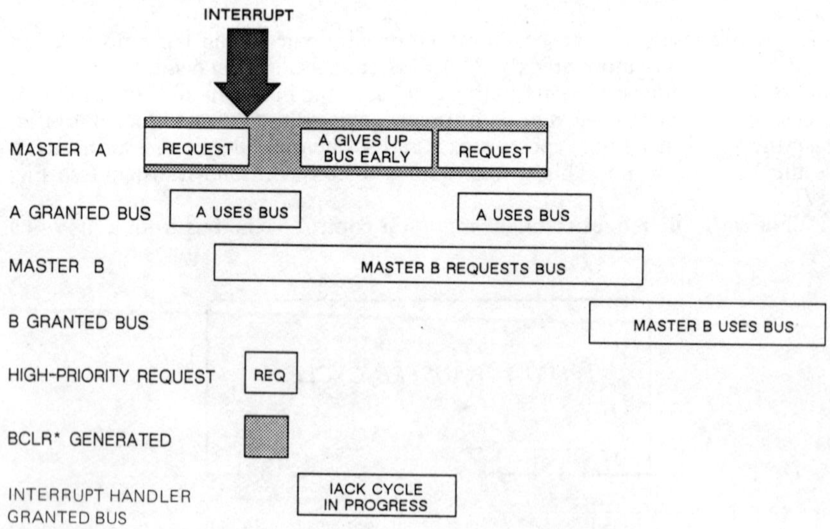

FIGURE 1.19 Using BCLR* to find the response time to real-time events.

To provide for this, VMEbus masters may monitor the ac failure and the bus clear lines. Both of these signals inform the master that the data transfer bus is needed for some higher-priority activity. The bus clear line is driven by the priority arbiter to inform the active master that a higher-priority request is pending (see Fig. 1.19). The active master's design determines how long it takes to release the bus when the bus clear signal is driven low. For example, a direct memory access (DMA) master might not be able to relinquish the bus during a disk sector transfer without loss of data, so it might keep the bus until the sector transfer is finished.

The ac fail signal is driven by the power monitor module and informs all bus masters that an ac power loss has been detected. The master who is currently in control of the bus is then required to relinquish it immediately, since whatever problems it will face in surrendering the bus are insignificant compared to the needs of the total system.

1.7.3 Portability of Software

In recent years there has been increasing emphasis upon portability and standardization of software, especially in the area of operating systems. As software standardization takes place, hardware engineers are being asked to design peripheral controllers whose command and status registers are tailored to the operating system's needs. This can be difficult since each operating system expects to see a different register interface.

The location monitor provides a solution to this problem by allowing the creation of *virtual status and control registers.* Figure 1.20 shows an intelligent peripheral controller board equipped with a location monitor. The board's software or firmware can create virtual status and control registers in global memory

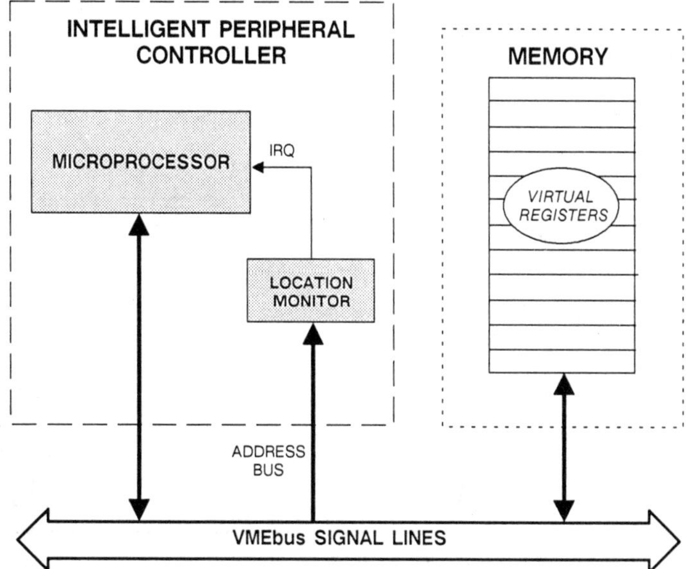

FIGURE 1.20 An intelligent peripheral controller with location monitor.

by simply programming its location monitor to "watch" a range of addresses. Any data transfers to or from those locations cause the location monitor to interrupt the peripheral controller's processor. Any master accessing these virtual registers will find them indistinguishable from "real" registers. Location monitors allow the creation of virtually any configuration of registers up to the limits of global memory. This flexibility allows a single intelligent peripheral controller board to be customized to meet the needs of a wide range of standardized software.

The example given above shows how the location monitor can be used to create VMEbus systems with *flexible architectures.* To cite a more elaborate example, suppose that each of the processor boards in a multiprocessing system are equipped with a location monitor. They can each establish their own *virtual message registers* in global memory for receiving messages from other processors. These message registers can be a single memory location or a block of locations, depending upon the size of the messages being exchanged.

Using location monitors to "decouple" the hardware architecture from the software architecture promotes portability of software. Two VMEbus boards with very different hardware architectures can be made to appear identical to the operating system. At the same time, software engineers are not faced with artificial contraints imposed by real-estate limitations on boards.

1.7.4 System Initialization and Diagnostics

The VMEbus protocol specifies the behavior of boards during the power-up process. This facilitates the synchronization of the various system resources prior to starting normal system operation. This is done using the system fail line, which is part of the utility bus. It allows the operating system to determine the status of intelligent system resources, such as CPUs and integrated printed circuits (IPCs). These intelligent boards drive the system fail line low when the system is powered up or when the system reset is activated, and maintain it low until they successfully complete their on-board self-test and/or initialization routines (see Fig. 1.21). By monitoring the system fail line, the operating system can determine the status of the various system components and when to start normal system operation. If any board in the system detects a failure after this point, it broadcasts this by driving the system fail line low. The operating system can then take the appropriate action.

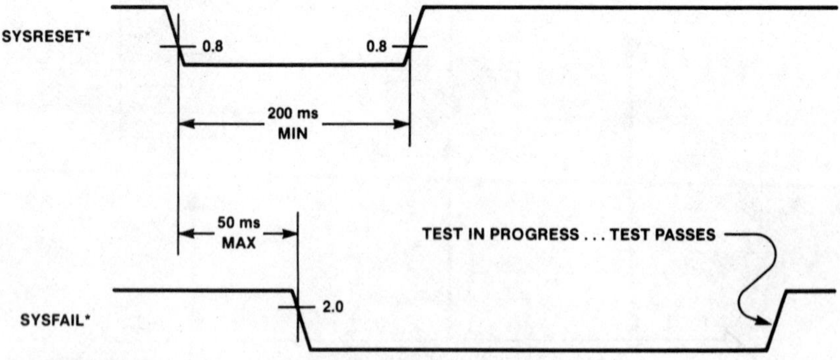

FIGURE 1.21 The timing of the system fail line.

1.8 SUMMARY

The VMEbus provides both the performance and versatility needed to appeal to a wide range of users. Its rapid rise in popularity has made it the most popular 32-bit bus. As a result, it is the first 32-bit bus to undergo formal standardization by both the Institute of Electrical and Electronic Engineers (IEEE) and by the International Electrotechnical Commission (IEC). This same versatility that has made it so popular will also ensure that as technology progresses to yet higher levels of performance, VMEbus systems will accommodate the inevitable changes easily and without making existing equipment obsolete.

LIST OF TRADEMARKS

Motorola and the Motorola symbol are registered trademarks of Motorola, Inc.

VERSAbus, VERSAmodule, and VMEmodule are trademarks of Motorola, Inc.

CHAPTER 2
MULTIBUS I

Mike Pritchard
Oregon Systems Division
Intel Corporation
Portland, Oregon

2.1 INTRODUCTION

Applications based on the IEEE 796 standard (Multibus I) architecture have been in use since 1976. Even though several bus architectures have been introduced since the advent of the Multibus I architecture, the strengths that encouraged the development of the IEEE standard still apply today, contributing to the continuing and growing popularity of Multibus I–based products.

Examples of these strengths are as follows:

Simplicity and ease of use. Whether the design engineer wishes to use only standard products or design special boards to augment the wide range of products from many manufacturers, the well-established Multibus I standard eases the design process.

Processor flexibility. The Multibus I architecture is processor independent, which means that diverse families and generations of microprocessor fit well on the bus. As the latest microprocessors are incorporated with large amounts of local memory accessible through 32-bit execution paths, the performance of single the Multibus I system bus boards tracks technology improvements. With the use of 16-bit data and I/O backplane connections, it is possible to create a high-performance functionally distributed system comprising multiple 32-bit microprocessors.

System flexibility. Various system architectures can be implemented using the Multibus I system bus as the interconnecting bus. These range from a small single master design to a large system with several processors all performing different tasks. Processors using 8, 16, and 32 bits coexist comfortably on the same backplane, in many cases running the same software. This allows a smooth migration as the performance needs of the design change. In a typical Multibus I system, the backplane itself is not the only standard bus implementation used. The iSBX expansion I/O bus makes it possible to add cost-effective options to any board that has iSBX connectors; this increases the range of configuration choices. The iLBX local bus extension is an off-board interface that allows memory, or memory-mapped I/O, to connect to a processor at a higher-performance rate than regular backplane speeds.

Suitability for harsh environments. Although reliability is not part of the IEEE 796 specification, Multibus I boards are typically very reliable, with over 150,000 hours mean time before failure (MTBF) in some cases. Reliability is one of the reasons why Multibus I–based systems are so popular in factories and other situations where normal office equipment would not be suitable. Some Multibus I products are capable of operating with no air flow, which permits creation of sealed enclosures for further increased reliability.

Ease of upgrading. Along with flexibility, ease of upgrading a system design is one of the most attractive reasons for choosing any standard bus architecture. The Multibus I architecture has been relatively free from compatibility issues that result in difficulty when integrating boards from different manufacturers; this also means fewer problems when upgrading one board in the system to increase performance or I/O connectivity. Many designs based on the Multibus I architecture have been competitive in production for far longer periods than would have been possible had upgrading various parts of the design not been accomplished.

These strengths have resulted in the wide acceptance of the Multibus I architecture as a way to build many different types of applications. From the automatic teller machine to the trader workstation, elevator controller to steel mill, blood analysis to phototypesetting, the Multibus I architecture is at the heart of many of the most successful products in use today.

2.2 CHAPTER ORGANIZATION

This chapter will cover the Multibus I family, which includes the IEEE 796 Specification (Multibus I), the IEEE 959 specification (iSBX expansion I/O bus), and iLBX (local bus extension). (Although the iSBX specification has been implemented on other bus structures, it was originally defined as an extension to Multibus I, so it is logical to cover it in the same chapter.)

Each specification will be discussed in terms of general characteristics, and the more detailed specifications will be given as needed to understand the operation, together with a brief description of some of the product categories available. This chapter is meant to serve as an introduction, not to provide detailed specifications. The more detailed specifications may be found in manufacturers' literature and the IEEE documents as described in the Bibliography.

2.3 DEFINITIONS

* An asterisk following a signal name indicates that the signal is active low. This is in accordance with the usage in the IEEE 796 specification.

Master — A bus master is a module (board) with the ability to control the bus. A bus master, once established as controlling the bus, can initiate a data transfer.

Slave — A slave is capable of responding to data requests on the bus, but cannot itself initiate such requests.

NBVI — Non-bus-vectored interrupt. A non-bus-vectored interrupt will cause the master processor to immediately start execution from the address as defined on the master processor board (typically a combination of wiring the interrupt matrix and setting up the interrupt controller). One backplane line is linked to a single source.

BVI — Bus-vectored interrupt. The first interrupt signal from the backplane line causes the master processor to transfer the interrupt vector information from the interrupting source. This allows multiple sources to be linked to a single interrupt line.

CPU — Central processor unit. The CPU is a Multibus I board (a master) that is running application software.

SBC — Single-board computer. As more of the I/O and memory were implemented on the same board as the microprocessor, the board became more independent of the system bus. A single-board computer is always a CPU, but the reverse is not necessarily true.

Dual port — Memory on a CPU board can be made accessible to the local microprocessor and the bus. This gives the best performance for the local processor, since acquiring the bus is not required.

2.4 THE MULTIBUS I (IEEE 796) SYSTEM BUS SPECIFICATION

2.4.1 General Multibus I Characteristics

A system based on the Multibus I architecture comprises one or more boards (each 12 in by 6.75 in) connected via a passive backplane.

The Multibus I architecture is processor independent and has attracted a variety of manufacturers to implement products with many different microprocessor types. At the time of writing this chapter, the current edition of the Multibus Buyers Guide (published by Control Engineering) describes CPU boards with microprocessors from manufacturers such as Intel, Motorola, National Semiconductor, NEC, Zilog, and Texas Instruments. Microprocessors ranging from the 8080 and Z80A to the 68030 and 386 are available. Manufacturers of Multibus I products have been, and continue to be, quick to incorporate advances in silicon technology into board products. Figure 2.1 shows the incorporation of very large-scale integration (VLSI) technology onto Multibus boards.

Partly because of the incorporation of differing microprocessors, but more importantly because of architectural flexibility, a wide range of system performance is available. An EPROM-based system (EPROM denotes erasable programmable read-only memory) with a CMOS 8086 SBC board at its heart, with perhaps a small amount of additional I/O on a separate Multibus I board or on an iSBX Multimodule, would be at one end of today's typical spectrum. At the other end, we might have a powerful multiprocessing system built from three 386-based CPU cards, each with 16 Mbytes of local memory. In this case we would probably have a high-performance disk controller, Ethernet connection, and graphics. Even with this wide divergence of system configurations, some of the hardware and software might be the same, which gives enormous flexibility in the design process.

Up to 24 address lines and 16 data lines are available. This gives a maximum common bus address space of 16 Mbytes. (Actual physical memory is not necessarily available to the bus, which may permit more than 16 Mbytes of physical memory in a system). Eight-bit and sixteen-bit data transfers on the bus are permitted, with a swapping facility that allows odd bytes to be transferred on the low-order data lines for compatibility between 8- and 16-bit systems. For I/O transfers, either 8 or 16 address lines are used to give up to 64K addresses separate from the data space. Up to 16 bus masters can be supported in a Multibus I system, using either serial or parallel priority schemes. Eight interrupt lines are available—these can be configured as direct interrupts or bus-vectored interrupts to increase flexibility.

Data transfer on Multibus is asynchronous, which means that transfers proceed at the speed of the slower agent involved. The maximum theoretical data rate is 10 Mbytes per second, using 16-bit transfers. This could be a sustained data rate if DMA were used, but without DMA data rates of 2 Mbytes are more common. If the backplane were still being used for code execution, this data rate would seem low in comparison with microprocessors such as the 386. (The 386 microprocessor running at 20 MHz can transfer data at 40 Mbytes per second.) However, as the speed of processors increased, memory and manufacturing technology combined to bring more of the code execution onto the same board as the processor. (The iLBX local expansion bus allows for 0 wait-state execution *off-*

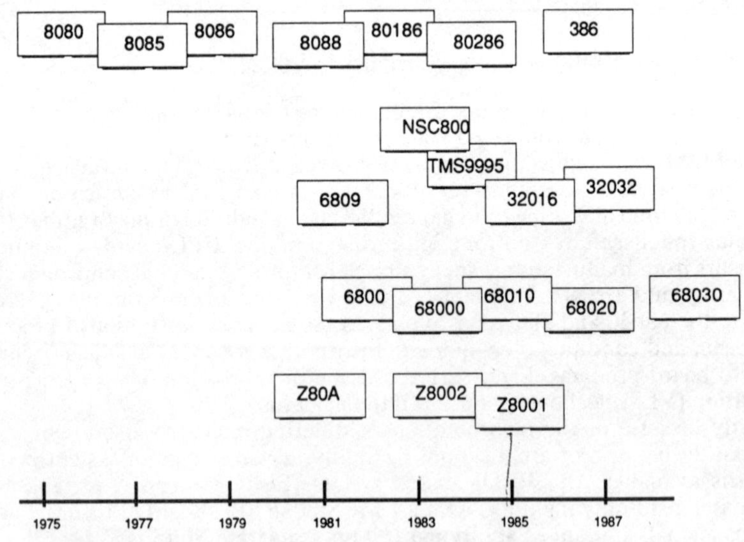

FIGURE 2.1 Microprocessors available on Multibus I architecture.

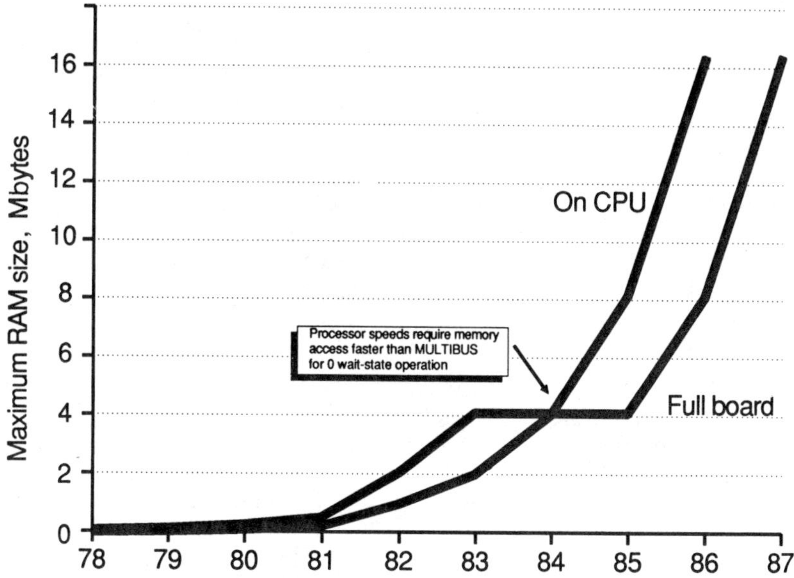

FIGURE 2.2 RAM available on Multibus I architecture.

board with an 8-MHz 80286 processor.) While it would not be completely true to say that the backplane on Multibus I is purely used as an I/O bus, the designer now has much more freedom of choice and can gain greater benefits from the faster processors now available. Figure 2.2 shows the amount of memory on dedicated Multibus I memory boards and on the CPU boards over time.

Some of the agents in a Multibus I system are slaves—not able to initiate data transfer. These would typically be the memory and simpler I/O controllers. The more complex I/O controllers may need to gain control of the bus to guarantee response to external devices such as a hard disk or an Ethernet packet. In this case the agent would be a master, but the more obvious example of a master is a CPU board. Multibus I can support up to 16 bus masters using parallel priority logic typically located on the backplane. A simpler serial priority scheme is also available; current implementations handle three bus masters.

An obvious difference when considering different buses is the board shape. However, this is not always seen as important in the decision process. Multibus I boards, at 6.75 in by 12 in, are among the largest of the standard open buses. The board size has implications both for architecture of the boards and the connectivity to the outside world. The combination of a large area and a simple bus interface makes it possible to create a very high performance system on a single board, even without resorting to on-board extensions such as the iSBX bus, or stackable memory. (Extensions like these require some real estate to support, so they are not entirely free.) A Multibus I board has 11.5 in of board edge available for connector mounting. This makes it very suitable for I/O intensive applications. For example, the AUTO32-00 board from Ariel Systems, Inc. provides 32 serial channels and connections in a single slot.

Software support is important in a bus decision. The majority of designers would prefer to concentrate on the application rather than the software to run the basic underlying machine. Excellent software support is available for Multibus I products, ranging from full operating systems to small kernels for simple designs. To integrate products from several vendors, drivers are available for the most popular real-time and non-real-time operating systems, and drivers can also be written for custom boards.

The IEEE 796 standard defines different levels of compliance; these varying levels should not imply difficulty in integrating different boards, since the different options are relatively few, well adhered to, and clearly described in most manufacturers' documentation. Compliance options cover such things as size of data and address paths and support for bus-vectored interrupts.

2.4.2 Bus Signals and Operation

The Multibus I bus signals and operation can be best understood by categorizing them into control lines, address and inhibit lines, data lines, and bus exchange lines.

All signals are active low and are terminated by pull-up resistors. This makes it easy to implement such features as differing address spaces, since if a signal is not driven it will appear as a logic 0. Figure 2.3 shows a simplified view of the signals connecting a Multibus I bus master and slaves.

2.4.2.1 Control Lines. Table 2.1 shows the Multibus I control signals.

Bus clock (BCLK)* is the signal used to synchronize the bus contention logic. It can be stopped or slowed down if necessary for debugging purposes. Since there must be only a single BCLK* within the system, each bus master must be able to optionally disconnect it from the bus. BCLK* normally operates at 10 MHz.

Constant clock (CCLK)* is a constant clock signal that may be used by masters or slaves as a master clock. CCLK* is commonly used by slaves for acknowl-

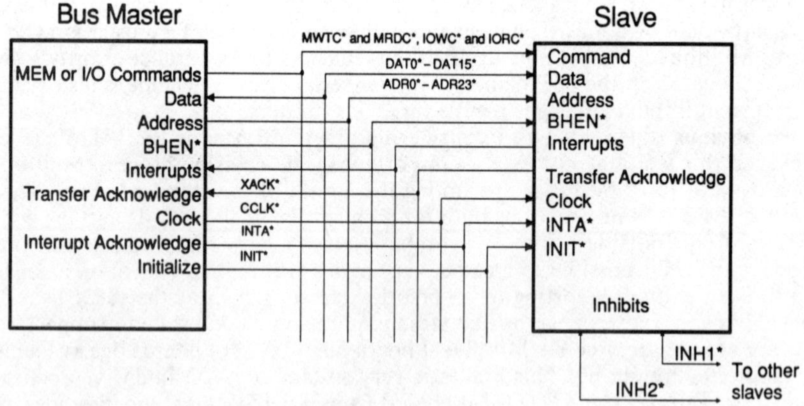

FIGURE 2.3 Simplified view of the Multibus I interface signals.

TABLE 2.1 Multibus I Control Signals

Function	Signal
Constant clock	CCLK*
Bus clock	BCLK*
Memory read	MRDC*
Memory write	MWTC*
I/O read	IORC*
I/O write	IOWC*
Transfer acknowledge	XACK*
System initialize	INIT*
Bus lock	LOCK*

edge generation logic. Since there must be only a single CCLK* within the system, each bus master must be able to generate CCLK* and must be able to optionally disconnect it from the bus. CCLK* is a 10-MHz clock.

Commands (MWTC, MRDC*, IOWC*, IORC*)* are signals driven by a master to transfer memory or I/O information to or from a slave. When the signals are active the master indicates to the slave that the address is valid. In a data write cycle, the active command line (MWTC* or IOWC*) additionally indicates that the data is valid on the bus. In a data read cycle, the transition of the command (MRDC* or IORC*) from active to inactive indicates that the master has received the data from the slave.

Transfer acknowledge (XACK)* is used by a slave to acknowledge commands from a master. XACK* indicates to the master that the requested action is completed and that the data has been placed on, or accepted from, the data lines.

Initialize (INIT)* is generated to reset the entire system to a known internal state. This signal is usually generated prior to starting any operations on the system. INIT* may be generated by any or all of the bus masters or by an external source such as a debounced and buffered front panel switch.

Lock (LOCK)* is generated by the master to indicate that the bus is locked. The purpose of LOCK* is to ensure that a multiple-processor system can guarantee the integrity of the shared memory used to communicate. A common way of communicating between multiple processors is to pass messages in shared memory. For this to be successful it must not be possible for one processor to write to memory while another processor is trying to read it. An indivisible *read-test-write* operation is essential. If shared memory were only accessible via the bus, the LOCK* signal would not be necessary since the indivisible instruction would be completed before the bus could be relinquished to another master. However, shared bus memory is not the only shared memory available. Dual-port memory allows memory on a bus master to be made available to its local processor and the bus. The LOCK* signal allows the dual-port memory to lock out the local microprocessor if necessary.

Figure 2.4 shows how the LOCK* signal can prevent the local microprocessor from gaining access to its dual-port memory, and how the local microprocessor's own lock signal causes the bus lock signal to be asserted.

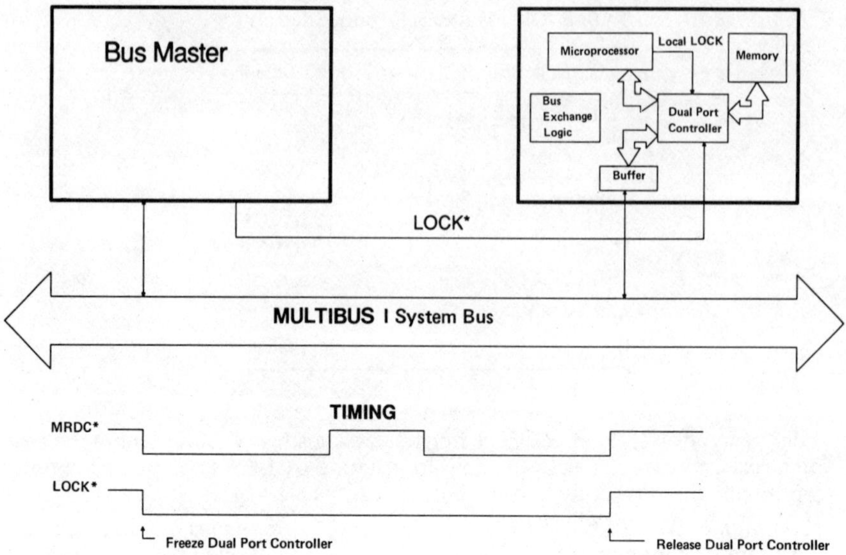

FIGURE 2.4 Multibus I lock operation.

2.4.2.2 Address and Inhibit Lines. Table 2.2 shows the signals used to communicate addresses and to inhibit areas of the address space.

Address lines (ADR0–ADR23*).* The 24 address lines specify the address of the referenced memory location or I/O device, allowing a maximum of 16 Mbytes (16,777,216 bytes) of memory to be accessed across the bus. This does not mean that 16 Mbytes is the maximum amount of memory in a Multibus I system, but 16 Mbytes is the maximum that is directly accessible from the bus. When addressing an I/O device, a maximum of 16 address lines (ADR0–ADR15*) are used, thus allowing a maximum of 64K I/O devices. An I/O module must also be able to be configured to decode only 8 address lines (ADR0*–ADR7*) and ignore the upper 8 lines.

Byte high enable (BHEN)* is used to enable the upper byte (bits 8 to 15) of a 16-bit word to drive the bus. The byte high enable signal is only used on 16-bit modules and permits 8- and 16-bit modules to coexist on the same bus without conflict.

TABLE 2.2 Multibus I Address and Inhibit Signals

Function	Signal
Address lines	ADR0*–ADR23*
Byte high enable	BHEN*
Inhibit lines	INH1* and INH2*

Inhibit lines (INH1 and INH2*)* can be invoked for any memory read or memory write signal. An inhibit line is asserted by a slave to inhibit another slave's bus activity during a memory read or memory write operation. The inhibit lines can be used to allow read-only memory (ROM) to override random access memory (RAM) in the same address space.

2.4.2.3 Data Lines. The 16 bidirectional data lines transmit and receive information to and from a memory location or an I/O port. DAT15* is the most significant bit, and DAT0* is the least significant bit. In 8-bit systems, only lines DAT0*–DAT7* are valid.

2.4.2.4 Interrupt Lines

Interrupt request lines (INT0–INT7*).* Interrupts are requested by activating one of the eight interrupt request lines with an open-collector driver. All interrupts are level-triggered, rather than edge-triggered. Requiring no edge to trigger an interrupt allows several sources to be attached to each line. INT0* has the highest priority and INT7* has the lowest priority.

Interrupt acknowledge (INTA).* In response to an interrupt request signal, a bus master with bus-vectored interrupt capability can generate an interrupt acknowledge signal. The interrupt acknowledge signal is used to freeze the interrupt status and request the placement of the interrupt vector address on the bus data lines.

2.4.2.5 Bus Exchange Lines. The bus exchange lines are used to transfer ownership from one bus master to another. Table 2.3 shows the exchange lines.

Bus busy (BUSY)* is driven by the master in control of the bus. All other masters monitor BUSY* to determine the state of the bus. BUSY* is a bidirectional signal, driven by an open-collector gate, and synchronized by BCLK*.

Bus priority in (BPRN)* is a nonbussed signal which indicates to a master that no master of a higher priority is requesting control of the bus. BPRN* is synchronized by BCLK*. In a serial priority scheme, BPRN* is the master's input from the priority chain. In a parallel resolution, BPRN* is the master's input from the parallel priority circuit.

Bus priority out (BPRO)* is a nonbussed signal that is activated by a master to indicate to the master of the next lower priority that it may gain control of the bus (i.e., no higher-priority requests are pending for control of the bus). This signal is used only in a daisy-chain serial priority resolution scheme, and

TABLE 2.3 Multibus I Bus Exchange Signals

Function	Signal
Bus request	BREQ*
Bus priority	BPRN*, BPRO*
Bus busy	BUSY*
Common bus request	CBRQ*

should be connected to the bus priority in (BPRN*) input of the next lower-priority bus master. BPRO* is synchronized by BCLK*. Each bus master must have the capability to allow its BPRO* signal to be disconnected from the BPRO* line on the backplane so that, if desired, a parallel priority resolution scheme can be used. This capability allows some bus masters to have their BPRN* inputs driven by a central parallel resolution circuit instead of driven by the BPRO* of the next higher-priority master.

Bus request (BREQ)* is used with the parallel priority resolution scheme and is a request of the master for bus control. The priorities of the BREQ* from each master are resolved in a parallel priority resolution circuit. The highest-priority request enables the BPRN* input of that master, allowing it to gain control of the bus. BREQ* is synchronized by BCLK*.

Common bus request (CBREQ)* is an optional signal that can be activated by any master that wants control of the bus. If CBREQ* is inactive, it indicates to the current bus master that no other request is pending and therefore bus control need not be relinquished. There are times when this can save the bus exchange overhead for the current master. This is because when a master is controlling the bus, quite often there are no other masters that are requesting the bus. Without CBREQ*, only BRPN* indicates whether or not another master is requesting the bus, and BPRN* is only active if the requesting master is of higher priority. Between the master's bus transfer cycles, in order to allow lower-priority masters to take the bus if they need it, the master must give up the bus. At the start of the master's next transfer cycle, the bus must be regained. If no other master has the bus, this can take approximately three BCLK* periods. To avoid this overhead of unnecessarily giving up and regaining the bus when no other masters need it, CBREQ* may be used. Any master that wants but does not have the bus must activate the line. The master that does have the bus can sense CBREQ* at the end of a transfer cycle. If CBREQ* is inactive, then the bus does not have to be released, thereby eliminating the delay of regaining the bus at the beginning of the next cycle. (At any time before the master's next cycle, any other master desiring the bus will drive CBREQ* and cause the master to relinquish the bus.) Masters that use CBREQ* must be able to disable the functions such that they can be used with masters that cannot use CBREQ*.

2.4.2.6 Data Transfer Operations. It is assumed in this discussion that there is only one master on the bus, and therefore no bus contention exists. (Bus exchange operations are discussed in Sec. 2.4.2.13.)

A data transfer is accomplished as follows. First the bus master places the memory address or I/O port address on the address lines. (If the operation is a write, the data would also be placed on the data lines at this time.) The bus master then generates a command (I/O read or write, or memory read or write), which activates the appropriate bus slave. The slave accepts the data if it is a write operation or places the data on the data lines if it is a read operation. A transfer acknowledge signal is then sent to the bus master by the bus slave, allowing the bus master to complete its cycle by removing the command from the command line and then clearing the address and data lines.

Read Operations. The read commands (MRDC* and IORC*) initiate the same basic type of operation. The only difference is that MRDC* indicates that the memory address is valid on the address lines, whereas IORC* indicates that the I/O port address is valid on the address lines. The address (memory or I/O

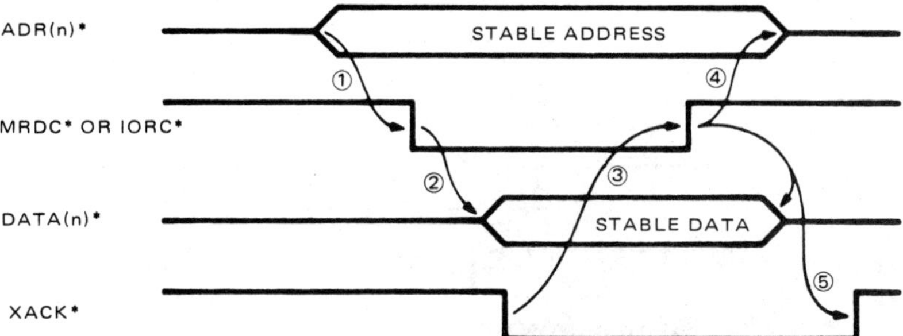

① ADDRESS SETUP TIME: 50 ns MINIMUM.

② TIME REQUIRED FOR SLAVE TO GET DATA ONTO BUS IN ACCORDANCE WITH SETUP TIME REQUIREMENT. XACK* CAN BE ASSERTED AS SOON AS DATA IS ON BUS.

③ TIME REQUIRED FOR MASTER TO REMOVE COMMAND.

④ ADDRESS AND DATA HOLD TIME: 50 ns MINIMUM

⑤ XACK* AND DATA MUST BE REMOVED FROM THE BUS A MAXIMUM OF 65 ns AFTER THE COMMAND IS REMOVED.

FIGURE 2.5 Multibus I memory or I/O read timing.

port) must be valid on the bus 50 ns prior to the read command being generated. When the read command is generated, the slave module (memory or I/O port) places the data on the data lines and returns a transfer acknowledge (XACK*) signal indicating that the data is on the bus. When the bus master receives the acknowledge, it strobes in the data and removes the command (MRDC* or IORC*) from the bus. The command signal must remain active for a minimum of 100 ns. The slave address (memory or I/O port) remains valid on the bus a minimum of 60 ns after the read command is removed. XACK* must be removed from the bus within 65 ns after the command is removed to allow for the next bus cycle. Figure 2.5 shows the timing for the memory read or I/O read command.

Write Operations. The write commands (MWTC* and IOWC*) initiate the same basic type of operation. MWTC* indicates that the memory address is valid on the address lines, whereas IOWC* indicates that the I/O port address is valid on the address lines. The address (memory or I/O port) must be valid on the bus 50 ns prior to the write command being generated. This requirement allows data to be latched on either the leading or trailing edge of the command. When the write command is generated, the data on the data lines is stable and can be accepted by the slave. The slave indicates acceptance of the data by returning a transfer acknowledge (XACK*) signal, allowing the bus master to remove the command, address, and data from the bus. The command signal must remain active for a minimum of 100 ns. XACK* must be removed from the bus within 65 ns after the command is removed to allow for the next bus cycle. Figure 2.6 shows the timing for the memory write or I/O write command.

2.4.2.7 Bus Time-outs. The asynchronous nature of the Multibus I interface permits data transfer operations to be extended to accommodate slower slaves. However, the system should be protected against the possibility of a data transfer extending indefinitely. If a bus master specifies an address that refers to a non-

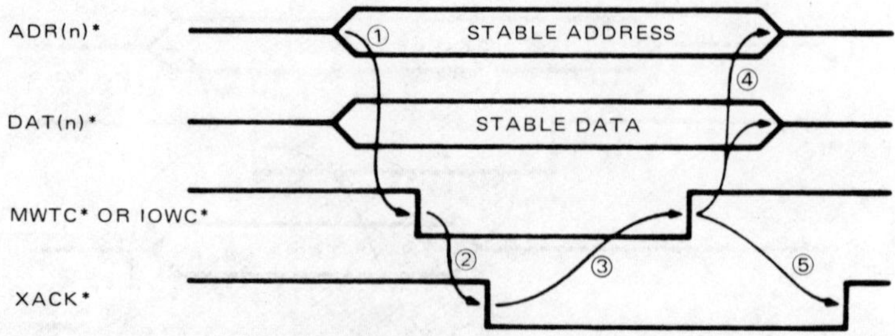

① ADDRESS AND DATA SETUP: 50 ns MINIMUM.
② TIME REQUIRED FOR SLAVE TO ACCEPT DATA.
③ TIME REQUIRED FOR MASTER TO REMOVE COMMAND FROM BUS.
④ ADDRESS AND DATA HOLD TIME: 50 ns MINIMUM.
⑤ XACK* MUST BE OFF THE BUS 65 ns AFTER COMMAND

FIGURE 2.6 Multibus I memory or I/O write timing.

existent or malfunctioning slave module, the transfer acknowledge signal will not be returned to the master. If this should occur without protection, the bus master would wait indefinitely for an acknowledge. A bus time-out function can be implemented on a bus master to terminate a bus cycle after a preset interval, even if no acknowledge has been received. The minimum allowable bus time-out interval is 1.0 ms.

2.4.2.8 Inhibit Operations. The inhibit lines can be invoked for any memory read or memory write operation (MRDC* or MWTC*). An inhibit line is asserted by a slave to inhibit another slave's bus activity during a memory read or write operation. The inhibit signal generated by the inhibiting slave is derived from decoding the memory address lines.

When inhibited, the slave module disables its drivers from the bus lines, although it may perform internal operations. A module issuing an inhibit signal cannot return the transfer acknowledge signal (XACK*) in less than 1.5 μs. This long delay is to give the inhibited slave 1.5 μs to complete its internal operations.

Use of inhibit signals during memory read operations must cause no adverse effect within the inhibited slave module; that is, data shall not be altered, and status registers shall not be affected.

Use of inhibit signals during memory write operations may or may not affect the data within the inhibited slave module. No data other than that located at the bus address shall be affected.

An inhibit signal must be generated within 100 ns of a stable address. A command may be generated as early as 50 ns after the address is stable. This timing can cause the inhibit to occur after the command has been received by the inhibited module. To prevent false acknowledges, modules that can be inhibited must not generate an acknowlege until the inhibit signals have had time to become valid (50 ns after the command).

There are two inhibit signals (INH1* and INH2*) that allow three priorities of modules to generate inhibit or be inhibited. The inhibit capabilities of Multibus I are designed to allow situations where RAM and ROM have the same address, such as diagnostics. Inhibit commands are not widely used during a normal oper-

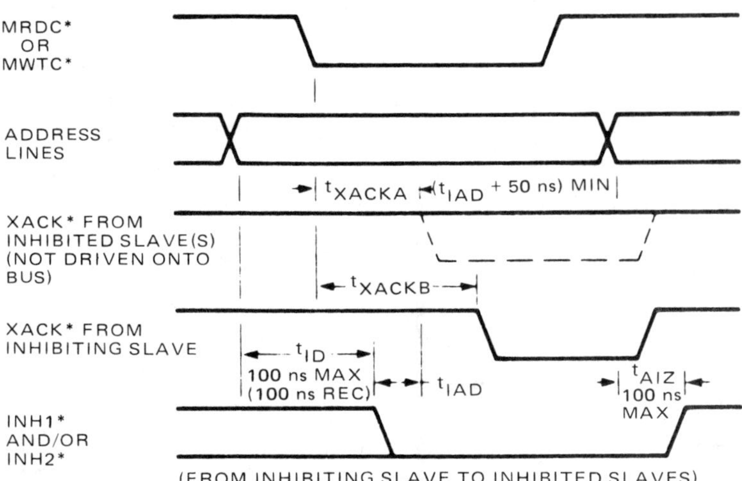

FIGURE 2.7 Multibus I inhibit timing.

ation, primarily because system performance is likely to suffer as a result of the timing imposed by inhibit operations.

Figure 2.7 shows the timing for an inhibit operation.

2.4.2.9 Data Transfers Between 8- and 16-Bit Modules. The Multibus I specification supports boards with 8- or 16-bit external data paths. Both 16- and 8-bit transfers can be accomplished by using only lines DAT0*–DAT7* (with DAT0* being the least significant bit).

There are three types of transfers that take place across the bus:

1. Transfer of an even byte on DAT0*–DAT7*
2. Transfer of an odd byte on DAT0*–DAT7*
3. Transfer of a 16-bit word

Figure 2.8 shows the data lines and the usage of these lines for the three types of transfers mentioned.

Two signals control the data transfers. The byte high enable (BHEN*) active signal indicates that the bus is operating in the 16-bit mode, and the address bit 0 (ADR0*) defines an even-byte or odd-byte transfer.

For an even-byte transfer, BHEN* and ADR0* are both inactive. The transfer takes place across data lines DAT0*–DAT7*.

For an odd-byte transfer, BHEN* is inactive and ADR0* is active. On this type of transfer, the odd byte is transferred through the swap byte buffer to DAT0*–DAT7*. The odd byte is transferred on the bus using DAT0*–DAT7* to make 8- and 16-bit boards compatible.

For a 16-bit transfer, BHEN* is active and ADR0* is active. On this type of transfer, the even byte is transferred across the bus on DAT0*–DAT7* and the odd byte is transferred on DAT8*–DAT15*.

The Multibus I data lines are always driven by three-state drivers.

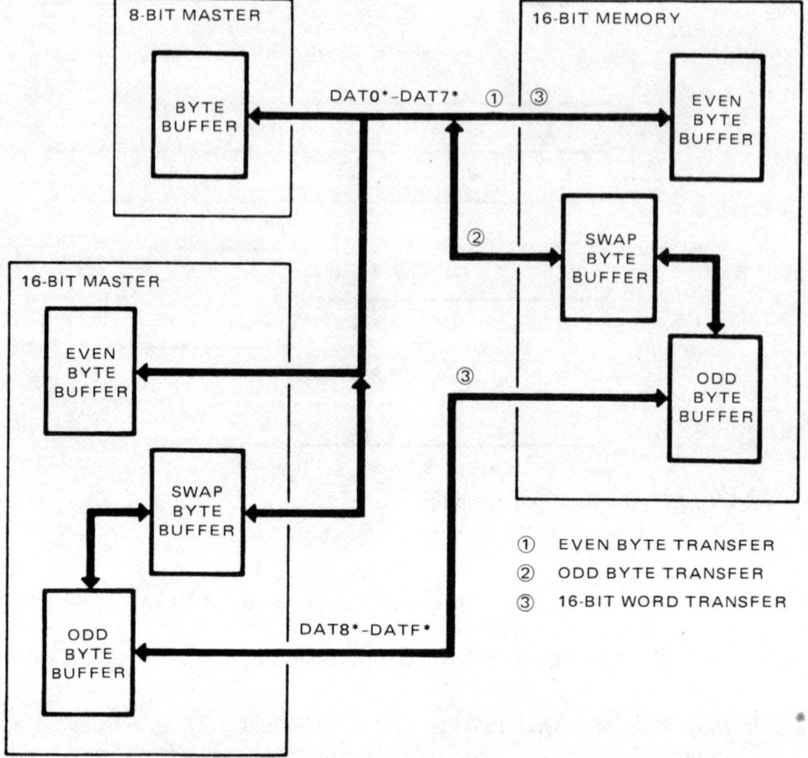

FIGURE 2.8 Multibus I data line usage.

2.4.2.10 Bus Performance. The maximum transfer rate for data can be calculated from the timing specifications for transferring data. The address must be set up for 50 ns before the control signal (MRDC*, IORC*, MWTC* or IOWC*) is activated. The control signal must remain active for 100 ns, and the address and data must be held for 50 ns after the control signal is made inactive. This means that the minimum time for a data transfer is 200 ns, which implies a maximum data rate of 10 Mbytes per second, with 16-bit transfers.

Since Multibus I is asynchronous, this maximum figure is not enforced upon the modules on the bus. A master or a slave can extend the time taken to transfer data, thus reducing the throughput. The maximum performance also reflects a burst situation, where the only bus activity is data transfer. In normal situations other activities such as bus exchange and interrupts are also using bus bandwith, so the system throughput will be somewhat less than the maximum data rate.

The highest-performance microprocessors would be constrained by the performance of Multibus I if instructions and data were to be transferred across the bus. More frequently the bus is used to transfer data such as information from a disk, normally by using DMA techniques to gain the maximum system throughput. (Bus utilization could be increased at the expense of *system* performance, if the system is not designed correctly.) When the rate of information flow required is greater than Multibus I can sustain, techniques such as the iLBX bus (described later) are used. However, the ability to integrate large amounts of memory on the CPU board has dramatically reduced the likelihood of overloading the bus.

2.4.2.11 Interrupt Operations. There are two types of interrupt implementation schemes: non-bus-vectored (NBV) and bus-vectored (BV).

Non-Bus-Vectored Interrupts. Non-bus-vectored interrupts are handled by the bus master without use of the bus for transfer of the interrupt vector address. The interrupt vector is generated by the interrupt controller on the master and transferred to the processor over the local bus. The source generating the interrupt can be on the master module or on other bus modules, in which case the interrupt request lines (INT0*–INT7*) are used to generate the interrupt requests to the bus master. When an interrupt request line is activated, the bus master performs its own interrupt operation and processes the interrupt. Figure 2.9 shows an example of NBV interrupt implementation.

Bus-Vectored Interrupts. Instead of the bus master determining the interrupt vector address locally, the bus master can interrogate the interrupting slave for the interrupt vector address. This process is called a bus-vectored interrupt.

When an interrupt request occurs, the interrupt control logic on the bus master interrupts its processor. The processor on the bus master generates the INT* command, freezing the state of the interrupt logic for priority resolution. The bus master also overrides the bus (retains the bus between bus cycles) to guarantee back-to-back bus cycles. After the first INT* command, the bus master's interrupt control logic puts an interrupt code on the bus address lines. This interrupt code is the address of the highest-priority active interrupt request line. At this point in the BV interrupt procedure, two different sequences can occur because the interrupt vector can be a one- or two-byte address, and hence the bus master must generate one or two further INTA* commands.

The second INTA* command causes the bus slave interrupt control logic to transmit the low-order byte (or the only byte) of its interrupt vector address on the bus data lines.

If there is a third INTA* command, the high-order byte of the interrupt vector address is placed on the bus data lines.

The interrupt vector address received from the slave is then used by the bus master to service the interrupt.

The Multibus I specification supports only one type of bus-vectored interrupt (two or three INTA* commands) in a single system. However, both bus-vectored and non-bus-vectored interrupts can exist within the same system. Figure 2.10 shows an example of the BV interrupt mechanism.

2.4.2.12 Flag Bytes. Flag bytes are not part of the Multibus I specification, and it is not necessary to understand them to grasp the Multibus I fundamentals. Nevertheless, flag bytes (whether known as flag bytes or by some other term) are in use in many Multibus I systems, and their use has some bearing on the interrupt capabilities achievable in a Multibus I system.

As described earlier, there are eight interrupt lines available on the Multibus I backplane. With the possibility of connecting multiple sources to the same line, or use of bus-vectored interrupts, the interrupt capabilities provide a good balance of speed and flexibility. Interrupt lines are normally used as inputs into the CPU boards, but many intelligent I/O boards utilize an interrupt technique for communications, albeit without dedicated interrupt lines.

The concept of the flag byte is that the action of writing to a location (I/O or memory) on a board can generate an interrupt to the processor on the same board.

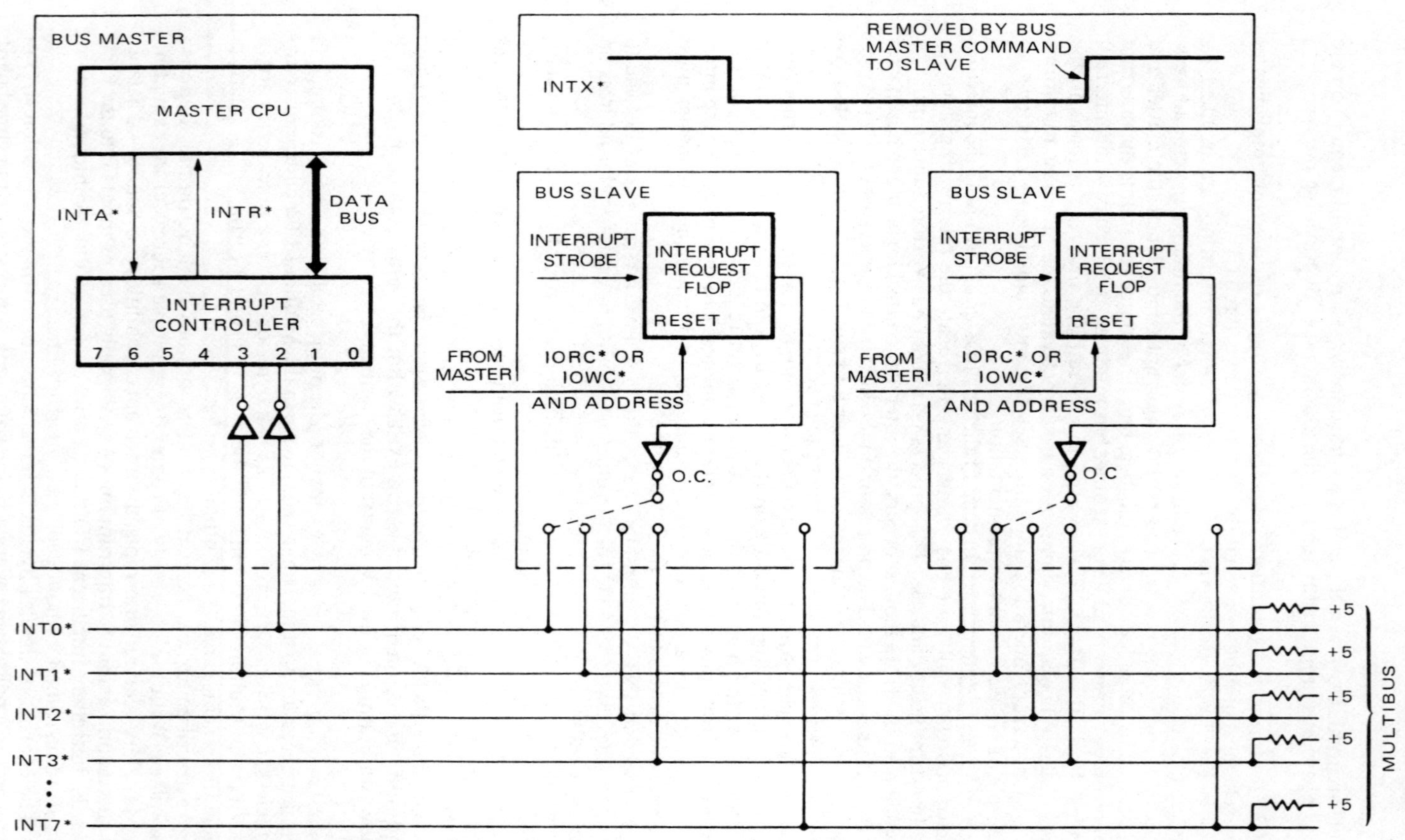

FIGURE 2.9 Non-bus-vectored (NBV) interrupt logic.

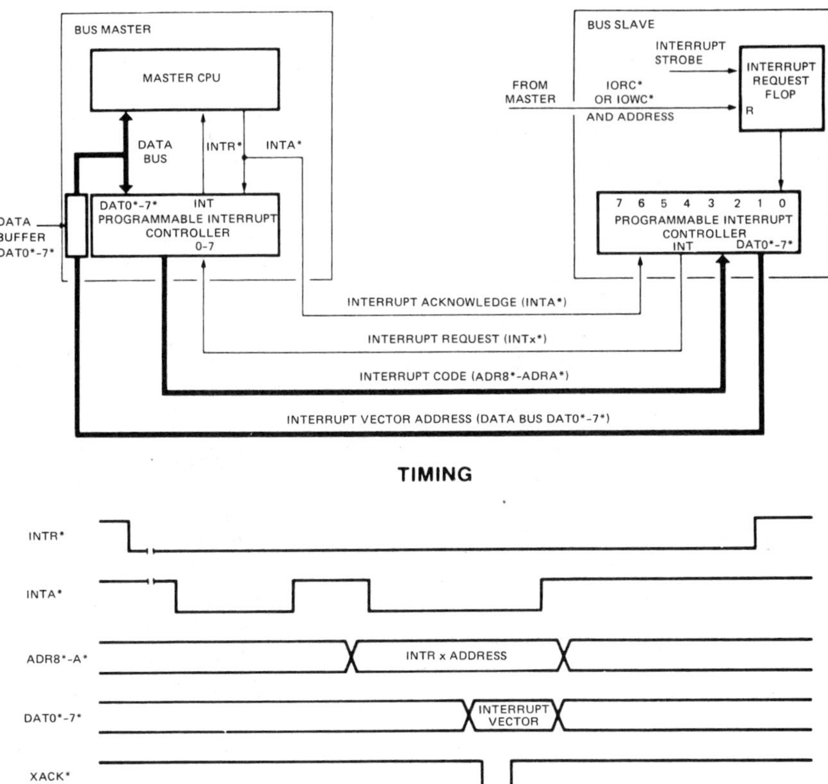

FIGURE 2.10 Bus-vectored (BV) interrupt logic.

This provides a mechanism to pass information such as parameters or commands to a peripheral controller.

2.4.2.13 Bus Exchange Operations. Multibus I systems can accommodate several bus masters in the same system, each taking control of the bus as it needs to effect data transfers. The bus masters request bus control through a bus exchange sequence.

Serial Priority Technique. Serial priority resolution is accomplished with a daisy-chain technique (see Fig. 2.11). With such a scheme, the bus priority out (BPRO*) of each master is connected to the bus priority in (BPRN*) of the next lower-priority master. The BPRN* signal of the highest-priority master in the serial chain shall either be always active or connected to a central bus arbiter as described in the next section. The latter connection would be used if a parallel-serial priority structure were used.

Serial priority is accomplished in the following manner. The BPRO* for a particular master is asserted if and only if its BPRN* input is active, and that master is not requesting control of the bus. Thus if a master requests control of the bus, it will set its BPRO* high, which in turn disables the BPRN* of all lower-priority masters. The number of masters that can be linked through a serial chain is lim-

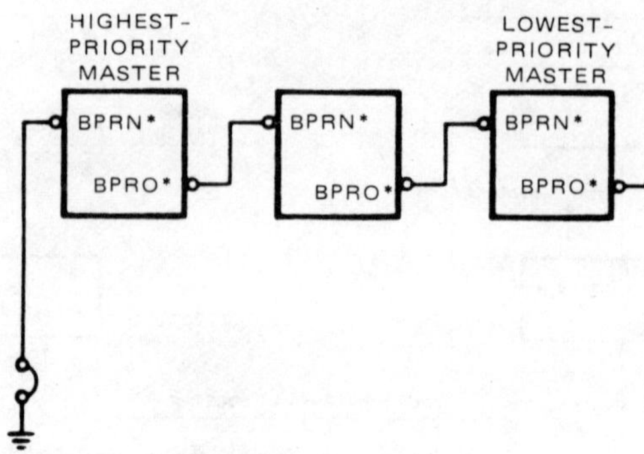

FIGURE 2.11 Serial priority technique.

ited by the fact that the BPRN* signal must propagate through the entire chain within one BCLK* cycle. For the maximum BCLK* frequency of 10 MHz, the number of masters in a serial chain is limited to three. Slowing down BCLK* would allow this number to be increased, but at the expense of a longer time for each bus exchange operation, and hence a reduction on overall throughput.

Parallel Priority Arbitration. In the parallel technique, the bus allocation is determined by a bus arbiter (see Fig. 2.12). This may be some priority scheme that determines the next master by a fixed priority structure or some other mechanism for allocation (e.g., sequential). The BREQ* lines are used by the arbiter to

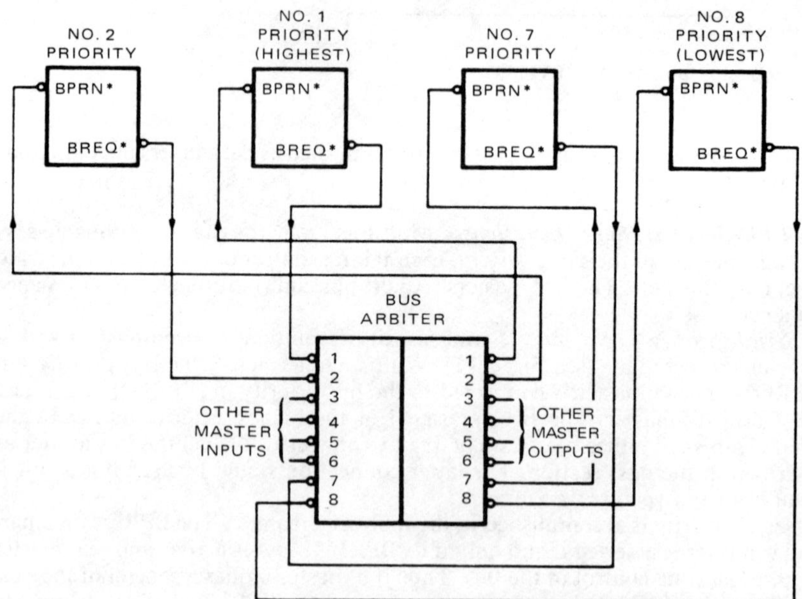

FIGURE 2.12 Parallel priority technique.

TABLE 2.4 Logical and Electrical State Relationships

Logical state	Electrical signal level	At receiver	At driver
	Active low signals (names end with *)		
0	H = TTL high state	5.25 V ≥ H ≥ 2.0 V	5.25 V ≥ H ≥ 2.4 V
1	L = TTL low state	0.8 V ≥ L ≥ −0.5 V	0.5 V ≥ L ≥ 0 V
	Active high signals (names do not end with *)		
0	L = TTL low state	0.8 V ≥ L ≥ −0.5 V	0.5 V ≥ L ≥ 0 V
1	H = TTL high state	5.25 V ≥ H ≥ 2.0 V	5.25 V ≥ H ≥ 2.4 V

signal the next master on the appropriate BPRN* line. The BPRO* lines are not used in the parallel allocation BPRN* scheme.

A parallel bus arbiter would normally be designed into the backplane.

2.4.3 Electrical Specifications

This section describes some of the additional electrical requirements for the Multibus I specification. For complete electrical specifications, including timing information, refer to the IEEE 796 specification or the other publications mentioned in the Bibliography.

2.4.3.1 Logical and Electrical State Relationships. All signals on the Multibus I backplane are active low. The logical-electrical state relationship is shown in Table 2.4.

2.4.3.2 Rise and Fall Times. Rise and fall times of the signals depend on which type of drivers are in use (as specified in Table 2.6). Rise and fall times for the specified devices are shown in Table 2.5.

2.4.3.3 Maximum Signal Propagation. The maximum signal propagation on the bus is 3 ns measured from the edge of one board plugged into the backplane to the edge of any other board plugged into the backplane.

2.4.3.4 Receivers, Drivers, and Terminations. Nontiming specifications unique to each signal line or to groups of signal lines are presented in Table 2.6. The requirements for the signal line receivers, drivers, and bus terminations, and the locations of the receiver, driver, and termination for each signal are given.

TABLE 2.5 Rise and Fall Times

	Open collector	Totem pole	Tristate
Rise time		10 ns	10 ns
Fall time	10 ns	10 ns	10 ns

TABLE 2.6 Bus Drivers, Receivers, and Terminations

	Driver[a]						Receiver[b]				Termination[c]			
Bus signals	Location	Type	I_{OL} min (mA)	I_{OH} min (μs)	I_{OH} max (μs)	C_O min (pF)	Location	I_{IL} max (mA)	I_{IH} max (μs)	C_I max (pF)	Location[d]	Type	R	Units
DAT0*–DATF* (16 lines)	Masters and slaves	TRI	16	−2000		300	Masters and slaves	−0.8	125	18	1 place	Pullup	2.2	kΩ
ADR0*–ADR17* BHEN* (25 lines)	Masters	TRI	16	−2000		300	Slaves	−0.8	125	18	1 place	Pullup	2.2	kΩ
MRDC* MWTC*	Masters	TRI	32	−2000		300	Slaves (memory, memory-mapped I/O)	−2	125	18	1 place	Pullup	1	kΩ
IORC* IOWC*	Masters	TRI	32	−2000		300	Slaves (I/O)	−2	125	18	1 place	Pullup	1	kΩ
XACK*	Slaves	TRI	32	−400		300	Masters	−2	125	18	1 place	Pullup	510	Ω
INH1* INH2*	Inhibiting slaves	OC	16		250	300	Inhibited slaves (RAM, PROM, ROM, memory-mapped I/O)	−2	50	18	1 place	Pullup	1	kΩ
BCLK*	1 place (master usually)	TTL	48	−3000		300	Masters	−2	125	18	Motherboard	To +5 V To GND	220 330	Ω Ω
BREQ*	Each master	TTL	10	−200		60	Central priority module	−2	50	18	Central priority module (not req.)	Pullup	1	kΩ

BPRO*	Each master	TTL	3.2	−200		60	Next master in serial priority chain at its BPRN*	−3.2	100	18	Not req.			
BPRN*	Parallel: central priority module; Serial: previous masters BPRO*	TTL	3.2	−200		60	Masters	−3.2	100	18	Not req.			
LOCK*	Master	TRI	32	−2000		300	All	−2	125	18	1 place	Pullup	1	kΩ
BUSY* CBRQ*	All masters	OC	20		250	300	All masters	−2	50	18	1 place	Pullup	1	kΩ
INIT*	Master	OC	32		250	300	All	−2	50	18	1 place	Pullup	1	kΩ
CCLK*	1 place	TTL	48	−3000		300	Any	−2	125	18	Motherboard	To +5 V To GND	220 330	Ω Ω
INTA*	Masters	TRI	32	−2000		300	Slaves (interrupting I/O)	−2	125	18	1 place	Pullup	1	kΩ
INT0*–INT7* (8 lines)	Slaves	OC	16		260	300	Masters	−1.6	40	18	1 place	Pullup	1	kΩ

[a]Driver requirements:

I_{OH} = high-output current drive
I_{OL} = low-output current drive
C_O = capacitance drive capability
TRI = three-state drive
OC = open collector driver
TTL = totem-pole driver

[b]Receiver requirements:

I_{IH} = high-input current load
I_{IL} = low-input current load
C_I = capacitive load

[c]±5%, ¼ W resistors.
[d]All termination resistors specified as "1 piece" are typically located on the backplane.

TABLE 2.7 Power Supply Specifications

	Standards*			
Parameter	Ground	+5	+12	−12
Mnemonic	GND	+5 V	+12 V	−12 V
Bus pins	P1–1, 2, 11, 12, 75, 76, 85, 86	P1–3, 4, 5, 6, 81, 82, 83, 84	P1–7.8	P1–79.80
Tolerance†	Reference	±1%	±1%	±1%
Combined line and load regulation	Reference	4.9 to 5.2	11.8 to 12.5	−12.5 to −11.8
Ripple (peak to peak)‡	Reference	50 mV	50 mV	50 mV
Transient response (50% load change)		100 μs	100 μs	100 μs

*Point of measurement is at connection point between motherboard and power supply. At any card-edge connector a degradation of 2% maximum (e.g., voltage tolerance ±2%) is allowed.

†Includes line, load, temperature, and ripple effects.

‡At 5 MHz bandwidth.

2.4.3.5 Power Supply Specifications. Table 2.7 shows all power supply specifications.

2.4.3.6 Temperature and Humidity. Bus specifications should be met with temperature and humidity within the following ranges:

Temperature	0–55°C (32–150°F) with free-moving air across modules and bus
Relative humidity	90% maximum without condensation

This represents the standard environmental specification for the Multibus I architecture. It may be desirable to create more (or less) severe environmental restrictions in some applications.

2.4.4 Mechanical Specifications

This section covers briefly the mechanical aspects of Multibus I boards and systems. For a complete specification refer to the IEEE 796 specification or to the other publications mentioned in the Bibliography.

2.4.4.1 Backplane Considerations. The maximum length of the backplane connecting modules is 18 in. Extender boards used within the system will not be supported by the bus unless the overall resulting length of the bus including the extender board is less than the 18-in maximum.

2.4.4.2 Board-to-Board Relationships. The minimum board-to-board spacing is 0.6 in.

1. *Board-to-board spacing (L_c)*—center to center of boards when plugged into backplane must be at least 0.6 ± 0.02 in.

2. *Board thickness (L_T)*—the typical board thickness is 0.062 ± 0.005 in.
3. *Component lead length (L_L)*—the length of the component leads below the printed circuit board cannot exceed 0.093 in.
4. *Component height (L_H)*—the following equation is used to determine the maximum height of the components above the printed circuit board:

$$L_H < L_C - L_T - L_L$$

$$L_H < 0.58 \text{ in} - 0.067 \text{ in} - 0.093 \text{ in}$$

$$L_H < 0.420 \text{ in including board warpage}$$

Figure 2.13 shows these relationships.

In practice, many of the backplane and chassis products have interboard spacing greater than 0.6 in. Spacing of 0.75 or 0.8 in is common, and some products have different spacing for different slots. There are a number of reasons for this:

Sufficient cooling for high-performance devices is difficult to provide.

Use of iSBX Multimodules to modify the functionality of the basic CPU board increases the height of a board.

Modular memory to improve performance increases the height of a board.

Increasing the interboard spacing is perfectly acceptable within the IEEE 796 specification; however, the system designer should ensure consistency between the backplane and the intended board set.

Other factors to bear in mind when choosing a backplane are the ease of access to the backplane signals, whether for iLBX on connector P2 or for special arbitration, etc., and the quality of construction particularly in terms of ground planes and multilayering. As performance of Multibus I–based systems has increased, the demands placed on the backplane have also risen.

2.4.4.3 Multibus I Board Form Factors. Figure 2.14 shows the standard outline for Multibus I–compatible boards. The nonbus edge of the board is not restricted.

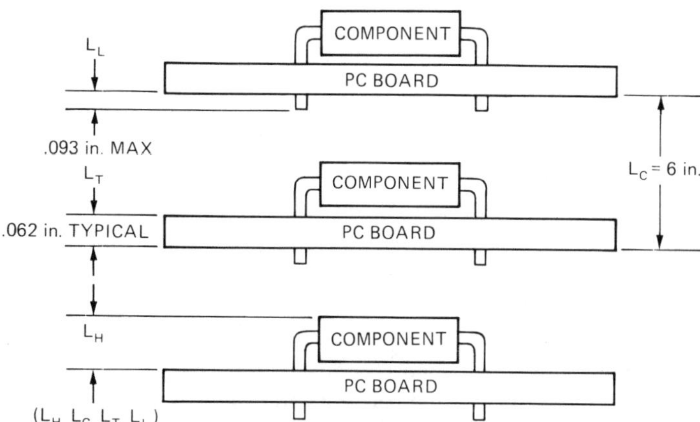

FIGURE 2.13 Multibus I backplane board to board specification.

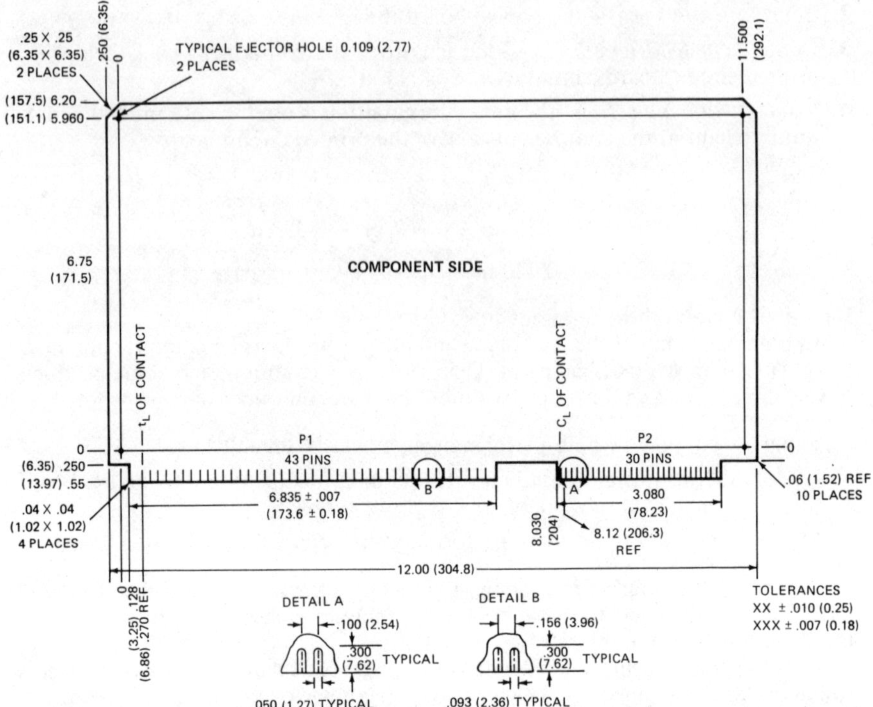

FIGURE 2.14 Multibus I standard board outline. Dimensions are in inches, with millimeters provided in parentheses for reference only; the inch measurements govern.

The remainder of the board including connectors P1 and P2 must adhere to the dimensions shown in Fig. 2.14.

Some boards conform to the Multibus I specifications in every way except the height of the board (the dimension from the backplane to the nonbus edge). While these boards are nonstandard, they have been used in situations where it was necessary to include more circuitry on a single board or to simplify the I/O connections. Designers of such systems are able to combine standard products with their own custom boards to gain the benefits of both.

2.4.4.4 Bus Connectors. The Multibus I backplane has connectors that mate to the P1 (43/86) board edge connector. The backplane uses 43/86 pins on 0.156-in center connectors.

The P2 connector is a 30/60-pin board edge connector with a 0.100-in center.

Edge connectors are numbered with odd-number pins on the component side of the board and in ascending order when going counterclockwise around the board.

2.4.4.5 Multibus I Edge Connector Assignments. Table 2.8 shows the signal and power assignments for the P1 connector on the printed circuit boards. Reserved signals on the P1 connector must be bussed as normal signal lines on the backplane. The wiring of the bus exchange lines (BPRO*, BPRN*, and BREQ*) is dependent on the priority scheme and implementation chosen. Table 2.9 shows the signal and power assignments for the P2 connector on the printed

TABLE 2.8 Multibus I Bus Signal Pin Assignments (P1)

	Component side			Circuit side		
	Pin	Mnemonic	Description	Pin	Mnemonic	Description
Power supplies	1	GND	Signal GND	2	GND	Signal GND
	3	+5 V	+5 V dc	4	+5 V	+5 V dc
	5	+5 V	+5 V dc	6	+5 V	+5 V dc
	7	+12 V	+12 V dc	8	+12 V	+12 V dc
	9		Reserved†, bussed	10		Reserved, bussed
	11	GND	Signal GND	12	GND	Signal GND
Bus controls	13	BCLK*	Bus clock	14	INIT*	Initialize
	15	BPRN*	Bus priority in	16	BPRO*	Bus priority out
	17	BUSY*	Bus busy	18	BREQ*	Bus request
	19	MRDC*	Memory read command	20	MWTC*	Memory write command
	21	IORC*	I/O read command	22	IOWC*	I/O write command
	23	XACK*	Transfer acknowledge	24	INH1*	Inhibit 1 (disable RAM)
Bus controls and address	25	LOCK*	Lock	26	INH2*	Inhibit 2 (disable PROM or ROM)
	27	BHEN*	Byte high enable	28	AD10*	
	29	CBRQ*	Common bus request	30	AD11*	Address
	31	CCLK*	Constant clock	32	AD12*	Bus
	33	INTA*	Interrupt acknowledge	34	AD13*	
Interrupts	35	INT6*	Parallel	36	INT7*	Parallel
	37	INT4*	Interrupt	38	INT5*	Interrupt
	39	INT2*	Requests	40	INT3*	Requests
	41	INT0*		42	INT1*	
Address	43	ADRE*	Address bus	44	ADRF	Address bus
	45	ADRC		46	ADRD*	
	47	ADRA*		48	ADRB*	
	49	ADR8*		50	ADR9*	
	51	ADR6*		52	ADR7*	
	53	ADR4*		54	ADR5*	
	55	ADR2*		56	ADR3*	
	57	ADR0*		58	ADR1*	
Data	59	DATA*	Data bus	60	DATF*	Data bus
	61	DATC*		62	DATD*	
	63	DATA*		64	DATB*	
	65	DAT8*		66	DAT9*	
	67	DAT6*		68	DAT7*	
	69	DAT4*		70	DAT5*	
	71	DAT2*		72	DAT3*	
	73	DAT0*		74	DAT1*	
Power supplies	75	GND	Signal GND	76	GND	Signal GND
	77		Reserved, bussed	78		Reserved, bussed
	79	−12 V	−12 V dc	80	−12 V	−12 V dc
	81	+5 V	+5 V dc	82	+5 V	+5 V dc
	83	+5 V	+5 V dc	84	+5 V	+5 V dc
	85	GND	Signal GND	86	GND	Signal GND

†All reserved pins are reserved for future use and should not be used if upwards compatibility is desired.

TABLE 2.9 Multibus I Bus Signal Pin Assignments (P2)

	Component side			Circuit side		
	Pin	Mnemonic	Description	Pin	Mnemonic	Description
	1		Reserved, not bussed	2		Reserved, not bussed
	3		Reserved, not bussed	4		Reserved, not bussed
	5		Reserved, not bussed	6		Reserved, not bussed
	7		Reserved, not bussed	8		Reserved, not bussed
	9		Reserved, not bussed	10		Reserved, not bussed
	11		Reserved, not bussed	12		Reserved, not bussed
	13		Reserved, not bussed	14		Reserved, not bussed
	15		Reserved, not bussed	16		Reserved, not bussed
	17		Reserved, not bussed	18		Reserved, not bussed
	19		Reserved, not bussed	20		Reserved, not bussed
	21		Reserved, not bussed	22		Reserved, not bussed
	23		Reserved, not bussed	24		Reserved, not bussed
	25		Reserved, not bussed	26		Reserved, not bussed
	27		Reserved, not bussed	28		Reserved, not bussed
	29		Reserved, not bussed	30		Reserved, not bussed
	31		Reserved, not bussed	32		Reserved, not bussed
	33		Reserved, not bussed	34		Reserved, not bussed
	35		Reserved, not bussed	36		Reserved, not bussed
	37		Reserved, not bussed	38		Reserved, not bussed
	39		Reserved, not bussed	40		Reserved, not bussed
	41		Reserved, bussed	42		Reserved, bussed
	43		Reserved, bussed	44		Reserved, bussed
	45		Reserved, bussed	46		Reserved, bussed
	47		Reserved, bussed	48		Reserved, bussed
	49		Reserved, bussed	50		Reserved, bussed
	51		Reserved, bussed	52		Reserved, bussed
	53		Reserved, bussed	54		Reserved, bussed
Address	55	ADR16*	Address bus	56	ADR17*	Address bus
	57	ADR14*		58	ADR15*	
	59		Reserved, bussed	60		Reserved, bussed

circuit boards. If a backplane is used then the *reserved and bussed* signals must be bussed as normal signal lines, and the *reserved but not bussed* signals shall have no connections. All of these reserved signals on P2 are used in the iLBX specification, as described later.

2.4.5 Compliance Levels

The Multibus I architecture was designed to allow systems to be constructed with boards of varying levels of capability. The IEEE 796 specification allows for variations in data path width, I/O address path width, and interrupt attributes. In addition, it is recognized that some vendor products have differing address path widths.

It is not necessary that all modules within a system have identical capabilities. One may, for instance, have a master with an 8- or 16-bit data path and a slave with an 8-bit data path. The system is completely functional, though the application must restrict itself to 8-bit access to the slave. In general, the microprocessors used in Multibus I–based systems mask such data path differences; some software and/or hardware configuration may be necessary for some of the other optional elements.

The key concept when constructing a Multibus I–based system is that of required capability versus supplied capability. Each product will provide some set of capabilities. A transaction between two such products will be restricted to use the capability that is the intersection of the sets of capability of the two products. It is the responsibility of the system designer to ensure the viability of this intersection.

2.4.5.1 Data Path. The Multibus I specification allows for both 8- and 16-bit data path products. The 16-bit data path products use the byte swapping technique described in Sec. 2.4.2.9, thus allowing the 8- and 16-bit modules to work together.

2.4.5.2 Memory Address Path. The Multibus specification designates a 24-bit address path. In many systems a 16-bit or 20-bit address path may be sufficient.

2.4.5.3 I/O Address Path. The Multibus specification allows for both 8- and 16-bit I/O address paths. Sixteen-bit path products must also be configurable to act as 8-bit path products.

2.4.5.4 Interrupt Attributes. As described in Sec. 2.4.2.11 the Multibus I specification allows for considerable variety in interrupt attributes. A product may support no interrupts, non-bus-vectored interrupts, two-cycle bus-vectored interrupts, and three-cycle bus-vectored interrupts. There are two methods of interrupt sensing: the preferred level-triggered, and for historical compatibility only, edge-level-triggered.

Level-triggered. The active level of the request line indicates an active request. Requiring no edge to trigger an interrupt allows several sources to be attached to a single request line. Sources for level-triggered sense inputs should provide a programmatic means to clear the interrupt request.

Edge-level-triggered. The transition from the inactive to the active level indicates an active request if and only if the active level is maintained at least until it has been recognized by the master. The requirement for a transition precludes multiple sources on a request line. However, edge-level-triggering removes the requirement that the source have a programmatic means to clear the interrupt request. (Note: Edge-level-triggering is only included for historical compatibility. New designs use level-triggered interrupt sensing.)

2.4.6 Range of Products Available

The range of Multibus I–based modules available today is immense. It is a tribute to the effectiveness of the concept and implementation of the Multibus I standard that many of these products have been available for over ten years. There are over 175 suppliers of Multibus I products listed in the latest issue of the *Multibus Buyers Guide.* Some of the suppliers are technology specialists, applying their expertise in, for instance, peripheral controllers to produce products on different standard buses. Other suppliers have a full range of Multibus I products and are able to supply most of the modules for an entire design.

Designs based on Multibus I modules have very long lifetimes, and so the modules that are used to build a system continue to be available. Thus there are still CPU boards with Z80A and 8080 microprocessors. These tend to be fairly simple boards with limited memory, as befitted the technology available when they were first designed. At the other end of the spectrum are powerful single-board computers with upwards of four millions of instructions per second (MIPS) performance, based on the 386 and 68030 microprocessors. The latest CPU boards have access to large amounts of memory and also various I/O interfaces ranging from simple serial interfaces to small computer system interface (SCSI) disk controllers on-board.

Memory technology spans a wide range, from battery-backed-up static RAM (SRAM), to EPROM and flash memory, to 8-Mbyte dynamic RAM (DRAM) boards. In addition to full-sized Multibus boards, there are also many boards that can be used to upgrade the memory on a CPU board.

Peripheral technology covers all the popular interfaces: ST506, QIC-02, ESDI, SCSI, SMD, SA450, etc. Many of the more modern peripheral controllers use microprocessors on-board to increase the performance of the system by taking high-level commands and by doing disk caching without involving the CPU. The higher-performance boards are bus masters, using DMA techniques to move information from a disk to memory.

Serial interface products on Multibus I boards range from multiple simple RS232 connections to intelligent communication controllers used to connect to wide area networks.

Around 2000 different products are available to give the Multibus I designer flexibility and choice, including analog and digital I/O (some designed for industrial connections), video controllers, backplanes, chassis products, etc.

2.5 The iLBX LOCAL BUS EXTENSION

The iLBX local bus extension is discussed here for two reasons. Originally defined as an extension to the Multibus I architecture for off-board memory when microprocessor memory speed demand first exceeded the Multibus bandwidth, the iLBX bus is used for execution memory. In addition, the iLBX interface has been used to provide a fast memory-mapped I/O interface, both for commercial products such as frame grabbers and also for custom I/O boards. Since the details of iLBX bus specification are primarily of interest to those designing boards rather than those designing systems based around the Multibus I architecture, this section is only a brief outline. More details will be found in the publications mentioned in the Bibliography.

2.5.1 History and Purpose of the iLBX Specification

When the Multibus I specification was first produced the microprocessors of the time had memory bandwidth requirements much lower than the 10 Mbytes/s achievable on the Multibus I backplane. It was natural to have main system memory on boards separate from the CPU. Component technology and manufacturing capabilities matched because it was difficult to create a highly integrated CPU board. Even in a multiple-CPU system, which was rare at the time, it was virtually impossible to saturate the backplane.

Initially, the demands for bandwidth were handled easily. The bus bandwidth was still adequate for most needs, and as memory technology improved it became possible to put more memory on a CPU board.

As the speeds of microprocessors increased, so did the demands for memory bandwidth. Complexity of applications also increased, so multiple-microprocessor systems became more common. A single microprocessor would soon be able to saturate the bus, even without any other masters consuming bus bandwidth. Memory size demands also increased, beyond what could be reasonably accommodated on a CPU board. This was the original reason for the iLBX specification.

Later on, memory technology and manufacturing capability began to catch up. The highest performance was achieved with a local 32-bit bus on a CPU board, accessing large amounts of surface-mounted DRAM. The iLBX bus remains useful for those designers who desire a fast memory-mapped interface.

2.5.2 General Description

The iLBX bus configuration uses the form factor of the standard Multibus I P2 connector. It occupies 56 of the P2 connector pins (55 defined signal lines and one reserved signal line). The four Multibus I address lines (pins 55 through 58) on the P2 connector retain the standard Multibus interface functions. Thus use of the iLBX specification is totally compatible with the Multibus I standard.

The iLBX bus is designed for direct high-speed master-slave data transfers and provides the following features:

A minimum of two and up to five devices can be connected over the iLBX bus.

The maximum length of an iLBX bus backplane is 10 cm (approximately 4 in).

Two (maximum) masters can share the bus, limiting the need for complex bus arbitration.

Bus arbitration is asynchronous to the data transfers.

Slave devices are defined as byte-addressed memory resources.

Slave device functions are directly controlled from iLBX bus signal lines.

Assuming 16-bit data transfers, a throughput of 19 Mbytes/s is achievable.

As can be seen from the maximum length of the backplane, the iLBX bus normally forms only part of a Multibus I system. The actual iLBX backplane can be implemented with ribbon cable or can be a rigid P2 connection formed with the main P1 backplane. Manufacturers of backplanes and card cages offer various different configurations to suit all needs.

2.6 THE iSBX EXPANSION I/O BUS (IEEE 959 SPECIFICATION)

2.6.1 Purpose

The iSBX bus concept was designed to allow low-cost flexible I/O expansion for computer boards. The iSBX specification was originally defined for use as an expansion capability for Multibus I boards, but has been implemented on many other buses.

The original purpose was to allow a board or system to be configured, with a lower level of granularity and cost than full-sized boards could offer, for differing I/O capabilities; in addition to I/O products, many manufacturers offer specialized memory capabilities using iSBX MULTIMODULES for such things as battery-backed-up SRAM.

In addition to purchasing standard products from the various vendors of iSBX MULTIMODULES, many system designers develop custom expansion modules. Using custom expansion modules is a simple way of introducing a specialized I/O capability to a design; because of the ability to use an iSBX module on a CPU board, it is possible to create a high-performance I/O capability without designing an entire board.

Most iSBX connectors are located on the CPU boards in an application. However, iSBX connectors are also found on high-performance peripherals to allow peripheral expansion, and also on simple I/O boards or dedicated iSBX expansion boards. The complete iSBX specification is most likely to be fully supported on the CPU boards, but lower compliance on other baseboards may well be adequate for simple, low-cost I/O expansion.

2.6.2 iSBX Bus Elements

There are two basic elements in the iSBX bus: the baseboard and the expansion module.

2.6.2.1 The Baseboard. A baseboard is any board that provides one or more I/O expansion interfaces (connectors) that meet the electrical and mechanical requirements of the iSBX specification. Logically, the baseboard is always the

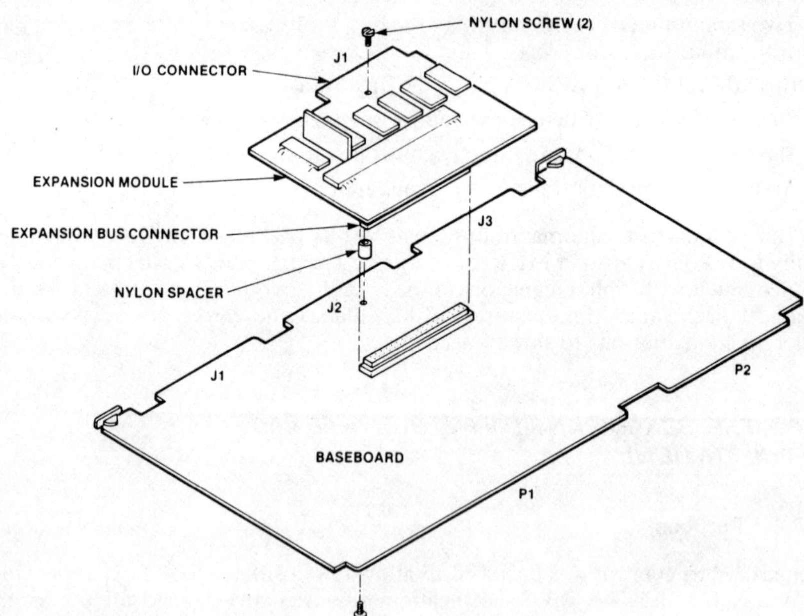

FIGURE 2.15 iSBX single-width expansion module on board.

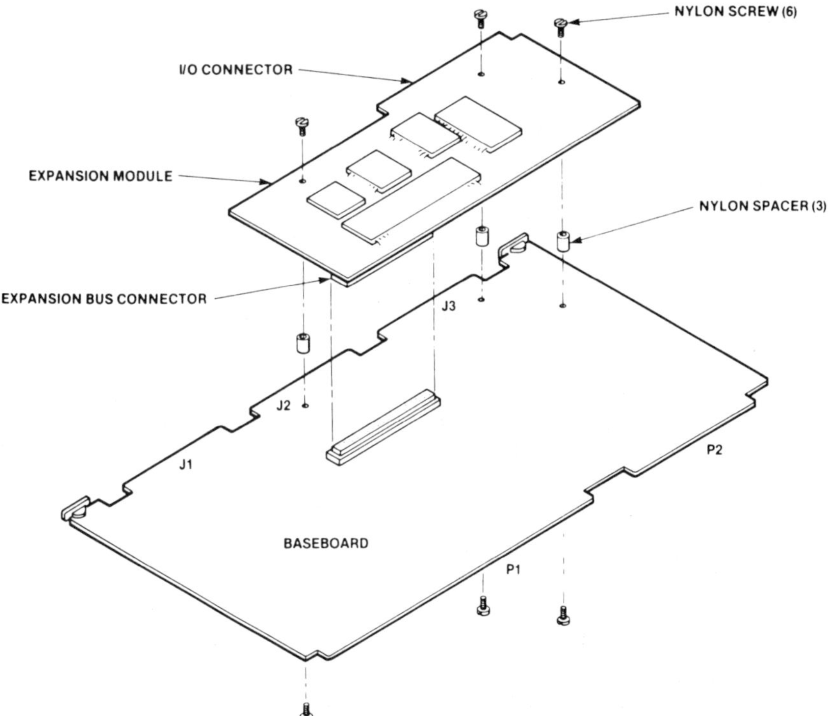

FIGURE 2.16 iSBX double-width expansion module on board.

master device, making it responsible for generating all addresses, chip selects, and commands. As a master device for DMA transfers, the baseboard is required to provide the DMA controller function (if DMA is needed). Mechanically, the baseboard shall supply the connector(s) and mounting hole(s) for attaching the expansion module with nylon screws and spacers. See Figs. 2.15 and 2.16 for mounting details. The baseboard typically views the devices on the iSBX expansion module as I/O devices; in many cases the interface is the same as if the devices were mounted directly on the baseboard.

2.6.2.2 The Expansion Module. An expansion module (or MULTIMODULE) is a small specialized board that attaches to a baseboard. Each expansion module can be one of two standard sizes: single width and double width. The modules are shown in Figs. 2.15 and 2.16. The purpose of an expansion module is to provide specialized functionality to the baseboard; an example of this would be an RS232 serial interface module. The iSBX bus is specifically designed to simplify the expansion module interface. In many cases peripheral components can connect directly to the iSBX interface bus.

2.6.3 iSBX Bus Signals

The iSBX bus signals can be grouped into seven classes based on the functions they perform.

2.6.3.1 Address and Chip-Select Lines. The function of these lines is different from most bus specifications. A typical bus would simply have address lines and require the slave device to create its own chip selects. The iSBX bus requires the baseboard to generate chip selects. This feature simplifies the expansion modules with only minimal impact to the baseboard.

Address lines (MA0, MA1, MA2). The address lines are active high signals generated by the baseboard from the low-order address lines. MA0 is the least significant address bit. For an 8-bit baseboard, these lines connect directly the least significant address bits A0, A1, and A2. For a 16-bit baseboard, the address line connections are MA1 to A1, MA1 to A2, and MA2 to A3 (A0 is used along with byte high enable to control byte or word transfers). During DMA operations, the state of the address lines is undefined.

Chip selects (MCS0, MCS1*).* The chip selects are active low signals generated by the baseboard to enable communication with the expansion module. These lines may undergo a transition when they are not required to be valid. It is the responsibility of the expansion module to qualify the chip-select signals with commands (note that this is done internally in many components). Chip selects will remain high during a DMA operation.

The chip-select lines are defined differently for 8- and 16-bit baseboards, as shown in Fig. 2.17. For 8-bit baseboards, each chip select enables eight consecutive ports as specified by the three address lines. For 16-bit baseboards, there are two cases: 8-bit expansion module and 16-bit expansion module. For a 16-bit baseboard driving an 8-bit expansion module, the chip-select operation is similar to the 8-bit baseboard. The 8-bit expansion module connects to the low byte on the data bus, which makes it only accessible through even-port addresses (odd-

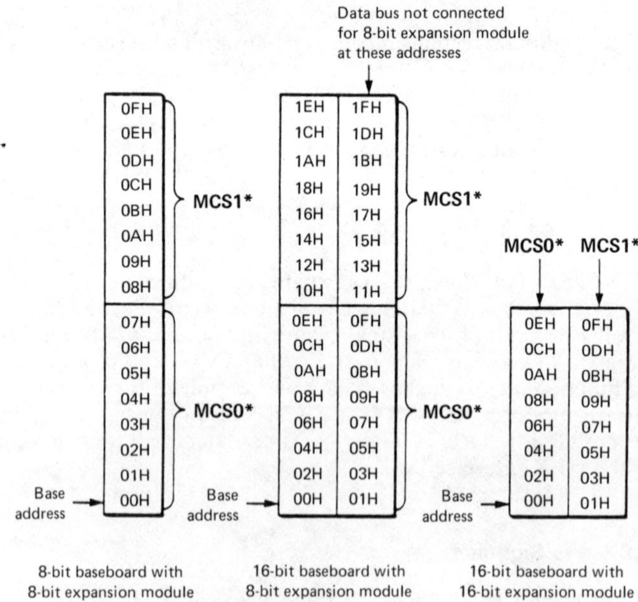

FIGURE 2.17 iSBX chip-select address ranges.

TABLE 2.10 iSBX Data Bus Functions for Different Configurations

Configuration	Lines used	
	MD0–MD7	MD8–MD15
8-bit baseboard	X	
16-bit baseboard with		
8-bit expansion module	X	
16-bit expansion module—even byte	X	
16-bit expansion module—odd byte		X
16-bit expansion module—word	X	X

port addresses transfer over the high byte). Each chip select therefore enables eight consecutive even ports as defined by the three address lines.

The chip selects on a 16-bit baseboard with a 16-bit expansion module have two functions. In addition to enabling communication, they control high-byte, low-byte, and word transfer modes. MCS0* is used to enable a low-byte transfer (even ports), MCS1* is used to enable a high-byte transfer (odd ports), and both are used for a word transfer. The three address lines determine which of eight 16-bit ports are being addressed.

2.6.3.2 Data Lines. The data lines are used to transmit or receive data to or from the expansion module ports. The 16 active high, bidirectional lines are organized in two groups (bytes) of eight lines each. The low-byte group (MD0+MD7) is used for all transfers on 8-bit baseboards and for all even-byte transfers on 16-bit baseboards. MD0 is the least significant bit of this byte. The high-byte group (MD8–MD15) is used for all odd-byte transfers on 16-bit baseboards. MD8 is the least significant bit of this byte. Table 2.10 shows a summary of the data bus functions for different configurations.

2.6.3.3 Control Lines. Table 2.11 shows the iSBX control lines.

Command lines (IORD, IOWRT*).* The command lines are active low signals generated by the baseboard. An active command line indicates to the expansion board that the address and chip-select lines are valid and that the selected expansion module (i.e., one with active chip select) should perform the specified operation. The I/O read operation (IORD*) is used by the base-

TABLE 2.11 iSBX Control Lines

Class	Function	Signal
Commands	I/O read	IORD*
	I/O write	IOWRT*
Direct memory access (DMA)	DMA request	MDRQT
	DMA acknowledge	MDACK*
	Terminate DMA	TDMA
Initialize	Reset	RESET
Clock	Expansion module clock	MCLK
System control	Expansion module wait	MWAIT*
	Expansion module present	MPST*

board to request data to be transferred from the expansion module. The I/O write command (IOWRT*) is used by the baseboard to transfer data to the expansion module.

Direct memory access lines (MDRQT, MDACK, TDMA).* The DMA lines control the communication link between a DMA controller on the baseboard and expansion module. The use of these lines is optional on both the baseboard and the expansion module.

The DMA request line (MDRQT) is an active high signal generated by the expansion module to request that a DMA cycle be initiated by the baseboard. Upon receipt of this signal, the DMA controller begins arbitration for the baseboard's local bus.

The DMA acknowledge line (MDACK)* is an active low signal generated by the baseboard to indicate that a DMA operation has been granted (DMA controller has the bus). Like a chip select, this signal may undergo a transition when not valid and shall therefore be qualified by commands on the expansion module.

Terminate DMA (TDMA) is an active high, two-directional DMA control signal. The specific direction shall be determined by configuration (i.e., jumper or three-state driver); once configured, TDMA may only operate in one direction. When generated by the expansion modules, TDMA is used to terminate the DMA transfer. When generated by the baseboard, TDMA is used to signal the end of a DMA transfer to the expansion module. Baseboards that support DMA shall be configurable to support TDMA in either direction. An expansion module may support or not support TDMA, as required.

Initialize (RESET) is an active high signal generated by the baseboard to put the expansion module into a know state. The baseboard shall generate a power-up reset (50 ms minimum width) when power is applied. During normal operation after a power-up reset sequence, the expansion modules may be reinitialized with a standard reset signal (50-s width).

Expansion module clock (MCLK) is a general purpose timing signal (9–10 MHz) that is generated by the baseboard; MCLK is asynchronous to all other iSBX bus signals.

Expansion module wait (MWAIT)* is an active low signal that is generated by the expansion module to extend the current data transfer operations. While MWAIT* is activated, the baseboard is forced to insert wait states into the current bus cycle, allowing the expansion module more time to complete the requested operation. The MWAIT* signal is generated or enabled by a combination of valid chip select(s) and addresses or by a valid DMA acknowledge signal. As these lines change MWAIT* may undergo a transition; however, it shall be stable no later than 75 ns after MCS0*, MCS1*, and MDACK* become stable.

Recognition of the MWAIT* signal by the baseboard is optional; however, it is strongly recommended. Only in cases where the process does not support the signal should it be omitted, as it will limit the number of modules that are compatible with the baseboard. Baseboards that do not support the use of the MWAIT* signal may perform only the full-speed operations as defined in Secs. 2.6.4.1 and 2.6.4.2. When it supports the MWAIT* signal, the baseboard shall guarantee (usually via a pull-up resistor) that the signal is inactive if not connected. Expansion modules shall support the MWAIT* signal if they cannot meet the full-speed operation specifications.

Expansion module present (MPST)* is an active low signal driven by the expansion module to inform the baseboard that the expansion module is present. Typically this signal is connected to ground on the expansion module and to decode logic on the baseboard. When the signal is not activated, the I/O address space normally reserved for the expansion module may be used elsewhere. One application of the MPST* signal is to allow an older product that did not include support for iSBX connectors to be upgraded with a new baseboard that includes iSBX capability. Without expansion modules, the I/O addressing for the new baseboard looks the same as that of the old one. If the new baseboard requires expansion modules, they can be added and their presence recognized by an active MPST* signal.

2.6.3.4 Interrupt Lines (MINTR0, MINTR1). These active high lines are driven by the expansion module to indicate an interrupt request to the baseboard. An interrupt line shall remain active until the baseboard services it. These lines are asynchronous to all other bus signals.

2.6.3.5 Option Lines. The option lines (OPT0, OPT1) are user defined. Their purpose is to provide connections for any unique system requirements. Examples would be to allow additional interrupt lines or another DMA channel. Baseboards shall connect these lines to wire-wrap posts for configurability.

2.6.3.6 Power Lines. All baseboards shall be capable of supplying +5 V dc at 3 A and ±12 V dc at 1 A.

2.6.4 Bus Operations

The iSBX bus supports I/O read, I/O write, DMA, and interrupt operations.

2.6.4.1 I/O Read Operations. There are two types of I/O read operations on the iSBX bus: the full-speed I/O read and the interlocked I/O read. Whether or not the expansion module generates the MWAIT* signal determines which type of operation is performed.

Figure 2.18 shows the full-speed I/O read operation. The baseboard generates

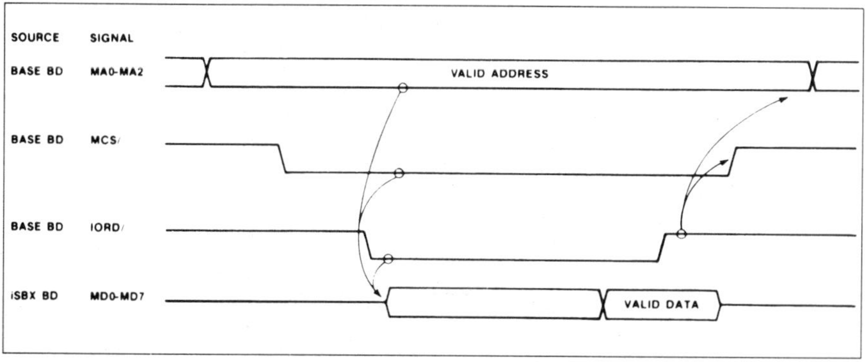

FIGURE 2.18 Full-speed I/O read operation.

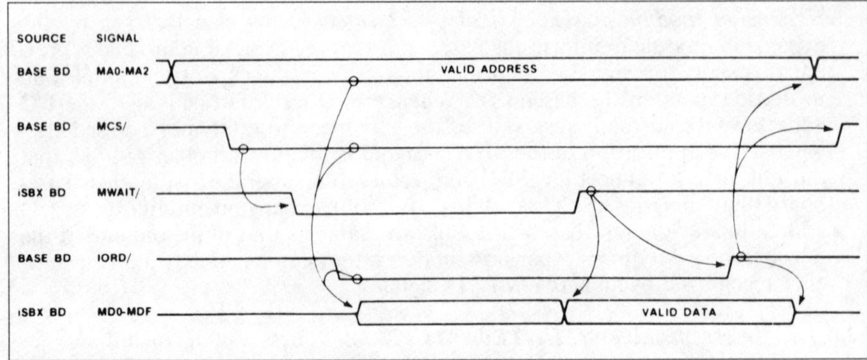

FIGURE 2.19 Interlocked I/O read operation

a valid address and chip select for the expansion module to initiate the operation. After the setup times are met, the baseboard activates the IORD* signal for a minimum of 300 ns. The expansion module shall generate valid data from the addressed I/O port within 250 ns after the IORD* line is activated. The baseboard then reads the data and deactivates the IORD* line. The baseboard is then free to change the address and chip-select lines for the next operation.

Figure 2.19 shows the interlocked I/O read operations. The baseboard initiates the operation by generating a valid address and chip select, just as in the full-speed I/O read. The expansion module then activates the MWAIT* signal, which in turn inhibits the ready signal to the baseboard microprocessor. The baseboard will activate the IORD* line and insert wait states as long as the MWAIT* signal from the expansion module is active. The expansion module will remove the MWAIT* signal when data is valid on the bus. The baseboard then reads the data and deactivates the IORD* line. The baseboard is now free to change the address and chip-select lines for the next operation. The interlocked I/O read operation shall be used by all expansion modules that require a read pulse width greater than 300 ns or that cannot guarantee valid data on the iSBX bus within 250 ns after the IORD* line is activated.

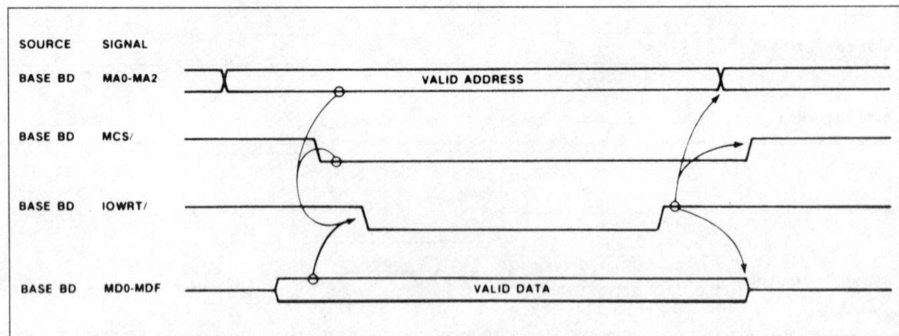

FIGURE 2.20 Full-speed I/O write operation.

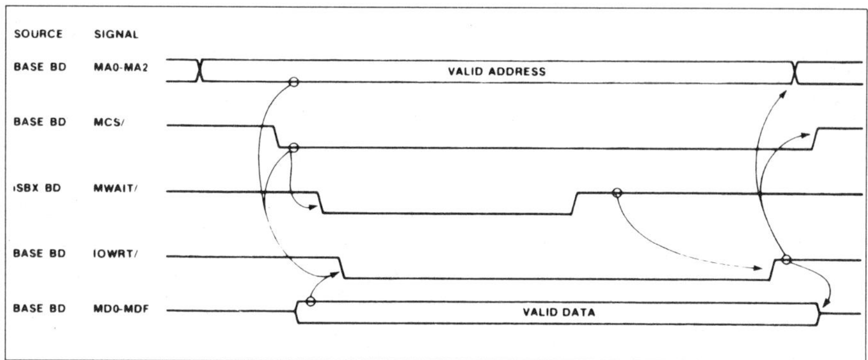

FIGURE 2.21 Interlocked I/O write operation.

2.6.4.2 I/O Write Operations. There are two types of I/O write operations on the iSBX bus: the full-speed I/O write and the interlocked I/O write. Whether or not the expansion module generates the MWAIT* signal determines which type of operation is performed.

Figure 2.20 shows the full-speed I/O write operation. The baseboard generates a valid address and chip select for the expansion module to initiate the operation. After the setup times are met, the baseboard activates the IOWRT* line and enables data. The IOWRT* line will remain active for at least 300 ns, and the data will be valid for at least 250 ns before the IOWRT* line is deactivated. After the IOWRT* line is deactivated, the baseboard is free to change the address and chip-select lines for the next operation.

Figure 2.21 shows the interlocked I/O write operations. The baseboard initiates the operation by generating a valid address and chip select, just as in the full-speed I/O write. The expansion module then activates the MWAIT* signal, which in turn inhibits the ready signal to the baseboard microprocessor. The baseboard will activate the IOWRT* line, enable data, and insert wait states as long as the MWAIT* signal from the expansion module is active. The expansion module will remove the MWAIT* signal when it is ready to receive the data. The baseboard then removes the data and deactivates the IOWRT* line. Data shall be stable at least 250 ns before the IOWRT* line is deactivated. The baseboard is now free to change the address and chip-select lines for the next operation. The interlocked I/O write operation shall be used by all expansion modules that cannot guarantee proper operation with a 300-ns write pulse width.

2.6.4.3 Direct Memory Access (DMA) Operations. DMA is a means of moving a block of data to or from an expansion module without the overhead of microprocessor intervention for every transfer. The source or destination of the data on the baseboard is typically a series of consecutive memory locations. For the expansion module, the source or destination is always an I/O port. The DMA process is always initiated by executing software on the baseboard that sets up the DMA controller and expansion module. This software determines the direction of data movement, the addresses of the sources and destination, and the length of the transfer. Once set up, DMA operations will be done automatically by the DMA controller, as requested by the expansion module.

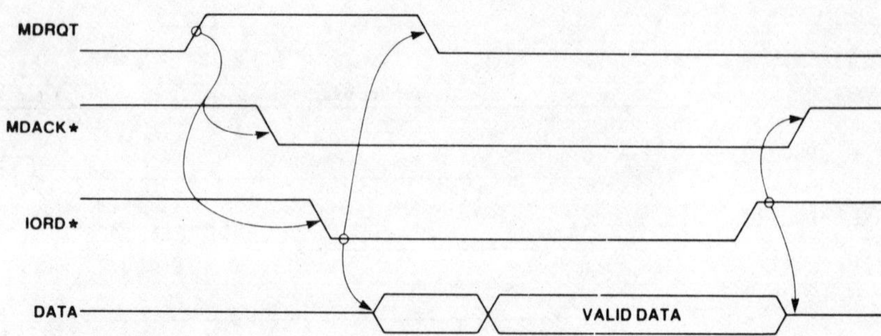

FIGURE 2.22 Full-speed DMA operation.

DMA operations are similar to I/O read and I/O write operations. Expansion modules that meet the requirements for full-speed I/O read and I/O write operations can perform full-speed DMA operations. Likewise, expansion modules that meet the requirements for interlocked I/O read and I/O write operations can perform interlocked DMA operations. Once the DMA controller is set up, a DMA operation is initiated by the expansion module activating MDRQT. The DMA controller then acquires the local bus on the baseboard (by arbitration) and activates the MDACK* line to the expansion module to acknowledge the request. The MDACK* line functions as a chip select for DMA operations. During a DMA operation, both chip selects (MCS0*, MCS1*) are deactivated and the address lines are undefined. The rest of the operation is the same as the I/O read and I/O write operations described previously. Figures 2.22 and 2.23 show full-speed and interlocked DMA operations, respectively.

DMA operations can be in two modes: cycle stealing and burst. In the cycle-stealing mode, the expansion module will deactivate the MDRQT line every operation after receiving a command. The DMA controller, in turn, releases the bus after completing the operation. In the burst mode, the expansion module will hold the MDRQT line active until the last operation of a transfer. The burst mode will always attain equal or greater throughput compared with cycle stealing, since

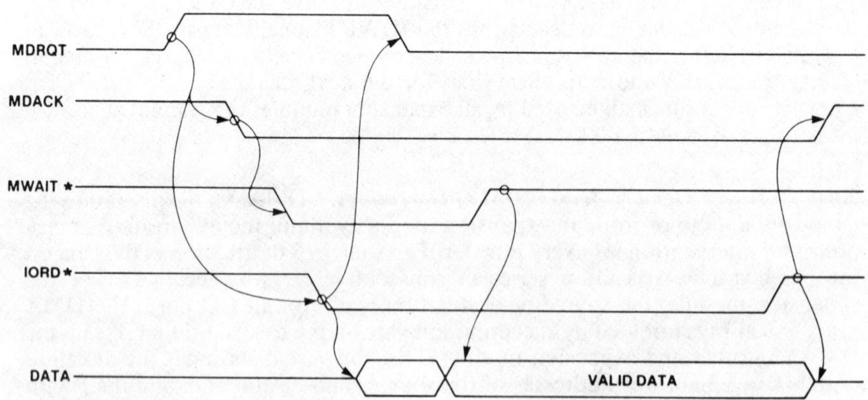

FIGURE 2.23 Interlocked DMA operation.

the DMA controller only arbitrates for the bus once per operation rather than once per transfer.

The TDMA line is provided for additional DMA control. This line is configurable either as an input to the expansion module or as an output from the expansion module.

As an input, the TDMA line identifies the end of a DMA transfer. In this mode, the baseboard activates the TDMA line after the last valid DMA operation is completed. If the expansion module is holding MDRQT active when the TDMA line is activated, it shall remove the MDRQT line as if it were a command. However, the baseboard need not wait for the MDRQT line to go active before activating the TDMA line.

As an output, the TDMA line shall terminate a DMA transfer in the baseboard. To accomplish this, the expansion module first deactivates the MDRQT line, and then activates the TDMA line.

2.6.4.4 Interrupt Operations. The expansion module initiates an interrupt operation by activating one of the interrupt request lines (MINTR0, MINT1). These signals will interrupt the baseboard microprocessor, causing it to execute an interrupt service routine. The interrupt service routine performs two functions. First it services the interrupt. This will typically consist of reading data from or writing data to the expansion module. Second, the service routine deactivates the interrupt line from the expansion module. In summary, from the expansion module's point of view, the expansion module initiates an interrupt by activating its interrupt line and removes the interrupt when the baseboard tells it to do so.

2.6.5 Environmental Specifications

Bus specifications should be met with temperature and humidity within the following ranges.

Temperature	0–55°C (32–131°F) with free-moving air
Relative humidity	90% maximum without condensation

2.6.6 Mechanical Specifications

This section describes the physical and mechanical specifications that a designer must be concerned with when designing a baseboard or an expansion module compatible with the iSBX bus.

2.6.6.1 Connector Specification. The connector used in the iSBX bus was specified as the bus was defined; it is a two-piece connector that was chosen for high reliability over 200 insertion cycles. Full definitions can be found in the IEEE specification and the iSBX manufacturer's documentation.

2.6.6.2 Connector Pin Assignments. There are two types of connector pairs used for the iSBX bus: a 36-pin 8-bit version and a 44-pin 16-bit version. The 36-pin male connector on the expansion module will mate with both the 36-pin (8-

36-pin version
(8-bit interface)

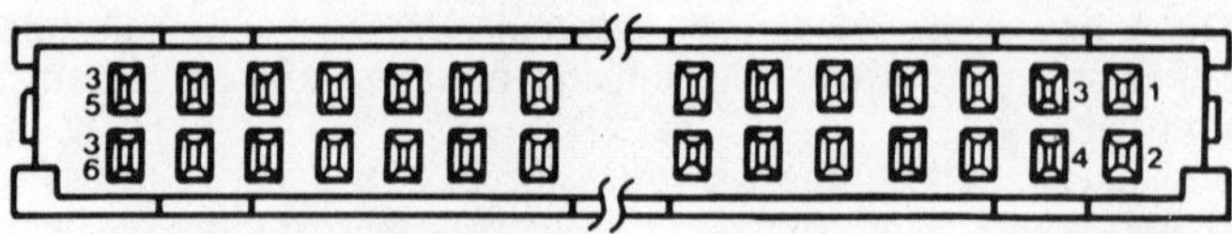

44-pin version
(8- and 16-bit interfaces)

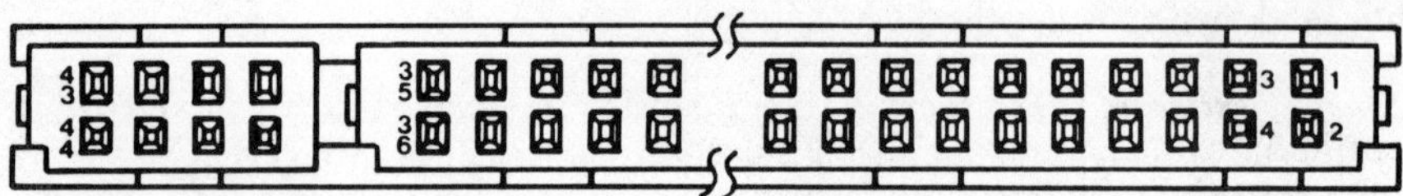

FIGURE 2.24 Connector pin numbering. Shown are top views of two baseboard connectors.

TABLE 2.12 Pin Assignments

Pin	Mnemonic†	Description	Pin	Mnemonic	Description
1	+12 V	+12 V	2	−12 V	−12 V
3	GND	Signal ground	4	+5 V	+5 V
5	RESET	Reset	6	MCLK	Expansion module clock
7	MA2	Address 2	8	MPST*	Expansion module present
9	MA1	Address 1	10		Reserved
11	MA0	Address 0	12	MINTR1	Interrupt 1
13	IOWRT*	I/O write command	14	MINTR0	Interrupt 0
15	IORD*	I/O read command	16	MWAIT*	Expansion module wait
17	GND	Signal ground	18	+5 V	+5 V
19	MD7	Data bit 7	20	MCS1*	Chip select 1
21	MD6	Data bit 6	22	MCS0*	Chip select 0
23	MD5	Data bit 5	24		Reserved
25	MD4	Data bit 4	26	TDMA	Terminate DMA
27	MD3	Data bit 3	28	OPT1	Option 1
29	MD2	Data bit 2	30	OPT0	Option 0
31	MD1	Data bit 1	32	MDACK*	DMA acknowledge
33	MD0	Data bit 0	34	MDRQT	DMA request
35	GND	Signal ground	36	+5 V	+5 V
37‡	MD14	Data 14	38‡	MD15	Data 15
39‡	MD12	Data 12	40†	MD13	Data 13
41‡	MD10	Data 10	42‡	MD11	Data 11
43‡	MD8	Data 8	44‡	MD9	Data 9

†Signals ending with an asterisk are active-low; signals not ending with an asterisk are active-high.
‡MD8–MD15 used only on 16-bit systems.

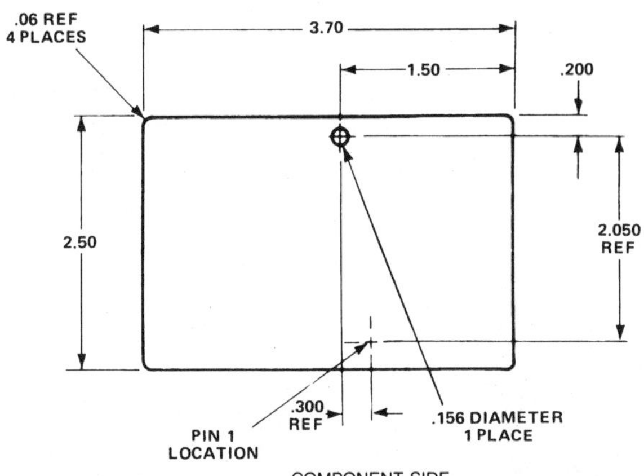

FIGURE 2.25 Standard outline for single-width Multimodule. All dimensions are in inches. Tolerances: to 2 decimal places, ± 0.01 in; to 3 decimal places, ±0.005 in.

bit) and 44-pin (16-bit) female connectors on the baseboard. The 16-bit 44-pin male connector on the expansion module will mate with only the 44-pin (16-bit) female connector on the baseboard. The pin locations are shown in Fig. 2.24. Table 2.12 shows the pin assignments.

2.6.6.3 Expansion Module Specifications. There are two standard outlines for expansion modules. The single-width outline is shown in Fig. 2.25 and the double-width outline is shown in Fig. 2.26. For each outline, either edge-finger connectors or pin-and-socket connectors may be used. When edge-finger connectors

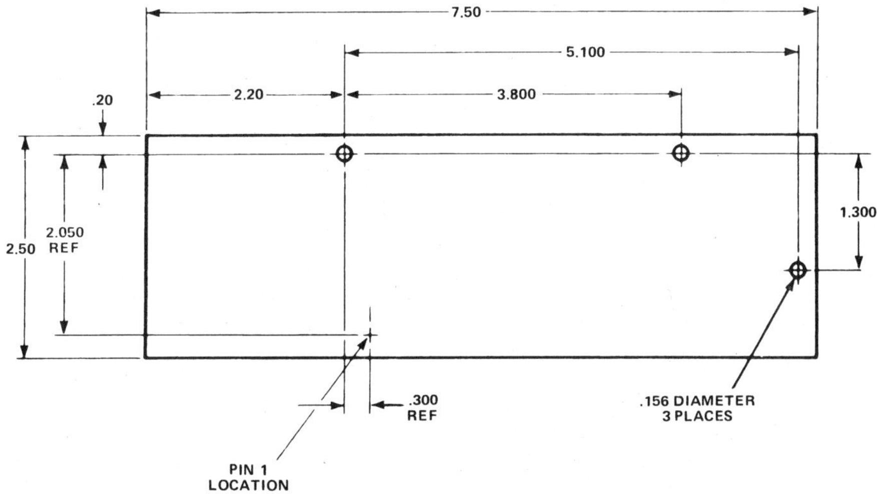

FIGURE 2.26 Standard outline for double-width Multimodule. All dimensions are in inches. Tolerances: to 2 decimal places, ±0.01 in; to 3 decimal places, ±0.005 in.

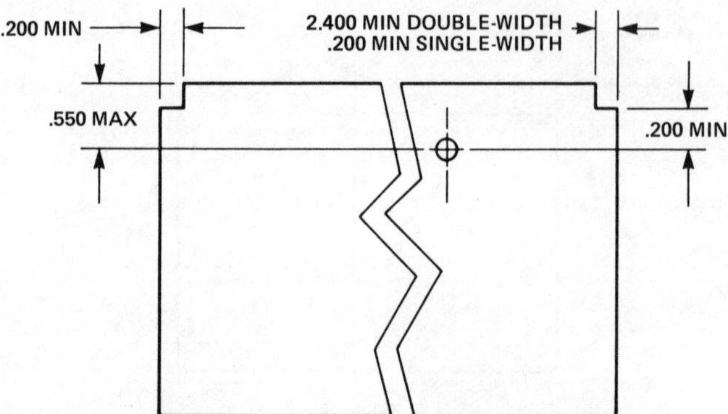

FIGURE 2.27 Edge-finger connector specification. All dimensions are in inches; all tolerances are ±0.005 in.

are used, they shall conform to the additional specifications shown in Fig. 2.27. For pin-and-socket connectors there are no additional restrictions.

2.6.6.4 Baseboard Specification. The absolute placement of the expansion connector(s) on the baseboard is not part of this specification. Only the relative position of the mounting holes with respect to the connector are specified. Figure 2.28 shows this relationship.

2.6.6.5 Board Height Specification. Figure 2.29 shows worst-case height parameters for the iSBX expansion bus system. Figure 2.28 shows the baseboard region for which an additional height restriction applies (necessary for edge-finger connectors).

2.6.7 Compliance

As with the Multibus I architecture, the iSBX expansion bus system allows for various different levels of compliance for products manufactured by diverse vendors.

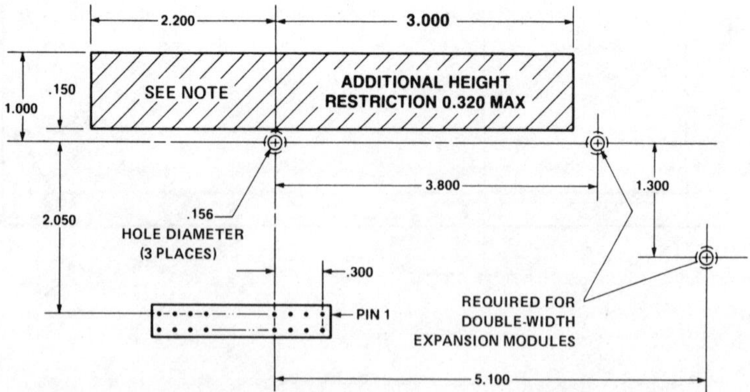

FIGURE 2.28 Relative mounting hole placement for baseboards. All dimensions are in inches; all tolerances are ±0.005 in. (*Note*: Required for edge-finger-type connector clearance.)

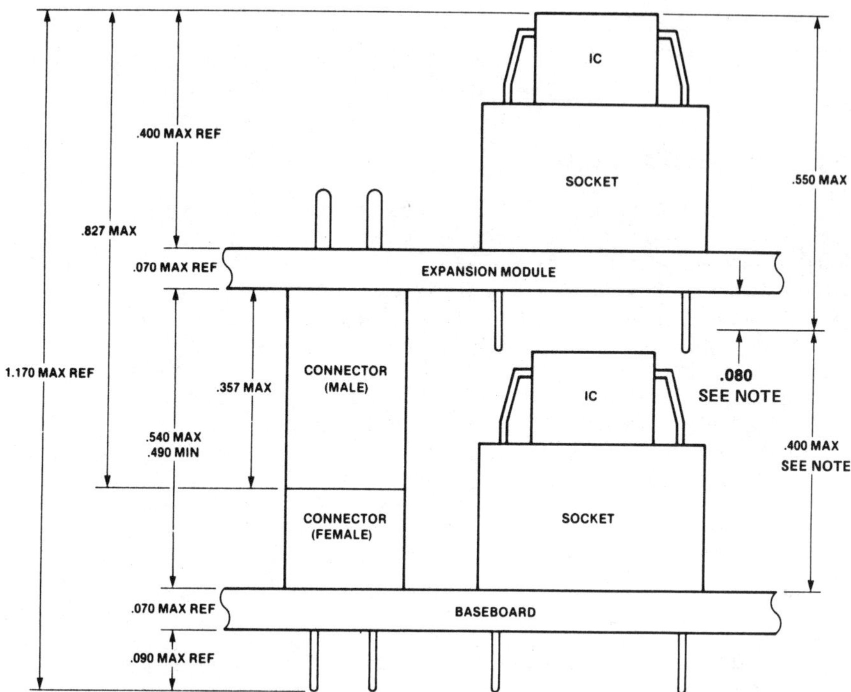

FIGURE 2.29 Maximum height requirement. All dimensions are in inches. Maximum connector dimensions allow for a 0.015 in maximum float from the PC board surface. All parameters listed as reference (REF) are not part of this specification. (*Note*: Except under clearance areas for edge-finger-type connectors.)

2.6.7.1 Data Path. Data path variations exist for both expansion modules and baseboards. Expansion modules may either support 8- or 16-bit data paths. Sixteen-bit baseboards may support only 8-bit data paths or both 8- and 16-bit data paths. Eight-bit baseboards may support only 8-bit data paths.

2.6.7.2 DMA Support. Both expansion modules and baseboards may optionally support DMA operations. In order for DMA to be used in a system, both the expansion module and the baseboard shall support the signals that are required (MDRQT, MDACK*, TDMA).

2.6.7.3 Interlocked Operation. Baseboards may optionally not support this feature. Expansion modules may optionally require this feature. The feature is implemented via the MWAIT* signal. Typically, the baseboard will support the interlocked operation and expansion modules will not require it. The purpose for not requiring interlocked operation from all baseboards is to allow the use of low-cost baseboards without a ready function.

2.6.7.4 Baseboards and Expansion Modules. When constructing an iSBX bus system, it is not necessary that all modules have identical capabilities. The only restriction is that the system will only support modes of operation supported by both the baseboard and the expansion module. For example, an expansion module that supports DMA can be plugged onto a baseboard that does not support

DMA; the result will be a system that does not support DMA. It is the responsibility of the system designer to guarantee that a required system feature is supported by all necessary system components.

2.6.8 Products Available

iSBX-bus-based products cover a vast range: standard system expansion capabilities with up to eight RS232C serial lines, or 48 parallel lines on one module; various interfaces using SCSI, QIC-02, BITBUS, floppy disk, IEEE 488 specification; analog and digital drivers and receivers; various combinations of battery-backed memory and clock-calendar. There are several iSBX modules with microprocessors, some designed as auxiliary microprocessor modules and some for video. As of this writing, the most highly integrated module contained three microprocessors, and over 1 Mbyte RAM, all used to provide a high-performance video display controller for real-time applications. In addition to standard, off-the-shelf modules, many system designers design their own iSBX modules for the unique interface requirements in their application.

The most usual way to provide iSBX capability in a system is from a connector on a CPU board (some boards carry up to three iSBX connectors), but the desirability of adding iSBX capability to a system has encouraged the addition of connectors to many different boards. These carrier boards may either be dedicated to the job of holding iSBX modules (up to six on a full size Multibus I board) or combining connectors with other features such as digital I/O.

There are currently over 200 iSBX modules available, providing over 50 distinct functions.

2.7 THE FUTURE

2.7.1 The Future for the Multibus I Architecture

The Multibus I architecture is well established in the marketplace with more products continuing to be introduced regularly by the vendors with ever-increasing performance and functionality. While some buses introduced since the advent of the Multibus I architecture have some advantages in some areas (such as high performance for multiprocessing), these advantages have not proved sufficient for users to abandon their Multibus I–based designs. The attractions of the Multibus I architecture—price, performance, breadth of compatible products, reliability—combined with a proven track record, continue to be major factors. For many designs needing one to three microprocessors, Multibus I boards will continue to be the answer.

Moving from one bus to another is no trivial matter, and it is rarely done for a design in production or evolutionary products based on existing designs. Manufacturers, recognizing the needs of the existing designs, are placing more and more emphasis on compatible upgraded products. The ability to increase CPU performance or I/O capability, with only minor design changes for the customer, has become more of a factor with most new product introductions. A 16-bit CPU board can simply be replaced by a new 32-bit board; an ST506 disk interface can be provided on a board with ESDI capability also to make the transition easier. This trend will continue and grow as newer devices become available, since this allows manufacturers to create products that can be quickly absorbed by their customers, and also allows customers a great choice in price and performance of a system.

Memory sizes will continue to increase; already the total memory in a single chassis can far exceed the Multibus addressability. As 4-Mbit DRAMs become available, it will soon be possible to create single boards with more than 16 Mbytes of memory.

Another trend is for increasing levels of integration on boards. In addition to memory and simple serial and parallel I/O, CPU boards are now becoming available with SCSI or Ethernet interfaces. With careful design, the performance of on-board I/O devices can approach or exceed that available through the iSBX interface or on a separate full-sized board. The latest microprocessors offer sufficient bandwidth to support a complex application and high-performance I/O using the same integrated circuit. There are opportunities for either cost reduction or increased overall performance, which in turn leads to increased competitiveness for the original equipment manufacturers using Multibus I–based products.

2.7.2 The Future for the iSBX Architecture

The iSBX architecture was originally created to increase the flexibility and capability of Multibus I boards; its applicability now has a much broader base, but the focus is still on the Multibus I architecture.

The range of iSBX expansion modules continues to expand; the simplest modules are used to provide extra serial lines for a CPU board, while at the other end of the spectrum all the latest device and manufacturing technology allows very complex boards to be produced. There is no reason for this divergence to narrow since the iSBX concept permits great flexibility. Use of ever greater performance on an iSBX board will result in the highest expression of the single-board computer.

LIST OF TRADEMARKS

Multibus, iSBC, and iRMX are registered trademarks of Intel Corporation.

iSBX, iLBX, Multimodule, 386, and 486 are claimed trademarks of Intel Corporation.

BIBLIOGRAPHY

Control Engineering, *Multibus® Buyers Guide,* Cahners, Des Plaines, 1988.

IEEE Standard Microcomputer System Bus ANSI/IEEE Standard 796-1983, Institute of Electrical and Electronic Engineers, New York, 1983.

IEEE Standard Specifications for an I/O Expansion Bus: SBX Bus IEEE Standard 959-1987. New York, Institute of Electrical and Electronic Engineers, 1988.

Intel Corporation, *Multibus I Architecture Reference Book.* Intel, Santa Clara, 1983.

Johnson, James B., and Steve Kassel, *The Multibus® Design Guidebook.* McGraw-Hill, New York, 1984.

CHAPTER 3
NuBus

Gerry Laws
Texas Instruments
Austin, Texas

3.1 OVERVIEW

The NuBus is an advanced 32-bit system bus that forms the backbone of several modern computer systems, including the Explorer from Texas Instruments and the Macintosh II from Apple. The bus is specified in a manner that will allow it to accommodate device technology advances well into the future.

The NuBus is based upon the concept that simplicity is the most effective way to optimize the cost-performance point of the system design. The entire system bus requires only 51 signals. This is only 19 more than the 32 needed for address and data. This simplicity, along with the synchronous nature of the NuBus, enhances system reliability and testability. During the design of the bus, only those features that demonstrated a significant benefit were included. This concept allows board designers to take full advantage of the bus' inherent performance without incurring the penalty of complex interface logic.

The NuBus meets the following objectives:

- System architecture independence

  Optimized for 32-bit transfers, but 8-bit and 16-bit nonjustified transfers supported.

  Not based on a particular microprocessor's control structure.

  Power-up and -down sequencing specified by the system rather than dictated by the bus structure.

- High bandwidth

  10-MHz basic cycle time provides 37.5-Mbyte bandwidth in block mode.

- Simplicity of protocol

  Simple master and slave architecture.

  Fair arbitration gives all masters equal use of the bus.

  Reads and writes are the only operations.

  I/O and interrupts are memory mapped.

A simple service request feature is provided for boards that do not have master logic.

The single large physical address space allows all addressable units to be uniformly accessed.

- Small pin count

  Multiplexed address and data.

  Only 51 signals, excluding power and ground.

- Ease of system configuration

  ID lines provide board-independent geographical addressing that enables the system to be free of switches and jumpers.

  Distributed, parallel arbitration eliminates daisy chains.

3.1.1 Basic NuBus Structure

The NuBus is a synchronous bus in that all signal transitions and samplings are synchronized to a central system clock. However, transactions may be a variable number of clock periods long. This provides the flexibility of an asynchronous bus with the design simplicity of a synchronous bus. Fig. 3.1 shows the major elements of a typical NuBus system.

Only read and write operations in a single large address space are supported: I/O and interrupts are accomplished within these mechanisms. The modules attached to the NuBus are peers; no card or slot position is the default master or "special slot." Each slot has an ID code hard-wired into the backplane. This allows cards to differentiate themselves without jumpers or switches.

A bus transfer consists of arbitration for access to the bus, transfer of the address and transfer of the data, and transfer of appropriate status information. Transfers may be 8-, 16-, or 32-bit transactions. All NuBus transfers are unjustified, as shown in Fig. 3.2.

The NuBus supports multiple-word block transfers of 2, 4, 8, or 16 words. The bandwidth of the bus is 37.5 Mbyte/s when block transfers are utilized.

Interrupts on the NuBus are implemented as write transactions. Interrupt operations require no unique signals or protocols. Any module on the NuBus can interrupt a processor module by performing a write operation into an area of memory that is monitored by that processor. Any address range that the processor module can monitor can be defined as its interrupt space. This allows interrupts to be posted to individual processors and allows interrupt priority to be software-specified by memory mapping the priority level.

For very simple boards that do not implement the logic required to become a bus master, a simple mechanism is provided to allow it to request service from another module in the system.

The NuBus fair arbitration mechanism differs from strict priority arbitration in that it prevents "starvation" of cards and distributes bus bandwidth evenly. It is implemented in a distributed manner and requires no daisy chains on the backplane.

The NuBus provides a linear address space of 4 Gbytes. The upper $\frac{1}{16}$ (256 Mbytes) of this address space is called *slot space*. As Fig. 3.3 shows, this area is further divided into sixteen 16-Mbyte pieces, which are mapped to the 16 possible NuBus card slots. Addresses of the form F(ID)XXXXXX belong to a card's slot

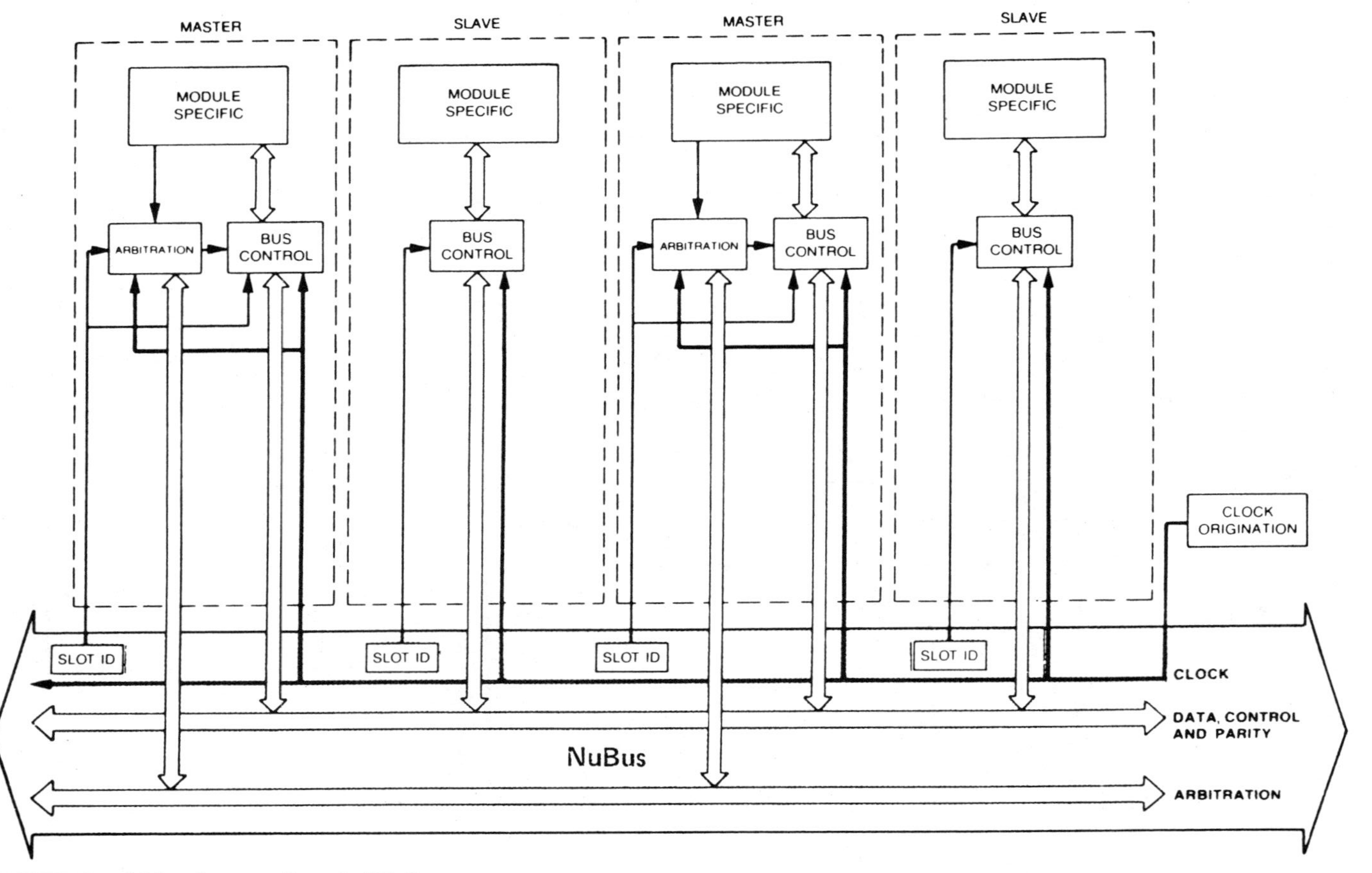

FIGURE 3.1 Major elements of a typical NuBus system.

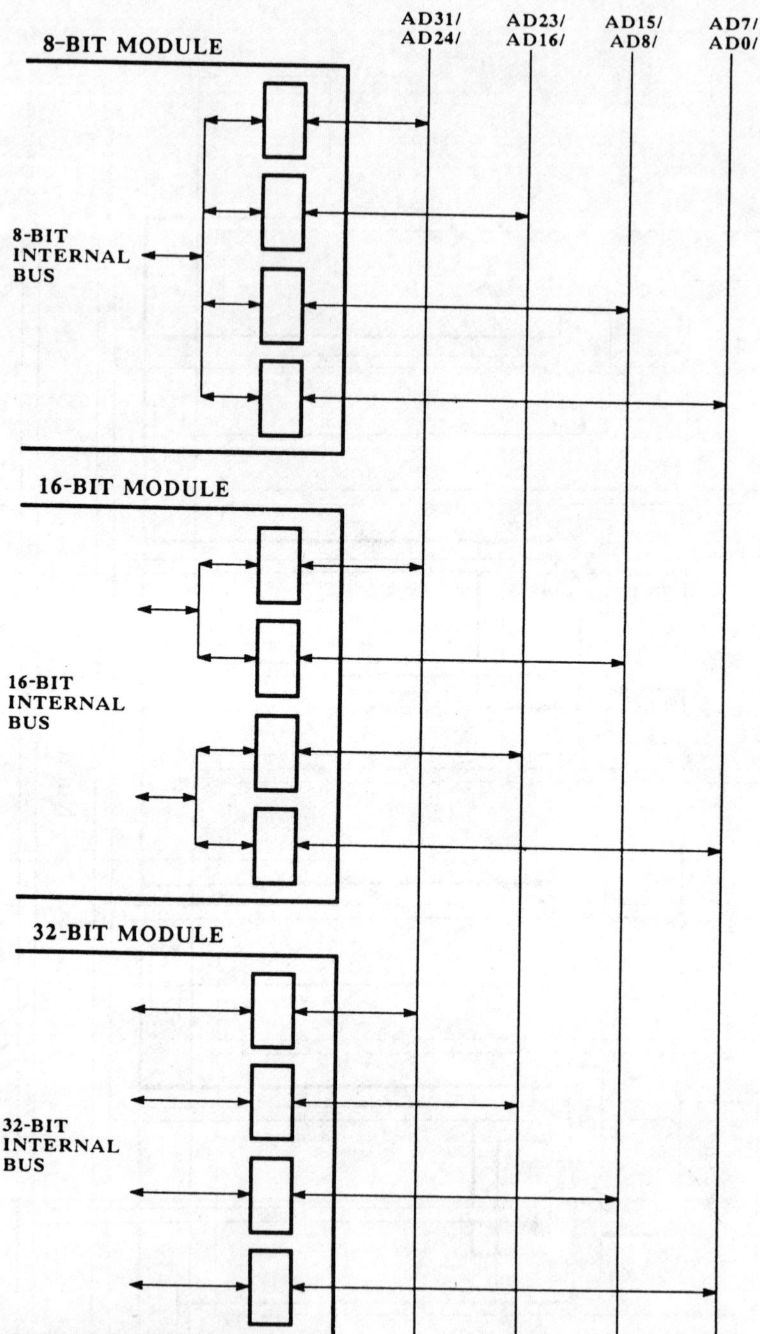

FIGURE 3.2 Data paths for 8-, 16-, and 36-bit devices. All lines indicate 8-bit paths. Boxes are 8-bit transceivers.

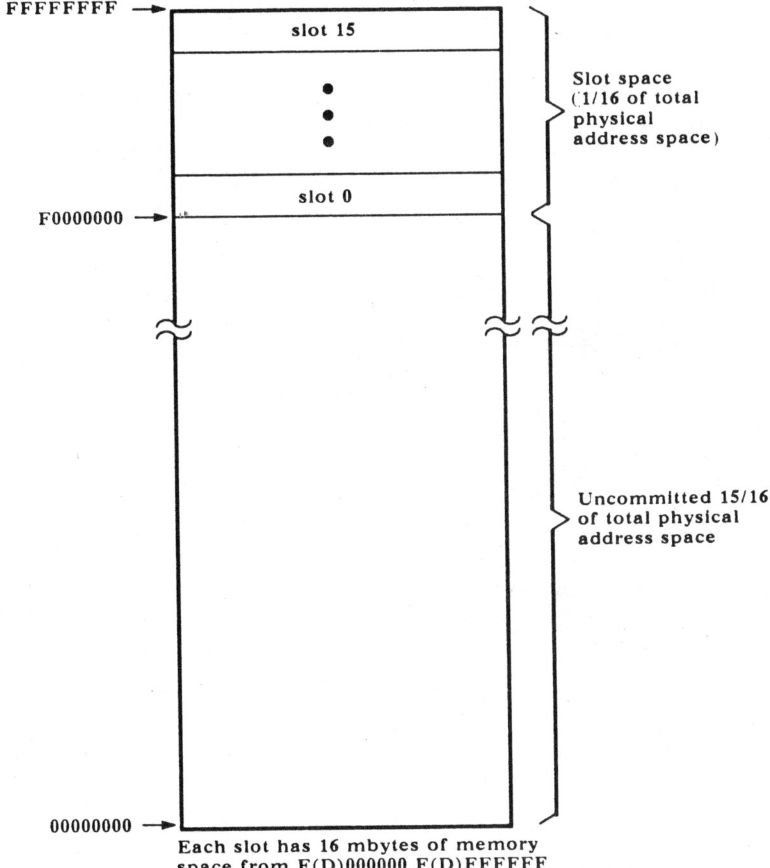

FIGURE 3.3 NuBus address space.

space. This fixed address allocation, based solely on a board's slot location, enables the design of systems that are free of jumpers and switches. The remaining $^{15}/_{16}$ of the address space is uncommitted and allocated as required. Any allocation of that space is programmable via registers in slot space.

Two board form factors are defined for two classes of systems: larger "minicomputer" systems, and smaller "desktop" systems. The Explorer and Explorer II LISP machines and the System 1500 multiuser business system from Texas Instruments use the Eurocard form factor boards, while the Macintosh II from Apple uses the desktop form factor.

The NuBus has been adopted by the Institute of Electrical and Electronic Engineers (IEEE) as a recognized standard. A detailed specification of the NuBus is published as IEEE 1196.[1]

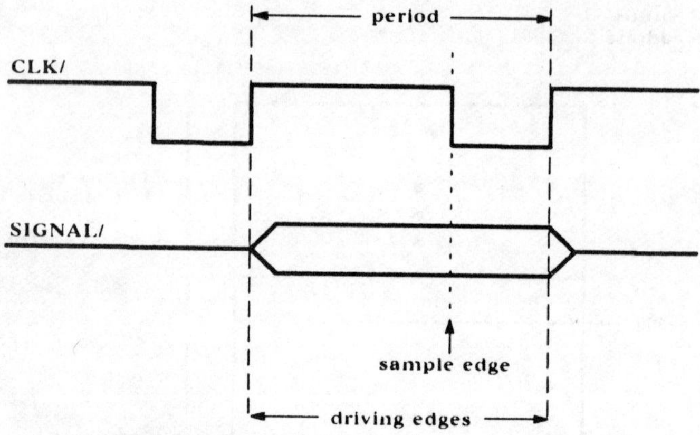

FIGURE 3.4 Basic NuBus signal timing.

3.2 DEFINITION OF TERMS

3.2.1 Basic NuBus Timing

The NuBus system clock has a 100-ns period with a 25% duty cycle. Figure 3.4 shows the basic timing for most NuBus signals. The low-to-high transition of the clock is used to drive signals onto the bus. Signals are sampled on the high-to-low transition of the clock. The asymmetric duty cycle of the clock provides 75 ns of propagation and setup time. With 25 ns between the sample and driving edges, bus skew problems are avoided.

3.2.2 Basic Definitions

Terms used throughout this chapter are defined below. The relationships between some of these terms are illustrated in Figs. 3.4 and 3.5. All NuBus signals are active when low and indicated by a SIGNAL* notation.

ACK cycle — Last cycle of a transaction (one clock period long) during which ACK* is asserted.

Address cycle — First cycle of a transaction (one clock period long) during which START* is asserted. This term is synonymous with START cycle.

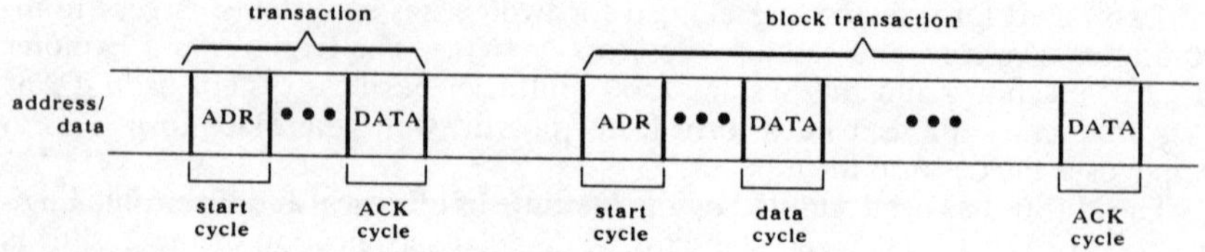

FIGURE 3.5 Cycle and transaction relationships.

Asserted	This term is synonymous with low and true. Note: Since all NuBus signals are active low (indicated by an asterisk following the signal name), the terms low, true, and asserted are synonymous. The terms true and false have been avoided in this chapter.
Cycle	A phase of a NuBus transaction. Address cycles are one clock period long and convey address and command information. Data cycles are also one period long and convey data and acknowledgment information.
Data cycle	Any cycle in which data is known to be valid and acknowledged. It includes ACK cycles as well as intermediate data cycles within a block transfer.
Driving edge	The rising edge (low-to-high) of the system clock (CLK*).
High	This term is synonymous with inactive, unasserted, and released.
Inactive	This term is synonymous with high, unasserted, and released.
Low	This term is synonymous with active and asserted.
Period	The 100-ns period of CLK* (shown in Fig. 3.4) consists of a 75-ns unasserted state and a 25-ns asserted state.
Released	This term is synonymous with high, inactive, and unasserted.
Sample edge	Falling edge (high-to-low) of the system clock.
Slot ID	The hexadecimal number (0–F) corresponding to each card slot. Each slot ID is established by the backplane and communicated to the card through the IDx* lines.
Slot space	The upper one-sixteenth of the total address space. These addresses are in the form F(ID)XXXXXX, where F, (ID), and X are hexadecimal digits of 4 bits each. This address space is geographically divided among the NuBus cards according to the slot ID numbers.
Start cycle	This term is synonymous with address cycle.
Tenure	Bus tenure is a time period of unbroken bus ownership by a single master. A master may lock the bus and during one tenure perform several transactions.
Transaction	A transaction is a complete NuBus operation such as read, write, block read, or block write. It is made up of one address cycle and one or more data cycles.
Unasserted	This term is synonymous with high, false, and released.

3.3 PHYSICAL LAYER

This section describes the physical components of the NuBus, including the signal lines and connector pins, the board form factor, and the backplane requirements.

3.3.1 Bus Line Definitions

3.3.1.1 Utility Signals. The eight utility signals provide functions that are not associated with any particular bus transaction.

Clock (CLK)*, driven from a single source, synchronizes bus arbitration and data transfers between system modules. CLK* has an asymmetric duty cycle of 25% and a constant nominal frequency of 10 MHz. In general, signals are changed at the rising edge of CLK*, while they are sampled at the falling edge.

Reset (RESET)* is an open-collector line that returns all cards to the initial power-up state. This signal may be asserted asynchronously to the CLK* line.

Power fail warning (PFW)* is an open-collector line that indicates that system power is about to fail. This signal may be asserted asynchronously to the CLK* line.

Identification signals ID0–ID3*)* are binary coded to specify the physical location of each module. The highest-numbered slot (15) has the four signals wired low. The lowest-numbered slot (0) has all ID signals open. The distributed arbitration logic uses the ID numbers to uniquely identify cards for arbitration contests. ID signals are also used to allocate a small portion of the total address space to each card. The upper 1/16 (256 Mbytes) of the entire 4-Gbyte NuBus address space is called *slot space*. As shown in Fig. 3.3, this area is further divided into sixteen 16-Mbyte pieces that are mapped to the 16 possible NuBus card slots (or ID codes). Addresses of the forum F(ID)XXXXXX belong to a board's slot space.

Nonmaster request (NMRQ)* is an open-collector signal that may be asserted to indicate that the board needs attention from another board in the system.

3.3.1.2 Bus Data Transfer Signals. The bus data transfer signals, including control, address and data, and bus parity, are all three-state signals.

Control Signals

Transfer start (START)* is driven for only one clock period by the current bus master at the beginning of a transaction. START* indicates to the slaves that the address and data signals are carrying a valid address.

Transfer acknowledge (ACK)* is driven for only one clock period by the addressed slave device and indicates the completion of the transaction.

Transfer modes 0 and 1 (TM0 and TM1*)* are driven by the current bus master during START* cycles to indicate the type of bus operation being initiated. They are also driven by bus slaves during ACK* cycles to denote the acknowledgment status (normal or error).

Address/Data. Address and data (AD0*–AD31*) signals are multiplexed to carry a 32-bit byte address at the beginning of each transaction and 1, 2, or 4 bytes of data later in the transaction.

Bus Parity

System parity (SP)* transmits parity information between NuBus cards that implement NuBus parity checking. Parity checking is an optional feature of NuBus systems.

System parity valid (SPV)* indicates that the SP* bit is being used. Cards that do not generate bus parity will never drive SPV* active, and cards that do not check parity will ignore SP* and SPV*.

3.3.1.3 Arbitration Signals

Arbitration signals (ARB0–ARB3*)* are open-collector binary coded lines driven by contenders for the bus. They are used by the distributed arbitration logic to determine bus mastership.

Bus request (RQST)* is an open-collector line driven low by contenders for the bus.

3.3.2 Bus Backplane and Module Requirements

The system clock, a bus time-out function, and signal line termination are provided by the backplane. The reset and power fail warning signals are generally driven by the power supply module. No other "central resources" are required from any system module.

The bus time-out prevents a NuBus system from "hanging" if a transaction is attempted to an address that does not exist. If a transaction is started, but not completed within 25.5 μs, the time-out logic will provide an ACK cycle to complete the transaction.

3.3.3 Board Form Factor

Two mechanical form factors are defined for NuBus systems: triple height and desktop. A triple-height card is derived from IEC specifications for connectors[2] and modules.[3] It conforms to the dimensions for a triple-height and triple-depth Eurocard and is approximately 11 in × 14.4 in with three 96-pin pin-and-socket type connectors (referred to as DIN connectors). Only one connector is required for the NuBus; the other two are used for I/O connections. This form factor is also referred to as *Eurocard style.* The desktop style card is 4 in × 12.875 in and contains one 96-pin pin-and-socket connector on the bottom edge. I/O connections are made to the back edge.

The desktop card form factor is intended for small systems that typically are placed on a desk or table. The triple-height card form factor is intended for use in larger systems that are typically packaged in racks or cabinets. Figures 3.6 and 3.7 illustrate the two form factors.

3.3.4 Pin Assignments

The pin assignments for the NuBus are listed in Table 3.1. The same connector and pin assignments are used for either card form factor.

3.4 DATA LINK LAYER

3.4.1 Protocol Requirements

The NuBus supports transactions of several different data sizes. Although optimized for transactions of 32-bit words and blocks of words, the NuBus also supports byte and halfword transactions. Figure 3.8 shows the relationship between bytes, halfwords and words. A byte of data is conveyed on the same signal line

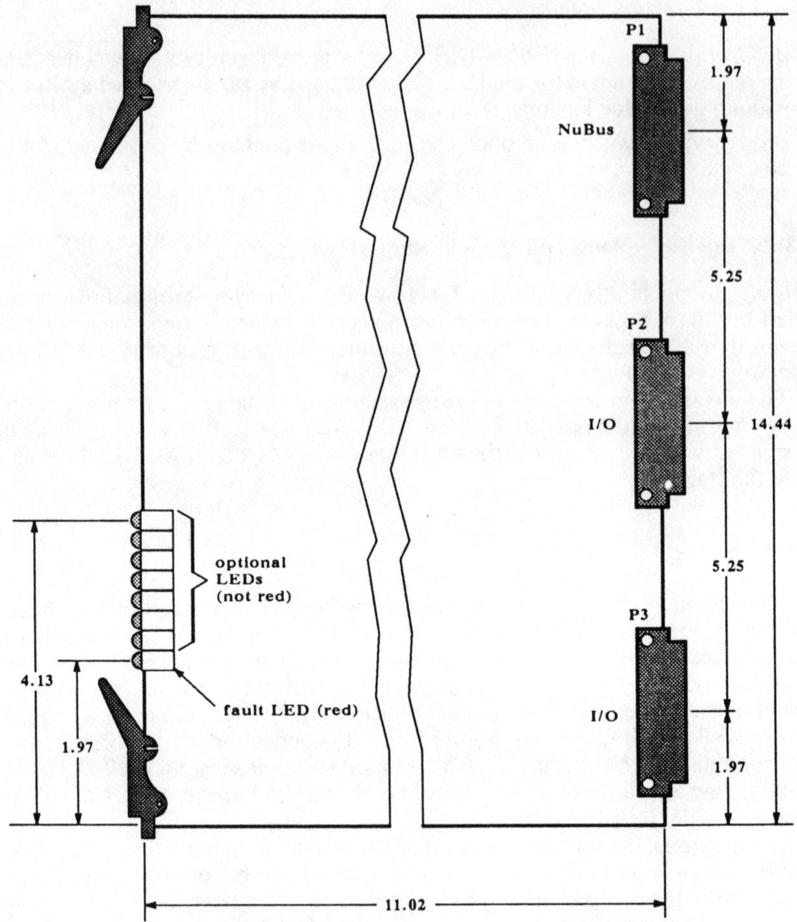

FIGURE 3.6 Triple-height NuBus board outline. Dimensions in millimeters.

regardless of the transfer mode. This unjustified data path approach allows straightforward connection of 8-, 16-, and 32-bit devices.

A NuBus transaction consists of a request made by a master and a response made by the addressed slave. Before a master can initiate a transaction, it must become the bus owner by winning an arbitration contest. Arbitration can occur in parallel with a transaction initiated by the prior bus owner.

Transactions consist of single-data cycle read or write transactions or multiple-data cycle read or write transactions, known as block transfers. All operations on the NuBus are accomplished using only these two simple types of transactions within a single address space.

3.4.2 Bus Detail Requirements

3.4.2.1 ***Single-Data Cycle Transactions.*** The simplest transactions on the NuBus convey one data item and consist of a START cycle and a subsequent

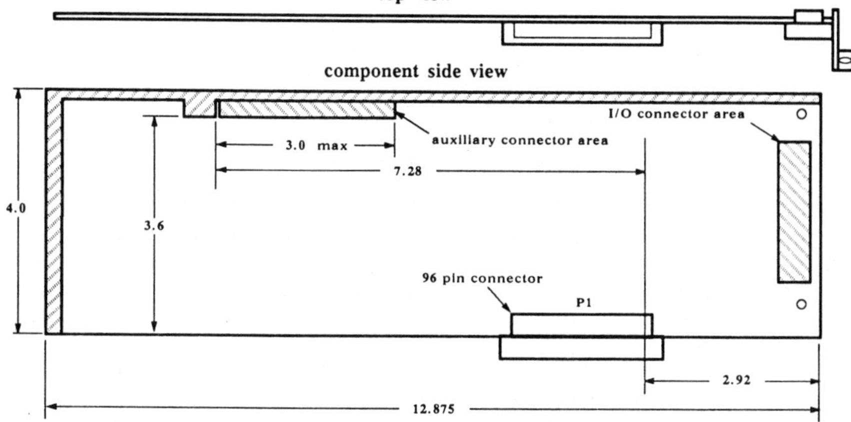

FIGURE 3.7 Desktop NuBus board outline. Dimensions in inches.

TABLE 3.1 Pin Assignment† for P1

Pin \ Row	A	B	C
1	−12	−12	RESET*
2	Reserved	GND	Reserved
3	SPV*	GND	+5
4	SP*	+5	+5
5	TM1*	+5	TM0*
6	AD1*	+5	AD0*
7	AD3*	+5	AD2*
8	AD5*	−5.2	AD4*
9	AD7*	−5.2	AD6*
10	AD9*	−5.2	AD8*
11	AD11*	−5.2	AD10*
12	AD13*	GND	AD12*
13	AD15*	GND	AD14*
14	AD17*	GND	AD16*
15	AD19*	GND	AD18*
16	AD21*	GND	AD20*
17	AD23*	GND	AD22*
18	AD25*	GND	AD24*
19	AD27*	GND	AD26*
20	AD29*	GND	AD28*
21	AD31*	GND	AD30*
22	GND	GND	GND
23	GND	GND	PFW*
24	ARB1*	−5.2	ARB0*
25	ARB3*	−5.2	ARB2*
26	ID1*	−5.2	ID0*
27	ID3*	−5.2	ID2*
28	ACK*	+5	START*
29	+5	+5	+5
30	RQST*	GND	+5
31	NMRQ*	GND	GND
32	+12	+12	CLK*

†As viewed from front edge of board.

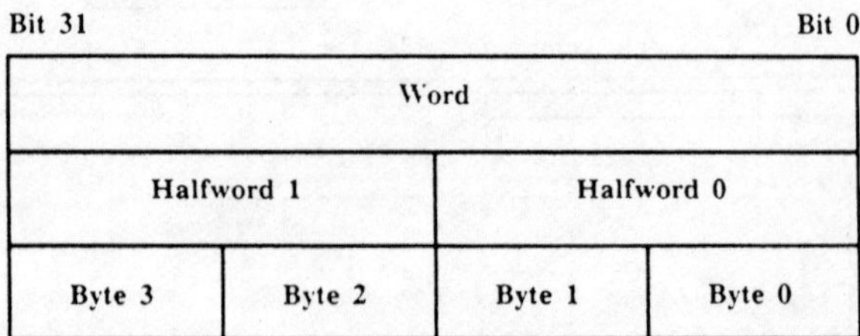

FIGURE 3.8 Layout of words, halfwords, and bytes.

ACK cycle. These transactions are either reads or writes of bytes, halfwords, or words.

All transactions are initiated by a bus master that drives START* active while driving the TMX*, AD0*, and AD1* signals to define the cycle type. Table 3.2 shows the encodings for the various types of transactions. The remaining ADX* signals are also driven to convey the address. The transaction is completed when the responding slave drives ACK* active while driving status information on the TMX* signals. For write transactions, the master must switch the ADX* signals from address to data information in the second clock period and hold that data until acknowledged. In read cycles, the slave drives the data simultaneously with the acknowledge in the last period.

Figure 3.9 shows the timing for read bus transactions other than block transfers.

During ACK cycles the addressed slave drives the TMX* lines while it drives ACK*. The TMX* lines provide status information to the current bus master as shown in Table 3.3. The four possible status conditions are described in the following.

TABLE 3.2 Transfer Mode Summary

TM1*	TM0*	AD1*	AD0*	Type of cycle
L	L	L	L	Write byte 3
L	L	L	H	Write byte 2
L	L	H	L	Write byte 1
L	L	H	H	Write byte 0
L	H	L	L	Write halfword 1
L	H	L	H	Block write
L	H	H	L	Write halfword 0
L	H	H	H	Write word
H	L	L	L	Read byte 3
H	L	L	H	Read byte 2
H	L	H	L	Read byte 1
H	L	H	H	Read byte 0
H	H	L	L	Read halfword 1
H	H	L	H	Block read
H	H	H	L	Read halfword 0
H	H	H	H	Read word

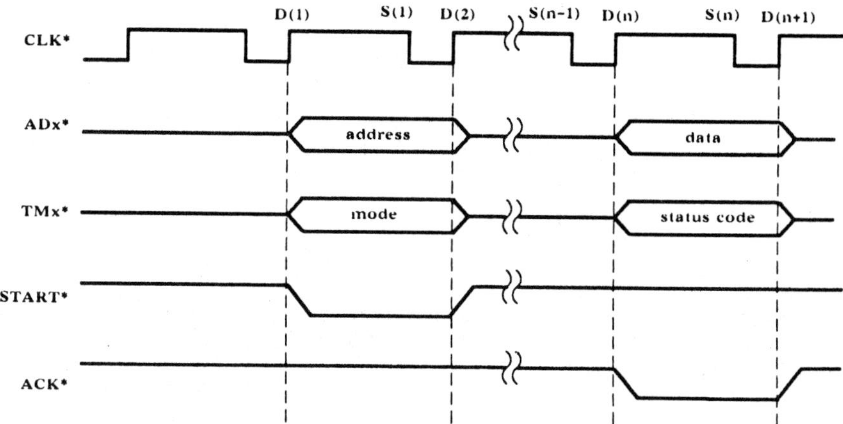

FIGURE 3.9 NuBus read transaction.

Bus transfer complete The bus transfer complete response indicates the normal valid completion of a bus transaction.

Error During a read or write operation, certain error conditions may occur. Examples of errors are an uncorrectable error during a memory read from a memory that performs error checking and correction (ECC) or a bus parity error. The transaction terminates in a normal manner, and the bus master has responsibility for handling the error condition.

Bus time-out If an unimplemented address location is summoned, the attempted transaction is acknowledged with a bus time-out response. Bus time-out responses are generated by the system time-out logic; therefore, time-out logic is not required on each card of the system.

Try again later An addressed slave may be unable to respond to a master's transfer request at the time of the request. Try again later indicates that the transfer cannot be accomplished at this time. The master should re-arbitrate for the bus later. This is not an error indication.

3.4.2.2 Block Transfers. Block transfers are transactions that consist of a START cycle, multiple-data cycles from or to sequential address locations, and an ACK cycle. The number of data cycles is controlled by the master and communicated during the START cycle. Allowed lengths of block transfers are 2, 4, 8, and 16 words. (Only word transfers are supported in block mode.) By restricting

TABLE 3.3 Transaction Response Status Summary

TM1*	TM0*	Type of attention cycle
L	L	Bus transfer complete
L	H	Error
H	L	Bus time-out error
H	H	Try again later

TABLE 3.4 Block Size and Starting Address Summary

AD5*	AD4*	AD3*	AD2*	Block size (words)	Block starting address
X	X	X	H	2	$(A_{31} \rightarrow A_3)000$
X	X	H	L	4	$(A_{31} \rightarrow A_4)0000$
X	H	L	L	8	$(A_{31} \rightarrow A_5)00000$
H	L	L	L	16	$(A_{31} \rightarrow A_6)000000$

block transfers to 16 words, system response time can be guaranteed, and low-cost interface buffering can be provided to allow fast transfers.

The AD0*, AD1*, and TMX* encoding for block transfers is shown in Table 3.2. The block's starting address must correspond to its size and is encoded by the AD2*–AD5* lines, as shown in Table 3.4.

During block transfers, each data cycle is acknowledged by the responding slave. The intermediate acknowledges are data cycles where TM0* is active and TM1* and ACK* are both inactive. For intermediate acknowledgments, TM0* has the same significance and timing as the ACK* signal for nonblock transfers. The final word transfer acknowledge is a standard ACK cycle. Status codes are the same as those for single-data cycles.

Figure 3.10 shows the timing for a NuBus block read operation.

3.4.2.3 ***Interrupt Operations.*** Interrupts on the NuBus are implemented as write transactions, which are referred to as *events.* Interrupt operations require no unique signals or protocols. Any module on the NuBus can interrupt a processor module by performing a write operation into an area of memory that is monitored by that processor. This allows interrupts to be posted to individual processors and allows interrupt priority to be software-specified by memory mapping the priority level. The memory that is used for event posting can be on the processor module or on some other module. Generally, a range of addresses on the processor module is implemented as a specially decoded event space. Any write transaction into this event space will activate an interrupt input signal to the processor.

For very simple modules that do not need the logic to become a bus master, but still need to request service, a simple service request mechanism is provided. Any module may drive the nonmaster request (NMRQ*) line, which indicates that service is needed. This feature is generally used only in systems that use the desktop form-factor boards. In these systems, a larger board, called the *system board,* contains a portion of the system hardware, such as the processor and memory. Connectors on the system board allow NuBus cards to be plugged into the system. An individual NMRQ* signal is connected from each NuBus connector to a priority encoder on the system board, thus allowing the identity of the module requesting service to be easily determined.

3.4.2.4 ***Bus Parity.*** Parity protects the integrity of all address and data transfers. Parity generation is optional on a cycle-by-cycle basis. Parity is useful only if the module driving the ADX* lines generates parity and the module capturing the address or data information checks it.

The two signals SP* and SPV* are used to communicate parity and parity valid, respectively. When SPV* is asserted (with the same timing as the address/data lines), parity is generated. Parity checking is optional. Modules that cannot

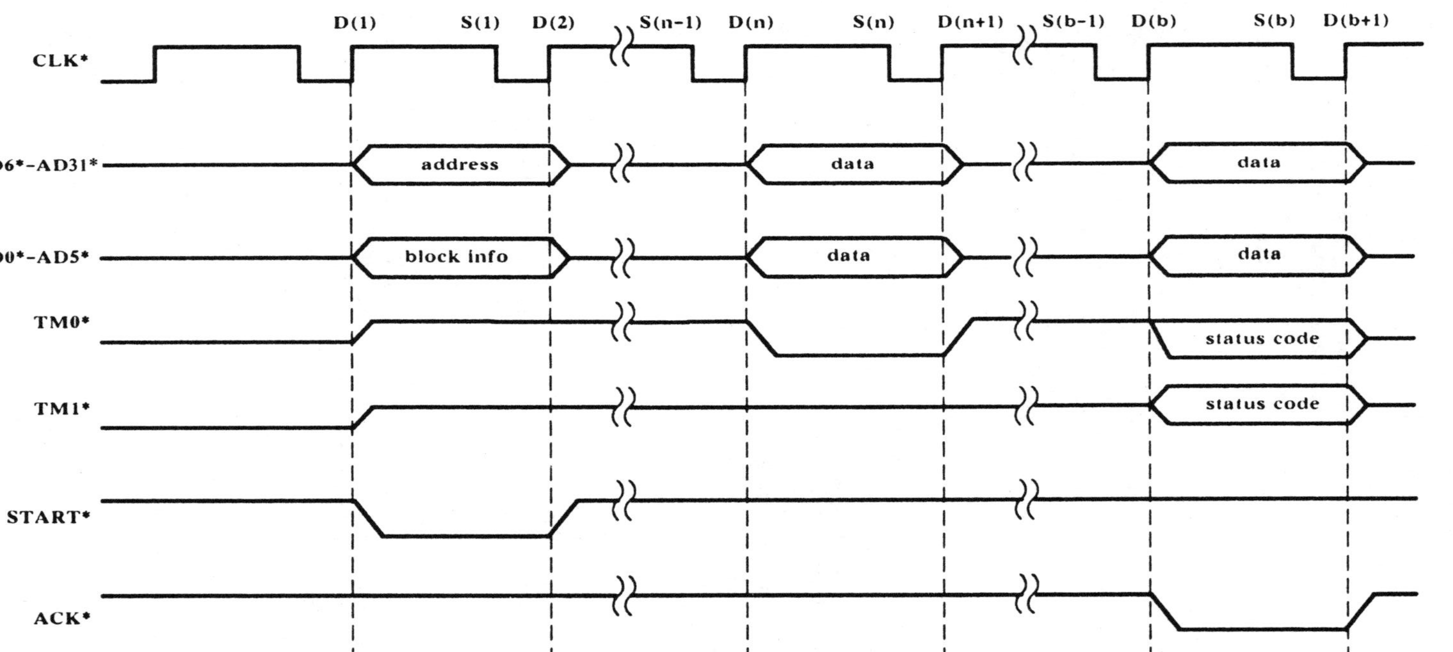

FIGURE 3.10 NuBus block read operation. The addressed slave is responsible for drawing TM0* to the desired state between D(n) and d(b + 1).

check parity normally ignore the SPV* and SP* signals. Although byte and half-word transfers are supported, parity is always calculated over the complete 32 bits of the ADX* lines, simplifying interface design.

Most systems that are currently available do not make use of the parity feature of the NuBus.

3.4.2.5 Arbitration. Arbitration is the mechanism used to determine the next owner of the bus. There is always a bus owner. Ownership can be viewed as a token that is always present and that is passed from module to module, as requested. The bus owner has certain privileges and a few responsibilities. The bus owner is the only module that can initiate bus transactions. The bus owner is responsible for ensuring that the START* signal is at the correct logic level on every bus cycle. The bus owner is also responsible for ensuring that the ACK* signal is driven to the correct logic level, normally unasserted, after it is asserted by a slave at the end of a transaction.

The NuBus fair arbitration mechanism differs from strict priority arbitration in that it prevents an unequal distribution of the bus bandwidth, which can result in "starvation" of cards that cannot get access to the system bus. This differs sharply from many buses that promote the idea of *priority*. Systems that employ priority-based arbitration often exhibit strange and nonrepeatable failures when one of the low-priority boards is prevented from obtaining access from or to the bus before a buffer overflows or a timer times out. Often, rearranging the position of the cards in the system causes the problem to go away, but one is never sure if the problem has been eliminated. Systems that use the NuBus are assured of a guaranteed maximum request latency for every card in the system. This allows adequate buffers to be designed into each card to avoid data starvation problems.

During arbitration, one or more modules contend for control of the NuBus. Modules that desire ownership of the NuBus must first assert the RQST* line. RQST* may only be asserted by a module if RQST* was in an unasserted state on the last sample edge of the CLK* signal. All modules that assert RQST* place their ID codes on the ARBX* lines and contend for the bus. The arbitration logic distributed among the modules determines which of the modules has ownership of the NuBus. After two clock periods, the contest mechanism settles. The contender with the highest ID code has its code on the ARBX* lines, has won bus ownership, and may initiate a transaction.

As long as the winner does not desire to lock the bus, the winning module removes its RQST* at the same time that START* is asserted and removes its ARBX* signals after the START cycle of its transaction. The release of START* initiates another contest between any modules that originally requested the bus in the same clock period, but that have not yet won. These modules will be granted ownership in turn from highest ID number to lowest ID number. The rule that RQST* must be unasserted before a module may assert it keeps other modules from participating in contests until all the original requesters have been served.

The longest request latency that a board should ever have would be when all sixteen bus modules simultaneously requested ownership of the NuBus, and each module did a sixteen-word block transfer, and each block transfer lasted for the maximum allowed bus transaction time of 25.5 μs. In this case the request latency would be 15×25.5 μs, or 383 μs. It would be possible for a longer request latency to occur if multiple locked transactions were done by one or more modules, but locked transactions are typically short.

The following logic equations describe how the arbitration logic on any given module works:

$$ARB3 = ID3 * arb$$
$$ARB2 = ID2 * arb * (ID3 + ARB3/)$$
$$ARB1 = ID1 * arb * (ID3 + ARB3/) * (ID2 + ARB2/)$$
$$ARBO = ID0 * arb * (ID2 + ARB2/) * (ID1 + ARB1/)$$

Notes:

For clarity, the equations are shown in positive logic.

ARB is a term that controls the arbitration process

* is logical AND

+ is logical OR

/ indicates inversion

According to these equations, after a short delay (arbitration period) the ARBX* lines will equal the ID code of the highest priority contender.

3.4.2.6 Bus Locking. Although modules generally use the bus for single transactions, sometimes a module must lock the bus. An example of this is an indivisible test-and-set operation performed in a multiprocessor environment. This is required to implement *semaphores,* or signal bits, that are used to control the allocation of resources that may be shared by the various processors in the system.

Bus locking is accomplished with no added mechanism. To lock the bus, a master simply continues to request and contend for bus ownership. Since it has the highest ID code of those modules present, it wins subsequent arbitration contests.

In many cases, just locking the NuBus is not sufficient to implement an indivisible test-and-set function. Boards that have private buses that allow a processor to communicate to memory on that board must be able to prevent the processor from accessing its own local memory during the test-and-set sequence. In order to easily lock the internal bus of a NuBus module, such as a board with a processor and memory, a resource lock mechanism is provided. A one-cycle transaction, called an attention-resource-lock cycle, is broadcast to all bus modules by a master that intends to lock the bus. Any module that is addressed after this knows that locked transactions are occurring. At the completion of the locked sequence, another one-cycle transaction, called an attention-null cycle, is broadcast by the bus owner to indicate to all bus modules that the locked sequence is completed.

3.4.2.7 Attention Cycles. The preceding paragraph introduced a special cycle, called the attention cycle. An attention cycle is a single bus cycle during which both the START* and the ACK* signals are asserted by the bus owner in the same clock period. The two TM* signals are also driven to indicate one of four types of attention cycles. Attention cycles are used to broadcast information to all modules on the bus. Table 3.5 summarizes the four types of attention cycles.

TABLE 3.5 Attention Cycle Summary

TM1*	TM0*	Type of attention cycle
L	L	Attention-null
L	H	Reserved
H	L	Attention-resource-look
H	H	Reserved

An attention-null cycle is used to end any pending action and cause a new arbitration contest to occur. This may happen if a bus module has requested the bus and won an arbitration contest but has decided not to perform a bus transaction.

An attention-resource-lock cycle is used to begin a sequence of locked transactions, as described in a previous paragraph.

The remaining two types of attention cycles have not yet been defined.

3.4.2.8 Bus Parking. In NuBus systems a bus master that has released RQST* "parks" on the bus and may use it at any time until another module asserts RQST*. When RQST* is finally asserted, the parked bus master finishes its current transaction and relinquishes the bus to the new winner. Bus parking reduces the average time period to acquire the bus in systems with a small number of contenders.

3.5 SYSTEM ARCHITECTURE

System architecture goes beyond the definition of the bus itself and describes how boards and components connected to the bus are structured so as to create a complete system. A system architecture is dependent on the type of system it is being used in. For example, a fault-tolerant multiprocessor system will have system constraints that are much different from a low-cost desktop workstation. This does not mean, however, that it is useless to suggest a "typical" system architecture that can be used for systems that do not have unusual or stringent requirements. In the case of the NuBus, two generally used architectures have developed. This is related to the two different board form factors and the differences in the character of the systems that use each type.

The larger triple-height Eurocard format is used in high-performance workstations and multiprocessor minicomputers. A system architecture that addresses the needs of this type of system is described in a document from Texas Instruments, *NuBus System Architecture.*[4] The desktop board format is used in systems that typically have a large system board that contains the system processor, memory, certain I/O controllers, and several NuBus connectors for optional peripheral controllers or coprocessors. A system architecture that addresses the needs of this type of system is described in a document from Apple, *Designing Cards and Drivers for Macintosh II.*[5]

3.5.1 NuBus System Architecture

The NuBus System Architecture, designed by Texas Instruments, provides a layer of definition on top of the NuBus that totally describes the operation and interaction of the various system components from power-up through self-test and booting procedures until the operating system(s) takes over operation of the system. A minimum board interface is defined that allows both intelligent and nonintelligent boards to be accessed to determine their function and to control their initialization. A self-test and booting scheme is defined that allows several different types of processors to be tested and initialized. This allows boards that are designed by different manufacturers to be combined easily into a system that may consist of several different types of processors and run one or more types of software operating systems.

3.5.1.1 System Configuration. A block of board-specific information must be contained in a ROM on each board. This ROM is referred to as the configuration ROM. This information identifies the function of the board, provides pointers to the various resources on the board, and provides other data such as the part number and revision level of the board. This ROM is always located in byte lane 0 and ends at the highest address of the slot space for each board. Several registers, such as the configuration register and the flag register, are also defined and must

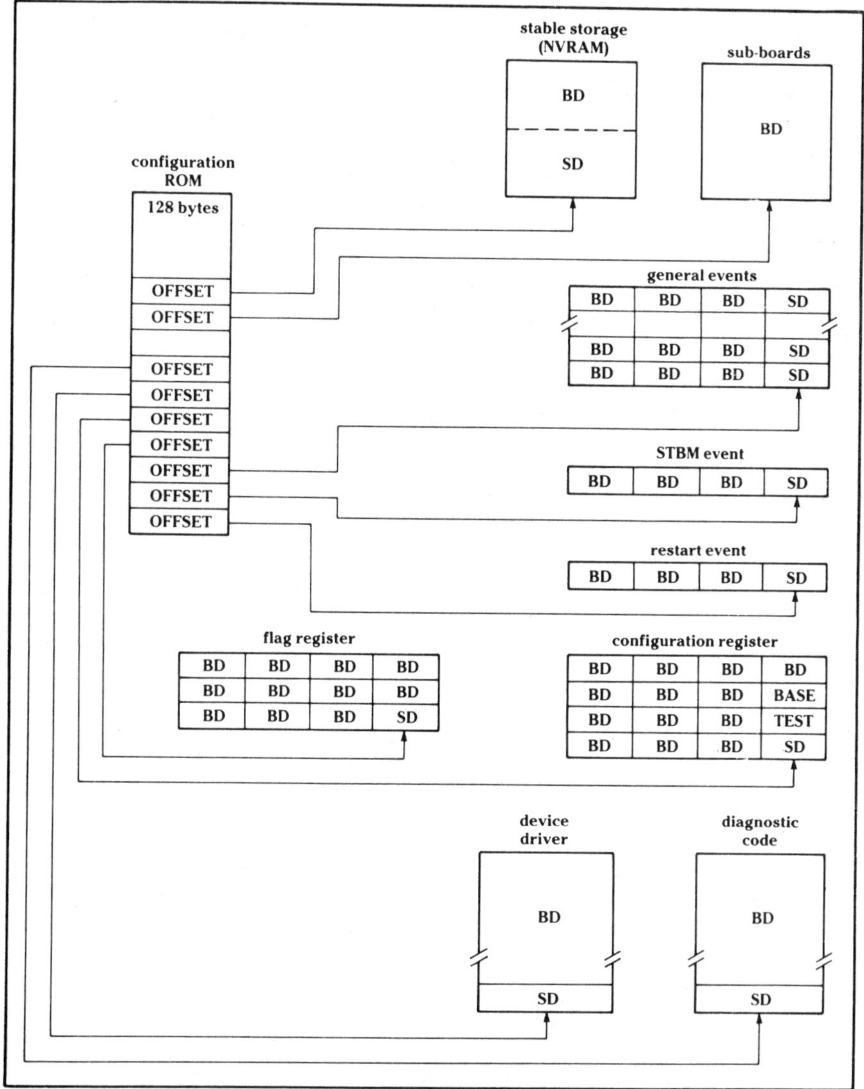

FIGURE 3.11 Texas Instruments configuration ROM structure. SD = system-defined byte; BD = board-defined byte.

exist on each board to provide a consistent control and status interface. Pointers in the configuration ROM point to the address of each of these registers. With use of these resources, each board in the system may be communicated with and its function determined, so that the system may dynamically configure itself. The structure of the configuration ROM and the required board interface registers are illustrated in Fig. 3.11.

3.5.1.2 Self-Test. A primary goal of the system self-test is to allow the user to identify and replace a failed system component. To aid in this, an LED is required on each board. This LED is illuminated whenever a failure on that board is detected. Each time the system is powered up or a system reset occurs, a defined self-test sequence is executed. If an error is detected, it is indicated by the LED and a message is sent to the system monitor.

The self-test sequence begins with each intelligent board in the system executing its own self-test code, contained in ROMs on that board. Upon successful completion, one of the boards must be designated to take control of the system and coordinate the remaining testing and booting operations. This processor is referred to as the system test and boot master (STBM). Each processor that can be an STBM indicates this fact with a certain bit in the configuration ROM. In order to be an STBM, the processor must have a small amount of additional code in its ROM that contains the STBM control routines. To select the STBM, each of the candidates that passed self-test polls all of the other boards in the system to determine if another potential STBM exists. The candidate in the lowest-numbered slot assumes control of the system.

The STBM now proceeds to test each of the nonintelligent boards that could not test themselves. This is done by executing the test code that is contained in ROM on each nonintelligent board.

In order for this code to be processor independent, a special diagnostic language has been designed for writing all diagnostics. Each STBM contains an interpreter to allow its particular processor to execute the individual board diagnostics. This interpreter is known as the diagnostic engine, and the language is referred to as diagnostic engine language (DEL).

The STBM locates the system console by examining the configuration ROMs of the system components. As the individual board tests are executed, the STBM displays a status message on the console so that the user can easily determine the condition of the system.

3.5.1.3 System Booting. Once the self-test has been completed, the STBM begins the process of booting the system software. As in the case of the self-test, a defined, processor-independent sequence is followed. This sequence will accommodate either single-processor or multiprocessor systems and will permit booting from a variety of sources.

The sequence begins by the STBM allowing the user to select a specific load device and load band or to accept as a default the setup specified by the nonvolatile RAM. If no choice is made within a short time period, the default setup is used. The STBM executes the load driver that is contained in ROM on the selected load device. This driver is also written in DEL, so that it is processor independent. The driver obtains a bootstrap program from the load device and sends it to the STBM, which begins executing it.

In a multiprocessor system, the just-booted program continues with the boot process. Each additional processor is identified by polling its configuration ROM and then is passed a command block that tells it which load source to boot from. The STBM then enables each processor, one at a time, to perform its own boot operation. Once all of the processors in the system have been booted, control is turned over to the system software.

During the booting procedure, status messages are displayed on the system console so that the user is made aware of any problems that occur.

3.5.2 Macintosh II System Architecture

Apple has defined a system architecture for the Macintosh II that is similar in function to that defined by TI for the Explorer, but different in many ways due to the inherent differences between a desktop system and a multiprocessor system. One major difference is the existence of the system processor on the system board. Since it is always there, it has been designated as the device that controls the system initialization process. Also, the test code is written in the system processor native code rather than in a processor-independent test language.

3.5.2.1 System Configuration. Each board must include a ROM that contains data which identifies the type of board and provides an initialization code for the board. This ROM is referred to as the declaration ROM. When the system is turned on, the system processor accesses the declaration ROMs on each board using a set of routines called the slot manager.[6] The slot manager determines the type of board in each slot, initializes the board with data provided by the declaration ROM, tests the board with code provided by the declaration ROM, and loads a driver for the board that matches the identification code in the declaration ROM.

The declaration ROM is organized in a hierarchical fashion with a format block in a well-known location that has a pointer to a directory structure, which, in turn, has pointers to all of the resource blocks contained in the ROM. Figure 3.12 illustrates the organization of the declaration ROM.

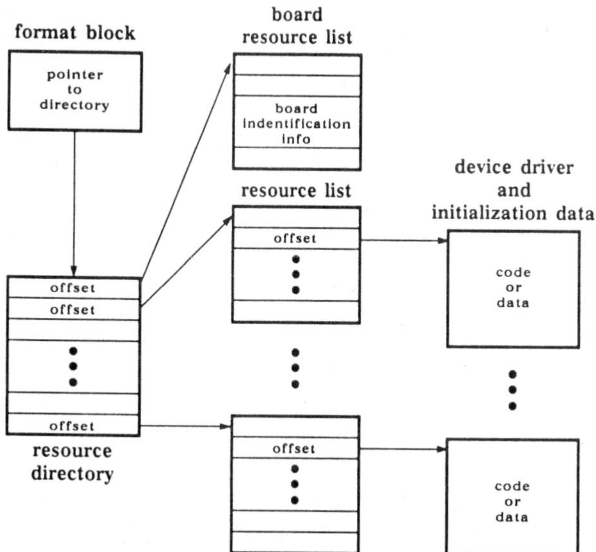

FIGURE 3.12 Apple declaration ROM structure.

3.5.2.2 System Test. The goal of the system test is to identify any malfunctions and indicate this condition on the system monitor. The slot manager executes the code provided by each board's declaration ROM to initialize the board and to determine if it is functional. This generally takes the form of a quick pass-fail test. Boards that require more extensive initialization are accommodated after the system has been booted.

3.5.2.3 System Booting. The system is normally booted from the internal disk drives that are contained within the system enclosure; however, the declaration ROM on a particular board may contain a field indicating that the system should be booted from resources controlled by that board. This allows system software to be obtained from any type of mass storage device.

During booting, a field in the declaration ROM on each board is checked to determine if a driver should be loaded for that board. The driver may be in one of three places: in the declaration ROM, in the file system with an identification code that matches a field in the declaration ROM, or anywhere that can be accessed by a loader routine contained in the declaration ROM.

Once all of the boards have been initialized, their drivers loaded, and the operating system software installed, control of the system is turned over to the operating system.

3.6 BUS APPLICATION EXAMPLES

The NuBus is uniquely suited for use in a wide range of computer and controller applications. The high performance of the bus allows it to be used in minicomputer class computers, where it forms the main system bus that is used for all communication and data transfer between components of the system. The simplicity and economy of the bus and the ease of configuration of a system make the NuBus the ideal expansion bus for a personal computer or workstation. Finally, the rugged construction of the pin-and-socket connector allows the NuBus to be used in harsh environments, such as industrial controllers and process control computers. The wide range of application of the NuBus is contributing to its popularity, since independent board manufacturers can create individual boards that can be used in a number of application areas. This in turn provides a wide selection of boards for system integrators to use to create systems for specific applications.

The NuGroup, which is the NuBus Manufacturers and User Group, was established to encourage the widespread use of the NuBus and products on which it is based. The NuGroup is open to any manufacturer or user of NuBus components and currently has members that are involved in the areas of minicomputers, personal computers, workstations, and industrial systems. The NuGroup sponsors many activities to promote the NuBus, including a product catalog, participation in seminars and conferences, and joint advertising and marketing. In addition, the NuGroup has a technical committee that provides a forum for the discussion of technical questions regarding the bus, including future enhancements.

In minicomputer applications, the NuBus is used as the main system bus. All I/O traffic is routed over the NuBus between the peripheral controllers and the system memory. Block transfer transactions are generally used to move large blocks of data from mass storage controllers to the system memory. If multiple processors are included in the system, data and commands are shared over the NuBus. Generally, it is not appropriate to use the system bus for instruction accessing, unless a cache is located on the processor. If all instruction accesses occur on the system bus, then the bandwidth available for I/O operations would be severely diminished. Section 3.6.1 describes a multiprocessor minicomputer system that uses the NuBus as its system bus.

In personal computer systems, the NuBus is used as the expansion bus to allow diverse specialty cards to be installed in the computer in order to tailor the capability of the system to a particular user's needs. Generally, a system board contains the processor, memory, and several I/O functions. The NuBus provides a high-bandwidth connection for additional I/O functions. The self-configuring features of the NuBus are especially attractive in this environment, since often the user of a personal computer wants to modify the capabilities of his or her machine, but may not wish to learn a complicated installation procedure that is required in other systems. The ability to "plug and play" is very valuable in this market. Since the NuBus is not oriented toward any one specific processor, it is equally usable for systems based on Motorola 68XXX processors, Intel 86XXX processors, or any other processor type. The NuBus desktop form-factor board size permits small, easily handled modules to be designed but is still large enough to allow complicated functions to be implemented on one board. Section 3.6.2 describes a personal computer that uses the NuBus as its expansion bus.

Industrial systems require all of the functional aspects of minicomputer and personal systems, with the additional requirement of the ability to operate in harsher environments. The 96-pin DIN connector used on NuBus modules provides reliable connection in the presence of vibration and airborne dirt or other contaminates. Since the same modules that are available for personal computers and workstations can also be used in an industrial setting, the NuBus provides a wide market opportunity for board vendors and a large selection of boards for system integrators.

The NuBus can also be used in "nonstandard" applications where a simple, high-speed bus is needed, but a different mechanical configuration is used to meet the requirements of the application. For military applications, for example, a NuBus-based prototype system has been built that uses a mil-specification, high-density connector and 6 in × 6 in aluminum core boards. Other special applications include telephone switch boxes and portable test equipment. These special applications cannot use standard cards but still benefit from using a well-defined, stable system bus.

3.6.1 Texas Instruments System 1500

The System 1500 is a general purpose multiuser-multiprocessor UNIX system with intelligent peripheral controllers. The System 1500 series depends heavily on the key features provided by the NuBus for multiprocessor support, which include fair arbitration, directed interrupts, indivisible transactions, high bandwidth, simplicity, and self-configuration. The System 1500 is constructed on Eurocard form-factor NuBus boards and is composed of three board types:

- Processor boards with local system memory
- Mass storage controllers for disk and tape
- Communication carrier boards (CCB) for all other I/O

The system memory is distributed with blocks of memory on each board in the system. The memory on each board is directly addressable in the NuBus slot space of the board. In normal operation only the memory located on the processor boards will be accessed by other boards in the system.

The processor board provides block slave support for NuBus accesses. The mass storage controller has block master capability. This allows mass storage data transfers to utilize the high transfer rate of NuBus block cycles.

The memory located on controller boards is for controller local program storage and data buffering. A controller's program may be down-loaded as part of the system booting process or after the operating system is running.

3.6.1.1 System 1500 Processor Board. The processor board is the heart of the System 1500 series. The processor consists of a Motorola 68030 processor, a floating point coprocessor, 64 kbytes of cache, 8 Mbytes of error correcting memory, a memory expansion connector, and 112 NuBus event locations. A simplified block diagram of the board is shown in Fig. 3.13. The physical address (PA) and data (PD) buses are part of the global NuBus address space.

The memory bandwidth available to the board's local processor has been optimized in several ways. There is a 64-kbyte cache memory that operates in the processor's address space. If the data is not available in cache, the physical address will be available to start a physical memory cycle. At the start of a cycle the physical address is compared to the board's slot address; if the address is within the board's slot space it is completed locally. Those cycles that cannot be completed locally are the only processor memory cycles that generate NuBus cycles.

3.6.1.2 System 1500 Software

Software Description. Each processor board contains a portion of main memory, in addition to its own cache. Since cache misses will be served more quickly

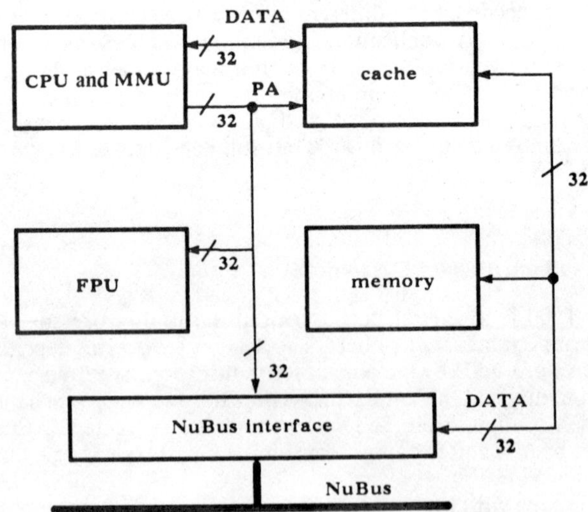

FIGURE 3.13 System 1500 processor block diagram.

by local memory than if a system bus request is required, it is desirable to keep a copy of all executing software in the local memory of each processor. For this reason, a copy of the operating system kernel is kept in each processor's local memory. Also, any task that is to be executed by that processor is also copied to its local memory. There are times, of course, when the processors must coordinate with each other since they are sharing various resources, including the system disk. When coordination is needed, they use a simple semaphore mechanism. For example, when one processor decides to communicate with a peripheral device, it first gains access to a semaphore associated with the device and then talks directly with the device, knowing that no other processor is presently talking with the same device.

There is one global area of memory, known as the kernel data area, where the system maintains various data structures for all processes in the entire system, all open files, etc. The semaphores for coordination also reside in this area. This kernel data area resides in the memory that is local to one of the processors, designated "processor 0." It is important to note that the NuBus' single large address space model allows all memory in the entire system to be accessible by every processor, but this kernal data area is the only area that has to be treated as shared memory. Each processor maps the shared kernel data into the same logical address location for its local copy of the operating system kernel. Therefore, the shared data appears in identically the same place for all copies of the operating system. This allows an application task to run transparently on any of the processors.

Since the kernel data for all tasks is in one place and since each processor can access any memory, any processor could execute any task. However, since local memory accesses are much faster than remote memory accesses, this is not allowed. There are distinct times when the system may decide to move a task from one processor to another:

- When a new task is started, it is assigned to the processor with the most available memory and the least load.
- When a task begins to do excessive paging because not enough physical memory is available, it is suspended and reassigned to another processor.
- When one processor is computation bound and another processor is free, tasks will be migrated from the busy processor to the more lightly loaded processor to balance the load.

Assigning each task to a specific processor simplifies the coordination that must take place between the independently running processors, but it does not eliminate it. Shared resources and data structures are protected by the semaphore mechanism. The NuBus supports this with two distinct mechanisms: bus locking and resource locking.

Bus locking is required when a test-and-set operation is performed to implement the semaphore test. By locking the bus, other processors are prevented from acquiring the bus during the test-and-set operation and simultaneously modifying the semaphore. Since the semaphore is located in one of the processors' local memory, that processor must also be prevented from modifying the semaphore by locking its local bus in addition to locking the NuBus. This is called resource locking. There is no need to inhibit any other processor from accessing its own local memory during this operation; therefore, resource locking is activated only on a resource that is accessed from the NuBus during a bus lock. The NuBus allows multiple resources to be locked, if needed, by accessing each during a continuous bus lock. All resources are released when the bus lock is canceled.

System Configuration. A typical System 1500 series is illustrated in Fig. 3.14. This system consists of three System 1500 processor boards, two mass storage controllers, and two communication boards. Any combination of the three board types can be configured, due to the flexibility provided by the NuBus.

3.6.2 Apple Macintosh II

The Macintosh II is a personal workstation that utilizes the desktop form-factor NuBus boards. The Macintosh depends on several key features provided by the NuBus to create a state-of-the-art cost-effective personal system, including high performance, simplicity, and self-configuration. The basic Macintosh II consists of a system board and a video controller board. Six NuBus slots are provided by the system board; the video card is installed in one NuBus slot, leaving five slots for other option cards.

3.6.2.1 Macintosh System Board. The system board consists of a Motorola 68020 processor, a memory management unit, a floating point coprocessor, sockets for up to 8 Mbytes of local memory, a controller for the floppy-disk drive, a

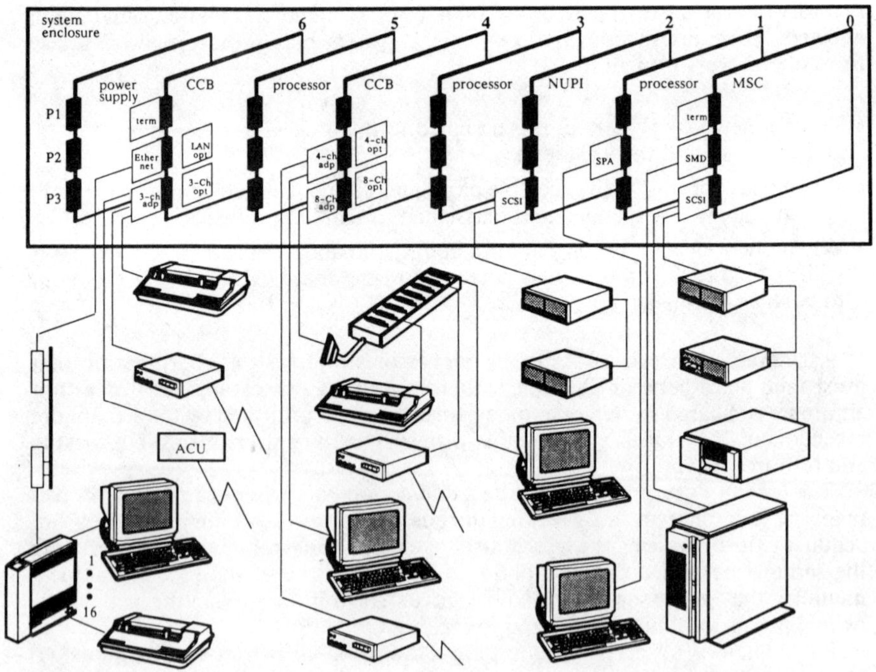

FIGURE 3.14 Typical system 1500 system configuration.

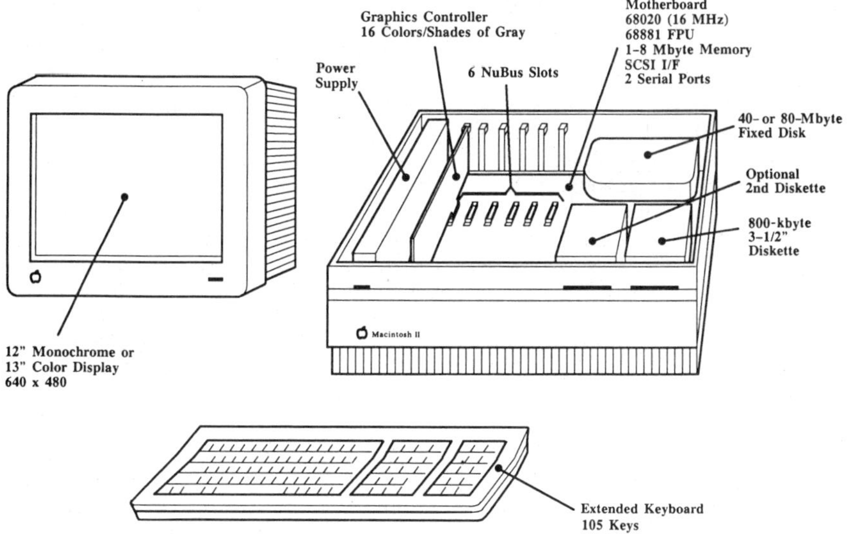

FIGURE 3.15 Typical Macintosh system configuration.

controller for the optional internal hard-disk drive and optional external mass storage devices, two serial ports, and two ports to connect the keyboard, mouse, and other optional user interface devices. The system board also provides connections for six NuBus option cards. Figure 3.15 illustrates the Macintosh configuration. The internal hard-disk and external mass storage devices are connected using the small computer system interface (SCSI) standard.

The system board appears as slot 0 on the NuBus. Option cards on the NuBus can address the local memory of the system board using any of the standard NuBus transactions except for block transactions. The system board does not support block transfers, but option cards may be designed that utilize block transactions between two option cards. The local memory on the system board is isolated from the NuBus so that none of the processor's local memory accesses appears on the NuBus.

The system board supports the nonmaster request (NMRQ*) signal on the NuBus by providing an individual signal from each NuBus connector to a priority encoder. The proccssor can determine which slot is requesting service by reading a register associated with the priority encoder.

3.6.2.2 Macintosh Option Cards. Six NuBus connectors are provided for option cards. These are designated as NuBus slots 9 through E. A video card is required, but there are several different types available from Apple or other vendors that cover a range of monitors from medium resolution (640 × 480 pixels) black and white to high-resolution color. Many other types of option cards are available, such as Ethernet controllers, data acquisition cards, coprocessor boards, etc.

The system processor accesses the option card address space in two different modes, determined by the memory management unit (MMU) that converts the logical addresses to physical address. The MMU is normally in the 24-bit mode for compatibility with old software. When in the 24-bit mode, the processor can only access a 1-Mbyte area in each of the six NuBus slots. This 1-Mbyte area is located in the first megabyte of the 16-Mbyte slot space of each NuBus slot. The MMU can be put in the 32-bit mode by a system utility call. When in the 32-bit mode, the processor can access all of the 16-Mbyte slot space of each NuBus slot.

Option cards that require more than 16 Mbytes of address space may use the 256-Mbyte "superslot" space that is also assigned to each of the NuBus slots. Superslot space is accessible by the system processor only when the mapper is in the 32-bit mode. Superslot space is a convention used on the Macintosh for dividing up and allocating to option cards the 4-Gbyte NuBus address space. Recall that the NuBus allocates 16 Mbytes to each slot, with an address of the form F(ID)XXXXXX, where ID is the slot number, from 0 to F. Since the Macintosh only uses slots 9 through E for option cards, an address of the form (ID)XXXXXXX can also be assigned to each slot. Notice that in a general NuBus system, this cannot be done since a superslot address for slot F, which would be FXXXXXXX, would overlay the normal NuBus slot space.

3.7 HISTORICAL RATIONALE

The NuBus had its origins at the Massachusetts Institute of Technology (MIT) in the late 1970s. In 1979 a paper by Ward and Terman[7] described an architecture for a personal workstation that was bus based rather than focused around a particular processor. MIT built a prototype system to demonstrate the concept of a simple, high-performance backplane bus.

In 1981, Western Digital became interested in using the NuBus concept and began a project to create a personal UNIX workstation based on the NuBus. This machine came to be known as the Nu Machine.

In early 1983, Texas Instruments acquired the Nu Machine project from Western Digital. The first commercial versions of the Nu Machine were delivered to MIT later that year. LISP Machines, Inc. purchased Nu Machine systems and added their own LISP processor to create the Lambda LISP machine. The Lambda systems made use of the multiprocessor aspects of the NuBus. Texas Instruments incorporated the NuBus system concept into the Explorer LISP machine and the System 1500 multiprocessor UNIX system.

The Computer Society of the IEEE was approached in 1983 with the proposal to create a standard based on the NuBus definition. The Futurebus activity was underway and shared many goals with the NuBus effort. It was envisioned that the NuBus would be a synchronous "kindred" bus to the Futurebus. As the Futurebus evolved, the supporters of the NuBus stood firm on the distinctly minimalist approach to bus definition. A separate study group for the NuBus was established by the Microprocessor Standards Committee in July, 1984. This study group refined the definition of the bus over a period of three years with input from several interested users. In June, 1987 the IEEE Standards Board adopted the work of the study group as IEEE Standard 1196.

One of the parties that participated in the refinement of the NuBus specification was Apple Computer. The NuBus was selected by Apple to provide a simple, high-performance bus for the Macintosh II desktop workstation, which began production in 1987.

In 1983, MIT licensed the use of the NuBus definition and technology to Texas Instruments. Later, MIT authorized Texas Instruments to provide sublicenses to any company interested in selling NuBus products. Texas Instruments has also

TABLE 3.6 Summary of NuBus Features

Feature	Description
Physical	32-bit multiplexed address and data Synchronous at 10 MHz 51 active signals, 5 V, -5.2 V, ± 12 V Single address space Distributed, parallel arbitration eliminates daisy chains Two board form-factors
Protocol	Simple master-slave architecture Fair arbitration Byte, halfword and word read and write transactions 2-, 4-, 8-, and 16-word block transfer transactions Memory-mapped I/O Memory-mapped events Slot addressing Configuration ROM Self-configurable
Interface	TTL levels Controlled impedence, terminated signals Separate assertion and sample clock edges
Performance	20 Mbytes/s using read or write transactions 37.5 Mbytes/s using block transactions
Status	IEEE standard 1196

obtained patents that apply to various aspects of the NuBus and now offers a combined license that covers the original technology license and Texas Instruments patents.

3.8 SUMMARY

The NuBus is a simple, high-performance system bus. It is applicable to a wide range of systems, including minicomputers, personal computers, workstations, industrial controllers, and process control computers. The NuGroup provides marketing and technical support for manufacturers and users. Table 3.6 summarizes the features of the NuBus.

LIST OF TRADEMARKS

NuBus, Explorer, Explorer II, and Nu Machine are trademarks of Texas Instruments Incorporated.

Apple is a registered trademark and Macintosh is a trademark of Apple Computer, Inc.

UNIX is a registered trademark of AT&T.

Intel is a registered trademark of Intel Corporation.

REFERENCES

1. IEEE Specification 1196, *NuBus—A Simple Backplane Bus,* Institute of Electrical and Electronic Engineers, New York, 1987.
2. IEC Specification for Connectors, IEC 603-2, International Electrotechnical Commission, New York, 1980.
3. IEC Specification for Printed Circuit Boards, IEC Publication 297-3, International Electrotechnical Commission, IEC, New York, 1984, and Supplement, IEC Publication 48D, IEC, New York, 1982, Sec. 16.
4. Part No. 2536702-0001, *NuBus System Architecture Specification,* Texas Instruments, Austin, Texas, 1987.
5. Apple Computer, Inc., *Designing Cards and Drivers for the Macintosh II and Macintosh SE,* Addison-Wesley, Reading, Mass., 1988.
6. Apple Computer, Inc., *Inside Macintosh,* Vol. V, Addison-Wesley, Reading, Mass., 1987.
7. S. Ward and C. Terman, "A New Approach to Personal Computers," MIT, Cambridge, Mass., 1979.

CHAPTER 4
UNIBUS, Q-BUS, AND VAXBI BUS

Atlant G. Schmidt
Digital Equipment Corporation
Tewksbury, Massachusetts

Since the introduction of the PDP-11 and VAX-11 family of computers, Digital Equipment Corporation has developed three major I/O buses. The first was the UNIBUS, first employed on the PDP-11/20 computer and released in 1970. The second was the Q-Bus, also known as the LSI-11 bus, and was released in 1975 along with the LSI-11 microcomputer. Both of these buses were subsequently made available on VAX-11 processors as well as on additional PDP-11 models. Recently, the VAXBI bus has addressed the ever-growing I/O needs of the VAX-11 family of computers.

All three buses are strongly related in a number of areas, although their implementation details vary. In addition, the VAXBI bus, being much newer, was able to use large-scale integration (LSI) technology to incorporate a great many more features than the two preceding buses. The similarities, however, make it convenient in this chapter to discuss all three buses together, highlighting their differences as necessary.

This chapter is not meant to be a design document—the available space does not permit adequate coverage of all of the necessary topics. Rather, it is meant to be a brief description of bus design at Digital, and is meant to give the main properties of the three principal buses currently in use at Digital.

Throughout this chapter, signals in timing diagrams are shown with "up" meaning asserted. This is usually in contrast to their actual polarities on the various buses.

4.1 A BRIEF HISTORY OF THE UNIBUS, Q-BUS, AND VAXBI BUS

At the time of the PDP-11 processor's development, it was common for computers to have totally separate paths for memory and I/O. Many computers did not even contain "buses" as we now commonly understand them. Rather, computers often contained dedicated I/O wiring for a variety of I/O adapters that were expected to be important by the CPU designer. This approach obviously limited the range of configurations that could be built from a given CPU model. Digital's 12-bit PDP-8 CPU (the "straight eight") was a hybrid of the two approaches and is relatively typical of the state of the art at that time: Memory was contained entirely in dedicated slots in the backplane—there was no memory bus per se. In addition, the CPU backplane contained dedicated wiring for a number of basic I/O devices such as the console terminal and the high-speed paper tape reader and punch. Finally, a simple I/O bus was implemented for programmed I/O and interrupt-driven I/O. Additional cabling permitted a simple form of high-speed access known as *data break*. It was *not* direct memory access (DMA), as all accesses still required that the CPU provide substantial assistance. A specific set of instructions was used to access I/O devices.

Looking into the future, it was clear that the users' needs would soon outgrow what a 12-bit computer could provide. An early proposal for a 16-bit computer strongly resembled its 12-bit predecessor, but for a variety of reasons (including limited I/O capability), this design was rejected. Instead, a computer was designed that was to represent a radical departure from previous practice.

This computer would not separate the memory and I/O subsystems. Instead, they would reside on a common, unified bus. I/O devices would consist of a series of registers assigned addresses in the same address space as memory cells. This is referred to as *memory-mapped* I/O. This had a number of advantages:

- The CPU did not require a specific set of I/O instructions. This, in turn, had several benefits:

  Programmers did not need to remember a specific set of I/O instructions.

  The CPU implementors did not need to waste valuable operation codes on I/O instructions. (In the PDP-8 processor, one eighth of the available operation codes were used for I/O instructions.) Instead, additional "basic" instructions could be designed.

  Very little additional hardware was required in the CPU in order to implement the I/O system.

- Direct memory access was an automatic feature of this bus design. Just as the CPU could access memory or I/O, an I/O device could access memory or other I/O devices. In fact, I/O devices could and eventually did take on all of the characteristics of the CPUs themselves. CPUs and I/O devices eventually became indistinguishable from the bus' point of view.

This bus was named the UNIBUS, standing for *unified bus*. All PDP-11 and VAX-11 processors have shared the basic features established by the UNIBUS. The bus was designed with the intent of minimizing, system-wide, the amount of logic required to implement the bus. As such, it is unmultiplexed and uses a relatively simple protocol with only five basic types of transactions.

As IC technology advanced, it became possible to integrate more and more of a PDP-11 CPU onto fewer and fewer chips. Using a microprogrammable chip set supplied by Western Digital, it finally became possible to implement a full PDP-11 CPU on just four chips: an 8-bit data path chip, a microcontrol chip, and two microcode storage chips employing a mix of ROM and programmed logic array (PLA). But as the CPU grew smaller, the UNIBUS became an economic stumbling block: It was physically large and had 56 signals, far too many to be accommodated by the IC packaging technology of the early 1970s. So a scaled-down version of the bus was developed. Called variously the Q-Bus or LSI-11 bus, this bus used multiplexed addresses and data and thus required little over half as many wires to implement. One of the tradeoffs, increased complexity of the interfaces, was easily accommodated by the advancing IC technology. Another tradeoff, decreased bandwidth, was addressed later by incorporating more advanced protocols into later Q-Bus products. These newer protocols were, of course, designed in a backwards-compatible fashion.

When the UNIBUS was originally designed, the only available processor had both a virtual and physical address space of only 64 kbytes. With an eye toward future expansion, the UNIBUS was provided with 18 address lines, providing an address space of 256 kbytes. Expansion, of course, proceeded much faster than any of the original designers had envisioned, and this allowance for the future was exhausted within two years of the first PDP-11 processor's appearance in the market: The second PDP-11 processor allowed the full 256-kbyte address space to be utilized.

The Q-Bus at first release also supported an 18-bit address but like the UNIBUS, its first processor only supported a 64-kbyte virtual and physical address space. But its second processor (the F11 as exemplified by the LSI-11/23 and PDP-11/23) allowed a 4096-kbyte address space.

At this point, the UNIBUS and the Q-Bus diverged. The UNIBUS had defined the top 8 kbytes of the address space as the addresses to be occupied by all I/O device registers; the rest of the address space had been given over to memory and memorylike functions. This placement of the I/O registers at the "top" of the UNIBUS address space fixed the physical size of the UNIBUS address space for all time. So in order to accommodate growing memory needs, the PDP-11/70 CPU introduced for the first time an address map between the UNIBUS and a now-separate memory bus. Architecturally, the system still had a unified bus and many of the same benefits as always, but I/O devices could no longer "see" all of memory at the same time. Instead, they could only see the portion of main memory that was visible through the address map.

To maintain program compatibility between UNIBUS and Q-Bus machines, the Q-Bus had also defined the top 8 kbytes of the bus address space as the location of the I/O registers, but with one *critical* difference: Where the UNIBUS had required that I/O devices decode their entire address from the generic bus address lines, the Q-Bus provided a single signal (BBS7 L, later renamed BBSIO L) that implied "address in the I/O space." All correctly designed Q-Bus interfaces use this signal instead of separately decoding all the bus address lines. This allowed the designers to embed the "I/O page" logic only in those Q-Bus devices (such as CPUs) that needed to access I/O space locations.

In addition, additional lines on the Q-Bus had been reserved for allowing address bits beyond the original 18. The basic design of the PDP-11 CPU conveniently allowed physical addresses as large as 22 bits, so the Q-Bus was designed with this limit in mind and later was officially expanded to that limit.

PDP-11 processors on the Q-Bus do not have address maps between the I/O devices and the memory—they maintain the full "unified bus" as originally implemented.

Most VAX-11 Q-Bus processors, however, *do* use I/O maps, as they have physical address spaces much larger than the Q-Bus 4096 kbyte (4 Mbyte) limit. In addition, there is no requirement in the VAX-11 that programs and data buffers occupy contiguous physical memory. Allowing long DMA transfers to discontiguous segments of physical memory requires either very sophisticated I/O devices or the presence of an address map to perform the scatter/gather operation. Only the original MicroVAX-I omitted such an address map, and, as a result, its I/O performance was seriously impaired as compared to later VAX-11 Q-Bus processors.

As scientific advancements were made, however, what was leading-edge technology had become mundane by the 1980s. It was clear by the late 1970s that Digital would need more powerful buses to keep the advancing line of VAX-11 CPUs well supplied with data. The internal bus of the VAX-11/780, the first VAX-11 CPU, provided a good example of what was possible:

- 32-bit data width (with a similar address width)
- Synchronous, very fast operation
- A limited number of nodes on the fast internal bus routed through adapters to slower external buses such as the UNIBUS

In addition, inasmuch as MOS IC technology had allowed whole CPUs to be integrated onto one or a few chips, further improvements in the technology now allowed whole I/O bus interfaces to be integrated into single chips, even with their requirements of controlled impedances and substantial drive capabilities.

The outgrowth of these converging forces was the VAXBI bus. Its single IC [the backplane interconnect interface chip (BIIC)] implements a wide variety of bus functions including:

- Distributed arbitration
- A variety of transaction types including all of the interlocked transactions required to implement VAX-11 processors
- Extensive error detection capabilities
- Incorporation into the chip of most of the bus interface logic that was previously designed by each implementor of a bus interface

This last point is particularly significant: By taking most of the bus interface design out of the hands of many individual implementors, the result is a bus where interoperability of all of the interfaces can more readily be ensured. It is no longer necessary that each individual designer be an expert on the bus. It is only required that the original designer of the interface chip do a correct job. As systems have become increasingly complex, they have also become increasingly difficult to test, so the "provability" of a correct design has become more and more important.

4.2 BUS CHARACTERISTICS

At this point, we will consider some of the attributes of buses in general, and the UNIBUS, Q-Bus, and VAXBI bus in particular.

4.2.1 Physical Characteristics

The UNIBUS was implemented as an outgrowth of the 18-pin, 0.125-in pitch, single-sided card-edge wire-wrapped connector block that had become the standard for Digital's line of logic modules. For the M series (TTL IC series) of logic modules, a new, double-sided card-edge connector was employed, and this

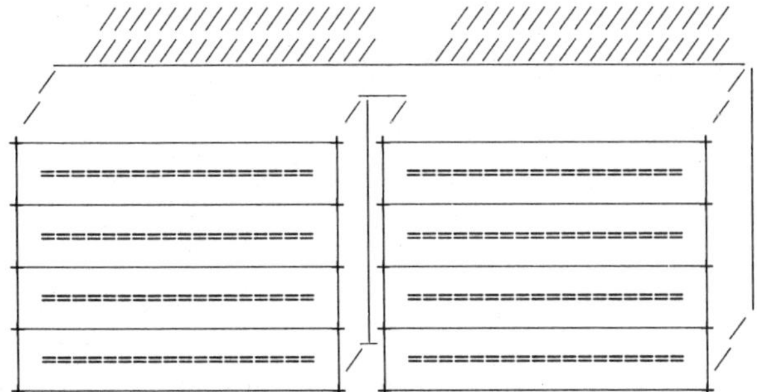

FIGURE 4.1 A Digital green-block module mounting block.

became the physical foundation of all UNIBUS products. Traditionally molded in dark green plastic, this connector is known within Digital as a *green-block* connector. Each block is two slots wide and four slots high (see Fig. 4.1). A variant of the block was two slots wide but only one slot high.

Assembled into cast metal mounting frames, these blocks formed the various backplanes used in the PDP-11/20 CPU. Each of these backplanes was six slots wide and four slots high. This subassembly was named a *system unit* (see Fig. 4.2). As with standard Digital practice, rows across the six slots were named A through F from left to right, looking at the wire-wrapped side of the backplane; slots were numbered from 1 upwards, counting back in the mounting box.

The PDP-11/20 mounting box had 8½ in of headroom over rows B, C, D, E, and F, but the fans obstructed most of the headroom over row A. This led to the CPU being implemented on modules that were 8½ in tall but only four connector rows wide (approximately 11 in). Because of their four rows of connector fingers, these modules are referred to as *quad* modules. These modules were plugged in such that they spanned rows C, D, E, and F, leaving rows A and B empty.

Some of the low-headroom space in the A rows was used to connect power to the backplanes with a very short paddlecard. At the first and last slots of most backplanes, the A and B rows were used to interconnnect the backplanes. Thus, the standard UNIBUS connection became the A and B rows of the first and last slots of all backplanes.

A rigid connector (the M920 module) was designed that could connect two adjacent backplanes, bridging from slot 4 of one backplane to slot 1 of the next. For connections outside of the mounting box, the BC11A UNIBUS cable (with small paddleboard connectors on each end) allowed similar easy interconnection.

The BC11A UNIBUS cable could carry the UNIBUS to any backplane built out of Digital green-block connectors, so many I/O controllers were not built in

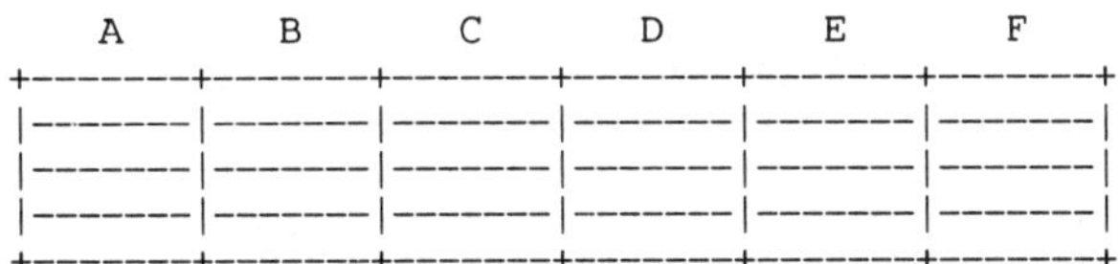

FIGURE 4.2 A Digital system unit (viewed from the wire-wrapped side).

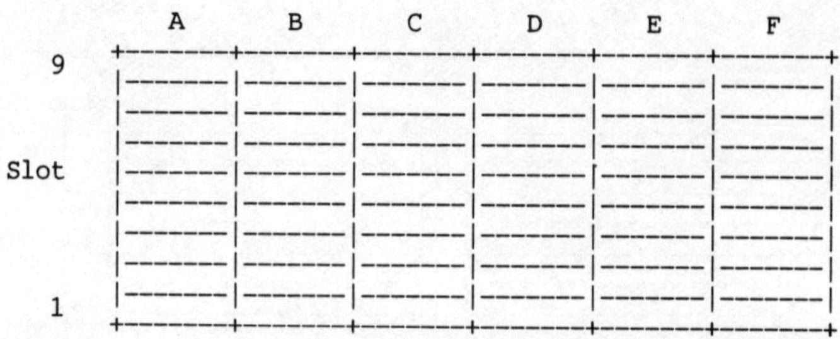

FIGURE 4.3 A Digital double system unit (viewed from the wire-wrapped side).

system units but rather in large or small arrays of green-block connectors mounted in standard 19-in Electronic Industry Association (EIA) rack cabinets. A single UNIBUS can contain combined BC11A UNIBUS cable and backplane wiring totaling up to 50 ft in length.

Later, a double system unit was introduced (see Fig. 4.3). This double-size frame provided a 6 × 9 mounting space. In addition, all PDP-11 mounting boxes after the PDP-11/20 CPU relocated the fans, eliminating the headroom constraint over the A rows. This allowed the use of *hex* modules, which are six slots wide.

Within these (double or single) system units, many slots (such as the multiple slots that contained the CPU) were wired for specific applications. Other slots contained more general wiring intended to support a number of different I/O controllers.

Many controllers share a few common logic elements such as address decoding and interrupt control. The controllers only differ in the specific "device" logic, and this is usually easily separated from the "bus" logic. Toward this end, two general-purpose modules were developed: the M105 address decoder and the M782 interrupt control. Each of these modules was 8½ in tall and a single slot wide.

Combined with some device logic [such as the M780 (KL11) serial line interface, the M781 (PC11) paper tape interface, or the M786 (DR11-A) general-purpose parallel I/O], the M105 address decoder and the M782 interrupt control formed a complete peripheral interface. These sets of M105, M782, and MXXX

```
+-------------------------++-----------++----------+
| Device Logic            || Address   ||Interrupt|
|                         || Decode    || Control |
|    - M780               ||           ||         |
|    - M781               || M105      || M782    |
|    - M786               ||           ||         |
|    - etc.               ||           ||         |
|                         ||           ||         |
|                         ||           ||         |
|                         ||           ||         |
|                         ||           ||         |
|                         ||           ||         |
|           __            ||           ||         |
 |_______| |_______|    |_______|    |_______|
```

FIGURE 4.4 A small peripheral controller.

were known as *small peripheral controllers* (SPCs) and many UNIBUS backplanes contained slots prewired to accept any of the MXXX device logic modules in rows C and D, the M105 module in row E, and the M782 module in row F. These prewired slots were naturally known as SPC slots (see Fig. 4.4).

Eventually, as production quantities increased, it became more cost effective to manufacture entire SPCs on single, quad-sized modules instead of assembling the three separate modules. Often, however, no logical change was involved but just a circuit-board relayout to put all the logic from the three individual modules onto a single large module.

In order to achieve lower costs, the Q-Bus design centered around smaller modules, although it still used the Digital green-block connectors. Many I/O modules were simple enough to be contained on a module only two slots wide (a *dual* module), and no individual component was too complex to be contained on a module four slots wide (a quad module). And, since generic I/O modules like the M105 and M782 were no longer being built, the intraslot wiring that was needed to support the module-to-module interconnections was no longer needed. This meant that all of the bus wiring for any module could fit into a dual-width slot (see Fig. 4.5).

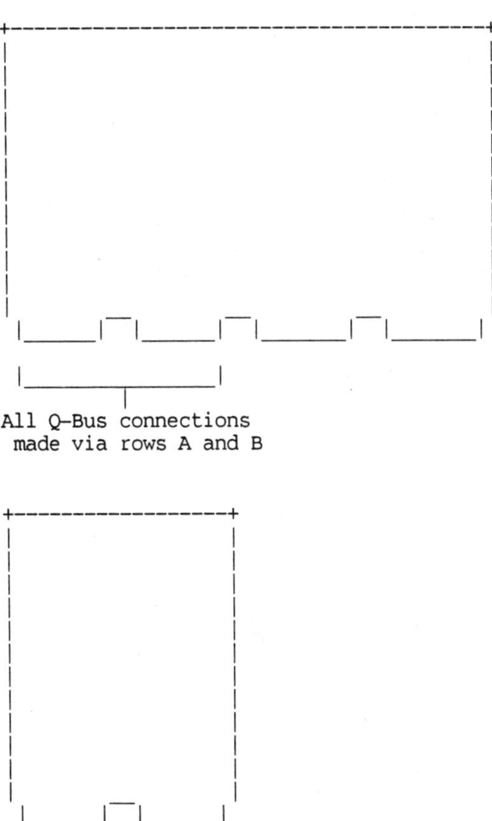

FIGURE 4.5 Q-Bus quad and dual modules.

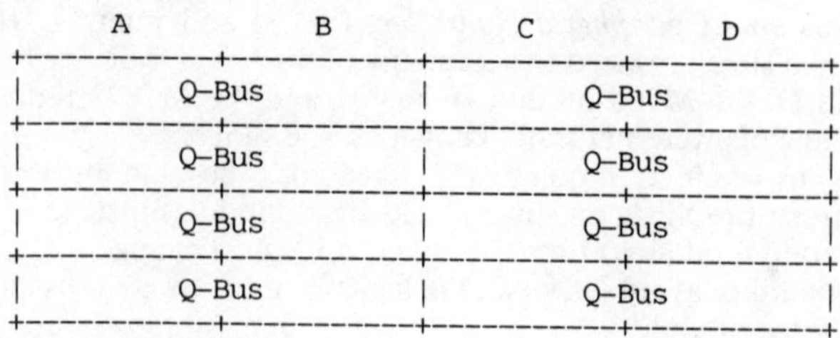

FIGURE 4.6 A Q-Bus backplane (viewed from the module side).

To allow efficient intermixing of dual- and quad-width modules in a single quad-width backplane, every pair of slots was wired with Q-bus signals (see Fig. 4.6). That is, the Q-Bus is duplicated in rows A and B and rows C and D. Quad modules only connect to the Q-Bus in rows A and B, while dual modules can connect in rows A and B or C and D, depending upon whether the module is mounted in the left or right halves of the backplane.

With the introduction of the RLV11 disk controller, it was finally necessary to split a controller across two logic modules. Since the designers did not want to use "over-the-top" connection cables, this required the design of a new backplane. In this backplane, rows C and D no longer carried Q-Bus signals. Instead, the pins on the bottom side of one slot were wired to the pins on the top side of the next slot, allowing two adjacent modules to intercommunicate. This was referred to as *C-D interconnect* (see Fig. 4.7). The original backplane arrangement with the Q-Bus on both sides became known as a *Q-Q backplane* while the new backplane arrangement became known as a *Q-CD backplane.*

Later, this C-D interconnect was used to connect processors to memory. The KDJ11-B PDP-11 and KA630 VAX-11 processors are examples of this technique. In these backplanes, only the first three or four slots are Q-CD slots; the rest of the backplane is pinned Q-Q (see Fig. 4.8).

A single Q-Bus can contain up to three backplanes and a total of 16 ft of interconnecting cable.

The VAXBI bus was a completely fresh start. (While some VAX-11 products had finally moved from the Digital green-block connectors to a more modern connector, they had maintained the same basic module form factors.)

The VAXBI bus introduced a new module form factor with dimensions of 9.18 in × 8.00 in (23.32 cm × 20.32 cm); see Fig. 4.9. In addition, new connector technology was introduced in the form of a 5-group, 60-pin per group zero-inser-

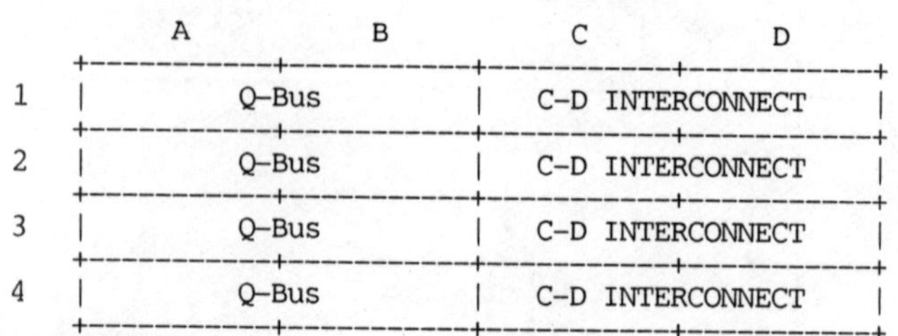

FIGURE 4.7 A Q-Bus backplane with C-D interconnect (viewed from the module side).

```
         A          B          C          D
    +----------+----------+----------+----------+
  1 |        Q-Bus        |  C-D INTERCONNECT   |
    +----------+----------+----------+----------+
  2 |        Q-Bus        |  C-D INTERCONNECT   |
    +----------+----------+----------+----------+
  3 |        Q-Bus        |  C-D INTERCONNECT   |
    +----------+----------+----------+----------+
  4 |        Q-Bus        |        Q-Bus        |
    +----------+----------+----------+----------+
```

FIGURE 4.8 A Q-Bus backplane with both Q-CD and Q-Q connections (viewed from the module side).

tion-force (ZIF) connector. The VAXBI bus itself only uses two of the five connector groups. The other three connector groups are available for user connections.

The VAXBI bus standardized the board layup, using a ten-layer technology suitable for TTL, CMOS, or emitter-coupled logic (ECL) power and logic levels. Of particular note is that the design standardizes the corner of all VAXBI bus modules that actually interfaces to the VAXBI bus. This helps ensure that all module designs will meet all VAXBI bus specifications. All licensed VAXBI bus developers are supplied with the exact layout of this VAXBI corner and must conform exactly. In this corner is mounted the BIIC, the heart of every VAXBI bus interface.

No switch packs or user-configuration jumpers are permitted on VAXBI bus modules. No cable connections are permitted to be made directly to VAXBI bus modules—instead, cable connections are made through the three user connector groups. Every module must contain two and only two yellow LEDs, one located on the front edge of the module and one located on the top edge. These LEDs are illuminated upon the successful completion of the module self-test procedure. (LEDs of other colors may be used for other purposes, but yellow is reserved for the self-test LEDs.)

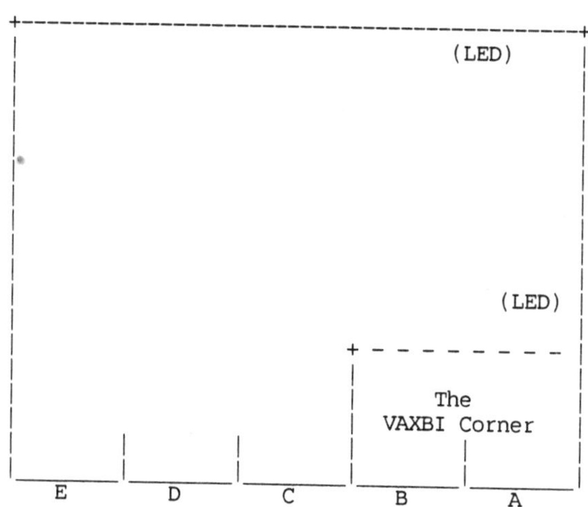

FIGURE 4.9 A VAXBI bus module.

VAXBI modules are assembled into card cages that contain up to six modules. Up to four card cages can be interconnected for a maximum of 24 VAXBI slots. (The VAXBI bus only allows 16 connections maximum, but certain designs require more logic than can fit on a single module. In these designs, only one module of the set actually connects to the VAXBI bus.)

If the VAXBI bus system employs multiple card cages, the card cages must be physically adjacent; they are connected by short jumper cables approximately 2 in long. No other VAXBI bus cables are permitted.

4.2.2 Power Availability

UNIBUS mounting boxes provide various voltage levels. Aside from +5 and ±15 V, the availability of other voltages depends upon the particular mounting box and, in some cases, the particular regulators installed in the mounting box.

- +5
- ±15
- +5B (battery-backed-up)*
- ±12†
- −5†
- +20†
- +8†

Q-Bus mounting boxes provide +5 and +12 V. Many Q-Bus modules contain a charge pump to produce −12 V from the +12-V source.

VAXBI bus mounting boxes provide various voltages. Aside from +5 and ±12 V, the availability of other voltage depends upon the particular mounting box and, in some cases, the particular regulators installed in the mounting box.

- +5
- ±12
- +5B (battery-backed-up)‡
- −5.2§
- −2.0¶

4.2.3 Electrical Characteristics

The UNIBUS consists of 56 signal lines and a number of ground (logic reference) lines. The individual lines are detailed in Table 4.1.

All lines on the bus employ open-collector drivers and pull-up resistors. The signal levels on the UNIBUS are approximately TTL voltage levels although specific driver and receiver ICs are required.

*May not be battery-backed-up in all boxes
†May not be available in all boxes
‡May not be battery-backed-up in all boxes
§May not be available in all boxes
¶May not be available in all boxes, but if −5.2 is available, −2.0 will also be available

Most of these signals are considered to be asserted (i.e., 1), while near ground and are considered to be deasserted (i.e., 0) while near 3.3 V. Signals of this type are indicated by the suffix L after the signal name. Any signal that is asserted while near 3.3 V is indicated by the suffix H.

Three different kinds of termination are used, depending on the particular signal line. The signals BUS AC LO L and BUS DC LO L are terminated by a resistor-capacitor network. In Table 4.1, this is indicated as "slow" termination. The grant lines (BUS NPG H, BUS BGX H) only connect from one module to the next and use a simplified termination on each module. In the table, this is indicated as "grant" termination. All other lines are terminated at each end of the UNIBUS into 120 Ω and 3.3 V. This is indicated as "fast" termination.

Driver saturation voltages and driver and receiver leakage currents are specified sufficiently close to allow at least 20 driver-receiver pairs to be connected to a single UNIBUS. (This driver-receiver pair approximately represents a so-called dc load.) Sufficient current is available from the terminators to support the ac loading (capacitance) that is normally associated with 20 dc loads.

The Q-Bus consists of 42 signal lines and a number of ground (logic reference) lines. The individual lines are detailed in Table 4.2.

All lines on the bus employ open-collector drivers and pull-up resistors. The Q-Bus uses the same voltage levels, drivers, and receivers as the UNIBUS. In addition, a number of specific medium-scale-integration (MSI) ICs were designed that integrated many of the Q-Bus subfunctions and may be connected directly to the Q-Bus.

Most of these signals are considered to be asserted (i.e., 1) while near ground and are considered to be deasserted (i.e., 0) while near 3.3 V. Signals of this type are indicated by the suffix L after the signal name. Any signal that is asserted while near 3.3 V is indicated by the suffix H.

Two different kinds of termination are used, depending on the particular signal line. The signals BPOK H and BDCOK H are terminated by a resistor-capacitor network. In Table 4.2, this is indicated as "slow" termination. All other lines are terminated at the processor end of the Q-Bus into 3.3 V and either 120 or 240 Ω (depending on the processor model). This is indicated as "fast" termination. On Q-Bus systems with cable connecting multiple backplanes, additional termination may be supplied at the various cable paddleboards.

As on the UNIBUS, up to 20 dc loads are permitted. The number of ac loads permissible is dependent upon the particular terminator arrangement contained in the system.

The VAXBI Bus consists of 52 signal lines and a number of ground (logic reference) lines. The individual lines are detailed in Table 4.3.

All lines on the bus except for the two clock pairs employ open-collector or open-drain drivers and pull-up resistors. All of these signals are considered to be asserted (i.e., 1) while near ground and are considered to be deasserted (i.e., 0) while near 3.3 V. Signals of this type are indicated by the suffix L after the signal name. All synchronous lines change state on the 5-MHz clock's leading (rising) edge.

The VAXBI bus clock signals are differential, emitter-coupled logic signals, but are driven and received by custom chips that use only positive voltages. (The signals may be thought similar to signals produced by ECL chips that have V_{ee} tied to ground rather than -5.2 V and V_{cc} tied to + 5V rather than ground.)

Any VAXBI bus module may contain clock drive circuitry. However, only the module in the first slot of the VAXBI bus may actually drive the VAXBI bus clock lines. To accomplish this, a hard-wired pin in every VAXBI bus slot determines whether the module in that slot should drive the clock lines. For all slots except slot 1, this pin is deasserted; it is only asserted in slot 1 of the first VAXBI bus card cage.

Only the BIIC is permitted to make connections to most of the VAXBI bus signals. Only the custom clock drivers and receivers are permitted to make connections to the VAXBI bus clock lines.

4.3 MULTIPLEXED VERSUS NONMULTIPLEXED BUSES

Most buses contain the concepts of address and data. All items on the bus are uniquely accessed by means of an *address* or a series of addresses. The address on the bus is very much like a telephone number or an address on an envelope. Once a unique device has been addressed (selected), *data* may be exchanged with that device. This data would correspond to the phone conversation or the letter itself.

Somes buses first use the same physical set of wires to carry the address, followed by one or more items of data. These buses are called multiplexed buses (see Fig. 4.10). Both the Q-Bus and the VAXBI bus are examples of multiplexed buses. Other buses use separate sets of wires to carry the address and data. These buses are called nonmultiplexed buses (see Fig. 4.11). The UNIBUS is an example of a nonmultiplexed bus.

Because an address and data can be carried simultaneously, a nonmultiplexed bus is usually faster than a multiplexed bus using the same technology, particularly if each new address bears no relationship to any preceding address. However, multiplexed buses share the same set of wires for address and data so they tend to be physically smaller and thereby less expensive. In addition, if addresses are usually presented in a particular order (e.g., ascending), the next address can be predicted rather than explicitly transmitted, and the performance of the multiplexed bus can approach the performance of the nonmultiplexed bus. Fortunately, long DMA I/O transfers almost always follow ascending order, so both the Q-Bus and the VAXBI bus take advantage of this address prediction: The Q-Bus implements a mode called *block mode* where a variable number of data words (up to 16 words or 32 bytes) can be delivered per single address; the VAXBI bus implements a variety of fixed transaction sizes (up to 8 words or 16 bytes).

4.4 STRICT MASTER-SLAVE RELATIONSHIP

Most transactions on the UNIBUS, Q-Bus, or VAXBI bus consist of a single device (called the *bus master* or *commander*) requesting another device (the *slave* or *responder*) to perform some operation. The UNIBUS and Q-Bus use the terms

```
Data
and      /addr\/data\/addr\/data\/addr\/data\/addr\/data\
Addr     \____/\____/\____/\____/\____/\____/\____/\____/
Wires
                     |<--------->|
                           |__ One Transaction
```

FIGURE 4.10 A Multiplexed bus (like the Q-Bus and VAXBI bus).

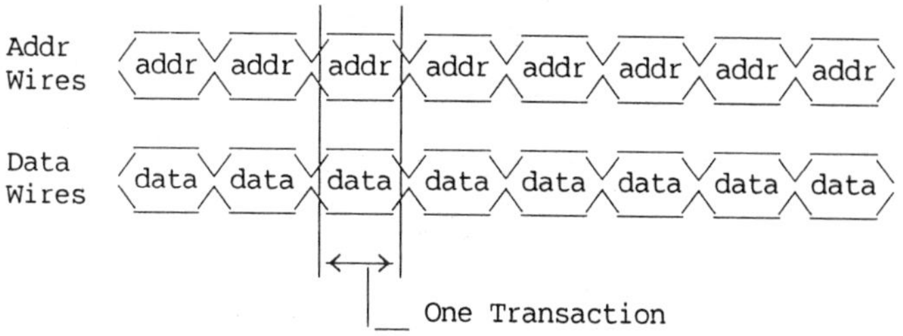

```
Addr   addr  addr  addr  addr  addr  addr  addr  addr
Wires

Data   data  data  data  data  data  data  data  data
Wires

                  One Transaction
```

FIGURE 4.11 A nonmultiplexed bus (like the UNIBUS).

bus master and slave, whereas the VAXBI bus frequently uses the terms commander and responder. No direction of data flow is implied here—the master may be requesting that the slave read *or* write data.

4.5 UNPENDED OPERATION

All three buses perform what is known as unpended operations—only one operation may be in progress at any given time, and it executes to completion before the next operation may be begun. No operation may be left "pending."

Other buses (such as those used within the CPUs) allow multiple simultaneous ongoing operations where, for example, several independent read operations may have been started and various memory modules are working in parallel, with all of the read operations pending. These are referred to as *pended* buses.

4.6 ASYNCHRONOUS OR SYNCHRONOUS OPERATION

A bus may be synchronous or asynchronous. Synchronous buses partition time into parcels of fixed duration, usually called cycles. These cycles are defined by one or more clocks on the bus. Every operation on the bus must take place in an integral number of these cycles. Some buses require that every operation take place within a single bus cycle. A synchronous bus of this sort is illustrated in Fig. 4.12. Here, every rising edge of the system clock implies that a valid address is

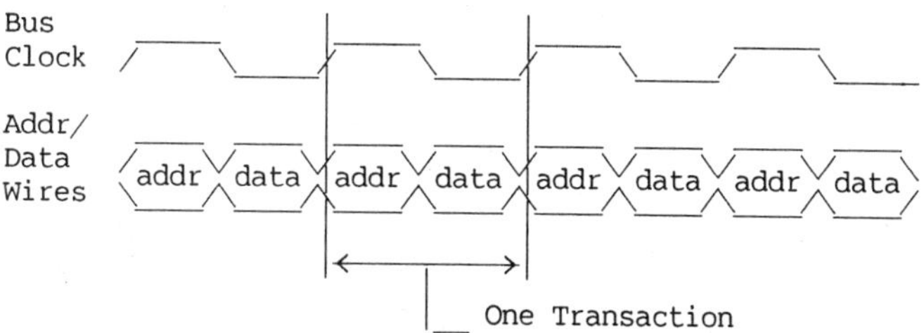

FIGURE 4.12 A single-cycle synchronous bus.

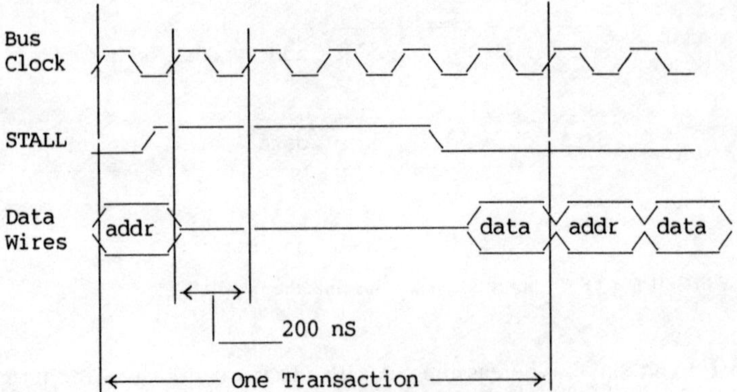

FIGURE 4.13 A multicycle synchronous bus such as the VAXBI (but ignoring arbitration here).

on the bus; every falling edge of the system clock implies that the data has replaced the address. Although synchronous buses may be very simple or very fast (although usually not both), this fixed timing imposes severe constraints on the system designer. The duration of the bus cycle must be long enough to allow for the slowest peripheral yet short enough to get reasonable system performance.

Other synchronous systems allow a device to take multiple bus cycles for one transaction. A bus of this sort is illustrated in Fig. 4.13. Here, a stall (or wait) line freezes the system, allowing slow slaves more time to process the data. This eases

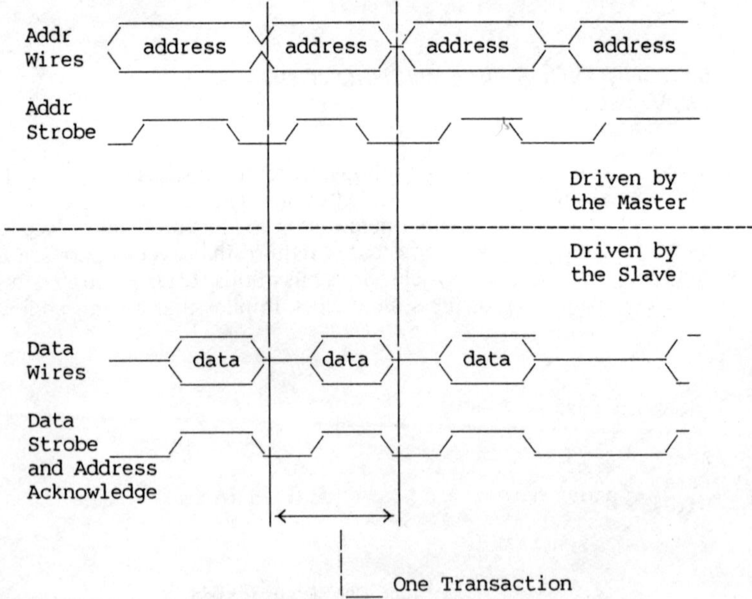

FIGURE 4.14 An asynchronous bus (like the UNIBUS).

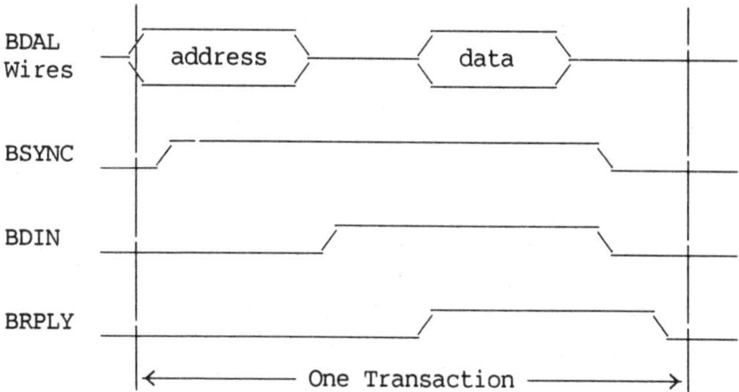

FIGURE 4.15 An asynchronous multiplexed bus (like the Q-Bus).

the timing constraints somewhat but does so at the expense of a more complex design. The VAXBI bus is an example of such a multicycle synchronous bus. The basic cycle time for the VAXBI bus is 200 ns.

The UNIBUS, on the other hand, is completely asynchronous. No master clock times the operations of the UNIBUS. Rather, the selected master and slave devices exchange handshaking signals to indicate the presence of information on the bus. This handshaking allows each bus transaction to run as quickly as the particular master-slave pair will allow. Figure 4.14 shows a series of read data transactions on the UNIBUS (i.e., the master has asked the slave to provide data to the master). Note that the master first asserts the address of the desired slave and then address strobe (actually called MASTER SYNC or BUS MSYN L). The slave then looks up the desired data and places it on the data lines along with a signal that combines the functions of data strobe and address acknowledge (actually called SLAVE SYNC or BUS SSYN L). No fixed timing is required between BUS MSYN L and BUS SSYN L; fast slaves can respond quickly while slow slaves can take more time to produce the requested data.

The Q-Bus is mostly asynchronous. Like the UNIBUS, no master clock times the operations of the Q-Bus. One operation, though, does have a fixed maximum time limit. That operation is the latching of an address. Because the Q-Bus is a multiplexed bus, the same set of physical wires is used to carry both addresses and data. When the bus master indicates that an address is present on the wires (by asserting BSYNC L), the master is also preparing to remove the address in preparation for the use of the wires by the data. No confirmation signal returns to the master, indicating that all possible slave devices have latched the address. It is simply assumed that by 200 ns after the assertion of BSYNC L all slave devices *have* latched the address. The bus master then asserts either BDIN L (DATA IN) or BDOUT L (DATA OUT) to command the beginning of the data portion of the read or write transaction. Figure 4.15 illustrates a read operation.

4.7 SKEW AND DESKEWING TECHNIQUES

One of the complexities of any bus design is skew. This is the phenomenon where signals that were placed on a bus exactly in phase arrive at their destination slightly out of phase (see Fig. 4.16). Skew develops whenever signals travel over

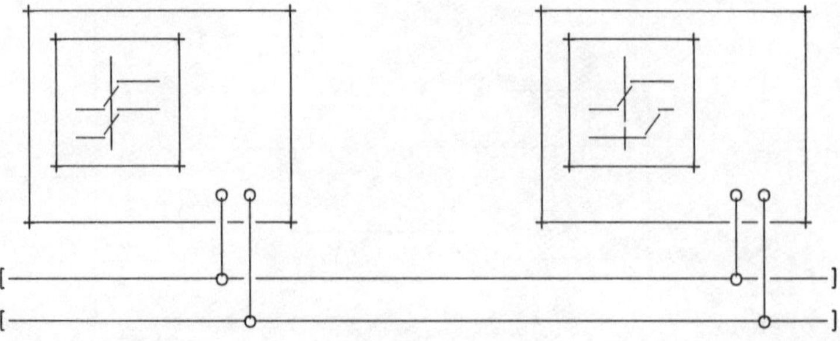

FIGURE 4.16 Skew.

paths of different lengths. It also develops if the paths have slightly different impedances, resulting in slight variations in the velocity of the electrical signals. For this reason, lumped capacitive loads frequently cause skew.

Skew is often the most critical parameter in the design of a bus. The VAXBI bus limits skew by strictly limiting the total physical length of the bus and the number of loads permitted to be attached to the bus. In addition, BIIC chips are the only type of connection that may be made to the VAXBI bus. Because of these factors, skew is thus limited to a small fraction of the cycle time, as a worst case.

The UNIBUS and Q-Bus, on the other hand, have a much less stringent set of physical configuration rules, and no single standard interface chip exists for these buses. They are thus much more subject to skew, and a designer of UNIBUS and Q-Bus interfaces must always consider skew and its effects. In general, the master is responsible for deskewing logic signals on either bus. For example, on the UNIBUS, the master must assert the address lines 150 ns prior to asserting BUS MSYN L, the address strobe signal. Out of the total 150 ns, 75 ns is allotted for deskew—during this time, a valid address should reach all points on the UNIBUS, even those connected by "slower" wires. (The other 75 ns is allotted for the various address decoders in the system to stabilize.)

Similarly, slaves are allowed to simultaneously assert read data and BUS SSYN L, the data strobe signal. But the data strobe signal may reach the master ahead of the actual data, so the data returned from the slave must not be sampled until 75 ns after the master observes the assertion of BUS SSYN L. This ensures that the master strobes in valid data, even data bits connected by "slower" wires.

Because of poorer control of impedances, deskew intervals on the Q-Bus are generally slightly longer than the analogous deskew intervals on the UNIBUS.

4.8 METASTABILITY

This is a problem that is generally unique to asynchronous designs. All logic design depends upon storage elements of varying types. D-type flip-flops are probably one of the most common examples, being frequently used to determine such things as which of two events occurred first. (Flip-flops are used as synchronizers in asynchronous designs.) And flip-flops, being built of real components, require a certain minimum activation energy to change state.

But by definition, in an asynchronous design, states may change at any arbitrary instant. For D-type flip-flops, this means that their data input may change at any time with respect to their clock input. As the transition edge of the data input approaches the transition edge of the clock input, less and less energy is available to flip the flop. If the flop were perfect, at a certain minimum energy level, the flip-flop would simply fail to change states.

But flip-flops are far from perfect, and many flip-flops behave very poorly as the activation energy hovers around the minimum required value. The flip-flop may flip and then revert to the previous state, it may oscillate, or it may assert both its Q and not-Q outputs simultaneously or it may assert neither. Eventually, the flip-flop will settle at one state or the other, but much data may have been lost in the meantime.

This phenomenon is known as metastability. Various techniques exist to combat its effects:

- Careful control (design) of the flip-flop's input signals can sometimes eliminate the "window of vulnerability"
- Good flip-flop design can minimize the tendencies of flip-flops to enter this indeterminate condition
- Maximum settling times can be specified
- Screening can test individual samples for good or bad tendencies
- Logic can be designed to not rely on the output state of the flip-flop during the expected period of metastability

Frequently, multiple ranks of synchronizers are used, as evidenced by the existence of master-slave flip-flops, where two sections are coupled together and data is latched into the first section on one clock edge and data from the first section is latched into the second section on the opposite clock edge.

Two cases in particular turn up frequently in UNIBUS and Q-Bus design:

- The CPUs are frequently synchronous machines interfaced to these asynchronous buses. All of the various asynchronous control signals must be synchronized prior to entering the synchronous CPU logic, and the CPU logic must not be affected by metastability in the synchronizers.
- Whenever an interrupt grant propagating along the bus reaches a device, that device must consider whether to accept the grant or to pass it onwards. The device must sample the instantaneous asynchronous state of its interrupt request logic, which frequently requires a flip-flop that is frequently subject to metastability. Over the years, reliable designs have evolved, but the penalty is that each device on the bus adds perceptible delay to the propagation of the grant along the bus. (This delay is frequently in the range of 75 to 150 ns.)

4.9 PARTIALLY DISTRIBUTED ARBITRATION

The UNIBUS, Q-Bus, and VAXBI buses, like most, allow only one device at a time to be the bus master. This implies that there must be some method of selecting a bus master from among all of the devices requesting the bus. The process that performs this selection is called *priority arbitration,* and the bus is usually granted to the requester with the highest priority (according to some prearranged scheme).

Arbitration on the UNIBUS and Q-Bus is performed using a two-dimensional

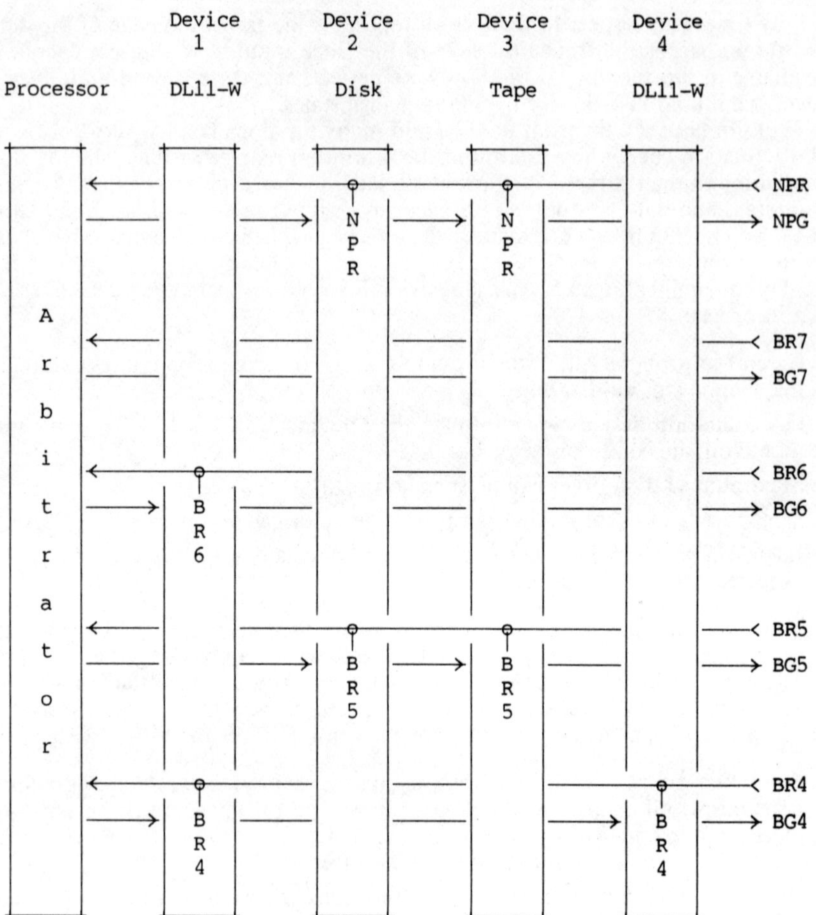

FIGURE 4.17 UNIBUS two-dimensional priority.

scheme. A typical example is shown in Fig. 4.17. The first dimension is the specific priority level of the request. The UNIBUS or Q-Bus may be requested at any of five different priority levels. The highest-priority level is named nonprocessor request (NPR) on the UNIBUS and direct memory request (DMR) on the Q-Bus. *Nonprocessor request* was so named because devices requesting use of the UNIBUS at this priority level do not need any assistance from the central processor. *Direct memory access* is the term that found more general favor, but it is somewhat incorrect because transactions on either bus are allowed between any two devices, not just between a device and memory.

The lower four levels are simply called bus request 7 (BR7) through bus request 4 (BR4) on the UNIBUS. On the Q-Bus these are known as interrupt request 7 (IRQ7) through interrupt request 4 (IRQ4). Devices request use of the UNIBUS via BR levels or the Q-Bus via IRQ levels in order to interrupt a processor (described later).

All requests are passed to a central bus arbitrator. This central bus arbitrator is usually included in the PDP-11 processor or VAX-11 bus adapter or interface. In any case, it is always located at the front end of the UNIBUS or Q-Bus. The arbitrator determines the highest requested level from among the five available and issues a grant for that level, if appropriate. The grant then travels toward the back end of the bus. On the UNIBUS, nonprocessor grant (NPG) is given in response to NPR, bus grant 7 (BG7) in response to BR7, and so forth. On the Q-Bus, direct memory grant (DMG) is given in response to DMR. A single interrupt acknowledge (IAK) signal is issued on the Q-Bus in response to any of the IRQ signals. The actual processing of the interrupt differs slightly between the UNIBUS and the Q-Bus.

The second dimension of the arbitration is performed when more than one device requests the UNIBUS or Q-Bus at the same priority level. Now, the grant is passed from device to device, toward the back end of the bus—this is referred to as daisy chaining. Each device, in turn, considers whether it wants to use the bus. A device that does not want to use the bus passes the grant on to the next device along the bus. A device that does want to use the bus does not pass the grant (i.e., it blocks the grant) and the device wins the arbitration. Thus arbitration among more than one device on a particular level is distributed among the devices. The example in Fig. 4.17 uses UNIBUS terminology but is equally applicable to the Q-Bus.

Figure 4.17 illustrates the beginning of a typical UNIBUS configuration. Here, the first DL11-W (device 1) can request the UNIBUS at priority levels BR6 or BR4; both the disk controller (device 2) and the tape controller (device 3) can request at levels NPR or BR5; the second DL11-W (device 4) can request only at level BR4. No device in this illustration uses BR7.

The UNIBUS arbitrator considers the five levels of priority and grants the highest-level request. So in our example, the disk or the tape requesting at the NPR level always has priority over either of the DL11-Ws requesting at either level BR6 or BR4.

On any given level (e.g., NPR), the grant is passed from device to device along the UNIBUS. At the NPR level, the disk has priority over the tape because the disk gets an opportunity to examine (and possibly block) the grant before passing it on to the tape. Similarly, at the BR4 level, the first DL11-W has priority over the second DL11-W.

4.10 FULLY DISTRIBUTED ARBITRATION

The VAXBI bus, on the other hand, uses fully distributed arbitration to determine which device will become the next master of the VAXBI bus. All boards connected to the bus share in the responsibility of arbitration and no special hardware exists at either end of the bus. (Curiously enough, the arbitration scheme harkens back to a scheme employed at least as early as the PDP-8E CPU and its OMNIBUS.)

Essentially, the VAXBI bus allows as many as 16 separate nodes to be connected to the bus. (Each node is an interface onto the VAXBI bus via a BIIC chip.) Each device is assigned a particular node number (its node ID) in the range of 0 through F hexadecimal, with node 0 having the highest priority. For fixed high-priority arbitration, each device has access to one data wire, determined by the node ID assignment (see Fig. 4.18).

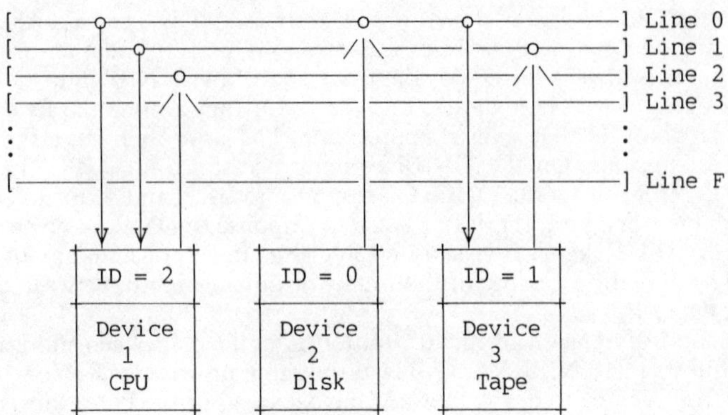

FIGURE 4.18 VAXBI distributed priority arbitration.

Here, we have three devices, using node IDs 2, 0, and 1, respectively. During an arbitration cycle, any device wishing to use the bus asserts its request line. At the same time, the device must monitor the state of all of the higher-priority arbitration lines. If the device is requesting use of the bus and it sees no higher-priority arbitration line asserted, the device concludes that it has won the arbitration.

Often, a strictly fixed priority scheme is not the best choice. Therefore the VAXBI bus actually implements three different, coexisting priority schemes. Once the system is up and running, any node can use any of the three schemes at any time, but at power-up time, all nodes must default to dual round-robin (fair) arbitration.

Fixed high priority. Nodes using fixed high-priority arbitration compete as described above. A node using fixed high-priority arbitration will always win the arbitration over a node using fixed low priority.

Fixed low priority. Nodes using fixed low-priority arbitration also compete as above but use a separate set of 16 wires and will always defer to nodes arbitrating at the fixed high-priority level.

Dual round-robin arbitration. This is a rotating priority scheme where all nodes compete with an equal chance (over time) of winning the arbitration. It is implemented by having nodes alternate in a fair way between the high- and low-priority arbitration methods based on the identity of the previous bus master.

A device can request either type of arbitration on a per-transaction basis, so a device could use rotating priority arbitration most of the time but revert to a fixed high-priority arbitration if, for example, it has critical data in its buffers and it detects that these buffers are on the verge of overflow.

Recently, the Q-Bus has begun using a variation on the fixed priority scheme described above to allow its single IAK (interrupt acknowledge) line to service four distinct IRQ (interrupt request) priority levels. Before accepting the grant, Q-Bus devices receiving IAK inspect the state of those IRQ lines that represent requests by higher-priority devices. If higher-priority requests are pending, the grant is passed. If no higher-priority requests are pending, the grant is accepted.

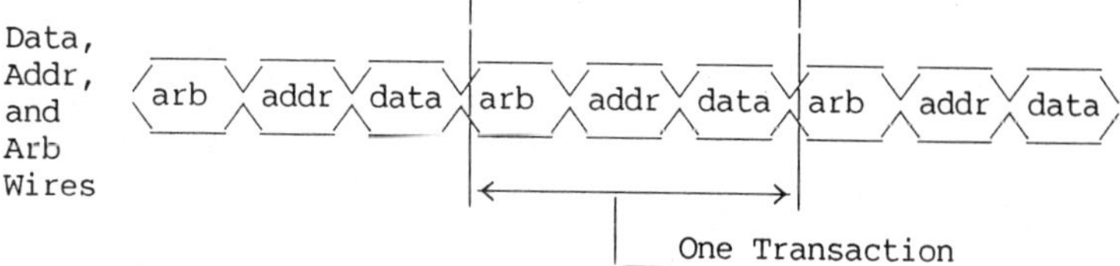

FIGURE 4.19 A nonoverlapped arbitration bus.

4.11 OVERLAPPED OR EMBEDDED ARBITRATION AND DATA TRANSFER

As mentioned previously, before a prospective bus master may use the bus, it must win the arbitration (ensuring that it is the highest-priority requestor of the bus). Some buses can do only one thing at a time, e.g., arbitrate or transfer data, but not both. This is illustrated in Fig. 4.19. Because it uses the same lines to arbitrate as well as carry addresses and data, the VAXBI bus is an example of such a bus. The UNIBUS and the Q-Bus, on the other hand, use separate lines to perform arbitration and to carry data and so allow the next master to be selected (arbitrated) while the current master is still transferring data. This is referred to as overlapped arbitration (see Fig. 4.20).

Overlapped arbitration greatly contributes to the performance of the UNIBUS and Q-Bus. The VAXBI bus, on the other hand, has much greater raw throughput, so lack of overlapped arbitration is not an impediment. In addition, unlike the picture shown in Fig. 1.4.19, most practical memories cannot deliver data quickly enough to fill the cycle immediately following the delivery of a read address (see Fig. 4.21). The VAXBI bus capitalizes on this dead time by usually embedding the arbitration for the next master in this cycle that would otherwise go to waste (see Fig. 4.22).

4.12 ADDRESS SIZE AND ADDRESS SPACES

The total number of unique data that can be addressed on any bus is dependent on the number of bits used to form the address as well as the basic unit addressed on the bus. The UNIBUS, Q-Bus, and VAXBI bus all address bytes as their basic unit.

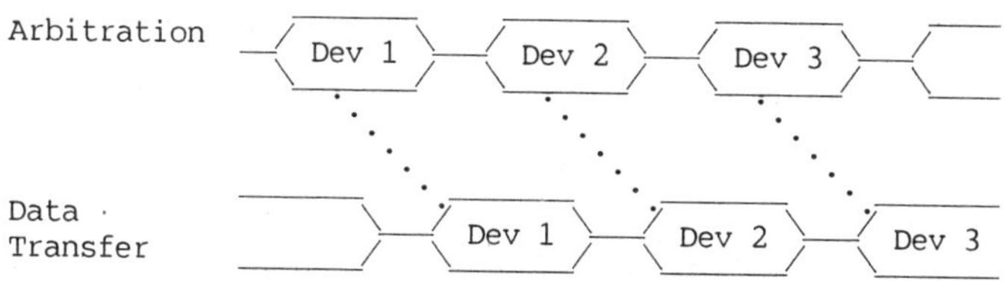

FIGURE 4.20 An overlapped arbitration bus (like the UNIBUS and Q-Bus).

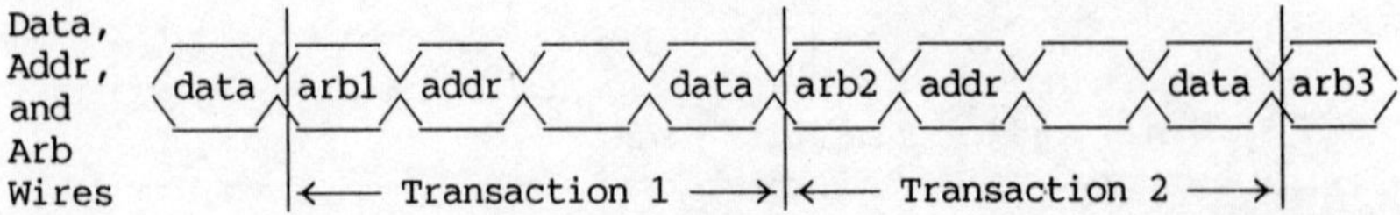

FIGURE 4.21 A nonoverlapped, nonembedded arbitration bus.

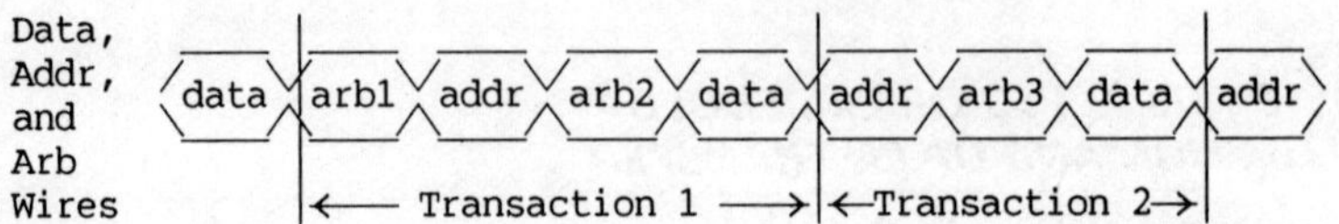

FIGURE 4.22 A nonoverlapped, embedded arbitration bus (like the VAXBI bus).

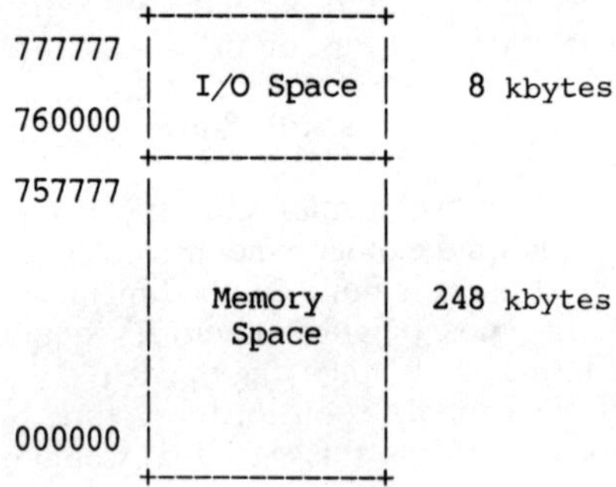

FIGURE 4.23 UNIBUS address space. Addresses are shown in octal.

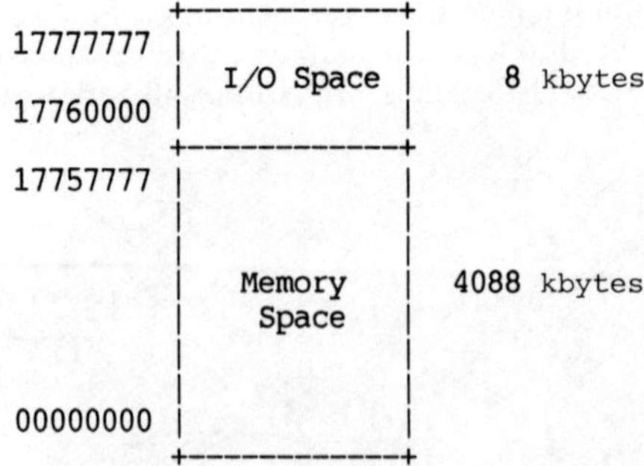

FIGURE 4.24 Q-Bus address space, as viewed from a PDP-11 processor. Addresses are shown in octal.

The UNIBUS uses 18 bits to specify an address. Because each address represents a byte of data, the UNIBUS allows

$$2^{18} = 256\text{K unique byte addresses}$$

Of these addresses, 248K are allotted for access to the system main memory and 8 K are allotted for access to I/O devices (see Fig. 4.23).

The Q-Bus uses 22 bits to specify an address *plus* the additional line that indicates the I/O space. As a result of this, the Q-Bus allows

$$2^{22} = 4096\text{K unique byte addresses for memory}$$

plus

$$2^{12} = 8\text{K unique byte addresses for I/O}$$

Only VAX-11 Q-Bus processors allow the full 4096 kbytes of Q-Bus memory space to be used for Q-Bus memory and access (through the VAX-11 address map) to the system main memory. PDP-11 processors with their limited 22-bit physical address reduce this amount by the number of bytes used for the I/O addresses. Therefore most PDP-11 Q-Bus processors actually allow 4088K byte addresses for memory and 8K byte addresses for I/O (see Figs. 4.24 and 4.25).

The VAXBI bus employs 30-bit addresses with the 1024-Mbyte address space broken up into two major divisions: The first half of the address space, 512 Mbytes, is allotted for access to the system main memory. The second half of the address space, 512 Mbytes, is broken up into a 16-Mbyte I/O space and a 480-Mbyte (15 × 32 Mbytes) reserved space.

The 32-Mbyte I/O space is further subdivided and allotted for various I/O space uses (see Fig. 4.26).

- Each node on the VAXBI bus is allotted 8 kbytes of node space. The CSRs implemented by the BIIC chip are in this space as are additional CSRs implemented by each VAXBI bus interface.
- 128 kbytes are allotted to multicast space. This space is currently reserved for use by Digital.

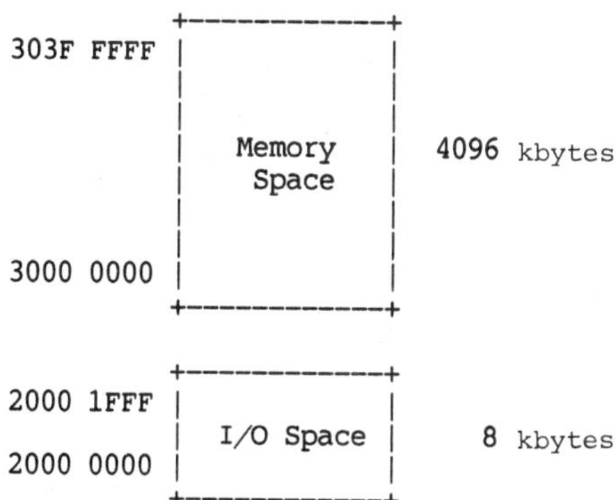

FIGURE 4.25 Q-Bus address space, as viewed from a VAX-11 processor. Addresses are shown in hex.

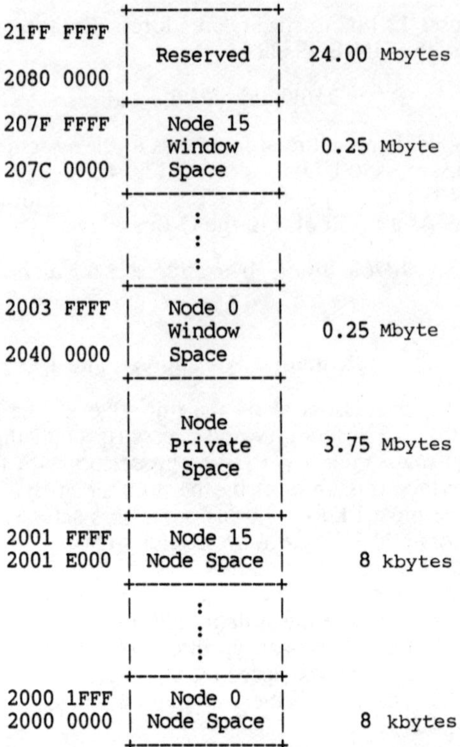

FIGURE 4.26 VAXBI bus I/O address space. Addresses are shown in hex.

- 3.75 Mbytes of the address space is allotted to node private space. VAXBI bus transactions in this address space will not be responded to by any VAXBI bus interface, although this address space may be visible from within a given VAXBI bus interface module. It can be used on a given module for such things as private RAM or ROM memory, I/O devices, etc., all of which would only be accessible from within the interface module.
- Each node on the VAXBI bus is allotted 256 kbytes of window space. This can be used for functions similar to those described in the node private space, but these addresses will be visible to all other nodes on the VAXBI bus, rather than hidden as in the node private space.
- A large piece of the address space (24 Mbytes) is reserved for future use by Digital.

Multiple VAXBI buses can be connected to a single VAX-11 system (see Fig. 4.27). When this is done, all the VAXBI buses on the system share the common 512-Mbyte memory address space.

But logic within the system takes addresses in the 512-Mbyte I/O space and allocates them to up to 16 individual VAXBI buses, 32 Mbytes per VAXBI bus.

```
               +--------------+
3FFF FFFF | VAXBI Bus 15 |
3E00 0000 |  I/O Space   |  32.00 Mbytes
               +--------------+
3DFF FFFF | VAXBI Bus 14 |
3C00 0000 |  I/O Space   |  32.00 Mbytes
               +--------------+
3BFF FFFF | VAXBI Bus 13 |
3A00 0000 |  I/O Space   |  32.00 Mbytes
               +--------------+
               |      :       |
                      :
               |      :       |
               +--------------+
25FF FFFF | VAXBI Bus 2  |
2400 0000 |  I/O Space   |  32.00 Mbytes
               +--------------+
23FF FFFF | VAXBI Bus 1  |
2200 0000 |  I/O Space   |  32.00 Mbytes
               +--------------+
21FF FFFF | VAXBI Bus 0  |
2000 0000 |  I/O Space   |  32.00 Mbytes
               +--------------+
1FFF FFFF |              |
               |              |
               |    Common    |
               |    Memory    | 512.00 Mbytes
               |    Space     |
               |              |
0000 0000 |              |
               +--------------+
```

FIGURE 4.27 Aggregate VAXBI bus address space as viewed from a VAX-11 CPU. Addresses are shown in hex.

Once the system decides which VAXBI bus should receive the transaction, then address bits ⟨28:25⟩ are discarded so that the actual transaction on the target VAXBI bus will take place in the 32-Mbyte range of physical addresses allotted to the I/O space. (That is, the system adapter never sends to a VAXBI bus an address in the 480-Mbyte reserved region. Instead, the system adapter first trims the address down to fit into the defined 32-Mbyte I/O space region.)

4.13 DATA SIZE

The basic unit of data transferred on both the UNIBUS and the Q-Bus is a word of 16 bits (two 8-bit bytes). Data on either bus must be read as a word with the bus master extracting a single byte if required. Data on either bus may be written as a word or a byte. Data must always be naturally aligned—that is, it is illegal to attempt to transfer in one transaction two bytes that are not part of the same word. Byte data must always be *justified,* that is, the data byte must always appear on the same wires that it would occupy if it were being sent as part of a word.

The basic unit of data transferred on the VAXBI bus is a longword of 32 bits (four 8-bit bytes). Data on the VAXBI bus must be read as a longword with the bus master extracting whatever number of bytes are required. Data may be written as one, two, three, or four bytes in a single longword. Similar to the UNIBUS and the Q-Bus, on the VAXBI bus, data must always be naturally aligned—it is illegal to attempt to transfer in one cycle two bytes that are not part of the same longword. And as on the UNIBUS and Q-Bus, byte data must always be justified.

4.14 PARITY ERROR INFORMATION FROM SLAVES

If the slave (e.g., a MOS memory) contains logic to detect parity errors, the slave can pass a parity error indication to the master via predefined UNIBUS or Q-Bus signals. The UNIBUS and Q-Bus themselves do not include parity checking of any bus signals.

The VAXBI bus, on the other hand, contains extensive parity checking for bus operations. In addition, it contains functionality similar to the UNIBUS and the Q-Bus whereby a slave device can signal that the data it has provided on the bus is corrected data (e.g., as in the case of a single-bit memory error) or that correction was not possible (e.g., as in the case of a double-bit memory error).

4.15 INTERLOCKING

The UNIBUS supports a transaction called data-in, pause (DATIP). Originally included to optimize core memory access (by holding off the unnecessary restore operation when the processor intended to modify the stored data), this transaction is also used as the basis for interlocking on the UNIBUS. Once an interlockable slave has been accessed by a DATIP transaction, it will reject subsequent accesses until unlocked by a data out (DATO/write) transaction. For most slave devices, it is also possible to achieve interlocking by becoming bus master and doing separate a read and write without releasing ownership of the UNIBUS, simulating an atomic read-modify-write operation.

The Q-Bus, on the other hand, supports two atomic read-modify-write transactions called DATIO (data in/out) and DATIOB (data in/out, byte). Because these operations are indivisible, the slave needs no extra logic to ensure correct interlocking.

The VAXBI bus was intended from its inception to fully support multiprocessor operations. As such, it contains a full set of explicit interlocking primitives. It does not implement an atomic read-modify-write transaction but the UNIBUS technique works here as well.

4.16 INTERRUPTS

The UNIBUS and the Q-Bus implement similar interrupt schemes. Both expect that a single processor will field all interrupt requests. This processor is referred to as the interrupt fielding processor (IFP), and while it need not be located at the front end of the bus, it must have special connections to the bus arbitrator. For this reason, the IFP is usually located at the front end of the bus and actually contains the bus arbitrator within itself.

Both buses support vectored interrupts. That is, each device on the device can pass the IFP the virtual address of its interrupt service routine(s) so that no device polling is required. The exact process of obtaining the interrupt vectors varies slightly between the two buses.

On the UNIBUS, a device makes an interrupt request by asserting one of the four bus request lines (BUS BR7 L through BUS BR4 L). When the IFP is willing to field the interrupt, the IFP (via the bus arbitrator) asserts the respective bus grant line (BUS BG7 H through BUS BG4 H). The interrupting device then becomes bus master and performs a special write transaction using the BUS INTR L line as both address and address strobe, supplying the interrupt vector as its data to be written. The IFP will be the selected slave and it will respond with BUS SSYN L as in any other transaction.

On the Q-Bus, a device makes an interrupt request by asserting one of the four interrupt request lines (BIRQ7 L through BIRQ4 L). When the IFP is willing to field the interrupt, the IFP becomes bus master via the arbitrator. The IFP then performs a special read transaction using the interrupt acknowledge (BIAK L) signal as both the address and the address strobe. The highest-priority interrupting device will supply the interrupt vector as the returned read data and supply BRPLY L as in any other transaction.

Note that on the UNIBUS, the highest-priority interrupting device became the bus master, and it wrote its vector to the IFP. On the Q-Bus, the IFP becomes the bus master and reads an interrupt vector from the highest-priority interrupting device. The Q-Bus method represents a substantial simplification in the design of I/O devices as they do not necessarily need any bus master logic. In addition, the Q-Bus scheme avoids the problem of bus hangs that can occur if an error occurs during the vector read—the vector read can be timed out like any other read using the same processor logic. (It is unclear why the original UNIBUS designers did not notice this optimization.)

Interrupts on the VAXBI bus represent a generalization of aspects of both the UNIBUS and Q-Bus concepts. A node desiring interrupt service becomes bus master and issues an INTR transaction. The transaction can be directed at any subset of the 16 nodes on the VAXBI bus. This transaction identifies the current interrupt priority level of the node desiring service. Any IFPs on the bus will latch the fact that some node at this priority level desires service.

When an IFP is ready to service an interrupt at the requested interrupt priority level, the IFP issues an IDENT request to obtain the interrupt vector from the highest-priority device that has interrupts pending to this IFP at the specified level. All such devices then arbitrate to determine the device with the highest priority; that device then sends its interrupt vector in response to the IDENT read and the interrupt operation has now been completed.

Since arbitration is fully distributed, there need not be a single system-wide interrupt-fielding processor. However, it is still general practice that individual I/O devices target their interrupt requests to individual processors rather than broadcasting them to all IFPS. Otherwise, multiple IFPs might respond to a single interrupt request. This would cause the IFPs that responded after the first IFP to waste valuable time as they each recognized that the interrupt was no longer pending.

4.17 TRANSACTION TYPES

The UNIBUS implements five basic transactions:

Mnemonic name	Mnemonic expansion	Explanation
DATI	Data in	Read word
DATO	Data out	Write word
DATOB	Data out, byte	Write byte
DATIP	Data in, pause	Read word (with write intent)
....	....	Interrupt vector write

The Q-Bus implements six basic transactions:

Mnemonic name	Mnemonic expansion	Explanation
DATI	Data in	Read word
DATO	Data out	Write word
DATOB	Data out, byte	Write byte
DATIO	Data in, pause	Read word and write word
DATIOB	Data in/out, byte	Read word and write byte
IAK	Interrupt acknowledge	Interrupt vector read

The VAXBI Bus implements 13 basic transactions. Read and write transactions can operate across three basic data widths: longword (4 bytes), quadword (8 bytes), and octaword (16 bytes) with byte-masked writes allowing writing to individual bytes within the longword, quadword, or octaword.

Mnemonic name	Explanation
READ	Read
RCI	Read with cache intent
IRCI	Interlock read with cache intent
WRITE	Write
WCI	Write with cache intent
WMCI	Write (byte-) masked with cache intent
UWMCI	Unlock write (byte-) masked with cache intent
INVAL	Invalidate (cached data)
INTR	Interrupt
IPINTR	Interprocessor interrupt
IDENT	Read interrupt vector
STOP	Stop a node
BDCST	Broadcast

4.18 TIME-OUTS

Buses employ time-outs to catch a variety of error conditions. For asynchronous buses like the UNIBUS and the Q-Bus, time-outs are used to set upper bounds on the time allowed for the various asynchronous events to occur. This avoids the problem of the bus becoming "hung" due to some handshaking failure such as trying to access a nonexistent slave device. Synchronous, stallable buses like the VAXBI also use time-outs in a similar fashion to ensure that the bus does not become hung in the event of a prolonged stall.

Aribtration time-outs on the UNIBUS and Q-Bus are the responsibility of the bus arbitrator. Usually, this is the PDP-11 or VAX-11 CPU or its bus adapter or interface. The arbitration time-out is usually set to 10 μs, and failure to assert BUS SACK L or BSACK L within 10 μs after issuance of BUS NPG H or BUS BGX H (on the UNIBUS) or BDMG L (on the Q-Bus) will result in removal of the grant.

Slave reply time-outs on the UNIBUS and the Q-Bus are the responsibility of each individual bus master—there is no centralized time-out facility as exists on some other buses. For the UNIBUS, the time-out used by CPUs, bus adapters and interfaces, and I/O devices varies but is usually in the range of 7–35 μs. VAX-11 CPUs with several levels of bus adapters between the UNIBUS and the actual system memory have brought about increased slave reply latencies on the UNIBUS and the subsequent need to lengthen the time-out period.

For the Q-Bus, the slave replay time-out is conventionally set at 10 μs. To date, no Q-Bus VAX-11 CPU has imposed substantial delay between the Q-Bus and the actual system memory so there has been no need to extend the time-out period.

4.19 UNIBUS SIGNAL DETAILS

The UNIBUS signals are partitioned into three groups:

- Initialization and shutdown signals
- Arbitration signals
- Data transfer signals

In addition to those signals that are actually part of the UNIBUS and controlled by the UNIBUS specifications, there are other standard signals that are present in most UNIBUS backplanes and follow UNIBUS-like conventions. These signals are documented under the heading of "miscellaneous signals" (see Table 4.1).

4.19.1 UNIBUS Initialization and Shutdown Signals

BUS DC LO L. This signal, when asserted, indicates that somewhere on the UNIBUS the ac power has failed for a sufficiently long time that all other bus signals are not to be trusted. Each power supply in the system can drive BUS DC LO L.

This signal may also be driven by any UNIBUS device that desires to restart the system as though power had just been applied. Network interfaces use this feature to cause down-line loading to begin.

BUS AC LO L. This signal, when asserted, indicates that somewhere on the UNIBUS, ac power has failed and the system will soon be inoperative. Upon the assertion of BUS AC LO L, the system processor will usually begin an orderly shutdown. Each power supply in the system can drive BUS AC LO L.

TABLE 4.1 UNIBUS Signals

Name	High or low	Termination type	Pin(s) in: UNIBUS cable	Pin(s) in: SPC backplane
		Initialization and shutdown		
BUS DC LO L	L	Slow	BF2	CN1
BUS AC LO L	L	Slow	BF1	CV1
BUS INIT L	L	Fast	AA1	DL1
		Arbitration		
BUS NPR L	L	Fast	AS2	FJ1
BUS BR7 L	L	Fast	AT2	DD2
BUS BR6 L	L	Fast	AU2	DE2
BUS BR5 L	L	Fast	BC1	DF2
BUS BR4 L	L	Fast	BD2	DH2
BUS NPG H	H	Grant	AU1	In: CA1; Out: CB1
BUS BG7 H	H	Grant	AV1	In: DK2; Out: DL2
BUS BG6 H	H	Grant	BA1	In: DM2; Out: DN2
BUS BG5 H	H	Grant	BB1	In: DP2; Out: DR2
BUS BG4 H	H	Grant	BE2	In: DS2; Out: DT2
BUS SACK L	L	Fast	AR2	FT2
		Data transfer		
BUS A00 L	L	Fast	BH2	EH2
BUS A01 L	L	Fast	BH1	EH1
BUS A02 L	L	Fast	BJ2	EF1
BUS A03 L	L	Fast	BJ1	EV2
BUS A04 L	L	Fast	BK2	EU2
BUS A05 L	L	Fast	BK1	EV1
BUS A06 L	L	Fast	BL2	EU1
BUS A07 L	L	Fast	BL1	EP2
BUS A08 L	L	Fast	BM2	EN2
BUS A09 L	L	Fast	BM1	ER1
BUS A10 L	L	Fast	BN2	EP1
BUS A11 L	L	Fast	BN1	EL1
BUS A12 L	L	Fast	BP2	EC1
BUS A13 L	L	Fast	BP1	EK2
BUS A14 L	L	Fast	BR2	EK1
BUS A15 L	L	Fast	BR1	ED2
BUS A16 L	L	Fast	BS2	EE2
BUS A17 L	L	Fast	BS1	ED1
BUS C0 L	L	Fast	BU2	EJ2
BUS C1 L	L	Fast	BT2	EF2
BUS D00 L	L	Fast	AC1	CS2
BUS D01 L	L	Fast	AD2	CR2
BUS D02 L	L	Fast	AD1	CU2, FE2*
BUS D03 L	L	Fast	AE2	CT2, FL1*
BUS D04 L	L	Fast	AE1	CN2, FN2*
BUS D05 L	L	Fast	AF2	CP2, FF1*
BUS D06 L	L	Fast	AF1	CV2, FF2*
BUS D07 L	L	Fast	AH2	CM2, FH1*

TABLE 4.1 UNIBUS Signals (*Continued*)

Name	High or low	Termination type	Pin(s) in UNIBUS cable	Pin(s) in SPC backplane
		Data transfer (continued)		
BUS D08 L	L	Fast	AH1	CL2, FK1*
BUS D09 L	L	Fast	AJ2	CK2
BUS D10 L	L	Fast	AJ1	CJ2
BUS D11 L	L	Fast	AK2	CH1
BUS D12 L	L	Fast	AK1	CH2
BUS D13 L	L	Fast	AL2	CF2
BUS D14 L	L	Fast	AL1	CE2
BUS D15 L	L	Fast	AM2	CD2
BUS PA L	L	Fast	AM1	CC1
BUS PB L	L	Fast	AN2	CS1
BUS BBSY L	L	Fast	AP2	FD1
BUS MSYN L	L	Fast	BV1	EE1
BUS INTR L	L	Fast	AB1	FM1
BUS SSYN L	L	Fast	BU1	EJ1, FC1*
		Miscellaneous		
BOOT ENABL L	L	NA	None	AR1
HALT REQ L	L	NA	None	CP1
HALT GRANT L	L	NA	None	CR1
LTC	NA	NA	None	CD1

*For forward compatibility, use the first pin rather than the second.

Note that this signal (and BUS DC LO L, as well) is usually derived from each power supply's bulk dc source, not from direct measurements of the ac power line. This means that a lightly loaded power supply may not assert BUS AC LO L for quite some time after the actual line power fails. This helps the processor ride through line transients but means that a system that must actually monitor the quality of the ac power line must not depend on BUS AC LO L. Other devices in the system may become inoperative prior to the assertion of BUS AC LO L.

This signal may also be driven by any UNIBUS device that would like to cause the system to perform its power-fail or power-recovery action. This is also used by network interfaces.

BUS INIT L. This signal, when asserted, indicates that all devices on the UNIBUS should reset themselves to the state they entered upon the initial power-up sequence. BUS INIT L is asserted each time the system is started, by the PDP-11 RESET instruction, and by specific commands to the VAX-11 UNIBUS adapters or interfaces.

4.19.2 Arbitration Signals

BUS BR4 L, BUS BR5 L, BUS BR6 L, BUS BR7 L—Bus Request. These signals request that the interrupt fielding processor (the IFP, usually the central processor) be interrupted at interrupt priority level 4, 5, 6, or 7, respectively (IPLs 14 through 17 for VAX-11 processors). Priority 7 is the highest priority. If the IFP is running below the priority of the request, the interrupt will be granted at the end of the current instruction. If the IFP is running at or above the priority of the request, the request will be deferred until the processor priority is reduced.

BUS BG4 H, BUS BG5 H, BUS BG6 H, BUS BG7 H—Bus Grant. These signals indicate that the IFP is willing to grant the interrupt at priority level 4, 5, 6, or 7, respectively. The interrupting device must now become bus master and pass its interrupt service vector address to the IFP.

Note that these signals are asserted high. They are also not used as wired-OR signals although they are driven with the same type of integrated circuits as all other lines. They are terminated in a slightly different manner than other UNIBUS signals.

BUS NPR L—Nonprocessor Request. This signal is used to request use of the UNIBUS (without causing an interrupt of the IFP). This signal is roughly analogous to the direct memory access (DMA) request signal defined by other buses.

BUS NPG H—Nonprocessor Grant. This signal indicates that the bus arbitrator is willing to allow use of the UNIBUS by one of the devices asserting BUS NPR L.

Note that this signal, like the BUS BGX H signals, is asserted high. It is also not used as a wired-OR signal although it is driven with the same type of integrated circuits as all other lines. Also like the BUS BGX H signals, it is terminated in a slightly different manner than other UNIBUS signals.

BUS SACK L—Selection Acknowledged. This signal is asserted by a device that has accepted a grant (whether a BG or NPG) to become the next UNIBUS master. As long as BUS SACK L is asserted, further arbitration is stopped. This ensures that only one device is designated as the next master of the UNIBUS.

4.19.3 Data Transfer Signals

BUS BBSY L. Also known as BUS BUSY L, this signal indicates that the UNIBUS data transfer bus is occupied (by the current bus master). The next bus master monitors this signal to determine when it can seize the data transfer bus.

BUS A17 L through BUS A00 L. These 18 signals are referred to as the UNIBUS address lines and supply the address that selects a slave device. BUS A00 L is the least significant bit and is ignored for all transactions except DATOB (write byte).

BUS C1 L, BUS C0 L. These two signals are referred to as the UNIBUS control lines and designate four out of the five types of operations of the data transfer bus. The operations are described in detail later in this chapter.

C1	C0	Transaction type
0	0	DATI (Read word)
0	1	DATIP (Read with intent to modify)
1	0	DATO (Write word)
1	1	DATOB (Write byte)
X	X	VECTOR WRITE (see BUS INTR L)

BUS D15 L through BUS D00 L. These 16 signals are referred to as the UNIBUS data lines and transmit the data word. BUS D00 L is the least significant bit. Byte data is not always transmitted on D07–D00. While the data for bytes at even addresses (A00 = 0) is transmitted on D07-D00, data for bytes at odd addresses (A00 = 1) is transmitted on D15–D08. This generally simplifies the design of word-oriented devices that may also read and write bytes.

BUS PA L, BUS PB L. These two signals are used to convey parity error information between the master and slave devices (e.g., memories assert BUS PB L to indicate that a parity error was detected within the memory).

PA	PB	Status
0	0	Good parity detected within slave
0	1	Bad parity detected within slave
1	X	Master should ignore PA (i.e., parity detection is disabled by someone on the UNIBUS). This combination is not used by Digital.

BUS MSYN L—Master Sync. This signal serves two purposes:

- As the UNIBUS address strobe, it indicates that the UNIBUS address lines contain a valid address and that BUS C1 L and BUS C0 L contain a valid function code and sufficient address deskew and decode time has elapsed.
- For write word and write byte operations (DATO and DATOB), BUS MSYN L also serves as the data strobe, indicating that the master has placed valid data on the UNIBUS data lines and sufficient data deskew time has elapsed.

BUS SSYN L—Slave Sync. This signal also serves two functions:

- As the UNIBUS address acknowledgment, it serves to inform the bus master that the requested address exists within some slave.
- For read operations (DATI and DATIP), BUS SSYN L also serves as the data strobe, indicating that the slave has placed valid data on the UNIBUS data lines and valid parity status information on BUS PA L and BUS PB L. After receipt of BUS SSYN L, the master must wait a minimum of 75 ns before latching the data to allow for data deskew.

BUS INTR L—Interrupt. This signal provides for a fifth kind of UNIBUS data transaction known as WRITE VECTOR. BUS INTR L acts simultaneously as the address, the address strobe, and the data strobe. The IFP is always the selected slave. The contents of the UNIBUS address lines, BUS C1 L, and BUS C0 L are ignored. After a 75-ns data deskew delay, the IFP then latches contents of the UNIBUS data lines as an interrupt vector. The IFP then returns BUS SSYN L, just like any other bus slave.

Note that even though the IFP was the slave, it was responsible for the data deskew. This is the one case where the slave is responsible for deskew.

4.19.4 Miscellaneous Signals

BOOT ENABL L. This signal indicates that memory contents are not valid. It is used by the processor logic after recovery from a power failure to determine whether to attempt a warm restart or a cold boot.

HALT REQ L. This is the signal from the "halt" switch on the front panel to the processor(s).

HALT GRANT L. This signal is the confirmation that the requested halt occurred.

LTC—Line-Time Clock. This line carries a square wave at the frequency of the power line.

4.20 Q-BUS SIGNAL DETAILS

The signals are partitioned into four groups:

- Initialization and shutdown signals
- Arbitration signals
- Interrupt requests
- Data transfer signals

A detailed list of these signals is given in Table 4.2.

4.20.1 Q-Bus Initialization, Shutdown, and Miscellaneous Signals

BDCOK H. This signal is exactly analogous to the BUS DC LO L signal on the UNIBUS.

BPOK H—Power OK. This signal is exactly analogous to the BUS AC LO L signal on the UNIBUS.

BINIT L. This signal is similar to the BUS INIT L signal on the UNIBUS. Unlike the UNIBUS signal, which consists of a pulse of from 10 to 100 ms, this signal on the Q-Bus usually consists of a pulse of 10 μs duration, followed by 90 μs of idle time on the bus.

BHALT L. The "halt" signal from the switch on the front panel to the processor(s).

BEVNT L. This signal is similar to BUS LTC L on the UNIBUS. This signal may be running at the power-line frequency or at a low, crystal-determined frequency such as 50, 60, 100, or 800 Hz.

SRUN L. This is the "run" signal from the processor module in slot 1 to the LED on the front panel.

4.20.2 Arbitration Signals

BDMR L. This signal is analogous to BUS NPR L on the UNIBUS.

BDMG L. This signal is analogous to BUS NPG H on the UNIBUS.

TABLE 4.2 Q-Bus Signals

Name	High or low	Termination type	Pin in backplane
	Initialization, shutdown, and miscellaneous		
BDCOK H	H	Slow	BA1
BPOK H	H	Slow	BB1
BINIT L	L	Fast	AT2
BHALT L	L	NA	AP1
BEVNT L	NA	NA	BR1
SRUN L	L	NA	AH1
	Arbitration		
BDMR L	L	Fast	AN1
BDMG L	L	Fast	In: AR2; Out: AS2
BSACK L	L	Fast	BN1
	Interrupt request		
BIRQ7 L	L	Fast	BP1
BIRQ6 L	L	Fast	AB1
BIRQ5 L	L	Fast	AA1
BIRQ4 L	L	Fast	AL2
	Data transfer		
BDAL00 L	L	Fast	AU2
BDAL01 L	L	Fast	AV2
BDAL02 L	L	Fast	BE2
BDAL03 L	L	Fast	BF2
BDAL04 L	L	Fast	BH2
BDAL05 L	L	Fast	BJ2
BDAL06 L	L	Fast	BK2
BDAL07 L	L	Fast	BL2
BDAL08 L	L	Fast	BM2
BDAL09 L	L	Fast	BN2
BDAL10 L	L	Fast	BP2
BDAL11 L	L	Fast	BR@
BDAL12 L	L	Fast	BS2
BDAL13 L	L	Fast	BT2
BDAL14 L	L	Fast	BU2
BDAL15 L	L	Fast	BV2
BDAL16 L	L	Fast	AC1
BDAL17 L	L	Fast	AD1
BDAL18 L	L	Fast	BC1
BDAL19 L	L	Fast	BD1
BDAL20 L	L	Fast	BE1
BDAL21 L	L	Fast	BF1
BSYNC L	L	Fast	AJ2
BBSIO L	L	Fast	AP2
BBWTBT L	L	Fast	AK2
BREF L	L	Fast	AR1
BDIN L	L	Fast	AH2
BDOUT L	L	Fast	AE2
BIAK L	L	Fast	In: AM2; Out, AN2
BRPLY L	L	Fast	AF2

BSACK L. This signal is similar to BUS SACK L on the UNIBUS, but is only asserted in response to BDMG L. (For Q-Bus interrupts, the IFP becomes bus master, not the interrupting device.)

4.20.3 Interrupt Request Signals

BIRQ4 L, BIRQ5 L, BIRQ6 L, BIRQ7 L. These signals are similar to BUS BR4 L through BUS BR7 L on the UNIBUS. Devices that interrupt at priority 5, 6, or 7 must follow additional protocols that allow the single BIAK L signal to unambiguously acknowledge any of the four requests.

4.20.4 Data Transfer Signals

BDAL21 L, BDAL20 L, BDAL19 L, BDAL18 L—Data/Address Lines. During address time, these four lines carry bits ⟨21:18⟩ of the Q-Bus address. During data time, these four lines are unused and reserved to Digital.

BDAL17 L, BDAL16 L—Data/Address Lines. During address time, these two lines carry bits ⟨17:16⟩ of the Q-Bus address. During data time, these two lines carry parity error information from the slave (analogous to the information on the BUS PA L and BUS PB L lines on the UNIBUS).

BDAL15 L through BDAL00 L—Data/Address Lines. During address time, these 16 lines carry bits ⟨15:00⟩ of the Q-bus address. During data time, these 16 lines carry the entire Q-Bus data word. As in the UNIBUS, byte data must be justified.

BSYNC L. This signal combines the functions of the UNIBUS's BUS MSYN L and BUS BBSY L signals. It indicates that a bus master now occupies the Q-Bus and has placed a valid address onto the Q-Bus BDALXX L lines.

BDIN L. This signal indicates that address time has ended and it is now time for the selected slave to supply read data on the Q-Bus BDALXX L lines.

BDOUT L. This signal indicates that address time (or data read time) has ended and the master is now supplying write data on the Q-Bus BDALXX L lines.

For read-modify-write transactions, BDIN L will be asserted first. After data has been returned by the slave, BDOUT L will assert as the bus master does the write-back.

BIAK L. This signal indicates that the IFP is willing to grant the highest-priority interrupt. The highest-priority interrupting device should place its vector on the BDALXX L lines and assert BRPLY L.

BWTBT L. "Write/Byte." If asserted during address time, this signal indicates that the operation will begin with a write rather than a read.

If asserted during data time during write transactions, this signal is used to indicate that a byte should be written (rather than a full word).

BBSIO L—Bank Select: I/O. If asserted during address time, this signal indicates that the values on BDAL12 L through BDAL00 L should be construed as an address in the 8-kbyte Q-Bus I/O page.

If unasserted during address time, this signal indicates that the values on BDAL21 L through BDAL00 L should be construed as an address in the 4096-kbyte Q-Bus memory space.

If asserted during data time, this acts as a harbinger that the master would like to perform an additional read cycle at the next sequential bus address and the master will soon reassert BDIN L. In other words, this signal requests Q-Bus block mode for reads.

BREF L—Refresh. If asserted during address time, this signal indicates that a read operation is being conducted solely for the purposes of refreshing dynamic RAM memory, and that each memory module in the system should access (and refresh) an entire row of memory. (Only the earliest Q-Bus memories were incapable of refreshing themselves and this signal is now relatively unused during address time.)

If asserted during data time, this signal indicates that the selected slave can deliver or accept an additional word of data from or to the next sequential address. In other words, this signal acknowledges the (continued) possibility of Q-Bus block mode.

BRPLY L. This signal is analogous to the UNIBUS BUS SSYN L signal.

4.21 VAXBI BUS SIGNAL DETAILS

The signals are partitioned into four groups:

- Clock signals
- Data path signals
- Synchronous control signals
- Asynchronous control signals

A detailed list of these signals is given in Table 4.3 on pp. 4.38–4.39.

TABLE 4.3 VAXBI Bus Signals

Name	High or low	Type	Explanation
		Clock signals	
BI TIME +	···	Diff. ECL	20 MHz (50 ns) clock
BI TIME −	···	Diff. ECL	20 MHz (50 ns) clock
BI PHASE +	···	Diff. ECL	5 MHz (200 ns) basic clock
BI PHASE −	···	Diff. ECL	5 MHz (200 ns) basic clock
		Data path signals	
BI D⟨31:00⟩ L	L	Open drain	Arbitration/address/data lines
BI I⟨3:0⟩ L	L	Open drain	Command codes, commander IDs, read status codes, write byte masks

Command code	Meaning
H H H H	Reserved
H H H L	Read
H H L H	IRCI
H H L L	RCI
H L H H	Write
H L H L	WCI
H L L H	UWMCI
H L L L	WMCI
L H H H	INTR
L H H L	IDENT
L H L H	Reserved
L H L L	Reserved
L L H H	Stop
L L H L	INVAL
L L L H	BDCST
L L L L	IPINTR

Read response code	Meaning
H X H H	Reserved
H X H L	Read data
H X L H	Corrected data
H X L L	Read data substitute
L X H H	Reserved
L X H L	Read data/don't cache
L X L H	Corrected data/don't cache
L X L L	Read data substitute/don't cache

Name	High or low	Type	Explanation
BI P0 L	L	Open drain	Parity on BI D⟨31:00⟩L and BI I⟨3:0⟩L

TABLE 4.3 VAXBI Bus Signal (*Continued*)

Name	High or low	Type	Explanation
		Synchronous control signals	
BI NO ARB L	L	Open drain	Inhibit arbitration
BI BSY L	L	Open drain	A transaction is in progress
BI CNF⟨2:0⟩ L	L	Open drain	Used to send responses to data cycles (note the implicit parity): Code — Meaning H H H — NO ACK H H L — Illegal H L H — Illegal H L L — ACK L H H — Illegal L H L — Stall L L H — Retry L L L — Illegal
		Asynchronous control signals	
BI DC LO L	L	Open drain	Analogous to BUS DC LO L on the UNIBUS
BI AC LO L	L	Open drain	Analogous to BUS AC LO L on the UNIBUS
BI RESET L	L	Open collector	Analogous to BUS INIT L on the UNIBUS
BI STF L	L	Open collector	Select the fast self-test rather than the extensive self-test
BI BAD L	L	Open collector	One or more VAXBI bus nodes failed self-test
BI SPARE L	L	. . . .	Reserved for use by Digital

CHAPTER 5
IBM MICRO CHANNEL ARCHITECTURE

Leslie F. McDermott
IBM Corporation
Boca Raton, Florida

5.1 INTRODUCTION

This chapter describes the purpose, structure, and use of IBM Corporation's Micro Channel architecture. The Micro Channel architecture is a set of signal specifications, timings, procedural definitions, and physical requirements necessary to maintain product compatibility. The material presented here will fundamentally focus on the architecture as implemented in IBM's Personal Systems/2 computer products. The Micro Channel architecture was developed by a group of IBM system developers and architects over several years. It was specified to be a computer bus or channel which can be enhanced by the specification of new procedures and the use of currently reserved signals.

The purpose of this architecture is to provide a flexible high-performance transfer medium that can be implemented at low cost. It was specified for use by many families of micro-, mini-, and mainframe computer products. This flexibility will provide a great deal of cross-product consistency and added product value to all Micro Channel–based products.

Micro Channel is a synchronous architecture. This structure was chosen to maximize the life and flexibility of the architecture and systems that use it. The structure was also chosen to minimize dependence on any processor or logic technologies. Computer systems utilizing this architecture have a well-defined transfer medium. This medium permits a mixture of attachment devices that operate at a wide variety of speeds. The specification of the bus or channel also enables the computer system's function and performance to be upgraded and enhanced. The systems can be enhanced by adding attachment cards with additional functions or increased performance levels. They can be upgraded by adding attachment cards that can control the system resources and increase the processing power of the system. Many years of effort were expended to ensure the flexibility, technology independence, and useability of the Micro Channel architecture.

The Micro Channel architecture was developed to be used in a wide variety and range of products. During the fundamental development of this architecture, all known computer bus and channel architectures were evaluated. The best features and functions were identified, and specifications were created and structured to enable system developers to provide the necessary set of functions without preventing others from being provided on attachment cards. The specification is written in a manner that permits end-users to purchase the features and functions needed, while enabling them to add others when their requirements change.

5.2 MICRO CHANNEL FEATURES

The IBM Corporation has three strategic Input/Output (I/O) bus or channel architectures. The first is the System 360/370 host computer I/O channel. It was developed in the early 1960s. The second is the system product division (SPD) I/O family of compatible attachment bus architectures. The third is the Micro Channel. The Micro Channel architecture was primarily developed for IBM's Personal Systems/2 family of microcomputers. However, it was also developed with the capability of being utilized in IBM's midrange and low-end mainframe environments. The use of the Micro Channel architecture in mini- and mainframe computer products will provide hardware cross-product consistency and added value to the purchase of any product produced to the Micro Channel specification.

The Micro Channel architecture is fundamentally a set of signal definitions, timing relationships, and use procedures. There is but one Micro Channel architecture specification. However, subsets of its features and functions can be implemented. These subsets can be implemented without eliminating the ability to add other features and functions to systems utilizing the architecture. What follows is a description of the features of the Micro Channel architecture.

5.2.1 Serial Third-Party Direct Memory Access (DMA)

The third-party direct memory access feature allows the transfer of data to and from an I/O device into a memory address under the control of a specialized logic device called a *DMA controller.* This feature provides full software compatibility with earlier IBM microcomputers (and compatible computers) while adding functional and performance enhancements. Third-party DMA allows more system throughput than central processing unit (CPU)–controlled I/O to memory transfer throughput. Micro Channel permits the DMA controller to execute a single transer or multiple transfers (Burst mode). The serial DMA specification allows the design of DMA controllers that can implement independent read and write cycles and data widths optimized to the target device. Serial DMA is a fundamental improvment over older parallel DMA, which required a read followed by a write operation that occurred at the data rate and width of the slowest device. Developers now have more options available to optimize their cost and performance objectives. For more information on specific implementations, please see the DMA controller section of the subject system's technical reference manual.

5.2.2 Level-Sensitive Interrupts

The interrupt feature of the Micro Channel architecture specifies that all interrupt (IRQ) signals are level sensitive. Level-sensitive interrupt structures require less logic to implement, are less susceptible to noise interference, and require less software support. These characteristics reduce implementation costs, improve system reliability, and improve performance.

5.2.3 Audio Sum Node

An audio subsystem feature is provided in the Micro Channel architecture. An analog audio signal and analog ground signal are specified. The bandwidth of the audio signal is 50 Hz to 10 kHz. The subsystem provides high-quality audio capability between devices and output over the system speaker. This subsystem eliminates the need for duplicate audio circuitry on devices added to a system.

5.2.4 High-Performance Transfers

A key feature of the Micro Channel architecture is its ability to support high-performance transfer cycles (instruction and/or data). The Micro Channel architecture signal timing specification defines a default transfer cycle of 200 ns to transfer 4 bytes of data. The default cycle timing equates to a 4-byte transfer rate of 20 million bytes of data per second. The specialized logic or a CPU and its support logic that can gain control of the Micro Channel bus or channel is called a *bus master* (or master). The actual default transfer rate of a system is determined by a maximum transfer rate of the bus master controlling the transfers, the limitations of the support logic, and the design constraints of the attachment devices on the bus or channel. (Device transfer constraints include transfer rates and transfer widths.) The architecture provides signals and procedures to allow all logic on the bus or channel to align and pace the device controlling the bus or channel to other devices.

5.2.5 Matched-Memory Procedure

The Micro Channel architecture has a specification that enables data to be transferred in cycles less than the default, 200 ns. Data can be transferred to or from system memory or memory-mapped I/O devices using the matched-memory signals and the matched-memory procedure. These signals and procedures permit specialized devices to be tuned to transfer characteristics of specific systems. This procedure also requires that devices designed to specific system characteristics also function with all other devices designed to the Micro Channel architecture specification.

5.2.6 32-Bit Address Bus

The architecture specifies a 32-bit address bus. This address width supports 4 Gbytes of memory or memory-mapped I/O addressing. The specification also permits a 24-bit subset of this bus to be implemented by system developers. The 24-bit address bus subset permits the addressing of up to 16 Mbytes of memory or memory-mapped I/O.

The 32-bit address bus and its 24-bit subset also act as a 16-bit I/O address bus. When used as a 16-bit I/O address bus, 64-byte I/O addresses can be accessed. The use of the address bus as a memory or I/O address bus is controlled by the +Memory/−IO signal.

5.2.7 32-Bit Data Bus

The architecture specifies a 32-bit data bus. This data bus can also be used as a 24-bit data bus, 16-bit data bus, or an 8-bit data bus. The Micro Channel architecture specification permits a 16-bit subset of the 32-bit data bus to be implemented when the 24-bit address bus is implemented. The 16-bit data bus can be used to transfer 16 bits or 8 bits of data.

5.2.8 Exception Condition Recovery

The Micro Channel architecture specification includes a feature called exception condition recovery. This feature includes a channel check signal, device condition bits (and optional status bits), and recovery procedures. An *exception condition* is defined as any error or status condition that cannot be resolved by typical computer recovery methods. The exception condition recovery feature permits hardware and software to be implemented that can correct the condition or disable the device creating the exception condition. This feature increases the system's ability to continue functioning.

In many high-performance bus or channel architectures, transfer status information is provided as part of the block transfer sequence or through special status query procedures. As circuit technology has improved, the need for transfer-by-transfer status checking has become less necessary. The Micro Channel architecture specification has chosen exception condition reporting as its method of minimizing system error detection overhead. Hardware is used to check the integrity of transfer cycles. With the Micro Channel architecture, the transfer time is typically insignificant in comparison to CPU instruction execution time. Therefore, the Micro Channel architecture has removed the burden of validating transfer cycle integrity from the system and application software. Exception conditions are only reported when they are detected by the hardware support. The error detection and correction code is only executed when it is needed. This significantly reduces system overhead and enhances system performance.

5.2.9 Programmable Option Select

The programmable option select (POS) feature of the Micro Channel architecture eliminates the need for hardware configuration switches, identifies devices, and provides flexible system and dynamic system configurability (when supported by an appropriate operating system and device driver software) and exception condition support (control and optional status information). POS hardware is used to configure devices attached to the Micro Channel. Because all devices attached to the bus or channel are identified and controlled by their POS registers, they can be dynamically reconfigured when supported by the appropriate software.

Each device on the Micro Channel can be enabled or disabled through a control bit in its POS registers. The exception condition indicator and the optional status information are also located in the POS registers. With this information, the system control software and device drivers can correct exception conditions detected by a device or disable the device. This action permits the system to continue providing full or diminished service. It can dramatically reduce problem determination and inoperative time.

5.2.10 Arbitration Bus

A 4-bit arbitration bus is specified by the Micro Channel architecture. Its purpose is to support up to 16 total bus masters and DMA slaves. Each bus master is assigned a unique priority level from the lowest priority level F to the highest priority level 0. Each system must have at least one bus master. At least one bus master must be assigned the priority level F. This bus master is referred to as the default bus master. It is given control of the Micro Channel bus when no other bus master owns the bus or channel or during an exception condition. A procedure for bus masters to gain control of the bus or channel is specified by the architecture. This process is controlled by an architecture-required logic unit called the system arbitration control point (SCP).

One of the most subtle features of the Micro Channel architecture is that it does not require the default master to be the system master. The default master is the bus master assigned arbitration level F. The system master is the bus master that allocates and administers system resources. The operating system that controls the system resources can be run on any bus master in the system. This allows multiple concurrent operating systems to be run. It also supports the tuning of systems to match the end-user's environment.

5.2.11 Bus Masters

One of the most significant features of the Micro Channel architecture is the support of bus masters. A Micro Channel bus master is any specialized logic or CPU and its support logic that can gain control of the bus or channel and drive the address, data, and control signals. Bus masters can be used to enhance or upgrade systems using the Micro Channel architecture. Bus masters can enhance a system by adding functions and increasing the amount of work that can be performed in any unit of time (performance).

Bus masters minimize the number of interrupts required to implement a function. This eliminates a significant amount of system overhead in servicing interrupts. Bus masters provide a significant advantage over third-party DMA transfers. A bus master implementing an I/O function can perform bursting direct memory access operations without the overhead of setting up and checking the status of third-party DMA controllers. These bus masters can enhance a system by providing optimized pair-to-pair transfers (I/O to I/O, memory to memory, and CPU subsystem to CPU subsystem). Bus masters can significantly enhance system performance by minimizing CPU support of block transfers and interrupt service support.

Bus masters can be used to upgrade the processing capability of systems. As all bus masters added to a system can have a higher priority than the existing CPU subsystem, the system is easily upgraded by the addition of a CPU subsystem that can be given control of the system resources after the default master has initialized the system. The default master can be made quiescent or relegated to supporting I/O functions. Because multiple bus masters are supported by the Micro Channel architecture, multiple-CPU subsystems can (with the appropriate operating system and software support) operate concurrently. This concurrent processing can provide significant system processing capabilities without wasting any existing system logic.

5.2.12 Architectural Enhancements

One of the key features of the Micro Channel architecture is the ability to enhance the architecture by defining compatible new procedures to add functions or increase performance. New and compatible procedures can be defined for the existing signals. The architecture currently defines several reserve signal pins that can be used with new procedures. The new functions and procedures can be provided to all Micro Channel–based systems by adding appropriate bus masters and attachment devices.

5.3 MICRO CHANNEL STRUCTURE

5.3.1 System Implementations

The Micro Channel architecture is structured in a manner that permits it to be implemented in a *card on board* or in a "Plainer" environment. In the case of the card on board implementation, provisions must be made to identify the system arbitration control point and the default bus master when the system is initialized. The system implementor can specify the slot location of the card that contains the SCP and the slot that contains the default master. The system developer can also implement a procedure that allows the SCP and default master to be located in any attachment slot. High-reliability and fault-tolerant systems can be produced by implementing systems that support multiple copies of the SCP and default bus master logic.

A requirement is that after the selection process is completed, only one SCP and only one default bus master (bus master assigned arbitration level F) be active in the system. The additional logic function necessary to implement this process must be compatible with all Micro Channel architecture specifications. At power-on time or system initialization, the default bus master is responsible for system configuration. Another consideration for card on board implementations is that provisions must be made to provide the logical OR functions for the card channel ready (CD CHRDY), card select feedback (−CD SFDBK), card data size 16 (−CD DS 16), and card data size 32 (−CD DS 32) signals from each attachment card. These signals must be OR and their respective card channel ready return (CHRDYRTN), card data size 16 return (−DS 16 RTN) and card data size 32 return (−DS 32 RTN) driven to the specified pin on the connector. The return signals are generated to eliminate timing skews caused by variable bus loading and logic circuits when detecting a signal from multiple sources. For a practical example of a Micro Channel card on board implementation, please see the technical reference manual for IBM's Electronic gearbox industrial computer.

In a "Plainer" implementation, the CPU subsystem built on the plainer is typically assumed to be the default master. It is typically given the fixed arbitration level F and assumes control of the system at power-on time or initialization. The required logical OR functions are typically performed on the plainer near the Micro Channel connectors. I/O devices, memory, and other special functions implemented on the plainer may or may not be direct bus- or channel-attached devices. If they are not attached directly to the bus or channel, they are accessed through the CPU subsystem's bus or channel interface logic. If they are directly attached to the bus or channel, they must follow all Micro Channel architecture requirements.

5.3.2 Signal and Power Groups

The Micro Channel can be divided into eight groups of signal and power pins. The definition of each signal and their signal pin location is contained in the signal definition section of this chapter. A description of each group is presented here to provide a foundation in the structure of the Micro Channel architecture.

5.3.2.1 32-Bit Address Signal Group. The 32-bit address bus comprises the following address signals:

+A0–+A23	Used as a part of the 32-bit and as the 24-bit memory bus subset and 16-bit I/O address bus
+A24–+A31	Used with +A0–+A23 as the 32-bit address bus
+M/−IO	Used to determine if the address is a memory or I/O address
+MADE 24	Used to indicate that a memory address exceeds 16 Mbytes

The architecture specifies a 32-bit address bus. This address width supports 4 Gbytes of memory or memory-mapped I/O addressing. The specification also permits a 24-bit subset of this bus to be implemented by system developers. The 24-bit address bus subset permits the addressing of up to 16 Mbytes of memory or memory-mapped I/O.

The 32-bit address bus and its 24-bit subset also act as a 16-bit I/O address bus. When used as a 16-bit I/O address bus, 64-kbyte I/O addresses can be accessed. The use of the address bus as a memory or I/O address bus is controlled by the +Memory/−IO signal.

5.3.2.2 32-Bit Data Signal Group. The 32-bit data bus comprises the following data signals:

+D0–+D15	Used as part of the 32-bit data bus and as the 16-bit data bus subset
+D16–+D31	Used with +D0–+D15 as the 32-bit data bus
−BE0–−BE3	Used to identify which of the 4 data bytes on the 32-bit data bus contain valid data
−SBHE	Used to enable transfer of bits +D8–+D15

The architecture specifies a 32-bit data bus. This data bus can also be used as a 24-bit data bus, 16-bit data bus, or an 8-bit data bus. The Micro Channel architecture specification permits a 16-bit subset of the 32-bit data bus to be implemented when the 24-bit address bus is implemented. The 16-bit data bus can be used to transfer 16 bits or 8 bits of data.

5.3.2.3 Control Signal Group. The control signal group comprises the following signals:

−ADL	Used to provide two gating edges early in the bus/channel cycles. Its primary use is gate-transparent address latches.
−CD DS 16	Used by I/O and memory slaves to indicate that their data port size is at least 16 bits.
−CD DS 32	Used by I/O and memory slaves with −CD DS 16 to indicate that their data port size is 32 bits.
−DS 16 RTN	Used by bus masters to determine the data port size of I/O and memory slaves.
−DS 32 RTN	Used by bus masters with −DS 16 RTN to determine the data port size of I/O and memory slaves.
−S0 or −S1	Used to indicate that the bus or channel cycle is a read (−S0) or a write (−S1) cycle.
−CMD	Used to indicate when to execute the transfer.
−CD SFDBK	Used by I/O and memory slaves to acknowledge that they have been selected by a bus master.
CH CHRDY	Used by I/O and memory slaves to indicate that they can execute a 200-ns cycle.
CHRDYRTN	Used by bus masters to determine that the selected slave can execute a 200-ns cycle.
−IRQ3- msIRQ7, −IRQ8-−IRQ12, −IRQ14-−IRQ15	Used to indicate an interrupt service request.
−CS SETUP	Used as a slot-dependent indication that the bus or channel cycle is a POS setup cycle.
−CHCH OSC	Used as 14.31818-MHz oscillator signal.
+CHRESET	Used as a bus or channel or system reset signal.
−REFRESH	Used to indicate that memory refresh cycles are being executed.
+TR 32	Used to indicate that a 32-bit bus master is controlling the bus or channel.

5.3.2.4 Arbitration Signal Group. The arbitration bus signal group comprises the following signals:

+ARBO-+ARB3	Used to indicate the arbitration level of the current bus master controlling the bus or channel and during arbitration cycles to determine the next bus controller
−PREEMPT	Used to indicate that a bus master wants control of the bus or channel
+ARB/−GNT	Used to indicate that an arbitration cycle is in progress or that the bus or channel control has been granted to the bus master with its arbitration level on the arbitration bus
−BURST	Used to indicate that the bus master controlling the bus or channel is executing multiple cycles

−TC Used to indicate that the terminal count of the current third-party DMA has been reached

A 4-bit arbitration bus is specified by the Micro Channel architecture. Its purpose is to support up to 16 total bus masters. Each bus master is assigned a unique priority level from the lowest priority level F to the highest priority level 0. Each system must have at least one bus master. At least one bus master must be assigned the priority level F. This bus master is referred to as the default bus master. It is given control of the Micro Channel bus when no other bus master owns the bus or channel or during an exception condition. A procedure for bus masters to gain control of the bus or channel is specified by the architecture. This process is controlled by an architecture-required logic unit called the system arbitration control point (SCP).

5.3.2.5 Audio Signal Group The audio signal group comprises the following signals:

AUDIO Used as an anlog audio sum node. This signal is used to communicate audio signals between devices on the bus or channel and to the system speaker circuits

AUDIO GND Used as an analog audio ground return signal

An audio subsystem feature is provided in the Micro Channel architecture. An anlog audio signal and analog ground signal are specified. The bandwidth of the audio signal is 50 Hz to 10 kHz. The subsystem provides high-quality audio capability between devices and output over the system speaker. This subsystem eliminates the need for duplicate audio circuitry on devices added to a system.

5.3.2.6 Matched-Memory Signal Group. The matched memory signal group comprises the following signals:

−MMC Used by bus masters to indicate that they can execute a matched-memory cycle

−MMCR Used by memory or memory-mapped I/O slaves to request a matched-memory cycle

−MMC CMD Used by bus masters in place of −CMD during a matched memory cycle

The Micro Channel architecture has a specification that enables data to be transferred in cycles less than the default 200 ns. Data can be transferred to system memory or system memory mapped I/O devices using the matched-memory signals and the matched-memory procedure. These signals and procedures permit specialized devices to be tuned to transfer characteristics of specific systems. This procedure also requires that devices designed to specific system characteristics also function with all other devices designed to the Micro Channel architecture specification.

5.3.2.7 Reserved Signal Pins. The Micro Channel architecture has several signal pins marked reserved. These signal pins were added to the structure to ensure that future enhancements which require new signals can be implemented.

5.3.2.8 ***Power and Ground Pins.*** The Micro Channel architecture is specified with 20 power and 26 ground pins (28 with the matched-memory extension connector). These power and ground pins are specified and arranged to minimize the potential of capacitive signal coupling and the effects of electromagnetic interference. This increases the reliability, data integrity, and transfer capability of systems implementing the Micro Channel architecture.

5.3.3 Micro Channel Bus Participants

The Micro Channel archtiecture specifies that only two types of devices can participate in transfer cycles. These are bus masters and slaves. All transfers are initiated and controlled by a bus master. Slaves respond to read and write data requests from bus masters. At any instant of time, only one bus master and one slave can participate in a transfer cycle. The Micro Channel architecture obtains its fundamental value and flexibility from the ability to define a variety of simple high-performance procedures for transferring data between bus masters and slaves.

A Micro Channel bus or channel attachment card can contain several types of devices. The attachment card is identified by the device type representing its principal function. However, the Micro Channel architecture does rank the bus or channel devices by priority. In order, the ranking is as follows:

1 Memory slaves
2 Bus masters
3 DMA slaves
4 I/O slaves

5.3.3.1 ***Bus Masters.*** One of the most significant features of the Micro Channel architecture is the support of bus masters. A Micro Channel bus master is any specialized logic or CPU and its support logic that can gain control of the bus or channel and drive the address, data, and control signals. It is important to note that bus masters *do not* require a processor to be bus masters. It is also important to note that bus masters must respond as slaves when accessed by another bus master. The only specified requirement to be a bus master is the ability to gain control of the bus or channel (through internal arbitration logic or through the specific actions of another device) and control the execution of a defined bus or channel cycle. By not utilizing a processor, the bus master developer can optimize the performance and reduce the cost of production. The ability to reduce system overhead, increase performance, and produce at a cost equivalent to third-party DMA slaves makes the bus master one of the most significant features of the Micro Channel architecture.

Bus masters can be used to enhance or upgrade systems using the Micro Channel architecture. Bus masters can enhance a system by adding functions and increasing the amount of work that can be performed in any unit of time (performance). There are three basic types of bus masters:

- Full-function bus masters
- Special-function controllers
- Programmable special-function controllers

The fundamental differences between the types of bus masters are flexibility, function, and cost. The full-function bus master is the most flexible, generally has the most functions, and has the highest production cost. The special-function controller has the least flexibility and generally has the least functions and lowest cost. The programmable special-function controller can span the range between the full-function bus master and the special-function controller.

The full-function bus master has a programmable CPU and is *capable* of controlling the system resources. These resources include the operating system software which controls and allocate system resources. IBM's Reduces Instruction Set Computer (RISC) upgrade (for its Personal System/2 educational computer) is an example of full-function bus masters. Multiples of the RISC processor bus master can be placed into a Micro Channel system to significantly upgrade the processing power of a computing system. Several different operating systems can be run concurrently on a system with these bus masters. This provides a broad range of software flexibility and compatibility while significantly increasing system performance.

Special-function controller bus masters are devices that have logic circuits to perform a specific function with little or no assistance from a full-function bus master. They have dedicated logic optimized to perform the function. They do not contain a CPU. Examples of special-function controllers are communication, direct access storage device (DASD), and printer controllers, which can move blocks of data and implement their functions with little or no support from a full-function bus master and with few (if any) interrupts. Special-function controllers can maximize system performance by minimizing system overhead and facilitating the optimal full-function bus master utilization.

Programmable special-function controller bus masters are devices that span the range between full-function bus masters and special-function bus masters. The fundamental difference between a special-function controller and a programmable special-function controller is the ability to modify the function and/or execution characteristics of the bus master. They can contain processing units, or their programmability can be as simple as setting a control register(s). Examples of programmable special-function controllers are third-party DMA controllers, DASD, and page-printer bus master controllers. With the possible exception of cost and performance, these bus masters have the same advantages as special-function controllers. However, they possess the ability to be attached to a variety of I/O devices.

Bus masters minimize the number of interrupts required to implement a function. This eliminates a significant amount of system overhead in servicing interrupts. Bus masters provide a significant advantage over third-party DMA transfers. A bus master implementing an I/O function can perform bursting direct memory access operations without the overhead of setting up and checking the status of third-party DMA controllers. These bus masters can enhance a system by providing optimized pair-to-pair transfers (I/O to I/O, memory to memory, and CPU subsystem to CPU subsystem). Bus masters can significantly enhance system performance my minimizing CPU support of block transfers and interrupt service support.

Bus masters can be used to upgrade the processing capability of systems. As all bus masters added to a system can have a higher priority than the existing CPU subsystem, the system is easily upgraded by the addition of a CPU subsystem that can be given control of the system resources after the default master has initialized the system. The default master can be made quiescent or relegated to supporting I/O functions. Because multiple bus masters are supported by the Micro Channel architecture, multiple-CPU subsystems can (with the appropriate operating system and software support) operate concurrently. This concurrent processing can provide significant system processing capabilities without wasting any existing system logic.

5.3.3.2 ***Bus Slaves.*** Bus masters execute read and write cycles to and from slaves. Slaves never initiate bus or channel cycles. However, a slave can initiate a service request. The most common method for a slave to request service is through the use of interrupts. A common misconception about Micro Channel bus or channel slaves is that they are merely passive devices. The misconception stems from the use of the word *passive* to mean not working or operating until triggered. An important concept is that slaves designed for the Micro Channel architecture *respond* to bus or channel cycles.

Slaves can be very active devices. In event-driven systems, the slaves typically initiate most of the system activity by requesting service. In direct pair-to-pair (non-third-party DMA cycles) information transfers, both pair components must be bus masters. One bus master controls the bus or channel while the other acts as a slave and responds.

There are three types of Micro Channel slaves. Micro Channel attachment cards can contain several types of bus or channel devices:

- Memory slaves
- I/O slaves
- DMA slaves

A Micro Channel memory slave is a bus or channel device whose principal function is to provide a block of system memory. The key word here is *system.* System memory is memory whose allocation is controlled by operating system software. Memory slaves are selected by memory addresses and respond to memory read and write cycles. It should be noted that memory-mapped I/O is also selected by memory addresses and respond to memory read and write cycles. However, the allocation of memory-mapped I/O memory is not controlled by operating system software.

A Micro Channel I/O slave is a bus or channel device that implements an input/output function. Slaves may respond to either memory or I/O addresses. They may contain non-system-memory blocks. They typically control or communicate with another piece of equipment. I/O slaves can be simple controlled response devices or complex subsystems.

The DMA slave is a special type of slave. It is the only slave that can request control of the bus or channel. The request is made for a third-party bus master (typically a DMA controller). To enable them to request bus control, DMA slaves are assigned an arbitration level. DMA slaves respond to their arbitration level, I/O addresses, or their memory addresses. Memory and I/O slaves can also be DMA slaves. DMA slaves can participate in third-party pair-to-pair transfer cycles. The instructions or data being transferred must, however, pass through the third-party bus master. Micro Channel serial DMA slaves can offer significant system performance enhancement over programmed I/O when blocks of bytes are to be transferred. The magnitude of the performance enhancement is determined by the size of the block and the implementation of the third-party bus master.

5.4 MICRO CHANNEL ARCHITECTURE TRANSFER CYCLE PROCEDURES

The Micro Channel architecture obtains its fundamental value and flexibility from the ability to define a variety of simple high-performance procedures to transfer instructions and data between bus masters and slaves. Bus Masters are responsible for beginning, executing, and completing all Micro Channel bus or channel cycles. (It should be noted that refresh cycles are typically executed by the default bus master's support logic.) All Micro Channel transfer cycle procedures are defined to be compatible, to be simple, and to maximize every opportunity to facilitate performance.

There are many types of Micro Channel cycles. All transfer cycles begin when the device address is placed on the bus or channel by the bus master. The Micro Channel–designed slaves use raw address decodes to continually check for their address ranges. The slave realizes that a transfer cycle has begun when it detects its address and a read or write status signal. This minimizes the address and device selection time. Transfer cycles are terminated at the trailing edge of the command signal (− CMB).

Designing to the Micro Channel architecture specifications maximizes the value and life of attachment cards by eliminating dependence on logic technologies and system implementations. The currently specified Micro Channel transfer cycle procedures are the following:

- Basic transfer cycles
- Synchronous extended cycles
- Asynchronous extended cycles
- Matched-memory cycles
- Third-party DMA cycles
- Refresh cycles
- Setup cycles

The purpose of this section is to describe the Micro Channel transfer cycle procedures. The relationships of the signal used and their effects will be described. For detailed timing specification and design requirements, please refer to the Micro Channel section (Chap. 2) of any IBM Personal System/2 Technical Reference Manual.

5.4.1 Basic Transfer Cycles

The basic transfer cycle is defined to be 200 ns long. This is the default Micro Channel cycle. Unless the specified Micro Channel signals are utilized to request a slower or faster transfer cycle, bus masters assume that 200 ns is the *minimum* bus or channel cycle time that can be executed. Figure 5.1 illustrates the basic transfer cycle signal procedure.

The basic transfer cycle begins when the bus master drives a stable memory or I/O address on the bus or channel. At the same time, the +M/−IO signal is driven to indicate whether the address is a memory or an I/O address. The + MADE 24 signal is driven if the memory address exceeds 16 Mbytes. The +TR

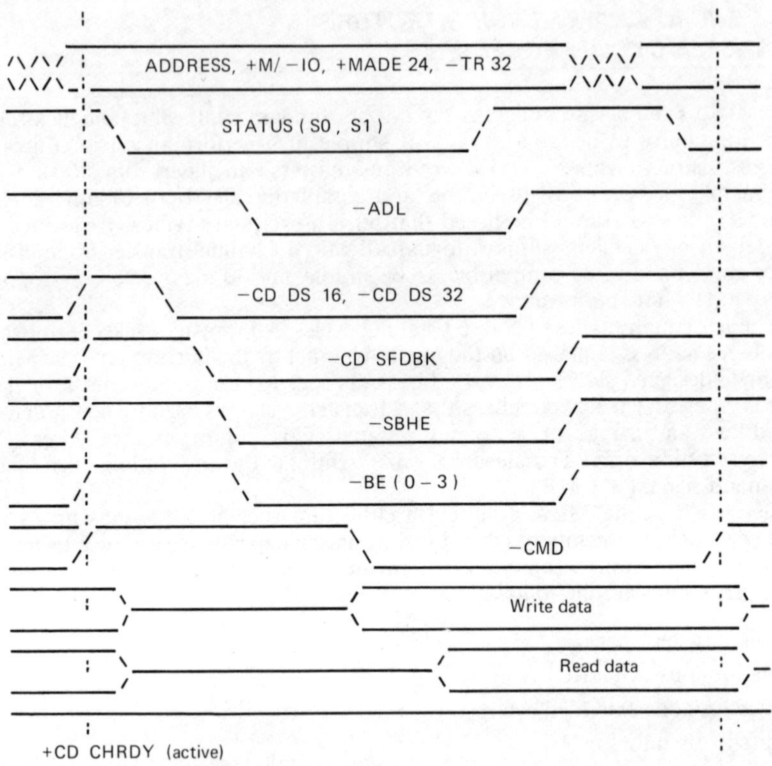

FIGURE 5.1 Basic transfer cycle.

32 signal is driven if the bus master is a 32-bit bus master. Slave designs are encouraged to use raw address decode logic to determine if the address on the bus is within their ranges(s). This is done to minimize device selection identification time.

Shortly after the address is driven (a minimum of 10 ns), the read (−S0) or the write (−S1) STATUS signal is driven to identify the type of cycle and direction of transfer flow. The slave has a maximum of 55 ns to indicate its data port size by driving −CD DS 16 and/or −CD DS 32. The slave has a maximum of 60 ns to indicate that it has been selected by driving −CD SFDBK.

The bus master uses −DS 16 RTN and −DS 32 RTN to determine the data port size of the slave. It is important to remember that the bus master controlling the bus or channel controls the number of bytes to be transferred during the cycle. When multiple cycles are to be used to transfer a block of bytes, the bus master can alter the number of bytes transferred on a cycle-by-cycle basis. The bus master's data port size and transfer efficiency, the slave's data port size, the byte address alignment, and potentially a CPU instruction determine the number of bytes transferred. Once the number of bytes to be transferred has been determined, the bus master drives the −SBHE appropriately to indicate to the slave if the high byte (+D8–+D15) of each two-byte transfer is valid. A 32-bit bus master will also drive the appropriate byte enable [−BE (0–3)] signals. The byte enable

TABLE 5.1 +A0, +A1, −SBHE, −BE Procedural Table

+A0	+A1	−SBHE	−BE (0–3)	Valid data bytes
0	0	0	0000	0,1,2,3
0	0	0	0001	0,1,2
0	—	0	0011	0,1
—	—	1	0111	0
—	—	1	1111	No valid data
0	0	0	1100	2,3
0	0	1	0101	0, 2
0	0	0	1010	1, 3

Note: A dash denotes "do not care."
Data byte 0 = Bits +D0–+D7
Data byte 1 = Bits +D8–+D15
Data byte 2 = Bits +D16–+D23
Data byte 3 = Bits +D24–+D31

signals provide a very efficient way for 32-bit slaves to gate transfers. Table 5.1 illustrates the +A0, +A1, −SBHE, −E procedure used by bus masters and slaves to indicate and determine where valid bytes are located.

At this point, an important decision must be made by the bus master. If the bus master wishes to prematurely terminate the cycle, it must be done before the leading edge of the address decode latch (−ADL) is driven. The −ADL signal is driven to provide two gating signals early in the cycle. Its two edges can be used to transparently latch the address, status, and internal device selected signals. (It is recommended that the internal devices selected be latched; not the raw address. This significantly reduces circuit count.) It can also be used to activate or deactivate other logic functions.

At a minimum of 40 ns after the leading edge on the −ADL signal, the bus master can drive −CMD active. In a write cycle, the bus master must drive the data bus at or before driving −CMD active. The leading edge of the −CMD signal is the indicator to the slave to execute the read or write command. The minimum −CMD pulse width is 90 ns. The leading edge of the −CMD pulse is typically used to latch the write data from the bus master. However, the leading or trailing edge of the −CMD can be used. Read data from the slave must be valid on the bus or channel a maximum of 60 ns after the leading edge of −CMD.

The bus or channel cycles end with the trailing edge of the −CMD signal. Write data must be held on the data bus for a minimum of 30 ns after the trailing edge of −CMD. Write data must be removed from the data bus or channel prior to the leading edge of the next −CMD signal or when the current bus master loses control of the bus or channel. Read data must be held on the bus or channel at least until the trailing edge of −CMD. Read data must be removed from the bus or channel a maximum of 40 ns after the trailing edge of −CMD. All address and control signals are removed from the bus or channel after the leading edge of −CMD and at or before the trailing edge of −CMD. The trailing edge of −CMD ends the cycle.

There is one special consideration with all Micro Channel transfer cycles. The address and status signals for the next cycle can be driven on the bus or channel prior to the end of the current cycle. Bus masters that execute these overlapped cycles must ensure that they do not become confused by slaves with fast response times. The responsibility for properly terminating the current cycle is the respon-

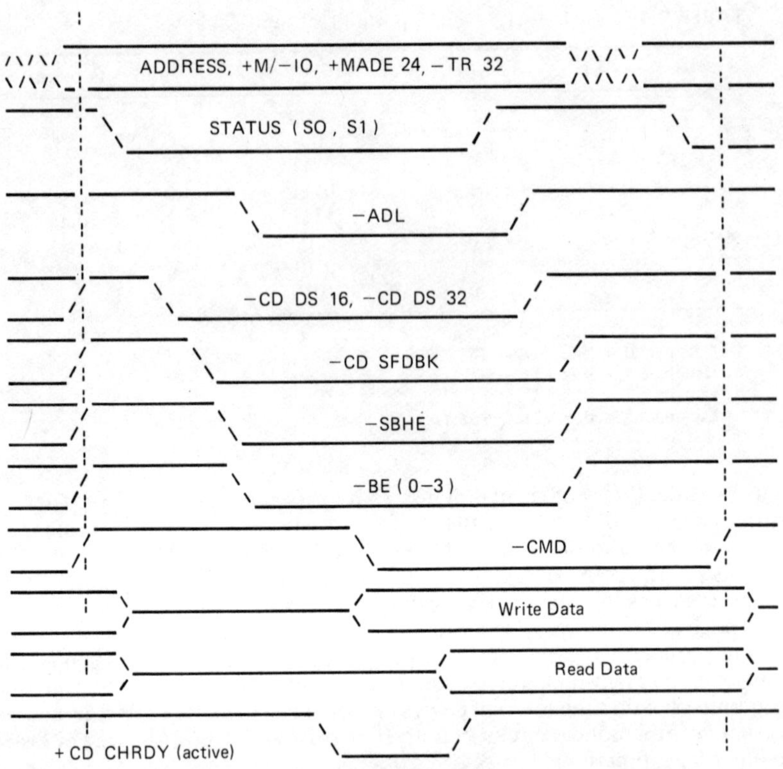

FIGURE 5.2 Synchronous extended cycle.

sibility of the bus master executing overlapped cycles. This consideration is of particular importance when executing transfer cycles other than the basic transfer cycle.

5.4.2 Synchronous Extended Cycles

The synchronous extended transfer cycle is specified to be 300 ns long. The primary difference between the basic transfer cycle and the synchronous extended cycle is that the −CMD pulse width is minimally 190 ns. This procedure is intended to help optimize the performance of slaves that require between 60 and 160 ns of data setup and hold time. Figure 5.2 illustrates the synchronous extended transfer cycle signal procedure.

The slave requests a synchronous extended transfer cycle by pulsing the channel ready signal (+CD CHRDY). Other than the pulsing of the +CD CHRDY signal and the extending of the −CMD pulse, the synchronous extended transfer is identical to the basic transfer cycle. To request a synchronous extended transfer cycle, the slave must drive +CD CHRDY inactive (low) a maximum of 30 ns after the status signal (−S0 or −S1) becomes active. The +CD CHRDY signal must be released a maximum of 30 ns after the leading edge of −CMD.

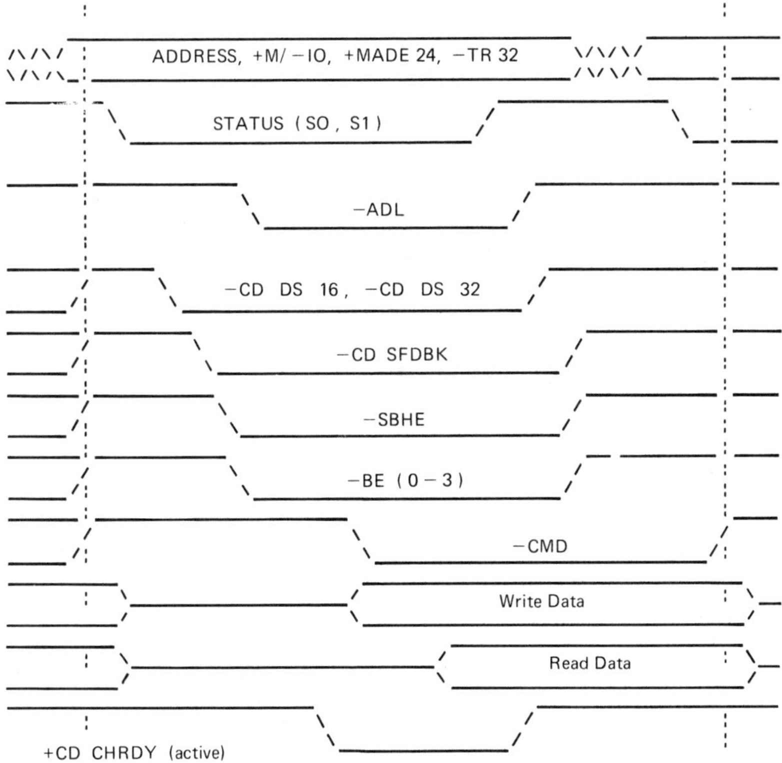

FIGURE 5.3 Asynchronous extended cycle.

5.4.3 Asynchronous Extended Cycles

The asynchronous extended transfer cycle is specified to be greater than 300 ns long. The primary difference between the basic transfer cycle and the asynchronous extended cycle is that the −CMD pulse width is minimally greater than 190 ns. This procedure is intended to help slaves that require more than 160 ns of data setup and hold time. Figure 5.3 illustrates the asychronous extended transfer cycle signal procedure.

The slave requests an asynchronous extended transfer cycle by deactivating the channel ready signal (+CD CHRDY). Other than the use of the +CD CHRDY signal and the extending of the −CMD pulse, the asynchronous extended transfer is identical to the basic transfer cycle. To request an asynchronous extended transfer cycle, the slave must drive +CD CHRDY inactive (low) a maximum of 30 ns after the status signal (−S0 or −S1) becomes active. The +CD CHRDY signal must drive +CD CHRDY active to permit the bus master to end the cycle. The slave cannot hold +CD CHRDY inactive for more than 3.0 μs.

5.4.4 Matched-Memory Transfer Cycles

The Micro Channel architecture has a specification that enables data to be transferred in cycles less than the default, 200 ns. Matched memory is the only pro-

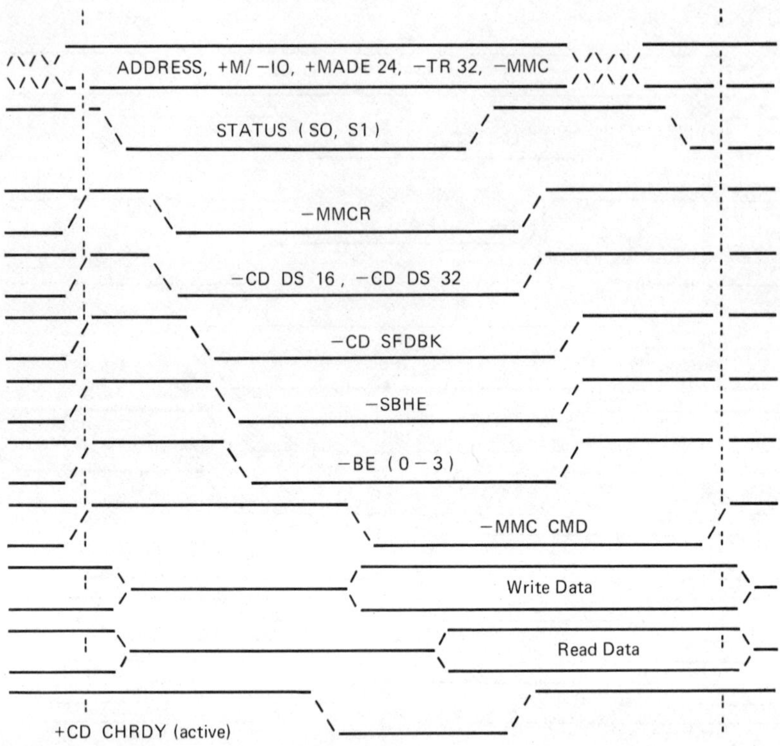

FIGURE 5.4 Matched-memory transfer cycle.

cedure specification that is system specific. Data can be transferred to or from system memory or memory-mapped I/O devices using the matched-memory signals and the matched-memory procedure. These signals and procedures permit specialized devices to be tuned to transfer characteristics of specific systems. This procedure also requires that devices designed to specific system characteristics also function with all other devices designed to the Micro Channel architecture specification. Figure 5.4 illustrates the matched-memory procedure.

Matched-memory transfer cycles are very similar to asychronous extended cycles. The primary differences are that −ADL and −CMD are not activated, and −MMC, −MMCR, and −MMC CMD are utilized. The matched-memory cycle (−MMC) signal is driven during all bus or channel cycles. The −MMC signal is driven with the address signals. It is driven to indicate to a slave capable of participating in matched-memory cycles that the bus master can drive such cycles. The slave indicates to the bus master that the current cycle can be a matched-memory cycle by driving the matched-memory cycle request (−MMCR) signal active. The −ADL and −CMD signals are held inactive. The matched-memory cycle command (−MMC CMD) signal is driven by the bus master to instruct the slave to execute the read (−S0) or write (−S1) transfer cycle.

During matched-memory transfer cycles, the slave can use the +CD CHRDY signal to extend the cycle. If +CD CHRDY is driven inactive (low), the −MMC

CMD pulse period is extended. Slaves can be used to extend the −MMC CMD period to enable them to drive or latch data and instructions.

5.4.5 Third-Party DMA Cycles

The third-party direct memory access feature allows the transfer of data to and from an I/O device into a memory address under the control of a specialized logic device called a *DMA controller.* This feature provides full software compatibility with earlier IBM microcomputers (and compatible computers) while adding functional and performance enhancements. Third-party DMA allows more system throughput than central processing unit (CPU)–controlled I/O to memory transfer throughput. Micro Channel permits the DMA controller to execute a single transfer or multiple transfers (burst mode). The serial DMA specification allows the design of DMA controllers that can implement independent read and write cycles and data widths optimized to the target device. Serial DMA is a fundamental improvement over older parallel DMA, which required a read followed by a write operation that occurred at the data rate and width of the slowest device. Developers now have more options available to optimize their cost and performance objectives. For more information on specific implementations, please see the DMA Controller section of the subject system's technical reference manual.

The third-party DMA transfer cycle procedure is fundamentally a specification for implementing block data or instruction transfers under the control of a third-party bus master. This third-party bus master is typically called a DMA controller. Third-party DMA transfers are basic, synchronous extended, or asynchronous extended transfer cycles controlled by the third-party bus master.

A full-function bus master is required to initialize the DMA controller with

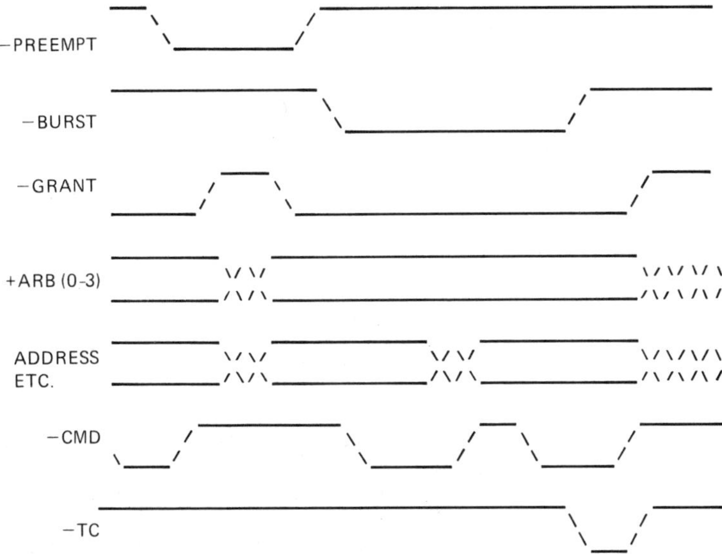

FIGURE 5.5 Third-party DMA read transfer cycle.

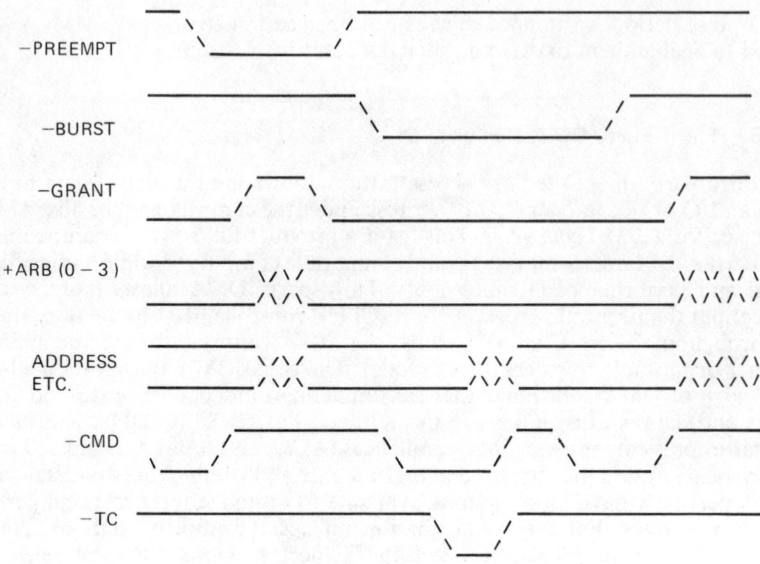

FIGURE 5.6 Third-party DMA write transfer cycle.

transfer directions, the starting address of the target area, and other control information required by the specific DMA controller design. This process can be initated by an interrupt from a DMA slave or application program. The DMA slave requests control of the bus or channel for the third-party bus master by activating the −PREEMPT signal. An arbitration cycle will eventually occur that gives bus or channel ownership to the DMA slave. Third-party DMA bus masters are responsible for recognizing that a DMA slave which it controls has gained ownership of the bus or channel. When this occurs, the DMA controller executes the necessary signal or multiple bus or channel cycles.

The third-party DMA transfer procedure requires the use of a special signal called terminal count (−TC). The −TC signal is driven by the third-party bus master to indicate the last transfer to the DMA slave. The −TC signal is driven during the last bus or channel cycle for DMA read operations. This operation is defined as reading from a memory address and writing to the DMA slave. This is illustrated in Fig. 5.5. The −TC signal is driven during the next to the last bus or channel cycle for DMA write operations. This operation is defined as reading from the DMA slave and writing to memory addresses. This is illustrated in Fig. 5.6.

5.4.6 Refresh Cycles

The Micro Channel architecture specifies a procedure for systems providing dynamic memory refresh. Typically, dynamic memory is refreshed by executing read (−S0) bus or channel cycles with the refresh (−REFRESH) signal active. By executing read cycles with the −REFRESH signal active, the dynamic memory controller refreshes a row of dynamic memory locations. The Micro Channel architecture supports single or multiple row refresh cycles in one operation. In the

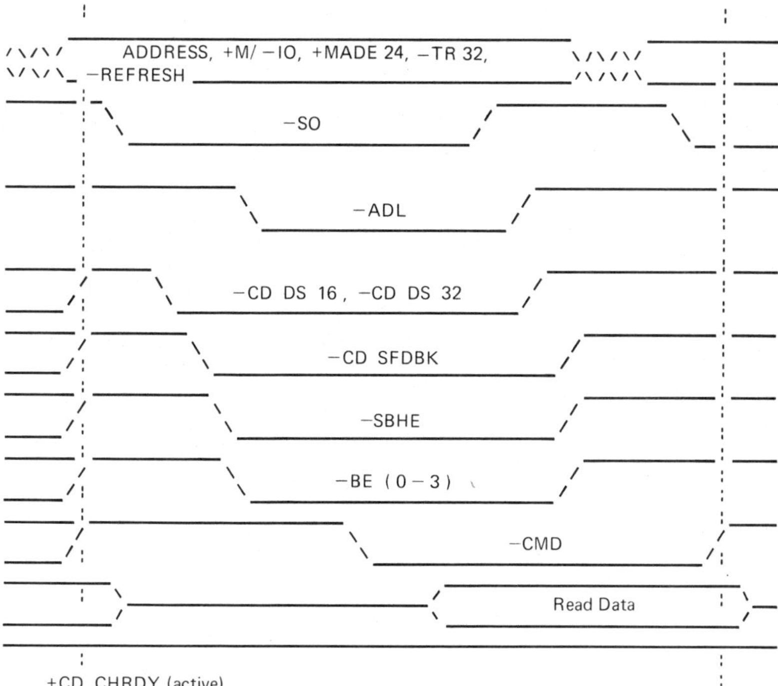

FIGURE 5.7 Refresh cycles.

Personal System/2, refresh cycles are performed during arbitration cycles (see Sec. 5.5, Bus Ownership). Refresh cycles are illustrated in Fig. 5.7.

5.4.7 Setup Cycles

Setup cycles are used to read or write programmable option select (POS) data from or into the POS registers. Setup cycles are nearly identical to asynchronous cycles. One difference is that each card slot (or device in a plainer implementation) has a unique *setup signal.* This signal is used to notify the device that its POS registers are being accessed. The other difference is that during setup cycles, only the three low-order address bits are used to address the POS registers. Figure 5.8 illustrates a setup cycle.

5.5 BUS OWNERSHIP

Understanding the concept of Micro Channel bus or channel ownership is important. This understanding is key to understanding the value of bus masters and the master-slave structure of the architecture. Only bus or channel participants assigned an *arbitration level* (during system configuration) can own the bus or

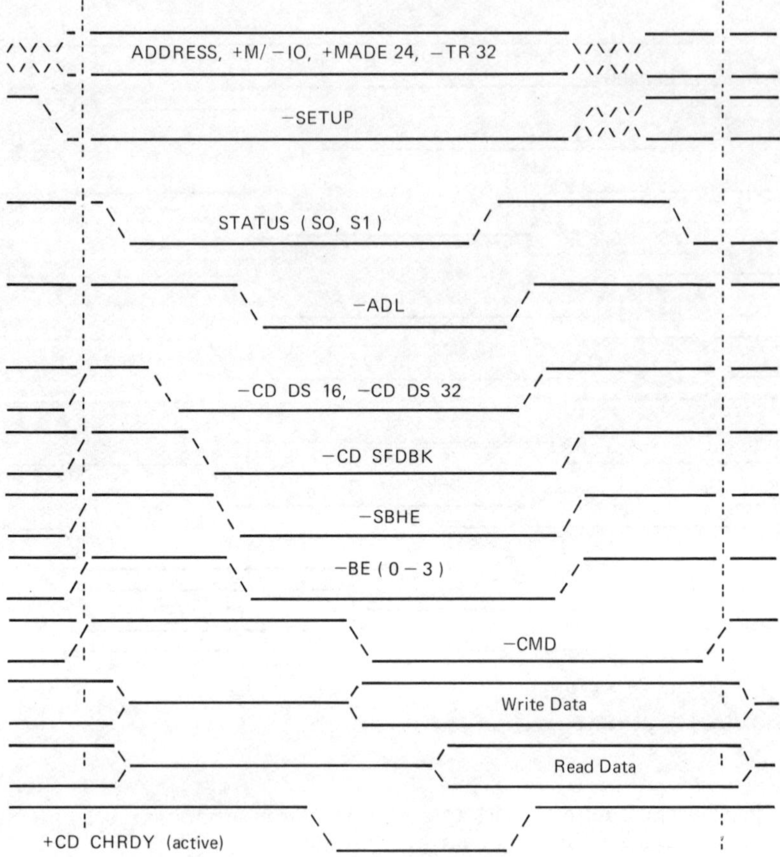

FIGURE 5.8 Setup cycles.

channel. As defined, the Micro Channel permits bus masters and DMA slaves to own the bus or channel. The bus or channel is owned when the arbitration bus contains the owner's arbitration level and the +ARB/−GNT signal is in the −GNT (grant) state.

At this point, it is important to note that only bus masters can drive the address and certain control signals. Therefore, when a DMA slave owns the bus or channel, a third-party DMA controller must act as bus master in its behalf. The third-party DMA controller must be programmed to recognize the arbitration levels assigned to the DMA slaves it supports. (The DMA slave and third-party DMA controller must also be programmed to use the same DMA channel.)

The Micro Channel architecture supports up to sixteen bus owners. At least one bus or channel owner must be a bus master and be assigned arbitration level F. This bus master is the default master. With the ability to support sixteen bus masters, the Micro Channel architecture supports very flexible system structures. Bus ownership is controlled by the system control point (SCP). Which bus or

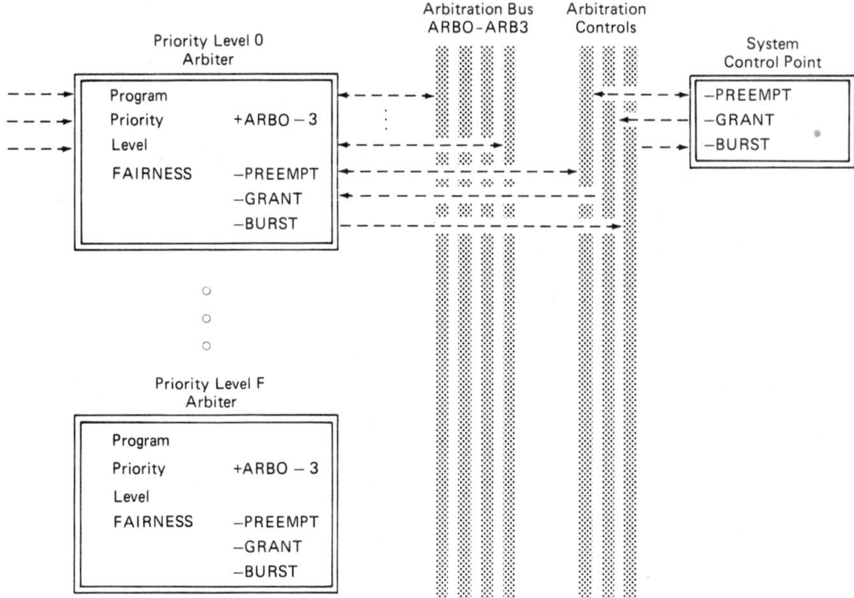

FIGURE 5.9 Arbitration logic.

channel participant owns the bus is determined by the arbitration cycle procedure.

5.5.1 Central Arbitration Control Point

The central arbitration control point is the logic that controls bus or channel ownership. It detects requests for ownership (−PREEMPT active) and the end of transfer condition (−CMD and −S0, −S1 inactive), and initiates an arbitration cycle. The arbitration cycle is started when the SCP changes the state of the +ARB/−GNT signal to +ARB. During the arbitration cycle, all bus participants wishing to own the bus or channel drive their arbitration levels onto the arbitration bus. All potential bus owners monitor the arbitration bus and remove their arbitration level if it is not the highest arbitration level on the arbitration bus. Once the highest-priority arbitration level is stable on the arbitration bus, the SCP grants ownership by changing the state of the +ARB/−GNT signal to −GNT. A block diagram of the arbitration structure is shown in Fig. 5.9.

5.5.2 Arbitration Cycles

Arbitration cycles are used to determine the next bus or channel owner. They are controlled by the system control point. They begin when the SCP detects an end of transfer condition and a request for bus or channel ownership. The cycle is terminated by the SCP when it detects a stable arbitration level on the arbitration bus. Figure 5.10 illustrates an arbitration cycle.

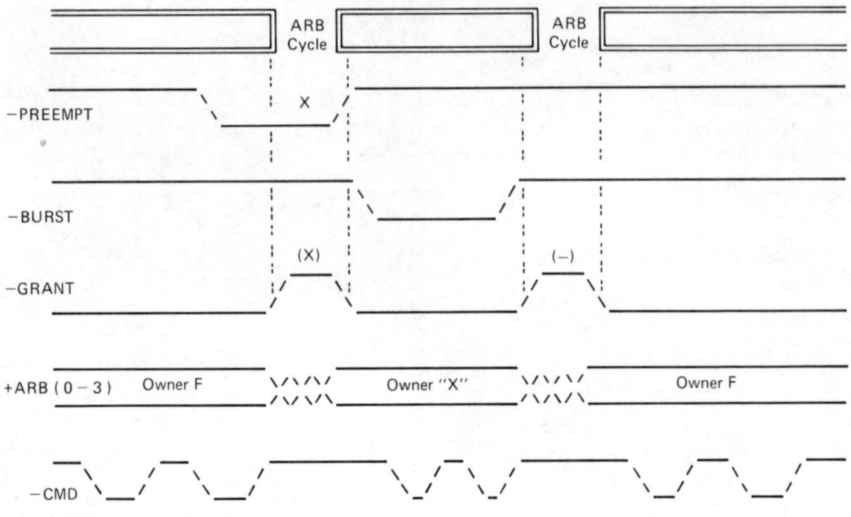

FIGURE 5.10 Arbitration cycles.

5.6 CONFIGURATION WITH PROGRAMMABLE OPTION SELECT

The programmable option select (POS) feature of the Micro Channel architecture eliminates the need for hardware configuration switches, identifies the device and its location, resolves resource assignment conflicts, facilitates installation of multiple identical devices, provides flexible system and dynamic system configurability (when supported by appropriate operating system and device driver software), and exception condition support (control and optional status information). POS hardware is used to configure devices attached to the Micro Channel. Because all devices attached to the bus or channel are identified and controlled by their POS registers, they can be dynamically reconfigured when supported by the appropriate software.

Each device on the Micro Channel can be enabled or disabled through a control bit in its POS registers. The exception condition indicator and the optional status information are also located in the POS registers. With this information, the system control software and device drivers can correct exception conditions detected by a device or disable the device. This action permits the system to continue providing full or diminished service. It can dramatically reduce problem determination and periods of inactivity.

Programmable option select information is contained in eight 1-byte registers. Figure 5.11 illustrates the structure of the POS registers. The POS registers contain ten types of information fields. There are three types of information fields: required, conditionally required, or optional.

Device ID Field (Required). The device ID field is contained in POS bytes 0 and 1. The device ID is a unique number provided upon request by the IBM Corporation. It identifies the type of bus or channel participant.

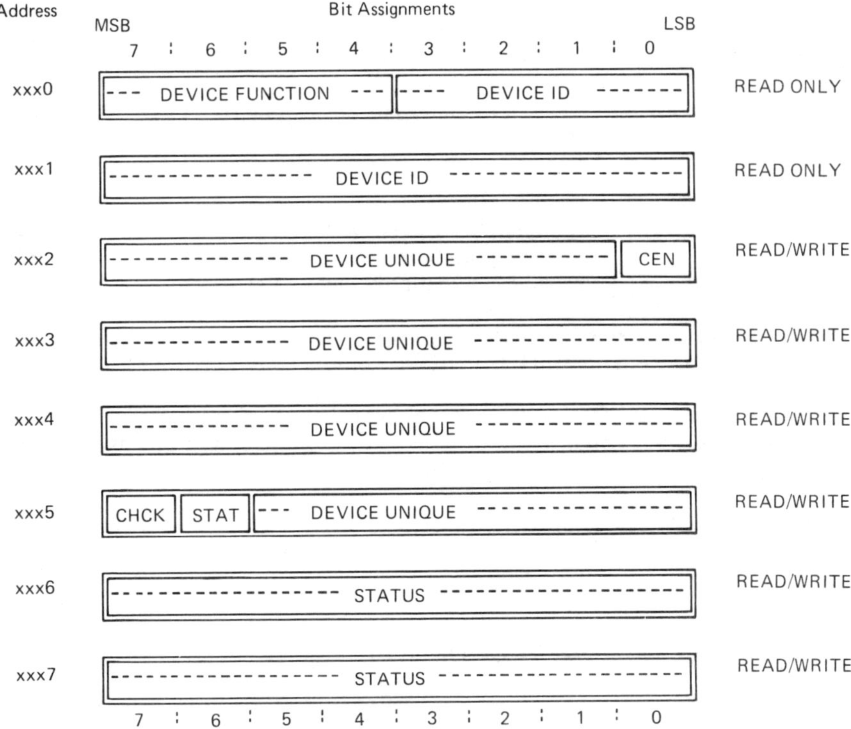

Note: Card Function will be defined as follows:

x 0 0 0 = MASTER
x 0 0 1 = RESERVED
x 0 1 0 = RESERVED
x 0 1 1 = RESERVED
x 1 0 0 = RESERVED
x 1 0 1 = DMA SLAVE
x 1 1 0 = I/O SLAVE
x 1 1 1 = MEMORY SLAVE or CARD w/SYSTEM MAPPED MEMORY

x = '1' for IBM Devices
x = '0' for Non-IBM Devices

FIGURE 5.11 System configuration bytes.

Device Enable Field (Required). The device enable field is located in POS byte 2, bit position 1. It is used to enable and disable devices.

Fairness Enable Field (Conditionally Required). The fairness enable field is conditionally located in a designer-determined device unique bit position. It is used to enable and disable the bus master fairness option. When the fairness option is disabled, a bus master can gain greater access to the bus or channel.

Arbitration Level Field (Conditionally Required). The arbitration level field is conditionally located in designer-determined device unique bit positions. It is used to hold the arbitration level assignment provided to bus owners.

I/O ROS Segment Address Field (Conditionally Required). The I/O ROS segment address field is conditionally located in designer-determined device unique bit positions. It is used to hold the I/O ROS segment address provided by the system.

I/O Device Address Field (Conditonally Required). The I/O device address field is conditionally located in designer-determined device unique bit positions. It is used to hold the I/O device address field provided by the system.

Device Unique Information Fields (Optional). The device unique information fields are used to hold control bits for device unique functions.

Channel Check Field (Optional). The channel check field is located in POS byte 5, bit position 7. It is used to indicate that an exception condition has occurred. Its use and implementation are optional.

Channel Check Status Information Field (Optional). The Channel check status information field is located in POS byte 5, bit position 6. It is used to indicate that device status information on the exception condition is contained in POS bytes 6 and 7.

Exception Condition Status Field (Optional). The exception condition status information is optionally located in POS bytes 6 and 7. This information (when provided) is used to identify the source of the reported exception condition.

LIST OF TRADEMARKS

Micro Channel, Personal Systems/2, and Electronic Gearbox are registered trademarks of IBM Corporation.

CHAPTER 6
FASTBUS

W. K. Dawson and Robert G. Skegg
TRIUMF
Vancouver, British Columbia, Canada

6.1 BACKGROUND

In the mid-1970s high-energy physicists were planning experiments to take place in the mid-1980s that would take advantage of the potential of the high-energy particle accelerators then on the drawing boards. One problem area was found to be in the availability of large, high-speed data acquisition systems with the required distributed processing power and addressing capacity. An initial study was carried out to specify general requirements that would satisfy all foreseen needs for a wide variety of experiments. The problem was then handed over to the National Instrument Methods (NIM) Committee of the U.S. Department of Energy (DOE) that had previously generated the widely used NIM[1] and CAMAC[2] instrumentation standards. The NIM Committee worked in close collaboration with its European counterpart European Standards on Nuclear Electronics (ESONE) in coming up with a suitable scheme.

While developed with a particular use in view, the nature of that use has led to the specification of a general, versatile instrumentation system that could have a wide range of applications. This high-speed data acquisition and control system is called FASTBUS[3,4] and is currently in use in many laboratories around the world.

6.2 SYSTEM OVERVIEW

The most basic component of a FASTBUS system is the segment. It is the electrical signal transmission medium that supports the FASTBUS protocol and to which FASTBUS devices are connected. There are two kinds of segments: the crate segment, which consists of a backplane mounted in a FASTBUS crate and has connections to mate with a multiplicity of FASTBUS modules, and the cable segment, which consists of a cable and the appropriate connectors for mating with devices. Modules, in order to fit into the crate, have closely defined dimensions, while devices that attach to the cable segment do not require dimensional definition.

Modules (or devices) are of two basic types: masters and slaves. Masters are capable of acquiring control of the segment to which they are attached and initiating operations. Slaves respond to the operations initiated by masters. A master may also act as a slave when responding to operations initiated by another master. The complexity of modules may vary enormously ranging, for example, all the way from simple counters or memories to sophisticated processors.

The data path is 32 bits wide. Address and data are multiplexed; hence primary addresses are also 32 bits wide. A secondary addressing scheme allows the addressing capability within each device to be expanded in 32-bit increments. Electrical constraints place an upper limit of 32 on the number of devices connected to a segment. However, the crate segment is physically limited to 26 modules in order that modules may have a reasonable width and yet have the crate fit into a standard relay rack.

There is some circuitry required for each segment, cable or crate, that is not part of any device. This ancillary logic plays a role in arbitration for bus mastership, identification of geographical addresses, broadcast addressing, and run/halt control. It also provides bus terminations. For crate segments this ancillary logic is located on two small boards that plug into the back of the backplane, near each end. One board, the geographical address control (GAC) board, is plugged into one end of the bus and the second, the arbitration timing controller (ATC), into the other end. Both boards supply bus terminations.

Many practical systems cannot be constructed within the confines of a single segment regardless of the functionality that can be placed on a single module. Therefore FASTBUS defines a technique for the interconnection of segments in a transparent way.[5] The master initiating the operation need not be concerned with whether the addressed slave is or is not on a different segment. This transparency is provided by segment interconnects that automatically come into play only when the master and addressed slave are not on the same segment. It is therefore possible for operations to be occurring simultaneously on several different segments, and when an intersegment operation is required, the necessary segments can then be connected and participate in the same operation. The FASTBUS specification defines a particular implementation of the segment interconnect that links a crate segment to a cable segment. With such a segment interconnect very general systems can be constructed. In particular, it is possible to have the topology of the FASTBUS system parallel the structure of a data acquisition or control system.

If the parallelism of operation afforded by the segment interconnect is not required, the less complex segment extender may be used to increase the number of modules in the system. Up to six segments may be interconnected by segment extenders.[6] As is the case for segment interconnects, masters need not be concerned about the particular segment to which the addressed slave happens to be connected.

Besides the possibility of having concurrent processing occurring on different segments, each segment may have several potential masters. The FASTBUS protocol includes an arbitration scheme that allows masters on a segment to determine which one will next gain use of the bus.

In the FASTBUS specification the protocol is defined in a way that is independent of any particular implementation. The appendices then provide implementation-dependent specifications. To date, only an ECL implementation has been defined. Data transfer rates of up to 160 Mbyte/s have been obtained with the ECL implementation.

6.3 THE SIGNALS

In this section the signals that are used to make up the FASTBUS protocol, and shown in Table 6.1, are described. A discussion of the actual use of the signals is postponed to later sections. Table 6.1 contains a list of all signals used by the FASTBUS protocols. The first 60 are used for both crate and cable segments, while the remainder are used for crate segments only. In addition to these signals there are many ground and power connections to each device.

6.3.1 Nomenclature

When referring to signals the following conventions are used. All signals are denoted by a two-letter mnemonic: AD, MS, RD, etc. The mnemonic by itself refers to all signals of that type if there is more than one. For example, AD refers to all 32 AD lines while RD refers to the one RD line. Specific signals within a group are indicated by the mnemonic followed by the particular line number or line number range in angle brackets (AD⟨07⟩ or AD⟨07:00⟩) or by the mnemonic followed by a single digit representing the binary weight of the signal [MS1 is the MS signal line with weight 2 ($=2^1$)].

An asserted signal is indicated by equating its mnemonic to 1 (RD = 1) and a deasserted signal by equating its mnemonic to 0 (RD = 0). A transition of a timing signal from unasserted to asserted and from asserted to unasserted is indicated by the signal mnemonic followed by (u) and (d), respectively [AS(u), AS(d)], while a transition in either direction is indicated by a (t) [AS(t)].

Signals are classified as described in the remainder of this section.

6.3.2 Timing

Timing signal transitions are used to delimit FASTBUS cycles involving either address, data, or arbitration information. Address cycles are delimited by a master's assertion of AS (address sync) and by the responding slave's assertion of AK (address acknowledge). Similarly, data cycles are delimited by DS (data sync) and DK (data acknowledge), and bus arbitration cycles by AG (arbitration grant), issued by the ancillary logic, and GK (grant acknowledge), issued by the master that is about to take over the bus.

6.3.3 Control

Control signals are used to specify further details of an operation. Their level is examined at the transition of a timing signal. Interpretation of the control lines is dependent upon the associated timing signal. For example, the three MS (mode select) lines are used to specify the address type at AS(u) and data type at DS(t). The EG (enable geographic) control line simplifies the implementation of geographical addressing. The direction of data flow is determined by the RD (read) line. The BH (bus halted) control line is used in conjunction with AK to indicate a halted state of the bus and that all devices should protect themselves from spurious signals caused, for example, by the insertion or removal of another device.

TABLE 6.1 FASTBUS Signals

Mnemonic	Signal name	Use*	Number	Comments
		Cable and crate segments		
AS	Address sync	T	1	For address and reporting status of connection
AK	Address acknowledge	T	1	
EG	Enable geographical	C	1	
MS	Mode select	C	3	For data and control of data transfers
RD	Read	C	1	
AD	Address/data	I	32	
PA	Parity	I	1	
PE	Parity enable	I	1	
SS	Slave status	I	3	
DS	Data sync	T	1	
DK	Data acknowledge	T	1	
WT	Wait	A	1	
SR	Service request	A	1	
RB	Reset bus	A	1	
BH	Bus halted	C	1	
AG	Arbitration grant	TA	1	For bus arbitration
AL	Arbitration level	IA	6	
AR	Arbitration request	A	1	
AI	Arbitration request inhibit	CA	1	
GK	Grant acknowledge	TA	1	
		Crate segment only		
TX	Serial line transmit	S	1	For FASTBUS serial protocol
RX	Serial line receive	S	1	
LX	LAN connection	S	1	
GA	Geographical address pins (position encoded, not bused)†	F	5	
TP	T pin (not bused)†	X	1	
DL	Daisy chain left	X	3	
DR	Daisy chain right	X	3	
TR	Terminated restricted use	X	8	
FP	F pins (free use, not bused)		4	
R	Reserved		4	

*Description of use symbols:

T = timing for address and data cycles
C = control for address and data cycles
I = information for address and data cycles
A = asynchronous—timing not directly related to data transfers
TA = timing for arbitration bus
IA = information for arbitration bus
CA = control for arbitration bus
S = serial data, timing independent of parallel bus
F = fixed information—constant
X = special purpose

†On cable segments switches are used instead of GA and T pins.

6.3.4 Information

The level of these signals at a transition of a timing signal conveys information that is defined by the control lines and the associated timing signal. The principal information lines are the 32 AD (address/data) lines. As implied by their name, address and data information are multiplexed. The full 32 bits are available for both addresses and data. The three SS (slave status) lines report on either the success or reason for failure of an address or data cycle. The PA (parity) information line is set to 1 if the AD lines have an even number of bits set to 1. The use of PA is optional and is indicated by the PE (parity enable) information line.

6.3.5 Asynchronous

Asynchronous signals indicate the occurrence of events that are not synchronized with the timing signals of the FASTBUS protocol. The WT (wait) signal is issued by slaves to prevent address or data time-outs when longer than usual times are required by a slave to generate a response. The RB (reset bus) line may be asserted at any time to force the bus and the devices connected to it into a defined state. Slaves can indicate to masters that they need attention by asserting the SR (service request) line and masters indicate their wish to gain bus mastership by asserting AR (arbitration request). Other asynchronous lines are the six AL (arbitration level) lines used by masters to indicate their priority when arbitrating for use of the bus. Indeed, all the lines associated with arbitration for bus mastership are classified as asynchronous since arbitration cycles can occur independently of address and data cycles.

6.3.6 Serial Data

There are three lines devoted to serial data. TX and RX (serial line transmit and receive) are intended for a serial network protocol and LX for an Ethernet-like connection. The object of these lines is to provide a way of probing and diagnosing systems that is independent of the main FASTBUS protocol. Such an ability is especially important for large systems.

6.3.7 Fixed

On a crate segment each module position has five GA pins that are encoded with the slot number. These play a role in geographical addressing. For cable segments these pins are replaced by switches.

6.3.8 Other Lines

In addition to power and ground lines there are another 16 defined lines. These include those that provide left- and right-running daisy chains, some terminated and unterminated restricted-use lines, and the T pin (TP), which is not bussed. At each module position in a crate the T pin is connected to the AD line that corresponds to the slot number. It is asserted, for example, by modules during broadcast polling operations to indicate that they are satisfying certain conditions. There are also some free-use F pins (FP) that are not bussed and a number of reserved bus lines (R).

6.4 FASTBUS TRANSACTIONS

A FASTBUS transaction starts with a potential master gaining bus mastership and carrying out one or more operations. It terminates when the master releases the bus. Each operation begins with a primary address cycle during which the bus master attaches to a slave (or more than one if it is a broadcast primary address cycle). Attachment is followed by one or more data cycles, and the operation is ended by a termination sequence in which the slave is released by the master. When releasing the slave the master need not release the bus. Once a master has gained control of the bus there is no automatic way for its activity to be preempted by another master that wants to become bus master. The current bus master can be aware that others may wish to use the bus, but it alone decides when to release the bus.

6.4.1 Arbitration

In order to gain bus mastership a master must participate in an arbitration cycle. The arbitration process itself takes place in circuitry in each master, but the process is initiated and timed by ancillary logic that must reside on each segment.

Each potential bus master is assigned a six-bit priority level. The high-order bit of this priority level determines if the priority is local (0) or global (1). Local priority levels do not propagate across segments whereas global ones do. Hence values of local levels may be reused many times in a multisegment system. Local levels may be changed by segment interconnects while global levels cannot. It is a typical, but not a mandated, practice for a segment interconnect to raise a local priority level to a global one for an operation that passes through it.

A master wishing to acquire bus mastership asserts the AR (arbitration request) signal at any time. When the current bus master indicates by deasserting GK (grant acknowledge) that it is about to release the bus, the arbitration timing controller of the ancillary logic initiates an arbitration cycle. This is done by asserting AG (arbitration grant). All masters asserting AR then also assert their priority onto the AL lines. They also monitor the actual levels onto the AL lines starting with the most significant one (AL⟨05⟩) first. If a difference between the level on the bus and the internal value is found (and this difference can only be a 1 on the bus and a 0 internal value) then the master ceases to assert all AL lines of lower significance. This process is allowed to continue for at least four bus delay times plus an allowance for internal logic delay times. At the end of this period, which is signaled by the ancillary logic deasserting AG, only one master, the one with the highest priority level, will see a match between its internal priority level and the one on the bus. It becomes the pending master and knows that when the bus is released, it may take over bus mastership. This is done by first asserting GK to indicate to the ancillary logic that as pending master it is indeed prepared to take over bus mastership. When the current master releases the bus the pending master proceeds with a primary address cycle.

Several points are worth noting: Because arbitration cycles can occur independently of addressing and data cycles, little or no time is lost in transferring bus mastership from one master to the next. Another is that if no rules are imposed on the issuance of AR, it would be possible for high-priority masters to indefinitely deny access to the bus to low-priority ones.

Two protocols concerning the assertion of AR have been defined. One, the assured access protocol, prevents starvation by making use of the AI (arbitration inhibit) line. AI is asserted by the ancillary logic wherever AR is also asserted, and masters that obey this protocol do not assert AR if AI is asserted. This results in a round-robin allocation of bus mastership in that all existing requests are satisfied in priority order before any new requests are allowed to be made.

The other, called the priority access protocol, allows a master only to assert AR if its priority is higher than that of the current master. Thus if the current master sees AR, it knows that if it releases the bus the ensuing arbitration cycle will be won by a higher-priority master.

6.4.2 Primary Address Cycle

A primary address cycle is carried out by a master to identify and attach to the slave with which it wishes to communicate. (Multiple-slave connections will be discussed later under broadcast addresses.) Figure 6.1 shows the sequence of events. The master starts a primary address cycle by asserting the slave's address on the AD lines and the address modifier on the MS lines (see the primary address type specifications in Table 6.2). It waits a segment skew time and then asserts AS, the address synch signal. This assertion of an address sets up a path, through segment interconnects if necessary, between the master and the specified slave. When the slave recognizes its address, it responds by issuing the address acknowledge signal, AK. The slave may also assert an SS (slave status) code before or along with AK to indicate that there were problems with the part of the address that relates to internal features of the slave. Should the address be that of an off-segment slave and the connection fail to be made, then a segment interconnect will respond along with an explanatory SS code. The protocol requires that the master continue to assert AS and the slave AK for the duration of the operation. All other devices upon seeing this AS-AK lock realize that a connection has been established and that they should ignore all subsequent bus activity until AS and AK both become deasserted.

Table 6.3 presents a list of SS codes along with their explanation. The responses SS = 1, 2, or 3 are issued by segment interconnects. SS = 7 indicates that, while a connection has been made to a slave, the internal address specified is not one that is implemented. This can only occur for logical addresses.

Note that both for address cycles and for data cycles (see below) the master asserts a time delay between the assertion of data on the information lines and the issuance of the synch signal. The master also introduces a similar delay between the time of receipt of an acknowledge signal and the later sampling of the information lines. Thus only masters, and not slaves, need be concerned with any variations in propagation times for signals on different bus lines (the segment skew time).

6.4.3 Address Spaces

During the primary address cycle one of two address spaces, data or CSR (control and status register), is selected by the MS code. This clear separation allows

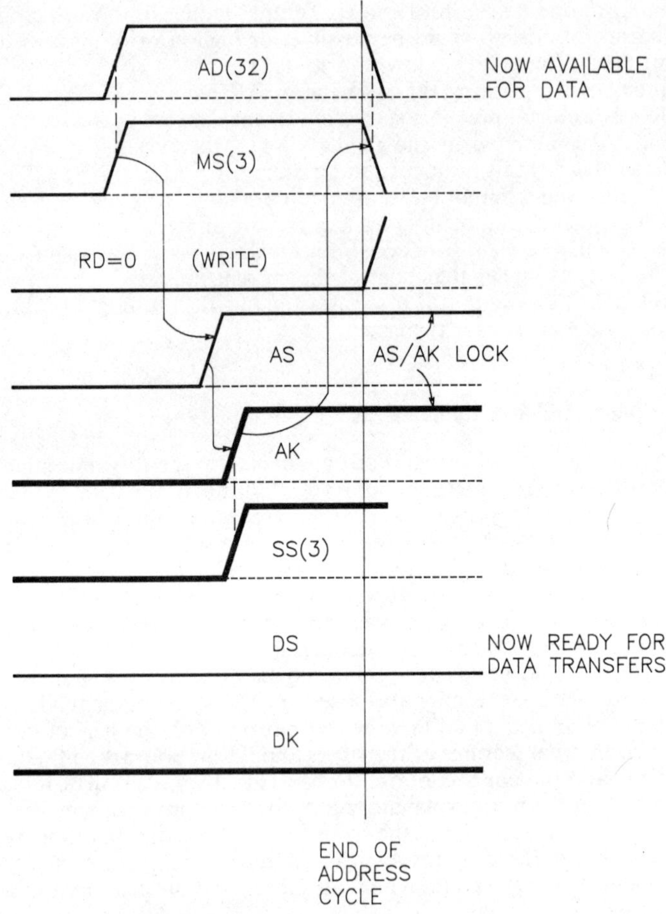

FIGURE 6.1 Primary address cycle. Prior to carrying out the activity shown here the master must have arbitrated for and gained bus mastership. The master inserts skew times between the assertion of information lines and the address synch (AS) to allow for bus characteristics. Similarly sensing of information lines (SS in this case) is delayed by the master for a skew time after receipt of the acknowledgment signal (AK). ——, asserted by master; ▬▬, asserted by slave.

TABLE 6.2 Address Type Specification

SS⟨2:0⟩	Address type
0	Specific device—data space
1	Specific device—CSR space
2	Broadcast—data space
3	Broadcast—CSR space
4–5	Reserved—specific device
6–7	Reserved—broadcast

TABLE 6.3 Address Time Responses

SS⟨2:0⟩	Interpretation
0	Address recognized
1	Network busy
2	Network failure
3	Network abort
4	Reserved
5	Reserved
6	Reserved
7	Invalid IA—address accepted

addressing of data from one module to the next to be seamless and unaffected by the necessary presence of registers containing control and status information. Also, because of techniques defined below, it allows a system-wide consistent definition of CSR registers and their usage to be made. Such a definition greatly simplifies software since common features and functions are always accessed in the same way regardless of device type. Allocation of registers in CSR space is described later.

6.4.4 Address Types

It is by means of a primary address that a master identifies the slave(s) with which it wishes to exchange data. Primary addresses are 32 bits wide. Three types are available: geographical, logical, and broadcast. The type of address is specified by the MS code (see Table 6.2) and the AD field. Identical address formats are used for data and for CSR space. The segment address is a common component of all three address types.

Each segment, crate or cable, is identified by a nonzero segment number that is in the high-order bits of the primary address. The number of bits devoted to the segment number is left as a design choice (and is typically eight). The field devoted to the segment number in the primary address is called the group field (GP). The group field is examined by segment interconnects during primary address cycles to determine if an off-segment address is being specified.

For geographical and logical addresses the remaining bits in the primary address are used to specify a specific device on a segment and, for logical addresses where appropriate, to also specify a register within a device. For broadcast addresses the remaining bits are used to further specify the type of broadcast.

6.4.5 Logical Addresses

Figure 6.2 shows the logical address format. It consists of two main portions: the device address field (DA) and an internal address field (IA). The IA field is used to specify an internal register of the device for data space cycles, but is ignored for CSR primary address cycles. Hence a secondary address data cycle is required to select any register in CSR space and may be necessary to select a data space register if the allocated IA field is too narrow. The width of the IA field is a design choice constrained somewhat by the GP field width. Because of secondary address data cycles the number of accessible registers in a device is, for all

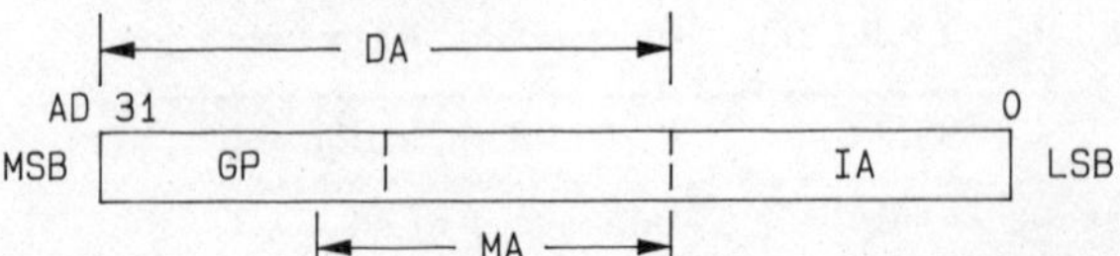

FIGURE 6.2 Logical address format. The 32-bit (AD⟨31:00⟩) address word consists of a device address (DA) and an internal address (IA). The boundary between them may move from device to device. The DA field in turn consists of a segment specifier (GP) and a module address (MA). There may be some overlap of these two fields.

practical purposes, unbounded. It should be noted that all internal addresses in data and CSR space refer to 32-bit words, not bytes.

The DA field consists of two possibly overlapping fields, GP and the module address (MA). This possible overlap expresses the fact that more than one GP field may be assigned to a given segment. If the segment itself has to be identified, for purposes such as geographic addressing, only one particular value of the GP field is used. This value is stored, during system initialization, in a CSR register in the GAC board associated with each segment. In order to remove any confusion between logical and geographical addresses the MA field must contain at least one nonzero bit.

Each device that implements the nonmandatory logical addressing scheme does so by implementing a defined logical address register in CSR space. During system initialization this register is loaded with the DA that is to be used for comparison with the AD lines during logical primary address cycles. This comparison is enabled and disabled by a bit in another defined CSR register.

6.4.6 Geographical Addresses

The first 256 logical addresses on each segment are called geographical addresses. Of these the first 32 are reserved for positional addressing of devices on a normal segment, the next 192 for positional addressing of devices on extended segments[6] and the last 32 are reserved for special purposes.

Position on a cable segment is determined by means of five binary switches. On a crate segment it is determined by the five encoded GA pins. When viewed from the front of the crate the rightmost module position has geographical position 0, and this position number increases by 1 for each position moved to the left.

The two forms for a geographical address are shown in Figure 6.3. They differ in that one contains a GP field and the other does not. The former is more general and is required if an off-segment slave is to be addressed geographically. The form with all high-order address bits zero can be used by a master to geographically address a slave on the same segment as the master.

During all nonbroadcast primary address cycles the primary address is examined by circuitry on the ancillary logic GAC board. If the 24 high-order address bits are zero or if a match is found between the segment number stored in the GAC and the GP field and all remaining bits down to bit 8 are zero, then the GAC asserts EG (enable geographic). Slaves sensing EG then examine only the eight low-order address bits. In order for a slave to attach to the master, the lowest five address bits must match the device's position as determined by the switches

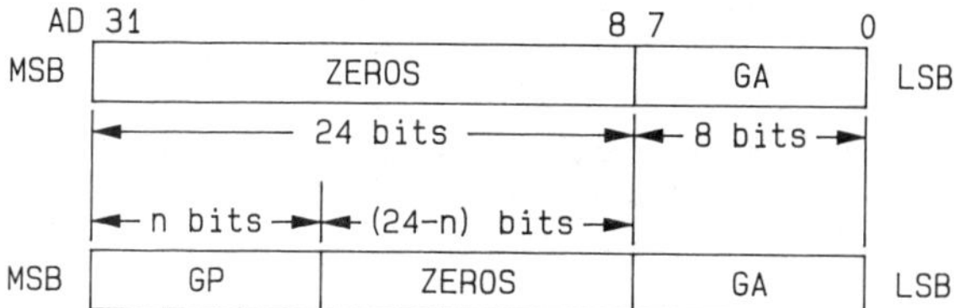

FIGURE 6.3 Geographical address format. There are two forms of geographical addresses, one of which specifies the segment address (GP) and the other which specifies that the location is on this segment. The GA field specifies a position on a crate segment or a switch specified device on a cable segment.

or GA pins, and the remaining three bits must be zero. In order to select a register within the attached device the master must next carry out a secondary address data cycle.

Extended segments are identified by nonzero bits in the three high-order geographical address bits. The patterns of all three bits clear or all three bits set are disallowed for extended segment addressing. During geographical addressing the extended segment connection device zeros these bits before passing them on to the specified extended segment, thus preserving the addressing mechanism.

Every device in FASTBUS must be capable of responding to geographical addressing. Note that while the EG mechanism may seem cumbersome and unnecessary, it does allow considerable simplification of devices designed to respond only to geographical addressing. Also, the overhead of an additional data cycle to convey internal address information generally has little impact upon performance since many applications make extensive use of block transfers.

6.4.7 Broadcast Addresses

Broadcast addresses are identified by the MS codes as shown in Table 6.2. By issuing a broadcast address, a master expects that more than one slave will become attached and participate in ensuing data cycles. If each slave that attached were to issue acknowledgment signals, it would be impossible for the master to understand what was going on. Hence slaves never issue acknowledgments to broadcast primary address or data cycles. Rather, acknowledgments are issued by the system handshake logic (SHL) on the ATC ancillary logic board.

The SHL reacts to all broadcast primary address and data cycles by waiting for implementation-dependent broadcast address or data response time periods and then, if WT has been 0 for at least two bus delays, issuing the appropriate response [AK(u) or DK(t)]. The SHL deasserts AK when AS has been deasserted for the broadcast address response time period. It is through the intervention of the SHL that the master receives timing acknowledgments, which indicate that the requested operation has had its full effect.

A broadcast address is used for two purposes: one is to specify the segments on which the broadcast is to be effective, and the other is to select on the affected segments either a function or test to execute or a class of devices that should attach. Segment selection is carried out by the GP, G (global), and L (local) fields in the broadcast address word (Figure 6.4). The segment interconnect plays an important role, other than the obvious one, in broadcast addressing. Under the appropriate circumstances it modifies the values of the GP, G, and L fields of the

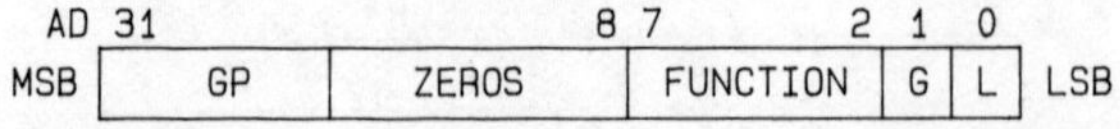

AD 31		8 7	2 1	0	
MSB GP	ZEROS	FUNCTION	G	L	LSB

FIGURE 6.4 Broadcast address format. The usage of the fields in the broadcast address format is described in Tables 6.4 and 6.5.

broadcast addresses so that the spread of the broadcast and the segments on which it is effective can be controlled, as shown in Table 6.4. The L bit must be set for a broadcast to be effective on a segment. The G bit along with the GP field determines how the broadcast propagates through the system. A zero GP field is used to indicate a general broadcast tree defined at system initialization time, which will be traversed if the G bit is set.

The interpretation of the function bits is shown in Table 6.5. This table shows a number of the uses of the T pin. At each position on a crate segment the T pin is connected to the AD line that corresponds to that position's geographical address on the segment. Thus at module slot position 5 the T pin is connected to AD⟨05⟩. Modules responding in the affirmative to a question asked by a broadcast address do so by asserting TP in the ensuing read data cycle, allowing an entire crate to be polled in one operation. Using this feature multiple devices asserting SR can be identified in a single operation and efficient sparse data scans may be carried out. Modules can also be set up by a broadcast address to attach to the master if their T pin is asserted in the ensuing write data cycle. This is done by the master asserting the appropriate AD line. The class N feature, implemented in conjunction with a defined register in CSR space, allows, for example, the clearing, resetting, starting, or stopping of a defined group of devices in a single operation.

6.4.8 Data Cycles

On receipt of AK from the attached slave the master removes the address information from the AD lines, which will be used for data during the ensuing data cycles. To initiate a write cycle the master asserts the data on the AD lines, asserts

TABLE 6.4 Propagation of Broadcast Addresses

GP field	G bit	L bit	System action
0	0	0	No operation
0	0	1	Broadcast effective on local segment only
0	1	0	Broadcast effective on broadcast (sub)tree below local segment
0	1	1	Broadcast effective on local segment and on broadcast (sub)tree below local segment
N≠0	0	0	Broadcast effective on segment N only
N	0	1	Broadcast effective on local segment, on segments traversed in reaching N, and on N
N	1	0	Broadcast effective on segment N and on broadcast (sub)tree below N
N	1	1	Broadcast effective on local segment, on segments traversed in reaching N, on N, and on broadcast (sub)tree below N

TABLE 6.5 Slave Response to Broadcast Address Function Codes

Function (AD bits*						
7	6	5	4	3	2)	Description
X	X	X	X	0	0	General broadcast—all devices respond to subsequent data cycles
N	N	N	N	0	1	Only devices of class N respond to subsequent data cycles.
E	E	E	0	1	0	Sparse data scan: Devices respond by asserting TP during following read cycle if data present. Pattern select: Devices sensing TP during the immediately following write data cycle are selected and respond to subsequent read or write cycles.
E	E	E	1	1	0	Device available scan: Devices respond by asserting TP if they contain no data or are available for use. Pattern select: Same as above.
0	0	0	0	1	1	Devices respond by asserting TP during following read cycle.
0	0	0	1	1	1	Assert TP during following read cycle if asserting service request.
0	0	1	0	1	1	Devices respond by asserting TP during the following read cycle if their SR flag bit is set.
0	0	1	1	1	1	Reserved.
0	1	X	X	1	1	Reserved.
1	X	X	X	1	1	Defined by manufacturer.

*Definition of bit labels: X = do not care; N = class code; E = optional extended segment number (zero for normal segment)

0 on the RD (read) line, asserts a data transfer–type code on the MS lines (Table 6.6), waits a segment skew time, and then asserts DS(t). The attached slave accepts the data and responds with the assertion of an SS code (Table 6.7) and finally DK(t). After seeing DK(t) the master waits a segment skew time and accepts the returned SS code, completing the operation.

For data cycles, each edge of DS issued by a master initiates an action in the slave that is determined by the state of the MS lines. Cleanup cycles have no

TABLE 6.6 Interpretation of MS Codes for Data Cycles

MS⟨2:0⟩	DS(u)	DS(d)	Comment
0	Transfer data	Cleanup	Single transfer
1	Transfer data, incl. NTA	Transfer data, incl. NTA	Block transfer
2	Transfer NTA	Cleanup	Secondary address
3	Transfer data, incl. NTA	Transfer data, incl. NTA	Pipelined transfer
4	Restricted use	Reserved	
5	Reserved	Reserved	
6	Reserved	Reserved	
7	Reserved	Reserved	

TABLE 6.7 Slave Status Codes at Data Time

SS⟨2:0⟩	Interpretation
0	Valid action
1	Busy
2	End of block
3	User defined
4	Reserved
5	Reserved
6	Data error (reject)
7	Data error (accept)

associated data and are needed in particular when during an address-locked sequence a read operation is followed by a write one. For block and pipelined transfers both edges of the timing signals are used to transfer data and incrementation (by 1 only) of the NTA is optional.

Each DK signal issued by a slave is accompanied by an SS code, with meaning as indicated in Table 6.7. On sensing a problem with data such as bad parity for write data or internal problems with read data, a slave may refuse to transfer the data (SS = 6) or allow the bad data to be transferred (SS = 7).

To initiate a read cycle (Fig. 6.5) the master asserts 1 on the RD line, a data transfer–type code on the MS lines, and waits a segment skew time before asserting DS(t). The attached slave responds by asserting the data specified by the previous address cycle on the AD lines, a status code on the SS lines, and finally DK(t). The master, seeing DK(t), waits a segment skew time and then strobes both the AD and SS lines.

6.4.9 The NTA

All but the simplest devices are required to have a next transfer address (NTA) register. As its name implies, this register points to the internal register that will participate in the next data transfer. The NTA register is accessible by read or write data cycles that are accompanied by MS = 2. Hence, once a primary address cycle has been carried out to cause the slave to attach to the master, secondary address data cycles can be used, if needed, to select particular registers in a device. Using such secondary address data cycles combined with normal data cycles, a master can carry out a series of data transfers involving different locations in the slave. Such a series of data transfers is called an address-locked sequence.

The NTA also plays a role in block and pipelined data transfers. Both of these transfer types involve sending the slave an internal starting address (during either the primary or a secondary address cycle) followed by a sequence of data transfers. The NTA may optionally be automatically incremented by one after each transfer, thus keeping track of the next internal address to be used. If difficulties occur because of data transmission problems, the NTA can always be interrogated by the master to learn more about the best way to resume operation. For devices such as first in–first out registers (FIFOs), which supply or accept many words of data at a single address, special precautions, such as the provision of protective buffers, have to be taken if error recovery is to be carried out.

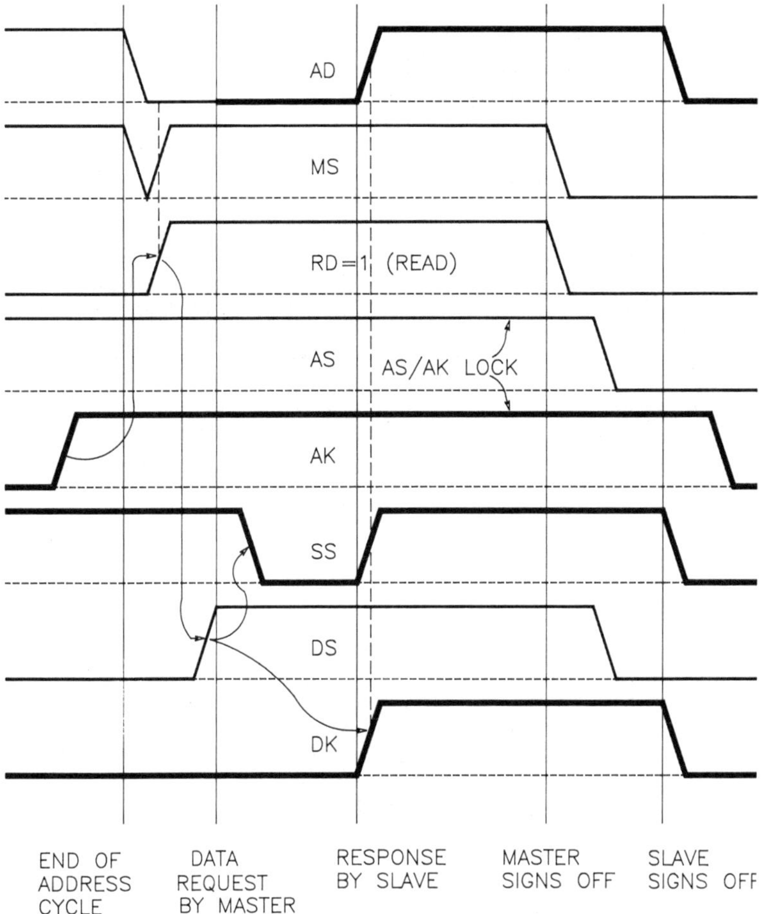

FIGURE 6.5 Read data cycle. Data is requested by the master asserting RD followed a skew time later by DS(t). The slave places the data pointed to by its NTA on the AD lines, asserts an SS code and issues an acknowledge [DK(t)], all of which are sensed by the master. The AS-AK lock, which indicates to all other devices that the bus is in use, is broken by the master deasserting AK, which when sensed by the slave causes it to cease asserting any information or timing signals. ———, asserted by master; ▬▬▬, asserted by slave.

Block and pipelined data transfers differ from single-word data transfers in that a transfer takes place on each edge of DS. Hence each time DS toggles a data transfer takes place. For a read block transfer, for example, a DS(u) transition will get a DK(u) response from the slave accompanied by data and an SS code, and a DS(d) transfer will get a DK(d) response again accompanied by data and an SS code. Block and pipelined transfers differ in that for block transfers the master always waits for the slave acknowledgment before initiating the next transfer, while for pipelined transfers the master simply initiates requests at a rate it considers reasonable without waiting for the slave's response. At any one time during a pipelined transfer the master may have many outstanding requests for data transfers that have not yet been acknowledged. While all acknowledgments are accompanied with status codes, it is usually difficult, if not impossible, to recover from error conditions should they occur.

6.4.10 Termination and Bus Release

A master signals a slave that it wishes to break the connection by dropping AS. The slave responds by ceasing to assert all bus lines, AK in particular. When AK(d) is seen by the master it may then, if it wishes, proceed to carry out a primary address cycle, thus reestablishing a connection with another slave, after which data cycles can again occur. A master that carries out a series of operations to a number of slaves without releasing its mastership of the bus is said to have carried out an arbitration-locked sequence.

A master signals that it is about to release the bus by deasserting GK. This causes an arbitration cycle to take place, the result of which is the selection of the pending master. The pending master then asserts GK and waits until the bus becomes quiescent, that is, until the AS-AK lock of the last operation has been broken, before starting a primary address cycle.

6.4.11 Time-outs and the Use of Wait

In asynchronous systems, system integrity requires that no device wait indefinitely for a response. Hence the need for time-outs at various levels. All time-outs are implemented in the master; therefore only masters need to be aware of the delay properties of the bus to which they are connected. Earlier we saw that the slave asserted or acted upon information and timing lines without regard to segment skew times. These skew times were allowed for by the master.

Each time a master issues a synch signal (As or DS) it starts a response timer. If the corresponding response (AK or DK) is not received within the time-out period the operation is aborted. Master time-out periods are meaningless unless compatible requirements are placed upon slave response times. For ECL implementations of the bus a slave must respond to AS in less than 500 ns and to DK(t) in less than 1000 ns. The corresponding master time-out periods are 900 and 1600 ns, respectively.

There are occasions, however, when the time-out periods will be recognized as being too short. Examples are primary address cycles or data cycles that have to traverse several segment interconnects or slaves, which because of infrequent special circumstances, may be slow to respond. In such cases the device, recognizing that extra time is required, asserts wait (WT), thus asking the master to stop and reset its active bus time-out timer. When the response is imminent, WT is deasserted and the sequence continues as if the delay had not been enforced. Slaves that anticipate a longer than usual delay before being able to respond to the requested data transfer operation may issue a temporizing response by setting SS=2 along with asserting data acknowledge. This is interpreted by masters as meaning that the operating should be requested again shortly with every expectation of success.

Protection is provided in masters in the form of a wait timer to prevent excessively long periods of assertion of WT. Similarly a timer in masters, the long timer, is provided to prevent a master from using the bus continually for too long a period. All these timers are implemented in and controlled by registers in CSR space (see below).

6.5 CSR SPACE

During a primary address cycle to CSR space (geographical, logical, or broadcast) no internal address information is conveyed to the slave(s). This must be done using a secondary address data cycle, which means that each device has 2^{32} addressable CSR locations. It is this large number that makes it feasible to define the usage of CSR registers.

One of the reasons for not allowing a primary address cycle to CSR space to convey internal address information is to allow further diagnosis of the state of a slave. Enforcement of this rule means that the process of attachment does not affect the contents of the NTA, whose contents before the attachment may then be determined as part of the diagnostic procedure.

The 2^{32} addressable CSR locations are subdivided into four equally sized groups. The lowest, starting at address 0, is called normal CSR space. It contains general as well as device-specific control and status registers. The next group, called program CSR space, starts at hex addresses 4000 0000. It contains programs and tables that may be down-loaded by a master and used primarily by the device and, possibly, used as data by other devices. The third region, parameter CSR space, starting at hex 8000 0000, contains static or rarely changing infor-

TABLE 6.8 Normal CSR Space Allocation

The assignments in this table must be followed if any of the described features are implemented. The asterisk is used to denote selective set and clear registers.

Hexadecimal address	Definition
0000 0000*	16-bit ID, 16-bit status and miscellaneous control
0000 0001	User-defined control/status register
0000 0002*	Auxiliary control/status register
0000 0003	Device logical address register
0000 0004	Device user address register
0000 0005	Word count register
0000 0006	Test selection register
0000 0007	Broadcast class selection register
Assignments associated with masters	
0000 0008	Arbitration level register
0000 0009*	Timer control
0000 000A	Source A interrupt destination device (address)
0000 000B	Source A interrupt destination secondary (address)
0000 000C	Source B interrupt destination device (address)
0000 000D	Source B interrupt destination secondary (address)
0000 000E	Source C interrupt destination device (address)
0000 000F	Source C interrupt destination secondary (address)
0000 0010–17	User defined
0000 0018–1B	Reserved
0000 001C–1F	Timer periods
0000 0020–3F*	SR source and mask bits

TABLE 6.8 Normal CSR Space Allocation (*Continued*)

Hexadecimal address	Definition
	Assignments associated with segment interconnects
0000 0040	Route table address register
0000 0041	Route table data register
0000 0042	SI near-side geographical address
0000 0043	SI far-side geographical address
0000 0044–6F	Reserved
	Assignments associated with resource management
0000 0070–7F	Address of device currently using subsection N of this device (N = 0 through Fh)
0000 0080*	Read⟨15:00⟩ allocated subsection Fh-0 Write⟨15:00⟩ allocate subsection Fh-0 Write⟨31:16⟩ deallocate subsection Fh-0
0000 0081	Read⟨15:00⟩ enabled subsection Fh-0 Write⟨15:00⟩ enable subsection Fh-0 Write⟨31:16⟩ disable subsection Fh-0
0000 0082-9F	Reserved
	Assignments associated with interrupt messages
0000 00A0–AF	Interrupt message source A
0000 00B0–BF	Interrupt message source B
0000 00C0–CF	Interrupt message source C
0000 00D0–FF	Reserved
	Assignments associated with interrupt receivers
0000 0100–10F	Receiver block 0 (lowest-priority interrupt)
0000 01N0–1NF	Receiver block N (N = 1 to Eh)
0000 01F0–1FF	Receiver block Rh (highest-priority interrupt)
0000 0200 through 3FFF FFFF	Reserved

*Selective set and clear registers.

mation such as calibration constants or manufacturer data applicable to the device. A technique for storing data in CSR space is specified. Finally, starting at hex C000 0000 is user CSR space, upon which no restrictions are placed.

From a device design viewpoint it is often desirable to control and record several device features in a single CSR register. Many control functions are implemented by setting or resetting bits. An appreciable overhead is required to do this without affecting other bits in the same register (e.g., read-modify-write). FASTBUS provides an alternative in the form of selective set and clear registers. Such registers are effectively only half the 32-bit word width. For such a register only the lower 16 bits, which represent its current status, are returned by a read cycle. Bit N is set by writing a 1 to bit N; it is reset by writing a 1 to bit $N + 16$. Hence single bits can be manipulated in the register without concern for the current state of other bits in the same register.

Table 6.8 presents the assignments of registers in normal CSR space. If any feature covered by a register in this table is implemented, then it must be implemented as described in the specifications. This rigid rule simplifies the software problem and allows commands such as clear data to be issued by a broadcast operation.

The only mandatory register in any device is CSR#0 (see Table 6.9). Within this register only the 16-bit manufacturer's identification code is mandatory. Contrary to recommended practice, this register overlaps the clear bits of the set/clear group with information bits in order to increase the possibility that it be the only CSR register needed even for moderately complex but only geographically addressed devices.

TABLE 6.9 Bit Assignments Within CSR Register 0

The letters S and C preceding a bit number indicate that the bit is part of a selective set and clear pair.

Bit	Read significance	Write significance
S00	Error flag	Set error flag
S01	Enabled	Enable
S02	RUNing	RUN
S03	Device allocated	Allocate device
S04	SR assertion enabled	Enable SR assertion
S05	SR flag	Set SR flag
S06	User-defined Status 0	User-defined set 0
S07	User-defined Status 1	User-defined set 1
S08	User-defined Status 2	User-defined set 2
S09	User-defined Status 3	User-defined set 3
S10	User-defined Status 4	User-defined set 4
S11	User-defined Status 5	User-defined set 5
S12	User-defined Status 6	User-defined set 6
S13	User-defined Status 7	User-defined set 7
14	Parity error	Set parity error
15	Active	SI route trace bit
C16	LSB of device type	Clear error flag
C17	Device type	Disable
C18	Device type	HALT
C19	MSB of device type	Deallocate device
C20	LSB of manufacturer's ID	Disable SR assertion
C21	Manufacturer's ID	Clear SR flag
C22	Manufacturer's ID	User-defined clear 0
C23	Manufacturer's ID	User-defined clear 1
C24	Manufacturer's ID	User-defined clear 2
C25	Manufacturer's ID	User-defined clear 3
C26	Manufacturer's ID	User-defined clear 4
C27	Manufacturer's ID	User-defined clear 5
C28	Manufacturer's ID	User-defined clear 6
C29	Manufacturer's ID	User-defined clear 7
30	Manufacturer's ID	Reset
31	MSB of Manufacturer's ID	Clear data

Note: LSB and MSB denote least and most significant bit, respectively.

6.6 SEGMENT INTERCONNECTS

Segment interconnects allow intersegment operations to appear to be the same to the originating master as those to slaves on the same segment as the master.[3] As far as the master is concerned there are no protocol differences, just a difference in the duration of the operation. The design of the segment interconnect allows many different structures to be built, including trees and stars or combinations of these.

A segment interconnect (SI) consists of two sections, called ports, connected to the two segments that it links. The port of the segment interconnect connected to the same segment as the initiating master acts as a slave for the duration of the operation and the port connected to the slave's segment acts as a master. If several segments are traversed by the operation, all intervening segment interconnects act in the same way. The port of each SI electrically nearer to the originating master (the near-side port) acts as a slave and the one further away (far-side port) acts as a master (see Fig. 6.6). All segments traversed must be devoted to the operation. The process of establishing an off-segment connection may be a lengthy one because of the serial process of gaining mastership of each needed segment. Once the connection has been established, data transfers only undergo circuit logic delays plus distance delays.

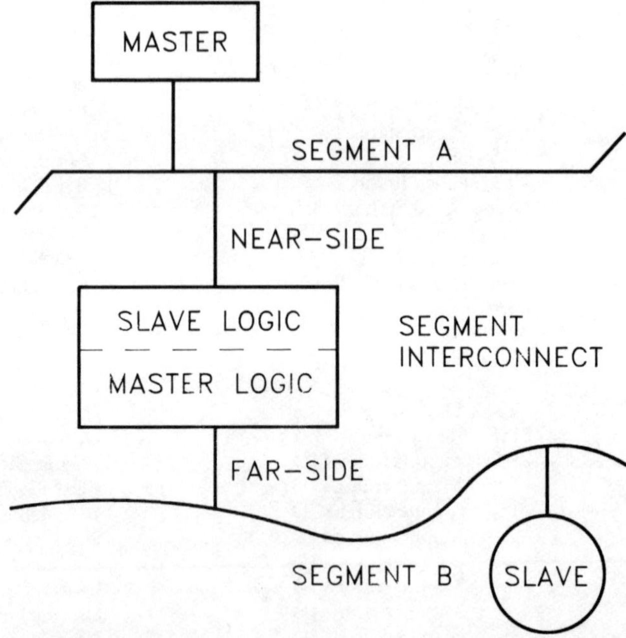

FIGURE 6.6 Segment interconnect. Primary address cycles flow from the near side to far side of a segment interconnect with the near side acting as a slave and the far side as a master. Once the connection has been established data can flow in either direction. For duplex segment interconnects, the only implementation defined in the specification, the connections to each segment have both near- and far-side capabilities.

Should it be required that the operation be driven in the reverse direction, that is, the master and slave be interchanged, then the FASTBUS specification mandates that the path taken for the operation in both directions be the same. Hence, while it is possible to define a unidirectional segment interconnect, the specification defines a duplex (bidirectional) one and gives an implementation that links a crate segment with a cable segment. Two unidirectional segment interconnects are not equivalent to a single duplex one because of differences in the way that conflicts in usage have to be resolved.

Each port of a duplex segment interconnect monitors all primary address cycles on the segment to which it is attached. The GP field of a primary address is used as an index into a route table to determine subsequent behavior of the segment interconnect. The number of route table entries is determined by the width of the GP field: for the typical 8-bit GP field there would be 256 entries. In the simple nontransforming SI, an entry consists of 3 bits: pass, destination, and base GP. Legal entries are either all bits clear or the pass bit set, the pass and destination bits set, or all three bits set. If all bits are clear for the entry corresponding to the current GP field, the operation is ignored by the segment interconnect. No further action is taken until the next primary address cycle.

Whenever the pass bit is set in the entry for the current GP field, the segment interconnect carries out a series of actions. First it asserts WT = 1 on the near-side port. This warns the master that extra time is required before an acknowledgment can be expected. Next it proceeds to arbitrate for use of the segment connected to the far-side port. The arbitration level used is that of the originating master if it is a system arbitration level or, if it is not, the arbitration level of the far-side port is used. Once a system arbitration level has been assigned to the operation either by the originating master or by an intervening segment interconnect, that level is used when arbitrating for all subsequent segments involved in the operation.

If the destination bit is also set, the segment interconnect realizes that the far-side segment is the destination segment (i.e., the one specified by the GP field). This information is used during broadcast primary address cycles as a signal to zero the high-order 24 address bits and set AD⟨00⟩ = 1 before passing the address on to the far-side segment. This is the mechanism that implements broadcasts to system subtrees. (Recall that a GP field of zero is used exclusively for broadcast routing.)

If, in addition, the base GP bit is set, the SI asserts EG = 1 if all bits from AD⟨08⟩ up to the GP field are zero and it is a nonbroadcast primary address. This feature enables initialization of segments via geographical addressing.

The designated slave responds to its address by issuing AK(u). A segment interconnect responds to AK(u) on its far-side port by releasing WT and issuing AK(u) on its near-side port. Thus the response and the AS-AK lock works its way back to the originating master. Data cycles then proceed using WT in the same way except that, of course, no time is lost arbitrating for the use of segments.

Broadcast primary address cycles and data cycles proceed in the same way with one exception. More than one segment interconnect connected to a given segment may pass the operation. This causes no difficulty, as each segment interconnect passing the operation will assert WT = 1 on the near-side segment. When responses come back to these segment interconnects they will release WT, and it is the last one to do so that allows the response to ripple back through the system.

There are a number of occurrences or situations that may make it impossible to reach the desired slave. The segment interconnect may not be able to gain access to the far-side segment because of higher-priority or conflicting operations on that segment. An address time-out may occur on the destination segment, perhaps because the device does not exist. Invalid arbitration levels may be found during contention resolution. All these conditions are indicted by the affected segment interconnect issuing an appropriate SS code (Table 6.3) and AK(u) and, of course, releasing WT.

Standardized assignments of registers in CSR space are made for segment interconnect route tables and other features (Table 6.9).

6.7 INTERRUPTS

FASTBUS defines two mechanisms whereby devices can request service or attention from other devices. Neither interrupt mechanism is capable of stopping an ongoing operation, then initiating and running to completion a new one (probably involving a different master-slave combination), before resuming the original operation at the point of interruption. Rather, both mechanisms rely upon a master becoming aware of the existence of an interrupt and arbitrating for and winning use of the bus in order to determine and carry out the desired actions. The current master can also become aware of the existence of the interrupt and may, if it chooses, release the bus prematurely with the intention of later requesting bus mastership in order to complete the operation.

6.7.1 Interrupt Operation

Only potential bus masters are capable of initiating interrupt operations since they involve the sending of a defined format interrupt message of up to 16 words in length to an interrupt service device. The format requires that the source of the message be identified. Sets of registers in CSR space are defined for the receipt of such messages (Table 6.9). The breaking of the AS-AK lock by the sending master generates an interrupt to the processor in the interrupt service device and also places the register set used into a state that will not accept further messages until explicitly enabled to do so. If FASTBUS operations are required to respond to the request contained in the message, the interrupt service device must participate in and win an arbitration cycle before carrying out the requested operations on the bus.

6.7.2 The Service Request Line

Devices with only slave capability can indicate their desire for attention by asserting the SR (service request) line. A single device may have up to 256 different internal sources of SR, all of which are controllable and testable using defined registers in CSR space. All enabled internal sources of SR are ORed then ANDed with an overall enable bit to form the external SR signal. Segment interconnects can be enabled to pass SR from their far-side to near-side segments.

The SR line is monitored by a service request handler which, when SR assertion is sensed, arbitrates for bus mastership and proceeds by means of polling using special broadcast operations (Table 6.5) to locate the devices asserting SR. The service request handler proceeds to deal appropriately with each device, usually under the umbrella of an arbitration-locked sequence.

6.8 FASTBUS SLAVES

A FASTBUS slave is usually organized as a set of registers that can be read or written to transfer data or execute control functions. It is connected to the segment by a coupler or interface that translates the FASTBUS protocol to simple control and data signals (Fig. 6.7).

The interface design determines which of the FASTBUS commands the slave will respond to. This may range from very simple application-specific examples meeting only the minimum FASTBUS requirements to general purpose complex semicustom implementations that respond to the full protocol.

6.8.1 Designing Slave Interfaces

A simple interface for a specific application may be realized in "discrete" logic chips and programmable array logic (PAL), but care has to be taken in a number of areas. For instance, while a geographic address may be safely recognized by the state AS = 1, AK = 0, EG = 1, AD⟨7:5⟩ = 0, AD⟨4:0⟩ = GA⟨4:0⟩, there is a pitfall in the use of the state AS = 1, AK = 0, AD⟨31:0⟩ = CSR#3⟨31:0⟩, Enable = 1 to recognize a logical address. Rather than using this state, the edge AS(u) should be used as an indication of a logical address cycle in order to avoid the following fault situation: If an address-locked operation is in progress and because of a failure in the slave it drops AK, then the condition AS = 1, AK = 0 exists on the bus together with some data. If that data happens to match the data in another slave's CSR#3, then that slave would assert AK and become attached. The master may not see any change in AK and would carry on as if nothing had happened. Such

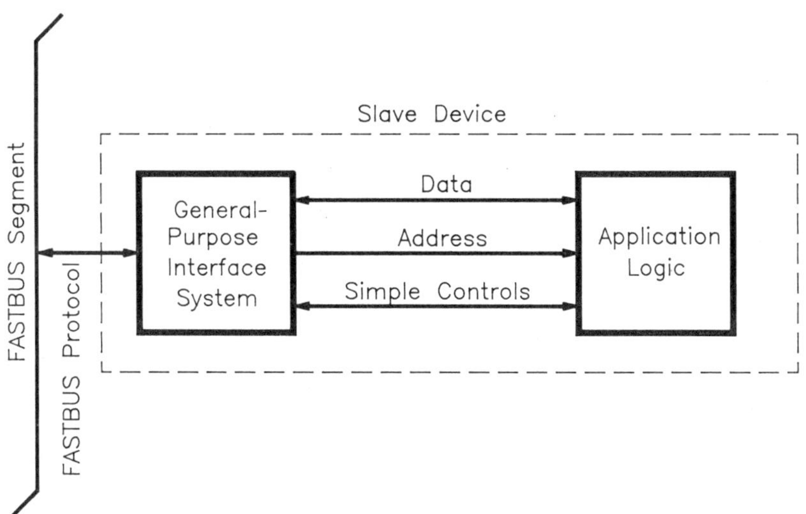

FIGURE 6.7 Structure of a typical FASTBUS slave. The application logic is connected to the segment via an interface which translates the FASTBUS protocol to simple data, address, and control signals.

happened. Such situations are very difficult to debug and can be avoided by careful design of the address recognition circuits.

It is advisable to latch any signals from the user part of a device that have a direct effect on segment signals (e.g., SS codes) to prevent them from changing during a FASTBUS operation. Likewise it is advantageous to latch FASTBUS segment signals such as MS and RD during an operation to reduce the effects of any noise that may be present on the segment.

The reset bus signal (RB) is both useful and powerful. Because noise on this signal would cause any slave to detach, it is required that RB be integrated before use in a slave. RB must also be ANDed with not BH to prevent spurious operation while modules are being replaced on the segment. Note that BH is not integrated.

6.8.2 General Purpose Interfaces

To ease the design construction of slave modules, much work has been done on general purpose interfaces. These interfaces convert the FASTBUS protocol to separate address and data buses and simple control signals. Other inputs and outputs are provided to customize the interface to the application logic and to handle FASTBUS special requests and responses. Standard interfaces use either programmable array logic or semicustom gate arrays to conserve board space.

6.8.3. The ADI-PCL Interface

The ADI (address and data interface[7]) and PCL (protocol control logic[8]) are gate arrays containing the majority of logic necessary for a complete general purpose interface. The ADI processes data on the AD lines into separate address and data, stores and recognizes primary addresses, and performs parity generation. It is contained in an 88-lead-pin grid ceramic package and is available from Fujitsu as part number MB114F307. One ADI handles 16 AD lines; therefore two chips are required for a FASTBUS interface. The ADIs contain the following:

- A 32-bit data latch that is used to pipeline operations and can be used as a protective buffer
- A 32-bit logical address register (CSR#3) with mask control inputs to select the required width
- A 16-bit Class N register (CSR#7), which may alternatively be used as a 32-bit register (eg. CSR#1 or CSR#4)
- All necessary logic to compare the AD signals with CSR#3 for logical address recognition, with the GA inputs for geographical address recognition and with CSR#7 for class N broadcast address recognition
- A 32-bit NTA register with loading from the full AD field (secondary address), selected width (internal address), or increment (block or pipelined operations)
- Parity generation

The PCL provides all the control signals for two ADIs, segment handshake and response signals, and simple read and write timing signals for the application

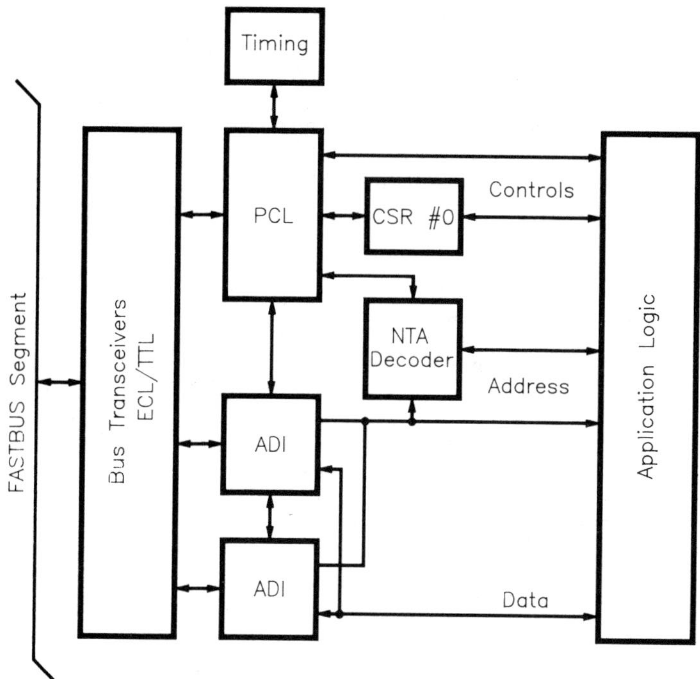

FIGURE 6.8 Slave interface using PCL and ADI semicustom devices. Translator-transceiver devices are required to convert segment ECL signals to TTL levels. CSR#0 and address decoding to suit the application must be implemented in discrete logic but all other registers necessary for FASTBUS operations are contained within the semicustom devices. Such an interface will respond to all FASTBUS protocols.

logic. It is manufactured by LSI Logic Corp., and uses a CMOS gate array in a 100-lead-pin grid package.

A complete slave interface (Fig. 6.8) can be constructed from two ADIs, a PCL, TTL-ECL translater-transceiver chips, and an address decoder configured for the application logic. The necessary parts of CSR#0 must also be implemented in discrete logic. This interface will provide the following: geographical, logical, and broadcast cases 1–6 and 8 addressing; multiblock addressing; all data transfer modes and optionally, advanced data transfer modes; external timing loops to set the read/write response time and the address access response time; automatic parity checking and generation; SS response generation; application-side arbitration logic to allow sharing of the application data and address buses with an on-board microprocessor; and use as the slave part of a master.

6.8.4 The FSI

The FSI is a FASTBUS slave interface single chip device being designed by Scientific Systems International,[9] which should be available in the fall of 1989. It is a complete single-chip interface using a Raytheon BIT1 ECL gate array in a 229 lead pin grid package. It can be connected directly to a FASTBUS crate segment and has either ECL or TTL application signals.

The FSI contains an NTA register, CSR#0⟨15,14,5:0⟩, CSR#3, CSR#7, and a protective buffer. It produces all necessary responses to segment timing and control signals and provides the application with read and write strobes and separate data and address buses. It will handle geographical, logical, and broadcast primary addresses, all standard and advanced data operations, and parity checking and generation.

6.8.5. Cable Segment Driver Device

The FASTBUS cable segment uses a balanced ECL bus, which is both driven and received at each device. The mechanism for doing this, using discrete components, is shown in the FASTBUS specifications.

In order to improve noise immunity, the recommended cable segment implementation makes use of differential signaling. A special five-channel cable transceiver (CSX) has been designed at the Stanford Linear Accelerator Center.[10] It should be generally available in the fall of 1989. The CSX makes use of differential current source-sink cable drivers, which leads to a linear superposition of signals from multiple drivers. This superposition eliminates the need for circuit delays introduced to avoid responding to switching glitches that can occur for wire-OR configurations.

6.9 SOFTWARE

Many benefits accrue from the existence of a software specification for FASTBUS.[11–13] In particular, it provides a common, unambiguous way for dealing with FASTBUS, thus enhancing the portability of both programs and programmers. The software specification can also be helpful to those designing modules and configuring systems. Standardization means that software is easier to maintain, understand, and share.

Though specific problems are apt to change, over time specific problem-oriented solutions do not cope gracefully with such change. The process of generating a standard involves many people with different points of view and problems to solve. To be acceptable the standard must therefore contain definitions and methods that represent a consistent global view of the overall potential and uses of FASTBUS. Hence, following the standard is a big step toward robust software.

The ultimate source of commands to and recipient of data from a FASTBUS system is usually a program running in a general purpose computer. This computer may be directly interfaced to a FASTBUS segment or may send instructions to a special FASTBUS engine that then carries out the requested actions on the segment to which it is attached. A convenient and effective way to prepare and issue FASTBUS instructions and examine their results is to make use of a general purpose language such as FORTRAN or C to which FASTBUS-related routines have been added. The FASTBUS Standard Routines document[9] defines routines that make available all the features of FASTBUS in a consistent and readable way.

In this document all routines are defined in terms of their names, calling sequences, and either the actions they have on a FASTBUS hardware system or their effects upon the FASTBUS software system. Parameters are named and defined that allow all possible variable features of the hardware implementation to be specified. Error codes are named and described that cover just about all conceivable conditions that can result from the execution of any defined routine.

All FASTBUS address types and data transfer modes are supported in the software specification. A number of compound routines such as those that load segment interconnect tables, move data between devices, read, modify, or write, and send interrupt messages are also defined. Primitive FASTBUS action routines that either generate single arbitration, address, or data cycles or manipulate individual bus lines are specified, in particular, to assist in preparing diagnostics. Not all FASTBUS controllers may be able to execute all routines and features described in the software specifications.

FASTBUS action routines specify in their calling sequences the environment in which they are to take place. An environment is the context in which actions take place and consists of many operational parameters, most of which are not changed from one operation to the next. Considerable simplification of calling sequences and increased readability of code result from the use of environments. A program may define a number of different environments, each of which is capable of later being put into effect. The operational parameters that describe an environment may be modified within an environment. Several classes of operational parameters are defined.

Protocol operational parameters define features such as arbitration protocol and level, whether a secondary address cycle occurs, whether the address connection is broken at the end of the current operation, and whether the master retains bus mastership. Time-out operational parameters specify all time-out periods and are also used to enable and disable selected timers. If errors occur, other operational parameters specify the maximum number of retries as well as an average delay time between retries of failed primary address cycles.

Another class of operational parameters controls features associated with automatic error handling and reporting. Since the acceptability of an error code can be context dependent (e.g., an end-of-block indication may be normal or abnormal), routines are provided to allow acceptable responses to be specified and context-dependent recovery procedures to be defined and invoked. Severity levels for each response may be defined and used as thresholds for various reporting and corrective activities.

Overall operational parameters define entities or activities not directly related to details of the activity on FASTBUS itself. Two such parameters are worthy of special mention. One determines whether the FASTBUS routines encountered in a program are executed immediately or held as part of the environment for later execution. The other determines if the return to the calling program is made after all requested actions have been completed or immediately after the requested actions have started.

ACKNOWLEDGMENTS

We wish to thank all our colleagues on the various working groups who, by their dedication, ingenuity, and hard work, have produced the FASTBUS specifications and who have shown the practicality and utility of the specifications by successfully implementing a wide variety of systems.

REFERENCES

1. Standard Nuclear Instrument Modules, AEC (now DOE) document TID-20893.
2. CAMAC Instrumentation and Interface Standards, ANSI/IEEE Standard 583-1982 and related documents. Available from IEEE Service Center—C87, 445 Hoes Lane, Piscataway, NJ 08854-4150.
3. Standard ANSI/IEEE 960-1986 (SH10223), FASTBUS, Modular High Speed Data Acquisition System, with Addenda and Errata of April 17, 1989, U.S. NIM Committee. Available from IEEE Service Center—C87, 445 Hoes Lane, Piscataway, NJ 08854-4150.
4. *FASTBUS Users' Guide,* U.S. NIM Committee. Available from L. Costrell, B119, Radiation Physics, National Institute of Standards and Technology, Gaithersburg, MD 20899.
5. R. Downing and M. Haney, "The FASTBUS Segment Interconnect," *IEEE Transactions on Nuclear Science,* **NS-29:** 94 (1982).
6. Donald Machen, "The FASTBUS Segment Extension as a Crate Coupling Concept," *IEEE Transactions on Nuclear Science,* **NS-33:** 800 (1986).
7. Robert Skegg and Andrew Daviel, "A General Purpose FASTBUS Interface Chipset," *IEEE Transactions on Nuclear Science,* **NS-32:** 305 (1985).
8. Robert Skegg and Andrew Daviel, "A Semi-Custom Protocol Control Logic Device for FASTBUS," *IEEE Transactions on Nuclear Science,* **NS-35:** 306 (1988).
9. Scientific Systems International, 3491B Trinity Drive, Los Alamos, New Mexico 87544.
10. H. V. Waltz, Boris Bertolucci, and David B. Gustavson, "Monolithic Transceiver for FASTBUS Cable Segment—CSX," *IEEE Transactions on Nuclear Science,* **NS-36:** 532 (1989).
11. *FASTBUS Standard Routines,* U.S. NIM Committee, DOE Report DOE/ER-0367, May 1988, with Addenda and Errata of April 19, 1989. Available from L. Costrell, B119, Radiation Physics, National Institute of Standards and Technology, Gaithersburg, MD 20899, or National Technical Information Service, U.S. Department of Commerce, Springfield, VA 22161.
12. Ruth Pordes, "Review of the Status of the FASTBUS Standard Routine Specification," *IEEE Transactions on Nuclear Science,* **NS-34**(1): 162 (1987).
13. T. Kozlowski and W. M. Foreman, "An Implementation of the New IEEE Standard Routines For FASTBUS," *IEEE Transactions on Nuclear Science,* **NS-34**(4): 800 (1987).

CHAPTER 7
FUTUREBUS

David Hawley
National Semiconductor Corporation
Santa Clara, California

7.1 INTRODUCTION

Futurebus is a high-performance 32-bit backplane bus designed by an IEEE committee and standardized as IEEE 896.1-1987 for use in a wide variety of multiprocessor architectures. Futurebus' high speed is due to a unique electrical specification, backplane transceiver logic (BTL), which is designed specifically to drive backplane transmission lines, solving many of the problems associated with TTL interfaces. All Futurebus transactions are governed by a technology-independent, asynchronous handshake protocol. This allows a module to be designed at the highest possible data transfer rate allowed by the technology used, while ensuring full compatibility with all other modules designed before and after. With today's technology, this corresponds to a maximum burst data transfer rate of 100 Mbyte/s.

Bus access contention is resolved in parallel with data transfers via a fully distributed arbitration mechanism providing both fairness and priority access. The data transfer protocol orthogonally supports read and write operations, single access and block transfers, and single-slave and multislave operations. Broadcast addresses and data transfer intervention make this the first standard bus to support efficient copy-back caching protocols. These protocols significantly enhance overall system performance.

A higher-level Futurebus firmware standard, 896.2, was under development at this writing. It standardized module identification, interrupt mechanisms, a message-passing format, and a general-purpose cache coherence protocol.

Of all the attributes described above, those most significant for the performance of a multiprocessing system are the electrical layer, the flexible and efficient data transfer mechanisms, and the caching protocol. Those that affect the potential life-span of the bus are its technology independence and extensibility. Each of these is discussed in detail in the following sections.

The seeds of Futurebus were planted in 1979, when the Microprocessor Standards Committee of the IEEE Computer Society attempted to create a 32-bit bus standard that would preempt the marketplace chaos which existed in the 16-bit world. Inevitably, differences in perceived system requirements and conflicting corporate pressures resulted in division both within the committee and in industry. No less than four different TTL-based 32-bit bus standards eventually emerged from the IEEE. Futurebus was unique, however, in that it continued to be designed by a core of dedicated volunteers guided by a set of "purist" principles that became the cornerstones of the standard. Its lack of corporate backing during this period, while delaying its completion and postponing its market acceptance, allowed 896.1 to emerge as an IEEE standard in 1987 with its principles intact. Its success can be measured by the fact that designers of other 32-bit buses are now looking to Futurebus to form the basis of their next-generation architectures.

Note: This chapter describes the 1987 Futurebus specification and its proposed companion firmware standard, not the Futurebus+ extension now under development. Refer to the IEEE standards for the authoritative specification.

7.2 MECHANICAL INTERFACE

Futurebus specifies the traditional Eurocard interface technology, using a 96-pin DIN connector (see Table 7.1). Although any board size is permitted, Futurebus recommends a triple-height (three connector), 280-mm-deep board as the primary size. Futurebus itself occupies only a single 96-pin connector. Six pins are for +5-V power, six for dc ground, ten for ac ground, and five for geographical addressing or slot identification. This leaves 67 signal lines upon which the protocol operates. Of these, 55 are used to implement the data transfer protocol, 12 are for arbitration and reset, and 2 are reserved for a serial bus that is currently being defined with the IEEE. The relatively high ratio of ground return paths to signal lines serves to enhance the integrity of the Futurebus backplane environment. Confining the interface to a single connector allows the user to place alternate or redundant buses on the other two connectors if desired.

7.3 ELECTRICAL CHARACTERISTICS

Futurebus gains a large measure of its speed through its incorporation of an entirely new bus electrical interface standard, known as backplane transceiver logic, or BTL. BTL provides the fastest possible backplane interface in a CMOS or TTL environment. It is a fundamental contribution to the state of backplane bus technology, and its characteristics are the foundation upon which the Futurebus protocol rests. In order to understand the benefits of the new technology, perhaps it is best to examine the limitations of a traditional TTL interface.

7.3.1 Limitations of TTL

In a typical PC board environment, TTL is an ideal interface. TTL devices can be built with short propagation delays, fast signal rise and fall times, and relatively high immunity to a noisy environment. This is possible only because the length of the traces is relatively short, and the number of devices driving any one line, and therefore the capacitive loading, is relatively low. In a typical backplane, however, a trace may be almost 20 in long, with as many as 20 devices attached via

TABLE 7.1 Futurebus Connector Pin Layout

0 V dc	0 V dc	0 V dc
+5 V dc	+5 V dc	+5 V dc
AD0*	**AD1***	**AD2***
AD3*	GA0*	**AD4***
AD5*	**AD6***	**AD7***
0 V	**BPZ***	**AD8***
AD9*	**AD10***	0 V
AD11*	**AD12***	**AD13***
AD14*	GA1*	**AD15***
BPY*	**AD16***	**AD17***
0 V	**AD18***	**AD19***
AD20*	**AD21***	0 V
AD22*	**AD23***	**BPX***
AD24*	GA2*	**AD25***
AD26*	**AD27***	**AD28***
0 V	**AD29***	**AD30***
AD31*	**BPW***	0 V
CM0*	**CM1***	**CM2***
CM3*	GA3*	**CM4***
CP*	**CM5***	**ST0***
0 V	**ST1***	**ST2***
AS*	**AK***	0 V
AI*	**DS***	**DK***
DI*	GA4*	**AP***
AQ*	**AR***	**AC***
0 V	**AB0***	**AB1***
AB2*	**AB3***	0 V
AB4*	**AB5***	**AB6***
SB0*	**RE***	**SB1***
TG*	**ST3***	**TP***
+5 V dc	+5 V dc	+5 V dc
0 V dc	0 V dc	0 V dc

connectors along its length. This greatly increases the capacitive loading on the bus, which in turn decreases the ac impedance of the backplane and requires much greater currents to cleanly drive a signal high or low within a specified rise or fall time. The propagation velocity of signals down the backplane also decreases, which, combined with the longer trace length, means that the signal transition time becomes much less than the propagation delay. This brings the digital designer into the often unfamiliar world of transmission line effects.

These effects are described in more detail elsewhere; suffice it to say that TTL devices are unable to drive a properly terminated signal line, and the most obvious remedies do not work. Using devices with faster rise and fall time characteristics only worsens the situation. Increasing the current capacity of the drivers to the point that they are guaranteed to cross the receiver thresholds causes the capacitive loading on the bus to increase even faster, in an upward spiral. TTL backplanes typically choose instead to increase the termination resistance at the ends of the backplane, allowing the reflections resulting from impedance mismatch to build the signal voltage over several round trips across the backplane. Any advantage gained by using faster drivers and receivers is lost waiting for these transmission line effects to dissipate.

7.3.2 The BTL Solution

Futurebus solves the bus driving problem from first principles. BTL devices use open-collector drivers with a significantly lower output capacitance than TTL. This is possible because the drive transistor is isolated from the bus by a series Schottky diode. The total output capacitance of these drivers is only 5 pF, which allows the combined connector, trace, and package capacitance to be limited to 10 pF.

Because a backplane is a tightly controllable environment, unlike a PC board, BTL can reduce the required signal swing to only 1 V (see Fig. 7.1). The backplane is terminated at 2.1 V, which represents the released, or high, state of the line. When any driver asserts a signal, it pulls the line down to 1 V. The receivers have a precisely controlled switching threshold halfway between for maximum noise margin. The result is that the backplane can be properly terminated at its fully loaded impedance of 39 Ω, while allowing the drivers to cleanly switch the bus signals with only 50 mA of drive current. (The PC-board side of these transceivers uses a standard TTL interface.)

The consequences of this new interface is that a bus designer can guarantee that a signal will cross the input thresholds of every receiver on the backplane on the incident edge of the propagating wavefront. A BTL bus never has to wait for reflections to dissipate before signals can be sampled. This allows Futurebus to implement a much more efficient and higher-performance data transfer protocol than any of its TTL competitors.

Futurebus allows some flexibility in terms of transceiver and therefore backplane design. If the user wants a simpler, lower-cost interface, a designer can use

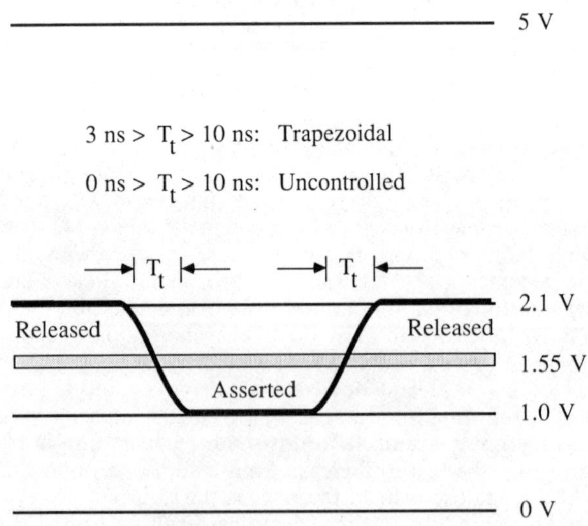

FIGURE 7.1 BTL signal wave form.

TABLE 7.2 Futurebus Electrical Characteristics

Power connections	+5 V dc, 0 V dc, and 0 V logic
Power supply variation	4.9 to 5.25 V
Power supply noise	50 mV peak-to-peak, 20 mV rms
Maximum connector current	1 A per pin
Minimum slot spacing	20.32 mm (0.8 in)
Maximum slot capacitance	10 pF per signal pin
Maximum signal propagation delay	12.5 ns (including 1 extender card)
Unloaded backplane trace impedance	55 to 65 Ω
Termination resistance	39 Ω ± 1%
Termination voltage	2.1 V ± 1%
Receiver threshold voltage	1.55 V ± 5%
Low signal output voltage	0.75–1.1 V under 19.3-Ω load
Maximum signal transition time	10 ns

drivers with controlled, or trapezoidal, rise and fall waveforms, and receivers incorporating noise filters, each of greater than 6 ns. This eliminates the crosstalk noise problem that is otherwise present in strip-line construction backplanes and reduces other transmission line effects.

If the user needs higher performance, a designer can use transceivers without these restrictions. The cost is an increase in interface design complexity. Microstrip backplanes are required to eliminate crosstalk. Trace lengths from the connector to the device must be kept to an absolute minimum to avoid stub-induced reflections. Careful ac grounding to the backplane is required to avoid ground bounce when the drivers are switching. Once these design precautions are taken, however, the resulting interface is quite reliable, with much higher performance than the equivalent TTL system. It is also perfectly compatible with the trapezoidal drivers.

The Futurebus BTL electrical standard may eventually be approved by the IEEE as an independent backplane standard, with some minor modification. The electrical characteristics of Futurebus are presented in Table 7.2.

7.3.3 Open-Collector Effects

Every signal on the Futurebus backplane is an open collector line. This has several important consequences that are exploited throughout the Futurebus protocol. Unlike a standard TTL totem-pole driver, no physical damage can occur when more than one device is driving a signal line.

When a BTL driver is turned on, it drives the line low by drawing current from the bus line and, once the low-voltage wavefront reaches the ends of the backplane, the termination network. When the driver is turned off, it does not "drive" the bus high. Instead, it merely shuts off the flow of current. The result is a high-voltage wavefront that propagates away from the driver. When this high voltage, the same as that set by the terminators, is absorbed at the ends of the backplane, the line will be at rest. Notice that the signal rise and fall times are independent of the capacitive load or the termination on the line. They are of roughly equal speed, dependent on only the switching speed of the bus drivers.

When a number of open-collector drivers are attached to a single bus line and any one of them is turned on, the line goes low (Fig. 7.2). If any other devices

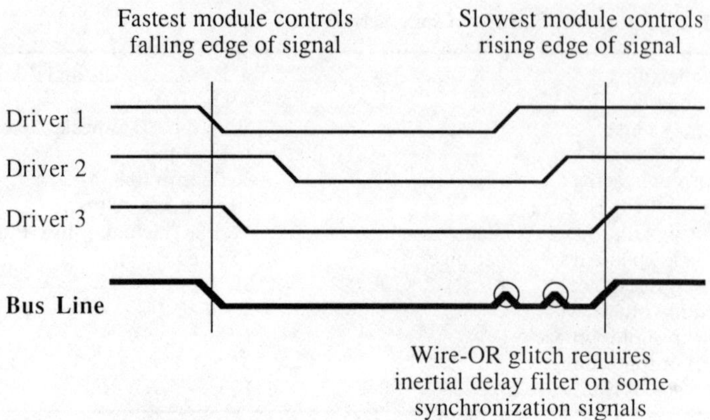

FIGURE 7.2 Wire-OR effects.

then drive the bus, they merely end up sharing the current necessary to keep the line at its low voltage. Thus, a shared bus line goes low with the first driving device. When one of these drivers switches off, the bus line remains low. Only when all of the drivers have turned off does the signal on the bus line go high. This characteristic is used in Futurebus whenever a multimodule handshake is required.

Since this is a transmission line environment, however, an unavoidable perturbation of the signal occurs when one driver releases an open-collector signal that is still being asserted by another driver. The current that is no longer passing through the released driver must now be sunk through a driver that is physically located elsewhere in the backplane. This current switch manifests itself as a voltage shift, called a wired-OR glitch, which has a duration and amplitude that are a function of the distance between drivers and the amount of current that is no longer being supplied by the released driver. Luckily, the wired-OR glitch problem is deterministically solved using an asymmetrical inertial delay line or low-pass filter (see Fig. 7.3). Any filter that rejects positive-going pulses of a duration less than the round-trip propagation delay time of the backplane is guaranteed to never pass any combination or superposition of glitches.

The round-trip propagation, or "glitch filter," delay specified by the Futurebus standard is 25 ns. This input filter, required on seven of the bus handshake lines, determines the maximum rate at which broadcast operations can take place. The

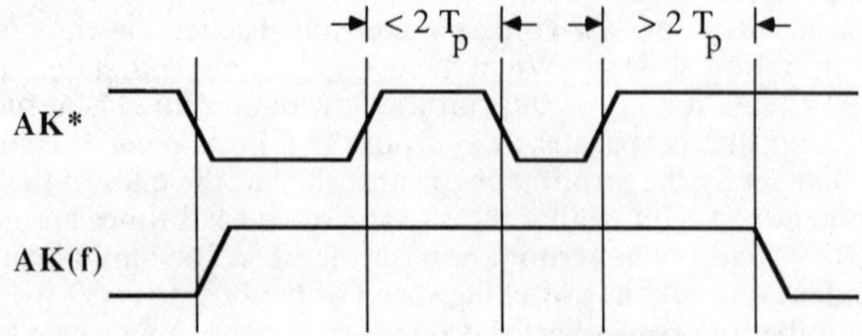

FIGURE 7.3 Glitch filter operation. T_p = bus propagation delay.

25 ns figure is only required for a maximum configuration system, however. Because of the possible performance impact, a user with a shorter backplane, and therefore smaller round-trip signal propagation delay, may wish to reduce the length of the glitch filter.

The above discussion, of course, only applies to signals being driven by multiple modules. The majority of data transfers on Futurebus take place with only one module driving each data handshake line and therefore are unaffected by this wire-OR effect.

7.3.4 Terminology

A word should be said about terminology before continuing. All signals on Futurebus are active low (represented by an asterisk). To reduce confusion, this chapter uses the terms *released* and *asserted* with the following meanings on the bus:

$$\text{released} = \text{false} = 0 = \text{high} = +2\text{ V}$$

$$\text{asserted} = \text{true} = 1 = \text{low} = +1\text{ V}$$

All Futurebus lines have a two-letter abbreviation. The signal that any one module is presenting to a bus line is designated by a lowercase label (**ai***). The wire-OR of all the signals asserted on that line (the value detected by any module) is represented by an uppercase label (**AI***). Finally, the name of a signal after it has passed through a module's internal glitch filter is followed by (f) [**AI(f)**].

7.4 PROTOCOL PHILOSOPHIES

In order to understand the Futurebus protocol, it is best to have a grasp of the philosophical guidelines adhered to (more or less) by the designers of the standard.

The first of these is simplicity. Although it may seem that this ideal was ignored almost as often as it was obeyed, complexity was not usually added to the standard without some compelling reason. Futurebus as a rule allows far fewer confusing options than any similar standard. Look first for orthogonality and symmetry as a key to understanding Futurebus.

Relatively low cost was also important. The long-term cost of any backplane system is proportional to the number of pins, particularly active signals, in the interface. Limiting the interface to a single connector forced the designers to economize in a very beneficial sense and reinforced the need for simplicity.

Decentralization is important for performance reasons in parallel systems and for reliability in fault-tolerant ones. Futurebus requires no central services except for the power supply. The bus will continue to function even if only one card remains in the backplane.

High performance was a requirement from the very beginning. It is the yardstick against which many of the proposals were measured, and often it determined the outcome of conflicts among competing philosophic standpoints.

Reliability is becoming a requirement in more and more systems. Although the BTL environment is very clean, permanent or transient module failures must be detected to maintain system integrity. Futurebus provides an odd-parity bit for every information signal for which it might be meaningful. Parity checking can be disabled for those systems that do not require it; in that case it is conceivable that those lines could be used to carry additional information.

Since Futurebus was designed with multiprocessing in mind, it was necessary that it provide support for all the basic functions, or primitives, required by parallel processing systems. The cache protocol, described in the 896.2 standard, is a case in point. All of the facilities necessary to support any combination of currently existing cache protocols are available in the 896.1 standard. It will be interesting to see whether this goal continues to be met as systems and architectures evolve.

7.4.1 The Asynchronous Interface

The choice of an asynchronous protocol was a difficult one at the time, but has proven to be enormously beneficial. In a synchronous system, a single, central source provides clocking for the synchronization of transactions on the entire interface. The validity of all other bus signals is referenced with respect to this clock. The speed of the clock is limited by the electrical length of the backplane, the distance of the clock relative to the source and destination of information being transferred on the bus, and the speed of the technology used to implement the interface. Once a clock speed is selected, these design parameters become locked into the protocol. Although a synchronous system may in general be faster than an asynchronous one for any particular design, this will almost certainly not be true as these parameters change over time. Furthermore, in a general-purpose system with different devices running at independently optimized clock rates, transfers over a synchronous backplane have to pay two resynchronization delay penalties with the associated metastablility hazards. An equivalent asynchronous interface introduces no additional points of synchronization.

In an asynchronous system, the source of synchronization is not fixed. In particular, for a Futurebus system, synchronization is provided at any instant by the current emitter of information on the bus. This eliminates one source of skew between the "clock" and transmitted information on the bus. In order to provide determinism and avoid metastability problems, Futurebus uses a fully compelled protocol.

In Futurebus, the transmitter of any type of information (data, for example) issues a synchronization signal to indicate that the information is now valid on the bus (see Fig. 7.4). The transmitter cannot remove this information from the bus, however, until the receiver(s) of it has issued a corresponding signal indicating reception of that data. Since each of the parties to any transaction can control the rate at which the information is transferred, the slowest party is guaranteed to participate successfully. This prevents older, or slower, Futurebus modules from ever becoming incompatible with faster ones, while allowing newer or faster modules to communicate between each other at their own higher speed. The overall performance of a Futurebus system grows with the advances in technology or increasing design sophistication incorporated by its individual components.

The Futurebus handshake is not only fully compelled, but also technology independent. There are no artificial timing parameters built into any handshake. The minimum setup time required for information emission before issuance of the validating synchronizer is 0 ns on the backplane. The minimum hold time guaranteed on the information after the acknowledge signal is issued is likewise 0 ns. This means that any module can truly be designed to the limits of the tech-

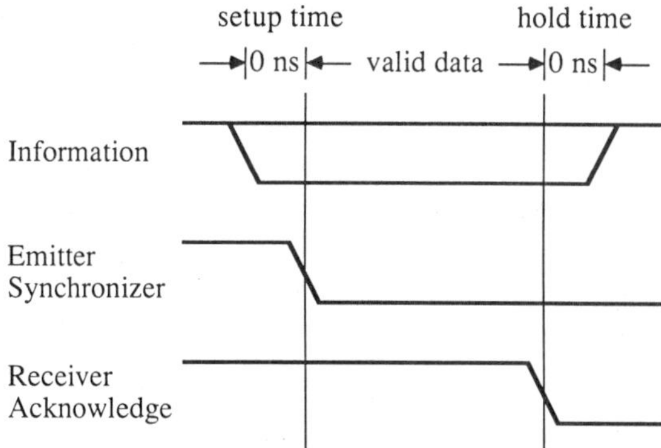

FIGURE 7.4 Fully compelled technology-independent handshake.

nology available to it, without assumptions about the requirements of other modules. The fully compelled handshake guarantees interoperability; technology independence removes all theoretical performance limitations but the speed of light on the backplane.

The 0-ns setup times ignore the possibility that backplane skews may shift the relative positions of the synchronizer and its associated information. The Futurebus specification therefore requires that the backplane and modules be constructed such that a synchronization signal never propagates faster than its associated information. This can be accomplished by making synchronizer traces marginally longer, wider, or of higher capacitance (with additional feedthroughs, for example), or any mechanism to guarantee a minimally longer electrical path for the synchronization signals.

7.4.2 Alternatives

There are alternative implementations that the designers of Futurebus rejected during its development. It is instructive to examine at least a few of these.

Futurebus implements a single 4-Gbyte address space. This allows a 32-bit microprocessor, or its memory management unit, to view the physical address of Futurebus in a context that is consistent with most high-level language models. A bus with multiple address spaces, although perhaps convenient for the hardware designer, often requires that the software be designed specifically for that bus' decode hardware. A single address space is both simpler and more flexible.

Futurebus has a multiplexed address/data path. Although a nonmultiplexed bus may allow some address pipelining to take place, the 32 additional pins devoted to the address generally remain idle. A multiplexed bus consumes less board space and power, and in the case of Futurebus, which assumes a large percentage of block transfers, the address transfer penalty is amortized over multiple data transfers.

Futurebus does not constrain the byte orientation of transfers on the bus. Most buses require that, during multibyte transfers, the least significant data byte correspond to either the most or least significant byte address. Different microprocessor families have also incompatibly chosen one of these two conventions. The designers of Futurebus, which is a manufacturer-independent standard, could not choose one format over the other. Although this might seem indecisive, it is true that merely specifying data ordering on the bus will not solely solve a system's data format issues. With Futurebus, the user and the software, rather than the bus, determine the data-base formats allowed and understood by the system.

Finally, Futurebus was given a standard read/write transfer protocol, rather than a write-only or split-cycle bus. Although a split-cycle bus can theoretically improve system throughput by eliminating memory access times from interfering with bus activity, it doubles the number of arbitration and address cycles required for each read transaction, greatly increasing the latency seen by each processing node. It also requires a far more complex interface. Since there are so many easier ways to optimize the performance of a Futurebus interface, it makes more sense to continue developing a much simpler protocol at the backplane level. A message-passing paradigm is more useful at the level of intercrate or intersystem communications.

7.5 ARBITRATION

The purpose of a backplane system is to allow the devices connected to it to transfer data among each other. Arbitration exists to prevent more than one module from trying to transfer data on the bus at the same time, and to optimize the scheduling of requests from multiple modules. Toward this end, Futurebus implements two arbitration algorithms, fairness and priority, as well as a preemption scheme, which reduces bus latency for urgent transfer requests. This arbitration takes place on its own set of lines from and parallel to data transfers.

The Futurebus arbitration mechanism also provides a number of other facilities, including error detection and recovery, parking, bus master identification, emergency messages, and synchronization during reset and the insertion or withdrawal of modules in a live system.

7.5.1 Fairness versus Priority

To some extent in a multiprocessing system, and to an even greater extent in a truly parallel environment, processors need to have approximately equal access to the bus. If a task has been divided among a number of processors, optimum performance results if all the subtasks are completed at roughly the same time. Bus latency (the time between when a processor requests the bus and when it is granted access) is not critical, however. The system will not fail if a task is stalled; it will only suffer a degradation in performance.

In the fairness mode, Futurebus requires that a winning module wait until all pending requests for the system bus have been serviced before making another request. This is a self-policing scheme that guarantees every module a portion of the overall bus bandwidth.

A real-time system has the opposite requirement. Here it is critical that certain data be recorded by the system as quickly as possible. The danger in any system with uncontrollable data input is that buffers may overflow and data may be lost while a module is waiting for access to the bus, or because access cannot be granted frequently enough.

In priority arbitration, the competing module with the highest priority always wins, and there is no limitation on the frequency of bus requests. Modules that are subject to real-time constraints are assigned priorities based on the maximum latencies they can tolerate. The drawback to this scheme is that modules with low priority may be completely shut out during periods of heavy bus usage.

A typical multiprocessing system may contain some examples of each type of module. Some I/O modules may require priority, but most bus transfers will take place under fairness arbitration.

7.5.2 Parallel Contention Mechanism

The basic arbitration mechanism used by Futurebus has become very popular, as variations of it are used in NuBus, Multibus II, and FASTBUS. The idea behind this pin-efficient asynchronous distributed scheme is very simple (see Fig. 7.5). Each potential bus master is assigned a unique 7-bit arbitration number (**an**⟨**6**· · ·**0**⟩).When arbitration begins, each competitor applies the number through its arbitration logic onto the open-collector arbitration bus (**AB**⟨**6**· · ·**0**⟩*). The arbitration logic in each competitor also senses the resulting wire-OR levels on the arbitration bus and modifies the number it is applying to the bus according to the following rule:

> If, for any bit of a module's arbitration number, the corresponding arbitration bus line shows a greater value, all lower-order bits of the number are withdrawn from the bus.

After a suitable settling period, the module with the highest arbitration number will find that its number matches the number remaining on the bus and is therefore the winner.

Remember that the signals on the bus itself are logically inverted and that the bus provides the wire-OR function of the signals applied to it. Only in the logic of the winning module will the arbitration request signal propagate all the way through to the bus grant output. The circuit required is, and in fact must be, purely combinational (no feedback paths or latching).

Notice that this algorithm results in a pure priority scheme. Rules to provide for fairness are superimposed onto the basic mechanism.

What is meant by a suitable settling time? This is the period that starts when the indication to begin arbitration is issued and ends when every module is guaranteed to have a valid state on the grant signal at the output of the arbitration circuit. For a k-bit parallel arbiter, this has been shown to be proportional to (k/

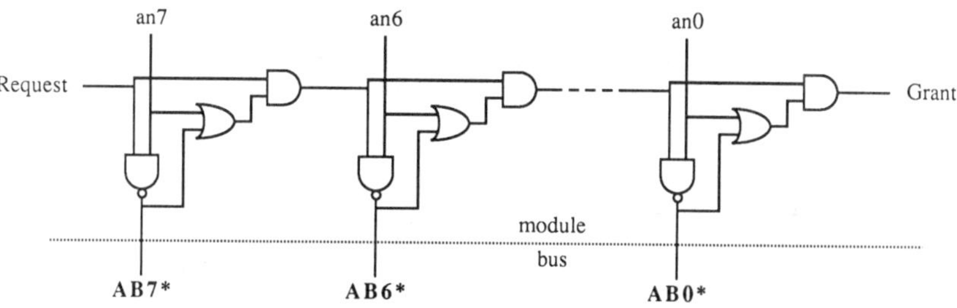

FIGURE 7.5 Distributed arbitration logic.

2)t_p, where t_p is the one-way propagation delay on the bus. For Futurebus, the worst-case settling time is only two signal round trips (50 ns, in the case of a full length backplane) on the backplane itself. All other delays are caused by signal propagation delays and skews within the logic on the modules themselves.

In Futurebus, each module is responsible for calculating its own worst-case arbitration settling time. It does not have to know anything about the arbitration timing of any other module. The speed of an individual module's arbitration logic can directly affect the overall performance of the system's bus arbitration, since it will only be as fast as the logic on the slowest participating module.

7.5.3 Arbitration Bus Signals

The arbitration competition takes place on a 7-bit arbitration bus(**AB⟨6· · ·0⟩***) (see Table 7.3). Each module is assigned a 7-bit arbitration number, which it may apply to the arbitration bus according to the rules described above. How are these arbitration numbers assigned?

Remember that Futurebus provides a fairness mode, even though the algorithm used is intrinsically prioritizing. Fairness arbitration is accomplished by requiring that once a fairness module has won arbitration, it be inhibited from reentering arbitration until all other pending requests have been satisfied.

In a system with a mix of priority and fairness modules, the former should always receive service before the latter. Since the arbitration number assigned a module determines its priority within a single competition, the most significant bit of the number, **an6,** is used to distinguish between the two modes. If this bit is set to a logic 0, the module is operating in the fairness class. A 1 in this position denotes a priority module. When modules of both classes are competing against each other, the winner will therefore always be a priority module.

An important requirement of the arbitration system is that all modules present unique arbitration numbers to the bus. In the fairness mode, it does not matter what specific values they have, and therefore **an⟨5· · ·1⟩** are generally derived from a module's geographical address, or slot position, which is encoded on a set of pins on the backplane itself. A priority module can set its arbitration number the same way or it can choose its own. The arbitration numbers are completely software configurable at any time. It is up to the system to guarantee uniqueness.

The least significant bit of the arbitration number, **an0,** is an odd-parity bit. This allows the detection of some types of errors in the arbitration process, improving the fault tolerance of the backplane.

Although there is no central timing element in Futurebus, the modules still need to know when to compete, when they have won arbitration, when to

TABLE 7.3 Arbitration Signals

Signal	Description
AB⟨6· · ·0⟩*	Arbitration bus
AB6*	Priority fairness
AB⟨5· · ·1⟩*	Arbitration number
AB0*	Parity
AP*, **AQ***, **AR***	Arbitration synchronization
AC*	Arbitration condition

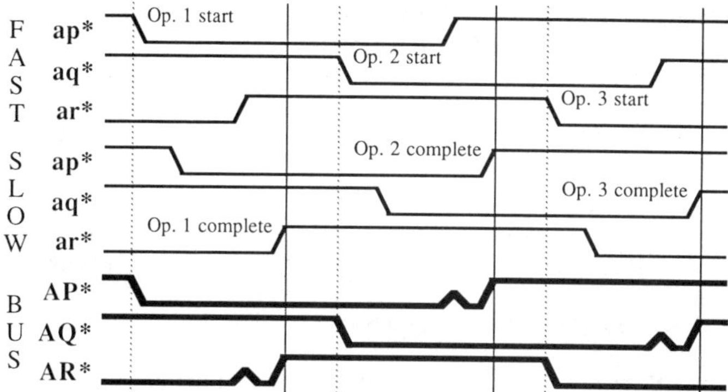

FIGURE 7.6 Arbitration synchronization handshake. FAST = fastest module; SLOW = slowest module; BUS = resulting wire-OR signal.

exchange mastership, and when to release their fairness inhibitions. This synchronization is provided by a *three-wire handshake* on the signals **AP*, AQ***, and **AR*** (see Fig. 7.6). They allow the modules to step through the various phases of arbitration in unison and adapt the speed of the protocol to the slowest participating module.

The synchronization handshake makes use of the wire-OR characteristic of BTL. The assertion of one signal is used to start an operation, and the release of another signals its completion. The fastest module, or the first module ready, will cause an operation to begin, and the last to finish that operation allows it to end. Because these are synchronization lines, a glitch filter is required on the rising edges of these three signals. This puts an upper limit on the performance of the arbitration process.

The three-wire handshake provides three distinct operations that can be used to describe the arbitration sequence (see Table 7.4). As will be described later, the arbitration sequence consists of either three or six operations, so two complete handshake cycles may be required to bring the system back to its original state.

The final arbitration control signal is the arbitration condition, or **AC***, line. This is used at two points in the arbitration cycle. One is to determine the status

TABLE 7.4 Sequence of Operations

AP*	AQ*	AR*	Operations
A	R	A	Operation 1 or 4 in progress
A	R	R	Operation 1 or 4 complete (Operation 5 wait)
A	A	R	Operation 2 or 5 in progress
R	A	R	Operation 2 or 5 complete
R	A	A	Operation 3 or 6 in progress
R	R	A	Operation 3 or 6 complete (Operation 1 wait)

Note: A = asserted, R = released

of pending requests, and the second is to flag errors or preemption. If one or more modules assert this bit, all modules react by branching appropriately in the control acquisition sequence.

7.5.4 The Control Acquisition Sequence

The control acquisition sequence describes a series of operations that provides for an orderly transfer of control of the bus, implements the fairness and priority algorithms, and allows a number of additional features which will be described later (see Fig. 7.7). The timing of these operations is controlled by the three-wire handshake described in the previous section.

7.5.4.1 Control Acquisition Cycle. The control acquisition cycle begins as a bystander module receives an internal bus request (see Fig. 7.8). At this point, either the module must wait until operation 1 (activation) arises or the bus itself will be waiting for a module to initiate operation 1. In either case, the module, if uninhibited (either a priority or an uninhibited fairness module), will become a competitor and assert **ac*** and then **ap***. The assertion of **AC*** indicates that an uninhibited module is making a request; the assertion of **AP*** tells all the other modules to start operation 1. This is one of the two decision points in the arbitration cycle that require synchronization to the arbitration handshake. The designer must take care to reduce potential metastability conditions.

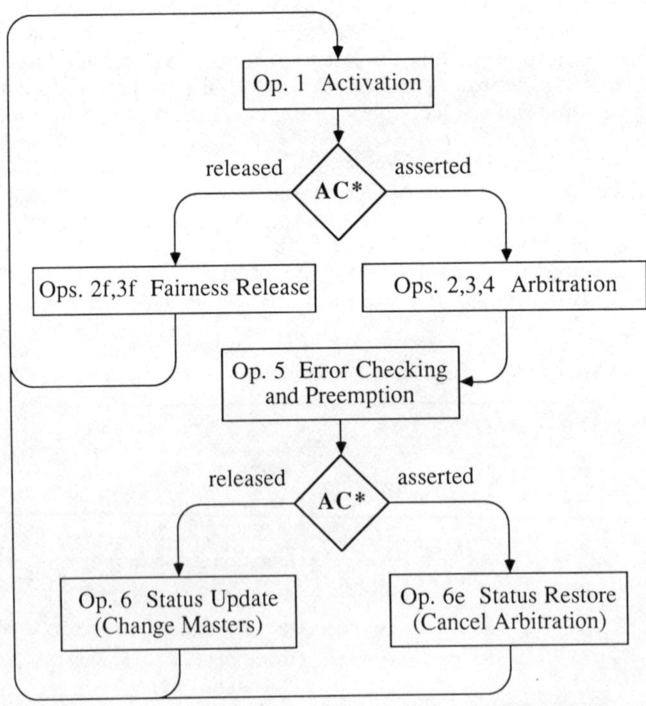

FIGURE 7.7 Control acquisition sequence.

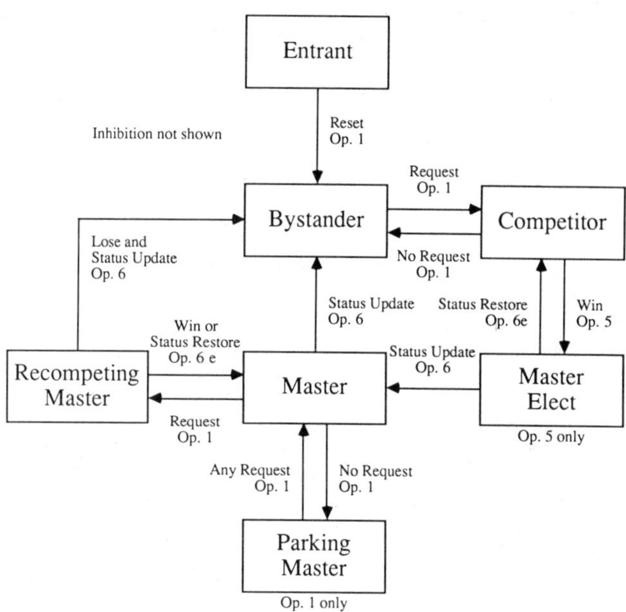

FIGURE 7.8 Module arbitration status transitions.

By the end of operation 1 [**AR(f)** detected released], all requests must be in. In this example, **AC*** is asserted, so all modules understand that this is a six-operation arbitration cycle. Modules that asserted **ac*** (uninhibited competitors) now enter into the arbitration competition, applying their arbitration numbers to the bus and timing their own arbitration intervals. This occurs as the bus steps through operations 2, 3, and 4 (arbitration).

When operation 4 is complete, the arbitration number of the winning competitors will appear on the **AB*** lines. Each competing module will know whether it has won or lost, and the winning module becomes the master-elect. Every module also checks for arbitration errors at this time. Assuming nothing unusual happened, the modules now release **ac*** and wait for the current master to finish its data transfers and assert **aq*** (beginning operation 5).

Since in this case, operation 5 completes with **AC*** released, operation 6 (status update) is used to pass control of the bus from the current master to the master-elect. Now the cycle can start over again.

Notice that all modules can read the arbitration number of the master-elect off of the **AB*** lines during operation 5. If operation 6 is a status update, causing a change of master, the new master may be identified. This allows a module to monitor the source of bus transactions. If operation 1 commences with all the **AB*** lines released, however, the modules know that there is no bus master, and they should initiate operation 5 themselves later on in the cycle, rather than waiting for a nonexistent master to do so.

The arbitration mechanism does not provide a means to forcibly evict the current master from the bus. It is up to the system designer to ensure that no master will hold the bus for too long. If all else fails, a faulty module can be removed by reinitializing the bus interface and initiating a recovery procedure.

7.5.4.2 Fairness Release Cycle. If the current master is a fairness module, it must become inhibited when it relinquishes mastership at the end of the control acquisition cycle. What happens now as the result of an internal bus request?

Once again, the module waits for operation 1. This time, however, it asserts **ap*** while keeping **ac*** released. If no uninhibited module is making a request, operation 1 will complete with **AC*** released, indicating that this is to be a three-operation fairness release cycle.

As the bus steps through operations 2f and 3f (fairness release), all modules remove their inhibitions (whether or not they have a request pending). Now when operation 1 arrives, the formerly inhibited competitor will be able to compete for access to the bus.

7.5.4.3 Error Recovery Cycle. One more branch point is shown in the arbitration flowchart. If, while waiting to begin operation 5 (error checking and preemption), a module detects a parity error or an unexpected arbitration number on the **AB*** lines, it can assert **ac*.** Instead of waiting for the current master to finish, it will assert **aq*** immediately. The assertion of **AC*** at the start of operation 6e (status restore) aborts the arbitration procedure and causes all modules to restore their original status. The master-elect reverts to an ordinary competitor, and the current master retains its status and returns its arbitration number to the **AB*** lines. This is the second decision point that requires synchronization within a module.

This error recovery mechanism will resolve transitory errors; it is up to the system to detect persistent (hard) errors and take action to recover from them.

7.5.5 Additional Features

The basic Futurebus arbitration protocol has been described in the preceding sections. There are two arbitration modes: fairness and arbitration. The three-wire cyclic arbitration handshake is used to step all the modules through a series of operations which allow for an orderly transfer of control of the bus. This mechanism, however, allows a number of other facilities that may not be obvious from the procedures outlined so far.

7.5.5.1 Parking. In a lightly loaded system, the bus may be paused, waiting for a request (the start of operation 1), for an extended period of time. In Futurebus, the current master retains control of the bus during this time and, if it has another request, may begin a new transaction without having to rearbitrate. This is known as *parking,* and it reduces bus latency in a lightly loaded or single-master system. The designer must allow for potential metastability when entering and exiting the parking master state.

7.5.5.2 Preemption. Futurebus also provides an opportunity to reduce bus latency for very-high-priority masters. Normally, a high-priority requestor may have to wait not only for the current bus master to finish, but, if it missed the start of the current arbitration cycle, also for the current master-elect to complete its bus transaction. The preemption mechanism guarantees a high-priority module that it will become the next bus master.

Remember that all modules can read the arbitration number at the beginning of operation 5 to identify the master-elect. If the high-priority module has a higher arbitration number than the master-elect, it is allowed to preempt the current arbitration cycle. It does this by simulating an error detection (asserting **ac*** and starting operation 5 immediately, rather than waiting for the current master to finish) and forcing a rearbitration. It may then enter and win the new arbitration cycle, thereby gaining access to the bus on the next period of mastership.

7.5.5.3 Emergency Messages. The arbitration number of the master-elect, since it is visible to all modules, can also be used to broadcast information to the entire system. With a maximum of 21 slots in a typical 19-in backplane, every module can be assigned a unique fairness and priority number with additional numbers left over. The very highest arbitration numbers can be used for emergency messages.

Most events in a Futurebus system are signaled using a virtual interrupt mechanism, requiring direct accesses to specific memory locations. Although this often has distinct advantages, it does require that an interrupting module possess the capability of assuming bus mastership. There are no physical interrupt signals in a Futurebus backplane. Emergency messages fill this gap, since they can be used to broadcast events quickly, without first obtaining bus mastership or disturbing transfers currently in progress.

As far as the arbitration process is concerned, an emergency message broadcast looks like any other priority request. The issuer of an emergency message may preempt the current arbitration cycle, if necessary, in order to hasten recognition of the event. The only difference is that the issuer of the emergency message does not assume bus mastership after winning arbitration but aborts the arbitration cycle immediately. All modules will read the emergency message number during operation 5, but the current master retains control.

It is up to the system to assign meaning to each arbitration number, including the emergency messages. If no priority numbers are needed, up to 32 emergency messages are available to the system. The only number reserved by the Futurebus standard is the highest arbitration number (all 1s), used to signal power fail.

7.5.5.4 Bus Reset and Live Insertion. Futurebus provides two reset facilities: initialization and reset. The former only affects a module's bus interface, whereas the latter restores the entire module to a known state. From the point of view of the arbitration protocol, however, these look identical. Each of these facilities can be applied to either the entire bus or an individual module. If applied to the entire bus, the system is starting in a known, quiescent state, so the synchronization required is fairly straightforward. If applied only to a single module, the rest of the bus may be actively engaged in transactions, or live. Because of its complexity, this type of resynchronization is optional in the standard. The arbitration protocol is used to synchronize a module to the rest of the bus in both of these situations; some form of live insertion can also be supported using either mechanism.

7.5.6 Performance Enhancements

Although they may not be strictly compatible with the 896.1 standard, there are a number of ways to increase the performance of a Futurebus arbitration cycle within the framework of the current protocol (see Table 7.5). The performance is limited by the handshake of the six-operation cycle, which requires a minimum of six glitch filter delays to complete, and the arbitration settling time, which requires calculation of two bus round-trip and worst-case internal logic delays.

TABLE 7.5 Bus Latency (Heavily Loaded System)

Fairness mode	$T_{arb} + (N - 1)T_m$
Priority mode	$T_{arb} + 2T_m$
Preemption	$T_{arb} + T_m$

Note: T_{arb} = arbitration time
T_m = time of bus mastership
N = number of competing masters

A system that does not support the complex synchronization required for single-module bus interface initialization can eliminate a 30-ns (technology-dependent) interval that has been added to operations 2 and 5. The assertion of the first address strobe after bus turnover can also be moved forward from operation 1 to operation 6, eliminating one glitch filter delay from the bus access latency.

In a shorter backplane, the glitch filter and arbitration delays can be reduced to account for the shorter maximum propagation delays of signals on the backplane. A module's arbitration logic delay can also be reduced according to the position of the most significant bit of the arbitration number being used by that module. These two items can cut arbitration times for some systems by more than half.

In a lightly loaded system, where the bus is typically idle, the arbitration cycle accounts for the entire bus access latency. Some work is currently being done to compatibly extend the protocol to allow faster idle bus arbitration. The bus access latency experienced by a module in a heavily loaded system, however, is only partly determined by arbitration. In a typical block-transfer system, it is likely that the average period of mastership will exceed the arbitration time. The choice of fairness, priority, or preemptive arbitration for any one module therefore has the greatest influence.

7.5.7 Protocol Limitations

Some might feel that the Futurebus arbitration mechanism is too complex for the fairly straightforward task it is required to implement. Although many of the features are very useful in certain applications, some have side effects that are undesirable. Recent studies have also shown that the fairness mechanism can be improved within the overall framework of the arbitration protocol. A system designer may want to take advantage of some of this accumulated hindsight.

The use of operation 5 for both error detection and preemption creates ambiguity about the reason for the assertion of **AC***. Although this is fine for transitory errors, the system must see an unusual number of **AC*** assertions before a real error can be verified. Because modules sending emergency messages also assert **ac*** to avoid gaining mastership, there is no way for the system as a whole to abort the reception of a message with bad parity. Each module must be responsible for detecting emergency message parity errors on its own. Of course, this has the advantage that a module with faulty error detection logic cannot prevent the rest of the system from receiving messages. This may be a useful way to alert the system to an otherwise crippling failure. Depending on how you look at it, this is either a bug or a feature.

Because both arbitration and fairness release take place in parallel with one module's period of mastership, according to a literal interpretation of the specification, the last fairness module in one "batch" will miss becoming uninhibited during the next batch. This means that the two fairness modules with the lowest arbitration numbers will only receive half the service that the rest receive during periods of heavy bus activity. This is easily solved by having the master inhibit itself at the beginning, rather than the end, of a period of mastership. Even after making this correction, there may still be a variation of up to 15 percent in the amount of access granted to each, module in a heavily loaded system. It is possible to replace the current fairness-priority protocol within the framework of the control acquisition sequence in a proprietary system, if necessary.

In a system with a bus that is usually idle, fairness modules will often have to pay the additional latency penalty of a fairness release cycle before obtaining bus mastership. This can be eliminated if the master, after completing its period of mastership, attempts a fairness release cycle before parking. When the next fairness module finally has a request, it will already have its inhibition released.

7.5.8 Summary

The Futurebus arbitration protocol provides the basic fairness and priority arbitration modes required by a high-performance multiprocessing system bus. The preemption mechanism increases the performance of high-priority bus requests. The distributed arbitration protocol maintains technology independence whenever possible, allowing future improvements in technology to increase system performance while ensuring compatibility with older designs.

Additional capabilities have been bundled onto the basic protocol. This includes the ability to transmit emergency messages, providing a simple interrupt mechanism, and support for bus reset and live insertion and withdrawal of modules.

Improvements in the performance of arbitration on Futurebus will come as increased integration is applied to the protocol. Other system implementation considerations also have a significant impact on the overall performance of the backplane environment.

7.6 DATA TRANSFER

Once arbitration has determined which module is to be the current bus master, the parallel protocol describes the manner in which data transfers are to be carried out. Each transaction consists of a broadcast connection, or address transfer, phase, followed by one of a variety of types of data transfer, and finally a broadcast disconnection. The connection formed can be either single slave, multislave, or three party. Data transfer can be either read or write, or single address or block transfers. This transfer tool kit provides the transactions necessary for applications ranging from the most basic to a high-performance multicache system.

7.6.1 Parallel Bus Information Signals

Futurebus allows the transfer of four types of information within the parallel protocol (see Table 7.6). Addresses are transferred from the master to all other mod-

TABLE 7.6 Data Transfer Signals

AD⟨31· · ·0⟩*	Address/data
BP⟨W· · ·Z⟩*	Bus parity
TG*	Tag
TP*	Tag parity
CM⟨5· · ·0⟩*	Command
CP*	Command parity
ST⟨3· · ·0⟩*	Status
AS*	Address synchronize
AK*	Address acknowledge
AI*	Address acknowledge invalid
DS*	Data synchronize
DK*	Data acknowledge
DI*	Data acknowledge invalid

ules on the backplane (the slaves) during connection. Data is transferred on the same set of lines between the master and selected or third-party slaves during the data transfer phase. Command information is transmitted from the master to the slave(s), and status from the slaves to the master. Addresses are transferred with the same timing as the address command, write data has the same timing as data command, and read data has the same timing as data status.

The address/data information path consists of 32 address/data lines (**AD⟨31· · ·0⟩***), divided into four 8-bit "lanes" (labeled W through Z to avoid byte sex favoritism), and one tag bit (**TG***), whose meaning is undefined by the standard. Each lane of the address/data path is protected by a single odd-parity bit (**BP⟨W· · ·Z⟩***), as is the tag bit (**TP***).

The command field consists of six bits (**CM⟨5· · ·0⟩***) that have different meanings during connection, data transfer, and disconnection (see Table 7.7). A single odd-parity bit (**CP***) provides error coverage here as well. The status field consists of four bits (**ST⟨3· · ·0⟩***), which are valid during address and data transfer only (see Table 7.8). Because the status lines are usually driven by many modules simultaneously, a parity bit here would lack meaning.

7.6.2 Parallel Protocol Handshake

The Futurebus parallel protocol uses six synchronization lines. Three of these, the address handshake lines, are used to establish and break a connection between a

TABLE 7.7 Command Field

Signal	Connection		Data transfer		Disconnection	
CM5*	**CC***	Cache command	**TH***	Three party		
CM4*	**IM***	Intent to modify	**WR***	Write		
CM3*	**LK***	Lock	**LW***	Lane W deselect		
CM2*	**BT***	Block transfer	**LX***	Lane X deselect	**DO***	Owner
CM1*	**BC***	Broadcast	**LY***	Lane Y deselect	**DE***	Error
CM0*	**EC***	Extended command	**LZ***	Lane Z deselect	**DB***	Busy

TABLE 7.8 Status Field

Signal	Connection		Data transfer	
ST3*	**CS***	Cache status	**CS***	Cache status
ST2*	**SL***	Selected	**SL***	Selected
ST1*	**ER***	Error	**ER***	Error
ST0*	**BS***	Busy	**ED***	End of data
DK*	Intervention/reflection			
DI*	Third-party transaction (nonbroadcast)			

master and one or more slaves. The other three, the data handshake lines, are used to transfer data between the master and the slaves that have established that connection. In Futurebus, information is usually transferred with every transition of these handshake lines.

The address handshake uses an address synchronization signal (**AS***), which is emitted by the master, and two address acknowledge signals (**AK*** and **AI***) of opposite polarity, which are emitted by both the slaves and the master. Because more than one module is driving the acknowledge lines, the master must receive them through a glitch filter.

The data handshake uses a data synchronization line (**DS***), which is also driven by the master. Only the slaves that have actually established a connection may drive the data acknowledge lines (**DK*** and **DI***). Unconnected modules must ignore everything that happens on the bus between connection and disconnection, as there is no guarantee that they can recognize any of the information being transmitted on the bus during the data transfer. This has important implications for future extensions to the standard; as long as the connected modules understand each other, they can perform any type of operation during the data transfer phase. Even during defined transactions, however, **DK*** and **DI*** do not always have the same meanings. Either or both may be used as the transfer acknowledge signal, depending on the transaction. Only during multislave transactions may they be driven by multiple slaves and therefore require glitch filtering. All other data transfers proceed without delay.

The two data acknowledge lines are also used during the connection phase as additional status lines and to set up for the data handshake. Although this may appear confusing, it is not as disadvantageous as it seems.

7.6.3 Transaction Phases (The Address Handshake)

There are four phases to every transaction on Futurebus, defined by the state of the address handshake lines (see Fig. 7.9). The first, most neglected phase, is the idle state. Here all the lines are released except for **AI***. Not only is this the interval between two transactions, but it also is the only place where bus mastership may be transferred (see Fig. 7.10). The bus must be idle before the current master can leave operation 5 in the control acquisition cycle, and the master-elect may not drive any of the bus lines until mastership has been assumed in operation 6.

When the current master asserts **as***, the connection phase begins. Prior to this, the master must have set up both the address and the address command on the bus. The command lines determine the type of transaction that is to take place. These command lines have the following meanings.

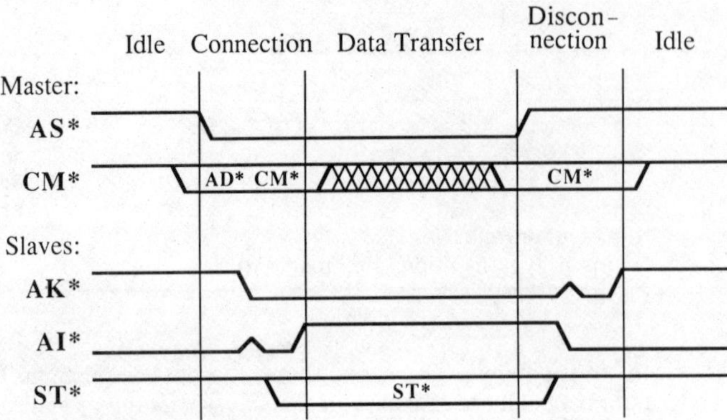

FIGURE 7.9 Data transfer phases.

CM5*—Cache Command (CC*): Ignored in standard 896.1, this bit is used in 896.2 to indicate that a caching master will be keeping a copy of the data to be transferred.

CM4*—Intent to Modify (IM*): This bit is asserted if the current transaction will change data as perceived by the system. It does not imply that the subsequent transaction will be either a read or a write, an important distinction in caching systems. For noncaching devices, however, it must be asserted if any part of the transaction may contain a write.

CM3*—Lock (LK*): Although a simple read-modify-write operation is permitted within a single transaction, more complex multitransaction or multislave indivisible operations require the assertion of this bit through the entire sequence to guarantee its inviolability. Those slaves selected by a locked operation remain locked until the locks are canceled, either by a transaction without this bit set or a change of mastership.

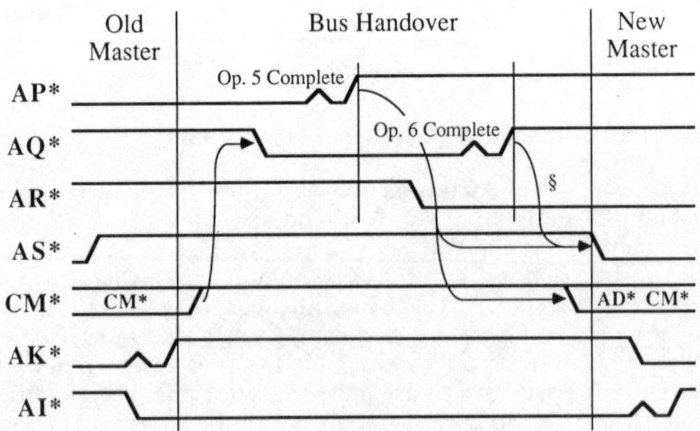

FIGURE 7.10 Exchange of bus mastership. §, requirement only for systems allowing 896.1 live module resynchronization.

CM2—Block Transfer (**BT***):* The assertion of this bit selects a mode of data transfer in which multiple data transfers access successively incrementing word addresses. A fast "two-edge" handshake is used. If not asserted, only a single address is accessed, and a slower "four-edge" handshake used.

CM1—Broadcast (**BC***):* The assertion of this bit selects a multislave access, requiring a "three-wire" glitch filtered handshake. The transaction must otherwise select only a single slave.

CM0—Extended Command (**EC***):* This bit is an escape mechanism that can be used to allow an as yet unspecified or proprietary data transfer protocol. Modules built according to the 896.1 standard simply remain unselected if they detect this bit set.

When a slave has finished decoding the address presented to it on the bus, it responds by driving the address status lines and then asserting **ak*** and releasing **ai***. These status lines have the following meanings.

ST3—Cache status (**CS***):* Not used in the 896.1 standard, an 896.2 caching module asserts this bit if it has and intends to retain a copy of the data being accessed.

ST2—Selected (**SL***):* A slave asserts this bit if it recognizes the address presented to it as its own and the parity on the address and command is correct. It must then participate in the subsequent data transfer.

ST1—Error (**ER***):* A slave asserts this bit if it detects any error condition associated with the address transfer, or if it has been selected but is unable to perform the operation requested of it.

ST0—Busy (**BS***):* A slave may assert this bit in order to noncatastrophically abort the transaction for later retry. It can be used for deadlock avoidance, to prevent unusually slow slave response from holding up the bus, or to maintain cache coherence, among other things.

The data acknowledge handshake lines may also need to be manipulated during this period. Normally, they will remain released. If the master has requested a broadcast transfer, the slaves that were selected must assert **di*** in order to prepare for the multislave handshake. If a copy-back caching module needs to participate in the transaction because it has internally modified the data being accessed (so that the selected slave has an incorrect copy), it must assert **di*** during nonbroadcast transfers. Futurebus provides two mechanisms with which a cache can interfere in a transaction, called intervention and reflection. If the cache intends to intervene, it must also assert **dk***.

The **AI*** signal will not go high until every slave has completed the address decode and presented its status to the bus. After a glitch filter delay, the master evaluates the accumulated status. If **CS*** is asserted, some other module holds a copy of the data about to be accessed. If **SL*** is not asserted, the master has accessed a nonexistent location (notice that no time-out is necessary). If **ER*** is asserted, there is something seriously wrong with the attempted transaction or on the bus. And if **BS*** is asserted, the master should end the transaction, relinquish bus mastership, and try again later.

The master must also examine the data acknowledge handshake lines if it did not request a broadcast transfer. If both **DI*** and **DK*** are asserted, a third party wishes to intervene in the transaction; if only **DI*** is asserted, the third party wishes to reflect. This will affect the subsequent data transfer handshake.

7.6.4 Data Transfer

The release of **AI(f)** marks the beginning of the data transfer phase of the transaction for the master. The modules that have been selected and any that have chosen to intervene or reflect participate in the data transfer handshake. These handshakes are described in more detail below.

Sometimes, the fact that a certain address was accessed transmits sufficient information across the system. In this case, or if there was an error, the master may choose to skip the data handshake entirely and perform an address-only transaction.

If data transfers do take place, the command and status lines take on new meanings, as follows.

CM5—Three Party (**TH***):* When a master detects that a third party wishes to participate in the data handshake, it asserts this bit. This lets the selected slave know, in a technology-independent fashion, that this is a three-party transaction; it must become either disabled or diverted according to the state of **DK*** (asserted or released, respectively).

CM4—Write (**WR***):* This bit determines the direction of data transfer; if asserted it is a write transfer, otherwise it is a read, from the point of view of the master.

CM⟨3 · · · 0⟩—Lane Deselects (**LW*, LX*, LY*, LZ***):* Each bit deselects one byte lane when asserted, where lane Z contains **AD0***. This allows data to be transferred on any combination of lanes.

Most of the status bits have the same meaning during the data transfer, partly because a nonselected slave will continue to assert them throughout the data transfer phase. A selected slave may also assert **ER*** in response to data transfer errors. Only **ST0*** changes meaning.

ST0—End of Data (**ED***):* A slave asserts this bit when another transfer will not access the next sequentially higher word address. This is to prevent a master from running past the end of one slave's address space, its address counter, or an internal FIFO. This rule is modified somewhat in the 896.2 standard to allow cache line wraparound.

7.6.5 Disconnection

For both slaves that have been participating in the data transfer and those that have been ignoring it, the data transfer phase ends when the master releases **as***. This signals the start of disconnection.

If the master supports the 896.2 standard, it may set up disconnection commands on the bus before releasing **as***. This allows copy-back caches to maintain system data coherence in the event of exception conditions that may occur during earlier portions of the transfer. The following bits are defined at the current time.

CM2—Disconnecting Owner (**DO***):* This bit is asserted by a caching master that intends to assume ownership of the previously addressed data.

CM1—Disconnecting Error (**DE***):* The master asserts this bit if it detected **ER*** asserted during the connection or data transfer phases of the transaction.

CM0*—Disconnecting Busy (DB*): The master asserts this bit if it detected **BS*** asserted during the connection phase of the transaction.

The master should have released all other information signals by this time. Likewise, the slaves must release all of their information lines by the time they assert **ai*** and release **ak*.** When the master detects **AK(f)** released, it knows that all of the slaves that required it have evaluated the disconnection command. It may then release the command lines and either go on to the next transaction or turn over the bus to the next waiting module.

Remember, there are four phases. All modules participate in the connection and disconnection; only the slaves that have connected actually participate in the data transfer.

7.6.6 Transaction Types

Futurebus supports three major types of transaction, determined by the **BC*** and **TH*** command bits. These are single-slave, multislave, and three-party (intervening or reflecting) transactions. Each has its own unique handshake, but all follow the same simple rules:

1. Commands and write data must be valid from a transition of the synchronizer signal, **DS*,** to the transition of the corresponding acknowledge signal, **DK*** or **DI*.**

2. Status and read data must be valid from a transition of an acknowledge signal, **DK*** or **DI*** as appropriate, to the next transition of the synchronizer, **DS*** (or **AS*** if it was the last transfer).

Now all that is left to describe is which participant drives which line under what conditions.

The single-slave transaction is the most common type of data transfer (see Fig. 7.11). The master handshakes with **DS*** and the slave with **DK*.** The speed of the handshake is limited only by the speed of the two modules and the distance between them, making this the fastest type of transaction as well.

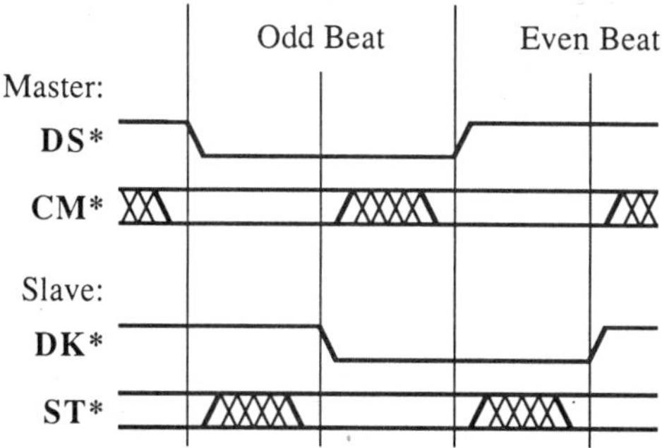

FIGURE 7.11 Single-slave handshake. Write data has same timing as CM*, read data has same timing as ST*.

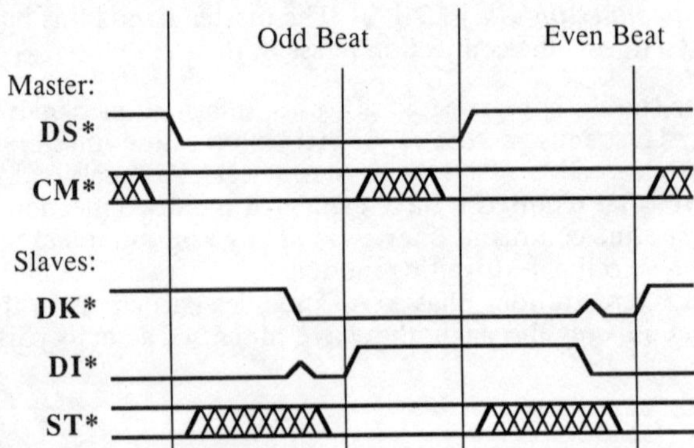

FIGURE 7.12 Multislave handshake. Write data has the same timing as **CM***, read data has the same timing as **ST***.

A multislave transaction is far less common, since it is only used when more than one module may have, or need, a copy of the data being broadcast (see Fig. 7.12). The handshake is the same as that used during address transfers: the master handshakes with **DS***, and each slave with both **DK*** and its inverse, **DI***. This means that there will always be a rising edge for the master to detect through a glitch filter, so that the slowest slave can limit the speed of each transfer. Since every transfer has to wait for the response of multiple slaves plus a glitch filter delay, this will in general be a much slower transaction than single slave.

Three-party transactions are more complex (see Fig. 7.13). They are required in copy-back caching systems when data in the selected slave may be incorrect, and a caching module is responsible for providing the correct data. In intervention, the third party blocks the selected slave from responding (it in fact becomes unselected) and handshakes in its place, driving **DI*** instead of **DK***. The polarity of **DI*** is the opposite of what **DK*** would have been, since the data transfer is entered with **DI*** asserted. This handshake is just as fast as a single-slave hand-

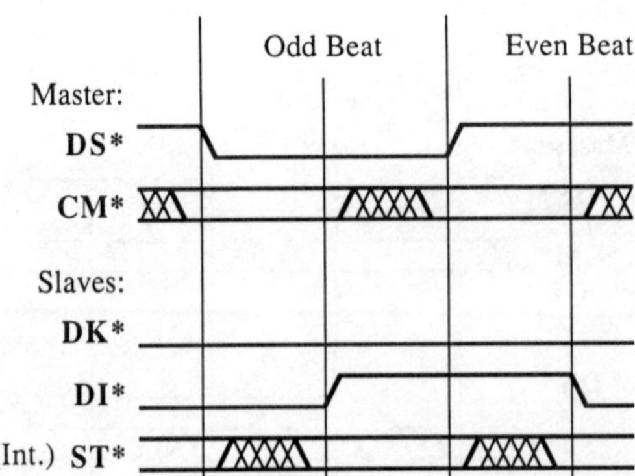

FIGURE 7.13 Intervening three-party handshake. The disabled slave releases **ST***; the intervening (Int.) slave drives **DK***, **DI***, and **ST***.

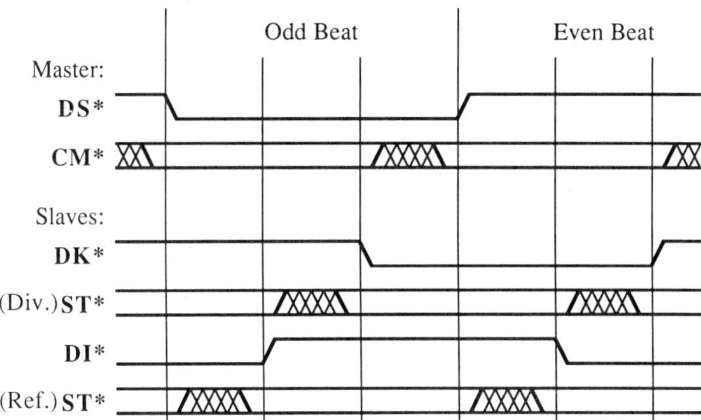

FIGURE 7.14 Reflecting three-party handshake. The diverted (Div.) slave drives DK* and ST*, the reflecting (Ref.) slave drives DI* and ST*.

shake, since once again, only two modules are involved. The difference is that the slave is now a third party, and the other acknowledge handshake line is used.

Since the data is already being placed on the bus, however, it may be more efficient to update the selected slave at the same time (see Fig. 7.14). Reflection involves a three-way handshake between the master, the third party, and the selected or "diverted" slave. The diverted slave treats the data as write information, regardless of the state of **WR*.** The master drives **DS*** and monitors **DK*.** The third party drives **DI*** and monitors **DS*.** The diverted slave drives **DK*** and monitors **DI*.** Despite this complex cycle, the command, status, and data information are always valid at the appropriate time for each module, as needed.

7.6.7 Transfer Modes

The handshakes described above made no reference to the polarity of a transition on a handshake line. This is because either edge can be used to synchronize or acknowledge the transfer of information; to put it another way, the "odd beat" and the "even beat" of a full handshake cycle can both be used to transfer data and information (see Fig. 7.15). Futurebus has two modes of data transfer selected by the **BT*** bit, which use these beats differently.

If the **BT*** bit is set, data is transferred on every beat. This is the most efficient way to transfer information across any medium—the clock changes at the same rate as the data. These burst transfers are used to transfer blocks of data from successive quadruplet addresses across the bus within a single transaction and at very high speeds. A single-slave burst transfer is the fastest possible technology-independent fully compelled data transfer protocol (see Fig. 7.16). It is expected that most bus transfers will use these burst transfers.

The limitation of burst transfers is that they must be all reads or all writes. There is no place in the handshake to turn the bus around. In order to allow efficient atomic operations, such as read-modify-write, Futurebus provides single-address transactions. When **BT*** is released, only the odd beat is used to transfer information. The even beat is unused, or *null.* Also, all transfers access the same

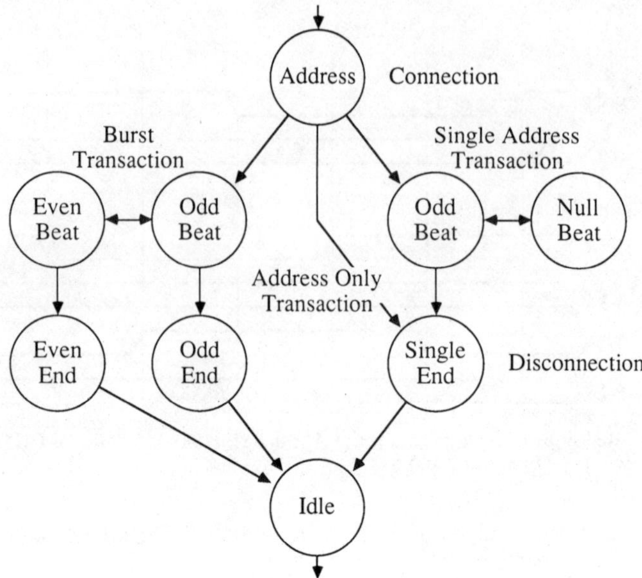

FIGURE 7.15 Data transfer sequence.

address location. This is similar to the traditional data handshake used by most other buses, but the increase in flexibility cuts the theoretical performance in half.

In either case, the number of data transfers contained within a transaction is not limited by standard 896.1, although a slave can always assert **ED*** to prevent a master from continuing. In a caching system, however, the memory space is broken up into *coherence blocks,* which are recommended by the 896.2 standard to be 16 32-bit words, or 64 bytes. Burst transfers cannot be allowed to cross a coherence line boundary, which places a limit on the block-transfer length.

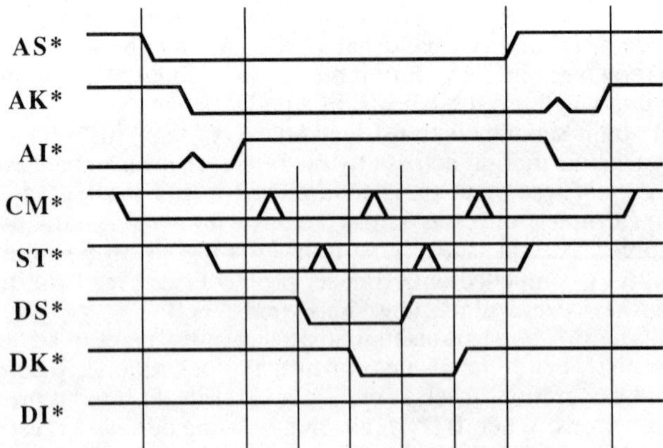

FIGURE 7.16 Example transaction: single-address single-slave burst transfer.

7.6.8 Exception Conditions

How should the master react when an exception condition occurs? Some are routine. **ED*** has already been discussed; the master merely ends the transaction and issues a new address. **BS*** has the same effect on the bus tenure level; the master should end its bus tenure and re-request the bus at a later time. The disconnecting busy signal (**DB***) allows the master to let the rest of the system know that the transaction was not completed successfully.

When **ER*** is asserted, or no module returns **SL***, a more serious error is indicated. It is likely that the system will have to enter a diagnostic mode to determine the exact cause of the problem. Either a master has tried to access a slave incorrectly or there has been some sort of information transfer error, either within a module or the bus. The disconnecting error signal (**DE***) provides the master with a means of rebroadcasting this condition as well.

If a module error is irreparable, the system must try to remove that module from the bus. As long as the bus interface has not been jammed, Futurebus provides a way to do this via a CSR (control and status register) access. If it is jammed, this condition can be detected by specifying a maximum transaction completion time (4–12 ms in standard 896.1) and issuing a bus initialize if it is exceeded. If a bus transceiver has experienced a hardware failure, it may be necessary to physically remove the module before the system can be restarted.

The 896.2 standard describes a mechanism that prevents one type of single-point failure from jamming the bus. When a module detects incorrect parity, the problem can be either with the data that was transferred or the detection logic itself. If one module has a fault in its parity detection logic for command or address, no module will be able to complete a transaction. Therefore a module that detects this type of error should go into a *parity suspect* state and ignore future transactions with parity errors until it has been reset by a diagnostic routine. This allows the rest of the system to continue functioning while the cause of the error is pinpointed. Note that emergency messages can be used to avoid single-point error lockups in the arbitration protocol.

7.6.9 Protocol Extensions

Two bits are reserved in the parallel protocol that may be used by a system designer to extend the Futurebus protocol. The first of these is the tag bit (**TG***). Tags are frequently used during the address phase to identify different types of data transfers, similar to an additional command line. Possible uses of the tag are to differentiate between instructions and data, I/O and CPU transfers, shared and single-processor data (to enable or disable cache monitoring), and cacheable or noncacheable data. During the data transfer phase, it could be used to identify pointers or data for LISP-style languages or provide other markers for extended data types.

With all these possible uses, it is reasonable to ask why only one tag bit was provided. A pragmatic reason was lack of space on the 96-pin connector, and a flippant reason was that one was a convenient number between zero and infinity. Both contain a fair amount of truth—given so many uses and given that most implementations will not use tags, one tag provides an escape with which any number could be generated on multiple or extended data transfers.

The second escape mechanism provided by Futurebus is the **EC***, or extended command bit. Its primary use is for future standard extensions to the protocol.

Two uses most often mentioned are for noncompelled, or source-synchronous, data transfers, and a wider address and/or data path. Both deserve more detailed review.

The only data transfer mechanism that is (theoretically) consistently faster than a fully compelled burst handshake is a source-synchronous transfer. Here, data is pipelined down the backplane at some predetermined maximum rate, accompanied by a two-edge clocking strobe signal. The source of data provides this synchronizer, and there is no return handshake. This is truly a packet-type transfer mechanism, since all transfers must be of a fixed length, and status can be returned only at the end of the transaction. An advantage of this protocol is that all modules that understand it can now monitor all data being transferred over the bus, allowing extensions to the current suite of transactions.

Theoretically, this protocol will always operate at twice the rate of the equivalent fully compelled protocol. Given today's technology, however, this is probably not the case. The source-synchronous protocol's maximum transfer rate is limited by the worst-case skews (a significant percentage of worst-case delay) throughout the bus interface logic. While the compelled protocol does have to insert delays to account for some of these skews, in other cases it runs at the typical speed of the devices used. The source-synchronous transfer rate of a system is determined by the lowest common denominator or the slowest module implementing that protocol. The fully compelled protocol runs as fast as the two modules currently communicating can operate. Finally, if one is willing to make the same packet-type assumptions on fully compelled transactions, it becomes questionable whether, using today's technology, the performance difference is worth the additional protocol complexity. On the other hand, a performance advantage of the source-synchronous protocol is that a maximum transfer rate is established, allowing the user to make assumptions about timing that are impossible in the technology-independent asynchronous protocol. As technology improves, it is likely that the source-synchronous protocol will provide a reasonable performance upgrade path.

Wider data and addressing modes are an obvious way to boost performance, although at considerable expense in bus interface cost and power requirements. Both 64-bit addressing and 64-, 128-, and 256-bit data paths have been considered. Multiple DIN or higher-density connectors are also required. These solutions, particularly in the case of wider data paths, have other hidden costs, however. The memory interface must be twice as wide for the same performance, and the cache line length and therefore cache size may also need to be doubled. A solution without these problems, and with a probable reduction in bus access latency, is to use parallel 32-bit Futurebuses on adjacent connectors. The choice, as always, depends on system design parameters.

7.6.10 Protocol Limitations

The data transfer protocol is, in general, a very clean interface. Because it has the philosophy that the master controls the bus interface, however, there are certain types of protocols that cannot be implemented directly. The only protocol of significance is one in which slaves may request that a normal data transfer be turned into a broadcast transfer. Given the speed penalty caused by going to a broadcast handshake, however, this does not seem unreasonable. It probably could be implemented in the future within a source-synchronous handshake.

A second performance limitation is that reliable read-write information is not available until the first data transfer. This is due to both the lack of a write bit in the connection phase and the existence of reflective data transfers. It will degrade the access latency of any transaction unless the slave can be built to initiate a read immediately and convert to a write only if proven wrong. The desirability of boosting performance in this manner depends on the ratio of reads to writes in any particular system environment.

7.6.11 Summary

The Futurebus parallel protocol defines an orthogonal set of data transfer mechanisms that provide both high-performance block transfers and flexible single-address transfers. The basic elements required for a multiprocessing system are all here: fully compelled, broadcast address transfer, and disconnection phases and single-slave, multislave, and three-party connections. The technology-independent interface allows the current protocol to increase performance compatibility as technology improves, and the independence of the data transfer phase allows other, higher-performance transfer protocols to be developed without interfering with current systems.

7.7 CACHE PROTOCOLS

Futurebus is the first 32-bit bus standard to provide the tools needed for a user to implement caching in a general manner. What is the purpose of caching, and what is its significance to a system?

A cache has three purposes. The first is to convert a microprocessor's semirandom reads and writes into efficient burst transfers on the bus. If a processor was allowed to execute single cycles directly over the bus, the frequency of requests would saturate the bus, in addition to the effect the bus latency would have on the processor's individual performance.

The second is to provide the microprocessor with a local window into the system memory space. For performance reasons, the processor should perform the majority of its accesses out of local memory. This fast memory is not usually large enough to store all of the data the processor may need to work with. What the processor wants, then, is the illusion that the entire system memory space is accessible and the effect that most of its transactions have the speed of local accesses.

The third purpose of caches is to provide the basis for a multiprocessing architecture. If multiple processors are working together within a single, shared memory space, a consistent, system-wide view of that space needs to be maintained. This requires that data be transferred among these processors and the shared memory according to shifting processor execution patterns.

A cache is able to do all of these things, and in a manner that is automatic and completely transparent to software.

7.7.1 How a Cache Works

A cache divides the memory space into fixed-length coherence blocks, or cache lines. This is the unit of data with which the cache associates a single address tag and maintains a set of cache attributes. When the microprocessor associated with

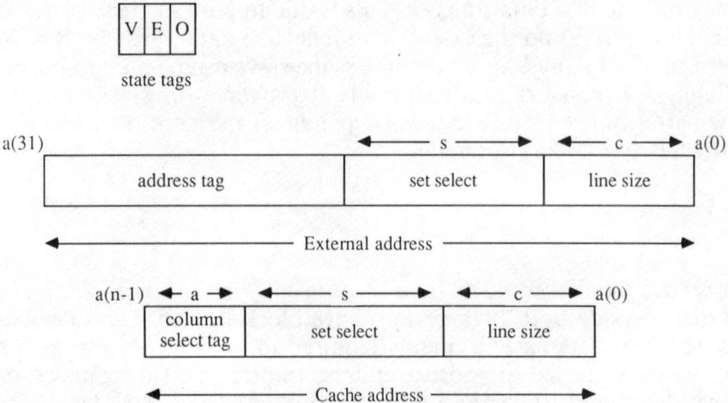

FIGURE 7.17 Cache address organization. 2^c = coherence line size (bytes per line); 2^a = set associativity (lines per set); 2^s = number of sets; 2^n = cache size (bytes).

a cache performs a single word read of data that does not exist in local (or cache) memory, for example, the cache fetches a full cache line from the system (or shared) memory, using a high-speed block transfer.

If a processor has accessed data at one location, it is likely to access the same or other nearby locations soon. These statistical principles of program behavior are known as spatial and temporal locality. They allow the fetching of an entire line in response to a single access to be good utilization of bus bandwidth.

The optimum cache line length varies between systems and architectures. For Futurebus over the next few years, a 16 transfer (64-byte) line size seems to be a reasonable value, and this size was recommended by the proposed 896.2 standard. Once this size is established, the entire system must adhere to it, and no transfer can be allowed to cross a cache line boundary.

A cache must maintain a directory to identify the cache lines that are stored in the cache memory (see Fig. 7.17). Each entry contains an address tag that consists of those address bits necessary to uniquely identify which address block is resident in a particular cache location. It also contains additional attribute bits that indicate the state of that cache line relative to the rest of system and cache memory.

With each processor read, the cache compares the processor-generated address with the tag in each directory location with which that particular address could be associated. (The number of eligible cache entries is called the associativity, usually limited to between one and four "columns" in most implementations.) If the address corresponds to a line already in the cache memory (a cache hit), the cache provides the processor with the correct data immediately. If the cache does not contain the addressed line (a cache miss), it holds off the processor while it fetches the line from shared memory. This will usually mean replacing a line that is already in the cache with the new one. For caches with multiple columns, one must be selected for replacement. The most common replacement algorithms are "least recently used" (LRU) and random replacement. The former is usually the most efficient, but under certain access patterns, the latter may result in more consistent performance. In either case, the cache automatically maintains for the processor a local copy of the data it is using at any one time.

Processor writes complicate the picture considerably. If the processor could guarantee that it was the only device that needed to access data being written, then writes could be treated as easily as reads. However, in the general case of a multiprocessing system, this is not possible. When one processor is allowed to write data privately, the data in shared memory is no longer correct. If another processor were to read from the same location in shared memory, it would receive an out-of-date copy of the data. Only Futurebus provides a general solution to the problem of maintaining data consistency, or coherence, across a multiprocessing system.

The easiest way to solve the problem is to avoid it. If the cache automatically passes every write on to the shared memory, it will never be incorrect. This is known as a write-through cache. Unfortunately, in a caching environment, the potential system performance is inversely proportional to the cache-miss rate. If writes are typically 20 percent of a processor's accesses, then the minimum cache-miss rate of a write-through system is 20 percent. If these writes are eliminated, the cache-miss rate can approach zero, and the system performance becomes theoretically unlimited.

The question, then, is how to allow multiple write-back or copy-back caches to exist in the same system. At the time the Futurebus caching specification was being developed, a number of isolated solutions existed as university and industry research projects. The proposed Futurebus protocol provides a superset of all of the previous solutions and allows any combination of them to coexist in the same backplane, including copy-back, write-through, and noncaching masters.

7.7.2 Cache Attributes

Every cache line may have associated with it three attributes: validity, exclusivity, and ownership (see Fig. 7.18). A cache must modify this state information in response to internal and external accesses, according to a specific set of rules described in the P896.2 standard.

If a cache line has the attribute of validity, then the client processor has *private read permission.* This means that the cache has a correct copy of the data, and the processor may read any part of the line without performing a bus access. If the

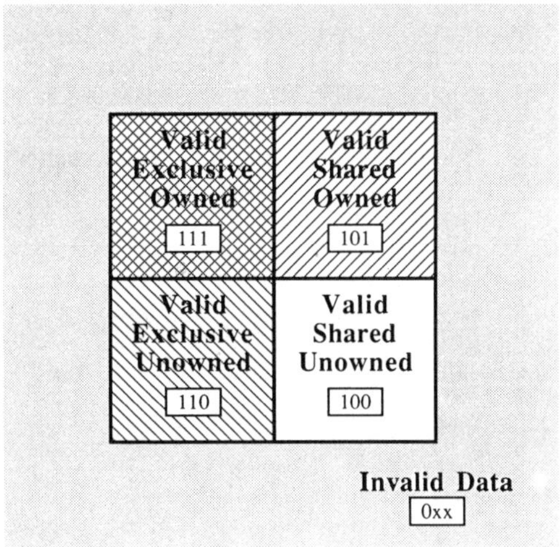

FIGURE 7.18 Cache attribute state diagram.

processor needs to read from a line that is currently invalid (does not exist or is incorrect within the cache), it must obtain validity by reading the full cache line from the bus with **CC*** asserted. In order to maintain a valid cache line, the cache must assert **CS*** in response to any external access to that line. A cache must therefore monitor every bus address, just as it monitors its own processor's requests. The cache must invalidate a line if there is an external access to it with **IM*** asserted (unless it is also a broadcast write to the full line). In order for a line to have either of the other two attributes, it must also have validity.

If a cache line has the attribute of exclusivity, then the client processor has *private write permission.* This means that the cache has the only cached copy of the data, and the processor may write to any part of the line without performing a bus access (the actual write also confers ownership). A cache may assign exclusivity to a line if no other slave asserted **CS*** when it obtained validity, meaning that no other cache has a copy of the same line. If a processor needs to write to a valid but nonexclusive (shared) copy of a line, it must first invalidate all other copies of the line by performing an address-only transaction on the bus with **IM*** asserted. A cache with an exclusive line may perform three-party transactions for performance, not coherency, reasons. A cache must relinquish exclusivity of a line if there is an external access to it with **CC*** asserted.

If a cache line has the attribute of ownership, the cache must assume that shared memory is incorrect. This means that not only does it contain the most recent copy of the data, but it also has the *responsibility* to maintain coherency by providing the correct data to any module that requires it. Only one cache in the system may have ownership of any one line. A cache must acquire ownership if its processor writes privately to an exclusive copy of a line. A cache can also acquire ownership of a line by asserting **DO*** at the end of a transaction. A cache owning a line must either respond as a third party to every bus transaction involving that line, or it must abort the transaction by asserting **BS*** and immediately write the line back to shared memory. A cache must relinquish ownership if a transaction to that line terminates with **DO*** asserted. It may relinquish ownership otherwise only by writing, or flushing, the entire line back to shared memory by any master transaction, or via reflection.

An action by one cache therefore affects every other cache in such a way that a consistent view of shared data is maintained. A processor that wants to read data acquires a valid copy of the line, either from shared memory or an owner (or exclusive) cache. If another cache had an exclusive copy, it reverts to being only valid. A processor that wants to write data first invalidates any other existing copies of the line, acquiring exclusivity. When the write is consummated, it assumes ownership of the line, which may then be passed from cache to cache before the line, and its ownership is passed back to shared memory.

Transactions by noncaching masters have no unusual effects on the system-wide state of a cache line. Owner caches still need to intervene or reflect, and nonowners still lose validity if the noncaching transaction is a nonbroadcast write. Write-through caches use only a valid bit, treating reads as caches do, but treating writes as if they were noncaching masters. And copy-back caches can use all three bits, choosing any subset of transactions required to maintain internal and external data consistency.

7.7.3 System Issues

There are real design considerations that affect the use of the bus in a caching system. It is worth discussing a few of these.

When a processor accesses a memory location that is not present in the cache, it is likely that the access will not be to the first word in the line. In order to provide the processor with the data it wants immediately, a cache may start reading the line at the point of processor access, rather than at the beginning of the line. When it reaches the end of the line, it has to wrap-around and read the rest of the line from the start. A typical shared memory module must assert **ed*** at a coherence line boundary, forcing the cache to issue a new address to complete the read. A module that supports implicit line wraparound, however, can automatically continue the transaction at the beginning of the line without breaking up the transfer. This higher-performance operation must be based on an understanding between the cache and the memory, and any other modules that might also access that memory.

As microprocessor chip sets appear with their own on-board caches, it may be necessary to reconcile differing bus and processor line sizes. If a processor cache with a smaller line size interfaces directly to Futurebus, it will have to invalidate multiple lines internally as a result of a single Futurebus transaction. This may require special on-board circuitry to simulate multiple transactions. However, since processor cache and line sizes are optimized for a completely different set of parameters than Futurebus cache and line sizes, the optimum high-performance solution requires a two-level cache. The external cache should be much larger than the processor cache and should perform the line size conversion and coherence maintenance required by the processor interface. This probably describes the high-performance bus-based cache architecture of the future.

7.8 CONTROL AND STATUS REGISTER SPACE

The Futurebus address space, although continuous, is divided into two areas (see Fig. 7.19). The majority of the address space is ordinary memory space, and the user is free to allocate it across a system in any appropriate fashion. The top 32 Mbytes, however, are reserved for control and status register (CSR) space.

The purpose of CSR space is to provide each module with a region in memory that has a fixed address, is based only on the physical slot location of that module, and is known by all other modules in the system. These "well-known addresses" allow the system both to begin initialization by reading an identification number for each module and to control its most basic functions by broadcasting com-

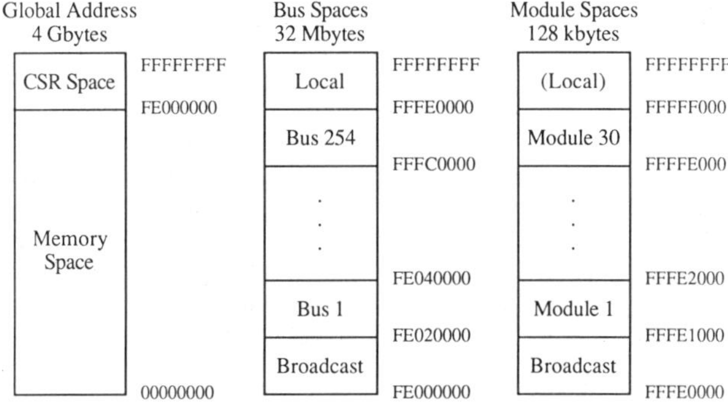

FIGURE 7.19 Futurebus CSR space.

mands to all of the modules in the system. It can also be used to allow the system to access any module's control space, either to write commands or to read status. The key is that these locations are always unique and fixed and therefore always available to the system.

The CSR space is broken down into several layers. At the highest level, it is divided into 256 equal segments. Each of these is known as a *bus space* and is primarily for use in systems connecting multiple Futurebus crates via bus repeaters. Once each crate has been assigned a unique number, either manually or automatically, a bus repeater on one backplane can access the memory-mapped CSR space of any other backplane in the system. The interconnect used is user-definable. Up to 254 backplanes can be accommodated with this mechanism. Bus space 0 maps into the CSR space of every backplane, allowing bus repeaters to send and receive system-wide broadcasts of control information. Bus space 255 always refers to the local backplane and is therefore a self-address space that does not require bus repeater intervention. In a single-crate system, only this segment of CSR space is used.

Each bus space is in turn divided into 32 equal segments, each called a *module space.* Every bus space is formatted identically, so only the local bus space need be described. Every slot in a Futurebus backplane has hard-wired into it a unique 5-bit geographical address. Every module therefore has a unique identifier ranging from 1 to 30. This defines the module space assigned to each card. Once again, module space 0 is reserved for broadcast (read or write) transactions to the equivalent locations on every module. If necessary, module space 31 can be assigned within any module for internal accesses to its own CSR space, regardless of slot position.

This mapping guarantees that any module in the system can access any other at a fixed location. The bus spaces allow this convention to be optionally extended across multiple crates through bus repeaters. This is a first step toward solving the traditional problems of system initialization and control.

7.8.1 The Primary ID

Each module's 4-kbyte CSR space is further divided into several fields (see Fig. 7.20). The bottom three-quarters is user-defined, and the top quarter defined by Futurebus. At the very bottom of a module's CSR space, however, are 4 bytes reserved for the module, or primary, ID.

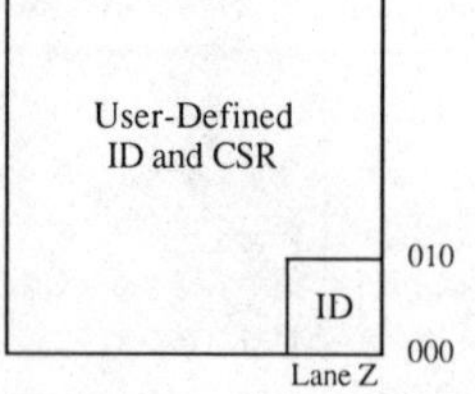

FIGURE 7.20 Module CSR space.

A traditional problem of system initialization is identification of system resources. Once a map of the system has been generated, the boot device can load the correct drivers and configure the system for normal operation. All too often, this configuration process required manual intervention every time the arrangement of modules within the system was changed. The P896.2 standard required that every module provide a 32-bit primary ID in the bottom 4 bytes in lane Z (for single-chip ROM implementations) of CSR space. Now the boot device can read the same location on every module in the backplane, identifying the software necessary to further configure and drive the device.

The primary ID is not a serial number; it defines a configuration standard. Additional software or an on-board code is obviously necessary to complete initialization. The primary ID merely serves as a pointer to that information. Although a more complete initialization standard may eventually be written, it is too early in the evolution of the standard to predict what range of system requirements need to be specified. A primary ID is sufficient to allow complete software control of system initialization.

The rest of user-defined CSR space can be used for additional identification, for module control and status registers, or for I/O ports.

7.8.2 CSR Functions

The top of module CSR space is used to control some basic module functions via addressable switches. Each 32-bit location functions as a single switch, set by a Futurebus access to its address with **IM*** asserted. Since they are at the same location in every module, an access to the broadcast module space will set the same switch on every module. No data need be associated with the transaction. For multiprocessing system integrity, a switch should not be set unless the transaction completes without **DE*** or **DB*** asserted during disconnection.

A module need only implement those switches that make sense for its application (although a configuration file should describe the set implemented). Those that had been defined by the P896.2 standard included targeted reset and initialize, parity check enable and disable, and a few additional switches for initialization and diagnostics. These switches occupy the top 32 locations in the module CSR space.

7.8.3 Targeted Interrupts

Futurebus has two major mechanisms for signaling events. The first, described in the arbitration section, is the emergency message. These are like shared interrupt lines; when one is triggered, the entire system is notified, but the sender remains anonymous. The second is the targeted interrupt. These are sent just like any ordinary transaction, but to a specific address location on a single module. The P896.2 standard described a primitive event notification mechanism which could be expanded to implement an arbitrary scheme of any complexity.

Futurebus reserves 32 locations, from $F00_{16}$ to $F7F_{16}$, in each module's CSR space for targeted events. They operate in exactly the same way as the CSR function switches, activated as the result of a Futurebus transaction to the location with **IM*** asserted. The target or slave may respond with **BS*** if the event was not recorded because the previous event had not yet been processed. The slave should not record the event if **DB*** or **DE*** are asserted during disconnection.

The minimum requirement for standard 896.2 modules was that at least one of the 32 locations be monitored for events. A more complex module could make the single location programmable or monitor more than one location. In the most general case, a location monitor can be programmed to look for accesses to any location in memory space. This allows one module to monitor a location for accesses no matter which modules are actively engaged in the transfer.

Location monitors can be of varying internal complexity as well. They can generate simple interrupts, be combined with counters or FIFOs for queuing, and even have data associated with them. A system can also broadcast these interrupts to a number of modules, possibly forming pools of processors with the ability to respond to any one interrupt.

These interrupt protocols, when combined with various types of locked transactions, are powerful enough to permit any type of multiprocessing event control system to be built on Futurebus. Once again, all of the primitive functions are in place, a minimum subset of operations is standardized, and the rest is up to the requirements of the individual system designer.

7.8.4 Reset and Initialization

One Futurebus signal has yet to be described. Although rarely used, the reset line (**RE***) is probably the most important in the system. Like all the other signals, **RE*** is open collector and can therefore be asserted by any module. Unlike any of the others, it has specific timing requirements.

There are two types of reset. The first, called *bus initialize,* resets only the bus interface, leaving the internal module functions undisturbed. This can be used if the bus interface is jammed, or to allow a module that has been inserted with power on to join the bus without elaborate synchronization procedures. The second, *bus reset,* is a traditional full reset of the entire system. This is used only at power-up time or in emergencies.

A module initiating a bus initialize must assert **re*** for 4 to 12 ms. To cause a reset, the signal must be asserted for 250 to 750 ms. The other modules should finish their transactions when **RE*** is asserted, but should not recognize a bus initialize until it has been asserted for more than 1 to 3 ms. If **RE*** continues to be asserted for more than 30 to 90 ms, a bus reset is in progress.

The response of the bus interface is the same for either type of reset. When a bus initialize has been detected, the module releases all bus signals, asserts **aq*,** and then asserts **ar*** and **ai*.** After **RE*** is released and the internal reset is complete, the module releases **aq*.** Now the bus should be in the idle phase of data transfer, and the arbitration state machine is ready to start operation 1.

The CSR function registers for targeted bus reset and initialize perform the same pair of functions, except on a single module only. They can be used to prepare a board for withdrawal with power on. Before the object of a targeted reset can release its bus signals, it must wait for the current transaction to finish and for the arbitration state machine to complete operation 6.

Once a module has joined the bus, the designated boot module must read that board's primary ID, initialize its operating parameters, and enable it using the standard CSR functions. Futurebus has been designed to allow this procedure to be fully software controlled. Manual intervention during reset or initialization no longer need occur.

7.9 CONCLUSION

Futurebus has generated significant advances in backplane technology throughout its long development. These include the creation of backplane transceiver logic, the exploration of the limits of technology-independent specification, and the formulation of a unified theory of cache coherence. It is designed for general-purpose multiprocessing systems and can support a wide range of performance requirements. It is currently being examined with great interest by the user community as a step beyond the current generation of 32-bit TTL standards. Although the 1987 standard may not become successful on its own, it forms the basis for its offspring, Futurebus+. One of these has the possibility of becoming the new universal standard bus. Wider address and data paths and even higher-performance data transfer protocols are all possible within the framework of the Futurebus philosophies. This is only the beginning for Futurebus.

ACKNOWLEDGMENTS

I would like to thank the following people, whose work, tutelage, and support allowed me to complete this Futurebus tutorial: R. V. Balakrishnan, Paul Borrill, Mike Evans, Jim Sutherland, Paul Sweazey, Matthew Taub, Mike Teener, John Theus, and Des Young.

REFERENCES

1. *ANSI/IEEE Standard 896.1-1987, IEEE Backplane Bus Specification for Multiprocessor Architectures: Futurebus,* Institute of Electrical and Electronics Engineers, New York, 1988.
2. R. V. Balakrishnan, "The Proposed IEEE 896 Futurebus—A Solution to the Bus Driving Problem," *IEEE Micro,* August 1984, pp. 23–27.
3. P. L. Borrill and J. Theus, "An Advanced Communications Protocol for the Proposed IEEE 896 Futurebus," *IEEE Micro,* August 1984, pp. 42–56.
4. P. L. Borrill, "Microstandards Special Feature: A Comparison of 32-Bit Buses," *IEEE Micro,* December 1985, pp. 71–79.
5. D. del Corso, H. Kirrmann, and J. D. Nicoud, *Microcomputer Buses and Links,* Academic, New York, 1986.
6. D. B. Gustavson and J. Theus, "Wire-OR Logic on Transmission Lines," *IEEE Micro,* June 1983, pp. 51–55.
7. D. Hawley, "The Futurebus Arbitration System," *Buscon UK,* October 1987, Conference Management Corp., Cerritos, California, 1987, pp. 78–85.
8. D. Hawley and R. V. Balakrishnan, "Timing Analysis of Synchronous and Asynchronous Busses," *Buscon West,* February 1988, Conference Management Corp., Tustin, California, 1988, pp. 237–245.
9. *IEEE Standard P896.2, Draft 1.0, Futurebus P896.2 Specification,* Institute of Electrical and Electronics Engineers, New York, April 1988.
10. C. J. T. Nichols, *A Guide to Futurebus,* Ferranti C. S. L., London, 1987.
11. P. Sweazey, "Shared Memory Systems on the Futurebus." *Digest of Papers, Spring Compcon '88,* IEEE Computer Society Press, New York, 1988, pp. 505–511.
12. D. M. Taub, "Arbitration and Control Acquisition in the Proposed IEEE 896 Futurebus," *IEEE Micro,* August 1984, pp. 28–41.
13. D. M. Taub, "Improved Control Acquisition Scheme for the IEEE 896 Futurebus, *IEEE Micro,* June 1987, pp. 52–62.
14. M. K. Vernon and U. Manber, "Distributed Round-Robin and First-Come First-Serve Protocols and Their Application to Multiprocessor Bus Arbitration," *Computer Architecture Conference Proceedings,* IEEE Computer Society Press, Washington, D.C., 1988, pp. 269–277.

CHAPTER 8
STD BUS (IEEE 961)

Matt Biewer
STD Bus Manufacturers Group
Pro-Log Corporation
Monterey, California

The STD bus is a powerful, rugged, modular, interconnect scheme for microprocessor industrial control applications. The modular card size, efficient form factor, and rugged bus connectors meet the reliability needs of the industrial environment. The I/O-oriented bus provides a simple, easy-to-implement interface between all popular microprocessors and a wide variety of I/O functions. The STD bus is rich in I/O functions, supported by many specialized interfaces created by a wide range of technical and scientific disciplines. Processing power on the STD bus ranges from simple 8-bit to powerful 32-bit processors with choices of single-master, master-slave, and multimaster environments. Software support includes MS-DOS and PC DOS operating systems on PC-compatible STD bus hardware.

8.1 STD BUS CHARACTERISTICS

The STD bus interface connector as shown in Fig. 8.1 is dedicated to microprocessor control of the card functions. Peripheral and I/O device connections are made at the user edge of the card. This layout gives an orderly signal flow across the card from the bus interface to the user interface. Peripheral and I/O devices are connected to the system using their own unique connectors and cabling. Complete modular functions are added to the system by simply installing a card with its cable.

8.1.1 Benefits of Modularity

The advantages of the STD bus lie in its efficient form factor (Fig. 8.2) that allows a cost-effective modular approach to microprocessor system design. These advantages apply particularly to control applications where modularity suits the need for design flexibility. Modularity allows the designer to select available functions

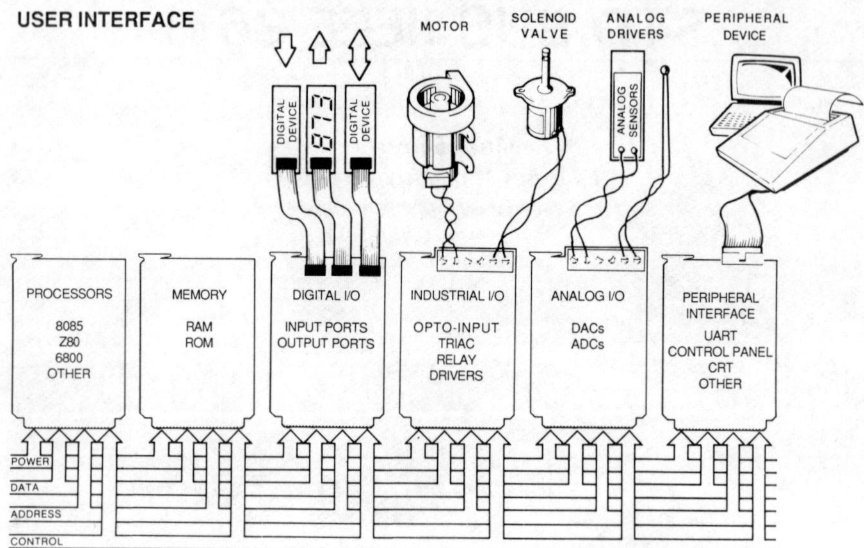

FIGURE 8.1 STD bus implementation.

and to tailor the solution for the application. Modularity also provides a solution for service and maintenance, where problems can be isolated at the module level and serviced quickly by board substitution. The STD bus form factor also provides ruggedness. The small card size (Fig. 8.3) resists shock and vibration and contributes to the reliability of the system.

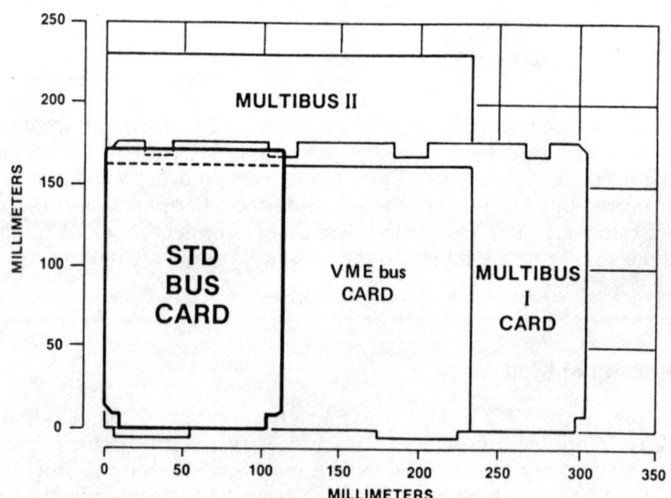

FIGURE 8.2 STD bus modular card size.

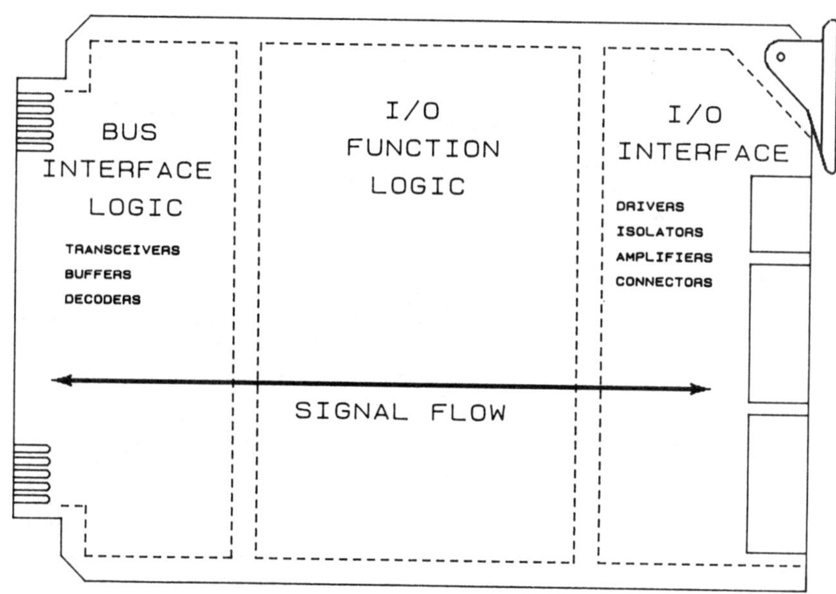

FIGURE 8.3 STD bus efficient form factor.

8.1.2 Reliability, Ruggedness, and Quality

Most STD bus products are aimed at the industrial market. Reliability is essential in industrial applications, where minutes of production time may be measured in thousands of dollars. Reliability is a function of ruggedness and quality. Ruggedness and quality determine how well a card survives in its operating environment. The ruggedness of a product can be specified in physical terms such as temperature, shock, and vibration. The quality of a product may be indicated by the specified warranty or MTBF figures. Quality, however, must be designed in and built in by the product vendor. Vendor procedures should be examined to assess the quality of a product. Quality is controlled through such processes as the use of standard components, worst-case design, automated manufacturing, product burn-in, functional testing, and electrostatic handling and packaging procedures.

The physical characteristics of the STD bus make it rugged. The small card size of the STD bus resists shock and vibration and minimizes thermal problems due to self-heating. The use of printed wiring edge connectors adds to the ruggedness and reliability of the system. These connectors can take abusive handling and can suffer severe misalignment without the danger of bent or broken pins.

8.1.3 STD Bus Power and Performance

The STD bus was originally designed as an 8-bit bus with 64K of addressing and was later expanded to become a 16-bit bus with 16 Mbytes of addressing. The expansion was accomplished through signal multiplexing with no wasted cycle time while maintaining backward I/O compatibility for the STD bus.

With changes in memory chip sizes and availability of application-specific integrated circuit (ASIC) chips for complex logic, we now see 8-, 16-, or 32-bit microprocessors with megabytes of memory on a single STD bus board. In this on-board configuration the processor operates at its full bandwidth without the limitations of the backplane bus but maintains full I/O compatibility on the STD bus. The STD bus has thus achieved wide-open processing power while maintaining the modular, rugged, simple I/O interface for the industrial environment.

8.2 STD BUS APPLICATIONS

The STD bus has been applied in all aspects of industrial control. General application areas include robotics, machine control, process control, factory control, instrumentation and testing, data acquisition, and data computing.

Robotics. Robotics in industrial control usually involve stationary machines with multiple-axis arms used to position goods or tools. An example of robotics is in a pick-and-place machine for surface-mount components. The STD bus system controls a component head that can be positioned, rotated, raised, and lowered. The component head selects the proper fixture and retrieves the designated component. The head is positioned and rotated over the printed wiring board and the component is lowered into place.

Embedded machine control. In embedded machine control the STD bus systems are built into large machines to automate the machine function. An example is injection molding machines. In this application the STD bus controls the feeding of raw materials into the machine, controls the hydraulics for clamping the mold, controls the heating and cycling of the injection process, and controls the robotics for unloading the molded parts. Future capabilities of this machine will include networked communication to a central control point for process monitoring, production data acquisition, and programming.

Process control. The STD bus has been applied as a control solution in areas such as food processing and chemical processing. A simple example of a food industry application is the use of the STD bus to control the refrigeration of produce warehouses (Fig. 8.4). This system controls multiple compressors and fans to reduce the peak energy requirements while it maintains the required temperature control.

Factory control. An example of a factory control system consists of multiple STD bus systems distributed at all workstations of an electronics assembly operation. All workstations are networked to a centralized file server that contains all programs and transaction data. Work orders issued to the system cause material to be processed on the assembly line. The STD bus systems use terminals and graphics displays to provide job information at each station. The materials and assemblies are tracked along the assembly line using bar-code readers and keyboards to provide on-line status. The STD bus systems are programmed wherever possible to interface directly to the production line processes.

Data acquisition. The small size and low-power requirements of CMOS STD bus cards allow implementation of portable and remote data collection systems. In one application a portable instrument was designed and implemented to locate and measure the depth of buried water pipes. The location and depth information were recorded in battery-backed RAM. The data was accessed by

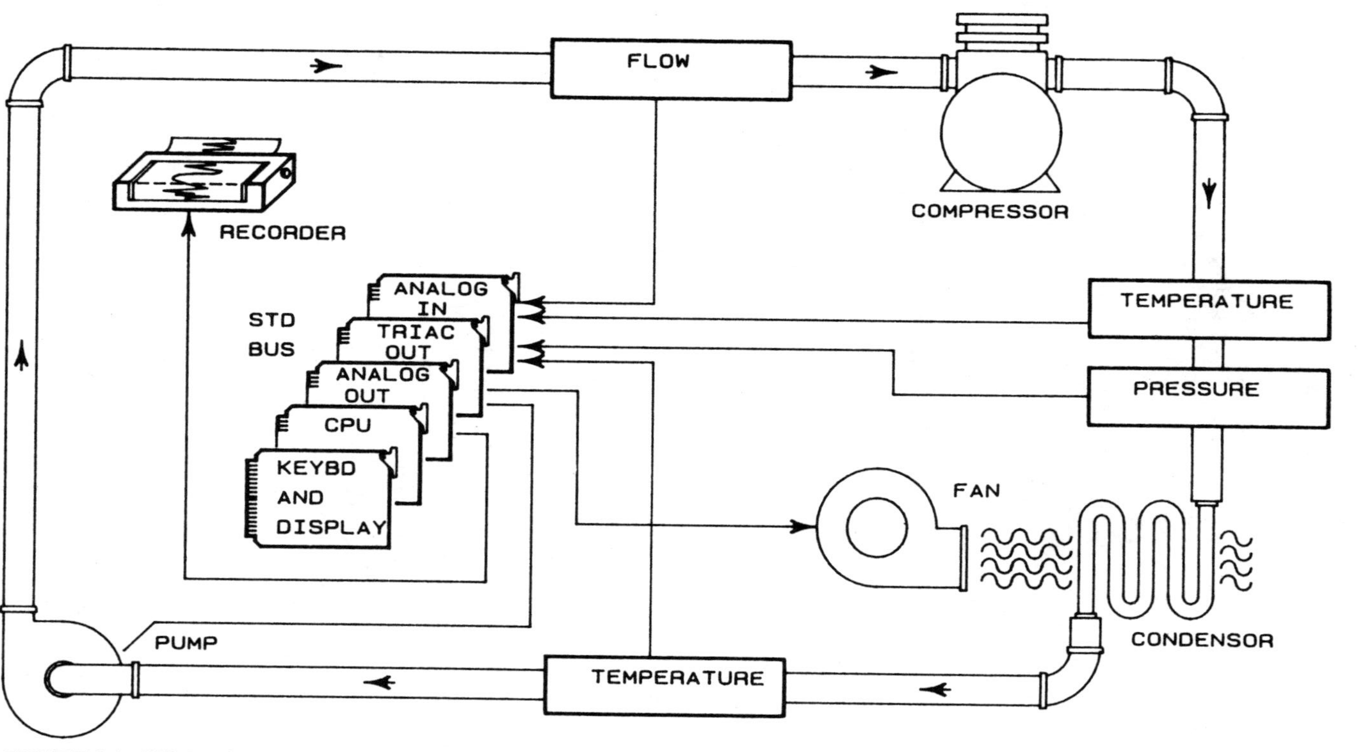

FIGURE 8.4 STD bus implementation: refrigeration process.

a computer at the completion of the mapping operation for the actual plotting of the information.

Instrumentation and testing. The use of the STD bus for instrumentation includes electronic component and board testing where test parameters are applied and measurements made to determine the pass or fail status. In more sophisticated applications, medical instruments use the STD bus for the analysis of blood and other body fluids.

Computing. Every application involves some form of computing. The STD bus has reached performance levels exceeding an 8-MHz AT computer using a single processor. With multiprocessing capability the STD bus can match the computing performance of the personal-computing industry as it progresses.

8.3 STANDARDS AND INDUSTRY SUPPORT

8.3.1 STD Bus Buyers Guide

There are hundreds of STD bus boards and support products. All STD bus products and manufacturers are conveniently listed in an industry publication called *The STD Bus Buyers Guide.* This guide is published semiannually by the microcomputer interface group of *Control Engineering* magazine. It lists all board-level and system products by manufacturer and model number in various product categories. This support publication simplifies the task of locating products and vendors.

8.3.2 STDMG

The STD bus is managed and maintained by an industry group called the STD bus manufacturers group (STDMG). The STDMG is an organization of STD bus manufacturers that cooperates for the benefit of its members, other manufacturers, and users. Its aim is to develop and maintain the STD bus standards and to promote the STD bus. A major objective is to help users get information to develop their systems and products using the products and services of the STDMG members. The STDMG creates technical specifications and practices for applying the STD bus. The group also sponsors joint promotion of the bus through trade shows, advertising, and press releases. The STDMG meets regularly, usually in conjunction with regional trade shows. The STDMG is incorporated with dues-paying membership.

8.3.3 Industry Standards

The STD bus is supported by the IEEE 961 standard. The STD bus also uses other IEEE standards, such as the IEEE 488 GPIB and IEEE 959 SBX standards, to extend its usefulness. By linking to industry standards the STD bus enhances its usefulness to the user. Because of its similar structure the STD bus has been able to link closely to the IBM PC standard, providing compatibility that allows use of the enormous PC software pool.

8.4 HISTORY AND EVOLUTION OF THE STD BUS

The STD bus was introduced in 1978 jointly by Pro-Log Corporation and Mostek as a planned industry standard. To encourage its acceptance as a standard the bus was made freely available to industry without patents, trademarks, or copyrights. An industry-supported manufacturers group (STDMG) was formed to manage and maintain the bus specifications and to encourage and enhance this modular method of applying microprocessors.

In 1980 the manufacturers group sought IEEE standardization to achieve more rigid control of the specification. In 1982 the IEEE authorized a Working Group to study the development of the P961 8-bit microcomputer bus standard, and in 1987 the IEEE 961 standard was approved.

The STD bus has evolved much like other classes of computers over history. Not unlike the recent evolution of the minicomputer, the STD bus feature set has expanded dramatically. Sophisticated peripherals, such as mass storage devices and easy-to-use interfaces, make it possible to develop programs directly on STD bus systems. High-level operating systems, powerful development tools, and device-driver libraries speed implementation and the sophistication of the final product or system. Intelligent I/O functions and multiprocessing have followed, increasing the performance of STD-based systems dramatically. Processors composed of 16 bits, soon to evolve to 32-bit units, were introduced to the bus. Finally, the implementation of compilers, source-level debuggers, and packaged systems bring the STD bus to a level where the less-than-expert user can use it in simple, more casual applications than previously.

8.5 STD BUS PROCESSOR SUPPORT

The STD bus is designed to support any microprocessor by using a simple I/O interface and by providing special peripheral interface timing signals on the bus. Simple port interfaces allow most I/O cards to work with any processor. Single-board computers with CPU, memory, and peripherals all on the same card remove the need for peripheral timing on the bus.

8.5.1 8085, Z80, 64180, and Z280 Processors

Early STD bus designs were predominantly Z80 and 8085. Many of these designs will continue to be supported in installed applications. The knowledge base and software libraries coupled with simplicity make the Z80 a viable choice for new designs in low-cost embedded applications. The frontier of this processor family is the 64180, which provides the Z80 with a more powerful single-chip architecture.

8.5.2 8088, 8086, 80186, 80286, and 80386 Processors

Processors using the 8088 appeared on the STD bus soon after the chip was introduced. However, it took the IBM PC to make the 8088 processor family popular.

The similarity of the PC architecture to the STD bus made it easy to create compatible hardware to take advantage of the large software pool. A growing segment of the STD bus market is developing around industrial PC-compatible systems. The ruggedness, modularity, and wide range of I/O functions on the STD bus coupled with PC compatibility have given the STD bus a strong position in industrial markets.

8.5.3 6800, 6500, and 68000 Processors

The 6800 and 6500 were some of the earliest processors to appear on the STD bus, followed a short time later by the 6809. When 16-bit chips became available, the 68008 and 68000 processors were also added to the bus.

8.5.4 Microcontroller Chips

Single-chip microcontrollers, such as the 8051 family, were originally designed for nonbussed embedded control applications. These devices have found their way onto the STD bus as intelligent I/O controllers.

8.6 MEMORY SUPPORT

The STD bus is supported by a wide variety of special memory cards and memory expansion cards. When memory chip sizes were small, it was necessary to have memory expansion cards to achieve reasonable memory capacity. In the lifetime of the STD bus many of these memory cards have become obsolete because the chip manufacturers have discontinued the memory devices. Control applications generally do not need large amounts of memory, and with the chip sizes of today STD bus cards place all the required memory on-board with the processor. An added advantage of on-board memory is that the processor can operate at greater speeds. All backplane buses suffer speed limitations due to transmission line characteristics and the loading from added modules. The trend for the STD bus is to place the operating memory on-board with the processor to achieve the maximum operating speed.

It is not possible in some situations to remove all memory from the bus. Cards requiring memory such as basic I/O software (BIOS) extensions, display memory, or shared memory in multiprocessor schemes must be on the bus. A solution for maintaining operating speed and the operating integrity of the bus is to run the on-board operating memory at full speed and to run bus-based memory at reduced speed by changing clock speeds or inserting wait states.

Specialty memory cards. With operating memory on-board there remains the need for special memory cards. There are static and dynamic memory expansion cards, battery-backed RAM cards, erasable PROM (EPROM) and electrically erasable PROM (EEPROM) cards, bubble memory cards, and ROM or RAM memory disk cards plus combination memory cards.

8.7 STD BUS I/O SUPPORT

The strength of the STD bus is the richness of its available I/O functions. The modular card size allows the user to select the exact I/O configuration by choosing from a long list of products. The simple interface of the STD bus makes it easy to design I/O interfaces; thus many specialized interfaces not available from card manufacturers are designed by the end-user.

8.7.1 Digital I/O Cards

Digital I/O cards (Fig. 8.5) are implemented with either TTL and CMOS 8-bit latches and gate chips or off-the-shelf programmable I/O (PIO) chips. Port cards with up to eight 8-bit I/O ports are some of the earliest cards that were available on the STD bus. These cards remain popular for driving control panel displays and sensing control switches. Programmable I/O devices are used when the inputs need to be interrupt driven.

8.7.2 Analog I/O Cards

Analog I/O cards fall into the categories of analog input (A/D) and analog output (D/A). The STD bus is well supported by analog functions including analog system cards containing both inputs and outputs. The analog input cards (Fig. 8.6) range from 8- to 16-bit resolution with 12 bits as the norm. Some analog input cards include signal conditioning and multiplexed inputs for specialized interfaces such as thermocouples. Analog output cards (Fig. 8.7) are available with either voltage output or 4 to 20 mA current outputs.

8.7.3 Industrial Control Interfaces

Industrial control interfaces are characterized by their ability to directly drive or sense high-current or high-voltage devices. Many industrial interfaces also provide circuit isolation to keep the high-powered signals from destroying the logic circuits during failures. Two implementations exist on the STD bus: in-rack functions and remote-rack module functions.

In-rack industrial interfaces. In-rack functions are implemented within the STD bus card rack. These include cards such as relays, relay drivers, optically isolated inputs, and optically isolated outputs for either ac or dc applications. In-rack implementation is ideal for embedded systems where the controlled devices are in the same package as the controller or in close proximity.

Remote-rack module interfaces. Remote-rack functions are implemented with industry standard, optically isolated plug-in modules mounted remotely from the STD bus controller (Fig. 8.8). Plug-in cards are available for the STD bus with the necessary cable interface and drivers for either serial or parallel protocols.

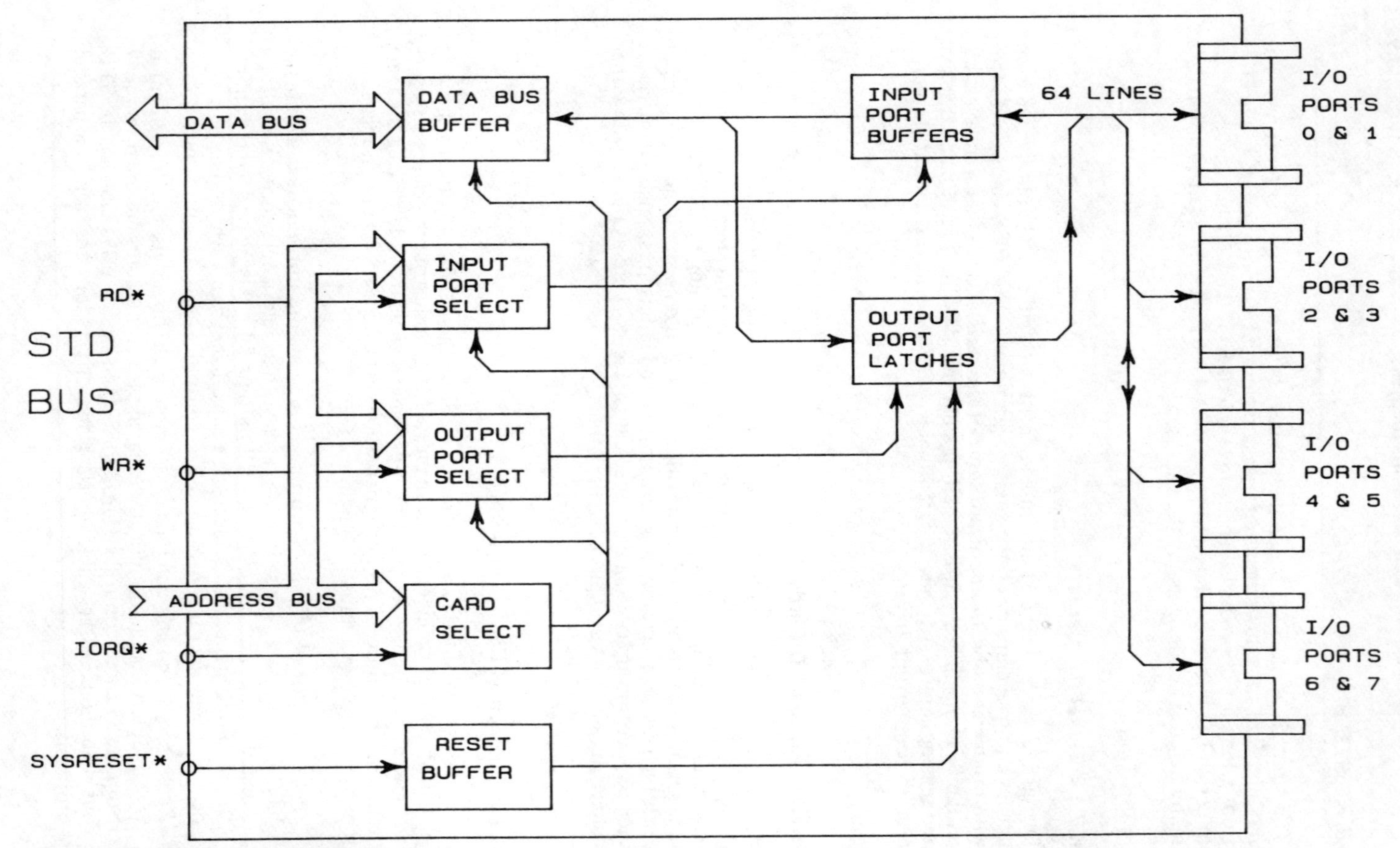

FIGURE 8.5 Digital I/O card block diagram.

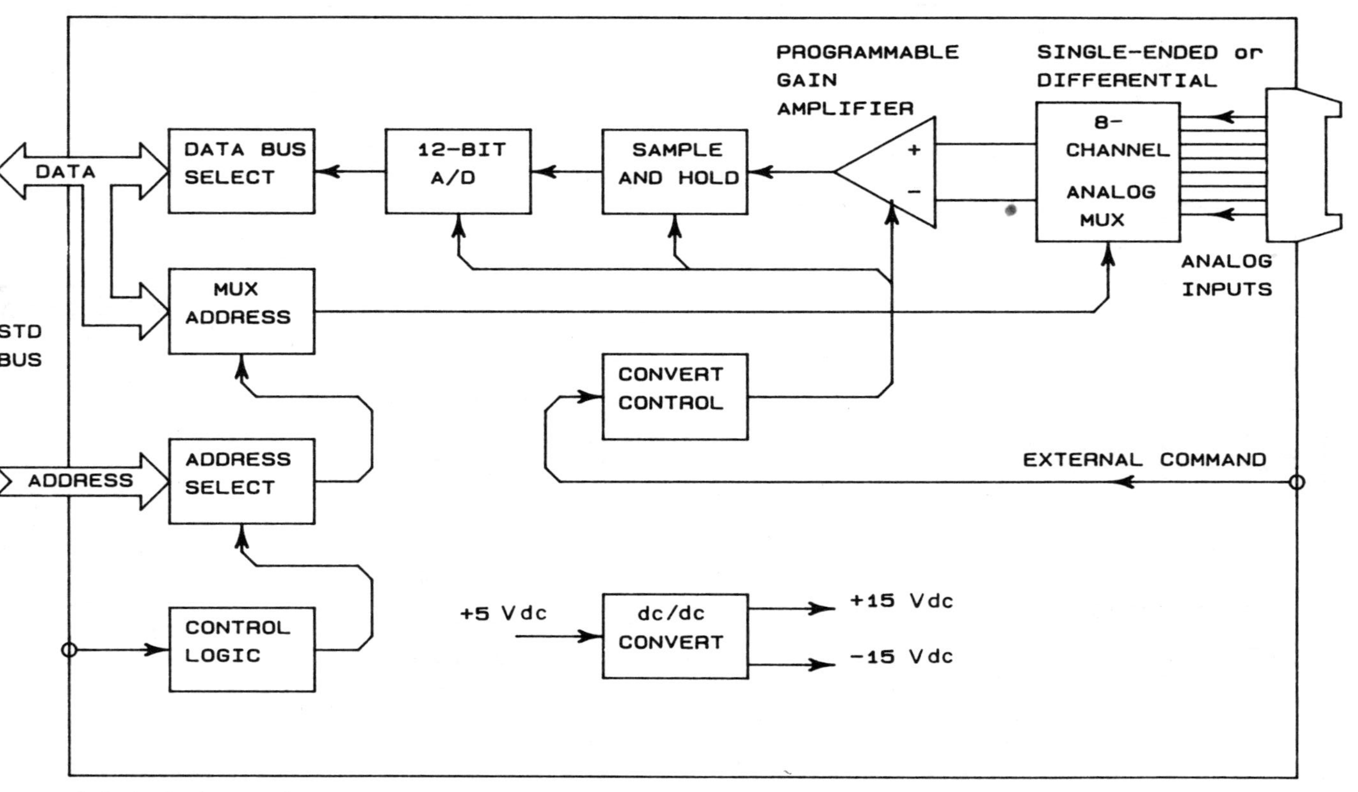

FIGURE 8.6 Analog input card.

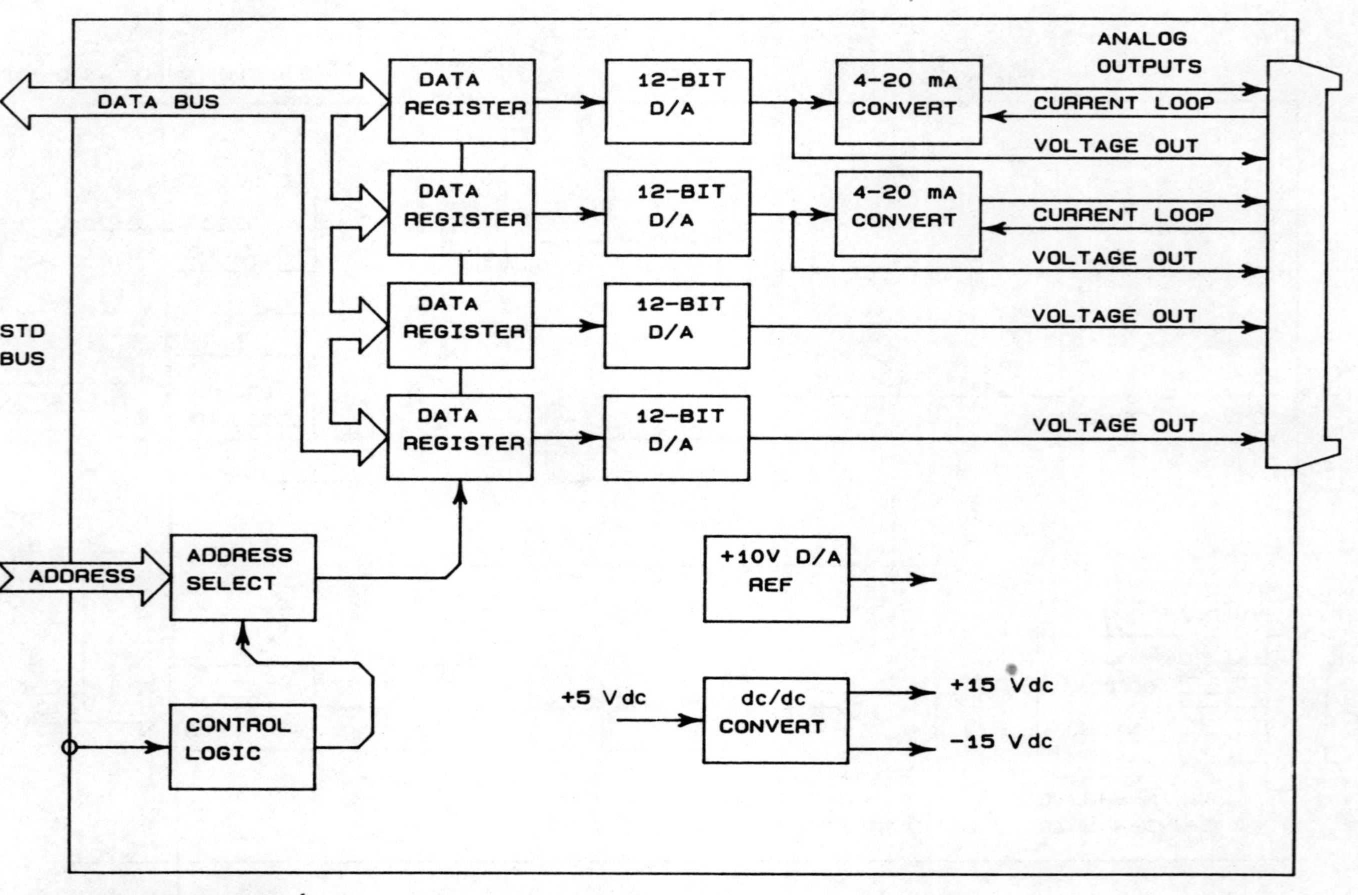

FIGURE 8.7 Analog output card.

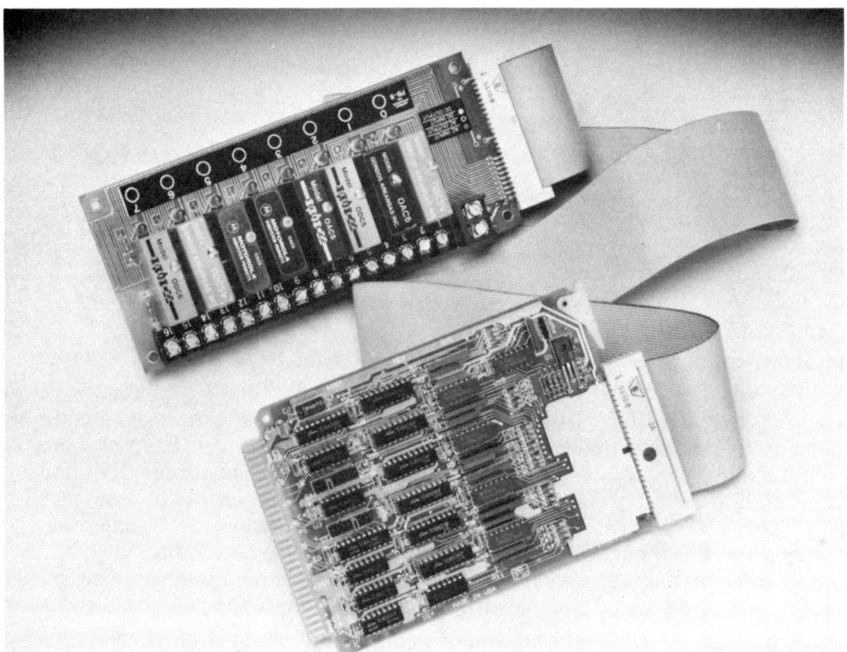

FIGURE 8.8 Remote-rack module interface.

8.7.4 Motion Control Interfaces

Motion control is an important part of industrial control. The STD bus supports motion control with both servo-motor and stepper-motor controllers. Applications range from simple on/off motor control and shaft encoder pulse counters to precise control with closed-loop servo or stepper motors.

On/off control. The common approach for on/off motor control (Fig. 8.9) is to use digital I/O to switch the motor current with a relay device. STD bus cards are available for both local in-rack switching or remote switching. The

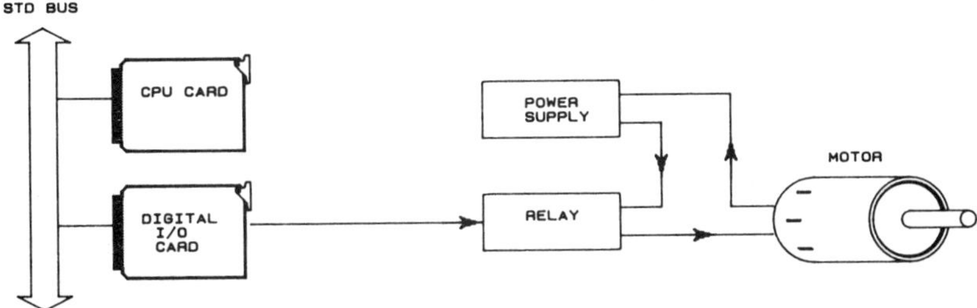

FIGURE 8.9 On/off motor control.

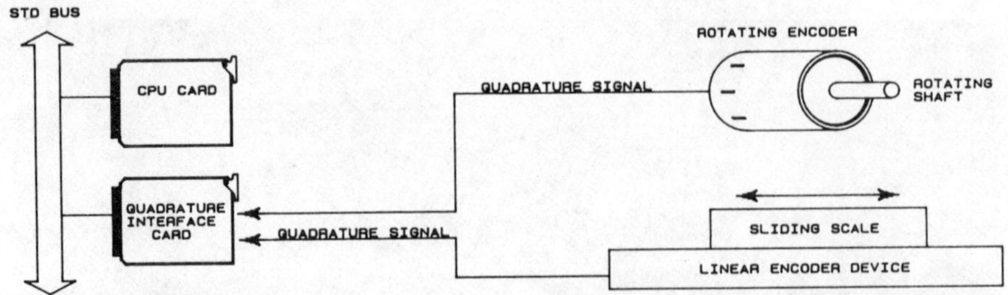

FIGURE 8.10 Motion sensing.

local switching applications include the relay on the STD bus card. Remote switching applications mount the relay close to the motor.

Position determination. It is often necessary in systems with moving components to precisely follow either linear or rotational travel. Examples are rotating shafts of machines, conveyor belts, and *X-Y* table positioning. Motion is generally tracked using quadrature encoders mounted on the moving part (Fig. 8.10). STD bus cards are available to decode the quadrature signals from rotating and linear encoders. These quadrature interface boards provide count values to be read by the processor or compared to user preset values. The resolution of the encoder device determines the precision of the position control.

Stepper-motor control. The control of stepper motors (Fig. 8.11) involves the generation of pulses to drive the motor and control direction. The step and direction pulses are generally amplified using a stepper-motor driver. Stepper-motor performance is optimized by shaped pulses that gradually accelerate to maximum velocity and then gradually decelerate. This pulse profile is referred to as the trapezoidal profile. Stepper motors also have no inherent position feedback; thus it is often important to consider end of travel and home limit switches. STD bus cards are available that generate the trapezoidal profile and provide home and limit switch sensing.

DC servo-motor control. The precise digital control of dc motors is possible using closed-loop servo controllers implemented on STD bus cards (Fig. 8.12). These cards input the motor velocity and position data from an encoder and calculate the motor control signal based on proportional, integral, differential (PID) parameters. The motor control signal is usually passed through a servo

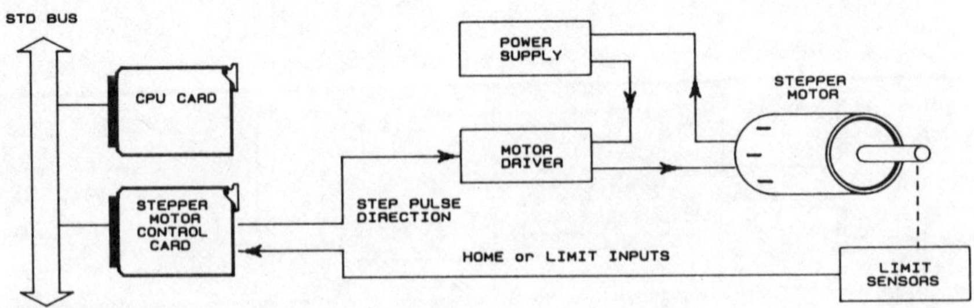

FIGURE 8.11 Stepper-motor control.

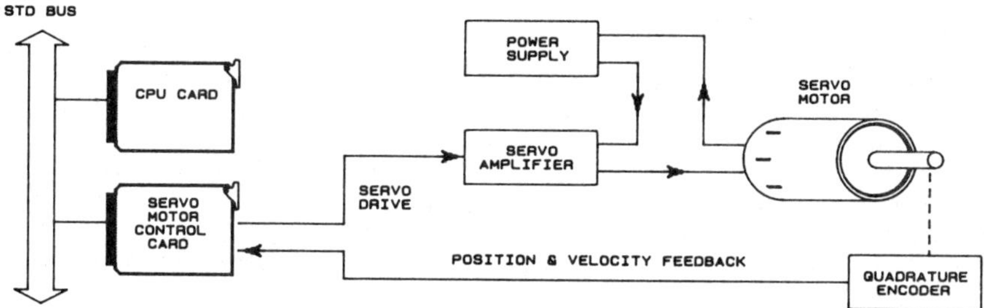

FIGURE 8.12 Servo-motor control.

amplifier to the motor. Servo control integrated circuits ease the implementation of digitally controlled servo motors.

8.7.5 Peripheral Interfaces

Peripheral devices such as keyboards, displays, printers, and disk drives provide the human interface in both the computing environment and the industrial environment. The STD bus offers a full range of peripheral interfaces with operating software such as CP/M or DOS for ease of use. Certain control areas involved with data acquisition can make full use of the data management features of standard operating software. The most common peripheral interface is the RS232 communications channel (Fig. 8.13). Many STD bus processor cards provide an RS232 channel packaged on-card to provide a communication channel for a terminal or PC. Other popular on-card peripherals are counter-timers and interrupt controllers. Packaging peripherals on-card with the processor and memory results in a single-board computer.

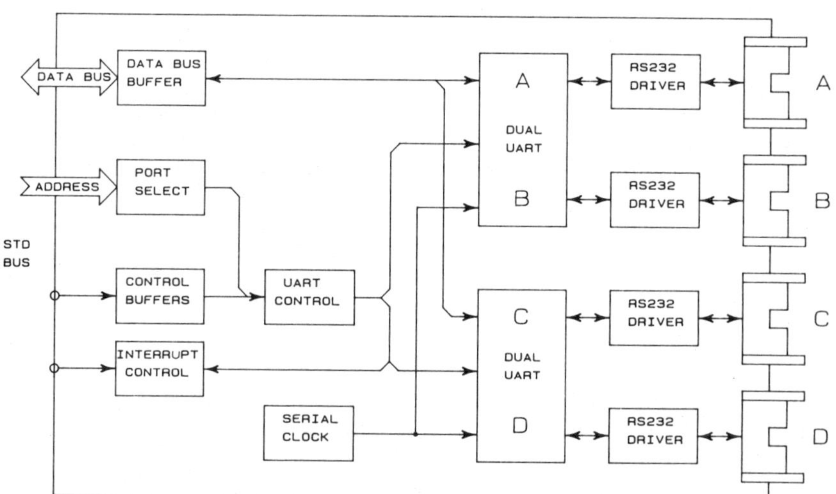

FIGURE 8.13 QUAD RS232 UART peripheral interface.

8.7.6 Instrumentation Interfaces

Instrumentation is an important aspect of the control environment especially in the field of test and measurement. The STD bus provides both in-rack instruments and remote instrument interfacing.

In-rack instruments consist of instruments and instrument functions, such as waveform generators, programmable power sources, and analog metering designed on STD bus boards. These cards operate directly on the STD bus and cable locally to the instrumented functions. In-rack instrumentation provides a low-cost solution for embedded applications.

Remote-instrumentation interfacing is used typically where a number of rack-mounted instruments are needed to monitor and control a process. Remote-instrument interfacing on the STD bus is accomplished using the industry standard IEEE 488 GPIB interface. In such applications STD bus GPIB solutions might serve both as a controller for other GPIB devices as well as a talker-listener implemented inside an STD bus–based instrument. With many STD bus manufacturers supplying IBM PC–compatible software and hardware solutions on the STD bus, existing PC instrument control applications can be run on the STD bus without change, thereby saving large amounts of programming time.

8.7.7 SBX Interface

The IEEE 959 SBX I/O expansion bus standard has been implemented on the STD bus to allow the use of the multimodule plug-in units available from many sources. SBX implementations on the STD bus provide local bus expansion on single-board applications. The single-board computers generally consist of a processor and local memory with on-board peripheral functions and a local SBX interface for pluggable I/O.

8.7.8 Smart I/O or Intelligent Controllers

It is quite common in microprocessor systems to use multiple processors to solve a problem. Complex tasks or very mundane, but time-consuming, I/O tasks are often assigned to separate processors. The modular characteristics of the STD bus make it well suited for intelligent controllers. These cards are generally specialized functions dedicated to a predictable I/O-intensive task. Examples of intelligent controller applications are stepper-motor controllers or network controllers. In the stepper-motor application the processor controls the timing intervals for stepping the motor, including the turn-on and turn-off characteristics, and manages the command and control interface to the bus. In networking the processor manages the complex communications protocol. An advantage of intelligent peripherals is that the software for these subtasks is often prewritten and usually independent of the application.

8.8 MULTIPROCESSING ON THE STD BUS

Intelligent peripherals are a form of multiprocessing limited to performing predefined dedicated tasks. A more powerful form of multiprocessing also exists on the STD bus as a solution for real-time processing. Real-time control is a common requirement on the STD bus because of its use in industrial applications.

Real-time response can be achieved either by multitasking software on a single processor or by using multiple processors that handle one or more tasks between them. The single-processor approach has a hardware cost advantage but is limited in the tasks it can handle by its serial architecture. As the number of tasks goes up, so does the complexity of the software, while the real-time activity of each task is reduced.

The multiple-processor approach has the advantage of speed. A given task can be broken into smaller tasks that are executed in parallel by the individual processors. Alternatively, separate tasks can be assigned permanently to each of the processors. Another advantage is the modularity and expandability of multiple-processor schemes. The distribution of tasks simplifies the writing of software for each processor and enables additional tasks (and processors) to be added after the original design process is complete.

There are essentially two types of multiple-processor schemes implemented on the STD bus: master-slave and multimaster.

8.8.1 Master-Slave Systems

Master-slave systems (Fig. 8.14) consist of a master CPU card and one or more slave CPU cards. The master CPU controls the STD bus and the resources on it, including the slave processors. The slaves operate exclusively with local on-board memory and I/O, running programs to perform some dedicated task. Data and control parameters are passed between master and slave on the STD bus, either through I/O ports or common memory. Dual-port memory, DMA, or local bus arbitration is provided on these types of boards for this purpose.

If common memory is used to communicate between master and slave, it may be mapped in one of two ways. Each slave may be mapped to a different memory address for the master, or all slaves may be mapped to the same address using an output port for bank selection. The linear mapping scheme gives quicker access to the master, but each slave consumes memory address space in the master map. The bank mapping scheme provides a fixed memory map for the master but requires port bank selection.

8.8.2 Multimaster Systems

Multimaster systems (Fig. 8.15) consist of multiple CPU cards, each capable of controlling the bus. Each CPU operates with local on-board memory and has the ability to access the STD bus for global memory and I/O. Any multimaster CPU may also have local on-board I/O. Data and control parameters are passed between masters through global memory on the bus. A full bus arbitration and priority scheme is implemented to allow this. The bus arbitration is performed by the hardware and does not affect the software.

Multimaster arbitration. Arbitration is handled by interface logic that uses normal STD bus control signals. Any master using the bus pulls the BUSAK* signal low to indicate that the bus is busy. Any master needing the bus pulls the BUSRQ* signal low to request access to the bus. A master always relinquishes control of the bus at the end of any machine cycle when another master

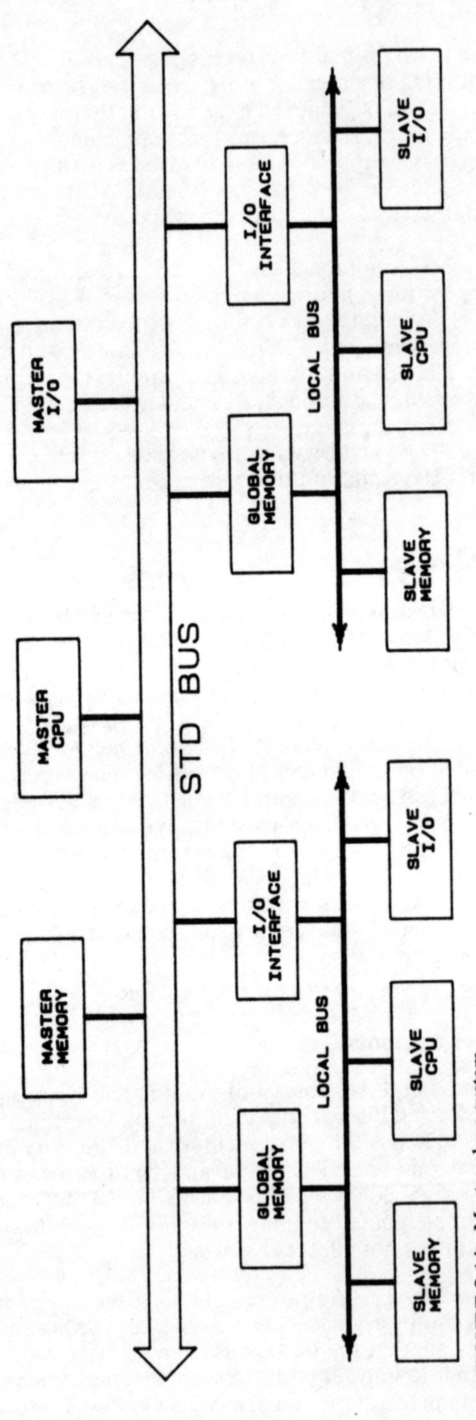

FIGURE 8.14 Master-slave system.

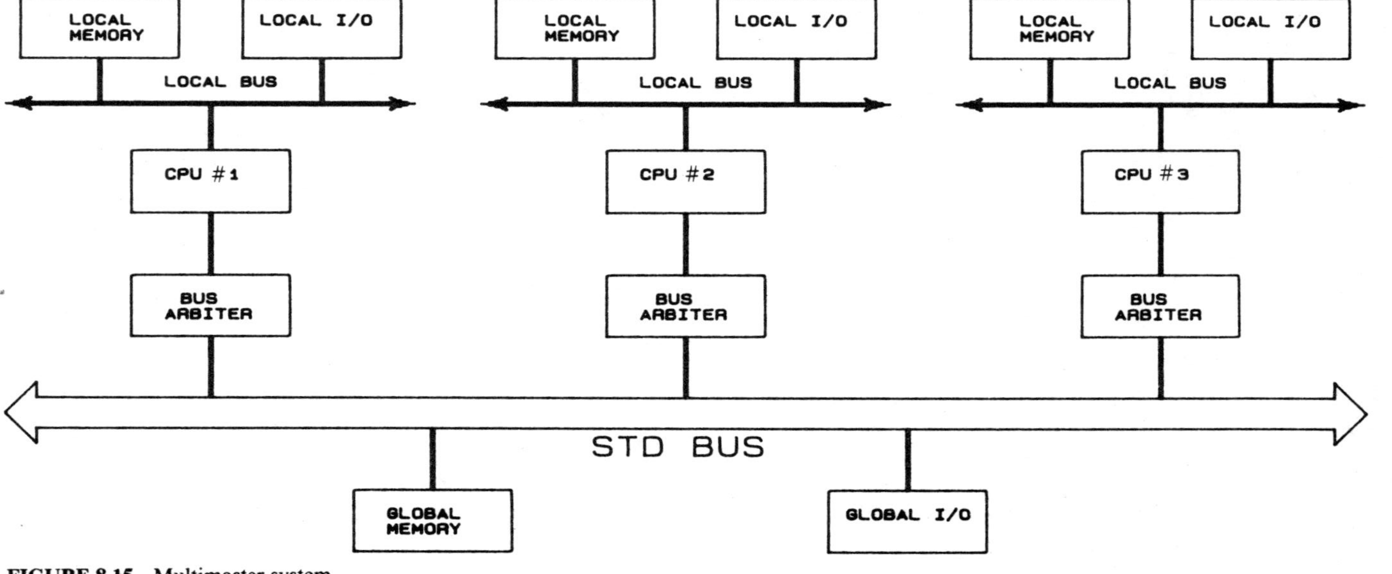

FIGURE 8.15 Multimaster system.

is requesting the bus. The bus priority chain (PCI, PCO) resolves simultaneous bus requests from more than one master. All arbiters are synchronized by a common clock signal on CNTRL*. The synchronized arbitration avoids metastability problems and allows a master to make continuous use of the bus without arbitration if no other master is requesting the bus.

Real-time recovery from certain types of system failure is possible in multimaster schemes in which each processor has access to the bus. Since each processor has access to all bus resources, any processor can take over the bus-related tasks of another.

8.9 DISTRIBUTED PROCESSING ON THE STD BUS

Distributed processing is a form of multiprocessing where multiple systems involved in a common task are located remotely from each other. Instead of communicating on a common backplane bus, distributed systems use some form of networked communication. Networking implies a communication implementation involving both hardware and multilevel software.

8.9.1 Networking on the STD Bus

The modularity and low cost of the STD bus makes it ideal for distributed systems. The STD bus is currently networked in factory environments for data acquisition, production, and machine control. There are many networking systems and protocols available in industry. Two of these networking environments, Bitbus and ARCNET, both suited for industrial control applications, are currently available on the STD bus.

8.9.1.1 Bitbus. Bitbus (Fig. 8.16) is a low-end networking scheme designed by Intel specifically for distributed control. In a fully networked factory Bitbus would be used as a subnetwork foundation for higher-performance networks such as Ethernet or ARCNET. Bitbus is built on the RS485 electrical standard with a synchronous data link communication (SDLC) line protocol implemented using the 8044 microprocessor chip. This network operates in a master-slave configuration and consists of a single master and up to 250 slave nodes. Bitbus offers performance to 2.4 Mbit/s for links up to 30 m. The speed of this network is dependent on the length of the cable. A 300-m link can accomplish 375 kbit/s while a 1200-m link is limited to 62 kbit/s. A Bitbus network can extend over 13 km using repeaters.

Bitbus software is implemented on the 8044 microprocessor for the master node and each slave node. This software includes a multitasking executive, task support for local I/O and memory, and implementation of the line protocol.

The master program communicates directly with the slave nodes using calls to linkable modules. Slave nodes autonomously control local I/O, executing a user-generated application code. At any time, the master may access the shared memory of the slave node to read or modify operating parameters or to down-load a new program. The master can also directly access I/O on the slave node to provide immediate real-time response.

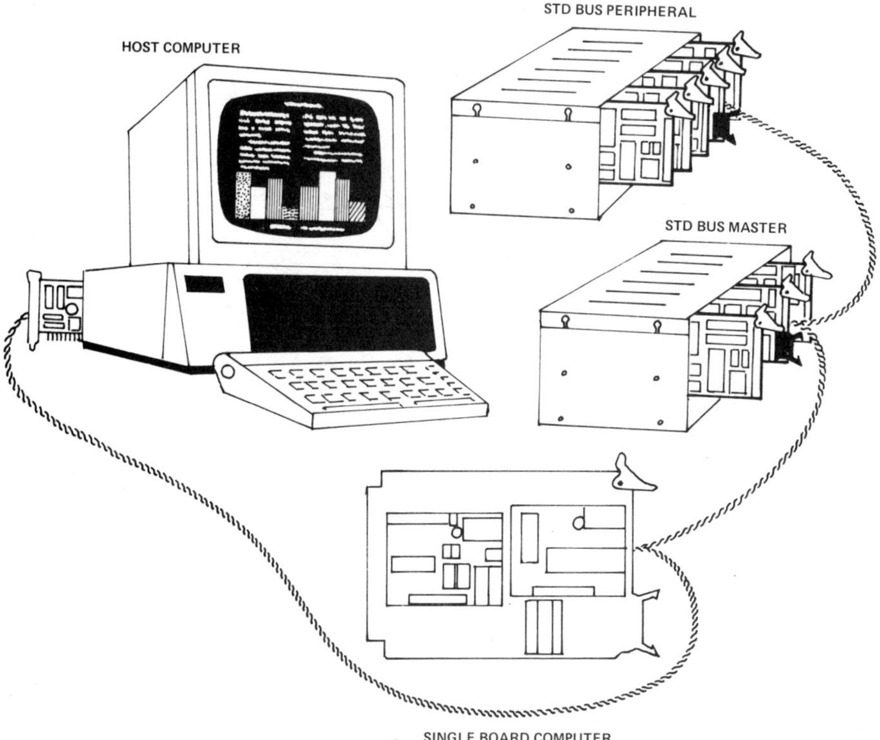

FIGURE 8.16 Bitbus system.

In STD bus implementations each card on the network contains a Bitbus controller. The STD bus card may contain both a host microprocessor controlling the STD bus and an 8044 processor controlling the Bitbus, or the 8044 may be controlling both the STD bus and the Bitbus.

8.9.1.2 ARCNET. ARCNET (Fig. 8.17) is a high-performance networking standard with characteristics that also suit the industrial control environment. Relative to other high-performance networks, ARCNET is inexpensive and easy to install and modify. The token-bus implementation allows nodes to be installed or removed on an active system without disrupting operation. It operates at up to 2.5 mbit/s and the network interface can be twisted pair wire, coaxial cable, or fiber optics. ARCNET uses a deterministic token-passing protocol and small message packets. *Deterministic* means that the user can predict precisely the expected delays for any operation at a given workload. The ability to move small messages quickly suits the real-time response needs of the control environment. These characteristics have proven to be desirable in the networked control environments.

An advantage of high-performance networks is that software from multiple sources has been written to create standard network operating systems. This software extends file-based operating systems over the network so that files can essen-

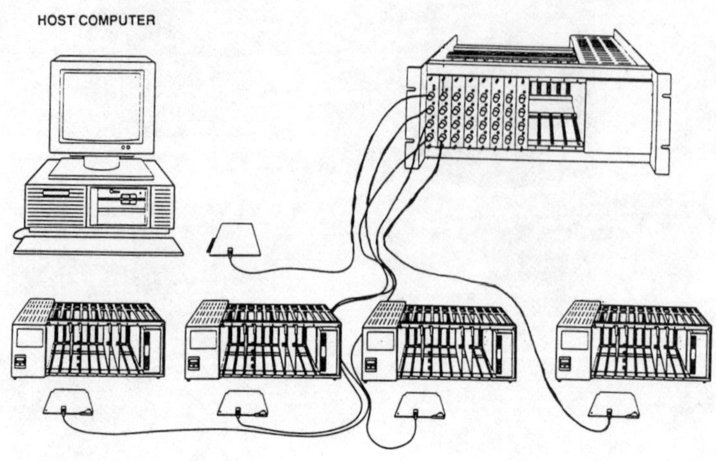

FIGURE 8.17 ARCNET system.

tially be shared between machines. These file-shared solutions are easily adapted to the control environment. Applications involving data acquisition and machine programming are natural for these solutions.

There are two types of network operating systems: shared resource and peer-to-peer. In a shared-resource network, files reside on a central file server that handles the distribution of files between nodes. In a peer-to-peer network, files reside at the various nodes and each node is involved in the file distribution. Shared-resource networks provide the highest performance with more easily managed data integrity. Peer-to-peer networks provide a lower-cost solution and lower performance.

STD bus ARCNET cards include node cards with the necessary drivers to use standard network operating software. Also available are in-rack STD bus repeater hub cards for network expansion. These cards are available with twisted pair, coax, or fiber optic network interfaces.

8.10 SYSTEMS AND OPERATING SOFTWARE

8.10.1 Device Drivers

Device drivers are needed in most applications and thus were one of the first software products to appear for the STD bus. Many STD bus functions are supported by device drivers. The more sophisticated devices such as disk, video, and networking have STD bus support built into the operating level software. Device-driver software is generally available from individual manufacturers. The

STDMG is standardizing a public domain device-driver library with a simple format.

8.10.2 ROM-Based Operating Software

Most simple STD bus implementations are intended to execute from firmware, making them more economical in terms of required memory as well as being restartable with the assurance that the program will always be intact. ROM-based systems for the STD bus can be built using almost any language if the tools produce ROMable code. Real-time operating system kernels such as VRTX, AMX or MTOS have been designed to operate from ROM and are commonly included in these "fixed" applications.

8.10.3 Multitasking Software

Multitasking operating software provides an operating environment that allows the user to add tasks with apparent ease. This software is often used to achieve simulated real-time operation. Since real-time control is essential in many industrial applications, multitasking is often sought as a solution. Task scheduling on a single processor is suitable for low-cost applications where the speed requirements of the real-time operation are not too high. Adding tasks to the multitasking system reduces the real-time response of all tasks.

Real-time multitasking implementations on the STD bus run from very sophisticated operating systems such as IRMX86 down to simple BASIC language implementations. Embedded STD bus control systems use small, real-time, multitasking kernels such as VRTX, AMX and MTOS.

8.10.4 Operating Systems

Just as the STD bus supports a variety of processor types, it also supports a variety of operating systems for those processors. The predominant operating systems are OS-9 for the 6800 and 68000 microprocessors, CP/M for the 8085 and Z80 processor family, and PC DOS and MS-DOS for the 8088 family of processors.

8.10.4.1 CP/M Operating Systems. 8085 and Z80 STD bus systems use the popular CP/M operating system primarily for the software development environment. Development systems are built using STD bus hardware, and the software tools and languages are used to create the embedded applications.

8.10.4.2 PC DOS and MS-DOS Operating Systems. The standard for operating system software shifted to DOS with the IBM PC and the 8088 family of processors. The similarity of the IBM PC and STD bus structure allows software and hardware compatibility. STD bus manufacturers have created STD DOS software that allows full use of the existing IBM PC software base. DOS brings to the STD bus the advantages of its familiarity, software availability, and its universal acceptance. The STD bus provides extensive I/O with the ruggedness and reliability needed in the control environment.

DOS is used extensively in the STD bus environment for software develop-

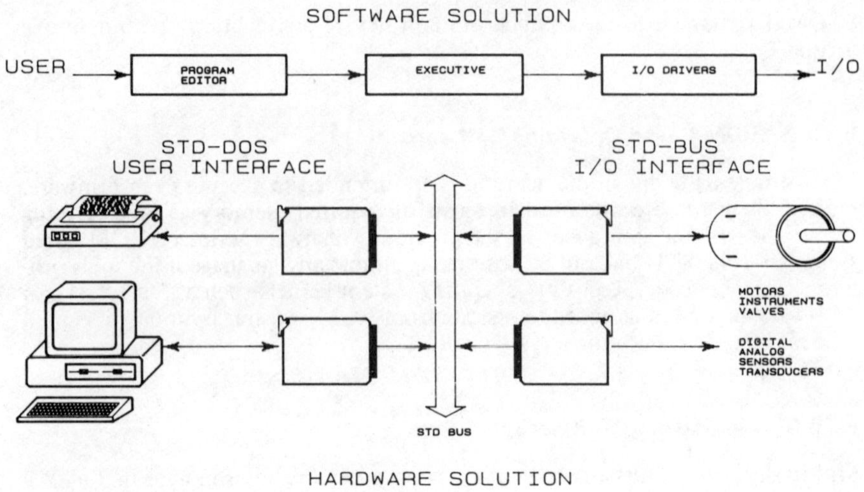

SOFTWARE SOLUTION

USER → PROGRAM EDITOR → EXECUTIVE → I/O DRIVERS → I/O

STD-DOS USER INTERFACE

STD-BUS I/O INTERFACE

MOTORS INSTRUMENTS VALVES

DIGITAL ANALOG SENSORS TRANSDUCERS

STD BUS

HARDWARE SOLUTION

FIGURE 8.18 Industrial control software solution.

ment, but it is also being embedded in the target applications. Many applications embed DOS in the target system to take advantage of the standardized user interface and its file and networking standards. Programs for file management and networking port directly to the STD DOS systems.

8.10.5 Software Solutions

Total solutions in a computing environment consist of applications software running on standard hardware with standard operating systems (Fig. 8.18). Software solutions in the industrial environment involve specialized hardware and specialized operating systems. These operating systems are usually referred to as *executives.* The executive interfaces on one end to a configurable I/O subsystem and at the other end to some form of editor or easily programmable human interface. The executive processes the "program" from the editor and translates it to the I/O system to cause some control operation. As an example, the control industry has used programmable logic controllers for years. These specialized computers exist with their user-oriented "ladder" language. Other easily used graphic languages are currently evolving.

The STD bus provides an ideal system for these I/O software solutions.

8.11 STD BUS LOGICAL SPECIFICATIONS

8.11.1 Bus Pin Assignments

The bus pin layout is organized into five functional groups:

Logic power bus	Pins 1–6
Data bus	Pins 7–14
Address bus	Pins 15–30
Control bus	Pins 31–52
Auxiliary power bus	Pins 53–56

The organization and pinouts are shown in Table 8.1. Signal flow direction is referenced to the current master.

TABLE 8.1 Bus Connector Pin Assignment

	Component side			Circuit side		
	Pin	Signal name	Description	Pin	Signal name	Description
Logic power bus	1	V_{cc}	Logic power	2	V_{cc}	Logic power
	3	GND	Logic ground	4	GND	Logic ground
	5	V_{bat}	Battery power	6	V_{bb}	Logic bias
Data bus	7	D3/A19	Data bus and address extension	8	D7/A23	Data bus and address extension
	9	D2/A18		10	D6/A22	
	11	D1/A17		12	D5/A21	
	13	D0/A16		14	D4/A20	
Address bus	15	A7	Address bus	16	A15/D15	Address bus and data bus extension
	17	A6		18	A14/D14	
	19	A5		20	A13/D13	
	21	A4		22	A12/D12	
	23	A3		24	A11/D11	
	25	A2		26	A10/D10	
	27	A1		28	A9/D9	
	29	A0		30	A8/D8	
Control bus	31	WR*	Write mem or I/O	32	RD*	Read memory or I/O
	33	IORQ*	I/O address select	34	MEMRQ*	Memory address select
	35	IOEXP	I/O expansion	36	MEMEX	Memory expansion
	37	REFRESH*	Refresh timing	38	MCSYNC*	Machine cycle sync
	39	STATUS 1*	CPU status	40	STATUS 0*	CPU status
	41	BUSAK*	Bus acknowledge	42	BUSRQ*	Bus request
	43	INTAK*	Interrupt acknowledge	44	INTRQ*	Interrupt request
	45	WAITRQ*	Wait request	46	NMIRQ*	Nonmaskable interrupt
	47	SYSRESET*	System reset	48	PBRESET*	Push-button reset
	49	CLOCK*	Processor clock	50	CNTRL*	Auxiliary clock timing
	51	PCO	Priority chain out	52	PCI	Priority chain in
Power bus	53	AUX GND	Auxiliary ground	54	AUX GND	Auxiliary ground
	55	AUX +V	Auxiliary positive (+12 V dc)	56	AUX −V	Auxiliary negative (−12 V dc)

*Low-level active indicator.

8.11.2 Signal Descriptions

8.11.2.1 Power Buses (Pins 1–6 and 53–56). The dual power buses accommodate logic and analog power distribution. As many as five separate power supplies can be used with two separate ground returns. Separate grounds allow analog circuits to be isolated from the digital ground. The practice is to connect all grounds at a single point, usually at the power source.

8.11.2.2 Data Bus (Pins 7–14). (There are eight lines, which are bidirectional, three-state and active-high.) The data bus direction is controlled by the current master and is affected by the signals read (RD*), write (WR*), and interrupt acknowledge (INTAK*).

All cards release the data bus to a high-impedance state when not in use. The current master releases the data bus in response to bus request (BUSRQ*) input from another master, as in DMA transfers or multimaster systems.

The data bus is extended to 16 bits by multiplexing eight additional data signals on the upper address lines. The data bus lines may also be multiplexed for address space expansion to give a total of 24 address signals. The pin assignment for address and data signal expansion is defined in Table 8.1.

8.11.2.3 Address Bus (Pins 15–30). (There are 16 lines, which are three-state, active-high.) The address originates at the current master. The current master releases the address bus in response to a bus request (BUSRQ*) input from another master.

The address bus is extended to 24 bits by multiplexing eight additional address bits on the data bus. The pin assignment for address expansion is shown in Table 8.1.

The address bus provides 16 address lines for decoding by either memory or I/O. Memory request (MEMRQ*) and I/O request (IORQ*) control lines distinguish between the two operations.

8.11.2.4 Control Bus (Pins 31–52). The control bus signal lines are grouped into five areas: memory and I/O control, peripheral timing, clock and reset, interrupt and bus control, and serial priority chain.

8.11.3 Memory and I/O Control Lines

Six signals are provided for fundamental memory and I/O operations. Simple applications may only require these six control signals. All cards support the memory and I/O control lines.

Pin 31—WR:* Write to memory or output (three-state, active-low). WR* originates from the current master and indicates that the bus data will be written to the addressed memory or output device. The selected device uses this signal to write the data to the memory or output port.

Pin 32—RD:* Read from memory or input (three-state, active-low). RD* originates from the current master and indicates that data will be read from memory or from an input device. The selected input device or memory uses this signal to gate data to the data bus.

Pin 33—IORQ:* I/O address select (three-state, active-low). IORQ* originates from the current master and indicates an I/O read or write operation. IORQ* may also be used to control processor-dependent peripheral devices.

Pin 34—MEMRQ:* Memory address select (three-state, active-low). MEMRQ* originates from the current master and indicates a memory read or write operation. MEMRQ* may also be used to control processor dependent peripheral devices.

Pin 35—IOEXP: I/O expansion (three-state, high expand, low enable). IOEXP originates from the current master and is used to expand or enable I/O port addressing. An active-low enables the primary (8-bit) I/O address space. All I/O cards decode IOEXP.

Pin 36—MEMEX: Memory expansion (three-state, high expand, low enable). MEMEX originates from the current master and shall be used to expand or enable memory addressing. An active-low enables the primary (64K) memory address space. All memory cards decode MEMEX. MEMEX may be used to allow memory overlay such as in bootstrap operations. A control card may switch out the primary memory to make use of an alternate memory.

8.11.4 Peripheral Timing Control Lines

Four bus control lines are provided for peripheral timing. These lines are defined specifically for each type of microprocessor, so it can serve its own peripheral devices.

Pin 37—REFRESH:* Refresh (three-state, active-low). REFRESH* may originate from the current master or from a separate control card and is used to refresh dynamic memory. The nature and timing of the signal may be a function of the memory device or the processor. In systems without refresh, this signal can be any specialized memory control signal. Systems with static memory may disregard REFRESH*.

Pin 38—MCSYNC:* Machine cycle sync (three-state, active-low). MCSYNC* originates from the current master to define the beginning of the machine cycle. This signal should occur once during each machine cycle of the processor. The exact nature and timing of this signal are processor dependent. MCSYNC* keeps peripheral devices synchronized with the processor operation. It can also be used for controlling a bus analyzer, which can analyze bus operations cycle-by-cycle. MCSYNC* is used to demultiplex extended addressing from the data bus.

Pin 39—STATUS 1:* Status control line 1 (three-state, active-low). STATUS 1* originates from the current master to provide secondary timing for peripheral devices. When available, STATUS 1* is used as a signal for identifying instruction fetch.

Pin 40—STATUS 0:* Status control line 0 (three-state, active-low).

8.11.5 Interrupt and Bus Control Lines

Interrupt and bus control lines allow the implementation of bus control schemes such as direct memory access, multiprocessing, single stepping, slow memory, power-fail restart, and a variety of interrupt methods. Priority for multiple interrupts or bus requests can be supported by either serial or parallel priority schemes.

Pin 41—BUSAK:* Bus acknowledge (active-low). BUSAK* originates from any master to indicate that the bus is available for use. The current master responds to a bus request (BUSRQ*) by releasing the bus and asserting a bus acknowledge (BUSAK*). BUSAK* should occur at the completion of the current machine cycle. This signal can be combined with a priority signal if multiple controllers need bus access.

Pin 42—BUSRQ:* Bus request (active-low, open collector-drain). BUSRQ* originates from a requesting master and causes the current master to suspend operations on the bus by releasing all three-state bus lines. The bus is released when the current machine cycle is completed. BUSRQ* is used in applications requiring DMA. This signal can be an input or output, or it can be bidirectional, depending on the supporting hardware.

Pin 43—INTAK:* Interrupt acknowledge (active-low). INTAK* originates from the current master to indicate to the interrupting device that it is ready to respond to the interrupt. For vectored interrupts, the interrupting device places the vector address on the data bus during INTAK*. This signal can be combined with a priority signal if multiple controllers need access to the master.

Pin 44—INTRQ:* Interrupt request (active-low, open collector-drain). INTRQ* originates from any slave function to interrupt the processor on the host master. It should be masked and ignored by the processor unless it is deliberately enabled by software. If the processor accepts the interrupt, it acknowledges by asserting INTAK*. Other actions depend on the specific type of processor, the interrupt handling software, and the hardware support of the interrupt mechanism.

Pin 45—WAITRQ:* Wait request (active-low, open collector-drain). WAITRQ* may originate from any master or slave and causes the current master to suspend operations as long as it remains low. The current master should hold in a state that maintains a valid address on the bus. WAITRQ* can be used to insert wait states in the processor cycle. Examples of its use include slow-memory and I/O operations and single stepping.

Pin 46—NMIRQ:* Nonmaskable interrupt (active-low, open collector-drain). NMIRQ* may originate from any master or slave and is used as an interrupt input of the highest priority to the permanent master. It should be used for critical processor signaling such as power-fail indication.

8.11.6 Clock and Reset Lines

Clock and reset lines provide the bus with basic clock timing and reset capability.

Pin 47—SYSRESET:* System reset (active-low, open collector-drain). SYSRESET* originates from any system reset circuit, which may be triggered by power-on detection or by the push-button reset. All cards with circuits requiring initialization should use SYSRESET*.

Pin 48—PBRESET:* Push-button reset (active-low, open collector-drain). PBRESET* may originate from any card and is used as an input to the system reset circuit.

Pin 49—CLOCK:* Clock from the permanent master. CLOCK* originates from the permanent master and is a buffered processor clock signal for use in system synchronization or as a general clock source.

Pin 50—CNTRL:* Control. CNTRL* may originate from any card for special clock timing. It may be a multiple of the processor clock signal, a real-time clock signal, or an external input to the processor.

8.11.7 Priority Chain Lines

Priority chain lines are provided for serial priority of interrupt or bus requests. Two bus pins PCI and PCO are allocated to the priority chain. Logic is required on each card that participates in the priority chain. Cards not needing priority simply jumper PCI and PCO on the card.

Pin 51—PCO: Priority chain out (active-high). PCO originates from every card as a signal sent to the PCI input of the next lower card in priority. A card that needs priority holds PCO low.

Pin 52—PCI: Priority chain in (active-high). PCI originates directly from the PCO of the next highest card in priority. A high level on PCI gives priority to the card sensing the PCI input. The PCI inputs have a pull-up resistance to +5 V on all cards participating in the chain to satisfy the highest-priority position.

8.12 ELECTRICAL SPECIFICATIONS

The STD bus has defined electrical specifications for both TTL and CMOS logic. Industry provides two types of CMOS: full-range CMOS and TTL-range-compatible CMOS. The CMOS specifications that follow define the full-range CMOS. TTL-compatible CMOS must conform to the TTL electrical specifications.

8.12.1 CMOS Logic Signal Characteristics

The CMOS bus is designed for compatibility with industry standard high-speed CMOS logic levels. All logic signals shall meet the voltage requirements given in Table 8.2.

TABLE 8.2 CMOS Logic Signal Voltage Ratings

CMOS parameter*	Test conditions	Minimum	Maximum
V_{OH}	V_{CC} = MIN, I_{OH} = −6 mA	3.76 V	
V_{OL}	V_{CC} = MIN, I_{OL} = +6 mA		0.37 V
V_{IH}	V_{CC} = MIN	3.15 V	
V_{IL}	V_{CC} = MIN		0.9 V

*V_{OH} = high-state output voltage; V_{OL} = low-state output voltage; V_{IH} = high-state input voltage; V_{IL} = low-state input voltage

TABLE 8.3 TTL Logic Signal Voltage Ratings

TTL parameter*	Test conditions	Minimum	Maximum
V_{OH}	V_{CC} = MIN, $I_{OH} = -3$ mA	2.4 V	
V_{OL}	V_{CC} = MIN, I_{OL} = 24 mA		0.5 V
V_{IH}		2.0 V	
V_{IL}			0.8 V

*V_{OH} = high-state output voltage; V_{OL} = low-state output voltage; V_{IH} = high-state input voltage; V_{IL} = low-state input voltage.

Each card should present only one load per bus signal. Bussed signal drivers should meet the current requirements given in Table 8.2. The capacitive input loading shall be 20 pF maximum.

Open-drain signals shall have a 1-kΩ pull-up resistor. The pull-up resistors should be located on the permanent master.

8.12.2 TTL Logic Signal Characteristics

The TTL bus is designed for compatibility with industry standard TTL logic levels. All logic signals shall meet the voltage requirements given in Table 8.3. TTL-compatible CMOS cards should conform to these specifications.

Each card should present only one load per bus signal. Bussed signal drivers should meet the current requirements given in Table 8.3.

Open-collector signals shall have a 470-Ω pull-up resistor. The pull-up resistors should be located on the permanent master.

TABLE 8.4 Circuit Board Parameters

Parameter	Minimum	Typical	Maximum
Conductor thickness	0.0028 in		
Conductor width, logic trace	0.012 in		
Conductor width, power trace	0.050 in		
Conductor spacing	0.013 in		
DC resistance, logic trace		20 mΩ/in	
DC resistance, power trace		5 mΩ/in	
Inductance, logic trace		0.028 μH/in	
Characteristic impedance, logic trace		100 Ω	
Signal propagation delay		2 ns/ft	
Contact current rating			3 A
Contact resistance, at rated current			8 mΩ
Capacitance per contact pair		0.3 pF	1 pF
Contact operating voltage		600 V ac	
Bus capacitance, logic trace to ground		3 pF/in	
Bus capacitance, logic trace to trace		2 pF/in	

8.12.3 Backplane Terminations

The distributed electrical characteristics of backplanes cause them to perform as transmission lines when operated with fast rise and fall times over long distances. The characteristics are a function of the length and layout of the backplane, the type of connector used, and the number and location of cards inserted into the backplane. These characteristics are generally controlled by terminating the backplane signals. Processors running at slow speeds can operate successfully on short backplanes without terminations. Fast processors and long backplanes require a properly designed and terminated backplane.

8.12.4 Circuit-Board Electrical Characteristics

The operating characteristics of STD bus circuit boards and motherboards can be determined from the parameters given in Table 8.4. These parameters present the worst-case conditions for two-layer circuit boards.

8.13 MECHANICAL SPECIFICATIONS

Card dimensions. STD bus circuit cards meet the dimensions given in Tables 8.5 and 8.6 and Fig. 8.19. The dimensions exclude the card ejector and I/O interface connections.

Card profile dimensions. Minimum card spacing requires a consideration for component height, lead protrusion, card clearance, and board thickness. Cards designed for minimum spacing shall meet the requirements of Table 8.6. Cards

TABLE 8.5 Card Dimensions

	Inches		Millimeters	
Parameters	Nominal	Tolerance	Nominal	Tolerance
Card length	6.500	±0.025	165.10	±0.64
Card height	4.500	+0.005, −0.025	114.30	+0.13, −0.64
Plated board thickness	0.062	+0.007, −0.003	1.58	+0.18, −0.08
Card spacing	0.500	−0.000	12.70	−0.000

TABLE 8.6 Card Profile Dimensions for Minimum Spacing

	Inches		Millimeters	
Parameter	Maximum	Minimum	Maximum	Minimum
Component height	0.375		9.52	
Component lead protrusion	0.040		1.02	
Adjacent card clearance		0.010		0.25

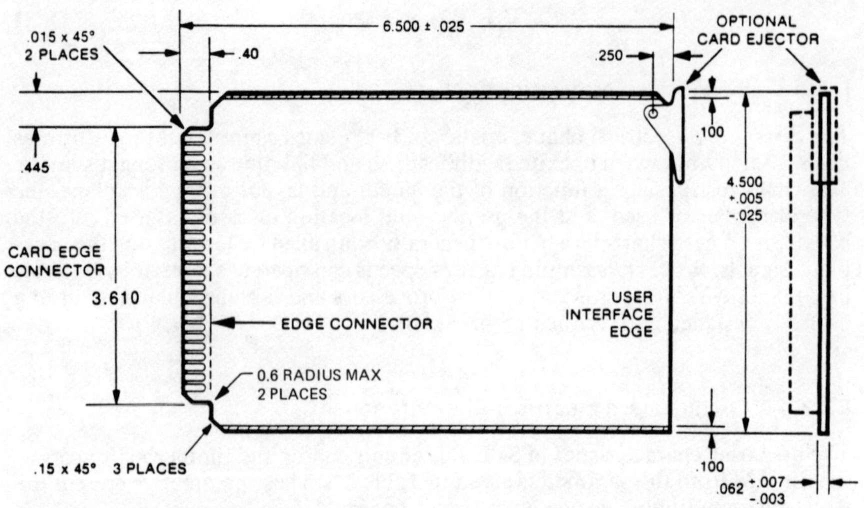

FIGURE 8.19 Bus card outline.

TABLE 8.7 Card-Edge Finger Specifications

Parameter	Minimum	Typical	Maximum
Nickel plating thickness	0.030 in		
Gold plating thickness in area of contact	0.010 in	0.015 in	
Insertion or extraction force per contact pair	2 oz		10 oz
Number of insertions	100		

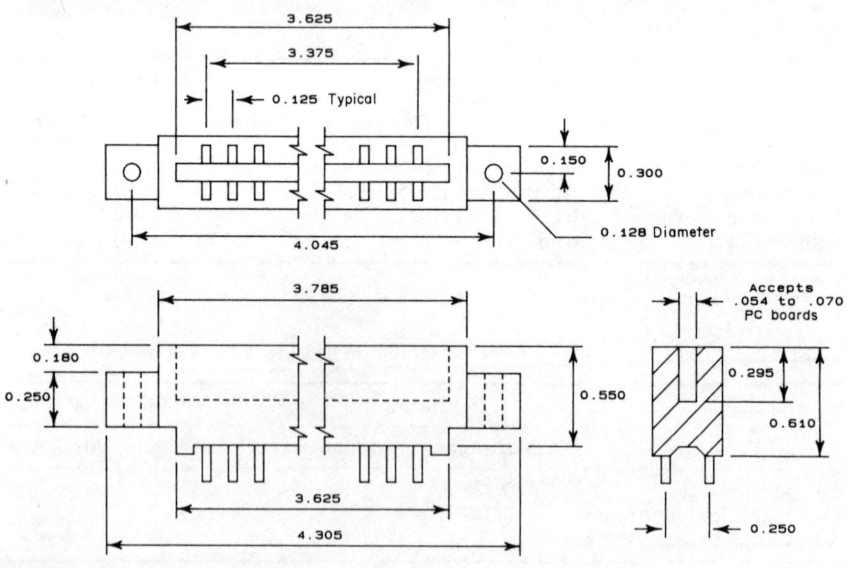

FIGURE 8.20 STD bus backplane connector.

that exceed the minimum spacing should specify the actual spacing requirements.

Card ejector. Each card uses one card ejector mounted on the top right corner.

Card keying. Cards are keyed for polarity to prevent upside-down insertion with a single, offset keyslot located between pins 25 (26) and 27 (28).

Card-edge fingers. Bus connections are made via a printed circuit-board edge connector. The connector contacts are gold plating over nickel plating over the etched copper finger. (See Table 8.7.)

Backplane connector. The bus backplane connector (Figure 8.20) is a 56-pin (dual 28) card-edge connector on 0.125-in (3.18-mm) centers.

LIST OF TRADEMARKS

ARCNET is a trademark of Datapoint Corp.

Bitbus is a trademark of Intel Corp.

CP/M is a trademark of Digital Research Corp.

IBM is a trademark of International Business Machines, as is IBM PC.

Intel is a trademark of Intel Corp.

IRMX 86 is a trademark of Intel Corp.

MS-DOS is a trademark of Microsoft Corp.

VRTX is a trademark of Ready Systems.

CHAPTER 9
THE MULTIBUS II BUS STRUCTURE

John Hyde
Intel Corporation
Hillsboro, Oregon

9.1 INTRODUCTION

Many people equate the phrase *Multibus II* with the parallel system bus defined within the IEEE/ANSI 1296 specification.[1] While this oversimplification is often useful, the failure to appreciate that *it is a contraction* of a more embracing architecture can lead one astray when comparing the Multibus II bus structure with other buses. Comparisons between the Multibus II parallel system bus and other buses are often completed in isolation, without full regard of the framework in which the Multibus II architecture was defined. This chapter rebuilds this framework, describes its hierarchical structure, and details how its features are *required* for multiple-microprocessor designs of today.

9.1.1 Customer Needs Define the New Bus Structure

Intel Corporation had had many years of experience with the Multibus standard before embarking upon the requirements for a next-generation bus structure. The first Multibus standard bus was introduced in 1974 and it was fundamentally a CPU and memory bus. It evolved along with microprocessor technology to become a multiple-master shared-memory bus capable of solving most real-time applications of the 1980s. The silicon trends throughout the 1980s were dramatic, with DRAM densities increasing by a factor of 2 every three years, so projecting exactly what customers would require in the late 1980s through the 1990s was particularly difficult. Intel therefore set up a consortium with 18 of its larger customers and other industry leaders who could see the potential within the single-board computer industry to define the scope and possibilities of what was to be called *Multibus II*.

It was known that the rate of silicon integration would allow a complete computer system including CPU, program memory, data memory, input/output, and bus interface to be fabricated upon a single board. With such a large transistor budget to be spent implementing a single-board computer, how could the technology best be utilized? Self-test and -diagnostics could now be considered—with so much silicon integration on a board it would be prudent to use some of the transistor count to test the remainder of the board. Since board manufacturers are integrating more and more very large-scale integration (VLSI) silicon circuitry onto their boards, the user needs some reassurance that the basic board functionality is intact before they load their value-added code—the user is *demanding* on-board diagnostics for these highly integrated boards. The bus interface itself, not a traditional candidate for high-integration silicon circuitry, could use transistors for added sophistication *if* this sophistication could make the single-board computers easier to use. A trend began to develop: transistors added to improve ease of use rose to the top of the implementation list.

With the increased silicon densities available, semiconductor manufacturers turned their focus on increased-capability peripheral components. Their use on single-board computers served to increase the board's complexity, and the single-board computer user was "rewarded" by having to wade through lengthy reference manuals and innumerable jumper options, often arriving at the final solution only by trial and error. Memory-mapping options, arbitration priorities, interrupt levels, and many other "tunable" parameters contributed to the problem leaving the system engineer confused and amazed. Often the only solution was to locate a board that had already been properly configured and was operating, and then make a duplicate from the jumper list.

Board manufacturers built in numerous options so that their products could be used in the broadest possible spectrum of applications. The number of options offered was not the core of the problem, but *managing* them was. Options allow interrupt routing, memory mapping, EPROM size selection, timing, and other user-installed components. When the jumper count exceeded 200, it no longer made sense to monopolize board real estate, since an inexpensive microcontroller could be used to manage the resources more effectively.

A system bus requires standardized system-wide configuration information to be made accessible to software, opening it to opportunities for centralized control and coordination. Ideally the end-users of these products will be completely unaware of the configuration process. They simply remove the board from its shipping container, install the proper firmware, put it into any free slot in the backplane, and apply power. Things work the first time without any configuration errors.

The consortium therefore placed focus on the system aspects of a single-board computer design. The developing model for a typical system built from these highly capable single-board computers was based upon functionally partitioned subsystems interacting across a standardized communication channel. This precipitated a change in philosophy for the traditional system development from the single-board computer outward to a higher-level system perspective, specified from the top down and bound together by disciplined interfaces.

The consortium quickly reached consensus that no single bus could be used to satisfy all aspects of a design of this type. Too many variables would have to be compromised, so a *multiple bus* structure was defined in a similar fashion to its predecessor, Multibus I (IEEE specification 796). Figure 9.1 shows the four sub-buses defined by the consortium: the iSBX bus was retained for incremental I/O expansion, a local CPU and memory expansion bus was proposed, and two versions of a system bus (serial and parallel) were defined. The concept of a system bus is an important one to grasp—all open buses to date were basically CPU-memory buses with little regard for system aspects. To have an open bus *specifically* designed to be a system bus was a bold step.

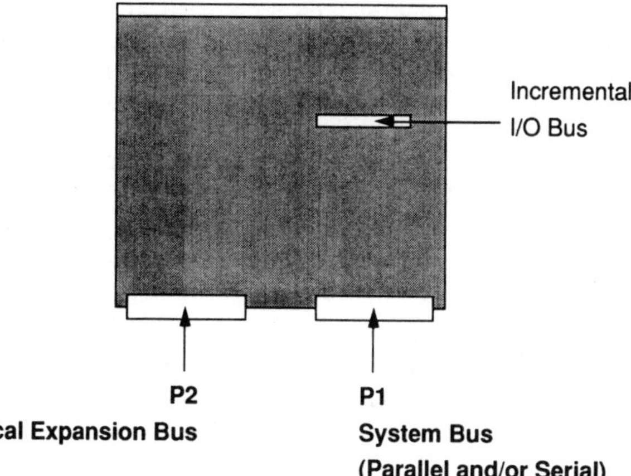

FIGURE 9.1 Since no single bus could solve the defined problem set, a multiple bus solution was proposed.

9.2 FUNCTIONAL PARTITIONING AS A SOLUTION FOR NONOBSOLESCENCE

Before detailing the attributes of each of the defined buses that make up the Multibus II system architecture, it is important to appreciate the model developed for the bus. Figure 9.2 shows a typical collection of systems connected to a local area network or LAN. This type of networked-system solution is very popular with system builders since it boasts a large array of benefits. The solution is functionally partitioned—separate systems are used to tackle different facets of an overall problem. These systems are independent of each other, and decisions made to optimize each of them for their individual task may be made in isolation with respect to the other systems in the network. This degree of freedom gives the system architect an unquestioned advantage when engineering tradeoffs are being made. The choice of hardware, options, and software may be made with the sole goal of solving the small part of the overall problem currently in focus. Each system is typically fitted for its task using specially configured hardware and software, and it is not uncommon to see multiple different operating systems within

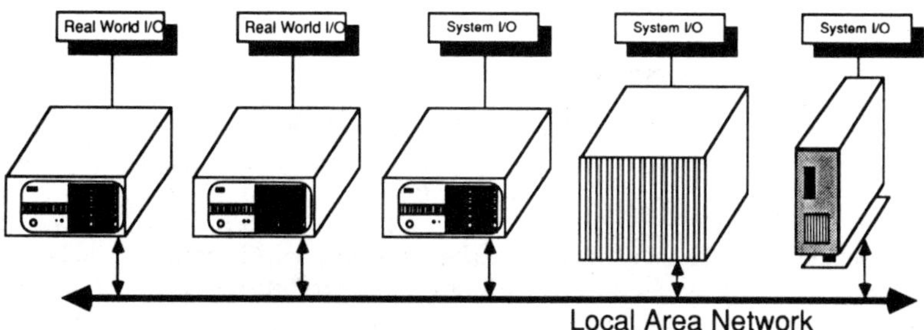

FIGURE 9.2 Multiple diverse systems can coexist on a local area network using defined protocols.

a single network. Systems that must respond in real time, for example, would use Intel's iRMX real-time operating system or their iRMK real-time kernel, while a data-base manager would use an industry-standard-operating system such as UNIX or DOS. The systems would probably contain a diversity of microprocessors.

Each of the systems is individually upgradeable. If something bigger, better, faster, or cheaper becomes available, it is easy to integrate this into a networked-system solution. New technology may be applied at strategic points on the network, and no major overhaul of the complete solution is ever required. Since the overall system is continuously upgradeable it will not become obsolete and will serve for many years.

The systems are independent in their own right, capable of completing their assigned task in isolation, and need not be connected to the LAN to function. The reason that they are connected to the LAN is to enable the sharing of data. The LAN defines a media type and details certain communication protocols that all the systems on the network must adhere to; in this way the diverse systems may share data in a consistent manner. Each system will require a hardware interface to the media and a software interface to the network protocols. Error recovery and retry algorithms are employed to ensure reliable communications between the individual systems on the network.

Application
Presentation
Session
Transport
Network
Data Link
Physical

FIGURE 9.3 A seven-layer intersystem communication model has been defined by the International Standards Organization.

The software model for this functionally partitioned solution is *protocol based* with *data movement*. In this type of model the computer population is split into server systems and consumer systems. A server system provides facilities and resources to the network such as file systems or access to a communications hierarchy. A consumer system does work using the facilities provided by the network servers. The consumer software model makes defined requests for data that a server will respond to. An intersystem comunication standard was developed by the International Standards Organization, and its seven-layer model is shown in Fig. 9.3. All interfaces are rigidly defined but the implementation is not—this allows many diverse systems to interact successfully.

9.2.1 A Major Breakthrough

Imagine now: keep the same network topology but use the advances in silicon integration to compress the systems into a single Multibus II chassis as shown in Fig. 9.4. We will use the parallel system bus as the network media. We will use protocols on the parallel system bus very similar to the protocols used over the local area network. Each of the networked systems will become a single-board subsystem (or a multiple-board subsystem if the circuitry exceeds the area of a single board). We have created a "very local" area network or a backplane LAN.

A Multibus II chassis with multiple boards operating as a backplane LAN is

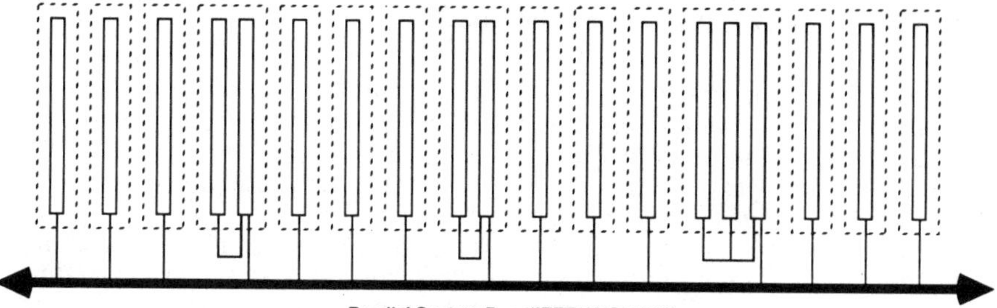

FIGURE 9.4 Applying higher levels of silicon integration allows a network toplogy to be used within a single system.

physically similar to a traditional system but its networked-subsystem philosophy realizes many benefits. This use of advanced Multibus II bus technology allows the system builder to tackle multiple-CPU designs with confidence.

Partitioning a multiple-CPU application into a set of networked subsystems allows us the opportunity to focus. We are able to break down a complex problem into solvable subproblems. These subproblems are also encapsulated; therefore they can be solved independently of the other problems. Encapsulation is an important attribute of a Multibus II subsystem. Encapsulation assumes that a subsystem is intelligent and that it has most of the resources required to complete its assigned task. These resources are exclusive and are under the sole control of the subsystem CPU(s). In a complex subsystem these resources may be spread over multiple boards as shown in Fig. 9.5. Even though there are three physical boards in this example it is important to appreciate that, at a system architecture level, they are treated as a single logical subsystem. The boards within a subsystem communicate using a local expansion bus defined on the P2 connector.

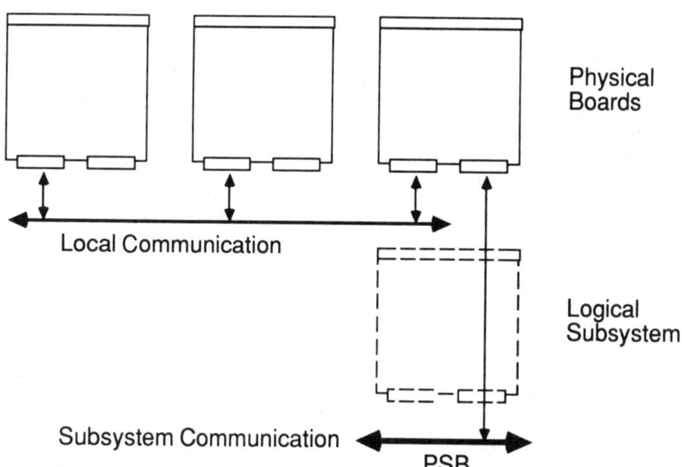

FIGURE 9.5 Multiple-board subsystems interact with each other across a private P2 bus and appear as a single logical subsystem.

9.3 IMPLEMENTING THE SUB-BUSES

The realization that a single bus could not solve all of the problems is an important first step. The requirements of each sub-bus are so different that compromising their features will result in a suboptimal system solution. The majority of this chapter will detail the system bus, but the other buses are discussed so that a context for decisions that are made will be evident.

The incremental I/O bus needs to be simple. Its role is to allow the addition of a small piece of input-output onto a single-board computer to customize it for a particular application. Performance is not an issue, but low interfacing costs are. More extensive I/O would be added on the local expansion bus or on the system bus if an accompanying microprocessor was appropriate.

The local CPU and memory expansion bus will always be dependent upon microprocessor technology. The interface between a CPU and its memory needs to be tightly coupled if we are to extract the maximum performance levels from a given microprocessor family. This bus will evolve with microprocessor technology and will typically exist for only two to four years before it has to be redesigned. If the CPU element requires more MIPs, then additional identical microprocessors could be closely coupled on this local expansion bus; if these microprocessors have on-chip or local caches, as do many of the higher-performance offerings, then this multiple-microprocessor CPU-memory bus must be cache coherent.

A major requirement of the system bus is a technology-independent communication media. Since this bus will remain constant throughout multiple generations of microprocessors, it must be decoupled from the microprocessor technology used on the single-board computer. This loosely coupled approach, whereby each single-board computer subsystem is independent, will enjoy all of the benefits of the systems networked on a local area network. Global system functions such as intialization, diagnostics, and configuration must be added in a standardized way to this long-lived system bus.

9.3.1 Physical Standards

A reasonably large card size with ample power is key to making the best use of the available levels of silicon integration. While no real data has proven that edge connectors should not be used, there is definite trend toward gas-tight pin-and-socket connectors. A double Eurocard format, the IEEE/ANSI 1101 standard, with dual 96-pin DIN connectors was chosen for the Multibus II standard. A U-shaped front panel, licensed from Siemens, West Germany, was chosen for its enhanced electromagnetic interference (EMI) and radio-frequency interference (RFI) shielding properties.

9.3.2 The Incremental I/O Bus

The large array of existing iSBX (IEEE 894) modules for the Multibus I family of products encouraged its adoption within the Multibus II standard. The iSBX strategy has proven itself with customers and vendors alike.

9.3.3 The Local Expansion Bus

The exact bus used for local expansion will vary according to the specific requirements for performance levels required in a subsystem design. As far as the IEEE/ANSI 1296 specification is concerned, this is an open option and any bus that is suitable may be used. Intel initiated a standard called iLBX II, which was optimized for a 12-MHz 80286 microprocessor, although other manufacturers have implemented this using members of the 68000 family. Siemens has implemented Multibus I on the P2 connector and called it the AMS bus. Intel has also offered the PC/AT bus[2] as a subsystem option on a range of PC-compatible products—while this subsystem bus is low performance, it is a low-cost method to add non-intelligent I/O to a Multibus II subsystem. The IEEE P896 committee is currently working upon cache-coherent extensions to Futurebus; this bus, discussed in Chap. 7, would be a good candidate for a high-performance local expansion bus.

9.3.4 The System Bus

The CPU-memory bus defined on most buses is inadequate to support system-level requirements so a *system space* was added to the definition of the Multibus II system bus. (A good analogy here, from the software world, is the user-supervisor spaces common in advanced operating systems). This system space is divided into two portions: interconnect space to fulfill the initalization, diagnostics, and configuration requirements and message space to fulfill the standardized communications requirements. Table 9.1 shows the four address spaces available on the Multibus II system bus. Note that the traditional CPU-memory space is retained for compatibility with existing buses and to aid migration of existing applications into the Multibus II environment. The system bus is optimized for system space operations, but CPU-memory space operations can perform well in their limited single-cycle mode.

TABLE 9.1 Address Spaces Available on Multibus II System Bus

Address space		Address space size	Sequence type	Transfer width (bits)	Block transfers	Number of replying agents
CPU/memory space	Memory	2^{32} bytes	Read/write	8, 16, 24, 32	Supported with increment	One
	Input/output	2^{16} 8-bit ports	Read/write	8, 16, 24, 32	Supported without increment	One
System space	Message	2^{8} agents 1 broadcast	Write only	32	Supported without increment	One or all
	Interconnect	2^{9} 8-bit registers each agent	Read/write	8	Not supported	One

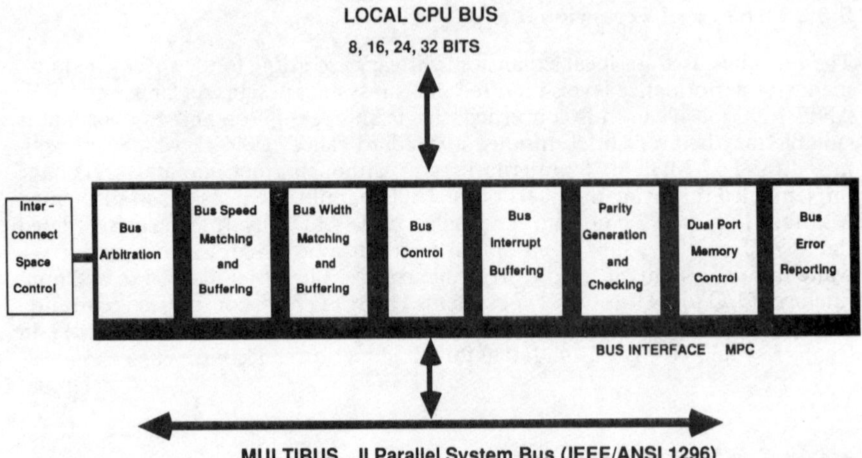

FIGURE 9.6 The MPC bus controller implements most of the IEEE/ANSI 1296 specification in silicon.

Intel's implementation of the Multibus II parallel system bus is contained in its VLSI bus interface device, the message–passing coprocessor (MPC or 82389), whose functional block diagram is shown in Fig. 9.6. The MPC bus controller is a 70,000-transistor single-chip device designed to minimize the board area required by the bus interface circuitry. By standardizing the bus interface in publicly available silicon, all users of the Multibus II standard can look forward to lowering costs and ensured compatibility. This standardization in silicon is similar to Intel's work with the IEEE 754 floating-point standard implemented in the 8087, 80287, and 80387 components and the IEEE 802.3 Ethernet standard implemented in the 82586 and 82588 components.

The 70,000 transistors that make up the MPC bus controller implement a variety of functions as shown in Table 9.2. As seen from this table most of the MPC bus controller deals with message space, either interrupt messages or data transfer messages.

The MPC bus controller contains almost all of the logic needed to interface any microprocessor to the parallel system bus—indeed, all of today's popular 32-bit microprocessors are available on Multibus II products. One of the few required external components is the high-current bus drivers shown in Fig. 9.7. Optional external logic to support dual-port memory selection and off-board memory and I/O references may be included if traditional bus functionality is required. All of Intel's Multibus II boards also include a microcontroller (8751) to implement interconnect space but some members of the Multibus Manufacturers Group have chosen to implement this using the host microprocessor or a simple state machine.

The alternate system bus, the serial system bus or SSB, is currently defined but is not implemented in silicon. The goal of this bus was to reduce the cost of coupling multiple boards together, and it was specified as a 2-Mbit/s serial link. All software interfaces to an SSB chip would be identical to that of the MPC parallel bus controller, so *no* software changes would be necessary to use the serial system bus. Performance would be much lower using this serial system bus but, for many designs, this would be acceptable. Other designs, however, would benefit from a

TABLE 9.2 Functions of Transistors within MPC Bus Controller

Functions	Number of transistors
Traditional bus functions	
Bus control	4,000
Bus arbitration	1,000
Dual-port memory control	2,000
Off-board references	1,000
Interrupts	20,000
Advanced bus functions	
Parity generation/detection	1,000
Interconnect space	6,000
Built-in self-test	1,000
Message passing	34,000
Total	70,000

200-Mbit/s link, and Intel has joined others on the IEEE P1394 serial bus standardization committee to produce this. This group of multiple vendors is driving for a standard that will allow *all* systems to interoperate. Implementation of the SSB interface chip awaits pending resolution and recommendation from this IEEE committee.

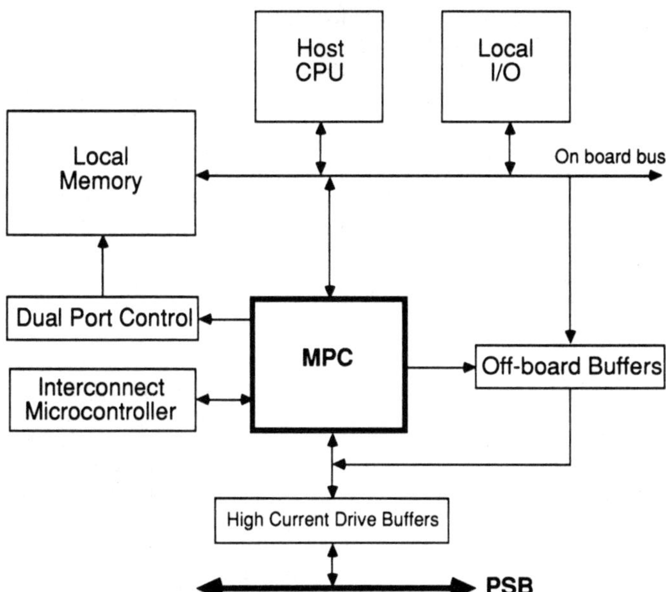

FIGURE 9.7 The MPC integrates all of the sysem bus functions into a single VLSI component.

9.4 INTERCONNECT SPACE

Interconnect address space is a fundamental part of the IEEE/ANSI 1296 specification, and it addresses three major customer requirements: board identification, initialization, configuration and diagnostics. Interconnect space is implemented as an ordered set of 8-bit registers on long word (32-bit) boundaries—in this way little endian microprocessors such as the 8086 family and big endian microprocessors such as the 68000 family access the information in an identical manner. One objective of interconnect address space is to allow higher-level software to gain information concerning the environment in which it operates, independent of the board's manufacturer, the functions it contains, and the card slot it is in. To accomplish this goal, a comprehensive interconnect interface specification that builds upon the concepts introduced within the IEEE/ANSI 1296 specification has been published by Intel Corporation and is available from the Multibus Manufacturers Group.

Board identification registers are read-only locations containing information on the board type, its manufacturer, what components are installed, and other board-specific functions. Configuration registers are read/write registers that allow the system software to set and change the configuration of many hardware options. In most cases hard-wired jumper options can now be eliminated in favor of software control. Diagnostic registers are used for the starting, stopping, and status reporting of self-contained diagnostic routines supplied with each board. These diagnostics are commonly known as built-in self-tests (BISTs).

Interconnect space is based on the fundamental principle that you can locate boards within a backplane by their physical slot position. This concept, known as geographic addressing, is a very useful tool during system-wide initialization. Each board in the system contains firmware that conforms to a standardized header format as shown in Fig. 9.8. At boot time, the system software will scan the backplane to locate its resources before loading device drivers. This approach eliminates the need for reconfiguring the software evey time a new board is introduced to the backplane. It also solves the problem of how to configure multiple controller and processor boards in large multiprocessing systems. Slot independence is achieved by having all boards in the system carry their own initialization and diagnostic functions on-board in firmware. Operating systems can generate a map showing the location of resources during initialization time and then use this list as the basis of message-passing addresses.

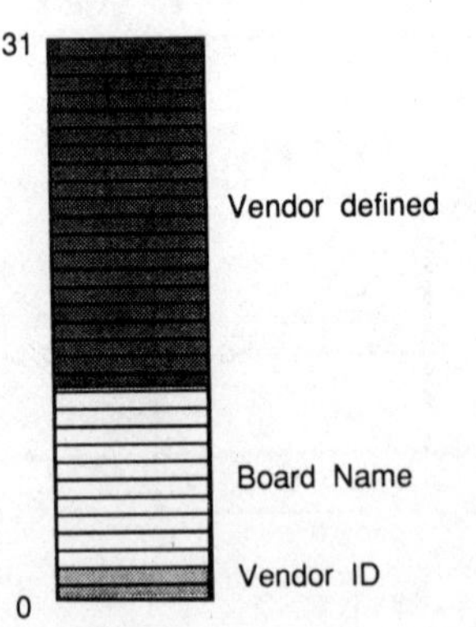

FIGURE 9.8 All IEEE/ANSI 1296–compatible boards contain an interconnect space header record.

In addition to the header record, a board manufacturer may also supply additional function records that make other features of the board accessible to the user through interconnect space. An example is shown in Fig. 9.9. Function records begin with a byte specifying the record type, followed by the number of bytes that the function record contains. The data contained in a function record is organized by the

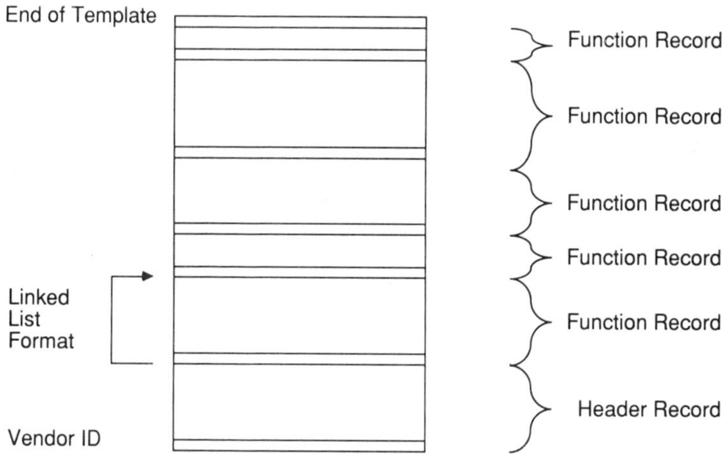

FIGURE 9.9 Extended records within interconnect space give system software knowledge of the hardware.

manufacturer according to published specifications that accompany the board. Many types of function records have already been defined. Some examples include memory configuration, parity control, serial I/O, and other commonly used functions. If there is no existing record type that adequately describes a given function, new record types can be defined, up to a maximum of 1020 different record types. System software will search for a particular record by starting with register number 32 (the end of the header record; start of the first function record), scanning the record type field, and then counting bytes to the next function record until either the correct record is found or an end of template record (hex value 0FFh) is encountered.

9.4.1 Diagnostic Philosophy within Interconnect Space

Intel has taken the usefulness and standardization of interconnect space one step further by embracing a standard diagnostic philosophy. Each intelligent board should have the capability to test itself and report error status in interconnect space if problems exist. There are two occasions when diagnostic testing can be invoked. A subset of the complete on-board diagnostics will be run during power-on initialization, and more extensive testing can be invoked from an operator's console. After turning the system on, most boards will go through a series of initialization checks where the basic functioning of the MPC bus controller and microcontroller is verified. These checks are followed by a power-on test suite which is controlled automatically by each local microprocessor. If a hardware failure is detected at this point, a yellow LED on the front panel will be illuminated so that the failing module can easily be identified and replaced by an operator; additionally, test results are posted in interconnect space to be read across the backplane. Note that a CPU board when scanning interconnect space can now discover the operational status of boards in the backplane as well as their identity.

If further testing is desired, extended diagnostics can be invoked by placing a diagnostic request in the BIST registers of interconnect space. Usually one board will operate as a master test handler and will request services from other boards in the system, which function as slaves while under test. A menu of available tests is accessible via interconnect space. This test philosophy can be applied on-site by the end-user or service representative, or remotely executed via modem from a regional repair center. In most cases, inoperative periods can be minimized by sending out a replacement board, thus avoiding an expensive repair call.

The firmware content of Multibus II boards is much greater than that of previous industry standard buses. In addition to the 8751 microcontroller, there are likely to be on-board EPROMs that contain the extended diagnostics, test handlers, reset initialization sequencing, debug monitors, and numerous other functions. The location of diagnostic firmware on a board will depend on the complexity of the code and the speed at which it runs. For simple replier agents, it may be that the on-board EPROM of the 8751 microcontroller contains enough program storage for rudimentary diagnostic functions as well as the interconnect core firmware. In contrast, most requestor-replier boards (those capable of becoming bus masters) are more complex, and most diagnostic codes are run by the microprocessor from on-board EPROM. In this case, the 8751 microcontroller serves primarily as the communications interface for diagnostics.

9.4.2 Interconnect Space—The Manufacturer's Perspective

From the perspective of a board designer, interconnect is a mixed blessing. The board manufacturer is certain to enjoy the benefits of reduced support costs, easier fault isolation in field repairs, and enhanced customer satisfaction, but a price has been paid for these advantages. One would anticipate longer development times, an increased number of on-board parts, and configuration in firmware to increase the amount of effort it takes to prepare a Multibus II board for market. Indeed this is so. In order to minimize this development time Intel has produced an applications note that details the steps and discusses the options available for a full-featured interconnect space implementation. The core microcontroller code is also provided on a DOS diskette and is designed to be user-extensible. It is now straightforward to add these advanced capabilities to any Multibus II board design.

9.5 THE MESSAGE-PASSING MECHANISM

While the previously described features make more reliable systems easier to build using the Multibus II standard, it is the innovative message-passing scheme that gives the parallel system bus its high performance in a multiple-microprocessor application.[3] The underlying theory behind message passing is simple—it decouples activities between the host microprocessor's local bus and the system bus. This decoupled-bus approach provides two major advantages. First, it allows increasing parallelism of operation—resources that would otherwise be held in traditional wait states while arbitration occurs are freed—and second, one bus bandwidth does not limit the transfer rate of another. The local microprocessor bus and the system bus can perform full-speed synchronous transfers indepen-

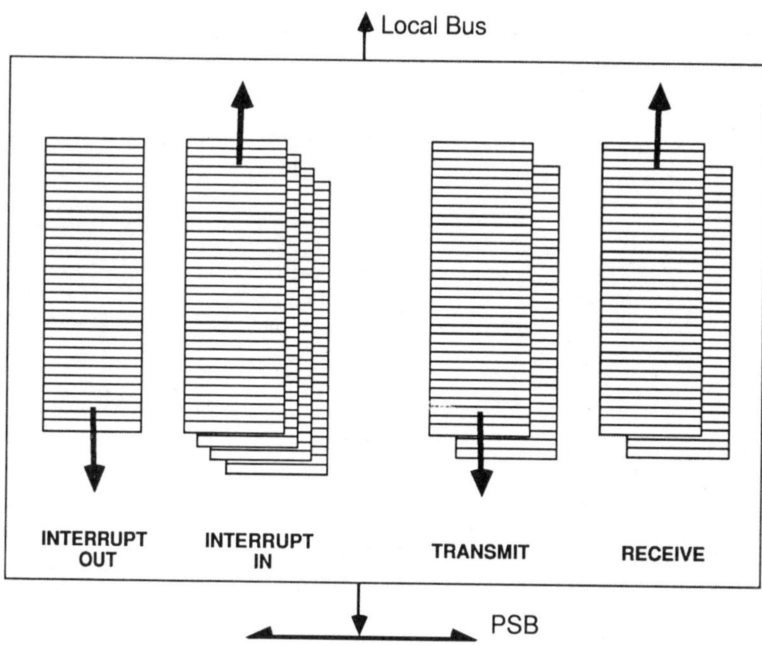

FIGURE 9.10 Decoupling of the local bus from the system bus is achieved with nine FIFOs within the MPC bus controller.

dently and concurrently. The decoupling is achieved within the MPC bus controller using very high-speed FIFO circuitry as shown in Fig. 9.10.

Nine 32-byte FIFO's are integrated into the MPC bus controller. Five of them are used for interrupt messages (one transmit and four receive messages) and four are used for the transfer of data blocks (two transmit and two receive messages). To understand the impact of message passing, let us consider a simple example of transferring a 1-kbyte block of data from CPU A to CPU B as shown in Fig. 9.11. We will first use a shared-memory method and then a message-passing method.

To use a concrete example let us assume that CPU A is a 186-based board and can transfer data at 1 Mbyte/s and CPU B is a 386-based board that can receive data at 10Mbyte/s. We will ignore DMA controller setup. DMA controller A will put a destination address onto the system bus and the address decode logic on board B will respond. We wait for the address to propagate through the dual-port controller on board B and then wait for the access time of the memory on board B. Data is transferred, and once accepted by board B a ready signal will be generated. DMA controller A will move on and generate the next address. This address-wait-data cycle repeats until the full 1 kbyte of data is transferred. The overall speed of the transfer will be 1 Mbyte/s (the slower of the two boards) so it will take 1 ms to transfer the complete 1-kbyte buffer. If the system bus was required by an alternate CPU, then the current data transfer would be delayed or the alternate CPU would have to wait.

Now let us consider the message-passing case. This time we have to set up both

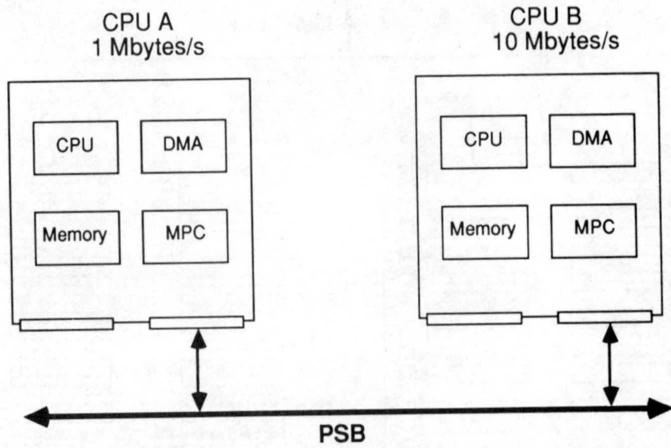

FIGURE 9.11 Let us move a 1-kbyte block of data from board A to board B.

DMA controllers. CPU A could probably transfer data faster than 1 Mbyte/s into a local I/O port (the MPC bus controller), but we will ignore this potential performance improvement. The speed of this transfer will still be 1 Mbyte/s, the speed of the slower board, and the total transfer time will still be 1 ms. What did we gain, then, for the overhead of setting up two DMA controllers?

Let us look in detail at what is happening inside the MPC bus controller. Figure 9.12 shows a fragment of each board with different areas of each MPC bus controller highlighted. Data is being moved into MPC A at 1 Mbyte/s and flows into one of the transmit FIFO pairs. Once 32 bytes have been received, the MPC automatically switches to the alternate-transmit FIFO and starts to fill that. The full-transmit FIFO empties across the system bus into a receive FIFO in MPC B. This transfer of a 32-byte packet occurs at the full bus bandwidth of 40 Mbyte/s. A data packet has a two-clock-cycle header that describes the source, destination,

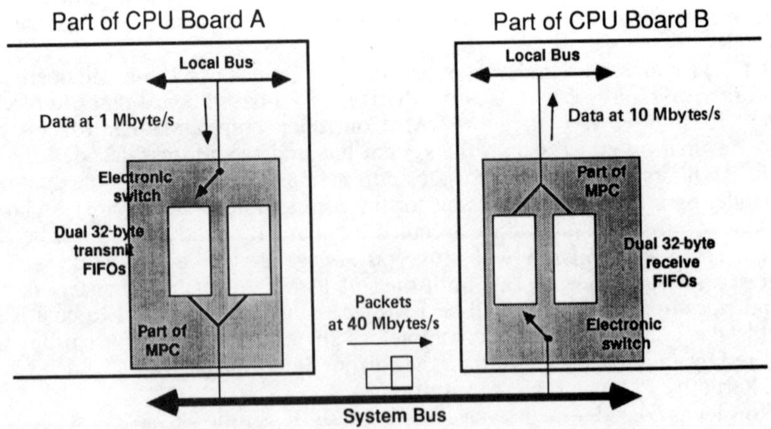

FIGURE 9.12 Looking closely at the message-based data transfer mechanism.

and type of this packet, which reduces the effective data transfer rate to 32 Mbyte/s. The packet therefore takes 1 μs to pass between the two MPC bus controllers. Bus arbitration is done in parallel with the packet transfer, so this does not add to the transit time. Once the packet is inside MPC B, then DMA B empties its receive FIFO at 10 Mbyte/s.

The transmit FIFO pair of MPC A alternates between filling from local memory and emptying into MPC B until the full 1 kbyte of data has been transferred. No programming, save the initial setup, is required. If we look at the system bus activity we see that 1-μs packets are being transferred at 32-μs intervals—the bus is only busy for 3 percent of the total data transfer. We have gained 97 percent bus availability. Compare this with the 0 percent bus availability in the shared-memory case. Message passing frees up system bus bandwidth to enable many other single-board computer pairs to interchange data with no loss in performance. In a multiple-microprocessor application the most precious resource will be system bus bandwidth, and the Multibus II message-passing scheme gives you much more.

We gain more than system bus bandwidth using message passing. Note that CPU A transferred data from its local memory into a local I/O port (the MPC bus controller). CPU A did not have to understand the memory layout or restrictions of memory on CPU B; this also allowed CPU B to do its own memory management and buffer allocations. Similarly CPU B is not restricted by the memory management of CPU A. We have isolated the data with respect to known memory locations and do not have to deal with semaphore flags or similar mechanisms. This simplifying step makes intercommunicating with multiple microprocessors as straightforward as communicating with a single microprocessor. This isolation of functions regarding the local environments of each board, through the use of a standardized data transfer mechanism, is especially important in the general case where each board is running a different operating system (probably on a different microprocessor). A real-time operating system can now simply exchange data with, say, UNIX using this standardized message-passing mechanism. Message passing also standardizes inter-CPU signaling since interrupts are special types of packet (discussed later).

This short explanation has oversimplified the transfer—some setup is required so that the sending MPC bus controller knows the message address of the receiving MPC bus controller, etc. This overhead is more than compensated for by the ignored increase in local transfer data rates. I also simplified the issue by having a receiving board much faster than the transmitting board (10 vs. 1 Mbyte/s). If I had transferred data in the opposite direction (from B to A) then MPC A would have rejected some packets because its receive FIFOs would be full and would have caused MPC B to retry some data transfers. No data would ever be lost, but bus activity would have increased. The MPC bus controller uses a logarithmic back-off algorithm on retries so the bus activity increase would not be excessive. Alternatively, MPC B could be preprogrammed to use a lower packet duty cycle if it knew that MPC A would always be slower.

Having the underlying architectural support to permit multiple-CPU solutions is, of course, only the first step. To build systems we need software. Intel, working with other vendors, has defined a transport protocol specification above the MPC bus controller that provides services such as large block transfers and acknowledged transactions. Data fragmentation at the sender or receiver is detailed so that large data buffers are neither assumed nor required. The implementation is efficient across all CPU architectures; indeed, Intel has supplied implementations on the iRMX real-time operating system, the iRMK real-time kernel, and the UNIX system V.386 operating systems; these are compatible with offerings from Digital Research (FLEXOS), Microbar (VRTX), and Tadpole technologies (UNIX68K).

9.6 *MESSAGE SPACE DETAILS*

The MPC bus controller introduces a hardware-recognized data type called a packet as shown in Fig. 9.13. The MPC contains FIFO circuitry such that these packets may be moved very efficiently between MPCs. Data is moved on subsequent clock edges of the 10-MHz synchronous bus; this defines the maximum bus occupancy of a packet to be 1 μs. Each MPC bus controller has an address in message space, and these are used in the message header (source and destination fields). Seven different packet types are currently defined and are summarized in Fig. 9.14. These are divided into two categories: unsolicited, or interrupt packets, and solicited, or data transfer, packets. The data fields within a packet are user-defined, and the length may vary from 0 to a maximum of 32 bytes (28 for an unsolicited packet) in 4-byte increments. Note that a packet with 0 data bytes will only consume two clocks or 200 ns of system bus time.

9.6.1 Unsolicited Packets

Unsolicited packets, as the name implies, are always a surprise to the MPC bus controller. Their arrival is unpredictable so each MPC has four FIFOs in which it can queue unsolicited packets. These packets are equivalent to the interrupts of a conventional bus with the added feature of having up to 28 data bytes provided with the signal. There are five different unsolicited packets: two are used for interrupts and three are used to set up solicited data transfers. A general interrupt request may be sent between any pair of single-board computers, and a broadcast interrupt may be sent to all boards in a system. The three special interrupts, buffer

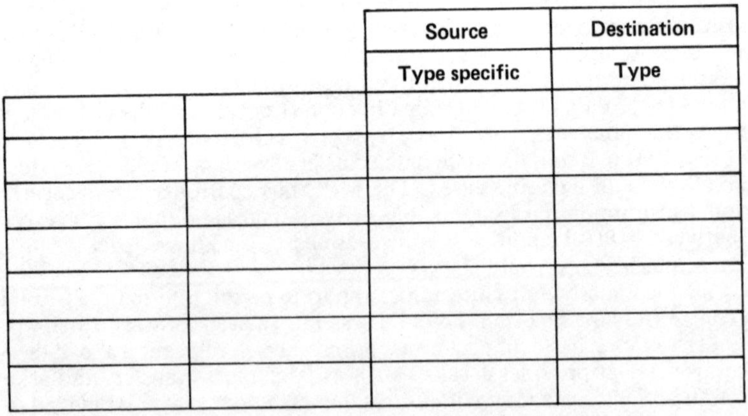

		Source	Destination
		Type specific	Type

FIGURE 9.13 The MPC bus controller introduces a hardware-recognized data type called a packet.

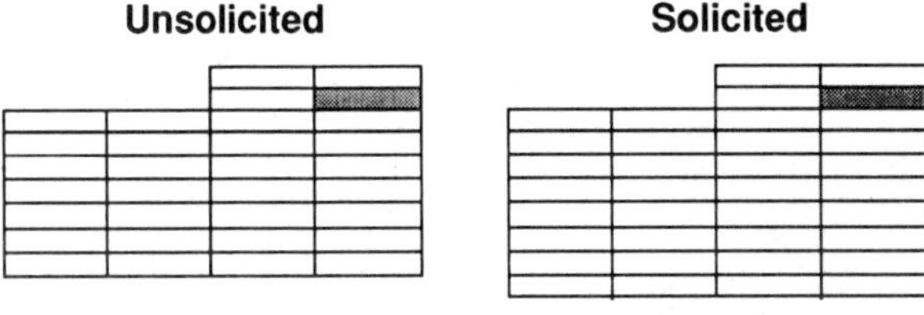

Unsolicited

- Intelligent interrupts
- Used for signaling
- User data 0 to 20 bytes
- Types
  - 00 General Interrupt
  - 01 Broadcast Interrupt
  - 36 Buffer Request
  - 52 Buffer Reject
  - 53 Buffer Grant

Solicited

- Negotiated arrival
- Used for data transfer
- User data up to 16 M bytes
- Types
  - 62 Data Packet
  - 63 Last Data Packet

FIGURE 9.14 There are seven types of packets subdivided into two categories.

request, grant, and reject, are used to initiate large data transfers (solicited messages) between pairs of single-board computers.

9.6.2 Solicited Packets

Solicited packets are never a surprise since their arrival is negotiated—the receiving MPC bus controller knows what to do with them. These packets are used for the transfer of data from one board to another, and the transfer is set up using unsolicited packets. To summarize the operation of solicited packets the MPCs cooperate in the moving of blocks of data between boards, they break the data into 32-byte packets, send them across the bus, and reassemble the data transparently to the sending-receiving boards. All operations such as packet creation, bus arbitration, and error detecting and recovery are handled by the MPC bus controllers—this is done transparently to the local microprocessors. The key to system performance is setting up data packets on the system bus that limits the maximum bus occupancy to 1 μs.

9.6.3 Bus Arbitration Guarantees Low Bus Latency

The Multibus II system bus uses a distributed arbitration scheme as shown in Fig. 9.15. Each board that requires access to the system bus contains the circuitry of this figure (note that this is contained within the MPC bus controller), and no active components are required on the backplane. The MPC bus controller uses a software-assigned identifier to request the bus, and the arbitration circuitry will indicate that the MPC is preparing for a bus cycle. The MPC supports two arbitration algorithms: fairness and high priority.

The fairness mode is used for data transfers and is "polite." If the bus is being used, the MPC will wait before requesting use of the bus; once the bus is not busy the MPC will request the bus and will wait for it to be granted; once the MPC uses the bus it will not request it again until all other requesters have used the

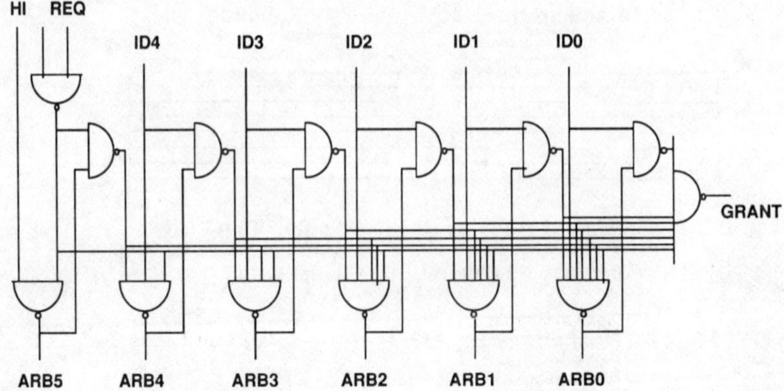

FIGURE 9.15 The arbitration scheme is distributed and supports priority and fairness modes.

bus. "Parking" on the bus is permitted: if no other board has requested the bus since the last time that this board accessed the bus (remember that the bus is continually monitored) then it may access the bus directly without executing an arbitration cycle. These algorithms ensure that a single board cannot monopolize the bus and keep others from using it. Remember that each MPC will only use the bus for a maximum of 1 μs and since the arbitration is being resolved in parallel there are no wasted clock cycles as bus ownership is transferred; all transfers operate back-to-back.

9.6.4 The System Bus Has Deterministic Interrupt Latency[4]

The high-priority mode is used for interrupts and is "impatient." The MPC bus controller, when in this mode, will "barge in" on an arbitration cycle and be guaranteed the next access to the bus. The MPC bus controller can set up interrupt packets specifically to operate in high-priority mode so these will only have a 1-μs latency to access the bus. In the rare instance that two MPCs try to initiate an interrupt packet within the same 1-μs window, the highest-priority board will be granted the bus, and the other board will have to wait a maximum of 2 μs for its bus access.

Interrupt packets and data transfer packets interleave on the bus (actually interleave within a single MPC too), with preference always going to the interrupt packet. A single MPC bus controller will operate with interrupt packets in high-priority mode and data transfer packets in fairness mode; this will ensure that interrupt packets have a deterministic bus transit time of 1 μs (sometimes 2 μs, and 20 μs for the conceivable worst case when all 21 MPCs try to initiate an interrupt packet within the same 1-μs window, a very rare occurrence).

9.7 SYSTEM BUS CHARACTERISTICS

Table 9.3 shows the pin-layout of the P1 connector. The complete parallel system bus can be implemented on a single 96-pin DIN connector. The signals can be

TABLE 9.3 Pin Outlay of the P1 Connector

Pin	Row A	Row B	Row C
1	0 V	PROT*	0 V
2	+5 V	DCLOW*	+5 V
3	+12 V	+5 V (battery)	+12 V
4	0 V	SDA	BCLK*
5	TIMOUT*	SDB	0 V
6	LACHn*	0 V	CCLK*
7	AD0*	AD1*	0 V
8	AD2*	0 V	AD3*
9	AD4*	AD5*	AD6*
10	AD7*	+5 V	PAR0*
11	AD8*	AD9*	AD10*
12	AD11	+5 V	AD12*
13	AD13*	AD14*	AD15*
14	PAR1*	0 V	AD16*
15	AD17*	AD18*	AD19*
16	AD20*	0 V	AD21*
17	AD22*	AD23*	PAR2*
18	AD24*	0 V	AD25*
19	AD26*	AD27*	AD28*
20	AD29*	0 V	AD30*
21	AD31*	Reserved	PAR3*
22	+5 V	+5 V	Reserved
23	BREQ*	RST*	BUSERR*
24	ARB5*	5 V	ARB4*
25	ARB3*	RSTNC*	ARB2*
26	ARB1*	0 V	ARB0*
27	SC9*	SC8*	SC7*
28	SC6*	0 V	SC5*
29	SC4*	SC3*	SC2*
30	−12 V	+5 V (battery)	−12 V
31	+5 V	SC1*	+5 V
32	0 V	SC0*	0 V

classified into five groups: 1. central control, 2. address/data, 3. system control, 4. arbitration, and 5. power.

9.7.1 Central Control

The parallel system bus is a synchronous design and great care is taken, especially within the backplane electrical specifications, to maintain a clean 10-MHz system clock. All other signals are referenced to the system clock for setup and hold times. The IEEE/ANSI 1296 specification details precisely what happens upon each of the synchronous clock edges so there is no ambiguity.[1] The specification also details numerous state machines that track bus activity and are implemented to guarantee compatibility.

A central services module (or CSM) in slot 0 generates all of the central control signals. This CSM may be implemented on a CPU board, a dedicated board, or on the backplane of a card cage. The CSM drives reset (RST*) to initialize a system; a combination of DCLOW* and PROT* is used to distinguish between cold start, warm start, and power failure recovery. Two system clocks are generated, BCLK* at 10 MHz and CCLK* at 20 MHz. RSTNC* and LACHn* are used for advanced facilities within the bus and their description is deferred.

SDA and SDB are reserved for a serial system bus (currently being investigated by the IEEE), and there are two pins reserved for future use.

9.7.2 Address/Data

The Multibus II parallel system bus is a full 32 bits (AD0· · ·31*) with byte parity (PAR0· · ·3*). The system control lines will define when address information or data is contained upon these multiplexed lines. Note that all transfers are checked for parity and, in the case of message packets, the MPC bus controller will retry an operation that failed due to a parity error. If, after 16 tries, the error is not recoverable, the MPC bus controller will interrupt its host microprocessor to ask for assistance.

9.7.3 System Control

Ten lines (SC0· · ·9*) are used for system control, and their functions are multiplexed too. SC0* defines the phase of the current bus cycle (request or reply phases), which then defines how SC1· · ·7 should be interpreted. SC8 provides even parity over SC4· · ·7 and SC9 provides even parity over SC0· · ·3. Table 9.4 shows the decoding of the status/control signals throughout a typical bus cycle.

9.7.4 Arbitration

All boards request use of the bus through a common bus request line, BREQ*. A distributed arbitration scheme is defined that grants the bus to the numerically highest requesting board as identified on lines ARB0· · ·5. Two arbitration algo-

TABLE 9.4 Decoding of Status/Control Signals throughout Typical Bus Cycle

Signal	Function during request phase	Function during reply phase
SC0*	Request phase	Reply phase
SC1*	Lock	
SC2*	Data width	End-of-transfer
SC3*	Data width	Bus owner ready
SC4*	Address space	Replier ready
SC5*	Address space	Agent status
SC6*	Read or write	Agent status
SC7*	Reserved	Agent status
SC8*	Even parity on SC<7· · ·4>*	
SC9*	Even parity on SC<3· · ·0>*	

rithms are supported: fairness, which gives each board an even portion of the available bus bandwidth, and priority, which permits a high-priority request (such as an interrupt) to be guaranteed the next access to the system bus.

9.7.5 Power

There are ample power and ground lines defined, and these are spread over the length of the P1 connector to minimize ground shift and other problems.

9.8 TYPICAL BUS CYCLE

The parallel system bus is particularly easy to interface to.[5] This section will cover the sequencing of a typical replier interface as an illustration of the bus timing. The IEEE/ANSI 1296 specification details numerous state machines that track bus activity and are implemented to guarantee compatibility. An I/O replier need only implement a single *replying agent* state machine. This is shown in Fig. 3.5-5 in the IEEE/ANSI 1296 standard and repeated here in Fig. 9.16 for reference. Remember that an application CPU (a requestor) will start the cycle that the replier will respond to.

In order to progress quickly through this dicussion, an assumption that the requestor always issues valid requests will be made. Error handling for invalid

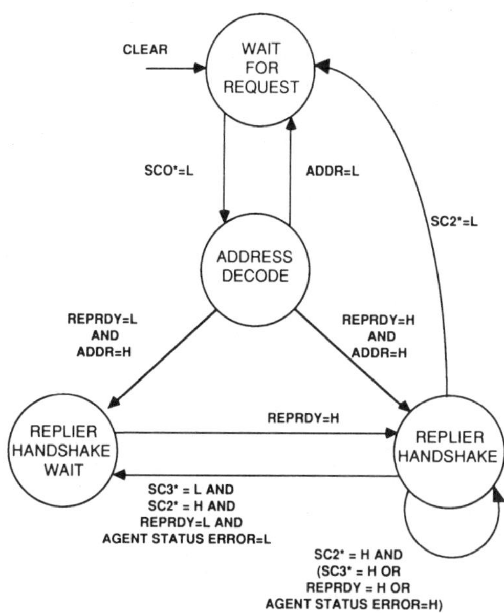

FIGURE 9.16 The IEEE/ANSI 1296 specification details numerous state machines. A replier is shown here.

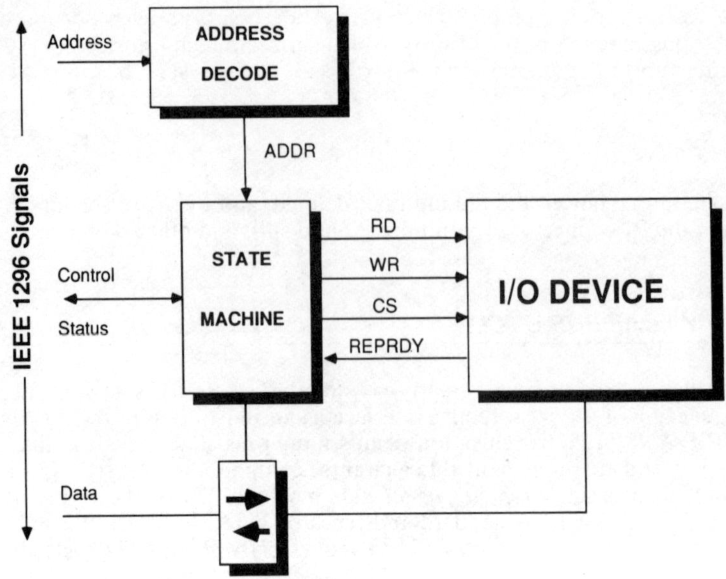

FIGURE 9.17 The design of a replier is fundamentally a bus monitor.

requests will be added later. Figure 9.17 summarizes the design task. The logic required to map the multiple signals and protocols from the Multibus II parallel system bus into the simple read strobe, write strobe, and chip select of an I/O device must be designed. In this example features will be kept at a design minimum but all essential circuitry will be discussed in detail.

The replying agent state machine is fundamentally a bus monitor. State transitions in Fig. 9.16 occur at the falling edge of bus clock. The state machine remains in the wait-for-request state until it detects the start of a requestor cycle on the system bus (the signal SC0* is low) and then it moves into an address decode state. If this requestor cycle is not ours (local decode signal ADDR is low), then it returns to the wait-for-request state. If the requestor cycle is detected as ours (ADDR is high), then there is a transition to a new state controlled by a local ready signal (REPRDY). If the I/O device is not ready (REPRDY is low), then the state machine waits until it is ready. Once ready, it then waits until the requestor is ready (SC3* is low) and provides or consumes valid data. The state machine checks to see if this is a multibyte transfer (SC2* is high), and if it is not, it returns to the wait-for-request state.

If a multibyte transfer is detected, then the state machine decides to accept or to ignore the data in the remainder of the cycle. If the additional data cannot be handled, it then signals an agent status error (continuation error) and waits for the requestor to terminate the cycle. If a multibyte transfer can be supported, it then oscillates between the replier wait state and the replier handshake state where data is strobed. Eventually the requestor will signal the last data element (SC2 set low) and return to the wait-for-request state.

At the start of each requestor cycle status lines (SC1* through SC6*) detail the type of cycle: SC1* signals a locked transfer, SC2* and SC3* encode the data width, SC4* and SC5* encode the address space, and SC6* signals a read or write cycle. A replier must latch these status lines with the address bus and use the information to control its subsequent cycle. A complete list of the status/control decoding is shown in Table 9.4.

An I/O replier has certain responsibilities that must be adhered to. A requestor expects an I/O replier to generate status information and to signal when ready so that the requestor may proceed with the cycle. The cycle will only terminate once both requestor and replier have signaled that they are ready (the IEEE/ANSI 1296 standard includes a time-out feature that prevents the bus from "hanging" if both ready signals are not generated). A replier drives SC4* low to indicate ready and status information is driven on lines SC5* through SC7*; SC8* must also be driven and identifies parity across lines SC4* through SC7*. If a replier is supplying data to a requestor, then correct data parity must also be driven onto the system bus.

9.9 SUMMARY

The Multibus II parallel system bus was designed to implement all of the *system features* of a single-board-computer-based system. The bus does have some CPU-memory attributes and these were included for compatibility and to aid entry into the Multibus II environment—comparing these CPU-memory features in isolation with those of other buses is a complete disservice to the Multibus II architecture and prohibits understanding of the complete design goals and motivation set forth for this standard.

The silicon revolution forced the design of the Multibus II parallel system bus. Technology was advancing faster than our abilities to use it, so we had to find new implementation strategies to utilize these advances. Functional partitioning with hardware-assisted data movement was chosen as the vehicle to embrace the technology; by partitioning the problems into smaller and smaller subproblems, we reach a point where the subproblems can be implemented. The Multibus II consortium chose this path and executed with precision; transistors were applied at strategic points to simplify implementations and enhance ease of use. The Multibus II architecture is completely defined, documented, and available.

ACKNOWLEDGMENTS

I would like to thank the complete Multibus II Marketing Staff at Intel Corporation for its support through the drafts of this chapter.

LIST OF TRADEMARKS

PC/AT is a trademark of IBM Corporation.
FLEXOS is a trademark of Digital Research Corporation.
VRTX is a trademark of Ready Systems.

REFERENCES

1. IEEE/ASNI 1296 Standard 1296-1987, *IEEE Standard for a High-Performance Synchronous 32-Bit Bus: Multibus II,* The Institute of Electrical and Electronics Engineers, Inc., New York, 1988.
2. Dave Redelfs, "PC/AT Compatibility Comes to Multibus® II Systems," *ESD Magazine,* December 1988, pp. 30–32, 35, 37.
3. Miriam Kim, "Migration from a Shared Memory Software Model to Message Passing Software Model," *AACE (Advanced American Control Engineers) Conference 1988 Proceedings,* November 1988, pp. 103–108.
4. Roger Finger, "The Multibus® II Parallel System Bus Designed for Real-Time," *iRUG (iRMX) Users Group Incorporated Conference Proceedings,* November 1988, pp. 249–258.
5. *Simple Multibus® II I/O Replier*, PLX Technology, Mountain View, California, September 1989.

P • A • R • T • 2

DIGITAL BUS ISSUES

CHAPTER 10
PRINTED-CIRCUIT INTERCONNECTION DESIGN

Samuel Gazit
Rogers Corporation
Rogers, Connecticut

The objective of this chapter is to present an analysis of the electronic interconnection concepts, problems, and solutions using printed circuits. An understanding of the capabilities and the limitations of printed circuits is necessary to properly design an optimal interconnection solution. Interconnection applications present a combination of electrical, mechanical, and environmental technical challenges that must be met by a proper choice of circuit design, materials, and fabrication processes. *Printed circuit* is a generic term to describe a wide range of electronic interconnection solutions. Printed circuits can be made from a wide range of circuit materials and by several different fabrication processes. This field, which utilizes numerous circuit materials and fabrication processes, offers a large combination of interconnection solutions. The choice of the most effective interconnection solution for a given application is a complex and often a difficult decision. In the competitive environment of the electronic industry, this decision is usually based on a set of compromises. Materials and processes must be carefully tailored to give the best performance and cost solution for the interconnection problem.

The design of interconnection solutions through printed circuits varies with the applications. Each solution should be based on an evaluation of the circuit materials and fabrication options for the specific interconnection need.

This chapter does not discuss circuit design from its electronic functional aspect. It primarily deals with circuit materials and circuit board fabrication issues.

10.1 INTRODUCTION TO ELECTRONIC INTERCONNECTION SYSTEMS

Electronic devices are assemblies of electrical and mechanical components that are interconnected to perform a required function. The hardware used to electrically wire together these components is termed the interconnection system. Rigid circuit boards, flexible circuits, cables, discrete wires and connectors are typical components of interconnection systems. Although discrete wires and cables are still important elements in interconnection systems, modern electronic interconnections are mostly accomplished by printed-circuit boards (PCB), which are also known as printed-wiring boards (PWB).

10.1.1 The Interconnection Concept

Various electronic interconnection methods have been developed, in the past several decades, to answer the growing and changing needs of the electronic industry.[1–4] The developments in the interconnection technology have been mostly driven by semiconductor technology, which has emphasized higher speed, higher gate densities, larger integration, and more sophisticated and lower-cost integrated circuits (IC). Similar advances have been made in the interconnection technology. A list of performance improvement milestones of the interconnection industry, as expressed by increasing circuit density, is presented in Table 10.1. As shown in the table, the density of an advanced multichip module interconnection system is about 30 to 50 times higher than the wiring density of a single-sided board. The overall performance improvement of the interconnection systems has been supported by the continuous developments of new packaging materials and by the modernization of circuit processing methods and equipment.

The growth of the electronic industry is steady, rapid, and diversified. The wide range of interconnection applications presents a need for different property requirements and performance priorities for circuits. To properly design and manufacture solutions for the various applications, the following aspects of the electronic interconnection system must be considered:[5]

1. Electrical (noise, speed, crosstalk, etc.)
2. Size (weight, volume, shape)
3. Reliability (components, process, materials, etc.)
4. Thermal dissipation (tooling, ambient component capability, etc.)
5. Environment (vibration, shock, temperature, humidity, etc.)
6. Producibility (automation, process, etc.)
7. Maintainability (field conditions, logistics, etc.)
8. Cost (labor, material, testing, etc.)

TABLE 10.1 Circuit Density Milestones, Expressed in the Number of Linear Inch Conductors per Square Inch of Board Real Estate

Interconnection type	Circuit density, in/in^2
Single-sided PWB	20
Double-sided PWB	40
Multilayer board—four layers	130
Multilayer board—eight layers	180
Multilayer board—eighteen layers	340
Microwire technology	150–400
Multichip module	600–1,000

As mentioned above, the priorities of these factors may vary from application to application.

10.1.2 Levels of Electronic Interconnection and Packaging

In modern packaging systems, dozens, hundreds and at times thousands of electronic components are interconnected to perform the required functions. To efficiently execute these functions, the individual components, or assemblies of these components, must be arranged in a hierarchical order. This hierarchy, or level of interconnection, is designed to optimize the overall performance of the device. Complex electronic packaging systems often combine various interconnection elements, which may be grouped in three major categories:

1. Rigid printed-circuit boards, which serve as the building blocks of the interconnection system. The two most important functions of the PCB are (*a*) to electrically connect and (*b*) to mechanically carry the components on the board.

2. Flexible interconnections, which, as a group, are represented by cables, flexible circuits, and discrete wiring. These interconnection elements are used to electrically connect the rigid elements of the system.

3. Connectors, the hardware that is primarily used to interface between rigid boards, flexible circuits, and cables. Connectors are also used to mount electronic and mechanical components on the various interconnection elements.

A schematic assembly of the three main interconnection categories is shown in Fig. 10.1.

To build electronic systems for diversified applications, the manufacturer of the equipment must often provide a product line with a variety of capabilities. This can be accomplished by a design for built-in expansion within the envelope of the equipment, without the need for remanufacturing. One frequent solution to this interconnection concept is achieved by the backplane and cards approach, as shown schematically in Fig. 10.2 This two-element packaging system consists of several rigid printed-circuit boards, which are commonly called cards or "daughter boards." These cards are connected to a bus system, which is commonly called a backplane or "motherboard." The connector mechanism involved with this approach includes a pad array on the edge of the rigid board cards, which by a zero-insertion-force (ZIF) is inserted into the card-edge connectors on the backplane.[6,7]

In more advanced interconnection systems, a third element has been added to the traditional cards and backplane hierarchy. This third interconnection element, which is often called "child board,"[8] is a small circuit board that carries an assembly of components and is parallel-mounted on a daughter-board card, as shown schematically in Fig. 10.3.

In the backplane and cards interconnection concept, the various rigid boards connect to each other via hard connectors without the use of flexible interconnection elements.

10.1.2.1 Rigid Printed-Circuit Boards (PCB). Rigid printed circuits, or wiring boards, are used where a rigid and planar electronic interconnection configuration is desired. The PCB serves as the basic interconnection building block and is primarily used to carry and interconnect electronic and mechanical components or their assemblies. The simplest PCB is the single-sided wiring board, while com-

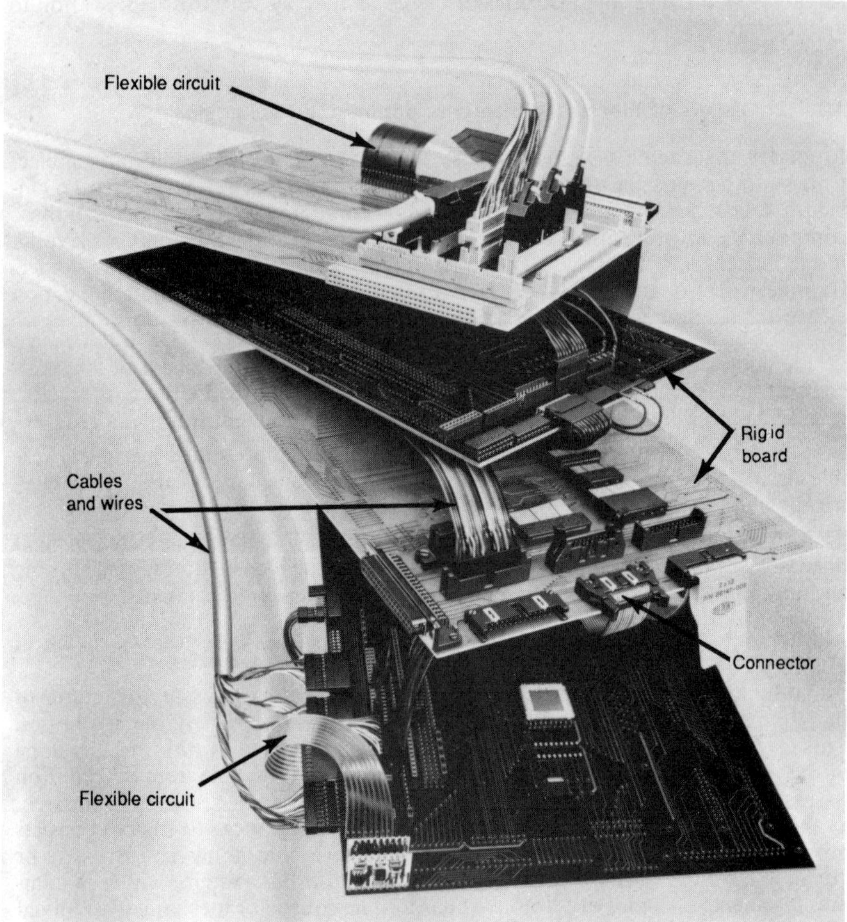

FIGURE 10.1 A schematic assembly of the various interconnection elements: rigid printed-circuit boards, flexible circuits, and connectors.

plex multilayer printed-circuit boards could contain more than 40 conductive layers laminated into a single rigid board.

The dielectric material of most printed-circuit boards is based on a polymeric matrix reinforced with fibers or particulate fillers. Specialty circuit boards are reinforced with different core materials that include metal and ceramic plates. The various commercial rigid printed-circuit board materials are discussed in more detail in Sec. 10.4.

10.1.2.2 Flexible Printed Circuits. Flexible printed circuits are wiring boards utilizing flexible base materials. The metal foil, in most cases copper, is normally bonded to the flexible dielectric material by an adhesive layer. In some flexible circuit laminates, the dielectric and the conductive materials are combined with-

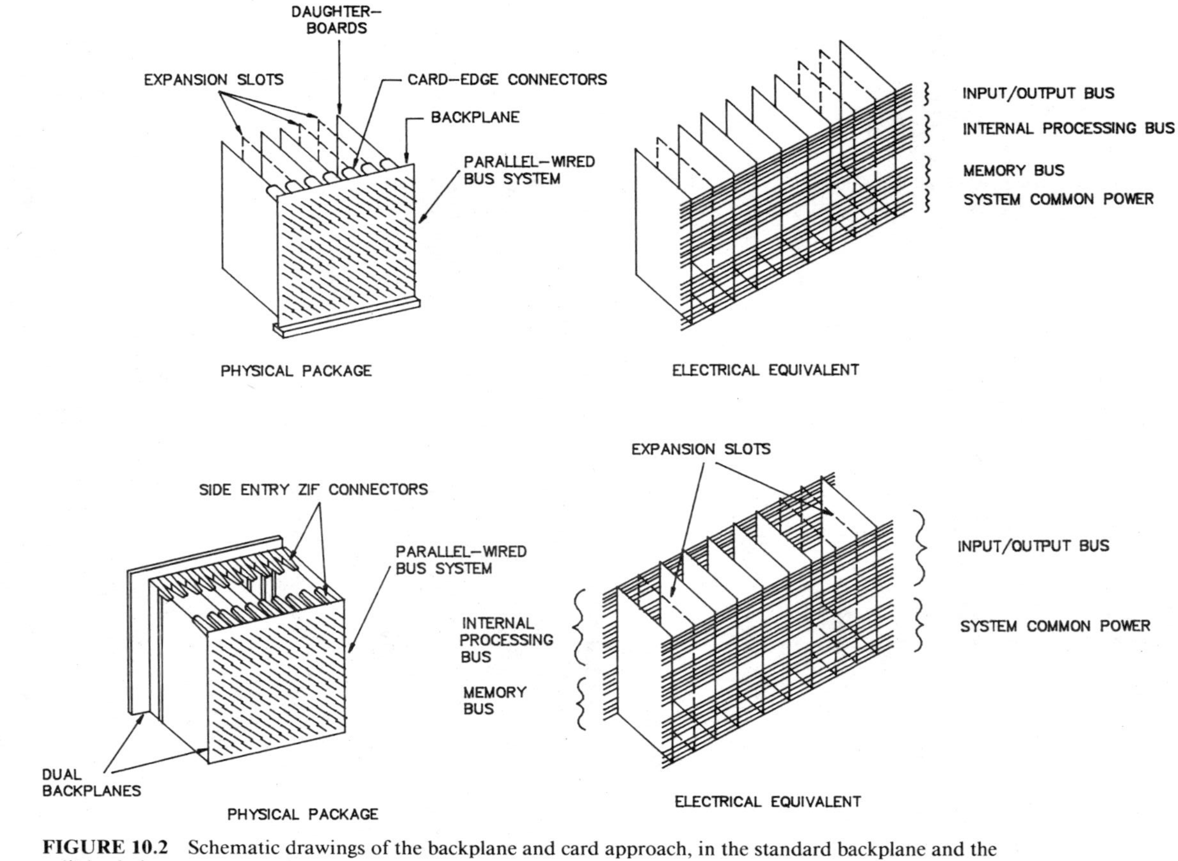

FIGURE 10.2 Schematic drawings of the backplane and card approach, in the standard backplane and the split backplane arrangements.

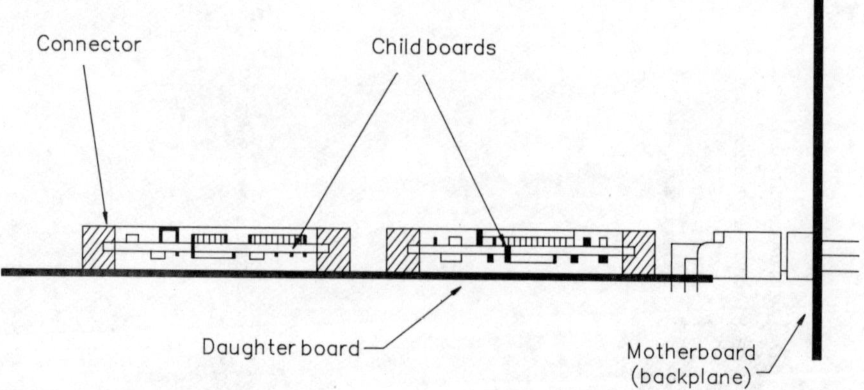

FIGURE 10.3 A schematic drawing of the hierarchical interconnection technology: motherboard, daughter-board, and child-board arrangements.

out the use of an adhesive. Flexible circuits are used to interconnect the rigid elements of interconnection systems.[9]

The conductive pattern of a flexible circuit is normally defined by processes similar to those used in the fabrication of rigid printed-circuit boards. For a detailed discussion of commercial flexible circuits, see Sec. 10.4.

10.1.2.3 Cables and Wires. Cables are primarily used to electrically interconnect rigid elements of interconnection systems.[10] This form of interconnection may be used within the "shell" of one system or when several systems are hooked together. Two or more wires can be combined into a single ribbon cable.[11] Advanced cables may be constructed with built-in shields and a ground layer to improve their electrical performance.[12–16] The choice of special dielectric material can further enhance the interconnection performance of the cable.

In addition to the three traditional interconnection systems (rigid boards, flexible interconnections, and connectors), there are several other interconnection elements that should be noted: hybrid microelectronics, multichip modules, bendable laminates, and injection-molded circuits. A brief summary of these concepts is presented in the following paragraphs.

10.1.2.4 Hybrid Microcircuits. In recent years, the increasing limitations on space and weight, especially in military and aerospace systems, have created the demand to achieve further reduction in the size of the interconnection elements, while maintaining overall high reliability and performance. For some applications, this higher degree of integration has been achieved by an advanced packaging technique that is termed *hybrid microcircuits.*[17] Hybrid microcircuits are a separate class in the technology of interconnections. This form of higher integration is also designed to handle high currents, high power density, and efficient dissipation of heat. A schematic drawing of a typical hybrid microcircuit is shown in Fig. 10.4. For more details, see Sec. 10.5.

10.1.2.5 Multichip Modules. The cost of high-end multilayer boards, which have been built in the late 1980s and which typically contain over 40 layers in large board sizes, exceeded $100,000 in 1986.[18] This type of board has been produced by pushing the conventional PCB technology to a peak in process difficulty. Cost and performance of such very complex PCBs have forced the circuit designers to look for alternative interconnection solutions. The interconnection industry started during the 1980s to experiment with new packaging concepts that use different technologies, to achieve higher performance and reliability at a low cost. The manufacturing techniques of these advanced interconnection concepts are most likely to mature during the 1990s. These advanced interconnection systems are known by different names—two of these are multichip modules (MCM) and high-density interconnections (HDI). Multichip modules are discussed in more detail in Sec. 10.5.

10.1.2.6 Bendable Laminates. Another interconnection concept was introduced in the mid-1980s—a bendable printed circuit board.[19,20] Portions of this bendable and formable board function as the rigid segment, while other portions of the same board function as the "flexible" connector in a multiplane configuration. A photograph of a typical bendable circuit is shown in Fig. 10.5. A more detailed discussion of bendable laminates is presented in Sec. 10.5.

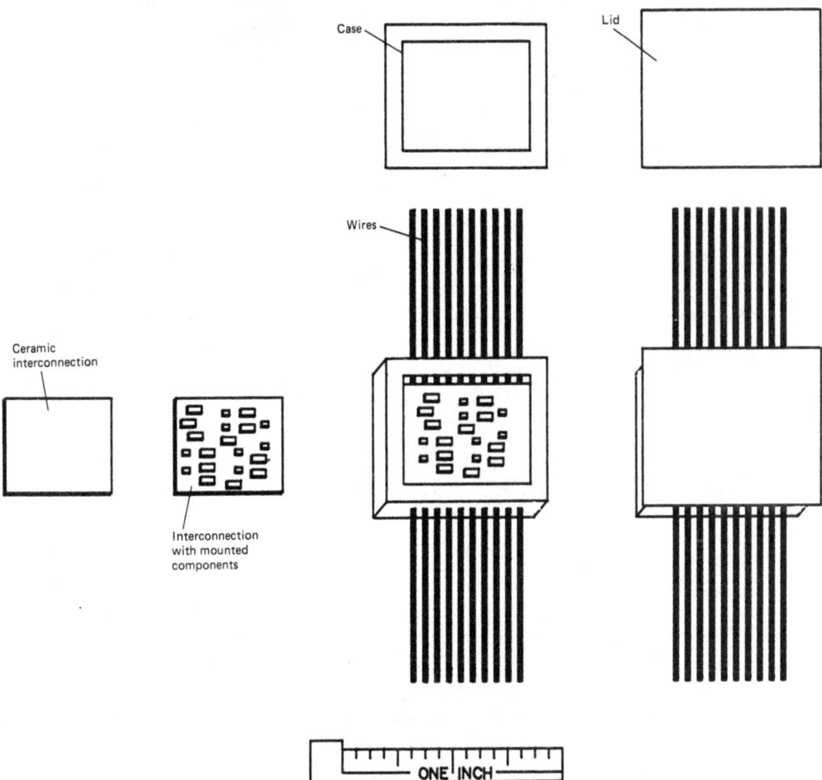

FIGURE 10.4 Schematic drawing of a typical hybrid microcircuit.

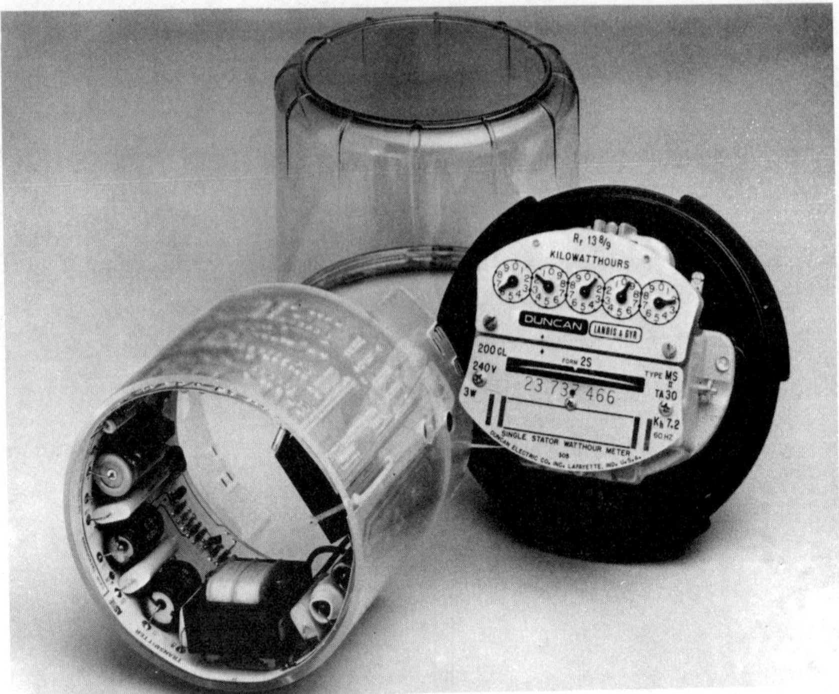

FIGURE 10.5 Photograph of a typical bendable circuit.

10.1.2.7 Injection-Molded Circuits. The idea of molding a three-dimensional circuit board was proposed in the early 1960s. However, the availability of materials, technology, and market has made the concept of injection-molded circuits a reality only in the late 1980s.[21] A photograph of a typical injection-molded circuit is shown in Fig. 10.6. Injection-molded circuits are discussed in more detail in Sec. 10.5.

10.2 THE CIRCUIT-BOARD CONCEPT

In concept, a circuit board consists of a conductive pattern that is bonded to a dielectric substrate. The methods to produce circuit boards can be classified by two general categories: (a) the subtractive technology and (b) the additive technology. The raw material for the subtractive circuit technology is a laminate of a conductive foil that is bonded to a dielectric material. Circuit fabrication with the additive technology starts with a bare dielectric layer. With the subtractive methods the circuit pattern is formed from a continuous conductive foil via an etching technique, while with the additive technologies the circuit is formed through deposition of the conductive material on the dielectric layer in a designed pattern. Some circuit fabrication methods combine the additive and subtractive technologies.

Commercial methods used to form circuit laminates are summarized in Secs.

10.2.1–10.2.4. These laminates are processed by subtractive circuit technologies. Additive circuit technologies are summarized in Secs. 10.2.5–10.2.9.

10.2.1 Lamination of a Metal Foil with a Dielectric Sheet

This is the basic and most common method used to fabricate circuit materials for both rigid and flexible applications. Conceptually, there are three ways to bond the dielectric material to the conductive sheet, as described in the following sections.

10.2.1.1 Lamination of a Metal Foil with a Prepreg Dielectric Sheet. The prepreg is a composite material of fibers which are impregnated with a B-staged (partially cured) thermosetting resin. Typical thermosetting resins are epoxy, phenolics, bismaleimides, etc. Upon lamination in a press or in an autoclave, the resin cures and simultaneously bonds to the metal foil. This process is described in *Printed Circuits Handbook*[22] and is shown schematically in Fig. 10.7. Key steps of the process include (1) resin application to the web, (2) drying and B staging of

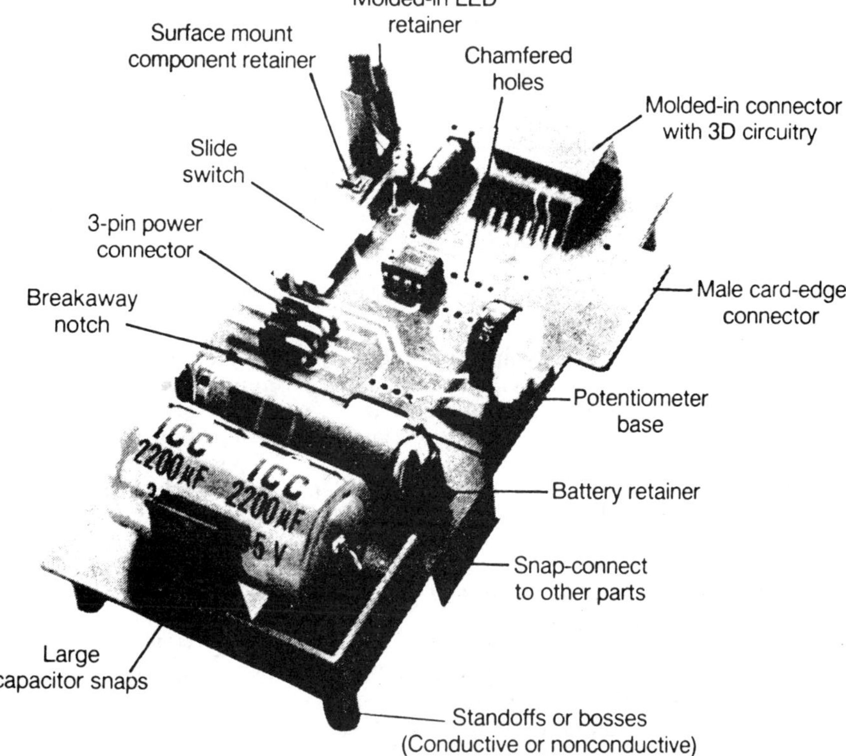

FIGURE 10.6 Design "demo" of a molded circuit board shows integral structural features and holes, eliminating need for several manufacturing operations.

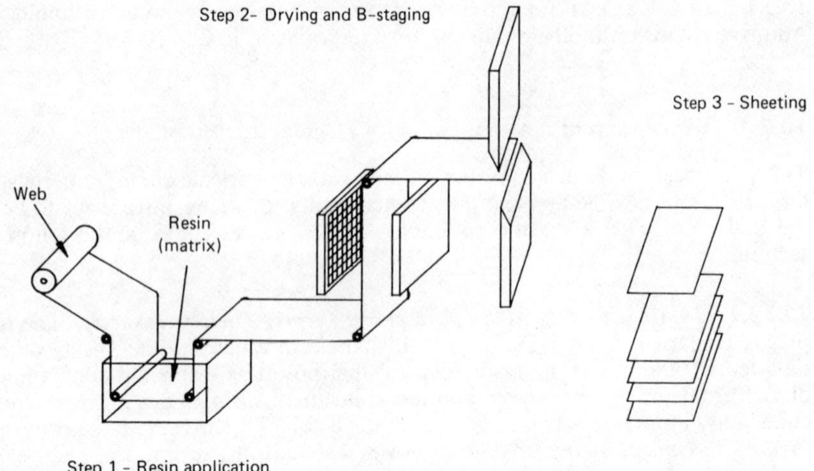

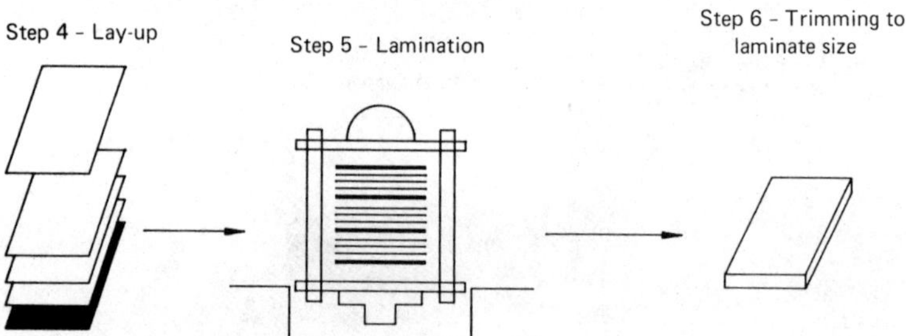

FIGURE 10.7 Schematic drawing of the fabrication process of circuit laminates.

the matrix, (3) sheeting, (4) lay up the B staged layers and the copper cladding to form the laminate structure, (5) lamination, and (6) trimming.

By choosing a quickly curing matrix and a different press mechanism, the batch lamination step can be replaced by a continuous lamination process. Continuous lamination has been used in the U.S. (Rogers Corporation, Sheldahl, and others) and in Europe (Perstrop Electronics, Sweden) since the early 1970s. Dwelling time of the laminate in the press is defined by the curing process and the kinetics of the resin chemistry.[23]

10.2.1.2 Lamination of a Metal Foil with a Thermoplastic Dielectric Sheet. Typical thermoplastic materials are fluoropolymers, acrylics, polyimides, etc. During the lamination process, the thermoplastic dielectric sheet bonds to the metal foil as the surface of the polymeric substrate melts. To obtain good circuit material properties, the thermoplastic dielectric sheet can be typically reinforced by a continuous web, short fibers, or by small particles.

10.2.1.3 Lamination of a Metal Foil with a Dielectric Sheet via an Adhesive Film. An adhesive film may be applied to the metal foil or to the dielectric sheet in the form of solution, solid film, or melt. Then, the dielectric and the conductive layers are bonded together in a lamination press. The adhesive could be either thermoset or thermoplastic.

10.2.2 Deposition of a Conductive Layer on a Dielectric Sheet in a Wet Chemistry Process

A metal layer can be deposited on a dielectric sheet as a continuous foil to form a circuit material. The metal deposition on the dielectric sheet can be done in one step using only an electroless process[22,24] or in two steps starting with an electroless deposition step followed by an electrolytic plating step. One of the key concerns of this technology is the bond strength between the metal and the dielectric surface. Surface preparation of the dielectric substrate is necessary to maintain adhesion at the metal-dielectric interface. Roughening or texturing the dielectric surface[25,26] promotes "mechanical interlock," while surface catalysis can improve the chemical bond between the deposited metal and the dielectric material.[22,27–29]

10.2.3 Deposition of a Conductive Layer on a Dielectric Sheet from a Gaseous Phase

This process is carried out in a vacuum chamber. The depositing metal is placed in a furnace, and the dielectric material is placed inside the vacuum chamber, in front and at a distance from the furnace. Under the conditions of high temperature in the furnace and low pressure in the chamber, the depositing metal evaporates from the furnace and immediately condenses on the surface of the dielectric material.[30]

As in the wet chemistry process, the vacuum-deposited conductive layer can be further electroplated to the desired film thickness. The thickness of the vacuum-deposited seeding layer is typically about 1000 Å.

10.2.4 Deposition of a Dielectric Layer on a Conductive Foil

In this form of circuit material the dielectric film is directly bonded to the copper foil without an adhesive layer. The dielectric material is typically nonreinforced, and it may be generally applied to the copper foil by one of the two following methods:

1. Cast the dielectric material (in solution) on the metal foil. Follow with drying and curing in the case of a thermoset polymer.[31,32]

2. Deposit the polymer on the metal foil from a gaseous phase. This process takes place in a vacuum chamber and is most suitable for thermoplastic polymers.[33,34]

10.2.4.1 Casting Dielectric on Metal Foil. This technology has been used by several laminate fabricators. Enka America Inc.[32] and Mitsui-Toatsu[31] offer polyimide-based laminates with different metals that are compatible with subtractive circuit processing. Typical metal foils are copper, nickel, aluminum, and stainless steel.

10.2.4.2 Deposition of Polymer on Metal Foil from a Gaseous Phase. Vapor deposition of dielectric materials is based on a fast evaporation of the polymer from a source and condensing it as a film[34] onto a metal foil. Vapor deposition polymerization (VDP) is another technique that has been employed for the preparation of a polyimide film using a conventional thin-film evaporator with a novel source design.[33]

10.2.5 Bonding a Conductive Wire onto a Dielectric Sheet to Form a Circuit Pattern

Historically, the concept of printed-circuit technology has replaced the old method of forming interconnections by discrete wiring. Printed-circuit technology is a more industrial and economical concept than the labor-intensive discrete-wiring method. However, the need to control electrical performance features, such as impedance and crosstalk, could not easily be met by the printed-circuit technology. These market needs combined with the availability of robotics and sophisticated software made, in some applications, the use of the discrete-wiring concept an economical interconnection solution.[35–39]

The use of discrete wiring has been industrially pursued by two approaches: (1) the stitch-wire technology and (2) the multiwire technology.

10.2.5.1 Stitch-Wire Technology. The stitch-wire method is a point-to-point wiring technique used to interconnect electronic components on a board. The process employs a reel of 30-gauge polytetrafluoroethylene (PTFE)-insulated nickel wire, which is discretely fed and bonded to stainless-steel pins or pads that are arranged on a dielectric substrate to form a circuit pattern. Stitch-wire cards can typically operate at clock rates from 100 to 250 MHz with twisted pairs.[39]

10.2.5.2 Multiwire Technology.[35–38] This technology was developed by Kollmorgen Corporation in the early 1980s. The advanced generation of this technology is called Microwire.* Microwire technology uses a 42-gauge (2.5-mil) copper wire, which is encapsulated in an insulator and bonded to a board to form the interconnection signal paths in the *X-Y* plane. The *Z*-axis interconnection is accomplished with 10-mil laser-drilled blind vias. Addition of a copper-Invar substrate may provide both the matched coefficient of thermal expansion (CTE) and high thermal conductivity. A schematic drawing of the layer structure of a Microwire board is shown in Fig. 10.8. Typical properties of Microwire circuitry are presented in Table 10.2.

10.2.6 Deposition of a Conductive Pattern on a Dielectric Sheet in a Wet Chemistry Process

The key process steps used to form a circuit pattern by an additive technology are shown in Fig. 10.9. The process starts with a bare dielectric surface, step (a). A thin layer of electroless is then deposited on the dielectric surface, step (b). A photoresist (normally dry film) layer is then applied to the electroless layer. By a lithographic or another method the photoresist layer is imaged and "developed," step (c), to form tracks in the shape of the circuit pattern in the photoresist layer on top of the electroless layer. In step (d), by an electrolytic process, the tracks are

*Microwire is a trademark of the Kollmorgen Corporation.

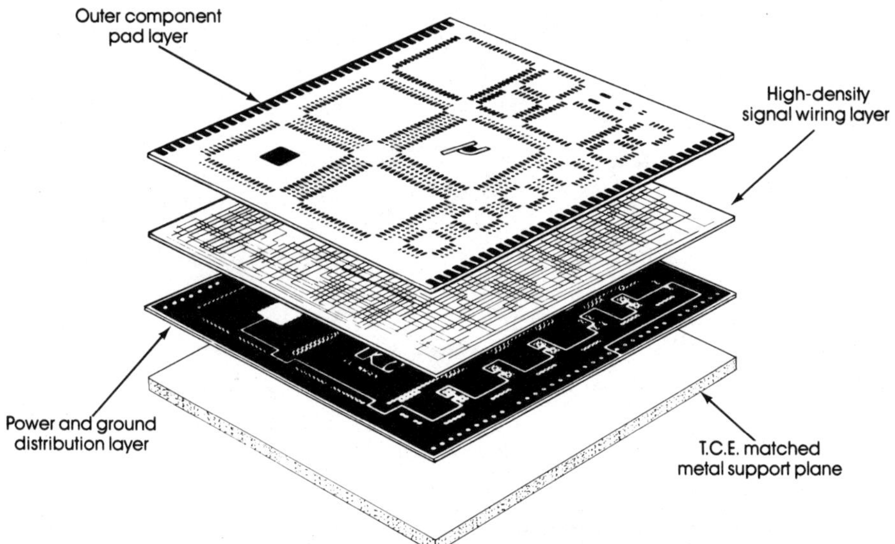

FIGURE 10.8 Schematic drawing of the layers structure of the Microwire concept.

plated with the conductive metal. The thickness of the plated traces is not usually larger than the thickness of the photoresist layer. Then, in step (f), the photoresist between the traces is dissolved, and the thin electroless layer between the electroplated traces is removed by a fast chemical etching process.[22,40–42]

10.2.7 Application of a Conductive Paste or Ink Pattern on a Dielectric Layer—Polymer Thick-Film Technology

Polymer thick-film (PTF) technology is an additive process in which the conductive features in the *X-Y* plane are applied directly on the dielectric layer by screen printing, spraying, or roller coating in the designed circuit pattern.[43–49] It has been

TABLE 10.2 Typical Properties of Microwire Technology (Ref. 38)

Physical properties		Electrical properties	
Dimensions	Up to 12 in × 14 in	Impedance	75 Ω ± 10%, typical
Thickness	Minimum 0.036 in	Line resistance	1.79 Ω/ft
Conductor size	0.0025-in diameter	Propagation delay	1.8 ns/ft
Wiring grid	Down to 0.010 in	Crosstalk	Backward <5.5%; forward <1%
Hole size	Blind laser via = 0.010 in diameter	Effective dielectric constant	3.2
Wiring density	200 linear in/in^2 level		
CTE	6.4×10^{-6} in/in °C		

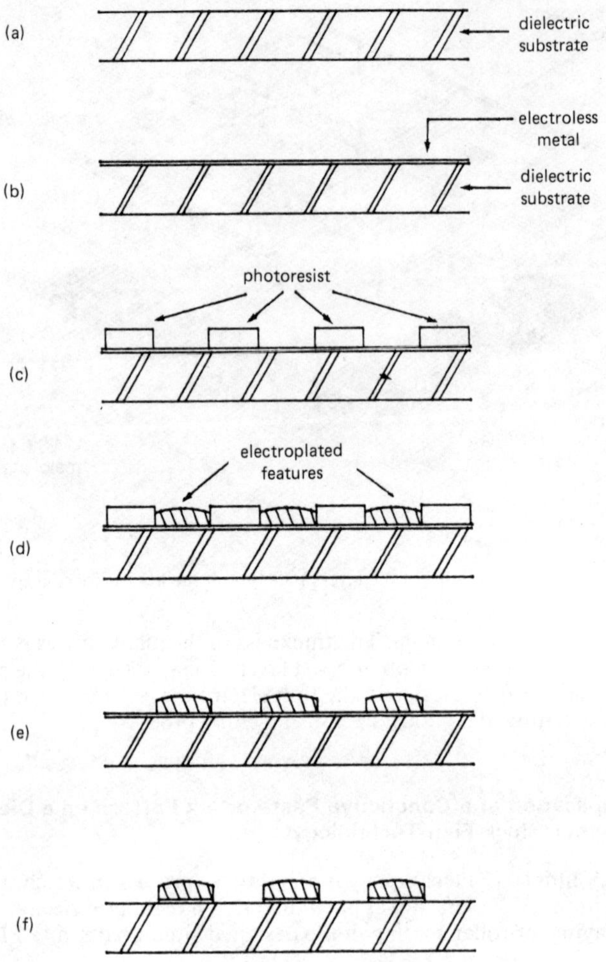

FIGURE 10.9 The key process steps to form a conductive circuit pattern on a dielectric sheet by an additive process, using wet chemistry.

mostly effective in forming circuit patterns with a linewidth of over 250 μm. The temperatures to cure these coatings can range from room temperature up to the temperature required for firing glass coatings. Other modern conductive inks are designed for UV and IR curing. PTF inks typically contain noble metals like gold, platinum, palladium, silver, and nickel.

10.2.8 Application of a Conductive Pattern on a Dielectric Material by Direct Writing

A computer-aided design and manufacturing (CAD/CAM) thick-film direct writing system consists of two components: (1) a precise ink-dispensing pen[53] and (2) a precision *X-Y* table.[50–54]

Key advantages of direct circuit writing are as follows:

- Prototype turnaround done in hours
- Design changes implemented in minutes
- Elimination of artwork, screen, and other tooling costs
- Significant savings of precious metal inks (compared to PTF technology)

10.2.9 Deposition of a Conductive Pattern from a Liquid Solution or a Gaseous Phase in a Laser-Assisted Process

This advanced circuit fabrication technique has received considerable attention since the early 1980s.[55–68] In concept, the method can be described as preferential and high-resolution maskless plating of electroless. The preferential plating results from exposing those regions where plating is sought to an energy beam, to increase the plating rate by a factor of 10^3–10^4.[55] The circuit substrate is placed in the plating solution, and a continuous focused beam is passed through the solution and illuminates regions on the surface of the substrate. Laser-enhanced plating has been demonstrated on metallic, polymeric, and ceramic substrates, using argon,[55,56,63,66] neodymium-doped yttrium aluminum garnet (Nd:YAG),[58,59] and UV excimer[64] laser sources.

Laser-enhanced metal deposition techniques have been further developed using a jet plating technique.[61,66] This new plating technique combines the laser effect with a pressurized jet of plating solution. Laser chemical vapor deposition of copper has been performed by decomposition of gas-phase compounds in the presence of the laser energy.[67] Another laser-assisted direct circuit writing process uses a conductive powder.[68]

10.3 CLASSIFICATION OF CIRCUIT BOARDS

A circuit board is basically an electronic package that consists of conductive traces (ground and signal lines) and conductive planes (ground and power), which are held together by a dielectric medium. The conductive portions of the circuit are logically routed in a two- or three-dimensional pattern to interconnect the various components on the board.

There are three generic types of printed-circuit structures:

1. Single sided
2. Double sided
3. Multilayer

10.3.1 Single-Sided Circuit

The simplest of all circuit boards, single-sided circuits have a conductive pattern only on one side of the dielectric board. Traces on a single-sided circuit are designed for both signal and ground functions. Depending on its mechanical and electrical functions, this board can be rigid, flexible, or bendable.

Schematic drawings of generic single-sided circuits are shown in Fig. 10.10 *a* and *b*. The conductive layer is patterned for the electrical and for the mechanical

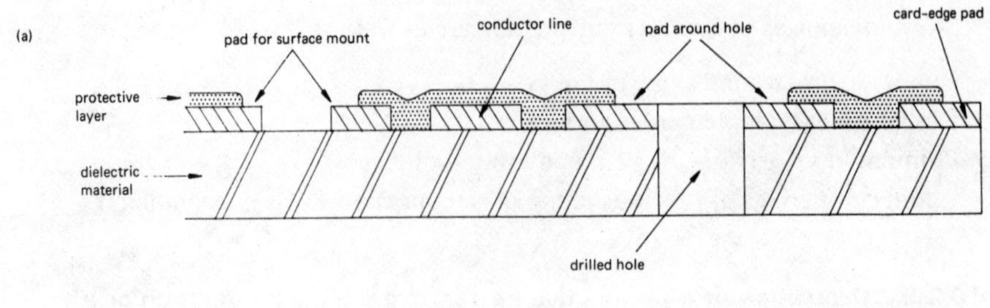

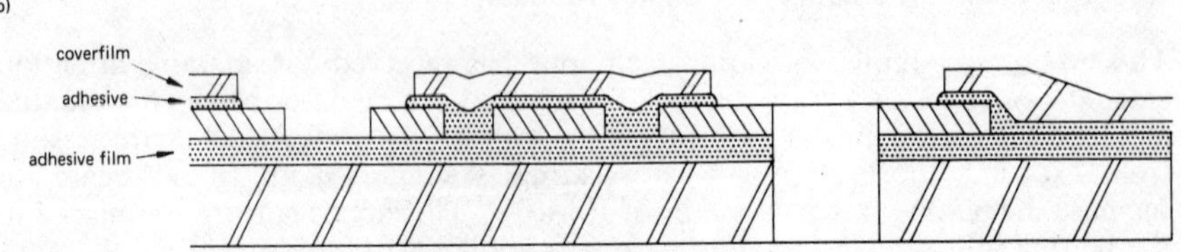

FIGURE 10.10 Schematic drawing of generic single-sided circuits boards: *(a)* conductors are covered by a protective film; *(b)* conductors are covered with a cover film.

function of the circuit. This pattern may include lines, pads around holes for pinned components, pads for surface-mounted components and card-edge pads. The conductive layer could be directly bonded to the dielectric layer, Fig. 10.10*a*, or combined with the dielectric layer by an adhesive layer, Fig. 10.10*b*. To protect the circuit mechanically or electrically, the conductive pattern is normally covered by a protective film or layer. This layer can be screened, sprayed, or laminated onto the patterned circuit. For flexible circuits, especially where the application requires a large number of flexing cycles (as in disk drive applications), the protective layer, which is also called the cover film, is designed to geometrically balance the structure of the circuit. This symmetrical structure, with the conductive traces at the neutral axis of the cross section, enhances the life of the flexible circuit during demanding dynamic flex applications. A typical process used to fabricate single-sided circuits via a subtractive process is shown in Fig. 10.11.

10.3.2 Double-Sided Circuits

Double-sided circuits have conductive patterns on both sides of the dielectric layer.

Double-sided circuits have two advantages over the single-sided circuit:

1. Interconnection density can be doubled.
2. Electrical properties can be better controlled in double-sided than in single-sided circuits.

To effectively use the routing capability of a double-sided circuit, the circuit patterns on the opposite sides of the board must be selectively connected by a conductive path along the *Z* axis. This conductive path can be achieved by several techniques, but the most important and practical industrial method is the plated-through-hole (PTH) technique. Another method used to form a *Z*-axis conductive path is by the blind via. A typical process flow chart for double-sided circuit fabrication is shown in Fig. 10.12.

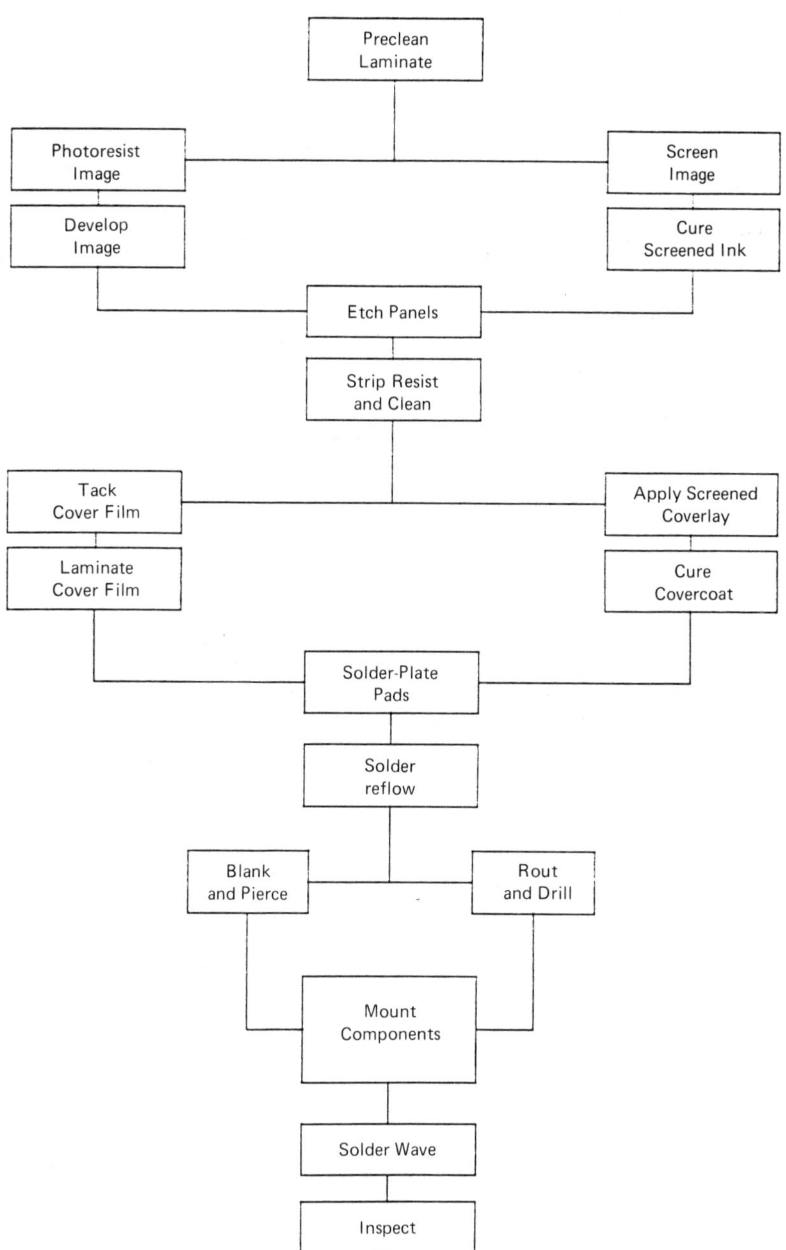

FIGURE 10.11 Typical process for flow chart for the fabrication of a single-sided circuit.

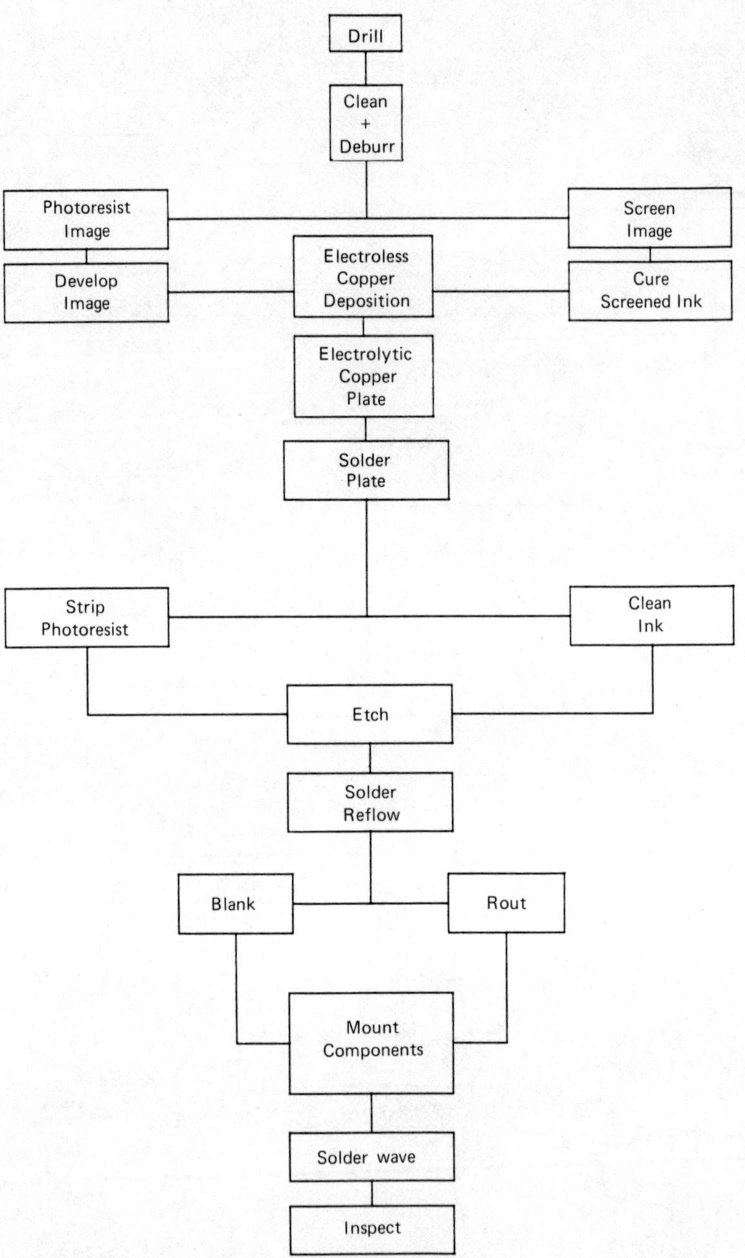

FIGURE 10.12 Typical process flow chart for the fabrication of a double-sided circuit.

TABLE 10.3 Sizes of Holes Drilled in Printed-Circuit Boards during the Years 1984–1986 (Ref. 71)

Hole size	1984	1985	1986	1985–86 change
Over 0.020 in	95.0%	93.2%	90.3%	−3.2%
0.019–0.015 in	4.0%	4.8%	6.9%	+41.7%
Under 0.015 in	1.0%	2.0%	2.8%	+40.0%

10.3.3 The Plated-through-Hole Process

The key fabrication steps of the plated-through-hole feature are drilling, smear removal, electroless deposition, and electroplating of the barrel in the hole.[22]

10.3.3.1 Drilling. Most of the drilling development work in the late 1980s has concentrated in drilling small holes.[69–73] This direction reflects the general trend to miniaturize electronic interconnection elements; see Table 10.3. Drilling circuit materials is a process that must be tailored for each individual case. Changing the key parameters, such as circuit materials, the aspect ratio of the hole, and the hole diameter, requires modifications in the drilling process. Table 10.4 lists several factors that affect the quality of the drilled hole.[70]

10.3.3.2 Smear Removal. Smearing of the dielectric material on the conductor surfaces occurs during the mechanical drilling operation due to the heating effects. Removal of the smeared dielectric before the electroless deposition step is necessary to ensure continuous plating of the hole.[22]

Using the proper drilling conditions can minimize or even eliminate the need for a desmearing step. However, many circuit fabricators choose to use a

TABLE 10.4 Factors That Affect the Quality of the Drilled Hole in Circuit Materials (Refs. 70 and 74)

Item	Considerations
Drilling machine	Positioning accuracy (registration) Vibration Spindle structure servo system Thermal stability (dimensional stability)
Drill bits	Material of the bit Shape Flute length Drill-bit wear
Drilling conditions	RPM Feed and retract rates Step drilling Number of boards in a stack
Entry and support material	Materials—top and bottom, thickness
Substrate material	Resin system Board thickness (dielectric and conductive layers) Reinforcement material

desmearing step prior to electroless deposition. Desmearing can be achieved by two methods:[75–80]

1. Wet process—chemical solutions
2. Dry process—plasma

Desmearing processes, whether wet or dry, must be tailored to the different circuit materials.

10.3.3.3 Electroless Deposition. After smear removal, the metal foils of the diclad material must be side-to-side electrically connected by a conductive material, usually copper. The electroless process steps include cleaning, metal microetching (surfaces of the metal foil), hole and surface catalyzing, and electroless deposition from solution.[22,81–84]

The electroless process is followed by an electroplating step, which forms a thick-walled conductive cylindrical path in the hole.

10.3.4 The Blind Via Process

The blind via is another method used to form a *Z*-axis conductive path. Blind vias are so called because they cannot be seen from one side of the board. A schematic process used to form a blind via is shown in Fig. 10.13. The via hole is formed, in step (b), from the dielectric side of the laminate by etching in a wet process, or by a laser-drilling process.[85–88]

A thin conductive layer is then deposited on the dielectric material and in the hole by a wet or a dry process, step (c), followed by an electroplating step to electrically connect the bottom and the top conductive layers.

10.3.5 Multilayer Circuits

Multilayer circuit wiring boards are designed and used because of one or two requirements: (a) the high density of the electronic interconnection requires more than two conductive layers, and (b) the need for electrical characteristics of the board that cannot be obtained from the single- or double-sided printed circuit.

A schematic drawing of a typical multilayer cross section is shown in Fig. 10.14. The individual internal (inner) layers are built separately on double-sided boards, as shown in Fig. 10.14*a*. Some copper foils of the internal layers may be designed to serve as signal layers and thus etched to form a circuit pattern, while other copper layers may serve as a ground layer and left unetched (top foil of the bottom inner layer in Fig. 10.14*a*). The inner layers and the outer laminates are then stacked with adhesive layers, while ensuring proper registration, and laminated to form a single multilayer board, as shown in Fig. 10.14*b*. After the multilayer has been laminated, the whole board is drilled, and side-to-side PTHs are formed. The side-to-side PTH can connect any two layers of the multilayer board, while the PTH features in the inner layers connect only across the individual layers—these inner layers vias are termed "buried" vias. After the multilayer PTHs are formed, the outer layers are imaged and etched in a process similar to the double-sided circuit board.

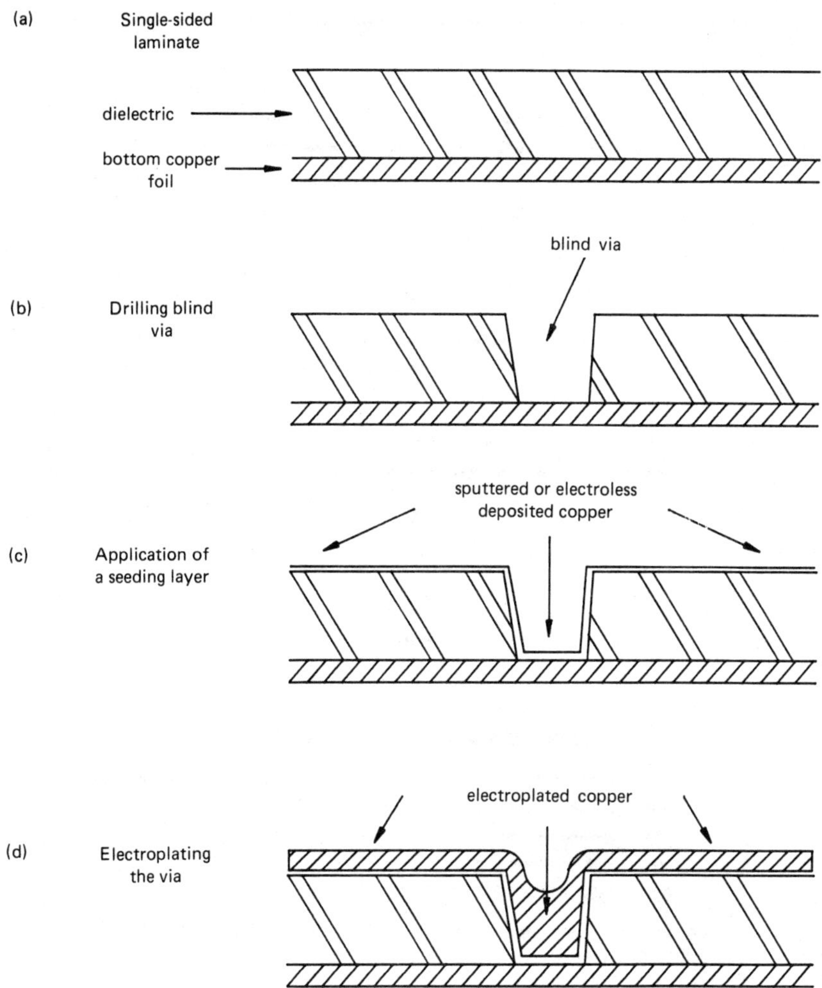

FIGURE 10.13 Schematic drawing of the process to form a blind via.

10.3.5.1 Layer-to-Layer Registration. Layer-to-layer registration is necessary to ensure correct positioning of the circuit features in the *X-Y* plane after the lamination step. The tolerance in registration defines how accurately the pads of the inner layers will be centered relative to the PTH. Multilayer registration is in most cases accomplished by a pin-and-slot alignment system, as shown schematically in Fig. 10.15. Hole location accuracy of this alignment system is ± 0.001 in at best.[89–91]

10.3.5.2 Lamination of the Multilayer Board. Some form of copper surface treatment is usually required to improve the bond between the layers in the multilayer stack. Mechanical abrasion of the copper by brushes and pumice are the

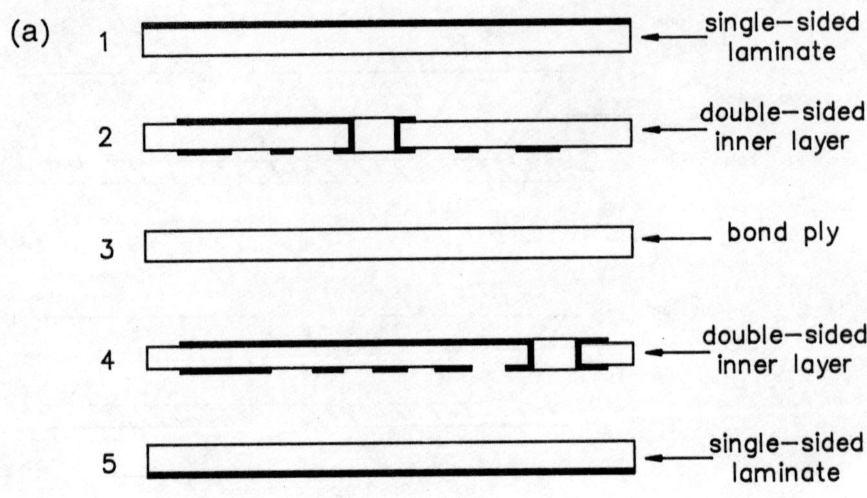

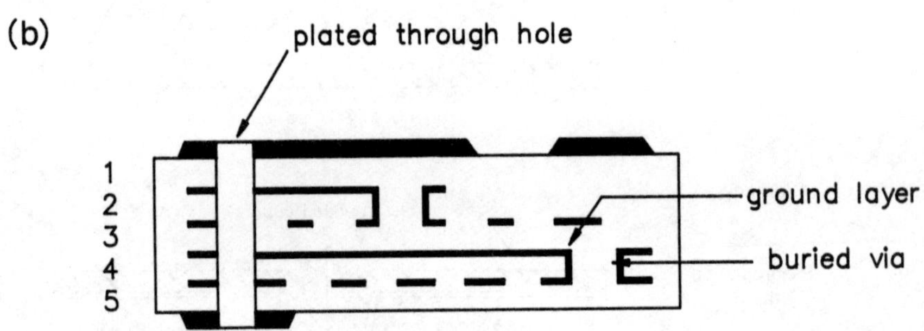

FIGURE 10.14 Schematic structure of a multilayer board with six conductor layers: *(a)* two double-sided boards and two single-sided laminates are stacked; *(b)* plated-through-hole connects the copper pads in the multilayer board.

most basic treatments. Abrasion of the copper surface by mild etchants such as the peroxide type or nitric acid has also been used successfully. Oxide treatments have also been used—"black," "red," and "brown" oxide treatments are coatings that can be deposited on the copper surface to promote bond strength between the layers in the stack.[92,93]

Multilayer lamination is best carried out in a vacuum hydraulic lamination process (VHL) or in a vacuum autoclave lamination process (VAL). Vacuum lamination reduces dimensional movement of the layers in the stack and removes air from the package more efficiently compared to hydraulic press lamination.[94,95]

10.3.5.3 PTH in a Multilayer Board. Buried vias are PTHs that connect circuit patterns side-to-side on a single inner layer. Multilayer plated-through-holes are designed to connect any two conductive layers throughout the entire stack of inner layers and outer layers.[96–101] In addition to the requirement to remove

1 Punch .032 FR4 panel on laminate punch

.1875

.280

2 Pin panel on drilling machine (soft tooling)

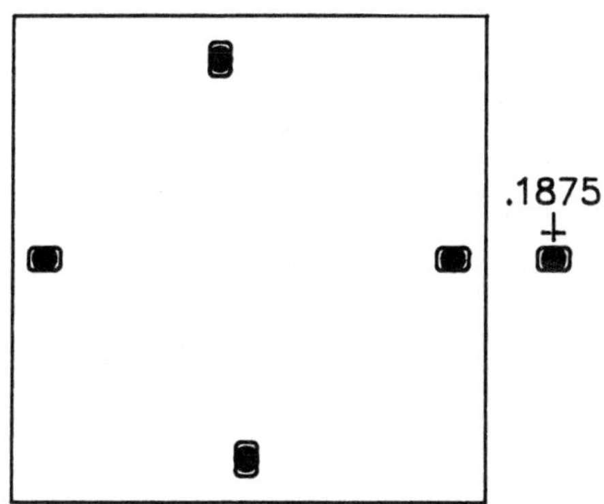

3 Drill all holes common to each layer (produce – optic master)

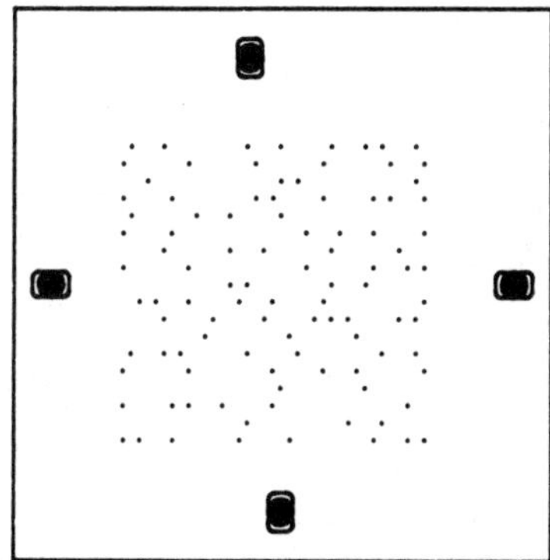

FIGURE 10.15 Major steps in registration artwork for multilayer circuits.

4 Punch clear Mylar on the laminate punch or pierce template

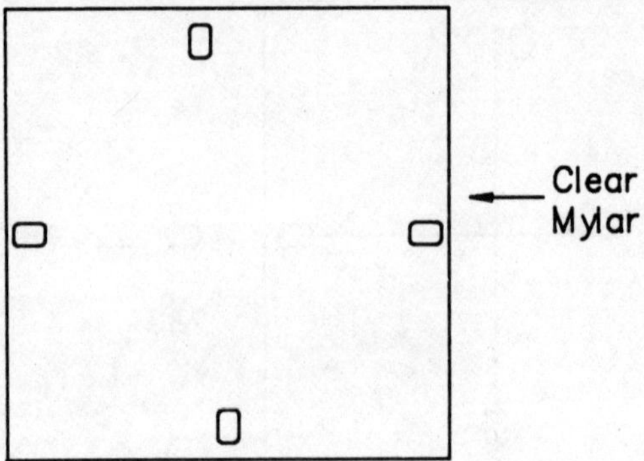

5 Using artwork pins (.1875 x .250) pin the clear Mylar to the optic master

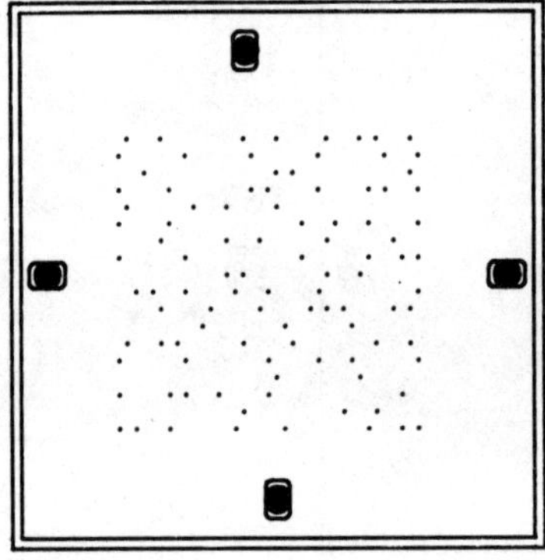

6 Cut the working film (actual artwork) inside the 4-slot area

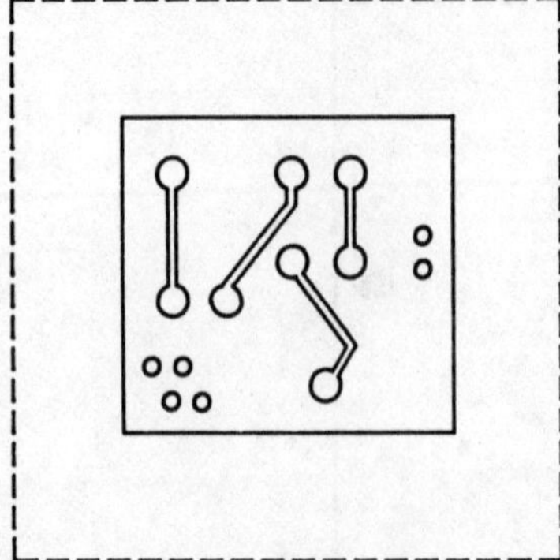

FIGURE 10.15 Major steps in registration artwork for multilayer circuits. (*Continued*)

7 Align artwork to optic master and tape in place

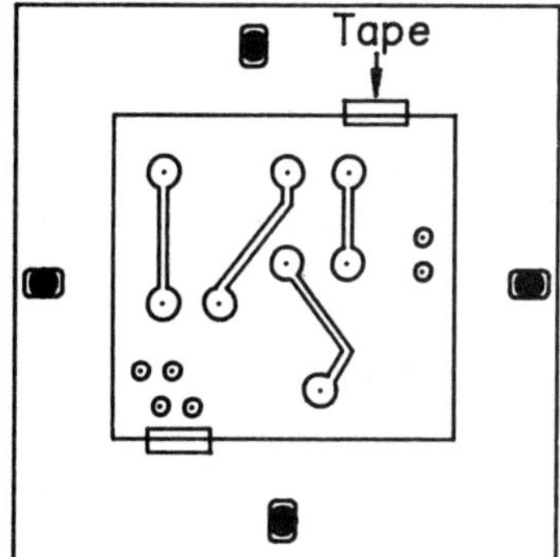

8 Remove the pins; the artwork is now taped on the Mylar in relationship to the 4 slots

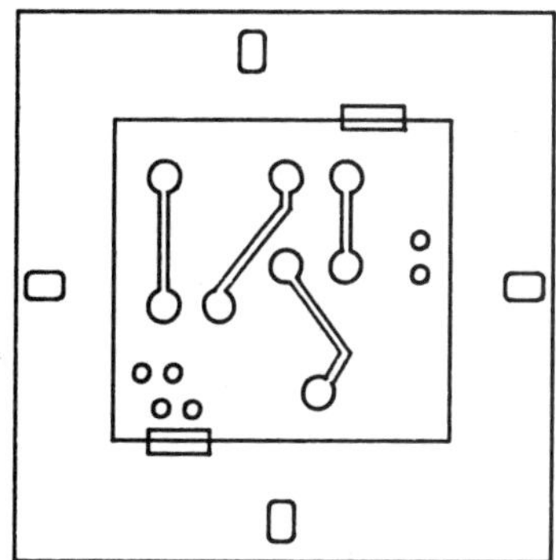

9 Punch unexposed film on laminate punch or pierce template

Unexposed Film

FIGURE 10.15 Major steps in registration artwork for multilayer circuits. (*Continued*)

10 Pin the Mylar and taped film to the unexposed film and contact print

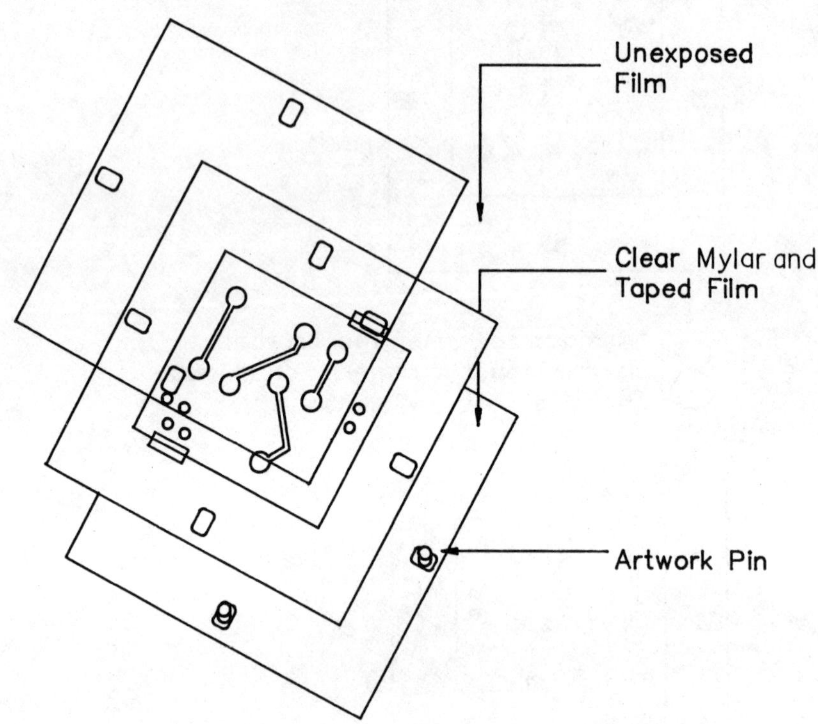

11 The result is an imaged art-work with 4 slots which can be pinned to the inner layers and exposed

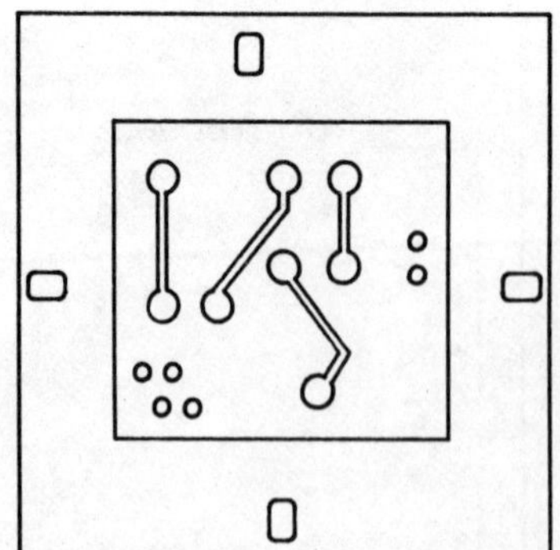

FIGURE 10.15 Major steps in registration artwork for multilayer circuits. (*Continued*)

smear, multilayer holes must be *etched-back*. Etch-back is required in multilayer PTH to form a sufficiently large interface between the inner-layer pads and the plated barrel in the hole, to ensure good bond and electrical contact.[22,96,97]

Plated-through-hole reliability is a major concern in multilayer boards. The reliability of a PTH is the measure of how well the electrical contact between the plated barrel and the pads is maintained under mechanical and thermal stresses. The right-hand side of Fig. 10.16 represents a perfect PTH, while the left-hand side emphasizes the common defects, discussed in the following.

1. *Stress crack:* This typically occurs in the corner of the hole, at the interface between the plated barrel and the plated section over the outer-layer pad. Stress cracking is caused primarily due to the mismatch of the coefficient of thermal expansion (CTE) between the dielectric material and the copper in the barrel.[97,99–101]

2. *Pad lifting (Z-axis expansion):* This mode of failure may occur during the solder operation. While the solder shrinks during crystallization, it may pull and lift the pads off the dielectric.[99]

3. *Reverse etch-back:* Wet etch-back may cause a reverse process, where the metal pad of the inner layer is etched faster than the dielectric material.

4. *Resin recession:* Excessive etch-back may result in the formation of a large void between the dielectric and the PTH barrel.

5. *Hole pull-away:* This results from poor bonding between the dielectric and the electroless copper.

6. *Laminate void:* Insufficient flow or damaged bond ply may result in laminate voids.

7. *Plating void:* Patches of dielectric that are not covered with electroless do not electroplate well and cause plating voids.

8. *Nail heading:* Poor drilling conditions may result in distortion of the pads.

9. *Smearing:* With the amount of heat generated in the drilling process, smearing of the dielectric is a common phenomenon.

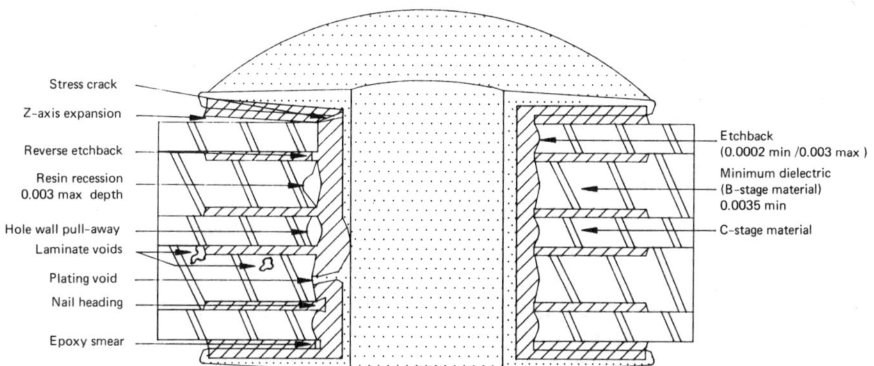

FIGURE 10.16 Schematic drawing of a plated-through-hole in a multilayer board shows common defects and their location.

10.3.6 Wiring Density of Interconnections—Summary

Tracking density of circuits is generally defined by (a) the size of the circuit features, (b) the thickness of the dielectric layers, and (c) the number of the conductive layers, in the case of a multilayer board. Tracking density is usually governed by the mechanical and the electrical performance limitations of the interconnection materials. Other critical limiting factors relate to the processing capability to form fine line features and small Z-axis vias. A list of maximum wiring densities of different interconnection systems is presented in Table 10.5.[102]

10.4 DESIGN CONSIDERATIONS OF DIELECTRIC MATERIALS

10.4.1 Overview

The choice of a circuit to solve an interconnection problem is a complex process that requires consideration of electrical, mechanical, environmental, fabrication, and cost aspects. These considerations can be grouped into two categories:

1. The properties of the circuit materials as they relate to the application, or more specifically, to the conditions in which the circuit is expected to operate
2. The fabrication processes of the circuit board, including the component mounting and the circuit assembly steps

The electronic circuit design is not the subject of this section and will not be discussed here. This section reviews the properties of circuit materials, and how these properties relate to circuit fabrication and the circuit performance in the application. The emphasis here is on the electrical, the mechanical, and the environmental properties of the dielectric portion of the circuit material. The information presented here relates to standard circuit materials as well as to generic dielectrics.

10.4.1.1 General Material Considerations. Circuit materials are often evaluated by standard test methods that are set by the industry. Some tests are specific to the application of the material (rigid boards, flexible circuits, multilayers, etc.), and other tests are intended to evaluate generic properties of the circuit material. Test methods of circuit materials are designed to evaluate both the conductive and the dielectric portions of the board. The relevance of the test results to the property required for the application is an engineering judgment. There are cases where new and specific test methods must be applied to properly address technical performance questions.

10.4.1.2 General Circuit Fabrication Considerations. Circuits are manufactured by processes that include, among other operations, exposure of the circuit material to chemicals, mechanical stresses, and high temperatures. Some of these circuit fabrication processes are directed at the conductive portion, while other processes are directed at the dielectric portion of the circuit material. However, a few circuit manufacturing operations, such as heat treatment, lamination, etching, and other operations, affect both the dielectric and the conductive portions of the circuit material simultaneously. Before defining a circuit fabrication process for a

TABLE 10.5 Maximum Wiring Density of Different Interconnection Systems (Ref. 102)

	Wiring density, in/in^2
Printed-circuit boards	
Single-sided	40
Double-sided	50
Multilayer— 4 layer, 2 signal	100
8 layer, 3 signal (insertion)	140
8 layer, 3 signal (surface mount)	200
8 layer, 4 signal	170
10 layer, 5 signal	220
12 layer, 8 signal	280
16 layer, 8 signal	300
Thick film	
Single-layer polymer thick film	40
Two-layer polymer thick film	100
Three-layer thick film hybrid	125
Co-fired ceramic (1 signal layer)	280
Microwire	
1 signal layer	
6.3-mil wire†	80
4.0-mil wire†	120
2.5-mil microwire†	240
Shielded wire†	≥240
2 signal layers	200
4 signal layers	380
Others	
Dual-in-line packages	36
Dual-in-line packages	80
Chip carrier	120
Chip carrier	180
Tape automated bonding	350
Thin film hybrid (1 signal layer)	300

†Only half these capabilities achievable in practice.

certain circuit material, the compatibility between the material properties and fabrication conditions must be well understood.

10.4.2 Classification of Generic Dielectric Materials

Polymers, ceramics, and glasses are the insulating materials to be considered as dielectrics for interconnection applications; see Fig. 10.17. Through composite material technology the properties of the dielectric materials can be optimized and tailored for the intended application. The dielectric materials of printed circuits have predominantly been composite material.

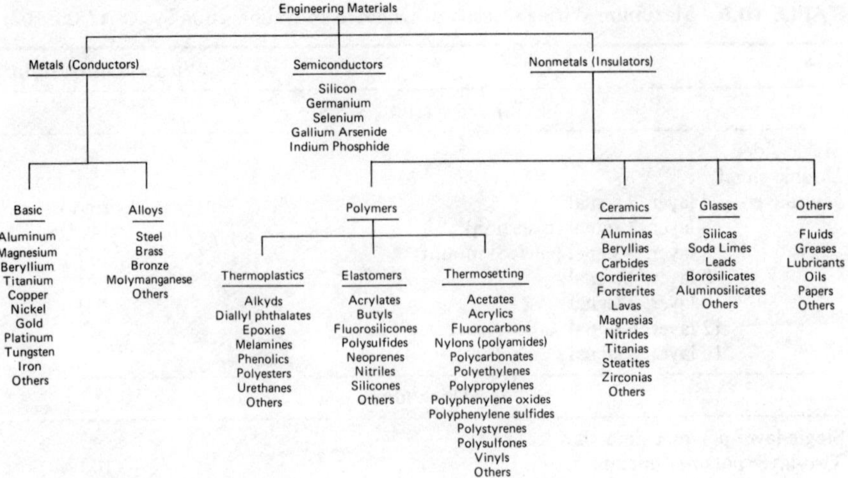

FIGURE 10.17 Engineering materials by categories.

10.4.2.1 Ceramic Materials. Ceramics are rigid and brittle inorganic polycrystalline solids, with softening temperatures typically above 1100°C. In general, ceramic materials have a relatively high dielectric constant and low coefficient of thermal expansion (CTE). Ceramic boards are fabricated from a paste of ceramic particles in an organic binder, commonly known as "green tape." The board is shaped in a molding or a sintering process and then fired at a high temperature to obtain the final geometry. Ceramic circuit boards are usually made by using polymer thick-film (PTF) technology to form the conductive paths.[103–106]

Ceramic materials are also used as reinforcement fillers for polymers. Their low CTE, high compressive modulus, and thermal conductivity are the major property advantages in formulating polymer-ceramic composites.

10.4.2.2 Glass. Glasses are not usually used as dielectric substrates for circuit boards. The most important use of glass in circuit materials is in the form of mechanical reinforcement. Glass fibers can be used as a reinforcement material in three forms: (1) short fibers, (2) nonwoven web, and (3) woven glass cloth. Glass particles or beads are also commonly used to reinforce plastic matrices.

10.4.2.3 Polymers. Polymers are the most important dielectric material class used in electronic packaging. Polymers are synthetic organic compounds, and as such, new polymeric materials are still being invented. Certain properties of polymers can be modified to a degree by manipulating the chemistry or the fabrication process of the polymer.

Thermoset Polymers. The term *thermoset* is applied to materials that, once heated, react irreversibly so that subsequent application of heat and pressure do not cause them to flow. This curing process is known as crosslinking, and it results in a three-dimensional rigid chemical structure of the polymer. Crosslinked polymers have a relatively high resistance to solvents.[107]

Thermoplastic Polymers. The term *thermoplastic* is applied to materials that soften and flow upon application of pressure and heat. This property limits the use of thermoplastics to temperatures under their softening point. Thermoplastic polymers are, as a rule, more sensitive to organic solvents.

Thermoplastic materials are used for interconnection applications because of their excellent electrical properties, and because they are easy to formulate and process. Composites of thermoplastic materials with fibers or particulate fillers have been widely used in interconnection systems. Since thermoplastic materials are easy to process and to machine they have been commonly named "engineering resins";[108,109] see Tables 10.6 and 10.7.

Standard industrial circuit laminates are composite materials of a polymeric matrix and fiber reinforcement. Most of the dielectric materials are based on thermoset polymers and glass fibers. A list of the industrial laminates identified by their NEMA (National Electrical Manufacturers Association) grade is presented in the Appendix.

10.4.3 Thermal Properties of Polymer-Based Dielectric Materials

Mechanical and electrical properties of polymers vary with temperature. Changes of these properties may affect the performance of the dielectric material during the circuit fabrication process and during service in the application.

10.4.3.1 Elastic Properties. At temperatures below the glass transition temperature (T_g) the polymer is rigid and glasslike, while above the T_g the polymer is soft and rubberlike. The elastic modulus of a polymer in the glassy state is typically three orders of magnitude higher than the elastic modulus of the same polymer in its rubbery state. At the transition the polymer is described as leather-like material. The glass transition phenomenon occurs in both thermoplastic and thermoset polymers;[107] see Tables 10.6–10.8.

Hence, the T_g is a property of polymers that defines the temperature at which the mechanical properties of a polymer change from rigid to soft. Knowledge of the T_g of the polymeric dielectric is important for the handling and processing of circuit material during fabrication processes. The same considerations apply to the environmental conditions in service. Heat deflection temperature is another measure of the mechanical usefulness of a polymer or a polymer composite relative to temperature. The method to measure the heat deflection temperature is described in ASTM D-1637. The UL temperature index (TI) is a third measure of the mechanical usefulness of a material over time. The temperature index defines the maximum temperature for continuous service of a polymer or a polymer composite; see Tables 10.6 and 10.7.

10.4.3.2 Volumetric Expansion. A typical volumetric expansion curve of polymers exhibits two distinct regions; the slope of the curve above the glass transition temperature is about 5 times the slope of the curve below T_g. In engineering terms, this means that the coefficient of thermal expansion (CTE) in the rubbery region is about 5 times the CTE of the polymer in the glassy state. Typical CTE values of selective polymers and composite circuit materials are presented in Tables 10.6 and 10.8.

10.4.4 Electrical Properties of Dielectric Materials

The electrical properties of the dielectric material, both of the bulk and the surface, have an important impact on the design of the conductive traces and the functionality of the circuit.[121] The electrical performance of a circuit is affected by (a) the dielectric material properties, (b) the design of the conductive pattern, (c) the circuit fabrication process, and (d) by the environmental conditions.

TABLE 10.6 Properties of Major Electronic Thermoplastic Polymers (Refs. 108 and 110–117)

Property	PTFE[a]	FEP[b]	PFA[c]	Tefzel[d]	Kynar[e]	Radel[f]	Udel[g]	
Ultimate tensile strength, N/m^2	$1.7–27 \times 10^7$	2×10^7	2.7×10^7	4.4×10^7	3.4×10^7	7.1×10^7	6.8×10^7	7.1×10^7
Ultimate elongation, %	300–600	300	300	200	140–250	60	50–100	
Tensile modulus, N/m^2	4.1×10^8	4.8×10^8	6.5×10^8	8.2×10^8	20×10^8	20×10^8	25×10^8	
Density, ASTM D-792, g/cm^3	2.14–2.21	2.15	2.13–2.16	1.7	1.76	1.29	1.29	
Heat deflection temperature, °C	52	70		104	88	204	174	
Glass transition temperature, T_g, °C							190	
Melting point, °C	327	260	310	270	300			
CTE, ppm/°C		82–160	67–200	90–140	110	55	58	
Flammability, LOI %	nonflammable	nonflammable	>95	[V-O]	44	38	30	
Thermal degradation, °C	260	200	250	150	>370		150	
UL temperature index, °C								
Dielectric strength V/mil	3400	6500	2000	7000	1280	1100	7500	
Dissipation factor		0.0005	0.0003–0.0005	0.0006–0.005	0.033–0.16	0.0001–0.0007		
Dielectric constant (at frequency, Hz)	2.1	2.1	2.06 (10^2)–2.05 (10^{10})	2.6 (10^1)–2.4 (10^9)	8.4 (60)–3.0 (10^9)	3.4 (60)–3.5	3.1–3.2	
Volume resistivity, Ω cm	$>10^{18}$	10^{17}	10^{18}	$>10^{16}$	2×10^{14}	9×10^{15}	2×10^{16}	
Surface resistivity, Ω	3.6×10^{16}	10^{16}	$>10^{17}$	5×10^{14}				
Arc resistance, s	>200	>165		75	60			
Water absorption, %	<0.01	<0.01	0.03	0.03	0.05			

Property	Ultem[h]	Victrex[i]	Peek[j]	Rayton[k]	TPX[l]	Lennite[m]	Propylux[n]
Ultimate tensile strength, N/m^2	10×10^7	7.0×10^7	9.1×10^7	6.5×10^7	2×10^7	2.2×10^7	3.4×10^7
Ultimate elongation, %	40–600	80	150	1.6	25	900	>200

Tensile modulus, N/m^2	26×10^8	25×10^8	11×10^8	38×10^8	0.13×10^8	1×10^8	11×10^8
Density, ASTM D-792, g/cm^3	1.27		1.32	1.3	0.83	0.94	0.90
Heat deflection temperature, °C	200		148	135	90	94	99
Glass transition temperature, T_g, °C	216	200	143	93		−85	−18
Melting point, °C			334	282	240	138	168
CTE, ppm/°C	56	50		48	120	200	68
Flammability, LOI %	27	34	24	44			
Thermal degradation, °C			260	200	250		
UL temperature index, °C	170	190	250				
Dielectric strength, V/mil	3500	400	480	380	1650	2200	660
Dissipation factor		0.001–0.006		0.0004–0.0007	0.00003–0.00007	0.0005–0.0006	0.0005–0.002
Dielectric constant (at frequency, Hz)	$3.1\ (10^5)$–$3.04(10^{10})$	$3.5\ (10^6)$–3.6	$3.2\ (10^6)$–3.3	$3.1\ (10^3)$–3.2	2.1–2.2	$2.3\ (10^5)$–2.4	$2.2\ (10^3)$–2.3
Volume resistivity, Ωm	$>10^{11}$	$>10^{17}$	$>10^{15}$		$>10^6$	$>10^{18}$	6.5×10^{16}
Surface resistivity, Ω	$>10^{10}$		3.6×10^{16}		$>10^{17}$	$>10^{13}$	
Arc resistance, s						melts	>13
Water absorption %		2.1	0.15	0.01	0.01	<0.02	<0.02

Property	Celcon[o]	Noryl[p]	PMMA[q]	Mylar[r]	Valox[s]	Lexan[t]	ABS[u]	Nylon 66[v]
Ultimate tensile strength, N/m^2)	6×10^7	4.5×10^7	7×10^7	20×10^7	5×10^7	6.2×10^7	6.1×10^7	60×10^7
Ultimate elongation, %	50–70		<10	120	100	85–105	20–50	300
Tensile modulus, N/m^2	50×10^8	23×10^8	31×10^8	40×10^8		20.7×10^8	27.6×10^8	33×10^8
Density, ASTM D-792, g/cm^3	1.41	1.06	1.19	1.33	1.41	1.20	1.1–1.2	1.15
Heat deflection temperature, °C	136	85	95		54	140	115	204
Glass transition temperature, T_g, °C			105	125		149		

TABLE 10.6 Properties of Major Electronic Thermoplastic Polymers (Refs. 108 and 110–117) (*Continued*)

Property	Celcon[o]	Noryl[p]	PMMA[q]	Mylar[r]	Valox[s]	Lexan[t]	ABS[u]	Nylon 66[v]
Melting point, °C	163		>200	255		225		250
CTE, ppm/°C	47	41	28–50	17	40	68	50–80	70–100
Flammability, LOI %								
Thermal degradation, °C			>250			132		
UL temperature index, °C	105					110		105
Dielectric strength, V/mil	1200	630	500	7500	>500	400	>350	400–450
Dissipation factor		0.0004–0.0009				0.007–0.010	0.0001–0.0006	0.02–0.04
Dielectric constant (at frequency, Hz)	3.8	2.6–2.8	3.7 (60)–2.5 (10^9)	3.3 (60)–3.7 (10^9)	3.3 (10^2)–3.1(10^6)	3.0 (60)–2.9(10^9)	2.4–4.5	3.6 (10^2)–3.0 (10^9)
Volume resistivity, Ωcm	10^{14}	10^{15}	10^{17}	10^{13}	10^{16}	10^{16}	10^{16}	4×10^{14}
Surface resistivity, Ω	10^{13}	10^{15}		10^{18}		$>10^{13}$		
Arc resistance, s	205					120		116
Water absorption, %	0.22	0.06		0.8	0.38	0.35	0.6–1.0	8

[a]Teflon-PTFE—polytetrafluoroethylene, Dupont.
[b]Teflon-FEP—fluorinated ethylene-propylene copolymer, Dupont.
[c]Teflon-PFA—perfluoroalkoxy, Dupont.
[d]Tefzel—ethylene tetrafluoroethylene, DuPont.
[e]Kynar—polyvinylidene fluoride, Pennwalt.
[f]Radel—polyphenyl sulfone, Union Carbide.
[g]Udel—polysulfone, Union Carbide.
[h]Ultem—polyether-imide, General Electric.
[i]Victrex PES—polyether sulfone, ICI.
[j]PEEK—polyetheretherketone, ICI.
[k]Rayton—polyphenylene sulfide, Phillips Petroleum.
[l]TPX—polymethyl pentene, Mitsui.
[m]Lennite—polyethylene, UHMW.
[n]Propylux—polypropylene.
[o]Celcon—polyacetal copolymer.
[p]Noryl—modified polyphenylene oxide.
[q]PMMA—polymethyl methocrylate.
[r]Mylar—polyethylene terphthalate.
[s]Valox—polybutylene terphalate.
[t]Lexan—polyarbonate.
[u]ABS—acrylonitrile butadiene styrene.
[v]Nylon 66—polyamide.

TABLE 10.7 Typical Properties of Thermoplastic–Glass Composite Dielectric Materials (Ref. 108)

Polymer–30 percent glass reinforcement	Tensile strength, psi	Flexural modulus, 10^6 psi	Heat-deflection temperature at 264 psi, °F	Dielectric strength, V/mil	Dielectric constant at 60 Hz	Dissipation factor at 60 Hz	Arc resistance, s	UL temperature index, °C
Inherent UL 94V-0								
Polycarbonate	19,000	1.0	300	450	3.50	0.0010	5	115
Polysulfone	15,000	1.1	360	480	3.65	0.0020	121	150
Polyethersulfone	20,000	1.25	415	460	3.80	0.0030	75	175
Polyetherimide	28,500	1.25	420	630	3.5	0.0015	85	180
Polyphenylenesulfide	23,000	1.8	500	375	3.83	0.0011	50	180
Polyetheretherketone	25,000	1.1	<540	500	3.71	0.0019	124	<240
Styrene-maleic-anhydride	9000	0.95	210	470	3.17	0.0083	30	
Polybutylene terephthalate	19,000	1.4	405	400	3.79	0.0031	15	120
Polyethylene terephthalate	23,000	2.0	435	550	3.8	0.0050	117	
Nylon 6/6	23,000	1.5	470	450	4.53	0.0375	12	120
Modified polyphenylene ether	14,500	0.33 to 0.75	300	400 to 630	2.7 to 3	0.0007 to 0.0047		
Nylon 6	22,000	1.35	410	450	4.40	0.0110	15	105

TABLE 10.8 Typical Properties of Circuit Materials (Refs. 5, 22, and 118–120)

Material type*	CTE, $\times 10^{-6}$/°C			T_g, °C	Maximum operating temperature, °C		Flexural strength, kpsi		Water absorption, %§
	Warp	Fill	Z direction		Elec†	Mech.‡	Warp	Fill	
XXXP	12	17			125	125			0.85
XXPC	12	17			125	125	10.5	12	
FR-2	12	25			105	105	10.5	12	0.65
FR-3	13	25			105	105	16	20	0.60
CEM-1	11	17			130	140	28	35	0.25
CEM-3	10	15			130	140	32	40	0.20
FR-6	10	10			105	105	15	15	
G-10	10	15	>100	100	130	140	50	60	0.20
FR-4	10	15	>100	125	130	140	50	60	0.20
G-11	10	15			170	180	50	60	0.20
FR-5	10	15	> 60	140	170	180	50	60	0.20
GI	10	12			260	260	40	50	
GT	10	25			220	220	10	15	0.09
GX	10	25			220	220	10	15	0.09
Aramid-polyimide	6.5	7.2	66	167					
Quartz-polyimide	8.5	9.8	34.6	188					
Aramid-epoxy	5.5	5.6	100.4	137					
Glass-polyimide	12.6	13.0	41.0	249					
Quartz–FR-4 epoxy	11.0	13.6	62.6	125					
Quartz-epoxy, polyimid	12.2	14.0	60.3	109					
PTFE-ceramic, glass	19	19	25						
BT epoxy–glass	13	13	90	220					

*See appendix, pages 10.55 to 10.57.
†Electrical factor.
‡Mechanical factor.
§Values for 3/32-in thickness.

The following sections review key electrical properties of dielectric materials and electrical phenomena that should be considered in the design of the circuit.[5,110]

10.4.4.1 Volume Resistivity. The volume resistivity is the electrical resistance between opposite faces of a cube of insulating material, commonly expressed in Ω cm.

Volume resistivity of polymers and polymer composites depends on humidity, temperature composition, and time. An increase in temperature results in a decrease in volume resistance of almost all polymers. Humidity usually reduces the volume resistivity of polymers and polymer composites. The volume resistivity of circuit materials exposed to humidity [typical tests are performed at 85–95 percent relative humidity (RH)] may drop several orders of magnitude in a few weeks.[121]

10.4.4.2 Surface Resistivity. The surface resistivity is the electrical resistance of a unit square surface of an insulating material, as measured between two coplanar conductors. Surface resistivity is commonly expressed in Ω and may vary with the measurement conditions.

The surface resistivity of polymers and polymer composites depends on the surface cleanliness and the surface quality of the dielectric material. Humidity degrades the surface resistivity of dielectric materials.[121]

10.4.4.3 Insulation Resistance. Insulation resistance is a measurement of ohmic resistance between two coplanar conductive patterns at a given condition. Several comb patterns are used in the industry to measure insulation resistance.

10.4.4.4 Dielectric Strength. Dielectric strength is the maximum voltage gradient a material can withstand before dielectric breakdown occurs. The dielectric strength is expressed in V/cm. The disruptive electric discharge through the dielectric material is commonly termed *breakdown.*

The thickness of the tested piece should be reported, since the dielectric strength of dielectric films is not linear with thickness. Dielectric strength of polymers normally drops with increasing temperature.[121,122] Moisture degrades the dielectric strength of polymers and polymer composites.[122]

Typical dielectric strength values of selected circuit material are given in Tables 10.6, 10.7, and 10.9.

10.4.4.5 Corona. Corona is the luminous discharge caused by ionization of the air surrounding a conductor around which exists a voltage gradient exceeding a certain critical value. Most organic materials are attacked by corona discharge.[121]

10.4.4.6 Arc Resistance (or Electrical Tracking). Arc resistance pertains to the time required for an arc to establish a conductive path in a dielectric material.

Arc resistance is a measure of an electrical breakdown condition along an insulating surface caused by the formation of a conductive path on the surface. Arc resistance is a surface-sensitive test that is greatly affected by cleanliness and dryness.[121]

The arc resistance values of selected dielectric materials are presented in Tables 10.6 and 10.7.

TABLE 10.9 Typical Thermal and Electrical Properties of Circuit Materials (Refs. 5, 22, and 120)

Material*	Thermal conductivity, W/°C m	Dielectric constant	Dissipation factor	Dielectric strength, V/mil
XXXP	0.17	4.1	0.028–0.030	740
FR-2	0.18	4.5	0.024–0.026	740
FR-3	0.16	4.3	0.024–0.026	550
FR-4	0.18	4.6	0.018–0.020	500
FR-5	0.18	4.3	0.019–0.028	500
FR-6		4.1	0.020–0.028	
CEM-1	0.18	4.4	0.027–0.028	500
CEM-3	0.18	4.6	0.020–0.022	500
G-10	0.18	4.6	0.018–0.019	570
G-11	0.18	4.5	0.019–0.020	600
GI		4.8	0.020–0.030	750
GT		2.8	0.005–0.006	
GX		2.8	0.002–0.002	
Polyimide-quartz	0.13			
Polyimide-Kevlar	0.12			
Polyimide-glass	0.35			
PTFE-glass	0.26			
PTFE ceramic, glass	0.44			
Alumina	16.8			
Copper	394.0			

*See appendix, pages 10.55 to 10.57.

10.4.4.7 Dielectric Constant (Relative Permittivity). The dielectric constant is the ratio of the capacitance of a device using the dielectric material to the capacitance of the same device in a vacuum. Common notations for dielectric constant are ϵ_r and *Dk*.

The dielectric constant characteristics of polar polymers are much more complicated than those of nonpolar polymers. The dielectric constant of polymers normally decreases with frequency.[121] The dielectric constant of most polymers varies from 2 to 10. By mixing polymers with fillers or reinforcing webs, the dielectric constant of the composite can be varied.[123,124]

Typical dielectric constant values of selected polymers and composites are presented in Tables 10.6, 10.7, 10.9, and 10.10. Low dielectric constant values are preferred for high-frequency or power applications to minimize power losses. Higher-dielectric-constant materials are preferred for capacitance applications. The dielectric constant is affected by temperature and frequency. These variations are unique to each material.[121]

10.4.4.8 Dissipation Factor. The dissipation factor is the ratio of power loss to power input of a dielectric material. More accurately, the dissipation factor is the tangent of the dielectric loss angle, abbreviated tan δ. In insulation materials, the dissipation factor is practically the equivalent of power loss.

The term *loss,* which is associated with a high dissipation factor, is defined as the decrease in signal power in transmission from one point to another.[121] The variations of the dissipation factor with frequency and with temperature are complex and difficult to predict. Typical values of the dissipation factor of selected polymers and composites are presented in Tables 10.6, 10.7, and 10.9.

10.4.5 Mechanical Properties of Dielectric Materials

10.4.5.1 Overview. The mechanical properties of circuit materials play an important role during circuit fabrication processes and during use in the application. Since most steps of modern circuit fabrication processes are automated, handling of the board has become an important aspect of the circuit material properties.

It is difficult (and may not be necessary) to separate the mechanical properties of the dielectric material portion of the circuit material and the mechanical properties of the laminate. In practical terms, it is important to understand the various fabrication processes of circuit boards to fully appreciate how they affect the circuit material. In its final state, however, only a small area of the board is covered with the conductive pattern; thus the mechanical properties of the circuit board are largely affected by the properties of the dielectric material.

Analysis of the mechanical properties of circuit materials should take into consideration the intended application of the material. While a rigid board, for example, is designed to carry components and to be attached firmly to a frame in the device, flexible circuits are designed to freely bend, roll or flex. These two functions are different in nature, and therefore the materials ficked for the applications should be evaluated and designed accordingly. Similar considerations should be given to the mechanical properties of circuit materials to be used in both the additive and subtractive circuit fabrication processes.

10.4.5.2 Machinability. The circuit material is usually drilled, tapped, punched, routed, cut, and sawed during the various steps of the circuit fabrication. One of the most important machining operations is the drilling step.[129]

TABLE 10.10 Dielectric Constant Values of Specialty Circuit Materials (Refs. 102, 109, and 125–128)

Dielectric material	Dielectric constant
Polystyrene foam	1.8–2.2
PTFE-microglass	2.4
PTFE-ceramic, glass	2.9
Polyether sulfone foam	1.5–2.5
PTFE-Kevlar	2.2–2.5
Polybutadiene-glass	3.2–4.2
Polybutadiene-quartz	3.0–3.2
Polybutadiene-Kevlar	3.5–3.6
Bismeleamide triazine–quartz	3.2–3.3
Bismeleamide triazine–glass	4.2–4.6
Polyimide-quartz	2.9–3.4
Polyimide-Kevlar	3.5–4.1
Epoxy foam	2.7–3.5
Epoxy-PTFE	2.6–2.8

A reinforcing cloth with a tight weave and large-diameter fibers, for example, is more difficult to drill than a loose weave of fine fibers. Abrasive fillers, mostly ceramics, usually cause drill bits to wear more quickly.

10.4.5.3 Rigidity and Toughness. These mechanical properties are measured by the tensile strength, elongation, and elastic modulus of the dielectric material. Rigidity and toughness are associated with the machinability of the circuit material and also with the capability of handling the circuit material during the process. Fixturing of the circuit material during the fabrication process, including the multilayer registration step, is affected by the rigidity and the toughness of the circuit material.

Mechanical properties of circuit materials may be evaluated by ASTM D299. Typical elastic properties of selected circuit materials are presented in Tables 10.6–10.8.

10.4.5.4 Dimensional Stability. This term is used to describe the dimensional changes of a circuit material during the circuit fabrication processes. More specifically, dimensional stability is the measure of the dimensional change of a circuit material after etching the copper foil (in a subtractive process), or the dimensional change of the material upon heating, exposure to chemicals, lamination, etc.[130–133]

Dimensional stability is an important property for all classes of circuit boards but is more important for multilayer circuit materials, where layer-to-layer registration is crucial.

10.4.5.5 Peel Strength. The bond strength between the conductor and the dielectric material must survive mechanical stresses during machining and thermal operations while the circuit is fabricated. During the circuit fabrication the board is exposed to chemicals that may attack the dielectric material and the interface between the conductive pattern and dielectric surface.

Typical peel strength values of standard circuit materials vary between 6 and 10 pli (pounds per linear inch), as measured by a standard test method IPC-TM-650, method 2.4.8. The Institute for Interconnecting and Packaging Electronic Circuits (IPC) has published various test methods for the evaluation of interconnection systems. At elevated temperatures and after chemical exposure these values usually drop.

10.4.5.6 Coefficient of Thermal Expansion. The CTE values of the dielectric material are an important property when considering (a) the reliability of a plated-through-hole in double-clad and multilayer circuits and (b) the reliability of the solder joints in surface-mount component approach.

The CTE of the dielectric material in the Z axis affects the PTH reliability. Mismatch of the CTE values between the plated metal (usually copper) in the hole and the CTE of the dielectric material is a major contributor to the tensile stresses that may develop in the plated barrel during thermal cycling; see also Sec. 10.3.5.3. The other contributing variables to the PTH reliability are discussed in Sec. 10.4.5.7. This mismatch of the CTE between the dielectric material and the plated metal in the hole may be further aggravated when the ambient temperature reaches the T_g of the dielectric material.

Surface-mount components are connected to the circuit-board surface via solder joints. To ensure high reliability of these joints, the X-Y plane CTE of the board should closely match the X-Y plane CTE of the component.[119,121,134]

Since most dielectric materials are composites of a polymeric matrix and a reinforcement element, the CTE of the circuit board may vary in the three dimensions of the dielectric material; see Table 10.8. Reinforcement with a particulate filler (low aspect ratio) will contribute to the composite properties isotropically, while the use of long fibers or woven reinforcement results in a directionality of the CTE values.[114,119,134]

Thus, the dielectric CTE of typical circuit materials depends on the composite properties in the three dimensions. The CTE in the *Z* axis is normally higher than that in the reinforced *X-Y* plane. Also, the CTE of a polymeric dielectric material above the glass transition temperature of the matrix is higher than the CTE below the T_g. Typical values of circuit materials are presented in Tables 10.6 and 10.8.

10.4.5.7 Reliability of PTH and Solder Joint of Surface-Mounted Devices. Reliability of PTH and of solder joints of surface-mounted devices (SMD) is a complex mechanical problem, which is affected by (a) the CTE, (b) the elastic modulus, and (c) the geometrical aspects of the materials in the vicinity of the hole or around the mounted device.[101,119,121,125,135–141]

PTH Reliability. When the plated-through-hole is exposed to a temperature variation, the metal and the dielectric materials around the hole expand. A typical mismatch between the *Z*-axis CTE of the dielectric material and the plated metal in the hole results in compression stresses in the dielectric material, while the plated metal in the hole is usually under tensile stresses. Assuming no fracture in the PTH, the strain in the plated metal is equal to the strain in the dielectric. The level of this strain is a function of the CTE values of the dielectric and the metal in the hole, of the aspect ratio of the hole, of the thickness of the plated metal, and of the elastic properties of the materials around the hole.[99] As a rule, PTH reliability increases with (1) decreasing *Z*-axis CTE mismatch between dielectric material and plated metal, (2) decreasing aspect ratio of the hole, (3) increasing plated metal thickness, and (4) decreasing ratio of dielectric to plated metal.

Solder Joint Reliability. Fracture of the solder joint between the component and the circuit board is the most common failure mode of surface-mounted devices. Mismatch between the *X-Y* CTE values of the board and the mounted component is a major contributor to solder joint failures. The CTE of the dielectric materials can be constrained, in the *X-Y* plane, by laminating the circuit material to a low-CTE metal core; see Fig. 10.18. Use of a metal core does not solve the CTE mismatch problem in the *Z* axis; thus PTH reliability is not improved by a metal-core approach. Copper-Invar-copper (CIC) and diclad molybdenum are among the metal cores that have been commonly used by the printed-circuit industry;[22,101,119,136,137,139,141] see Table 10.11.

The CTE of a polymeric matrix in the *X-Y* plane can also be reduced by an aramid fiber (Kevlar) reinforcement.[142] Kevlar has a negative CTE of −2 ppm/°C, which makes it possible to construct an epoxy-Kevlar board with a composite CTE similar to ceramics.[119,125,136,141] CTE values of typical polymer-aramid composites are presented in Table 10.8. Another approach for improving the reliability of surface-mounted devices makes use of a compliant layer between the solder joint plane and the bulk of the rigid board.[22]

10.4.6 Thermal Properties of Dielectric Materials

The trend to miniaturize interconnection systems has resulted in excessive heat generation on the advanced high-density circuit boards. Increased conductor den-

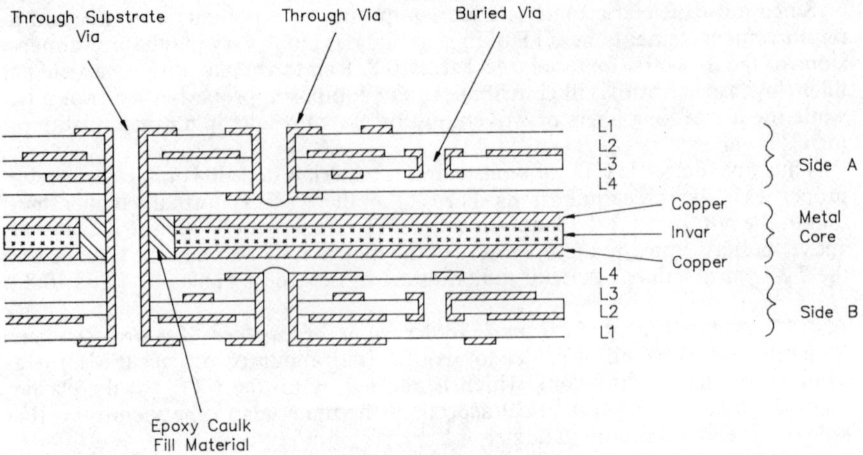

FIGURE 10.18 Schematic design of a circuit board with a constraining metal core.

sity, reduced conductor cross section, and use of high-power ICs are the major contributors to this problem. Removal of the heat from the board can be enhanced by conduction, convection, and radiation.[136,143] The engineering field that deals with controlling temperature in the device is commonly termed *thermal management.* Heat may be generated by the conductive patterns of the board or by the electrical components that are attached to the circuit board. While the components are external, the conductive features of a multilayer board may be embedded inside the circuit board. Heat generated by the components, especially ICs, could be removed directly off the component.

10.4.6.1 Conduction. Heat transfer by conduction through the circuit board may be enhanced by (1) using circuit materials that incorporate metal cores with high thermal conductivity, and (2) designing effective paths of heat from the board to a heat sink.

Heat conduction through standard dielectric boards is poor, since polymers are inherently poor conductors of heat. Typical matrix reinforcing materials, such as glass and ceramics, only slightly improve the coefficient of thermal conductivity of the composite. Direct heat conduction in the *X-Y* plane of the board can be enhanced by laminating a metal core to the dielectric materials. The metal-core layer, which is usually "buried" inside the multilayer board, serves as a heat sink.[137,144,145] Typical coefficients of thermal conductivity of selected core materials are presented in Table 10.11.

To fully benefit from a laminated heat sink, thermal energy generated on the board must be funneled from the surface of the board to the buried metal core. This can be accomplished by *thermal vias.* Thermal vias are plated posts that originate on the surface of the board and terminate at the heat sink layer.[146]

10.4.6.2 Radiation. Radiation of heat can be enhanced by (1) using materials with high emissivity, (2) building the radiator elements for maximum radiation area, and (3) raising the temperature of the radiating medium. Radiation can be effectively used to remove heat from the heat sink.[137,147]

TABLE 10.11 Properties of Core Material; Thermal and Mechanical Parameters

Material	CTE, $\times 10^{-6}$ °C	Thermal conductivity, W/°C in	Density, lb/in^3	Specific thermal conductivity, W in^2/lb °C	Relative cost	Young's modulus E 10^6 psi
Aluminum	23.6	219	0.098	56.0	1	10
Copper	17.6	394	0.323	30.7	1.2	17
Alloy 42	5.3	15.8	0.28	1.41	3.3	21
Molybdenum	4.9	148	0.369	10.1	5.0	47
Invar	1.3	10.5	0.30	0.88	3.3	21
Copper-Invar 20-60-20	6.5	165*	0.31	13.3	.2	18.5
Copper molybdenum 13-74-13	6.5	213†	0.36	14.8	4	31.2
Boron aluminum MMC‡ 20%	12.7	186§	0.095	48.9	100	27
Graphite aluminum MMC 0–90° crossply	5.8	163	0.087	46.9	400	21
SiC aluminum MMC	16.2	140	0.103	34.1	200	15

*Conductivity in normal direction is 0.430 W/°C in.
†Conductivity in normal direction is 4.43 W/°C in.
‡MMC stands for metal matrix composites, a class of exotic metal matrices reinforced with ceramics such as boron, silicon carbide, or graphite.
§Conductivity in normal direction is 1.93 W/°C in.

*10.4.6.3 **Convection.*** Convection cooling can be enhanced by (1) increasing the flow of the cooling substance over the element to be cooled, (2) increasing the surface area to improve heat transfer, and (3) using turbulent flow around the surface to be cooled to improve heat transfer. Air forced cooling[147] and liquid cooling[148,149] are used to remove heat from electronic systems that use VLSI devices. For high-density interconnection systems liquid convection cooling has become an effective solution.

10.4.7 Environmental Effects on Dielectric Materials

The term *environmental* is used here to describe the effects of chemicals, water, and fire on the interconnection system. Of these environmental aspects, the effect of water is the most critical to the performance of the circuit board in the application due to the changing humidity conditions in the air. The effect of chemicals is most important during the fabrication processes of the circuit board.

*10.4.7.1 **Effect of Water.*** Water, and especially water at elevated temperature, affects the circuit board in three different ways: (1) water corrodes the conductors, (2) water and chemical solution deteriorates the dielectric material, and (3) absorbed water in the dielectric material affects the surface and the bulk electrical properties of the dielectric material.

To minimize corrosion, the copper conductors are usually covered by a polymeric coat or by a layer of solder (tin/lead). Although slow, water does react with certain polymers. Epoxies, polyimides, and BT-epoxy resins are among the standard circuit materials that are chemically affected by water. Fluoropolymers have a high resistance to water. Polymer-fiber interfaces of composite materials are sensitive to water penetration and absorption. The rate of water corrosion increases with temperature.

Ions embedded as contaminants in the polymeric matrix become mobile in the presence of water and usually degrade the electrical properties of the dielectric material.[150] Water absorbed in the bulk also affects the dielectric constant and the dissipation factor of the dielectric material. Typical water absorption levels of selected polymers and circuit materials are presented in Table 10.6.

*10.4.7.2 **Effect of Chemicals.*** During the circuit fabrication processes, the circuit material is exposed to corrosive chemicals. Etching, plating, photoresist, developing, cleaning of solder flux, and etch-back solution are the major process steps in which the circuit board comes in contact with active chemical solutions. These chemicals may be organic or inorganic, and they may be dissolved in water or in organic solvents.

*10.4.7.3 **Effect of Fire.*** Regulations and fire codes require that the electrical device be properly rated for a *flame class.* There are several methods to evaluate the effect of flame on circuit materials. ASTM D228-77 defines two methods; the burning rate and the flame resistance tests, to evaluate flammability of insulation materials. Underwriters Laboratories, Inc. is one of the recognized institutions that develops test methods and performs industrial tests to classify the properties of interconnection materials when exposed to flame and high temperatures.

10.5. ADVANCED INTERCONNECTION TECHNOLOGIES

10.5.1 Multilayer Circuits by Sequential Processes—Multichip Modules

Conventional multilayer circuits are constructed by laminating a stack of several double-sided circuits, using bond ply between the individual circuit layers, into a single board. The *Z*-axis conductive paths can be formed by buried vias, blind vias, or side-to-side plated-through-hole vias; see Sec. 10.3.5.

Multilayer circuits can be also built using a sequential layer-by-layer process.[151–160] Generally, the additive multilayer circuit is built a layer at a time, dielectric or conductive, from bottom to top or vice versa. A typical process to build a multilayer circuit by the sequential technology is shown schematically in Fig. 10.19. These multilayer circuits, which are frequently identified as multichip modules (MCM) or as high-density interconnects (HDI), are characterized by high wiring density.

10.5.1.1 Circuit Substrate. The use of a substrate or a carrier is common to the various multilayer circuits built by sequential techniques. The substrate may be left attached to the circuit and used in the application as a heat sink, or it can be removed from the multilayer circuit at the end of the process. The substrate has two major functions: (1) carry the multilayer structure and (2) maintain dimensional stability of the board during the circuit fabrication process.

10.5.1.2 Generation of the Conductive Pattern. Accuracy of line width and spaces by the subtractive technology is a function of the pattern imaging and the etching step capabilities. It has been the industry experience that the subtractive technology is limited to features about 3 mil in size.[161] Smaller conductive patterns with higher tolerances can be better formed by an additive plating process; see Fig. 10.19, steps (a)–(e). The conductive layer may be also formed by the polymer thick-film (PTF) technology.[154,155,157]

10.5.1.3 Deposition of the Dielectric Layer. The dielectric layer is also applied in an "additive" process. Two major methods have been demonstrated: (1) lamination of a thermoplastic or a B-staged film,[151,154] and (2) application of a solution of the dielectric material by a coating process.[152,156] After the dielectric layer has been applied, the excess material may be removed by a planarization process, Fig. 10.19, step (f).

10.5.1.4 Application of the Seeding Layer. To form the next layer of the conductive pattern, the surface of the dielectric material and the top surface of the conductive features, which are embedded in the dielectric, are covered by a conductive thin film, called a seeding layer, Fig. 10.19, step (g). This layer may be applied by a wet or dry process. To build more layers, this sequential process is repeated to achieve a multilayer circuit, as shown schematically in Fig. 10.19, step (h).

10.5.1.5 Alternative Process. An alternative method to form multilayer circuits by a sequential process is shown schematically in Fig. 10.20. In concept, this process is based on forming the vias by a "drilling" step, which may be accomplished by a laser, by a reactive ion etching (RIE) process,[152] or by a chemical etching process. Lines and vias are formed simultaneously through a plating process. After the second dielectric layer is applied, a full process cycle has been completed. The steps (e)–(g) shown in Figure 10.20 illustrate the formation of the second conductive layer. The process may be repeated several times.

10.5.2 Tape Automated Bonding

Tape automated bonding (TAB) is the concept of using a miniature printed circuit to interconnect between an IC and a board. TAB is a flexible printed circuit, which is normally supplied in a continuous sprocketed film formation. The inner leads of the tape are bonded to an IC die, while the outer leads are bonded to a board. This interconnection concept offers a higher packaging density compared to the dual-in-pin (DIP) approach or the surface-mount technology. Typical TAB can increase the packaging density of the chip by a factor of 5 to 12.[162,163] TAB also provides the circuit assembler with a convenient construction to evaluate and test the functionality of the die before mounting it on the board.[162–169]

Terms commonly used by the TAB technologists are described in the following sections.

10.5.2.1 Single-Layer Tape. This tape is made of copper that is imaged and etched to form the interconnect pattern. Leads are held together in a pattern by

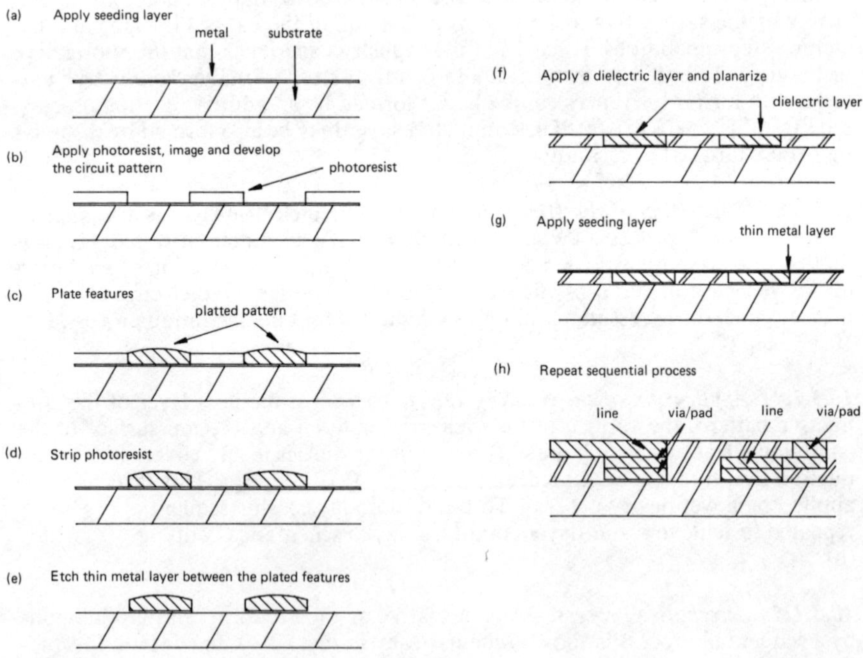

FIGURE 10.19 Schematic drawing of the steps to build a multilayer circuit by a typical sequential process.

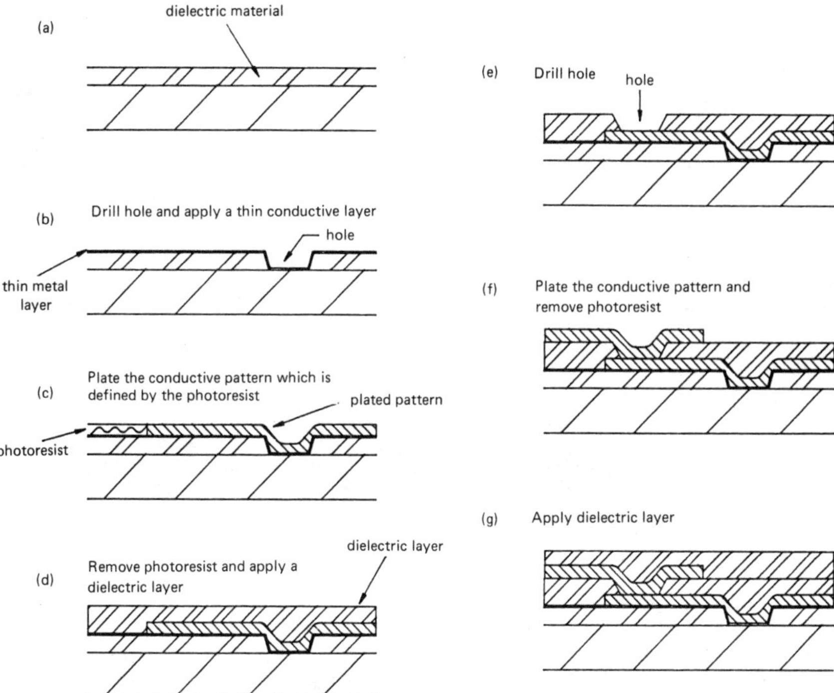

FIGURE 10.20 Schematic drawing of the steps to build a multilayer circuit by a typical sequential process.

tie bars. After bonding, the tie bars are excised. The leads of a single-sided tape are not attached to a dielectric layer.

10.5.2.2 Two-Layer Tape. The two-layer tape consists of a conductor layer and a dielectric layer. One method used to form the two-layer tape is by coating copper foil with a liquid polyimide film, and then imaging and etching the copper and the polyimide to the required pattern.

A two-layer TAB can also be formed by the deposition of copper on a polyimide film, followed by patterning and etching the conductive and the dielectric layers. The polyimide provides support to the fragile copper leads.

10.5.2.3 Three-Layer Tape. The three-layer TAB consists of a copper layer bonded to a dielectric layer by an adhesive layer. The dielectric of this thin three-layer laminate is usually made of a polyimide film, which may be punched to form window and sprocket holes. The copper is etched as the last step in the process.

The leads of the TAB can be bonded to the die pads or to the board in one step. This simultaneous bonding process, commonly termed "gang bonding," has been demonstrated for lead counts exceeding 200.[166] After bonding the outer leads to the board, the perimeter of the TAB is excised from the tape. In some applications, copper bumps are formed at the end of the inner leads as an alternative to bumps formed on the die. Bumps are needed to keep the inner leads above the

TABLE 10.12 Comparison of Wire Bond and TAB Electrical and Thermal Properties (Ref. 168)

Parameter	Wire bonding*		Tape bonding†
	Aluminum	Gold	Copper
Lead resistance, Ω	0.142	0.122	0.017
Lead-to-lead capacitance, PF (6-mil spacing)	0.025	0.025	0.006
Lead inductance, nH	2.621	2.621	2.10
Lead conduction, °C/mW	79.6	51.6	8.3
Lead convection, free, °C/mW	336.5	336.5	149.5

*0.001-in diameter × 0.10-in long wire bond.
†0.001 in × 0.004-in × 0.100-in long TAB lead.

surface of the chip, and to provide a specific bond area. Bumps are usually formed by a plating process.[162,167] The electrical properties of TAB packaging are compared to wire bonding properties in Table 10.12.

10.5.3 Hybrid Microcircuits

The ability to integrate ICs, resistors, and capacitors by using additive technologies to form the conductors on a ceramic-based board, while providing design flexibility and reliability, is the major characteristic of hybrid microcircuit technology. Hybrids have become an important electronic interconnection format for various applications including: digital, analog, power, RF, and microwave.[17,170–181]

While the dielectric materials of conventional circuit boards are based on polymer composites, single-sided and multilayer hybrid interconnections are based on ceramic dielectric materials; see Fig. 10.21. The inherent rigidity of ceramic materials and their low coefficient of thermal expansion are compatible with the needs for surface-mount technology in hybrid microcircuits.[110,171] Hybrid multilayer circuits can be fabricated by two processes: (a) co-fired ceramic and (b) thick film. Features of thick-film and co-fired technology are compared in Table 10.13. With co-fired technology the individual ceramic circuit layers are built separately and then laminated in one step to form a multilayer board. Multilayer boards using the thick-film approach are built in a sequential layer-by-layer process on a substrate.

10.5.3.1 Multilayer Co-Fired Technology. The dielectric material used in the co-fired multilayer approach is a sheet of alumina quartz or beryllium oxide particles held together by a binder. This thin and fragile sheet is commonly termed *green tape* and is normally carried on a carrier film.[170]

The tape in a co-fired ceramic process is first blanked to the proper dimensions by a die. Hybrid circuits that measure 5 × 5 in^2 have been processed successfully. Registration holes and vias are then punched in each layer of the multilayer stack. Laser drilling of vias has also been demonstrated. With use of a screen printing process, the vias are filled with a conductive paste. The tape with the filled vias is then dried and prepared for the circuit pattern printing. Screen printing or other additive circuit techniques can be used to deposit the conductive pattern on the

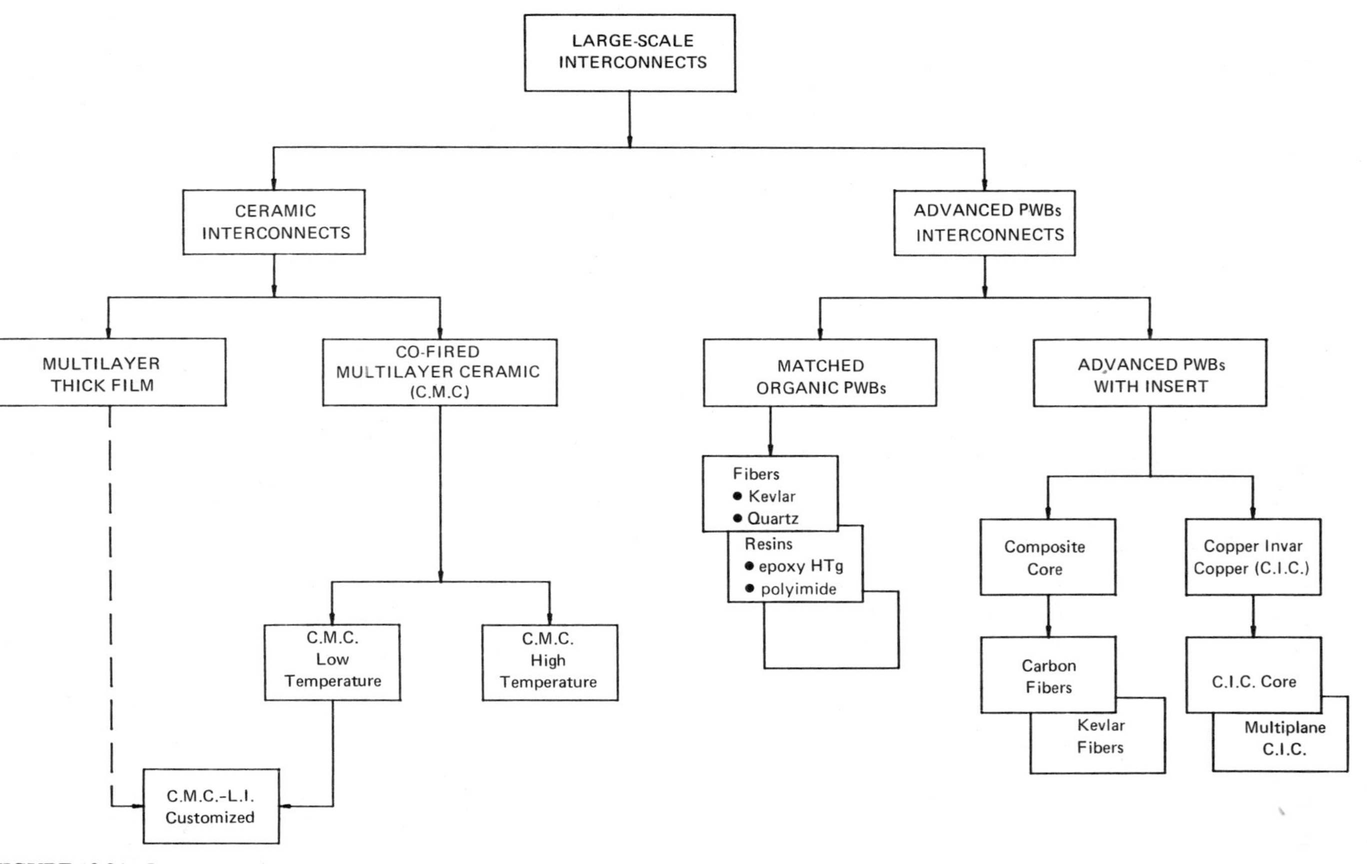

FIGURE 10.21 Interconnection techniques.

TABLE 10.13 Comparison of Thick-Film and Co-Fired Technology (Ref. 170)

	Thick film	High temperature co-fired
Dielectric	Paste composition glass + fillers	Tape 90–96% Al_2O_3
Dielectric constant	7–10	9.5
Conductor metallurgy	Ag, Au, Pd-Ag, Cu	W, Mo, Mo-Mn
Sheet resistance, mΩ □ 12.5 μm	2–4	16–30
Firing	800–950°C 45–60 min Air (precious metals) N_2 (Cu)	>1500°C >24 h H_2 atmosphere
Vias	Screen printing 0.010-in diameter 0.025-in center	Punching 0.005-in diameter 0.010-in center
Line resolution, line/spaces	0.006/0.006 in	0.004/0.004 in
Multilayer process	Sequential, many steps	Co-fired, fewer steps
Substrate required	Yes	No
Lead attachments	Direct	Plating required
Resistor compatibility	Yes	No
Capital investment	Low	High

ceramic tape. The individual layers are then dried, inspected, and registered for the lamination step. The stack is then pressed at high pressure and low temperature to combine the layers into a single board. The organic binders are then removed in a burn-out process at a moderate temperature, <500°C, and then the multilayer stack is co-fired in a high-temperature oven to complete the sintering process of the ceramic dielectric layers. The outer-layer conductors and resistors are deposited by screening or by a direct writing process, followed by a post-firing process to complete the fabrication of the interconnection system. Components are then mounted on the surface of the hybrid microcircuit.[170,172,178,180]

10.5.3.2 Multilayer by Thick-Film Technology. Hybrid multilayers by thick-film technology are built sequentially on a substrate or carrier. The multilayer is built layer by layer using consecutive printing and firing of the conductive and the insulating layers. This process requires several printing and firing sequences for each layer. Although the dielectric material is applied in thick layers, the conductive pattern can be applied by thick-film technology or by thin-film deposition; see Sec. 10.2.3.[176]

Thick-film technology makes use of lasers for accurate resistor trimming. Line width and spaces of thick-film technology are not as good as those achieved in co-fired hybrids.[174] A comparison of ceramic multilayer fabrication by thick-film and co-fired processes is presented in Table 10.14.

10.5.4 Bendable Circuits

In today's applications there is a growing need for multiplane circuitry designs that combine rigid and flexible elements. Multiplane circuitry can be achieved by the following:

1. Combinations of two or more rigid board segments interconnected by flexible jumper cables
2. The mother-daughter board arrangement, using edge card connectors
3. Building a flexible circuit, which is then selectively stiffened in sections that are designated for component mounting

A new class of formable or bendable laminates can be used to solve the problems of multiplane interconnections at a relatively lower cost than the conventional techniques. In concept, portions of the formable board function as the rigid segment and other portions of the same board function as the "flexible" interconnection in a multiplane configuration. One such formable or bendable board is BEND/flex*.[19,20] This laminate is based on a nonwoven reinforced epoxy dielectric material. It can be processed by most conventional printed-circuit processing techniques and then bent into the desired geometrical shape. Typical applications for these laminates are those which require a nondynamic multiplane interconnect system. A major advantage of this formable laminate is that it is sufficiently rigid to carry electrical components without buckling, yet is flexible enough to bend into various multiplane geometries without breaking.

Formable laminates are essentially processed in the same way as rigid boards for single- or double-clad applications, using the same equipment. These laminates can also be processed by conventional circuit fabrication methods that are currently used by flexible PCB circuit houses. After the circuit has been fabricated

*BEND/flex is a trademark of Rogers Corporation.

TABLE 10.14 Comparison of Ceramic Multilayer Fabrication Methods (Refs. 170, 178)

Thick film		High temperature co-fired Al_2O_3	
Negative	Positive	Positive	Negative
Multiple printing steps	High-conductivity metals (Ag, Au)	High print resolution to conductors	Low-conductivity metals (W, Mo, Mn)
Multiple firing	Low-K dielectric	Single firing	Complex process
Thickness control of dielectric	Low processing temperature	Good dielectric thickness control	High capital investment
Limited number of layers	Low capital investment	Low surface roughness	
		Unlimited number of layers	

and the components mounted, the board may be then bent to the desired configuration. Proper bending rules must be used to ensure the copper integrity.[19,20]

Bendable laminates may be used in two modes: curved and bent. The curve mode is defined as a circuit application that has a radius of curvature greater than 70 times the laminate thickness. At this curvature the tensile strain that develops in the curved copper conductors is about 0.7 percent. This low strain is mostly reversible and allows the circuit to be laid flat or curved repeatedly without affecting the conductors. The bent-mode application is one in which the radius of the circuit curvature is between 10 and 70 times the laminate thickness. In this mode, the circuit is allowed to bend only once. Bending around a radius of less than 10 times the laminate thickness increases the risk of fracturing the conductor lines in the bend area.

10.5.5 Injection-Molded Interconnections

The substrate of molded interconnections is fabricated by an injection-molding process. The circuit patterns are then placed on the molded substrate by an additive circuit technique. Molded circuits are often fabricated as a three-dimensional multifunctional board, using thermoplastic-based composite materials.[21,182–188]

Molded circuits or molded wiring board can be classified into three molded-feature categories:[186]

Category A: Two-dimensional (planar) substrate with conductive patterns on one or both sides of the board with plated-through-holes, slots, or other molded-in through-board features.

Category B: Three-dimensional molded features are formed only on one side of a substrate. The circuit pattern is placed on the flat, nonsculptured, side of the substrate. The board may include PTH slots and other molded-in through-board features.

Category C: Three-dimensional molded features and circuitry on both sides of the substrate with molded-in through-board features. This type of molded circuit provides a high degree of freedom in circuit design.

Injection molding is an inexpensive, precise, reproducible and fully automated process. The ability to create three-dimensional sculptured substrates, rather than conventional two-dimensional layouts, is an effective tool in designing complex molded printed circuit board structures. Molded-circuit technology is supported by a wide range of thermoplastic polymers and their composites.[21,182,183,187]

The dielectric substrate is fabricated by a single molding step, which forms the substrate to the designed shape including the holes of the PTH process. The conductive pattern is then deposited on the dielectric by an additive circuit technology; see Sec. 10.2.2. The drilling, deburr, and desmear steps of the hole are eliminated by the use of circuit molding technology. The location, the size, and the wall quality of a molded hole are more reproducible. The pattern plating process includes surface preparation, electroless plating on the substrate and in the holes, imaging for pattern generation, and electroplating the circuit pattern.[16] Conductive pattern placement on the molded substrate has also been demonstrated by conductive ink, direct circuit writing, and other additive technologies.[184]

APPENDIX Identification of Standard Circuit Laminates

NEMA grade	Fabric-resin base	Comments
X	Paper-phenolic	Primarily intended for mechanical applications where electrical properties are of secondary importance. Should be used with discretion when high-humidity conditions are encountered. Not equal to fabric-base grades in impact strength.
XX	Paper-phenolic	Good machining, punching, and threading qualities. Not as strong mechanically as grade X rolled tubes but better in moisture resistance. Better for low dielectric losses, particularly on exposure to high humidity.
XXP	Paper-phenolic	Better than grade XX in electrical and moisture-resisting properties and more suitable for hot punching. Intermediate between grades XP and XX in punching and cold-flow characteristics.
XXX	Paper-phenolic	Suitable for radio-frequency work, for high-humidity applications. Has minimum cold-flow characteristics.
XXXP	Paper-phenolic	Better in electrical properties than grade XXX and more suitable for hot punching. Intermediate between grades XXP and XX in punching characteristics. This grade is recommended for applications requiring high insulation resistance and low dielectric losses under severe humidity conditions.
XXXPC	Paper-phenolic	Similar in electrical properties to grade XXXP and suitable for punching at lower temperatures than grade XXXP. With good punching practice, sheets up to and including 1/16 in in thickness may be punched at a temperature not less than 23°C (73.4°F) and, in thicknesses over 1/16 in up to and including 1/8 in, when warmed to temperatures up to 60°C (140°F). This grade is recommended for applications requiring high insulation resistance and low dielectric losses under severe humidity conditions.
N-1	Nylon-phenolic	Nylon cloth base with phenolic resin binder. Excellent electrical properties under high humidity conditions. Good impact strength, but subject to flow or creep especially at temperatures higher than normal.
FR-1	Paper-phenolic (flame resistant)	Paper-base laminates with a phenolic resin binder. Similar in all properties to grade XP but formulated to have a flame resistance of at least class 1 when tested in accordance with LI 1-7.12.

NEMA grade	Fabric-resin base	Comments
FR-2	Paper-phenolic (flame resistant)	Paper-base laminates with a phenolic resin binder. Similar in all properties to grade XXXPC but formulated to have a flame resistance of at least class 1 when tested in accordance with LI 1-7.12.
FR-3	Paper-epoxy (flame resistant)	Paper-base laminaets with epoxy resin binder. Has higher flexural strength than grade XXXPC and is formulated to have a flame resistance of at least class 1 when tested in accordance with LI 1-7.12. Has low dielectric loss properties with good stability of electrical properties under conditions of high humidity. With good punching practice, sheets up to and including 1/16 in in thickness may be punched at temperatures not less than 27°C (80°F) and, in thicknesses over 1/16 in up to and including 1/8 in, when warmed to a temperature not exceeding 65.5°C (150°F).
FR-4	Glass-expoxy (flame resistant)	Continuous-filament glass cloth with an epoxy resin binder. Similar in all properties to grade G-10 but formulated to have a flame resistance of at least class 1 when tested in accordance with LI 1-7.12.
FR-5	Glass-epoxy (flame resistant)	Continuous-filament glass cloth with an epoxy resin binder. Similar in all properties to grade G-11 but formulated to have a flame resistance of at least class 1 when tested in accordance with LI 1-7.12.
FR-6	Glass-polyester (with fillers)	Random-laid glass-fiber reinforcement with polyester resin and suitable fillers. Intended for use as a flame-resistant printed-circuit board.
GPO-1, GPO-2, GPO-3	Glass-mat polyester (with fillers)	Track-resistant laminates.
G-3	Glass-phenolic	High impact and flexural strength. Bonding strength is the poorest of the glass-base grades. Good electrical properties under dry conditions. Electric strength perpendicular to laminations is good. Good dimensional stability.
G-5	Glass-melamine	Highest mechanical strength and hardest laminated grade. High degree of heat and arc resistance. Excellent electrical properties under dry conditions. Low insulation resistance under high humidities. Good dimensional stability.
G-7	Glass-silicone	Extremely good dielectric loss and insulation-resistance properties under dry conditions and good electrical properties under humid conditions, although the percentage of change from dry to humid conditions is high.

NEMA grade	Fabric-resin base	Comments
		Excellent flame, heat, and arc resistance. Good impact and flexural strength. Electric strength perpendicular to laminations is the best of the silicone grades.
G-9	Glass-melamine (heat resistant)	High mechanical strength and one of the hardest laminated grades. Excellent electric strength properties under wet conditions. Good dimensional stability.
G-10	Glass-epoxy	Extremely high mechanical strength (flexural, impact, and bonding) at room temperature. Good dielectric loss and electric strength properties under both dry and humid conditions. Insulation resistance under high humidity is better than that of G-7.
G-11	Glass-epoxy (heat resistant)	Properties similar to those of grade G-10 at room temperature; in addition, the material retains at least 50% of its room-temperature standard flexural strength when measured at 150°C after 1 h at 150°C. Insulation resistance is similar to that of grade G-10.
GT, GX	Polytetrafluorethylene	Low electrical loss sheets.
CEM-1, CEM-2	Composite-epoxy	Laminate with continuous-filament glass cloth surfaces and a cellulose paper core, all with a flame-resistant epoxy resin binder. With good punching practice, sheets up to and including 3/32 in in thickness may be punched at temperatures not less than 23°C (73.4°F) and, in thicknesses over 3/32 in up to and including 1/8 in, when warmed to a temperature not exceeding 65.5°C (150°F). CEM-1 is flame resistant.
CEM-3, CEM-4	Composite-epoxy	Laminate with continuous-filament glass cloth surfaces and a nonwoven glass core, all with a flame-resistant epoxy resin binder. Property values approach those of FR-4. With good punching practice, sheets up to and including 1/16 in in thickness may be punched at temperatures not less than 23°C (73.4°F) and, in thicknesses over 1/16 in up to and including 1/8 in, when warmed to a temperature not exceeding 65.5°C (105°F). CEM-3 is flame resistant.
CRM-5, CRM-6	Composite-polyester	A sandwich of random glass mat core and glass fabric surfaces, using polyester resin binder. CRM-5 is flame resistant.
PL	Glass-polyimide (MIL-P-13949, grade PL)	A high-thermal-stability laminate also having low *Z*-axis thermal expansion. Glass-triazine also fits this category, but has no industry or government standard specification.

REFERENCES

1. Francis J. Dance, "Printed Wiring Boards: A Five Year Plan," *Circuits Manufacturing,* June 1986, p. 23.
2. Gerald L. Ginsberg, *The Impact of New Semiconductor Developments on Printed Board Technology,* Institute for Interconnecting and Packaging Electronic Circuits, Lincolnwood, Illinois, 1986.
3. Robert Meehan, "Design Utilizing ICs and Circuit Boards Can No Longer Be Thought of as a Collection of Components, But Must Now Be Viewed as a Whole with Limitations Imposed by the Interaction of the System's Elements and their Interconnections," *Electronic Packaging and Production,* February, 1985, p. 139.
4. George Messner et al., "New Technology Inspires New Competition," *Electronic Packaging and Production,* December 1987, p. 66.
5. Charles A. Harper, *Modern Electronic Packaging,* Technology Seminars, Lutherville, Maryland, 1986.
6. George J. Lawrence, "Packaging Primer," *Circuits Manufacturing,* November 1982, p. 48.
7. George Lawrence, "Connectors Boost System," *Electronic Week,* January 1985.
8. Peter W. Derbyshire, "Hierarchical Interconnection Technology," *Electronic Packaging and Production,* April 1987, p. 26.
9. Steve Gurley, *Flexible Circuits—Design and Applications,* Marcel Dekker, New York, 1984.
10. Herb Van Deusen, "Improved Interconnections for High Speed Digital Systems," *Connection Technology,* December 1986, p. 27.
11. Hirosuke Suzuki, "Foamed Plastics," U.S. Patent 4,379,858, April 1983.
12. *Chabin—The Transmission Line Specialists* Technical Brochure, Chabin, Chico, California, 1983.
13. Chris Shmatovich, "Constructing Reliable Vehicles for Digital Signal Transmission," *Electri-Onics,* August 1984, p. 51.
14. Murray Olyphant, "Shielded Ribbon Cable," U.S. Patent 4,475,006, October 1984.
15. Joseph Marshall, "Flat Multi-Signal Transmission Line Cable with Plural Insulation," U.S. Patent 3,763,306, October 1973.
16. Joseph Marshall, "Flat Multi-Signal Transmission Line Cable with Plural Insulation," U.S. Patent Re. 31,477, December 1983.
17. Edward T. Lewis, "High-Density High-Impedance Hybrid Circuit Technology for Gigahertz Logic," *IEEE Transactions on Components, Hybrids, and Manufacturing Technology,* **CHMT-2** (2): 441 (1979).
18. *Chip Module—The New Interconnection Technology,* BPA, Technology and Management Ltd., Surrey, England, 1986.
19. Samuel Gazit, "Bendable Laminates—A New Concept in Circuit Design," PC Fabrications Technical Seminar, San Jose, California, May 1985.
20. Donald Greene, Samuel Gazit, and Connie S. Jackson, *Printed Wiring Board Laminates for Multiplane Applications,* International Society for the Advancement of Material and Process Engineering Electronics Conference Series, Covina, California, June 1987.
21. Ed Galli, "Molded Thermoplastic PWBs: Multifunctional 3-D Boards Are Here," *Plastics Design Forum,* May/June 1984, p. 21.
22. Clyde F. Coombs, *Printed Circuits Handbook,* McGraw-Hill, New York, 1988.
23. Ragnar Eliasson, "How to Make Better FR-4," *Electronic Packaging and Production,* October 1987, p. 76.

24. J. F. Dennis-Browne, "Circuit Board Technology," *PC Fab,* July 1985, p. 28.

25. Chin-An Chang, J. E. E. Baglin, A. G. Schrott, and K. C. Lin, "Enhanced Cu-Teflon Adhesion by Presputtering Prior to the Cu Deposition," *Appl. Phys. Lett.,* **51** (2): 103 (1987).

26. Chin-An Chang, "Enhanced Cu-Teflon Adhesion by Presputtering Treatment: Effect of Surface Morphology Changes," *Appl. Phys. Lett.,* **51** (16): 1236 (1987).

27. Philip D. Knudsen and Daniel P. Walsh, "Metal Coated Laminate Products Made from Textured Polyimide Film," U.S. Patent 4,725,504, February 1988.

28. Anthony J. Polak, "Method for Increasing the Peel Strength of Metal-Clad Polymers," U.S. Patent 4,382,101, May 1983.

29. K. L. Mittal, "Adhesion Aspects of Metallization of Organic Polymer Surfaces," *J. Vac. Sci. Technol.,* **13** (1): 19 (1976).

30. Linda A. Hoitt and Darrell Stoddard, "Metalized Film Flex Circuits Yield Fine Lines," *Electronic Packaging and Production,* June 1986, p. 64.

31. *Polyimide Flexible Copper Clad Laminates (Non Adhesive),* brochure by Mitsui Toatsu Chemicals, Inc., Tokyo, Japan.

32. *Polymer Clad System,* Technical Brochure, Enka America, Inc., Vernon, Connecticut.

33. J. R. Salem, F. O. Sequeda, J. Duran, W. Y. Lee, and R. M. Yang, "Solventless Polyimide Film by Vapor Deposition," *J. Vac. Sci. Technol.,* **A4**(3): May/June 1986.

34. Bruce A. Banks, James S. Sovey, Thomas B. Miller, and Karen S. Crandall, "Ion Beam Sputter Etching and Deposition of Fluoropolymers," NASA Report No. TM-78888, Eighth International Conference of Electron and Ion Beam Science and Technology, Seattle, May 1988.

35. Thomas J. Buck, "A Discrete-Wired Solution for High Speed Surface-Mount Packaging," *Electronic Packaging and Production,* June 1985.

36. Charles L. Lassen and Marc Motazedi, "High Density Discrete Wiring Offers a Solution to Chip Carrier Design," *Electronic Packaging and Production,* January 1983.

37. Philip Plonski, Thomas Buck, and Samuel Smookler, "Multiwire Boards Complete with Microstrip and Stripline Packaging," *Electronics,* September 8, 1981, p. 143.

38. *Microwire™,* brochure by Kollmorgen Corporation, Melville, New York, 1982.

39. Gerald F. Hammel, "Discrete Wiring Technique for High Speed Logic Systems," *Connection Technology,* August 1986, p. 24.

40. S. Leonard Spitz, "After Subvactive—Semi and Fully Additive Processes," *Circuit Manufacturing,* January 1981, p. 69.

41. J. Kanou, A. Endou, and K. Ikari, "A New Type of Semiadditive Process for Manufacturing Reliable and Low Cost Printed Circuit Boards," *New Materials and New Processes,* Vol. 2, p. 424 (1983).

42. *The Semi-Additive Unclad™ Process,* Technical Brochure, PCK Circuit Products Group, Lindenhurst, New York.

43. Gerald A. Keitel, "The Other Thick-Film Technology," *Microelectronic Manufacturing and Testing,* October 1980.

44. E. Ralph Egloff, "New Thoughts on Design and Manufacture of High Volume, Low Cost Polymer Thick Film Circuits," *International Printed Circuits Conference,* New York, New York, April 1980.

45. Nikita Andreiev, "New Transfer Process Applied 3-D Circuitry to Molded Substrates," *Electronic Packaging and Production,* December 1984, p. 40.

46. F. Wayne Martin, "Polymer Thick Film Updating Today's Technology," *Electri-Onics,* July 1983, p. 27.

47. James M. Kelly, Cornelius Y. D. Huang, and Sidney J. Stein, "Low Cost Resin-Based Thick Film Materials," *ISHM,* Vol. 4, No. 2 (1981).

48. *DuPont Thick Film Materials,* Technical Brochure, DuPont, Electrical Materials Division, Wilmington, Delaware, 1980.

49. David L. Diepholz, "An Introduction to Polymer Thick Films," *Hybrid Circuit Technology,* October 1986, p. 29.

50. Walter Mathias, "Direct Writing Technology Applications Update," *Hybrid Circuit Technology,* June 1986.

51. Carl E. Drumheller, "Dynamic Pen Control in Synchronous Positive Displacement CAD/CAM Thick Film Writing Systems", Poster paper at the International Society for Hybrid Microelectronics Meeting, Reno, Nevada, November 1982.

52. *Micropen Direct Writing and Precision Dispensing Systems,* Technical Brochure, Micropen, Inc., Pittsford, N.Y.

53. *Wire Ink™,* Technical Brochure, Additive Technology Corporation, Chelmsford, Massachusetts.

54. William J. Havey, "The Formation of Conductive Pattern on Hybrid Circuits and PWBs Using Alternative Techniques," *Hybrid Technology,* August 1985, p. 27.

55. Samuel E. Blum, Zlata Kovac, and Robert J. Von Gutfeld, "Masking Method for Electroless Plating Patterns," U.S. Patent 4,239,789, December 1980.

56. Larysa H. Kulynych, Lubomyr T. Romankiw, and Robert J. Von Gutfeld, "Laser Enhanced Maskless Method for Plating and Simultaneous Plating and Etching of Patterns," U.S. Patent No. 4,349,583, September 1982.

57. Abraham Auerbach, "Method for Deposition of Elemental Metals and Metalloids on Substrates," U.S. Patent 4,526,807, July 1985.

58. Michael J. Halliwell and Joseph Zahavi, "Laser Induced Deposition on Polymeric Substrates," U.S. Patent 4,578,155, March 1986.

59. Michael J. Halliwell and Joseph Zahavi, "Laser Induced Deposition on GaAs," U.S. Patent 4,578,157, March 1986.

60. Robert L. Melcher, Lubomyr T. Romankiw, and Robert J. Von Gutfed, "Method for Maskless Chemical and Electrochemical Machining," U.S. Patent 4,283,259, August 1981.

61. R. J. Von Gutfeld, M. H. Gelchinski, L. T. Romankiw, and D. R. Vigliotti, "Laser-Enhanced Jet Plating: A Method of High-speed Maskless Patterning," *Appl. Phys. Lett.* **43** (9): 876 (1983).

62. A. Auerbach, "On Depositing Conductors from Solution with a Laser," *J. Electrochem. Soc. Electrochemical Science and Technology,* **132** (1): 130 (1985).

63. R. J. Von Gutfeld, R. E. Acosta, and L. T. Romankiw, "Laser-Enhanced Plating and Etching: Mechanisms and Applications," *IBM J. Res. Develop.* **26** (2): 136 (1982).

64. Art R. Elsea and Otto L. Draper, "Advances in Laser Assisted Semiconductor Processing," *Semiconductor International,* April 1987, p. 152.

65. J. Zahavi, S. Tamir, and M. Halliwell, "Laser-Induced Deposition on Semiconductor and Polymeric Substrates," *Plating and Surface Finishing,* February 1986, p. 57.

66. M. H. Gelchinski, L. T. Romankiw, D. R. Vigliotti, and R. J. Gutfeld, "Electrochemical and Metallurgical Aspects of Laser-Enhanced Jet Plating of Gold," *J. Electrochem. Soc. Electrochemical Science and Technology,* 132 (11): 2575 (1985).

67. C. R. Moylan, T. H. Baum, and C. R. Jones, "LCVD of Copper: Deposition Rates and Deposit Shapes," *Appl. Phys. A* **40**: 1 (1986).

68. P. Soszek, "How to Avoid Web Processing," *Circuit Manufacturing,* May 1988, p. 21.

69. Yasuhiko Kanaya and Kunio Arai, "Small Hole Drilling: The Japanese Way," *Circuit Manufacturing,* December 1987, p. 33.

70. Hayao Nakahara, "Small Hole Drilling in Japan," *Electronic Packaging and Production,* February 1988, p. 68.

71. Michael Flatt, "Small Hole Drilling from a Business Perspective," *PC Fab,* March 1988, p. 14.

72. Hans Vandervelde, "The Game Is Small Hole Drilling. The Rules are Strict," *PC Fab,* March 1988, p. 19.

73. Hidwo Tsuzaki and Tim L. Taylor, "The Big Picture of Drilling Small Holes," *PC Fab,* March 1988, p. 25.

74. Russ Elias, "Optimization of Drilling Process for Teflon Printed Wiring Boards via Fractional Factorial Experimentation," Report IPC-TP-620, San Diego, September 1986.

75. Francesco Tomaiuolo, "Etchback/Desmearing Overview," *PC Fab,* April 1988, p. 68.

76. Anthony Piano and Katherine Pallone, "Solvent Swell," *PC FAb,* April 1988, p. 63.

77. Philip Pendleton, "Effect of Epoxy Smear Removal Process on the Locus of Failure of Electrolytic Copper Plated Hole Walls in a Printed Circuit Board," *J. Adhesion Sci. Technol.* **2**: 137 (1988).

78. Glenn W. Cupta and Anthony M. Piano, "Process for Preparing the Through Hole Walls of a Printed Wiring Board for Electroplating," U.S. Patent 4,718,993, January 1988.

79. Michael T. Mocella, "The Fine-Tuning of Plasma Desmearing," *Electronic Packaging and Production,* August 1986, p. 55.

80. R. D. Rust, R. J. Rhodes, and A. A. Parker, "The Road to Uniform Plasma Etching of PCBs," *PC Fab,* March 1985, p. 48.

81. Saad Nakhla and Robert Herberger, "Control of Electroless Copper," *PC Fab,* September 1988, p. 69.

82. Jerry Murray, "Plating, Part 1: Electroless Copper," *Circuit Manufacturing,* February 1985, p. 116.

83. William J. Amelio, David W. Hume, Donald G. McBride, and Robert G. Rickert, "Process for Preparing a Substrate for Subsequent Electroless Deposition of a Metal," U.S. Patent 4,639,380, January 1987.

84. J. R. House, B. C. Jackson, S. K. Nagi, and C. Courduvelis, "A Deeper Insight Into Electroless Copper Deposition," Report IPC-TP-437, San Diego, October 1982.

85. Darcy Poulin, John Reid, and Thomas Znotins, "Excimer Lasers," *PC Fab,* June 1988, p. 70.

86. Samuel Blum, Karen H. Brown, and Rangaswamy Srinivasan, "Far UV Patterning of Resist Materials," U.S. Patent 4,414,059, November 1983.

87. A. L. Kenney and J. W. Dally, "Laser Drilling of Very Small Electronic Via Holes in Common Circuit Board Materials," *Circuit World,* **14** (3): 31 (1988).

88. Larry W. Burgess, "Laser Vias—Today's Answer to Interconnect Density," *Proceedings of Nepcon West,* 1984.

89. Michael Angelo, "Multiplayer Registrations: Simple to Sophisticated," *PC Fab,* June 1986, p. 84.

90. Michael Angelo, "Multilayer Registration Tooling—The Full Spectrum," *PC Fab,* July 1987, p. 24.

91. Robert Keeler, "Scanning the Field for MLB Registration Solutions," *Electronic Packaging and Production,* July 1988, p. 48.

92. Allen G. Osborne, "An Alternate Route to Red Oxide for Inner Layers," *PC Fab,* August 1984, p. 28.

93. Linda Smith-Vargo, "Give New Strength to Multilayer Bonding," *Electronic Packaging and Production,* February 1987, p. 52.

94. Paul Marx, Bob Forcier, and Dwight Naseth, "An Overview of Vacuum Systems for Multilayer PWB Fabrication," *Electri-Onics,* June 1986, p. 19.

95. Howard W. Markstein, "Vacuum Fills the Voids in Lamination," *Electronic Packaging and Production,* February 1987, p. 62.

96. R. Menzel, "Optimizing the Drilling and Etch-back Parameters in Flexible Multilayer Manufacture," *Circuit World,* **13** (3): 21 (1987).

97. Leonard Spitz, "Plated Through Hole Reliability," *Electronic Packaging and Production,* October 1986, p. 34.

98. J. K. Hagge and J. C. Mather, "Machining Multilayer Circuit Boards," *Circuit World,* **11** (1):18 (1984).

99. Keiji Kurosawa, Y. Takeda, K. Takagi, and H. Kawamata, "An Investigation of the Reliability Behavior of Plated Through Holes in Multilayer Printed Wiring Boards," *IPC Technical Review,* April 1982, p. 11.

100. Louis Zakraysek, "Rupture Testing of Copper," *Metal Finishing,* April 1987, p. 29.

101. F. Gray and M. Elkins, "Reliability, Thermal and Thermomechanical Characteristics of Polymer-on-Metal Multilayer Boards," *Circuit World,* **14** (3): 12 (1988).

102. J. C. Curtis, K. J. Lodge, and D. J. Pedder, "The Limitations of High Speed, High Density PWB Substrates," *Circuit World,* **14** (3): 4 (1988).

103. David W. Boss and Derry J. Dubetsky, "Process for Minimizing Distortion in Multilayer Ceramic Substrates and the Intermediate Unsintered Green Ceramic Substrate Produced Thereby," U.S. Patent 4,677,254 June 1987.

104. S. J. Stein, P. Bless, and C. Huang, "Low-Cost, High Reliability Multilayers Made with Silver-Containing Thick Films," *Hybrid Circuit Technology,* August 1988, p. 30.

105. Pawel Chadzynski and Carl Milner, "Designing SMT Applications for Ceramic Substrates," *Surface Mount Technology,* August, 1988, p.18.

106. Ronald Pound, "New Ceramics Fill Performance Gaps," *Electronic Packaging and Production,* September 1987, p. 30.

107. Ferdinand Rogrigues, *Principles of Polymer Systems,* McGraw-Hill, New York, 1970.

108. Victor Wigotsky, "Engineering Resins Spark New Compact E/E Designs," *Plastic Engineering,* January 1986, p. 17.

109. David C. Frisch, "New PCB Substrates Expand Packaging Engineer's Choices," *Electronic Packaging and Production,* February 1985, p. 194.

110. Charles A. Harper (ed.), *Handbook of Electronic Packaging,* McGraw-Hill, New York, 1969.

111. T. C. Stening, C. P. Smith, and P. J. Kimber, "Polyaryletherketone: High Performance in a New Thermoplastic," *Modern Plastics,* November 1981, p. 86.

112. Donald J. Willats, "Advances in the Use of High Performance Continuous Fiber Reinforced Thermoplastics," *SAMPE Journal,* Sep./Oct. 1984, p. 6.

113. P. M. Hergenrother, B. J. Jensen, and S. J. Havens, "Thermoplastic Composite Matrices with Improved Solvent Resistance," *SAMPE Journal,* Sep./Oct. 1984, p. 18.

114. "Materials Selector 1987," *Materials Engineering,* December 1987.

115. Jane M. Crosby, "Melt-Processible Fluoropolymer Composites," *Plastic Design Forum,* Sep./Oct. 1983, p. 77.

116. J. Brandrup and E. H. Immergut, *Polymer Handbook,* Wiley, New York, 1975.

117. "Plastics for Electronics," *Desk-Top Data Bank,* The International Plastics Selector, Inc., San Diego, California, 1979.

118. "National Copper-Clad Laminates for High Reliability and High Density Mounting," Technical Brochure, Matsushita Electric Works, Ltd., Osaka, Japan

119. Larry Hayes, "Polymer Multilayers for Chip Carrier Applications," *PC Fab,* December 1984, p. 49.

120. Stewart Lee, "Low Dielectric, High Temperature Substrate for the Super Computer," Report IPC-TP-503, San Francisco, California, 1984.

121. D. J. Arthur, "Electrical and Mechanical Characteristics of Low Dielectric Constant Printed Wiring Boards," *IPC Technical Review,* **27**: 10 (1986).

121. K. N. Mathes, "Electrical Properties," *Encyclopedia of Polymer Science and Technology,* Vol. 5, p. 528, Wiley, New York, 1966.

122. *Kapton Polyimide Film—Summary of Properties,* Technical Brochure, DuPont, Wilmington, Delaware, 1982.

123. T. D. Newton, "Predicting Dielectric Properties," Report No. IPC-TP-587, Massachusetts, April 1986.

124. Richard J. Holmstrom, "Predicting the Dielectric Constant for FR-4 Laminates," IPC Technical Paper, San Francisco, California, September 1984.

125. Charles A. Harper and William W. Stanley, "Materials Meet Modern Electronic Packaging Trends," *Electronic Packaging and Production,* November 1985, p. 52.

126. David J. Arthur, "Composite, Process Development Keyed to Increasing PWB Demand," *Electri-Onics,* April 1986, p. 19.

127. Rhymer B. Rigby, "Polyetheretherketone PEEK," *Polymer News,* **9** (11): 326 (1984).

128. *Gore-Clad Laminates and Gore-Ply Pre-Pregs,* Technical Brochure, W. L. Gore, Newark, Delaware.

129. Paul E. Bern, "Another Look at Drilling Rigid Epoxy/Glass Laminate," *IPC Technical Review,* November 1980, p. 10.

130. B. A. Ballert, "Factors Which Influence Dimensional Stability of Multilayer," Report IPC-TP-295, California, 1979.

131. Phillip Hinton, "Controlling Dimensional Change during MLB Polyimide Lamination," *PC Fab,* June 1986, p. 47.

132. John Bartholomew, "Dimensional Stability of Epoxy Glass Laminates," *PC Fab,* December 1984, p.64.

133. Gary B. Roush, "Dimensional Stability, Part One," *PC Fab,* June 1986, p. 78.

134. Robert A. Reynolds, "SMDS Invade Military and Commercial Equipment," *Electronic Packaging and Production,* February 1985, p. 130.

135. Robert W. Wright, "Polymer/Metal Substrates Minimize SMD Thermal Expansion Problems," *Electronic Packaging and Production,* February 1984, p. 110.

136. George M. Mesner, "Impact of New Devices on PWB Design and Material Selection," *Printed Circuit Design,* November 1985, p. 4.

137. Louis J. Boccia, "Constructing PWB's with Copper-Invar-Copper," *PC Fab,* July 1986, p.34.

138. Fred Fehrer, "Plated Through Hole Reliability," *PC Fab,* March 1985, p. 76.

139. D. P. Bloechle, L. N. Schoenberg, and M. U. Rao, "A Low Expansion MLB Structure for Leadless Chip Carrier Applications," *PC Fab,* December 1985, p. 26.

140. Chester L. Guiles, "Polyimide PWPs—Materials and Process," *PC Fab,* June 1985, p. 47.

141. Gerald L. Ginsberg, "Design, Materials Selection Criteria for Packaging/Interconnection Structures," *Electri-Onics,* November 1984, p. 35.

142. Joseph D. Leibowitz, "Non-Woven PWB Construction Controls CTE," *Electronic Packaging and Production,* July 1988, p. 66.

143. Richard B. McPhillips, "Advanced Ceramic Materials for High Thermal Conductivity Substrate Applications," *Hybrid Circuit Technology,* August 1988, p. 21.

144. Dave Frish and Francis J. Nuzzi, "Improving PCB Performance with Thermoplastic and Metal-Core Substrates," *PC Fab,* February 1985, p. 90.

145. Foster Gray, Linda Cartwright, and Scott Lindblom, "Copper Clad Invar as a Constraining Core for Reliable LCC Applications," *PC Fab,* February 1986.

146. Marvin Moore, "Heat Sink for Gate Arrays," *Electronic Packaging and Production,* January 1988, p. 96.

147. Itoh Kinshi, "Heat Management Faces Demand of High Thermal Density," *Electronic Packaging and Production,* January 1987, p. 136.

148. Tom Dewey, "Developments in Liquid Immersion Cooling," *Electronic Packaging and Production,* April 1988, p. 59.

149. Howard W. Markstein, "Liquid Cooling Optimizes Heat Transfer," *Electronic Packaging and Production,* April 1988, p. 46.

150. Robert J. Boudreau, "Glass Fabric Finishes: Effects on the Kinetics of Water Absorption and Laminate Physical and Electrical Properties," *Printed Circuit World Convention II,* Germany, June 1981.

151. Sanford Lebow, Daniel Nogavich, and Eugene Nogavich, "Method of Manufacturing High Density Fine Line Printed Circuitry," U.S. Patent 4,159,222, June 1979.

152. Hideki Tsunetsugu, Akihiro Takagi, and Kunio Monya, "Multilayer Interconnections Using Polyimide Dielectrics and Aluminum Conductors," *International J. for Hybrid Microelectronics,* Vol. 8, no. 2, June 1985, p. 21.

153. T. Nakano, H. Yasuno, and K. Nishio, "Multilayer Printed Circuit Board," U.S. Patent 4,673,773, June 1987.

154. I. Shirahata, S. Shiga, H. Hori, and T. Jinbo, "Multilayer Printed Wiring Board and Method for Producing the Same," European Patent Application 0,247,575, May 1987.

155. Yamahiro Iwasa, "Method for Forming Electric Circuits on a Base Board," U.S. Patent 4,735,676, April 1988.

156. Shun-Ichiro Uchimura, Hiroshi Suzuki, and Hidetaka Sato, "Process for Producing a Multilayer Wiring Board," U.K. Patent Application 2,188,191, September 1987.

157. Yamahiro Iwasa, "Method for Forming Electrically Conductive Circuits on Base Board," U.S. Patent 4,734,156, March 28, 1988.

158. Harshadrai Vora, "Module for Packaging and Electrically Interconnecting Integrated Circuit Chips on a Porous Substrate, and Method of Fabricating Same," U.S. Patent 4,721,831, January 1988.

159. Charles E. Bauer and William A. Bold, "Multilayer Interconnect Circuitry Using Photoimageable Dielectric," European Patent Application 0,167,344, June 1985.

160. Yamahiro Iwasa, "Producing Multilayer Circuits on a Base Board," U.K. Patent Application 2,186,433, August (1987).

161. Marshall I. Gurian, "Reliable Fine Line," *PC Fab,* December 1987, p. 26.

162. Hayao Nakahara, "Japan's Swing to Chip-on-Board," *Electronic Packaging and Production,* December 1986, p. 38.

163. Howard Markstein, "TAB Rebounds as I/Os Increase," *Electronic Packaging and Production,* p. 42, August 1986, p. 42.

164. Robert Keeler, "Chip-on-Board Alters the Landscape of PC Boards," *Electronic Packaging and Production,* July 1985, p. 62.

165. Howard W. Markstein, "TAB Leads as COB Format," *Electronic Packaging and Production,* October 1987, p. 46.

166. Philip W. Rima, "TAB Gains Momentum," *Connection Technology,* August 1987, p. 26.

167. Tom Dixon, "TAB Technology Tackles High Density Interconnections," *Electronic Packaging and Production,* December 1984, p. 34.

168. Pieter Burggraaf, "TAB for High I/O and High Speed," *Semiconductor International,* June 1988, p. 72.

169. Ken Gilleo, "Future Directions for Tape Automated Bonding," *Connection Technology,* March 1988, p. 16.

170. A. L. Eustice, S. J. Horwitz, J. J. Stewart, A. R. Travis, and H. T. Sawhill, "Electronic Packaging Using Low Temperature Co-Fireable Ceramics," *Hybrid Circuit Technology,* June 1987, p. 9.

171. R. N. Merryweather and J. A. Solanky, "Substrate Development for Hybrids," *Hybrid Circuit Technology,* November 1986, p. 31.

172. Howard Markstein, "Hybrid Circuits: An Overview," *Electronic Packaging and Production,* February 1988, p. 90.

173. Haim Taraseiskey, "Custom Power Hybrids," *Solid State Technology,* October 1985, p. 111.

174. John W. Woulbroun, "Hybrid Module Manufacturing Techniques Yield Improved Packaging Alternatives," *Electri-Onics,* March 1985, p. 28.

175. Scott David, "Manufacturing Hybrid Circuits with a Co-fired Green Tape System," *Hybrid Circuit Technology,* January 1988, p. 18.

176. Don Mennie, "Hybrid Circuits Meeting Tough Challenges in Tough Environments," *Electronic Design,* June 1986, p. 65.

177. G. Menozzi, "Large Scale Interconnects for Aerospace Applications," *Hybrid Circuits,* January 1988, p. 18.

178. Robert Keeler, "Co-fired Ceramic Multilayers: When Reliability Counts," *Electronic Packaging and Production,* May 1987, p. 40.

179. Richard R. Langhoff, "Hybrid Microelectronics Packages: Metallographically Speaking," *Hybrid Circuit Technology,* December 1986, p. 23.

180. A. L. Eustice, S. J. Horwitz, J. J. Stewart, A. R. Travis, and H. T. Sawhill, "Electronic Packaging using Low Temperature Co-firable Ceramics—Part 2," *Hybrid Circuit Technology,* July 1987, p. 15.

181. Jim Angeloni, "VSLI Hybrids are Built with Modular Parts," *Electronic Packaging and Production,* September 1986, p. 28.

182. Jack Travis and John Ganjei, "Injection-Molded Thermoplastic Boards," *PC Fab,* July 1986, p. 89.

183. Carl Kirkland, "Injection Molding Circuit Boards: Understanding the Realities," *Plastics Technology,* November 1985, p. 68.

184. William Jacobi and Michael Kirsch, "Molded Wiring Board Materials and Processes," *PC Fab,* July 1986, p. 50.

185. D. L. Love, "Using Injection Molded Polymers for PCB Substrate Applications," *Electronics,* December 1984, p. 35.

186. David C. Frisch and Yu-Ling Teng, "Molded Circuits Enhance Use of Additive Process," *Electronic Packaging and Production,* February 1986, p. 176.

187. James P. Bright, "Injection Molded PWB's: New Generation of Interconnections," *Electri-Onics,* April 1985, p. 45.

188. David Frisch and Tom McNamara, "Resins and Tooling for Injection-Molded Circuit Boards," *Electronic Packaging and Production,* June 1986, p. 46.

CHAPTER 11
TRANSMISSION LINE REFLECTIONS

Stacey G. Lloyd
BiiN
Hillsboro, Oregon

11.1 INTRODUCTION

Computers are continuing to increase in frequency of operation at an accelerating pace. This is especially true of microprocessor-based systems that utilize many of the buses in Part 1. As a result, local and backplane buses are being pushed to higher and higher frequencies. Time allowed for signal "settling" can no longer just be guessed and the bus design must be optimized for minimal data transfer time. This in turn requires that phenomena such as reflections, crosstalk, ground shift, etc., be understood and minimized. Failure to do this can result in unreliable systems with higher manufacturing defects and increased field-service problems.

Reflections in transmission line networks are basically the result of impedance discontinuities: mismatched loads, connectors, line stubs, device inputs, and board layer changes. The impact a discontinuity has on a signal depends on the signal source impedance, source edge rate, length of the irregularity, and type of irregularity. These are all addressed by this chapter, beginning with an ideal network and progressing toward reality.

11.2 BASIC REFLECTION RELATIONSHIPS

A transmission line with line impedance Z_0 and delay per unit length (unit propagation delay) T_{pd} is shown in Fig. 11.1. The transmission line may physically be a coaxial cable, twisted pair, or PC board trace, etc. It is driven by an ideal unit step voltage source V_i through a source impedance Z_s at point A. It is terminated at point B, L units away from point A, by a load impedance Z_t. Initially, Z_s is 0 Ω ($V_s = V_i$) and Z_t is a resistive load. At time t=0, a unit step of amplitude V_i is applied to the line. The current step I_i determined by V_i and Z_0 propagates down the line. At $t = T_{pd} L = T_{prop}$ the step arrives at B. In order to satisfy Ohm's law

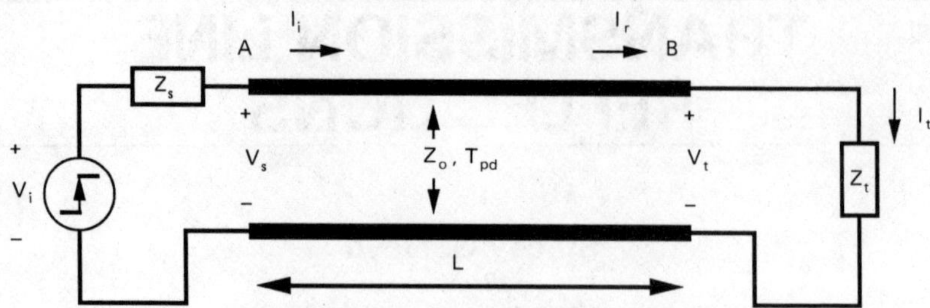

FIGURE 11.1 Basic transmission line with load.

for both the load and line impedance, an instantaneous adjustment of the voltage and currents must occur. This correction takes the form of a reflected electromagnetic (EM) wave composed of V_r and I_r.

Applying Ohm's Law at point B, with the polarities defined in Fig. 11.1, we have

$$Z_t = \frac{V_t}{I_t} = \frac{V_i + V_r}{I_i + I_r} \quad \text{and} \quad Z_0 = \frac{V_i + V_r}{I_i - I_r} \tag{11.1}$$

Therefore

$$Z_t(I_i + I_r) = Z_0(I_i - I_r) \tag{11.2}$$

rearranging,

$$I_r(Z_t + Z_0) = I_i(Z_0 - Z_t) \tag{11.3}$$

yields

$$\frac{I_r}{I_i} = -\frac{Z_t - Z_0}{Z_0 + Z_t} \tag{11.4}$$

the reflection coefficient for current.

More commonly, the reflection coefficient (r) is defined in terms of voltage.

$$r = \frac{V_r}{V_i} = \frac{(Z_t - Z_0)}{(Z_t + Z_0)} \tag{11.5}$$

This coefficient holds true at any impedance junction along a transmission line. As demonstrated, the incident signal will be split into the reflected and transmitted signals. The ratio of this division is defined by the reflection coefficient (r). It is positive for the reflected voltage and negative for the reflected current and can have a value from -1 to 1 for a load impedance of zero to infinity, respectively.

Examining the three cases, $Z_t = Z_0$, $Z_t > Z_0$, and $Z_t < Z_0$, will better illustrate the application of the reflection coefficient.

Case 1: $Z_t = Z_0$. In this case, when the incident wave (V_i, I_i) arrives at point B, Ohm's law is met without any correction. The waveforms at points A and B are as shown in Fig. 11.2*a*. Observe that applying Eq. (11.5) yields $r = 0$ and thus $V_r = 0$ and $I_r = 0$.

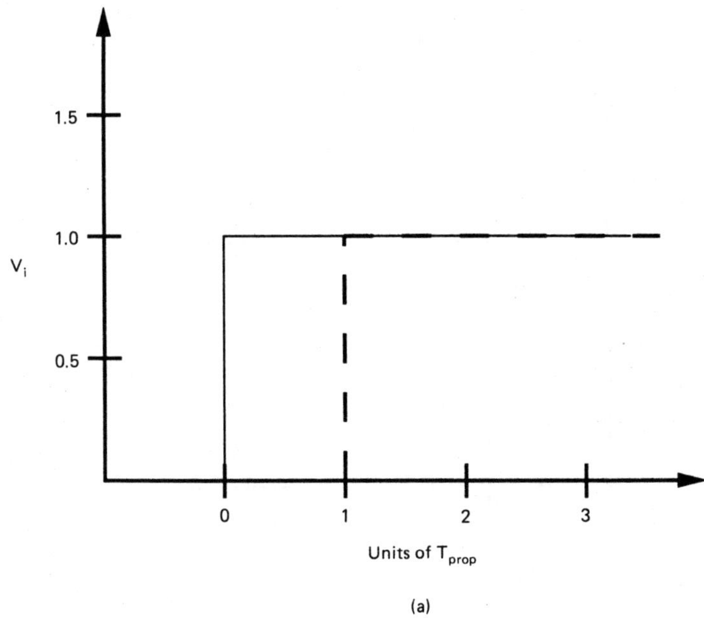

(a)

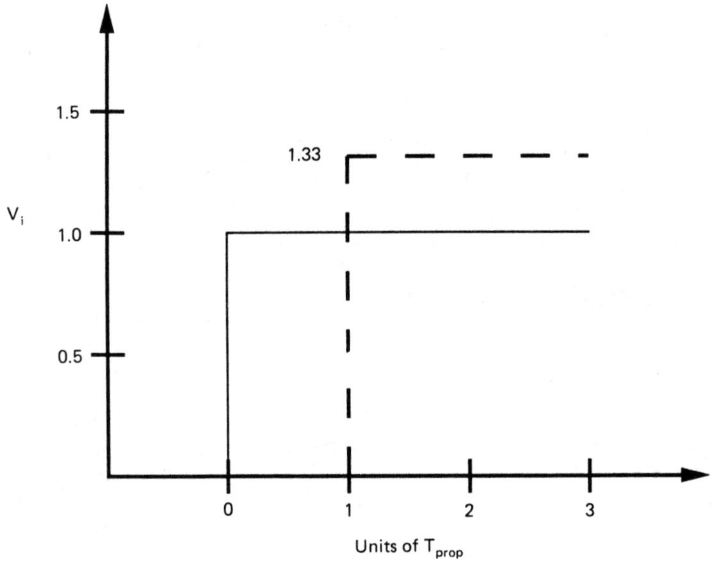

(b)

FIGURE 11.2 (*a*) Case 1: $Z_t = Z_0$; (*b*) case 2: $Z_t > Z_0$; (*c*) case 3: $Z_t < Z_0$. ——, at point A; – – –, at point B.

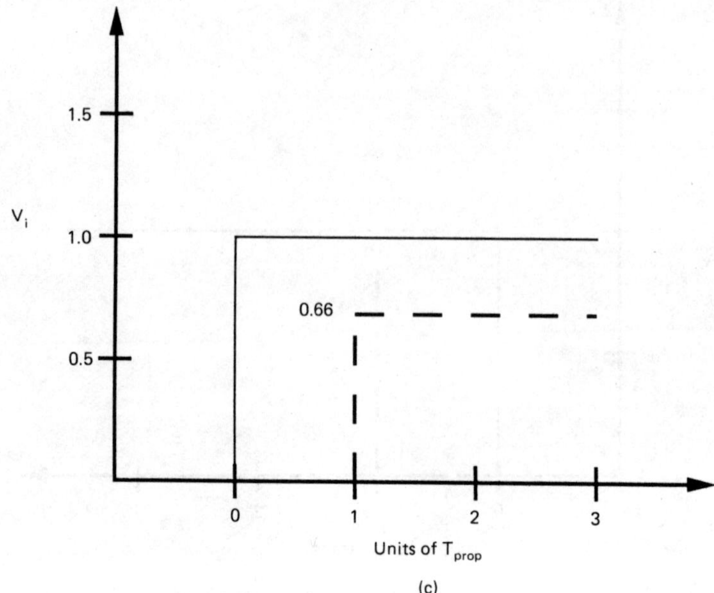

FIGURE 11.2 (*a*) Case 1: $Z_t = Z_0$; (*b*) case 2: $Z_t > Z_0$; (*c*) case 3: $Z_t < Z$. ———, at point A; – – –, at point B. (*Continued*)

Case 2: $Z_t > Z_0$. This time, when the incident wave arrives at point B, a reflection must occur to satisfy Ohm's law. If $Z_t = 2Z_0$, the reflection coefficient is +0.33, per Eq. (11.5). Therefore, at point B, the voltage is $V_i + V_r = 1.33V_i$ and the current into the load is $I_i - 0.33I_i = 0.66I_i$ as shown in Fig. 11.2*b*.

Case 3: $Z_t < Z_0$. Again, a reflection must occur at point B. Assuming $2Z_t = Z_0$, the reflection coefficient equals −0.33. At point B, the voltage is 0.66 V_i and the current into the load is $1.33I_i$ as shown in Fig. 11.2*c*.

11.3 THE NONIDEAL SOURCE

To this point, the line has been driven by an ideal unit step voltage source. Source resistance, inductance, capacitance and a finite edge rate were not taken into account. These nonideal characteristics not only impact the initial signal transition at point A, but the reflected waveforms at point A (due to reflections at B). As previously stated, a reflection coefficient exists for each impedance junction. This is true of the line-source junction. When a reflected wave returns to the source the reflection coefficient is

$$r_s = \frac{Z_s - Z_0}{Z_s + Z_0} \tag{11.6}$$

If we have an ideal line driver, $Z_s = 0$, then $r_s = -1$ and the voltage step reflected from B, V_r, is totally canceled and the voltage at A is still V_i.

11.3.1 Finite Source Resistance

When Z_s has a finite resistance, two things occur: a voltage division takes place on the initial transition and there are secondary reflections at the source.

First, a voltage division occurs between the source resistance and the line impedance; V_s no longer equals V_i

$$V_s = V_i \frac{Z_0}{Z_s + Z_0} \tag{11.7}$$

$$I_i = \frac{V_i}{Z_s + Z_0} \tag{11.8}$$

As Z_0 approaches Z_s, V_s approaches $V_i/2$. This limits the initial step voltage to where it may not reach a valid logic level. This effect is sometimes referred to as *back porching.*

Second, the reflection coefficient at the source is no longer -1 and some fraction of V_r is reflected back toward point B. Assuming that $Z_s = 0.33Z_0$ and $Z_t = 2Z_0$, the reflection coefficients at A and B are -0.5 and $+0.33$, respectively. This produces an initial step at V_s of $0.75V_i$. At point B the initial step voltage is

$$V_t = V_s(1 + r_t) = 0.75V_i(1 + 0.33) = V_i \tag{11.9}$$

The reflected voltage

$$V_r = 0.75V_i(0.33) = 0.25V_i \tag{11.10}$$

will travel back to A and the new voltage at A will be

$$V_s + V_s(r_t)(1 + r_s) = 0.75 \text{ V}_i + (0.25 \text{ V}_i) [1 + (-0.5)] = 0.825 \text{ V}_i \tag{11.11}$$

The step reflected from A will travel back to B and so forth, until the steady-state voltage is reached at A and B. This is shown in Fig. 11.3. The steady-state voltage is defined by the voltage division between the source impedance and the load impedance.

$$\text{V}_s \text{ or } V_t \text{ (steady state)} = \frac{Z_t}{Z_t + Z_s} = 0.86V_i \tag{11.12}$$

Calculating the voltage increments at points A and B can be quite cumbersome as the number of reflections become large. For example, by the second reflection at the source, the equation becomes

$$V_s = (0.75 \text{ V})(1 + r_t + r_t r_s + r_t^2 r_s^2) \tag{11.13}$$

Two techniques presented in Secs. 11.4.1 and 11.4.2, lattice diagrams and Bergeron diagrams, can be used to ease this calculation problem.

11.3.2 Nonlinear Sources

While linear resistances provide good approximations of reflection behavior, they may not adequately model the characteristics of real devices. Plots of high and low output voltages V_{oh} and V_{ol} given in many vendor catalogs reveal two impor-

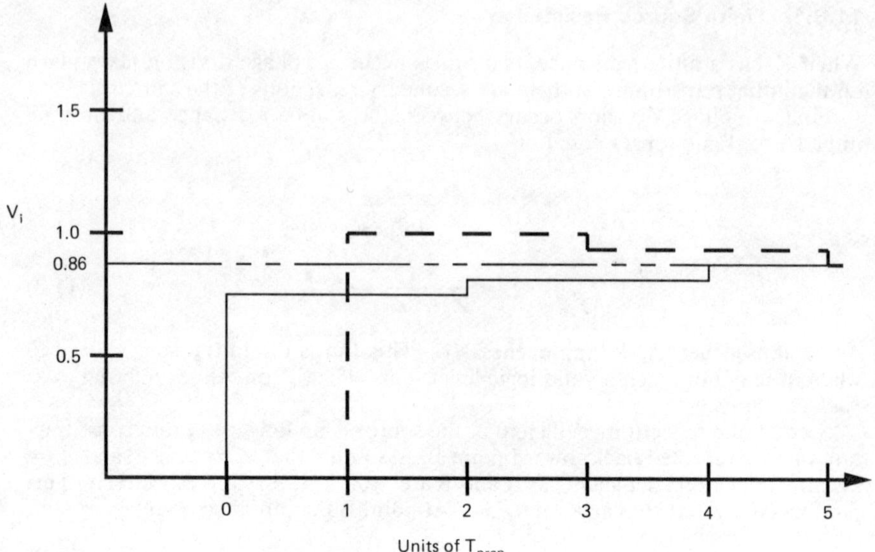

FIGURE 11.3 Impact of source resistance.———, at point A; – – –, at point B.

tant aspects of real line drivers: one, they are nonlinear and two, V_{ol} and V_{oh} are not symmetrical. An example of a TTL source is shown in Fig. 11.4. When the nonlinear characteristics of a driver or load become important, Bergeron diagrams can be used to easily analyze the transmission line.

When linear models are sufficient, the linear regions of the driver, highlighted in Fig. 11.4, are quantified (based on the slope) and used to calculate the reflection coefficients at the source. The linear region of V_{oh} is used as the source impedance for low-to-high transitions and the linear region of V_{ol} for high-to-low transitions. The linear region of V_{oh} is usually between 45 and 90 Ω and between 5 and 25 Ω for V_{ol}.

11.3.3 Source Inductance and Capacitance

Line drivers in the real world are not only resistive, but inductive and capacitive as well. This capacitance and inductance is present due to the driver's physical packaging and semiconductor junctions. Neither is typically a problem when looking at reflections at the source.

On the other hand, source capacitance becomes important when several sources are connected to a single transmission line (three-state buses and wired logic signals). The impact of multiple capacitive loads is discussed in Sec. 11.6, Capacitive Loads.

Source inductance can impact driver performance when the transmission line is heavily loaded. Backplane buses and clock lines often fall in this category. If a driver's effective inductance (L_{eff}) is significant relative to the effective impedance (Z_{0eff}) of the line, the transition time t_r or t_f can limit interconnect performance.

$$t_r \quad \text{or} \quad t_f \geqq 2.2 L_{eff}/Z_{0eff} \tag{11.14}$$

For example, a typical octal TTL driver in a DIP package may have 15 nH of loop inductance. Assuming half the loop inductance is in the ground path and shared with eight other drivers, the effective inductance (for a single-driver model) with all the lines switching simultaneously from high to low is 60 nH (7.5 nH × 8). If the loaded backplane impedance is 20 Ω (not unusual), the transition time will be at least 6.6 ns from the 10–90 percent levels regardless of the driver's semiconductor technology. The increased transition time is the result of the driver's internal ground shifting (bounce). Additionally, any quiescent drivers on this common ground will exhibit a glitch. High-speed octal drivers are especially bad.[1]

11.3.4 Finite Transition Time

Previously, all examples assumed a unit step for the voltage source function. With this unit step function all interconnects exhibit transmission line behavior regardless of length. In reality, the output of line drivers is more exponential in nature. With this finite edge time, not all interconnects will require reflection analysis.

Defining the point at which an interconnect should be treated as a transmission line and hence reflection analysis applied has no consensus of opinion. Classically, when the propagation time is greater than half the signal rise time ($t_r/T_{prop} = 2:1$), transmission line analysis is applied.[2] However, as Table 11.1 indicates, trouble can arise at ratios of 4:1 with 10 percent overshoot at the load.

Based on a finite transition time, three classes of interconnects can be defined.

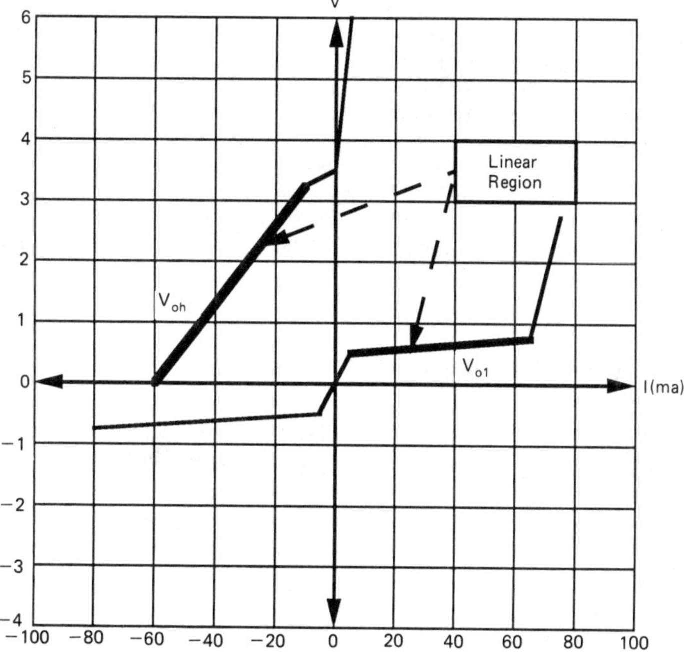

FIGURE 11.4 Typical nonlinear source.

TABLE 11.1 Effect of Signal Rise Time on Waveforms (Ref. 3)

t_r/T_{prop}	Percent overshoot at Z_l
1:1	87
2:1	63
3:1	30
4:1	10
6:1	5
8:1	0

Note: $R_s = 5\ \Omega$, $R_t = 4.6\ \text{k}\Omega$, and $Z_0 = 75\ \Omega$.

The classical definition will be used as the dividing line between short lines and long lines and a slightly more arbitrary line drawn to define lumped interconnects.

Lumped: $t_r/T_{prop} \geqq 4$
Short line: $4 > t_r/T_{prop} > 2$
Long line: $t_r/T_{prop} \leqq 2$

Long lines and short lines will both be analyzed using transmission line analysis. Lumped interconnects may be analyzed using classical circuit analysis (i.e., Kirchoff's voltage-current laws, etc.).

As noted, the output of real drivers is exponential, but for the purpose of simplifying analysis a ramp is typically substituted. In order to translate the rise times specified by manufacturers, 10 to 90 percent and 20 to 80 percent, to linear ramp times (0 to 100 percent), they must be multiplied by 1.25 and 1.67, respectively.[4] Table 11.2 provides the rise time for most logic families and includes this translation. Also included are the maximum interconnect lengths that should be treated as lumped.

Figure 11.5 shows a typical point-to-point interconnect with a high-impedance load ($Z_L = \infty$). If the rise time (t_r) is 2 ns, $L = 12$ in and $T_{pd} = 2$ ns/ft, then $T_{prop} = 2$ ns and $t_r/T_{prop} = 1$ (less than 2), which meets the long line requirement. Therefore, transmission line analysis must be used to evaluate the interconnect in Fig. 11.5.

11.4 REFLECTION ANALYSIS TECHNIQUES

Besides the equations described in Sec. 11.2, two other techniques can be used to analyze the interconnect, lattice diagrams and Bergeron diagrams.

11.4.1 Lattice Diagrams

A lattice diagram for Fig. 11.5 is shown in Fig. 11.6 with $Z_s = 0.33Z_0$. The diagram is constructed as follows:

- Vertical lines are drawn to represent the impedance boundaries. They are

TABLE 11.2 Unterminated Interconnection Lengths for Common Logic Families (Ref. 4)

Logic family	Published rise or fall time (10% to 90%) (ns)	Equivalent t_r maximum (0% to 100%) (ns)	Maximum interconnection	
			$t_r/T = 4$	$t_r/T = 3$
ECL 100K	1	1.25	2.1 in	3 in
ECL 10K	3.5	4.4	7.5 in	10 in
ECL 10KH	1.8	2.3	3.9 in	5.5 in
TTL	4	5	9.0 in	12 in
STTL	1.5	2	4 in	4.8 in
LTTL	4	5	9.0 in	12 in
AS	1	1.3	2.3 in	3.1 in
ALS	6	7.5	14 in	18 in
FAST	2	3	5.5 in	7.2 in
CMOS (5 V)	90	113	17 ft	23 ft
CMOS (15 V)	50	6.3	9.0 ft	13 ft
High-Speed CMOS	10	12.5	23 in	30 in
FACT	3	3.8	6.5 in	9.1 in
HC (Motorola)	8	10	17 in	24 in
AC (TI)	2.4	3	5.1 in	7.2 in

spaced in proportion to the delay time between each boundary (this becomes more important when more than two boundaries exist).

- At the top of each boundary, the calculated reflection coefficient is marked for each direction with which the wave may approach the boundary (again this becomes more important when more than two boundaries exist). In this example, $r_{ba} = -0.5$ and $r_{ab} = +1.0$.
- Tics on each vertical line mark off time in increments of T_{prop} ($T_{\#}$) for the pre-

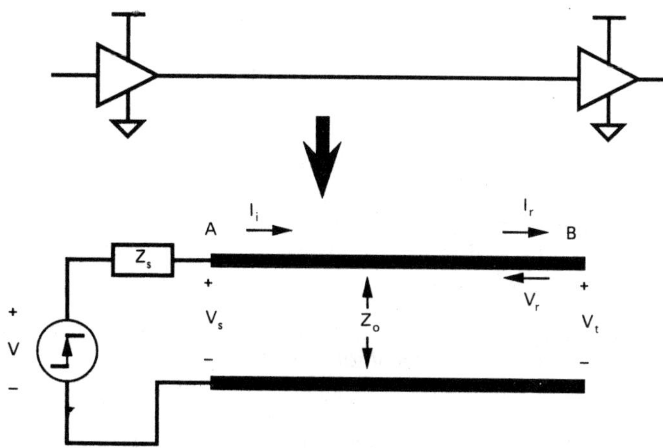

FIGURE 11.5 Point-to-point interconnect.

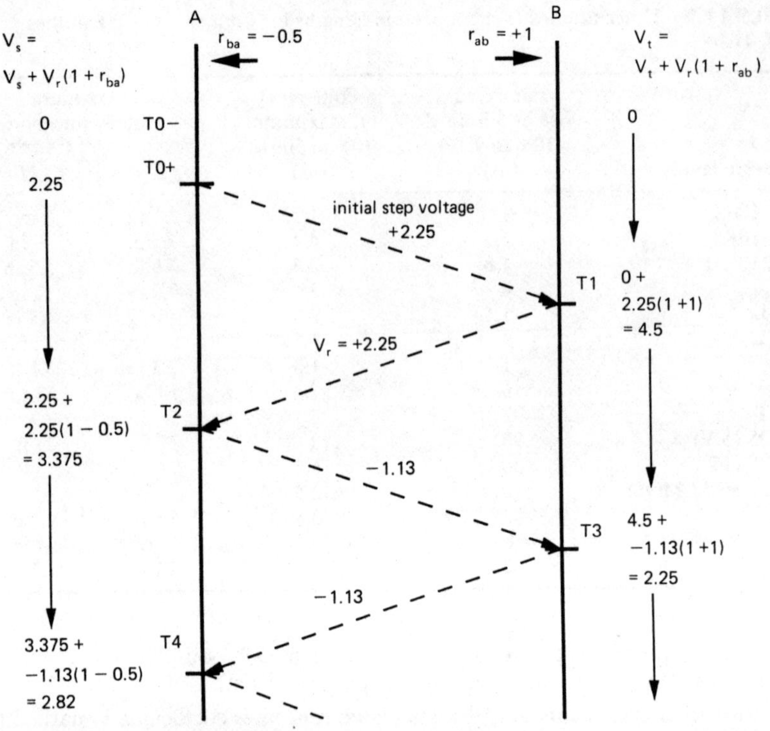

FIGURE 11.6 Lattice diagram for unterminated line.

vious transmission line segment. Begin with T_{0+} at $t = 0$, the source boundary, and T_1 at $t = T_{prop}$, the load boundary.

- Next the initial step voltage is written near T_{0+}.
- Then beginning at T_{0+} (at the source), a diagonal line is drawn to T_1 and labeled with the initial step voltage as determined by Eq. (11.7), $V_s = 0.75V_i$ (the example assumes $V_i = 3.0$).
- The sum of the existing voltage at V_t (initially 0 for this example), the incident voltage and reflected voltage, is written next to T_1, $V_t + 0.75V_i(1 + r_t) = 1.5V_i$, where $r_t = r_{ab} = +1$.
- A diagonal line is then drawn from T_1 to T_2 and labeled with the reflected voltage V_r.
- The sum of the existing voltage at V_s, the incident voltage and reflected voltage, is marked next to T_2, $V_s + V_r(1 + r_s)$, where $r_s = r_{ba} = -0.5$.
- The process continues as needed.

This procedure can be easily expanded to more than two impedance boundaries. Evaluating lattice diagrams as a technique yields the following.

Strengths

- Can be used for transmission line analysis when multiple impedance boundaries are present
- Easily converted to computer program

Weaknesses

- Limited to linear line drivers and loads
- Long and tedious to perform by hand, especially for more than two boundaries (see Fig. 11.23)

11.4.2 Bergeron Diagrams

Bergeron diagrams provide a graphical technique for simultaneously solving the equations that describe the source, line, and load *V-I* characteristics during a transition. The source and load may be nonlinear and include multiple discrete physical elements. Thus the source may not only include a TTL driver, but any near-end terminations (resistors, diodes, etc.). Equally, the load may include a TTL input clamping diode and far-end termination elements. A Bergeron diagram for the point-to-point interconnect (Fig. 11.5) with $Z_0 = 50\ \Omega$, $Z_s = 0.33Z_0 = 16.5\ \Omega$, and $V_i = 3.0$ V is shown in Fig. 11.7.

Construct a Bergeron diagram as follows:

- Draw the voltage and current axis perpendicular to each other. For convention, current will be on the x axis and voltage on the y axis.
- Establish a consistent sign convention for current. Current into the line driver will be positive and current to source will be negative.

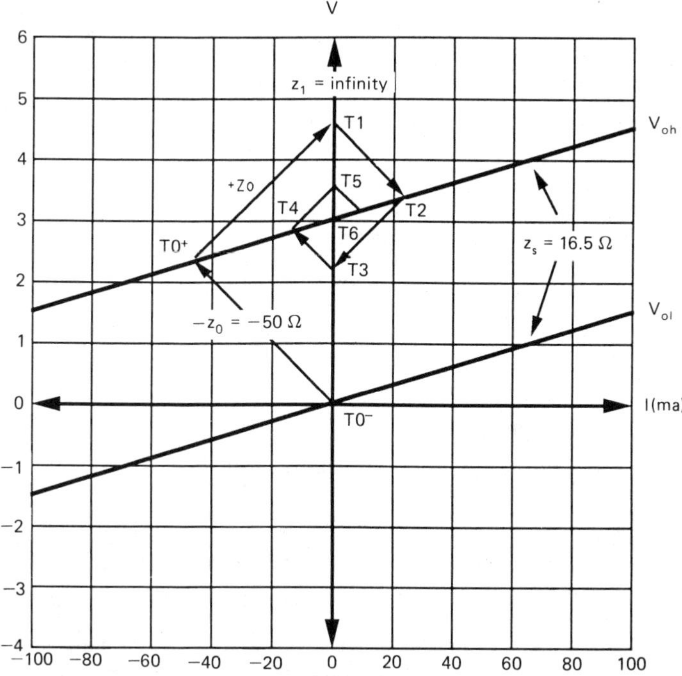

FIGURE 11.7 Bergeron diagram for unterminated line.

- Using the sign convention, draw the V_{ol} and V_{oh} curves for the driver (including the impact of near-end terminations) and then the load impedances (including the impact of clamping diodes, etc.).

For a high-to-low transition:

- Start at the intersection of the V_{oh} curve and the load line (T_{0-}). Draw a line with a slope of $-Z_0$ to the V_{ol} curve (T_{0+}). This establishes the initial voltage and current step at the driver.
- Draw a line with a slope of Z_0 from T_{0+} to the load line (T_1). This is the initial voltage and current at the load including the reflection at time T_{prop}.
- Draw a line with a slope of $-Z_0$ from T_1 to the V_{0l} curve (T_2). This is the voltage and current at the driver after the first reflection returns to the source at time $2T_{\text{prop}}$.
- Repeat until the steady state is reached (where the V_{ol} curve and load line intersect).
- Plot source and load waveforms based on the intersections. The source waveform starts at the T_{0-} voltage level and changes to the T_{0+}, T_2, and T_4 levels at times $0+$, $2T_{\text{prop}}$ and $4T_{\text{prop}}$, respectively.

For a low-to-high transition:

- Starting at the intersection of the V_{ol} curve and the load line (T_{0-}), draw a line with a slope of $-Z_0$ to the V_{oh} curve (T_{0+}). This establishes the initial voltage and current step at the driver.
- Draw a line with a slope of Z_0 from T_{0+} to the load line (T_1). This is the initial voltage and current at the load, including the reflection at time T_{prop}.
- Draw a line with a slope of $-Z_0$ from T_1 to the V_{oh} curve (T_2). This is the voltage and current at the driver after the first reflection returns at time $2T_{\text{prop}}$.
- Repeat until the steady state is reached (where the V_{oh} curve and load line intersect).
- Plot source and load waveforms based on the intersections. The source waveform starts at the T_{0-} voltage level and changes to the T_1, T_3, and T_5 levels at times T_{prop}, $3T_{\text{prop}}$, and $5T_{\text{prop}}$, respectively.

Evaluating Bergeron diagram analysis yields the following:

Strengths

- Can be used for transmission line analysis when nonlinear loads and drivers are present
- Easily performed by hand
- Presents a lot of information in a concentrated format

Weaknesses

- Not easily programmed but can be done using a piecewise linear solution
- Cannot be used when more than two impedance boundaries are present

The resulting waveforms from the lattice and Bergeron diagram analysis is shown in Fig. 11.8. In this case, the results are identical. However, if the driver had more

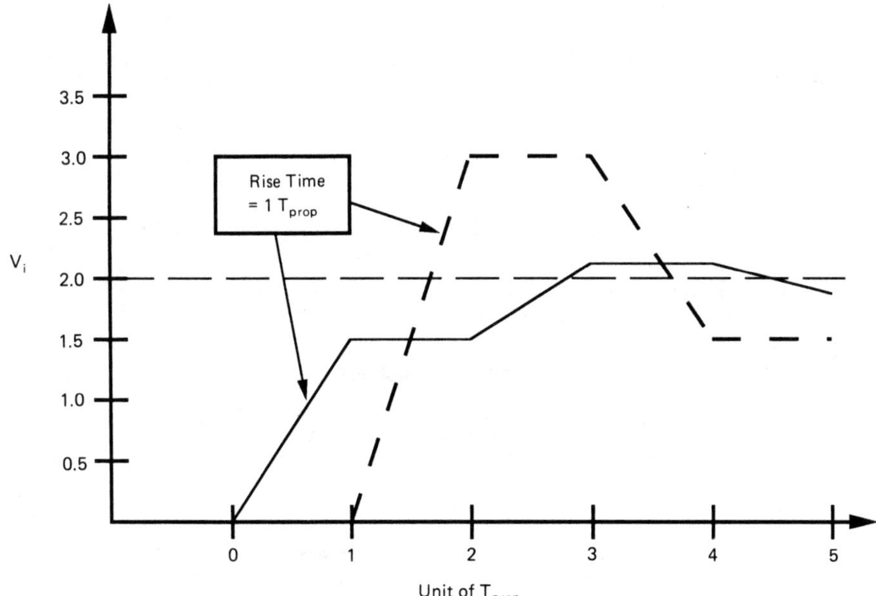

FIGURE 11.8 Reflections on an unterminated line.———, at point A; – – –, at point B.

realistic characteristics, like Fig. 11.4, the Bergeron diagram would yield different and more accurate results. The reader should perform the Bergeron diagram analysis for the high-to-low transition to verify this.

11.5 TERMINATIONS

Without any termination the interconnect of Fig. 11.5 exhibits the damped oscillation shown in Fig. 11.8. To correct this, some form of termination is required. Series (or back-end) and parallel resistive termination are the two most common.

11.5.1 Series Termination

Series termination, as shown in Fig. 11.9, places a resistor in series with the source output on an open-ended line. Ideally, the sum of the resistor plus the source impedance equals the impedance of the driven line, or

$$R_s = Z_0 - Z_s \tag{11.15}$$

With the source and line impedance matched, the initial voltage at V_s is $V_i/2$, per Eq. (11.7). When the wave reaches the open-ended line, a +100 percent reflection occurs ($r_t = +1$) and thus $V_t = V_i$. The reflected wave is then absorbed at the source since $r_s = 0$. The waveforms for the line are shown in Fig. 11.10.

As previously illustrated in Fig. 11.4, most line drivers do not have symmetrical output impedances, and Eq. (11.15) cannot be met for all cases (Z_{ol}, 5–25 Ω,

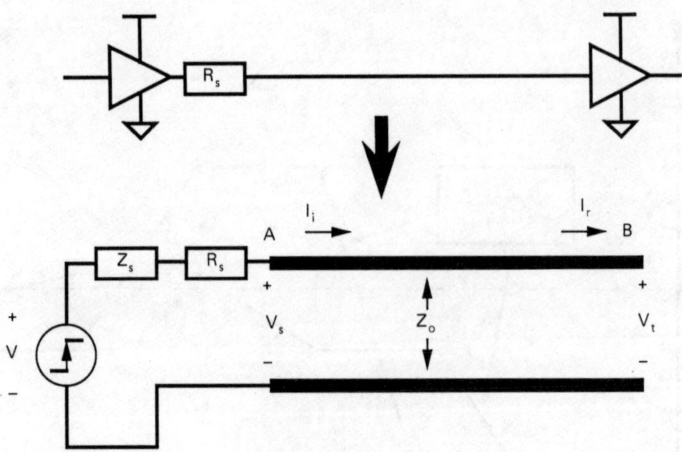

FIGURE 11.9 Series termination.

is usually much lower than Z_{oh}, 45–90 Ω). However, satisfactory results can be achieved with intermediate values for the resistor.

$$Z_0 - Z_{oh} < R_s < Z_0 - Z_{ol} \tag{11.16}$$

Examining series termination yields the following:

Strengths

- Has low power consumption between transients
- Can be implemented with one resistor or internal to the bus driver

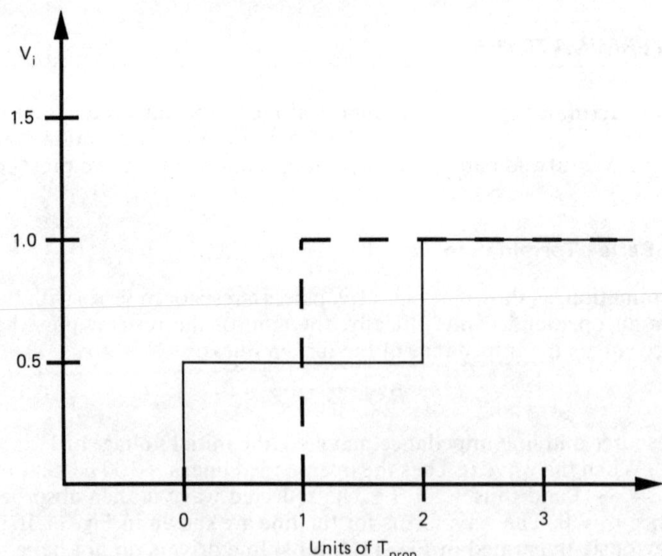

FIGURE 11.10 Series termination waveform.——, at point A; – – –, at point B.

Weaknesses

- Degrades the edge rate more per unit of capacitive load. See Sec. 11.6.
- Requires transmission line round-trip delay ($2T_{\text{prop}}$) to achieve full step level with distributed loads.

11.5.2 Parallel Termination

Placing a resistance at the receiving end of the transmission line is termed parallel termination. In order to eliminate reflections, the resistance value must match the effective impedance of the line. It is quite common to implement parallel termination using a split resistor network as shown in Fig. 11.11. Here, the Thevinin resistance, R_{Th}, should equal Z_0. The Thevinin equivalent resistance is found by shorting the independent voltage source, V_{cc}, and is determined per Eq. (11.17).

$$R_{\text{Th}} = \frac{R_1 R_2}{R_1 + R_2} \tag{11.17}$$

The Thevinin voltage is found by creating an open circuit by disconnecting the resistor network from the line and calculating the voltage.

$$V_{\text{Th}} = V_{\text{cc}} \frac{R_2}{R_1 + R_2} \tag{11.18}$$

Many times it is not possible to match R_{Th} to Z_0 because of the line driver's limited dc drive characteristics. However, depending on the receiver's noise margin, a limited reflection is usually acceptable. Equations (11.19) and (11.20) can be

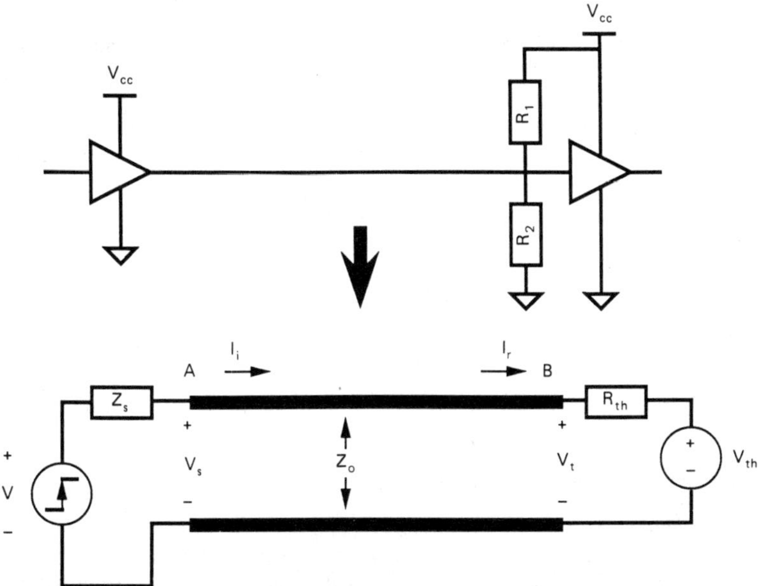

FIGURE 11.11 Parallel Thevinin termination.

used to determine the limits on the Thevinin equivalent network set by the line driver's dc limits.

$$I_{ol} \geqq \frac{V_{\mathrm{Th}} - V_{ol}}{R_{\mathrm{Th}}} \tag{11.19}$$

$$I_{oh} \geqq \frac{V_{\mathrm{Th}} - V_{oh}}{R_{\mathrm{Th}}} \tag{11.20}$$

Bergeron diagrams provide a good graphical technique for determining the reflection amplitudes and the best R_{Th} and V_{Th} values that meet the driver's dc limits. Using the nonlinear source in Fig. 11.4 and a 50-Ω line, Fig. 11.12*a* and *b* illustrates how varying the values of R_{Th} and V_{Th} impact interconnect performance. Only the falling edge analysis is performed. The reader should execute the analysis for the rising edge to check for changes there as well.

Other forms of parallel termination include single pull-up resistors, single pull-down resistors, and ac termination. A single pull-up resistor to V_{cc} only dissipates power when the driver output is low. Likewise, a single resistor to ground only dissipates power when the driver output is high. These variations are shown in Fig. 11.13.

ac termination, which involves placing a capacitor in series with a pull-up or pull-down resistor, is used to gain the benefits of parallel termination without paying as large a power penalty. The capacitor value should be chosen such that

$$C \leqq \frac{2T_{\mathrm{prop}}}{Z_c \pi} \tag{11.21}$$

where Z_c is the maximum impedance desired for the capacitor. Z_c should be less than 10 percent of Z_0 with the pull-up or pull-down resistor, R_t, equal to Z_0. This limits the reflection to less than 5 percent [i.e., applying Eq. (11.5) with $Z_t = Z_c + R_t$].

In summary, parallel termination has the following strengths and weaknesses.

Strengths

- Since the initial step voltage is not divided in half as for series termination, inputs can be distributed anywhere along the line. All inputs see the initial step within one propagation delay (T_{prop}).
- Can be used for bidirectional bus termination.

Weaknesses

- Loads the driver more heavily
- Has considerable power dissipated by the resistors in the steady state unless ac form is used
- Typically requires two resistors per termination versus one for series

11.5.3 Diode Clamp Termination

Most TTL devices and many CMOS devices have input protection diodes.[5,6] They not only protect the device from electrostatic discharge damage, but help limit reflections. Figure 11.14 shows a possible protection setup. The diodes will clamp

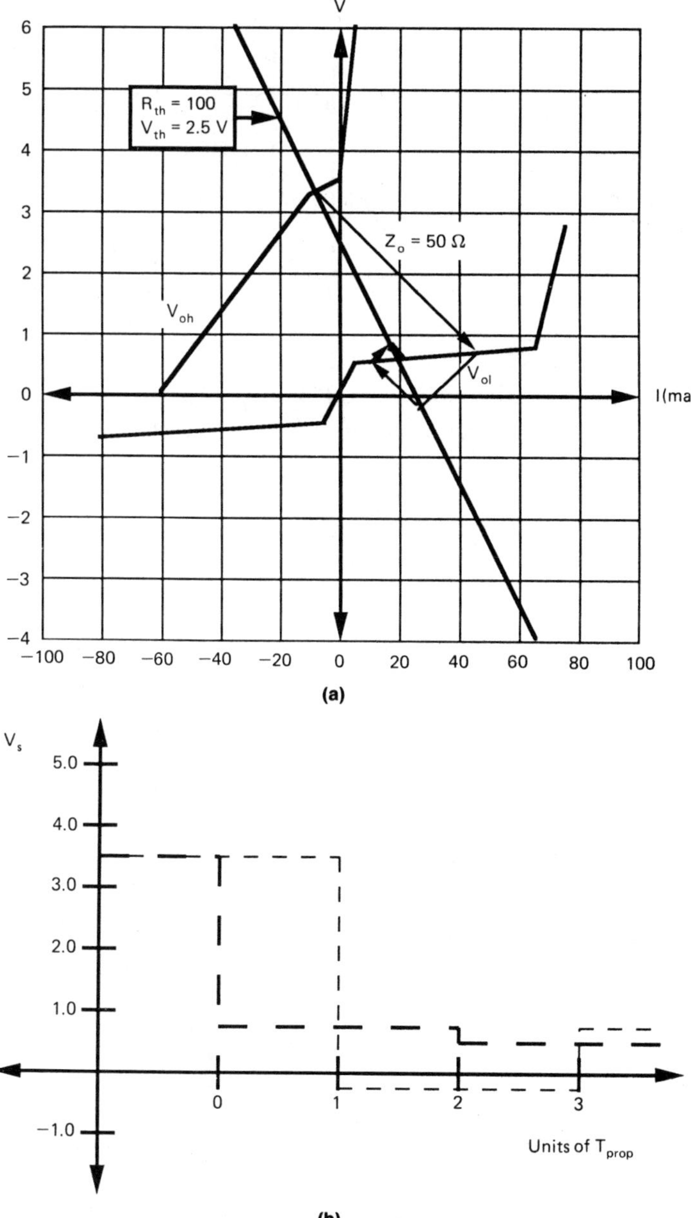

FIGURE 11.12A Variation of R_{Th} and V_{Th}.- - -, at source; – – –, at load.

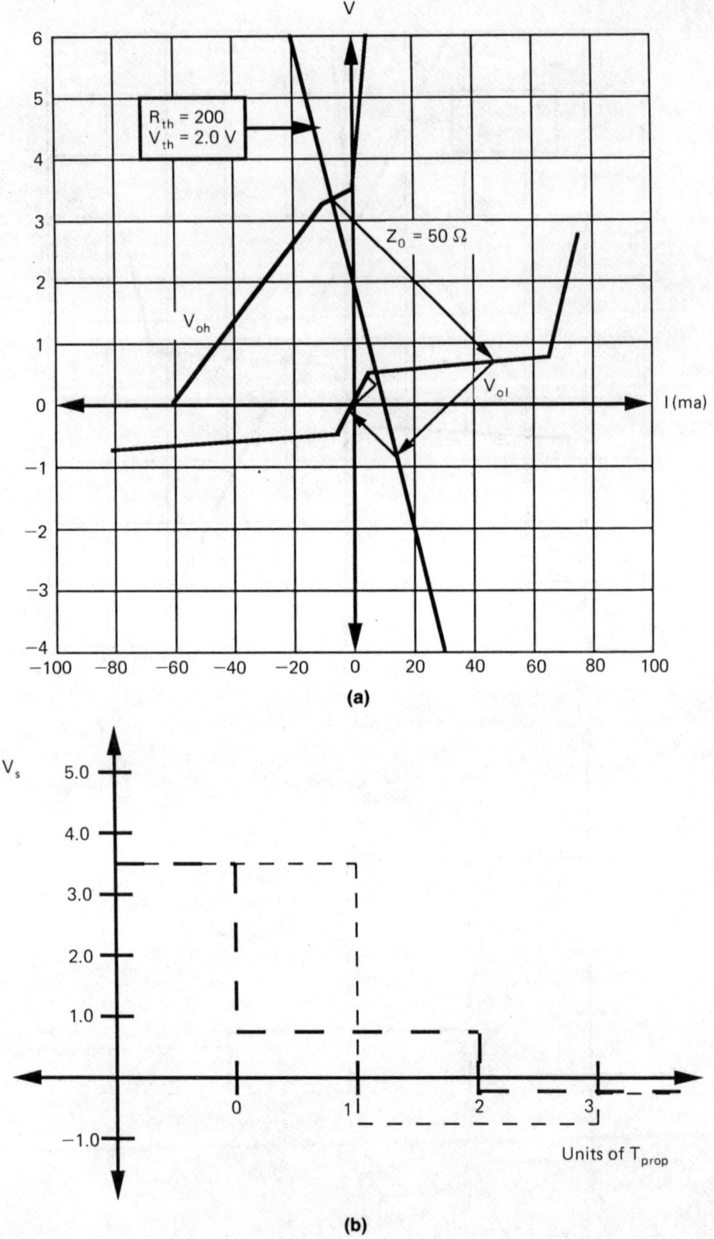

FIGURE 11.12B Variation of R_{Th} and V_{Th}.– – –, at source; – – –, at load. (*Continued*)

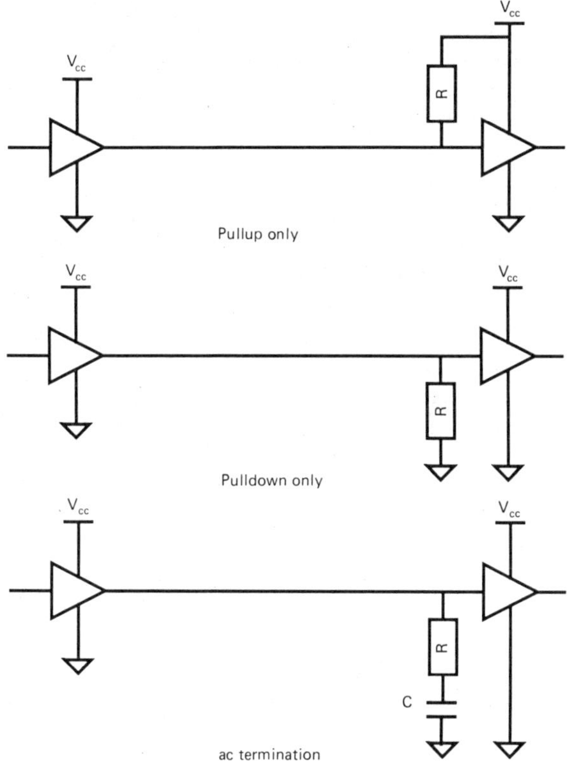

FIGURE 11.13 Alternative parallel terminations.

the input voltage at 0.5–1.5 V (Ref. 5) below ground and 0.5–1.5 V above V_{cc}, depending on the logic family and forward bias current. Note that pin inductances and diode reaction times may allow higher voltages momentarily.

With bipolar TTL circuits, the diode to V_{cc} is not typically present and would have little impact on interconnect performance. However, the diode to ground can be very important. A Bergeron diagram for the high-to-low transition of the circuit shown in Fig. 11.5 with and without clamping diodes is shown in Fig. 11.15. Note the reduction in the secondary reflection at the load. The result is a much cleaner and desirable signal.

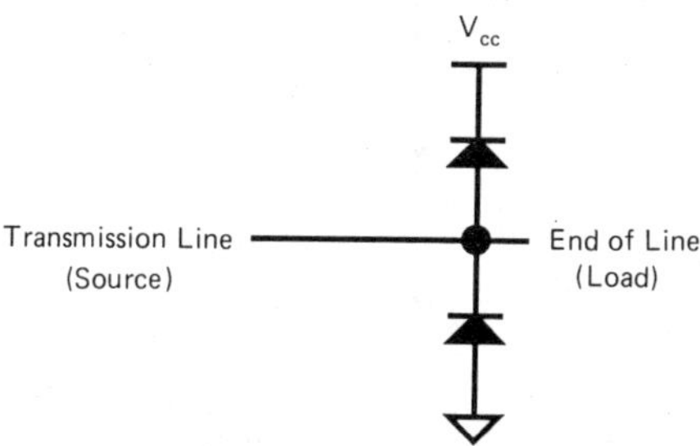

FIGURE 11.14 Input protection diodes.

In cases where no input clamping diode is present or further improvement is necessary, a discrete high-speed Schottky diode can be added to ground (and V_{cc} if needed). Improving further, a circuit that clamps at near 0 V as shown in Fig. 11.16 can be used.

The strengths and weaknesses of diode termination are as follows.

Strengths

- Diodes are commonly present on the input of many devices.
- Clamping diodes can reduce undershoot and overshoot without adding dc load.
- A controlled impedance interconnect is not required to be effective.

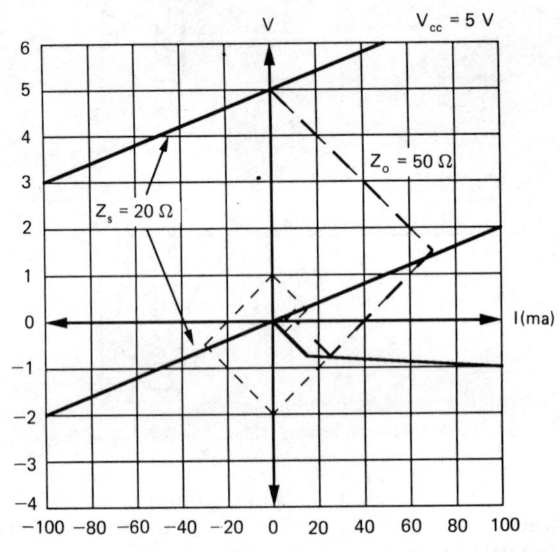

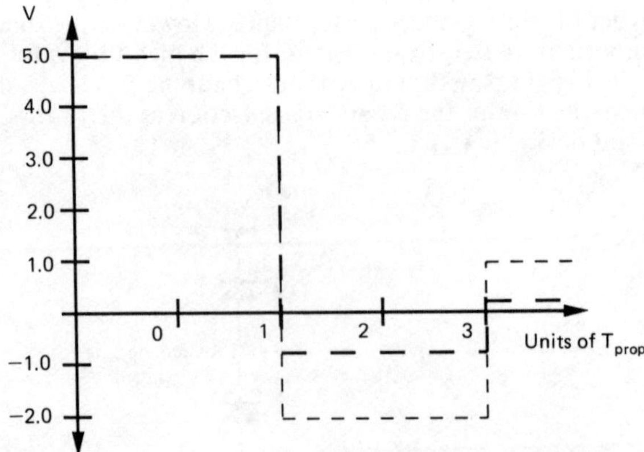

FIGURE 11.15 Impact of diode clamps.- - -, without diodes; ---, with diodes.

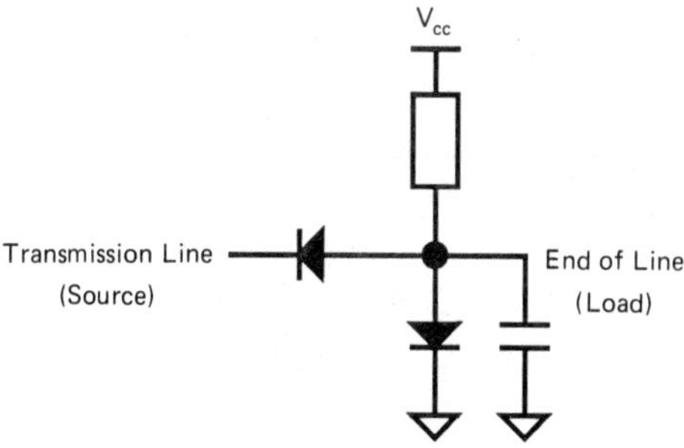

FIGURE 11.16 Improved diode clamp.

Weaknesses

- Costs more than resistors
- Has response times that may limit effectiveness
- Certain diodes when forward biased become quite capacitive and degrade interconnect performance

11.6 CAPACITIVE LOADS

Thus far the load impedance attached to the transmission line has been purely resistive. While resistors are added to transmission line networks to limit reflections, input buffers, three-state output buffers, and other circuit elements add capacitive loading to transmission lines. Because the resistance of these inputs and three-state buffers is usually much greater than the line impedance, they are simply represented by capacitors for ac analysis. These loads may be lumped at the end as shown in Fig. 11.17*a* or distributed along the transmission line as shown in Fig. 11.17*b*.

11.6.1 End-of-Line Load Capacitance

When the loads are lumped at the end of the line as shown in Fig. 11.17*a* the interconnect performance depends on its type: long line, short line, or lumped.

With a *long line,* the waveforms at the input and output of the line are impacted as shown in Fig. 11.18. The rising edge at the load is degraded, adding more delay to the signal propagation, and a glitch occurs at the source.

The amount of edge degradation at the load depends on the type of termination. Measuring from the 50 percent point the additional delay is as follows:[8]

$$T_{\text{deg}} = 0.7 Z_0 C_l \qquad \text{for series termination} \tag{11.22}$$

and

$$T_{\text{deg}} = 0.35 Z_0 C_l \qquad \text{for parallel termination} \tag{11.23}$$

These additional delays should be added to T_{prop} to calculate the total interconnect delay, $T_{\text{delay}} = T_{\text{prop}} + T_{\text{deg}}$.

As Fig. 11.18 also indicates, the end of line capacitance causes a glitch at the source: negative for rising edges and positive for falling edges. This reflection is

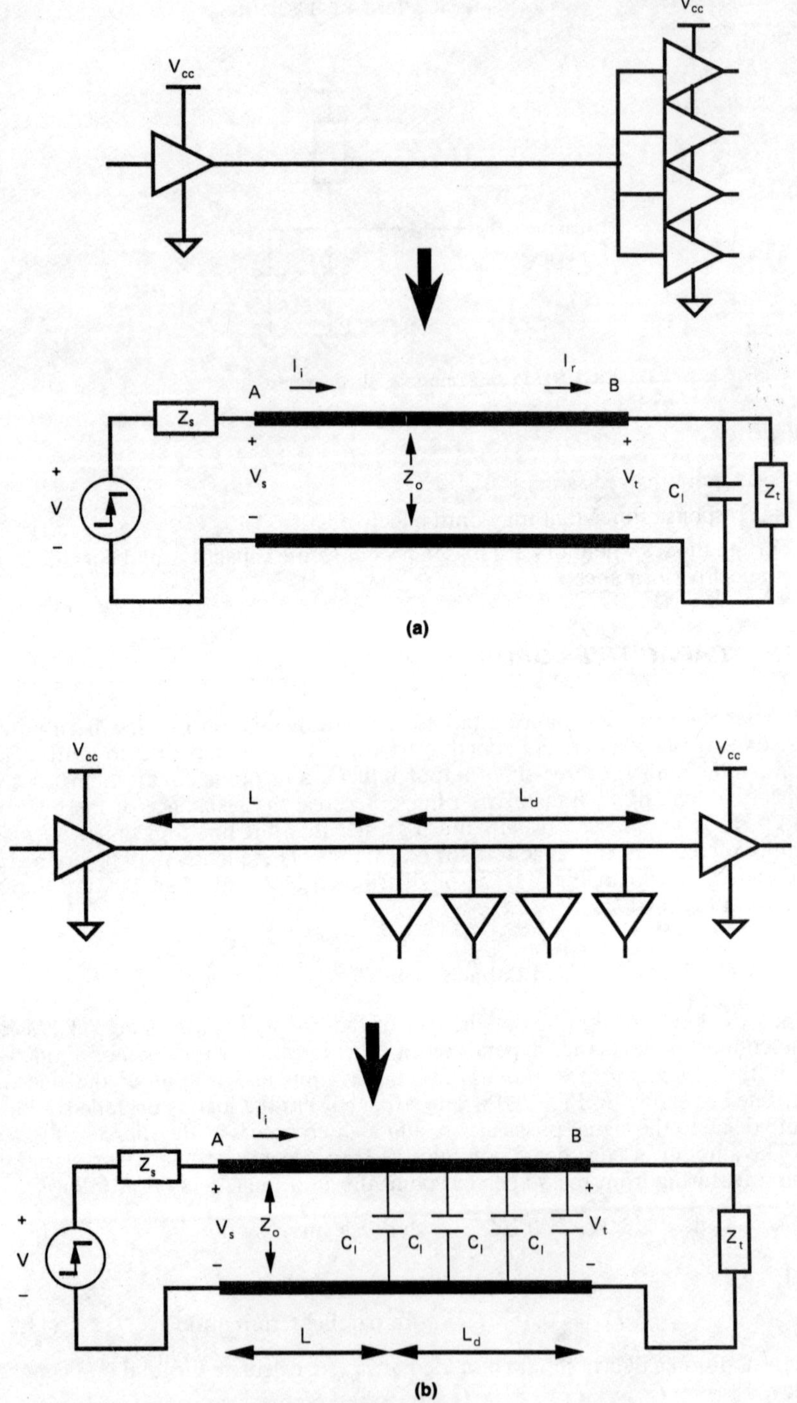

FIGURE 11.17 (*a*) End-of-line capacitance; (*b*) distributed capacitance.

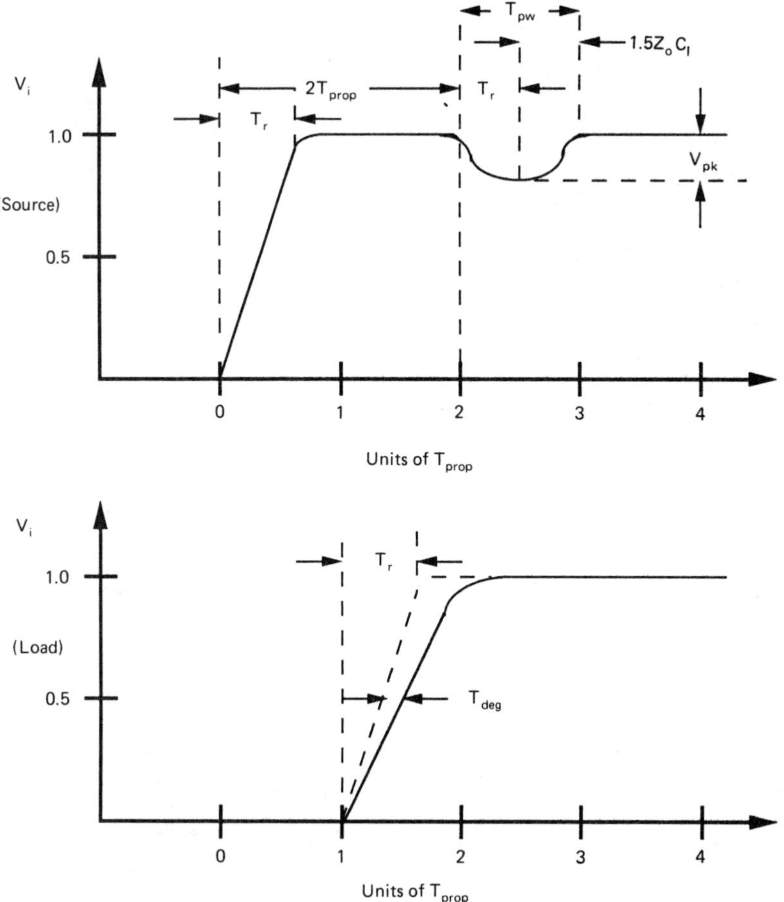

FIGURE 11.18 Impact of end-of-line capacitance.

due to the temporarily lowered impedance at the end of the line while the capacitance is charged. The glitch has a pulse width[2]

$$T_{pw} = (t_r \quad \text{or} \quad t_f) + 1.5Z_0C_l \tag{11.24}$$

and an amplitude[9]

$$V_{peak} = \frac{C_l Z_0 V_s}{2(t_r \quad \text{or} \quad t_f)} \tag{11.25}$$

where t_r and t_f are the signal rise and fall times, respectively.

With a *short line,* the edges at both the source and load will be degraded. A conservative estimate of the degradation can be made using a lumped-load model plus standard circuit analysis. In this case, the transmission line's capacitance,

$$C = T_{prop}/Z_0 \tag{11.26}$$

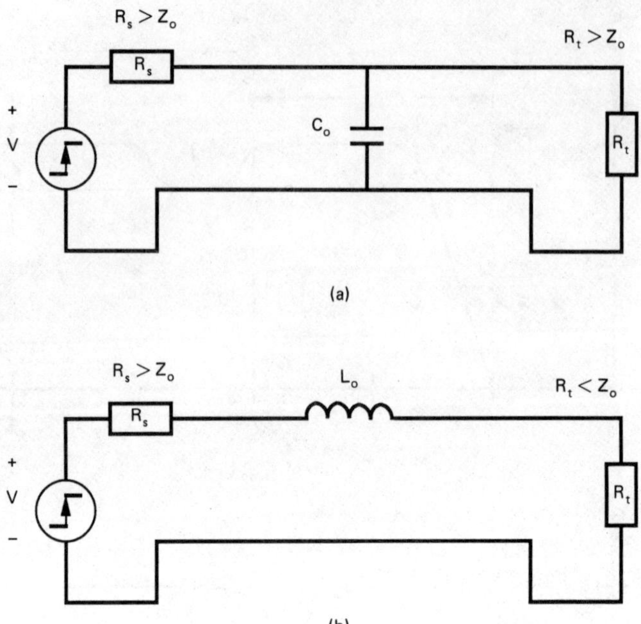

FIGURE 11.19 (*a*) Lumped line model ($R_s > Z_0$); (*b*) lumped line model ($R_t < Z_0$).

plus the load capacitance C_l equals the total lumped capacitance. Alternatively, the degradation can be determined from the long line case plus 7 percent.[10]

For a *lumped* element use a lumped-load model plus classical circuit analysis. To calculate the interconnect's equivalent lumped elements, do the following:[4]

- Determine the characteristic impedance of the line, Z_0.
- Determine the source and load impedances, R_s and R_t.
- If $R_s > Z_0$, then include only the interconnect capacitance, $C_0 = T_{\text{prop}}/Z_0$, when analyzing the circuit (Fig. 11.19*a*).
- If $R_t < Z_0$, then use only the interconnect inductance, $L_0 = T_{\text{prop}}Z_0$, for your analysis (Fig. 11.19*b*).
- If both $R_s > Z_0$ and $R_t < Z_0$, then include only the inductance as calculated above.
- If neither $R_s > Z_0$ nor $R_t < Z_0$, then do not use the capacitance or inductance.

11.6.2 Distributed Load Capacitance

When capacitance loads are connected along a transmission line as in Fig. 11.17*b*, "each one causes a reflection with a polarity opposite to that of the incident wave. Reflections from two adjacent loads tend to overlap if the time required for the incident wave to travel from one load to the next is equal to or less than the signal rise time."[10] When the load reflections overlap, they effectively change the transmission line characteristics to one whose intrinsic capacitance C_0 has been increased in the region where the loads are attached (L_d): The effective impedance $Z_{0\text{eff}}$ decreases and the effective unit propagation delay $T_{\text{pd eff}}$ increases. Figure 11.20 plots this relationship.

To calculate the new line characteristics over the loaded region, the added distributed capacitance (C_d) must be calculated. If the loaded region is L_d in length then

$$C_d = C_t/L_d \tag{11.27}$$

where C_t is the total distributed capacitive load ($C_l + C_l + C_l + \cdots$).

The new effective line impedance and unit propagation delay are

$$Z_{\text{oeff}} = \sqrt{\frac{L_0}{C_0 + C_d}} = \sqrt{\frac{L_0}{C_0(1 + C_d/C_0)}} \tag{11.28}$$

and

$$T_{\text{pd eff}} = \sqrt{L_0(C_0 + C_d)} = \sqrt{L_0C_0}\,\sqrt{1 + C_d/C_0} \tag{11.29}$$

where,

$$L_0 = Z_0T_{\text{pd}} \qquad \text{and} \qquad C_0 = \frac{T_{\text{pd}}}{Z_0} \tag{11.30}$$

Therefore, the relationship between Z_0 and $Z_{0\text{eff}}$ is

$$Z_{0\text{eff}} = \frac{Z_0}{\sqrt{1 + C_d/C_0}} \tag{11.31}$$

And T_{pd} and $T_{\text{pd eff}}$ is

$$T_{\text{pd eff}} = T_{\text{pd}}\,\sqrt{1 + C_d/C_0} \tag{11.32}$$

These equations indicate two important facts. One, the line impedance is reduced

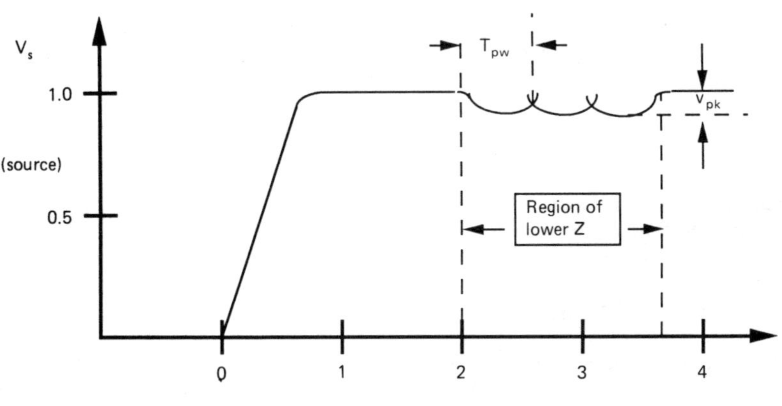

FIGURE 11.20 Impact of distributed capacitance.

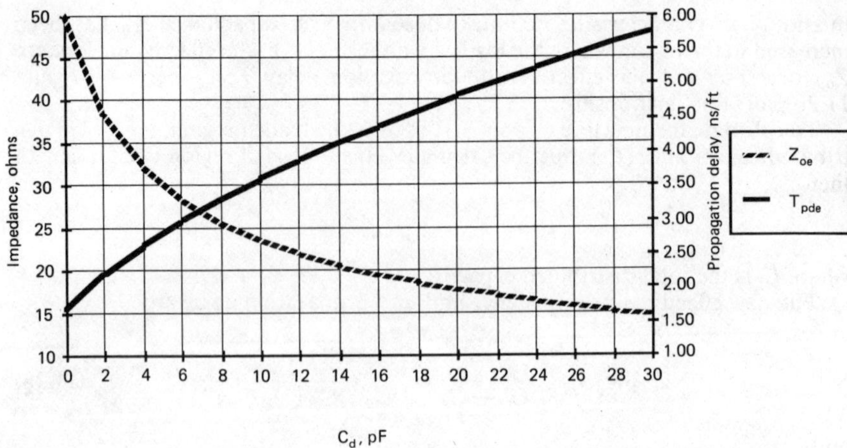

FIGURE 11.21 $Z_{0\text{eff}}$ and $T_{\text{pd eff}}$ vs C_d.

by adding distributed loads. As the density of these loads increases, the impedance decreases. Two, the line unit propagation delay increases with increasing load density. Figure 11.21 plots $Z_{0\text{eff}}$ and $T_{\text{pd eff}}$ as a function of increasing C_d for a 50 Ω line.

For example, given the circuit in Fig. 11.17*b*, if $Z_0 = 50\ \Omega$, $T_{\text{pd}} = 2.0$ ns/ft, $t_r = 2$ ns, $C_l = 6$ pF (not uncommon for TTL inputs), $L = 6$ in and $L_d = 6$ in, applying Eqs. (11.26), (11.31), and (11.32) yields $Z_{0\text{eff}} = 34\ \Omega$ and $T_{\text{pd eff}} = 3.0$ ns/ft. At the impedance boundary resulting from the uneven distribution of loads, the reflection coefficient is −20% per Eq. (11.25). If C_l is changed to 12 pF (some TTL clock inputs), then $Z_{0\text{eff}} = 27\ \Omega$ and $T_{\text{pd eff}} = 3.7$ ns/ft. The resulting reflection coefficient is −30 percent.

When the capacitive loads are separated by more than the rise time, the individual reflections will possess the amplitudes and pulse widths calculated for the end of line capacitance determined by Eqs. (11.24) and (11.25), respectively.

11.7 REFLECTIONS DUE TO LINE DISCONTINUTIES

Reflections can result not only from line to load mismatches but from multiple impedances along a line. This may occur as the result of board-to-board connections, board layer changes, discontinuities in cable shielding, stubs, gaps in PC board power planes, etc.

11.7.1 Board-to-Board Connections

Board-to-board connections may take the form of coaxial cables, twisted pair, backplanes, etc. When the impedance of all the interconnect elements do not match, reflections will occur at all the interfaces. Figure 11.22 shows a clock line traveling from one board to another across a backplane. The boards have 6 in of trace at an impedance of 75 Ω while the backplane has 12 in of trace at 50 Ω. A 75-Ω series termination is used at the source to damp out reflections. Figure 11.23 illustrates how a lattice diagram would be set up for this problem with multiple impedance boundaries. Note that the boundaries on the lattice diagram are spaced proportional to the different line delays, 1 ns for the boards and 2 ns for the backplane. The resulting waveform is shown in Fig. 11.24.

11.7.2 Board Layer Changes

Board layer changes can result in similar reflections to those in Fig. 11.24. This can be avoided by defining board layer stackings that keep equal impedances on all signal layers.

11.7.3 Bends in Transmission Lines

Bends in transmission lines on PC boards have often been pointed out as causing reflections, but this is generally not the case. For typical PC board traces, 6–12 mil wide, there is only a drop in impedance for a very short time, $T_{\text{prop}} < 10$ ps. Applying the line length criteria with any of the rise times in Table 11.2 indicates that a lumped-capacitive-load model should be used for analysis. Such a small capacitance produces a negligible glitch with any of the listed rise times.

Bends in cables can sometimes cause reflections as well. This occurs when the bend forces a long region of the cable to have a decreased signal conductor to ground shield spacing, lowering the impedance. A reflection then results from this impedance discontinuity.

11.7.4 Stubs

Stubs along tansmission lines occur frequently on PC boards. They often allow for the shortest interconnect between devices on the board. However, if care is not taken, substantial reflections from the stubs can occur along the transmission line. First, it should be determined whether or not the primary interconnect is long enough to be considered a transmission line. If it is, the attached stubs should be kept to a length defined by the 4:1 ratio of t_r or t_f to T_{prop} (for the stub).[4] This allows the stub to be treated as a simple capacitor attached to the primary transmission line, as in Fig. 11.17*b*. Whenever possible, avoid designing with stubs.

One place where stubs are typically unavoidable is the daughter-board to motherboard connection in backplane-based systems. Again, the stubs should be kept under the length defined by the 4:1 ratio. Note that the daughter-board stub is not just the PC trace but the entire interconnect from the driver to the primary backplane trace (i.e., IC package lead, PC trace, and board-to-backplane connec-

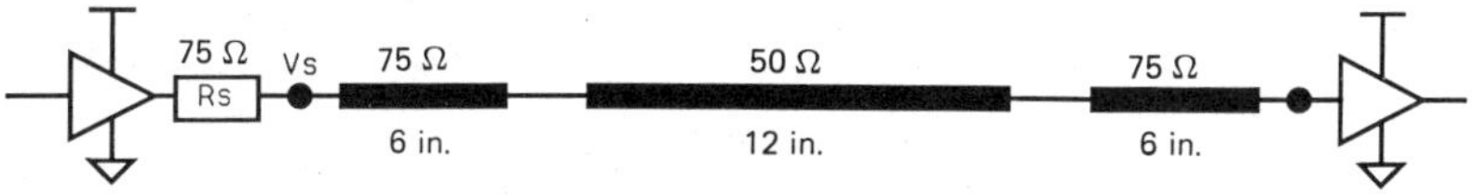

FIGURE 11.22 Multiple-impedance interconnect.

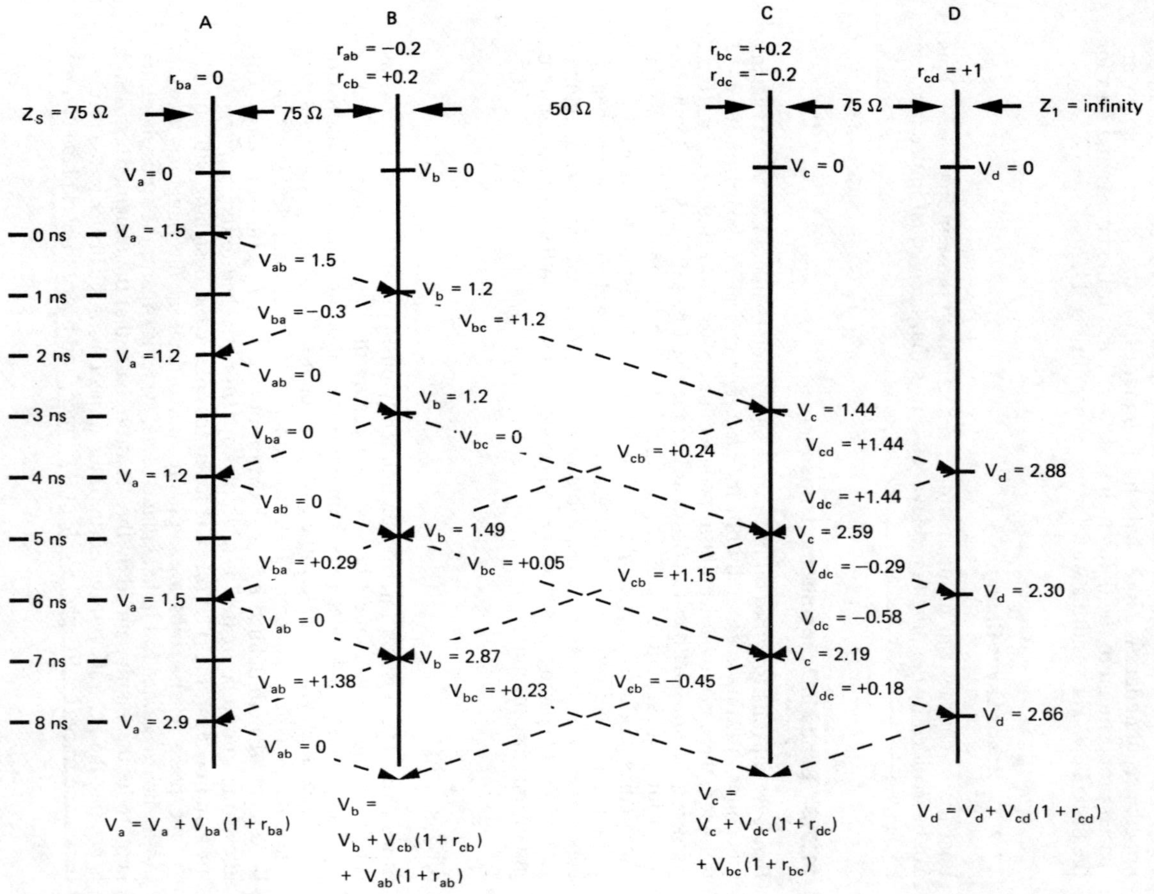

FIGURE 11.23 Multiple-impedance lattice diagram.

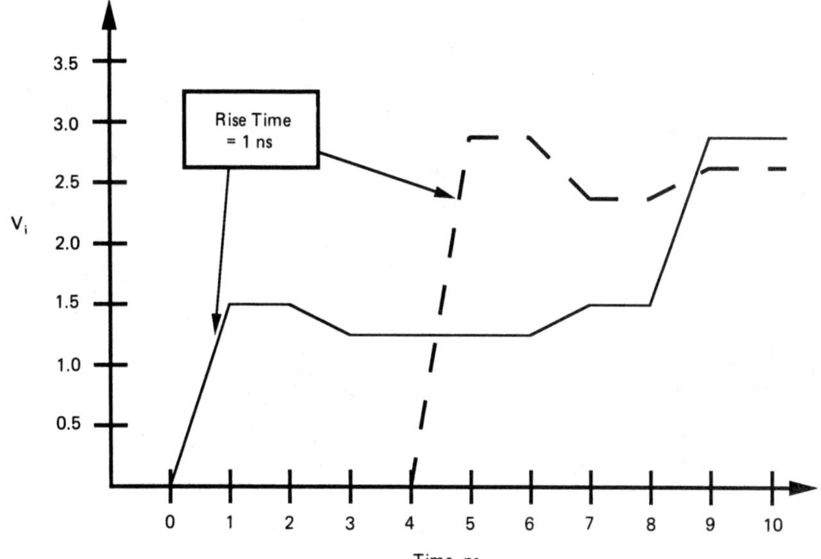

FIGURE 11.24 Multiple-impedance waveform.——, at point A; – – –, at point D.

tor). Violating this stub length limit allows for oscillations within the stub similar to the open-ended line in Figs. 11.5 and 11.8. In this case, Z_s is the effective backplane impedance (typically 15–30 Ω) and Z_0 the stub impedance (typically 50–90 Ω). V_s is the initial backplane voltage step. Since in most cases the stub will fall into the short line case, superposition techniques which take into account edge rate can produce a more accurate picture of the signal ringing.[10] Figure 11.25 illustrates the use of superposition for the line in Fig. 11.5 with a rise time of three times T_{prop}.

11.8 SIMULATION

Ultimately, evaluation of interconnects using simulators such as SPICE with the appropriate models can provide results more accurate than those obtained using Bergeron diagrams plus superposition. SPICE simulation models can be generated for most any interconnect geometry and can include models for skin effect and other lossy line phenomena.[11]

Simulation is becoming more common now in the development of backplane buses. Such an example can be found in Ref. 7. Information such as maximum backplane size, maximum daughter-board loading, termination requirements, and bus-driver requirements gained from these simulations can prove extremely important when developing new buses and systems.

The greatest difficulty in producing accurate results with simulators is obtaining and/or generating accurate models for drivers, connectors, etc. Recently, however, some vendors are making a few SPICE models available for various drivers

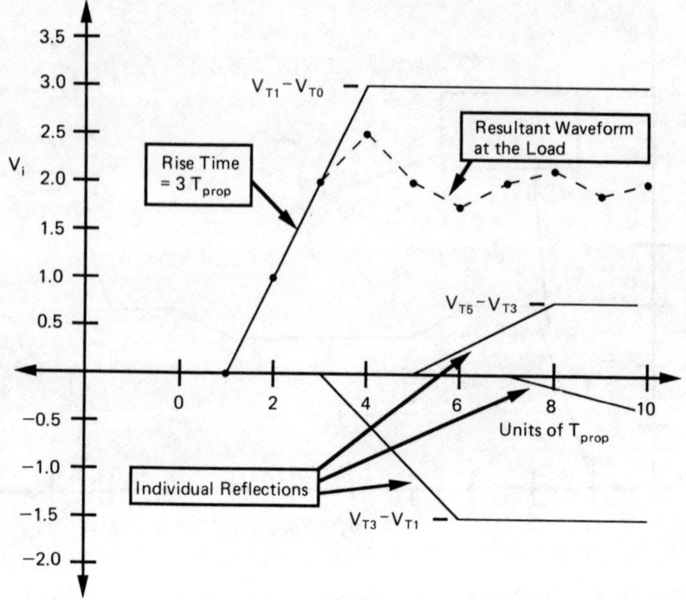

FIGURE 11.25 Stub response with finite edge rate.

and connectors. In addition, there are several papers available describing computer modeling techniques.

REFERENCES

1. David Shear, "EDN's advanced CMOS logic ground-bounce test," *EDN,* March 2, 1989, pp. 88–114.
2. A. Feller, H. R. Kaupp, and J. J. Di Giacomo, "Crosstalk and Reflections in High-speed Digital Systems," *IEEE Proceedings—Fall Joint Computer Conference,* 1965, pp. 511–525.
3. K. M. True, "Reflections: Computations and Waveforms," *The Interface Handbook,* Fairchild Corporation, Mountain View, California, 1975.
4. David Royle, "Designer's Guide to Transmission Lines and Interconnections," *EDN,* June 23, 1988, pp. 131–160.
5. *ALS/AS Logic Data Book,* Texas Instruments Inc., Dallas, Texas, 1986, pp. 4-9 to 4-44.
6. Larry Wakeman, "High-speed-CMOS designs address noise and I/O levels," *EDN,* April 19, 1984, pp. 285–296.
7. Roger Shelton, "Backplane Simulation," *ESD,* May 1988, pp. 87–95.
8. William R. Blood, Jr., *MECL System Design Handbook,* Motorola Semiconductor Products, Inc., Mesa, Arizona, 1988.
9. IPC Standard Proposal IPC-D-317, "Design Standard for Electronic Packaging Utilizing High Speed Techniques," The Institute for Interconnecting and Packaging Electronic Circuits, 1985.

10. *FAST Applications Handbook,* Fairchild Semiconductor Corporation, South Portland, Maine, 1987, Chap. 9.

11. Zvonko Fazarinc, Richard L. Wheeler, and Chu-Sun Yen, "Time-Domain Skin-Effect Model for Transient Analysis of Lossy Transmission Lines," *Proceedings of the IEEE,* July 1982, Vol. 70, No. 7, pp. 750–757.

CHAPTER 12
PULSE CROSSTALK

J. F. McDonald
Center for Integrated Electronics and the Department of Electrical, Computer and Systems Engineering
Rensselaer Polytechnic Institute
Troy, New York

12.1 INTRODUCTION

When two signal-carrying conductors lay parallel and in close proximity to each other over some distance, the electric field from one conductor will intersect the other, inducing a charge. Similarly, the magnetic flux from one conductor can envelop the second conductor. Any temporal change in this flux can induce a current in the second conductor. The result is that a signal on one line will result in an unwanted signal on the second line. We call this crosstalk or coupling noise.

This is not the only source of electrical noise in a system. Another source of noise occurs when a driver of a line attempts to charge that line in a short time. For example, this occurs when driving a terminated transmission line with a step-function signal, or a pulse. In this case we expect to charge up the transmission line in the time it takes for the signal to travel to the receiving end of the line. During this period the driver calls upon the voltage distribution system to supply this charge quickly. Any parasitic inductance in the power distribution system (even in the "on-chip" power grid) can cause the voltage supplied to the driver to drop during this time. The result can be seen as a drop in driver output voltage even as it attempts to rise. The effect becomes more annoying when several drivers depend on the same power distribution net. Then this inductive drop resulting from one driver's switching activity can actually be seen on latent or inactive driver outputs. IBM calls this kind of noise *delta-I* noise.

Unfortunately, the situation where coupling noise is most bothersome arises when a very wide bus must have its signals changed simultaneously on all lines. A bus containing 32- or 64-bit lines in which all but one line must be charged, while the remaining line must be held low, represents a worst-case situation for both types of noise. The channel to be held low will receive the delta-I noise from all the other drivers, sharing the same power distribution system, and in addition will have induced on it all the coupling noise from the adjacent bus paths. Sometimes it is impossible to distinguish between these two effects in practice. However, careful provision for well-regulated power with low inductance in the voltage distribution paths can minimize the delta-I noise. We now explore means for minimizing coupling noise.

12.2 THE DISTRIBUTED-PARAMETER MODEL

We consider for analysis two parallel coupled transmission lines (see Fig. 12.1). The extension to more than two coupled lines is straightforward but tends to obscure the simpler picture. The lines are considered to be of identical cross-sectional geometry, which is called the symmetric line case. Furthermore, nothing is assumed to change about this geometry as we move along the length of the coupled lines. This is called the constant-geometry case. In this situation the lines can be imagined to consist of sections lines of infinitesmal length, dx. Each "slice" taken along the length of the lines (in this case this distance is along the x axis) is taken to have a self-inductance and self-capacitance for each line. These are also infinitesimal quantities, $L\,dx$ and $C\,dx$, since the line segments are of infinitesimal length. In addition to the self-inductance and self-capacitance of each line, there is a mutual capacitance, $-\beta\,dx$, and a mutual inductance, $M\,dx$, resulting from the interplay of common field lines between the two conductors. The result is a lumped-parameter model of an infinitesimal section of the actual distributed transmission line as given by Dworsky[1] (shown in Fig. 12.2). The L and M are inductance per unit length, and C and $-\beta$ are capacitance per unit length parameters for the lines. The sign of the mutual capacitance is actually negative as we have shown it here. The argument for this is given in the reference by Frankel[2] on multiconductor transmission lines. In addition, it is easy to add a series conductor resistance $R\,dx$ and dielectric shunt leakage conductance $G\,dx$ to each line, where R and G are the per unit length resistance and conductance, respectively.

We can set up a set of partial differential equations that describe the voltage $V_1(x,t)$ and $V_2(x,t)$ and the currents $I_1(x,t)$ and $I_2(x,t)$ that appear at various points, x, along these lines. These are given by the following:

$$\frac{\partial V_1}{\partial x} = -RI_1 - L\frac{\partial I_1}{\partial t} - M\frac{\partial I_2}{\partial t} \tag{12.1a}$$

$$\frac{\partial V_2}{\partial x} = -RI_2 - L\frac{\partial I_2}{\partial t} - M\frac{\partial I_1}{\partial t} \tag{12.1b}$$

$$\frac{\partial I_1}{\partial x} = -GV_1 - C\frac{\partial V_1}{\partial t} + \beta\frac{\partial V_2}{\partial t} \tag{12.1c}$$

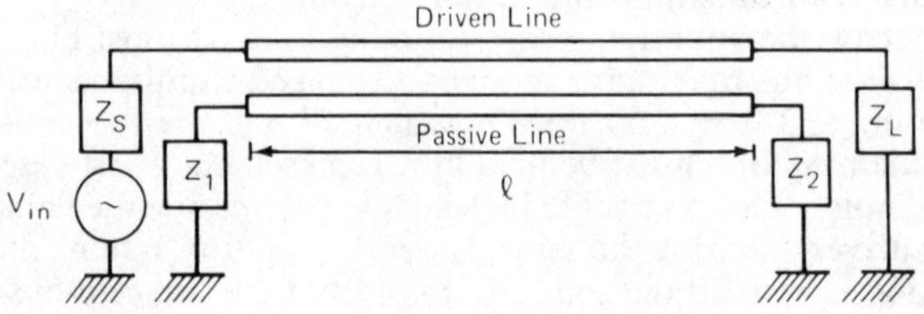

FIGURE 12.1 Two parallel coupled transmission lines. ℓ = length.

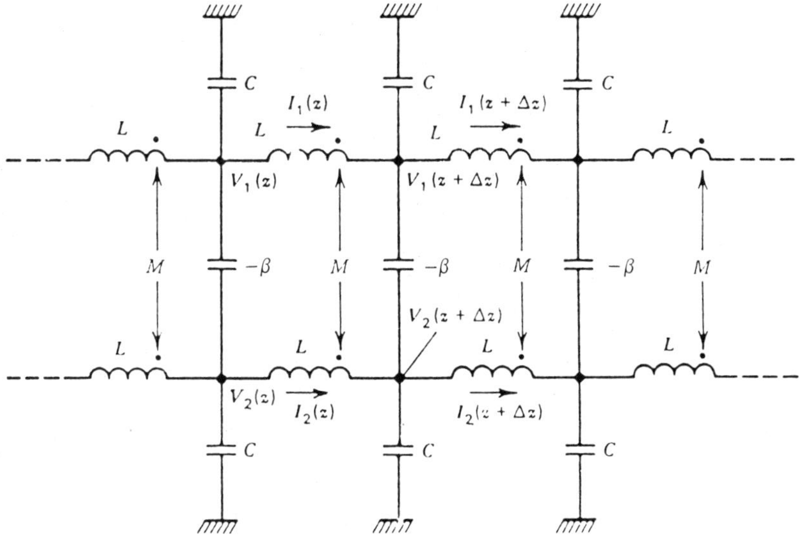

FIGURE 12.2 Lumped parameter model for an incremental section of two symmetrical coupled lines.

$$\frac{\partial I_2}{\partial x} = -GV_2 - C\frac{\partial V_2}{\partial t} + \beta\frac{\partial V_1}{\partial t} \tag{12.1d}$$

The first two equations are a result of Ampere's laws, giving the rate of change of voltage along the length of the line as a function of the time rate of change of magnetic flux produced by the two currents. The last two equations show the change in current along the line required to permit the accumulation of charge at a point along the lines, which is reflected in a change in voltage over time. Note the sign of the term containing the mutual capacitance. These four equations are the so-called telegrapher's equations for a coupled pair of lines.

These four equations are linear partial differential equations, and the exact solution for them is known.[2] However, that exact solution is in the form of sums and differences of waves propagating on the lines, and it is difficult to gain much insight from them concerning the effect of coupling without resorting to computations. However, we will mention here that the solution actually contains waves traveling at two distinct velocities. One component corresponds to an even mode of excitation of the two lines (say with identical sources). The second component corresponds to an odd-mode excitation of the two lines with the two sources, one of which is the negative of the other. This is a surprising result, which in very long lines or in situations with strong coupling can actually result in pulses separating into slow and fast pulse components. These even and odd modes also possess different characteristic impedances, resulting in additional complications when trying to terminate the lines.

However, these theoretical complications arise when the coupling signals become large. This can occur when the mutual inductive or capacitive reactance becomes large relative to the lines' characteristic impedance or when the length of the lines becomes very great. In such situations the coupling noise will be very unacceptable, and something will have to be done to reduce the coupling. Either

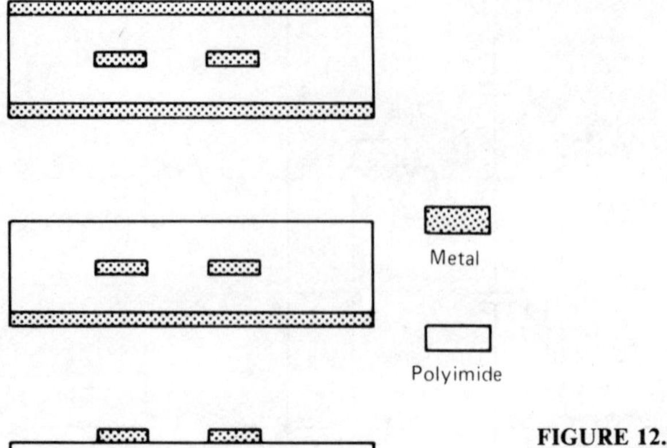

FIGURE 12.3 Three examples of the use of ground planes to reduce coupling between two conductors.

the lines must be moved farther apart spatially so the field lines will not interfere with each other, or some other means must be found to constrain these coupling fields, such as the use of a ground plane near the conductors as shown in Fig. 12.3. In the latter case some of the electric field lines are attracted away from the adjacent signal conductor toward the ground plane, and the magnetic flux around either conductor is confined between the conductor and the ground plane. Both mutual capacitance and inductance are reduced by this strategy, but at the expense of increasing the self-capacitance of the lines and reducing the self-inductance. This leads in turn to a general lowering of the level of characteristic impedance of the lines. These things are unattractive when they occur because they increase both the static and dynamic power dissipated and aggravate the current spiking, leading to the delta-I noise. Consequently, anything else that would make the self-capacitance even higher, such as a high dielectric constant for the insulator between the conductors, would discourage us from reducing coupling by simply introducing a nearby ground plane. Hence, using low-dielectric-constant insulators will help reduce coupling noise. Use of low-dielectric-constant insulators will also help increase propagation velocities. We note, however, that the improvement of propagation velocity with reduction in dielectric constant is a square-root relationship. That is, reducing the dielectric constant by a factor of 2 would only increase the velocity of propagation by a mere 30 percent. On the other hand, reductions in the dielectric constant are linearly reflected in reduction of the self-capacitance and mutual capacitance. As we shall see it is the reduction of self-capacitance (not necessarily the mutual capacitance) with lower dielectric constants that indirectly helps us reduce coupling voltage waveforms. This result is usually somewhat surprising to the novice, who would probably assume the reverse to be the case. Exactly how this occurs will be explained shortly.

12.3 WEAK-COUPLING APPROXIMATION

By restricting our attention to the case of weak coupling we can obtain a solution to the telegrapher's equations that is free of the complexities of the even- and odd-mode wave formulation and that gives a result with a pleasing intuitive simplicity. In the weak-coupling approximation the even and odd wave components can be shown to propagate at essentially the same velocity.[3] Furthermore, weak coupling permits us to ignore the secondary effects of coupling. Ordinarily the current and voltage induced in a line by coupling are themselves capable of recoupling back to the signal line causing the initial disturbance. The currents and voltages resulting from this recoupling are capable again of inducing additional coupling back to the disturbed line. This process of recoupling is included in the exact solution in a way that is not obvious. However, when the lines are not strongly coupled we find that the telegrapher's equations can be simplified. The original discovery of this approach is due to Jarvis.[4] Jarvis considers that line 1 is driven by a signal generator and has a significant voltage output. Line 2 is assumed undriven and hence should be quiet. However, a small voltage is assumed to be introduced into line 2 by weak coupling. Line 1 is unterminated at the source, but is either semi-infinitely long or terminated at the end opposite from the source with a characteristic impedance. The coupled line 2 is assumed terminated at both ends with characteristic impedances. This is shown in Fig. 12.4.

Evidently, when recoupling is weak (which will certainly be the case when coupling is weak), all terms in the telegrapher's equations corresponding to the line 2 signal terms in line 1's equations are ignored (set to zero). If in addition we take Laplace transforms of the telegrapher's equations in this form, we obtain the following simplified ordinary differential equations:

$$\frac{\partial \overline{V}_1}{\partial x} = -(R + pL)\overline{I}_1 \tag{12.2a}$$

$$\frac{\partial \overline{V}_2}{\partial x} = -pM\overline{I}_1 - (R + pL)\overline{I}_2 \tag{12.2b}$$

$$\frac{\partial \overline{I}_1}{\partial x} = -pC\overline{V}_1 \tag{12.2c}$$

$$\frac{\partial \overline{I}_2}{\partial x} = -p\beta\overline{V}_1 - pC\overline{V}_2 \tag{12.2d}$$

where from now on in the analysis we will assume G is zero (this is a pretty good approximation in many digital systems). Here we define the Laplace transform operator and Laplace variable as follows:

$$\overline{V}_1 = \mathcal{L}(V_1), \qquad \overline{I}_1 = \mathcal{L}(I_1),$$

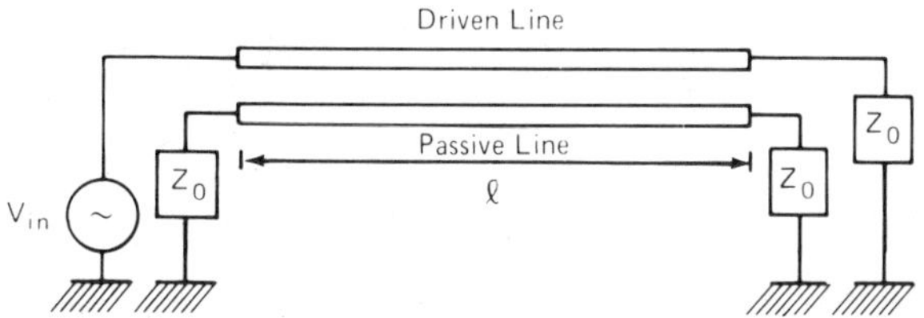

FIGURE 12.4 Coupled transmission lines where the driven line is semi-infinitely long and the passive line is terminated in Z_0 at both ends. ℓ = length.

where $\mathcal{L}$ is the Laplace transform operator and
p is the Laplace transform variable

By differentiating Eq. (12.2*a*) and Eq. (12.2*b*) with respect to x and substituting Eq. (12.2*c*) and Eq. (12.2*d*) for the appropriate quantities, we see that we have the following two equations:

$$\frac{\partial^2 \overline{V}_1}{\partial x^2} - \gamma^2(p)\overline{V}_1 = 0 \tag{12.3a}$$

$$\frac{\partial^2 \overline{V}_2}{\partial x^2} - \gamma^2(p)\overline{V}_2 = q\left(\frac{p^2}{v^2}(K-1) - pRC\right)\overline{V}_1 \tag{12.3b}$$

where

$$\gamma(p) = \sqrt{(R + pL)pC} = \sqrt{\frac{p^2}{v^2} + pRC}$$
$$= \text{propagation constant} \tag{12.4}$$

where

$$v = \frac{1}{\sqrt{LC}} = \text{signal velocity} \tag{12.5}$$

$$q = \left(\frac{\beta}{C}\right) = \text{capacitive coupling coefficient} \tag{12.6}$$

$$K = \left(\frac{M}{L}\right)\left(\frac{C}{\beta}\right) = \text{ratio of inductive coupling coefficient to the capacitive coupling coefficient.} \tag{12.7}$$

The first equation [Eq. (12.3*a*)] is the ordinary differential equation corresponding to the usual wave equation on a single isolated line. This is to be expected since all the recoupling effects have been ignored, and nothing occurring on line 2 shows up in this equation. On the other hand, the second equation [Eq. (12.3*b*)] appears in the form of a wave equation with driving terms on the right-hand side. The driving terms come from the voltage on line 1. This becomes one of the mechanisms for the voltage on line 1 to affect the voltage on line 2. The second way for information about line 1 to affect line 2 is through boundary conditions, which must be satisfied at the ends of the lines where the terminators are located. Here the telegrapher's equations are needed, and additional coupling information is introduced.

12.4 THE SOLUTION

Line 1 is governed by the simple wave equation with no interaction felt from the nearby line 2. The solution in general can be written as follows for the voltage and current on that line:

$$\overline{V}_1(x,p) = Ae^{-\gamma(p)x} + Be^{\gamma(p)x} \tag{12.8}$$

$$\bar{I}_1(x,p) = \frac{1}{Z_c}(Ae^{-\gamma(p)x} - Be^{\gamma(p)x}) \tag{12.9}$$

where

$$Z_c = \sqrt{\frac{R + pL}{pC}} = \text{characteristic impedance} \tag{12.10}$$

The line 1 voltage then acts as a distributed generator in the "wave equation" for line 2. Using straightforward Laplace transform techniques we obtain

$$\bar{V}_2(x,p) = \left[\mathcal{A} - \frac{qx}{2}\frac{Z_0}{Z_c}\left((K-1)\frac{p}{v} - \frac{R}{Z_0}\right)\mathcal{C}\right]e^{-\gamma(p)x} + \left[\mathcal{B} + \frac{qx}{2}\frac{Z_0}{Z_c}(K-1)\frac{p}{v} - \frac{R}{Z_0}\Big)\mathcal{D}\right]e^{\gamma(p)x} \tag{12.11}$$

where $\mathcal{A}$, $\mathcal{B}$, $\mathcal{C}$, and $\mathcal{D}$ are unknown constants for the expression for the voltage along line 2. These must be determined by employing the boundary conditions at the ends of the lines. Using the telegrapher's equations it is then possible to obtain a general expression for the current on line 2:

$$\begin{aligned} Z_c\bar{I}_2(x,p) = &\left[\mathcal{A} - \frac{q}{2}\frac{Z_0}{pL + R}\left((K+1)\frac{p}{v} + \frac{R}{Z_0}\right)\mathcal{C}\right. \\ &\left. - \frac{qx}{2}\frac{Z_0}{Z_c}\left((K-1)\frac{p}{v} - \frac{R}{Z_0}\right)\mathcal{C}\right]e^{-\gamma(p)x} \\ &- \left[\mathcal{B} - \frac{q}{2}\frac{Z_0}{pL + R}\left((K+1)\frac{p}{v} + \frac{R}{Z_0}\right)\mathcal{D}\right. \\ &\left. + \frac{qx}{2}\frac{Z_0}{Z_c}\left((K-1)\frac{p}{v} - \frac{R}{Z_0}\right)\mathcal{D}\right]e^{\gamma(p)x} \end{aligned} \tag{12.12}$$

Thus far we have not taken into account the effect of terminating the transmission lines in their characteristic impedances (except at the driving end). If we do this on the driven line (line 1) employing the two boundary conditions on each end, we obtain for the voltage wave $V_1\ (x,p)$ on this line

$$\bar{V}_1(x,p) = \bar{V}_{\text{in}}(p)e^{-\gamma(p)x} \tag{12.13}$$

where $\bar{V}_{\text{in}}(p)$ is the Laplace transform of the driving voltage at $x = 0$. This is the expression for a forward traveling wave. The current in this line $\bar{I}_1(x,p)$ is just this voltage divided by the characteristic impedance, since there are no waves propagating in the negative x direction. Two of the coefficients, namely $\mathcal{C}$ and $\mathcal{D}$, in the equations for the general solutions on the second line are determined by the satisfaction of the boundary conditions on the first line.

The other two coefficients are determined by meeting the two boundary conditions on the ends of the second line:

$$\begin{aligned} \bar{V}_2(0,p) &= -Z_0\bar{I}_2(0,p) \\ \bar{V}_2(l,p) &= Z_0\bar{I}_2(l,p) \end{aligned} \tag{12.14}$$

We now specialize the equations for the solution to the case $R = 0$. In this case we obtain the following expression for the voltage waveform on line 2:

$$\overline{V}_2(x,p) = q\,\frac{\overline{V}_{in}(p)}{2}\,(e^{-p(x/v)} - e^{-p[(2l-x)/v]})\,\frac{K+1}{2} - q\,\frac{K-1}{2}\left(\frac{Lx}{Z_0}\right)p\overline{V}_{in}(p)e^{-p(x/v)} \qquad (12.15)$$

It is this expression we are seeking for an interpretation of the results. We note that it is in the form of a transfer relation (with p as the frequency parameter) from the applied voltage on line 1, $\overline{V}_{in}(p)$, to the voltage observed on line 2 at any coordinate x, written in transform notation.

12.5 GRAPHICAL FORM OF THE SOLUTION

The previous expression [Eq. (12.15)] for the transfer relation from the driving input on line 1 to the various points along line 2 has a rather interesting interpretation. To study it, let us assume that a voltage step waveform with a finite rise time is applied as the time-domain equivalent of $\overline{V}_{in}(p)$.

Note that the second term is zero at $x = 0$. Therefore the coupling noise voltage at the end of line 2 nearest the driver on the first line is due completely to the first term. This is termed the near-end (NE) noise, and it has a distinctive behavior. At $x = 0$ the first exponent in the first term is unity. It represents a scaled replica of the input waveform. The second exponent in the first term represents for $x = 0$ an identically scaled replica of the input waveform but is time shifted by a round-trip delay on line 2 and changed in sign. As a result the coupled waveform is a trapezoidal shaped pulse with an initial rise time identical to the applied voltage rise time, which begins simultaneously with the application of the input pulse. The time duration of the coupling noise pulse is 2 times the rise time of the input pulse plus 2 times the one-pass delay down the line. The trailing edge of the trapezoidal coupling pulse descends with a fall time identical to the rise time since at this point the second exponent in the first term of the coupling expression becomes active at this point. In between the rise and fall slopes the coupling voltage "saturates" at a value that is the value of the step height of the input voltage multiplied by the capacitive coupling ratio q, multiplied by the factor $(K + 1)/2$, where K is the ratio of the inductive coupling ratio to the capacitive coupling ratio. In graphing this response, which is shown in Fig. 12.5, we have assumed that the round-trip delay on line 2 is longer than two rise times. If this is not the case, then the trapezoidal pulse becomes a triangular one, and the saturation voltage level is not reached by the coupling waveform.

The coupling noise waveform [Eq. (12.15)] at the far end (FE) of line 2 where $x = \ell$ is now examined. Note that in this case it is the first term in the transfer expression which is exactly zero, and the second term prevails. Upon examining this term we see that its effect is to delay the input step with finite rise time by a single-pass delay down the line (which is reasonable since the wave on the first line is just passing the end at that point). In addition to this delay we see that the second term contains the factor p, which indicates that a time derivative is taken of the input waveform. The time derivative of the input step waveform with a finite rise time delayed by the single-pass delay is a narrow rectangular pulse

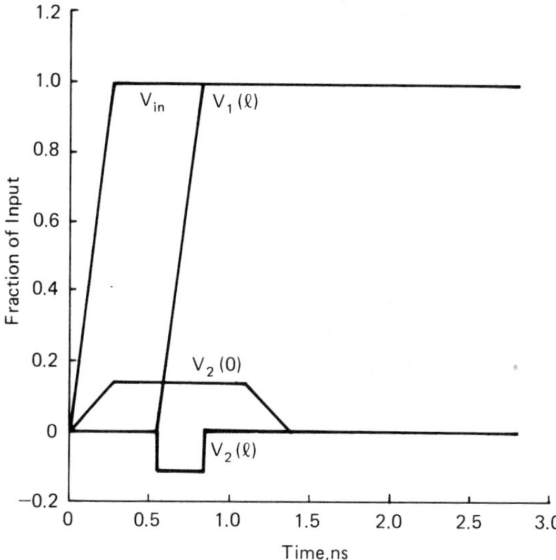

FIGURE 12.5 Step waveform response for an inhomogeneous dielectric (K = 1.5) at the front and back ends of lines 1 and 2.

whose width is equal to the rise time (see Fig. 12.5). The height of this pulse is the amplitude of the input waveform negated and scaled by capacitive coupling ratio q, multiplied in this case by $(K - 1)/2$, and the ratio of the one-pass delay time T, to the rise time t_r. Note that the ratio of the self-inductance to the characteristic impedance is the inverse of the propagation velocity on the line. We see that the height of this pulse worsens (grows more negative) if the length of the line increases, or if the rise time shortens. For extremely short rise times and sufficiently long lines, the amplitude of this pulse can be almost any height and could readily exceed logic thresholds, especially in situations involving multiple coupling to several lines, or when mixed with ground and power rail noise. However, since the width of the pulse is equal to one rise time it is quite a narrow spike of voltage. What is unclear is whether the pulse is present for a long enough time to switch devices. Because of its high-frequency nature, various parasitic conditions and losses we have not included here can help to mitigate its effect. For example, line loss, which we have ignored in these simplified expressions, can affect the coupling spike. One source of loss that we must mention is the skin effect, which tends at high frequencies to inductively confine current to flow in the outermost few micrometers of the conductor surfaces. This acts like a low-pass filter on the spike. In addition, almost any switching device has some parasitic capacitance that will tend to damp out the coupling spike. However, in some circumstances this spike can be surprisingly high and may not be sufficiently mitigated by losses. In such cases devices may respond to the FE noise spike.

Nevertheless, this second term in the coupling expression [Eq. (12.15)] contains an extraordinary surprise. Note that the factor $K - 1$ multiplying this term can be made identically zero when K is unity. This is shown in Fig. 12.6 for identical excitation waveform for that used in obtaining Fig. 12.5. Note that the FE noise spike is absent. Hence by choosing the conditions necessary to make the ratio of capacitive coupling and inductive coupling ratios equal to 1 one can com-

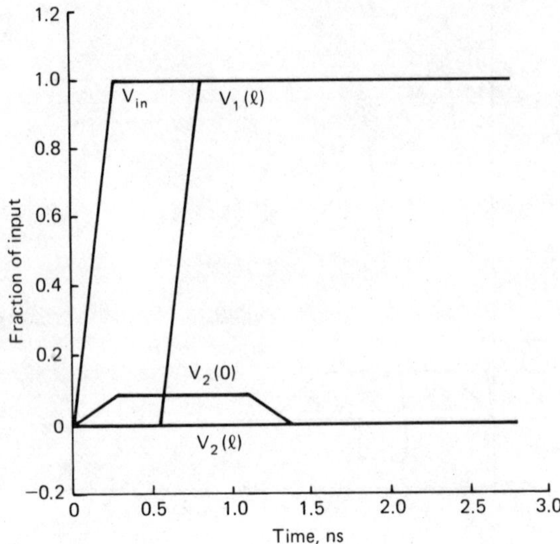

FIGURE 12.6 Step waveform response for a homogeneous dielectric ($K = 1$) at the front and back ends of lines 1 and 2.

pletely suppress the FE noise pulse, which is the most annoying because its height would otherwise worsen for fast rise times and on long lines. The conditions necessary to achieve a $K = 1$ condition are discussed in the next section.

12.6 SOME INTERPRETATION OF THE WEAK-COUPLING SOLUTION

Note that the height for the NE saturation voltage pulse is not greater for longer lines, but only has its width increased in proportion to line length. So if the saturation voltage is sufficiently below any logic threshold it will not be "seen" by any line receiver. Additionally we note that the scale factor giving the saturation coupling value is dependent only on the capacitive coupling ratio, and on the ratio of the inductive coupling ratio to the capacitive coupling ratio. Since both self-capacitance and mutual capacitance are linearly dependent on the dielectric constants of the insulator materials, in the case of a homogeneous dielectric (which uses the same insulator everywhere), it is clear that the dielectric constant cancels out in these ratios. Hence only the geometric shapes of the conductors, their spacings, and their distances to various ground planes affect the peak saturation voltage. The fact that only the ratio of capacitances is important in the expression for the coupled line voltage is akin to the voltage-divider-like relation that exists between these lines through their capacitances.

We must be careful not to draw the false conclusion from this that the dielectric constant of the insulator is not important in reducing coupling. Rather, the effect is felt indirectly, for as we attempt to reduce coupling by the introduction of ground planes, as was discussed earlier in the chapter, we find that self-capacitance for the lines is increased. Hence the total amount of charge one must transfer to these lines to raise their voltage to a given level increases with this dielectric constant. This also results in larger peak currents during line charging and larger dynamic power dissipation as the lines are charged and discharged, which is undesirable. Also, as spacings to the ground planes are reduced self-inductance decreases and since the self-capacitance increases, the characteristic impedance decreases. Large dielectric constants just make the problem worse. Lines with small characteristic impedance require small termination resistances, leading to increased static power losses in these resistors. Add to this the undesirability of the slower propagation velocity in high-dielectric-constant insulators and one has a strong argument for using the lowest-dielectric-constant materials possible, consistent with other needs. Of course the effect of dielectric constant on propagation velocity is proportional only to the square root of this quantity, whereas the mutual capacitance and self-capacitance are linearly proportional to this quantity.

Hence, the largest impact of high-dielectric-constant materials, such as ceramics, is on the coupling problem since it prevents us from employing ground screening to maximum advantage. The practical implication of this is the need to use generally larger conductor-to-conductor spacing, thereby decreasing the wiring density. This forces the use of more wiring planes, which increases cost and can also greatly increase the vertical thickness of these wiring planes.

Now the FE noise spike can be totally eliminated by achieving the situation where K is unity. K is the ratio of the inductive coupling ratio to the capacitive coupling ratio. Ordinarily one would expect that the calculation of K would demand complex calculations involving the conductor geometries and separations. However, one particular instance produces the value of $K = 1$, without any detailed inductance and capacitance calculation. This arises when the dielectric is homogeneous throughout the regions between the conductors. That is, the dielectric has the same dielectric constant everywhere. In strip lines one must be cautious, because even the transition from a dielectric insulator to air can cause a problem. It has been known for a long time that under this homogeneous dielectric condition not only is K unity, but that the matrix of capacitances per unit length multiplied by the the matrix of inductances per unit length is a diagonal matrix whose elements are all equal to the inverse of the propagation velocity squared:

$$\underline{L} \cdot \underline{C} = \epsilon\mu \underline{I} \tag{12.16}$$

For the details of this derivation the reader is referred to the book by Frankel.

Interestingly, when the dielectric is not homogenous this formula relating inductance and capacitance still has some utility. Provided the conductors are perfect (no loss), the inductance calculated by substituting an arbitrary homogeneous dielectric will still apply even when the dielectric is changed to a nonhomogeneous one. Hence, inductance can be calculated readily once capacitance values are available. When losses occur in the conductors, the magnetic field lines can penetrate into these metals, and the details of the dielectric makeup can affect the outcome. In many cases this effect is only very slight and inductance remains readily approximated by Eq. (12.16). However, for nonhomogeneous dielectrics K can depart sufficiently from unity that the perfect FE coupling suppression does not take place. Values for K in typical nonhomogeneous environments can range from 1.5 to 3.

When $K = 1$ physically we can visualize what is happening in the following manner. When a pulse is applied to line 1, it capacitively induces charge on line 2 that is similar when observed at both ends of line 2, and demands similar directions of current in each case. Inductive coupling, on the other hand, tends to promote current flow in line 2 which is opposite in orientation everywhere from that in line 1. The currents for each of these components are directed such that they might cancel if balanced right at the far end of line 2. The condition of homogeneous dielectric is that which is required for perfect balance. The physical balance is directly traceable to cancellation of inductive and capacitive terms in the expression for FE noise.

12.7 CASES OF LOSS AND OTHER METHODS OF TERMINATION

The previous discussion of coupling has ignored line losses and other arrangements of terminators or loads on the various ends of the lines. In the case of nonzero line loss the expression for coupling on line 2 (corresponding to Eq. 12-15) in the weak-coupling approximation becomes

$$
\begin{aligned}
\overline{V}_2(x,p) = {} & \frac{1}{A'}\frac{q}{2}\left(1+\frac{Z_0}{Z_c}\right)\left(\frac{Z_0}{Z_c}\right)^3\left((K+1)+\frac{R}{pL}\right)\overline{V}_{\text{in}}e^{-\gamma(p)x} \\
& - \frac{qx}{2}\frac{1}{Z_c}[(K-1)pL - R]\overline{V}_{\text{in}}e^{-\gamma(p)x} \\
& + \frac{1}{A'}\frac{q}{2}\left(1-\frac{Z_0}{Z_c}\right)\left(\frac{Z_0}{Z_c}\right)^3\left((K+1)+\frac{R}{pL}\right)\overline{V}_{\text{in}}e^{-\gamma(p)(x+2l)} \\
& - \frac{1}{A'}\frac{ql}{2}\left(1-\frac{Z_0}{Z_c}\right)^2\frac{1}{Z_c}[(K-1)pL - R]\,\overline{V}_{\text{in}}e^{-\gamma(p)(x+2l)} \\
& - \frac{1}{A'}q\left(\frac{Z_0}{Z_c}\right)^3\left((K+1)+\frac{R}{pL}\right)\overline{V}_{\text{in}}e^{\gamma(p)(x-2l)} \\
& + \frac{1}{A'}\frac{ql}{2}\left(1-\frac{Z_0}{Z_c}\right)\left(1+\frac{Z_0}{Z_c}\right)\frac{1}{Z_c}\{(K-1)pL - R\}\overline{V}_{\text{in}}e^{\gamma(p)(x-2l)}
\end{aligned}
\tag{12.17}
$$

where

$$
A' = \left(1+\frac{Z_0}{Z_c}\right)^2 - \left(1-\frac{Z_0}{Z_c}\right)^2 e^{-2\gamma(p)l} \tag{2.18}
$$

As can be seen here, the presence of losses in the form of some nonzero value for R creates some additional terms for the coupling. One problem is that some FE noise begins to appear even when the lines are terminated by matching to the characteristic impedance, as was in the case of the lossless analysis due to Jarvis. However, none of these new loss-related terms in the coupled waveform contains a rise-time-sensitive component, which is a pleasant result. This is discussed in a longer paper.[3]

Perhaps more significantly, this more general solution permits one to analyze what happens if the situation of perfect termination is not possible at all the undriven ends of the lines. DeFalco[5] presented an extremely useful summary of the kinds of waveforms that can arise in these situations.

Lack of termination can occur for various reasons. For example, a driver on one end of line 2 which is not "source" terminated (characteristic impedance resistor is not used in series with the driver) would lead to a situation where one end of this line is incrementally terminated in a short circuit. Source termination was not used is line 1, and symmetry would probably demand that any driver on line 2 would also not have a series terminator.

Other situations occur where the lines are too short to worry about terminating them with characteristic impedance resistors. This arises when the rise times of the pulses are smaller than the "single-pass" delay time down the line. Another way of saying this is that the lines are very short and do not exhibit discrete reflections that significantly lengthen the time for the step response to settle down. In such situations we would like to avoid putting resistor terminators at the far end of the line that are matched to the characteristic impedance of the lines. However, even in these situations coupling could be significant. So it is desirable to examine a few of these just to see what one can expect.

Two of the more easily analyzed configurations involve placing short-circuit terminations at either end of line 2, which simulates having a low-impedance driver at that end (incrementally we treat the source as a short circuit since we can superpose a second source's response in the linear system). Any end that has such a short on it obviously has no noise voltage (the voltage is exactly zero). So we only have to examine the coupling noise seen at the end of line 2 which does not have short-circuit termination.

We consider here just one of the many alternative terminations for line 2, namely placing a short circuit at the near end of line 2 as shown in Fig. 12.7. In this case the only differences in mathematics arise at the boundary condition for $x = 0$, from which we conclude that

$$\mathcal{B} = -\mathcal{A} \tag{12.19}$$

and at the far end where

$$\overline{V}_2(l) = +Z_0\overline{I}_2(l) \tag{12.20}$$

The solution for this condition (again with $R = 0$ and $G = 0$) is given by the following expression:

$$\overline{V}_2(x,p) = \overline{V}_{\text{in}}(p)\left\{\left[\frac{(K+1)q}{4} + \frac{p}{2}\left(\frac{l}{v}\right)q\right]e^{-p(x+2l)/v} - \left[\frac{p}{2}\left(\frac{x}{v}\right)q(K-1)\right]e^{-p(x/v)} - \left[\frac{(K+1)q}{4} + \frac{p}{2}\left(\frac{l}{v}\right)q(K-1)\right]e^{+p(x-2l)/v}\right\} \tag{12.21}$$

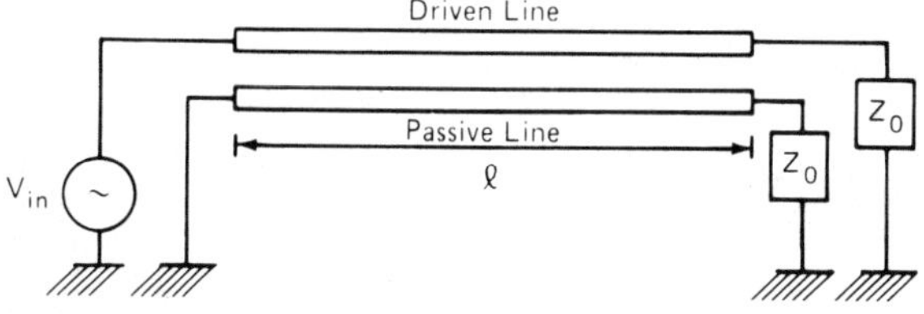

FIGURE 12.7 Coupled transmission lines with a short at the near end of line 2. ℓ = length.

This is obviously zero for $x = 0$, but at $x = l$ we obtain

$$\overline{V}_2(l,p) = -q\,\frac{\overline{V}_{\text{in}}(p)}{2}\,(e^{-p(l/v)} - e^{-3p(l/v)})\,\frac{K+1}{2} - q\,\frac{K-1}{2}\left(\frac{l}{v}\right)p\overline{V}_{\text{in}}(p)(2e^{-p(l/v)} - e^{-3p(l/v)}) \qquad (12.22)$$

This expression has the following interpretation. The first term in parentheses is very similar to the first term in parentheses of Eq. (12.15). It corresponds to a negated and scaled version of the input step (where the scale factor is the same as before) delayed by the one pass delay time down the line. This is reasonable since the rising edge of the pulse on line 1 has to propagate toward the far end before line 2 can respond at that end. At a time corresponding to three passes over the line, a delayed version of the scaled pulse begins to be added to the first term, thereby canceling it. The result is once again a trapezoidal pulse of time duration equal to a round-trip delay. Thus we have an FE noise result (for the case of a short at the near end), which is similar to the fully terminated NE noise case, but with a sign change and obviously a change in the arrival delay. The magnitude of the "saturation" amplitude of the trapezoidal pulse is the same in both cases. As before, the full trapezoidal pulse is only observed if the rise time is shorter than the one pass delay on the line.

The second term in Eq. (12.22) is a derivative term since it involves the Laplace p factor. It also is delayed by the line's one-pass delay time. It is a negative rectangular pulse of width equal to the rise time, and its magnitude is q times $K - 1$ multiplied by the input pulse voltage step height, times the ratio of the one-pass delay time divided by the pulse rise time. This is very similar to the result for the FE noise in the fully terminated case analyzed previously. The magnitude of this pulse is just twice that given for the earlier result. Rather than standing alone, this negative pulse is added to the broad trapezoidal pulse exactly at its leading edge, resulting in the "peak" at the beginning of the pulse.

The third term in Eq. (12.22) is also a derivative term, but involves an arrival time of three one-pass delay times. It is a positive rectangular pulse exactly aligned with the trailing edge of the trapezoidal pulse term.

The second and third terms, which are those whose magnitude is inversely proportional to rise time and linearly proportional to the line length, all include the factor $K - 1$ and as in the terminated case would be suppressed if $K = 1$, as in the homogeneous dielectric.

From the discussion it can be seen that the various alternative termination conditions produce a combination of the broad trapezoidal pulses and narrow rectangular rise-time-sensitive spikes. In all terms where rise-time dependency is observed for the magnitude of a pulse component, the same magnitude is multiplied by the factor $K - 1$. Hence setting $K = 1$ as in the case of the homogeneous dielectric is a very powerful method of reducing the coupling "spikes."

12.8 CONCLUSIONS

We have shown that coupling between two transmission lines can be modeled in the "weak-coupling" approximation as a simple transfer relationship between the voltage applied to a driven line and the voltage appearing at various points on the undriven line. This transfer relationship contains some terms that just delay, scale, and replicate the input waveform, and some terms that also involve the derivative. The former class of terms leads for step excitation with a finite rise time to low but broad trapezoidal pulses that are not rise-time sensitive in magnitude (provided the rise time is short compared to the one-pass propagation delay down the line) nor proportional to length. The second class of terms involves narrow rectangular pulses (or "spikes") whose amplitudes increase with line length and are inversely proportional to the input pulse rise time. Fortunately, all the latter terms contain the factor $K - 1$, which means that these spikes can be suppressed by simply making the dielectric insulator out of one homogeneous material. Both classes of pulses are reduced by reducing the factor q, which can be accomplished by introducing a ground plane under the transmission line conductors. However, in order to avoid unsatisfactory increases in self-capacitance by doing this, it is desirable to have the dielectric constant of the insulator be as low as possible.

REFERENCES

1. L. N. Dworsky, *Modern Transmission Line Theory and Applications,* Wiley-Interscience, New York, 1979.
2. S. Frankel, *Multiconductor Transmission Line Analysis,* Artech House, Dedham, Mass., 1977.
3. J. S. Kim and J. F. McDonald, "Transient and Crosstalk Analysis of Slightly Lossy Interconnection Lines for Wafer Scale Integration and Wafer Scale Hybrid Packaging—Weak Coupling Case," *IEEE Trans. on Circuits and Systems,* **CAS-35** (11): 1369–1382 (1988).
4. D. B. Jarvis, "The Effects of Interconnections on High Speed Logic," *IEEE Trans. Electron. Computer,* **EC-12:** 476–487 (1963).
5. J. A. DeFalco, "Reflection and Crosstalk in Logic Circuit Interconnections," *IEEE Spectrum,* **7:** 44–50, July 1970.

BIBLIOGRAPHY

Catt, I., "Crosstalk (noise) in Digital Systems," *IEEE Trans. Electron. Computer,* **EC-16:** 743–763 (1967).

Chang, F. Y., "Computer-Aided Characterization of Coupled TEM Transmission Lines," *IEEE Trans. on Circuits and Systems,* **CAS-27:** 1194–1205 (1980).

Djordjević, Sarkar, T. Harrington, R.F. Bazdarm, "Time Domain Response of Multiconductor Transmission Lines: Software and User's Manual," Artech House Press, Boston, Massachusetts, (1989).

Feller, A., H. R. Kaupp, and J. J. DiGiacomo, "Crosstalk in Logic Interconnections," Proc. IEEE F.J.C.C., 1965, pp. 511–525.

Paul, C. R., "Solution of the Transmission Line Equations for Three Conductor Lines in Homogeneous Media," *IEEE Trans. on Electromagnetic Compatibility,* **EMC-20:** 216–222 (1978).

Tripathi, V. K., and Rettig, J. B., "A SPICE Model for Multiple Coupled Microstrips and other Transmission Lines," *IEEE Trans. on Microwave Theor. and Techniques,* **MTT-33:** 1513–1518 (1985).

CHAPTER 13
CONNECTOR DESIGN

Scott S. Simpson
Rogers Corporation
Rogers, Connecticut

13.1 INTRODUCTION AND GENERAL TRENDS

Interconnections for digital systems and electronics in general include a tremendous range of design types. Much of this is due to the system specific requirements placed on connectors in input/output (I/O) count, contact spacing, environmental requirements, electrical requirements, and size. The number of connection schemes available has increased greatly in recent years due, in part, to the user's desire to limit the number of interconnection levels.

The primary driving forces on system design are higher electrical speed and greater complexity, meaning higher I/O counts and higher density. Of course, cost is still a primary factor. As both speed and density increase, heat dissipation becomes very important. The connection system must now at least accommodate, if not contribute to, the dissipation of heat. The importance of these forces will require significant changes in connector design, especially in creating higher interconnection density and in improving electrical performance at high frequencies.

Electrical connectors, with a few exceptions, can be viewed as belonging to one of two categories. The first category comprises fused, or soldered, interconnections, which are not readily disconnected but provide a relatively high level of reliability. The second category is separable, or pressure-mated, interconnections, which provide a normal force on the metal-to-metal contact using a hardware assembly. There are two types of pressure-mated connectors. The most common type uses the metal contact itself as a spring element to produce the contact force. The second type uses a separate contact-force generator, which might be a metal or elastomeric spring element, shape memory alloy, or other contact-force-generating mechanism.

Fortunately, when considering connector designs and requirements, the wide variety of interconnections used have many characteristics in common. A good single reference source covering connectors and connector technology is *The Connectors and Interconnection Handbook*[1] published in five volumes by the Electronic Connector Study Group.

This chapter reviews basic electrical contact phenomena and connector design requirements. Following descriptions of the various test methods used to evaluate connectors, the chapter describes connector types used for chip package to board, board-to-board, and backplane applications. Reference listings are included as a resource for more detail.

13.2 CONTACT PHENOMENA[2–5]

13.2.1 Contact Resistance

The resistance of a conductor is described by

$$R = \rho \times L/A \tag{13.1}$$

where R = resistance, Ω
ρ = resistivity, Ω·cm
L = length, cm
A = cross sectional area, cm^2

When an interconnection is inserted into the electrical path, however, a contact resistance is added, giving

$$R = \rho \times L/A + R_{cn} \tag{13.2}$$

where R_{cn} = contact resistance, Ω

The contact resistance has two main constituents, the constriction resistance (R_c) and the film resistance (R_f).

$$R_{cn} = R_c + R_f \tag{13.3}$$

The constriction resistance results from the microscopic roughness of the contact surfaces. The surfaces are in direct contact only on the asperities as shown in Fig. 13.1. Because of this the actual load-bearing area is generally several orders of magnitude less than the apparent contact area, the remainder of the contact area being occupied by gas. This relationship between actual and apparent contact area depends on the load and the Young's modulus of the contact materials.[2]

Most connectors have constriction resistances on the order of mΩ (μΩ for power connectors). For crossed rods or spherical to flat contacts the constriction resistance is generally proportional to the inverse of the square root of the contact

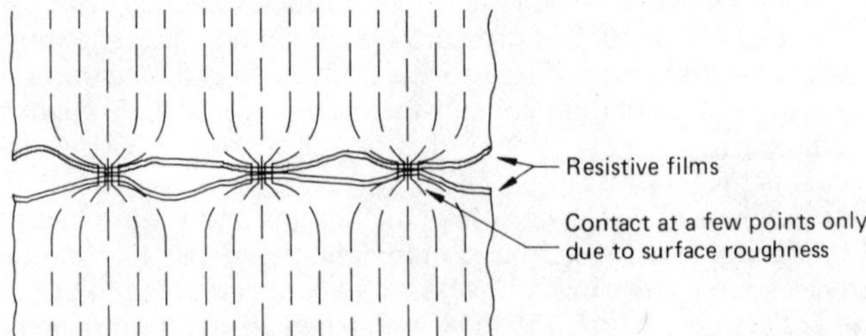

FIGURE 13.1 Contact resistance: constriction resistance (contact asperities) and film resistance. Pictured is a cross section of a contact region showing lines of current flow.

load if the contact asperities are plastically deformed. The constriction resistance is proportional to the inverse of the third root of the contact load if the contact asperities are elastically loaded. For well-aligned flat-to-flat contacts, however, the number of contact spots, rather than their size, tends to increase with load, and the constriction resistance is directly proportional to the inverse of the contact load.

The film resistance results from the semiconducting or nonconducting tarnish (oxide) films that form on the contact surfaces. Certain of these films, if thin enough, can be electrically punctured. The presence of these films means that the bulk of the load-bearing area in a contact region is primarily nonmetallic in nature. Williamson[3] uses the term *microspots* to describe the areas of metal-to-metal contact that occur between cracks in the opposing oxides. It is through these microspots that the majority of the current flows.

Wiping or sliding between contact surfaces during mating breaks through oxide films. In contrast, between nonwiping contacts the films are cracked due to the concentrated stress at the contacting asperities. Wiping has the additional advantage of dislodging particulates. These particulates, whether from deposited airborne dust or fragments of oxide film, reduce the actual contact area and can lead to deterioration of the contact due to wear by abrasion or, if the particles are hygroscopic, by corrosive and/or localized galvanic action.

Soldering, or any connection made by fusing the metallic interface, virtually eliminates the constriction resistance by equalizing the effective and apparent contact areas.

13.2.2 Contact Degradation and Healing[6,7]

The primary mechanism for connector failure is a loss of intermetallic contact due to oxidation.[6] Initially after mating, only the noncontacting surfaces oxidize. Over time, however, ambient gases diffuse into the contact region and the oxide films begin to attack the periphery of the contact spots. Eventually there is a significant loss of contact area and the contact resistance increases dramatically.

The degradation process can be slowed by self-healing,[3] which results from the heating produced by a resistance increase. The small mass of the material in the contact spots can develop high temperatures with small heat inputs. This results in a softening or melting of the metal at the interface. The contacting regions then respond to the applied contact force by deforming, which creates a larger contact area and lower resistance.

Another important degradation process is known as fretting corrosion.[7] In this case the oxidative mechanism is the same as that described above but is accelerated by relative micromotion between the contacts caused by vibration or thermal fluctuations. This micromotion causes wear of the surface, breaking down the oxide layer and exposing new metal. The freshly exposed metal oxidizes and again is broken down by the micromotion. This process builds up the volume of nonconductive oxide material, which becomes trapped between the contacts and increases the contact resistance.

13.2.3 Contact Materials[8–13]

The primary objectives for contact materials are low contact resistance and high corrosion resistance. In addition, for nonsoldered connections, it is seldom advisable to use different metals at the pressure-mated interface. This can form a bimetallic couple and will provide a prime location for the development and growth of a corrosion layer.

13.2.3.1 ***Base Metals.***[14,15] The primary base metal for electronic components is copper. It is very conductive (resistivity of about 1.8 $\mu\Omega\cdot$cm), ductile, and is available in sheet form for laminating. Copper can be easily electroplated, electroless plated, or vacuum deposited. Sheet laminated copper is generally either rolled and annealed or electrodeposited (ED) for higher bond strength. Unfortunately, copper has very poor corrosion resistance, resulting in nonconductive oxides and sulfides. An additional problem is the capability of these tarnish films to creep over the surface of adjacent plating.

The major exceptions to the use of copper as base metal occur in integrated circuits (ICs) and ceramic IC packages, hybrids, or multichip modules (MCM's). Integrated circuits use aluminum because it has a higher bond strength when sputtered onto the silica substrate. Ceramic packages or ceramic multichip modules use a fireable paste of glass frit and molybdenum or tungsten. These can be screened onto the unfired ("green") ceramic, forced into via holes, and fired to a solid at the same time as the ceramic is fired (cured). This results in a continuous sold metal-glass conductor pattern with resistivities of about 15$\mu\Omega\cdot$cm.

Hybrids use evaporatively deposited metal (thin film) and/or screen printed pastes (thick film) on a ceramic substrate.[14,15] These films are used in hybrids to create resistive and capacitive elements as well as conductive patterns. Thus, a wide range of materials are used in both the evaporative and thick-film deposition techniques. Thick-film compositions are of two types: cermet, which uses a fireable glass frit carrier (as with the ceramic packages and modules described above) and polymer thick-film (PTF) inks that use low-temperature curable polymer carriers.

13.2.3.2 ***Spring Contacts.*** Spring contacts provide both the contact force and a contact surface in one piece. The spring force requirement has led to the almost exclusive use of phosphor bronze or beryllium copper for these applications. Both of these alloys consist primarily of copper with either tin and small amounts of phosphorus (phosphor bronze) or beryllium and small amounts of cobalt and nickel (beryllium copper). These alloys are suitable for spring applications because they have higher plastic yield strength and elastic modulus compared to pure copper. These materials are 4 to 5 times less conductive than copper, however.

13.2.3.3 ***Undercoats.*** Nickel is the primary undercoat used in connector applications. Nickel has low interdiffusion rates with copper and gold (the most common top coat), thus preventing the migration of copper to the surface where it will corrode. In addition, the use of nickel as an undercoat has allowed the use of thinner top coats, specifically thinner gold top coats, because the nickel barrier reduces or eliminates problems caused by the porosity of thin plating layers over copper. Typical nickel plating thicknesses are on the order of 50 to 100 μin. Depending on the plating conditions, electroplated nickel can be very brittle. This can cause cracking and peeling of the coating. Also, the nickel surface passivates (i.e., oxidizes), which causes inadequate bonding of top coats such as gold. To prevent this, nickel undercoats are usually depassivated by an acid dip before plating of top coats. The acid dip is sometimes accompanied by a galvanic assist.

13.2.3.4 Coatings for Pressure-Mated Connections.[16–23] Gold is the most common top coat for creating the mating surfaces between pressure-mated contacts. It has low contact resistance, in part because of its low modulus, and it is extremely corrosion resistant. Because of the low modulus of gold, however, it has poor wear resistance in multiple-insertion applications where wiping between the contacts is used. This has led to the use of cobalt- or nickel-alloyed gold compounds, which have higher moduli and therefore greater wear resistance. A nickel underplate has also been shown to increase the wear resistance of gold top coats. The primary disadvantage of gold has been cost. This has also led to the use of nickel undercoats to reduce the thickness of gold required. If a nickel underplate is used, typical gold plating thicknesses range from 50 to 150 μin. Gold plating without an underplate is usually thicker.

Silver has the highest conductivity known and has been frequently used as a contact material. Silver readily corrodes in a sulfiding atmosphere, however, forming a highly insulating film. Thus, its use has diminished significantly.

Tin and tin-lead alloys are now being successfully used despite the fact that they readily oxidize to a nonconductive film. These connections require high normal forces on the contacts to maintain a seal around the contact regions ("gas tight"). Tin and tin-lead connectors also rely on the brittleness of the oxide layer on top of the soft base metal. Strong wiping action is used to break through the oxide layer. Examples of this technology are the Burndy GTH connector and the Molex HPT connector. These connectors also need to prevent micromotion between the contacts, which would cause fretting corrosion. Pure tin has the additional disadvantage of spontaneously growing metallic whiskers, which can short to adjacent conductors.

A useful comparison of gold versus tin contacts as a function of contact force, contact wipe, and cycle life can be found in Ref. 1, Vol. 2, Sec. 2.3.3.

Palladium and palladium-silver alloys are also used as top coats for pressure-mated contacts because the corrosion resistance of palladium is similar to that of gold.

13.2.3.5 Undercoats for Soldering. Undercoats are used for soldered connections to protect the base metal from oxidation and to promote adhesion to the solder. Three categories of solder undercoats are used. The first category is fusible coatings, which are compatible with the solder materials used. In this case the undercoat melts with the solder during interconnection. Generally these are tin and tin-lead electrodeposited undercoats.

Soluble undercoatings partially or completely dissolve during the soldering step. These can be silver or cadmium but most common have been thin coatings of gold. Gold forms a very brittle alloy with tin, however, and if sufficient gold is present can cause solder joint embrittlement.

Nonsoluble and nonfusible undercoats are used to prevent alloying of the solder with the base metal. Electrodeposited nickel and tin-nickel alloy are used, especially when soldering to aluminum base metal. The same passivity problems as discussed above for bonding to nickel still apply. Organic coatings, especially antioxidant coatings such as benzotriazole types, are used when the environmental or time requirements are less stringent because they are lower in cost.

13.2.3.6 Solder Materials. The most common solder materials are tin-lead alloys, predominantly at or close to 63% tin–37% lead composition, which is the eutectic point. The eutectic composition has a single melting point (183°C), which is less than either of the pure components. Other compositions have a pasty range over which the composition is partly liquid and partly solid. This condition occurs at temperatures higher than the eutectic melt point.

While tin-lead compositions are the most common, tin-bismuth, indium-tin-lead, indium-lead, and tin-antimony alloys are also used.

13.2.3.7 Contact Lubricants.[24] Contact lubricants are used in pressure-mated connectors to improve wear resistance and to inhibit corrosion by acting as a barrier layer. Many different waxes, oils, and greases have been used both with and without antioxidant additives. The most commonly used lubricants are polyphenyl ether and microcrystalline waxes. A combination of both materials has been shown to be very effective as long as the melting point of the wax is not exceeded after application.

13.3 CONNECTOR DESIGN REQUIREMENTS

13.3.1 Mechanical Design Requirements

Connectors of all types must provide a metal-to-metal contact for electrical continuity. If the connection is not a fused (e.g., soldered) connection, then continuous contact force between the metal surfaces must be provided. The amount of contact force required can vary greatly. Minimum reliable contact forces for gold-plated contacts are in the range of 50 to 100 g while minimum values for tin plated contacts are 100 to 150 g or more. The normal load is used to characterize the contact force for most connectors because the actual contact area is proportional to this load and the Young's modulus of the contact material (see Sec. 13.1.1). Unfortunately, the absolute value of the normal contact load has been overused in industry to directly compare and specify different connector designs. The relationship between normal load and actual contact area differs, depending on the contact materials and the nature of the contact design. Pin-and-socket or post-and-box connectors have different relationships than flat-pad to flat-pad contacts.

A large number of factors affect the design of a connector since they bridge the gap between two different components with different capabilities and limitations. A primary purpose of connectors is to combine components of greatly different contact densities. This is especially true in the case of integrated-circuit chips (ICCs) and circuit boards, where the feature size varies by about two orders of magnitude.

Connectors must withstand physical handling during interconnection as well as vibration and mechanical shock during use. Environmental and other evaluative testing generally follows vibration and mechanical shock exposures.

Environmental requirements determine if wiping is needed in a connector. Relative motion between the contacts upon mating is used to clean the contact surfaces by breaking down and removing nonconductive oxides and dust particles. When wiping is used the number of wear cycles can be an important limitation. Thus, the amount of wiping and the contact force versus wipe profile can vary greatly from connector to connector. The wiping itself can be generated by any number of different mechanical schemes.

The need to limit or eliminate micromotion between contacts can be an important design constraint when the potential for fretting corrosion is high. This is especially true for tin-plated contacts, which are significantly more susceptible to fretting problems than gold-plated contacts.

13.3.2 Electrical Requirements

13.3.2.1 Contact Resistance.[25] Contact resistances for electronic connectors are almost always less than 25 mΩ and generally in the range of 1 to 10 mΩ prior to environmental exposure. It is interesting to note that values in this range correspond to the resistance of only about 0.2 to 2 mm in length of a typical circuit-board trace. A connector test criterion after environmental aging of 3 times the original contact resistance was originally proposed by J. H. Whitely.[25] A useful criterion, it highlights the importance of a low initial contact resistance value to ensure sufficient long-term metal-to-metal contact area.

It is important to note that during environmental aging the range of contact resistance values tends to increase before the average contact resistance increases. This important characteristic can be used to infer imminent failure or instability of a group of connections.

13.3.2.2 Electrical Strength.[26] The important characteristics of a connector relative to electrical strength are directly related to the power transmission capability and the insulation resistance. The ability to carry current without excessive heat generation and the ability of the connector dielectric to withstand high voltages without breakdown are important, especially as the package level increases or if the connectors are used for power transmission. In most cases the insulation resistance is measured both before and after a high-humidity aging to evaluate possible moisture absorption by the dielectric.

13.3.2.3 Signal Integrity.[27–33] Signal speeds are increasing rapidly in electronic applications. This trend has led to the use of low dielectric constant and low dielectric loss circuit-board substrates. The signal path lengths are long in most circuit boards. Because of this it has become important to reduce crosstalk (noise) between signal lines and increase propagation speeds by providing a low dielectric constant substrate. It is also important to reduce transmission line losses and rise-time degradation by providing a low-loss dielectric. Regardless of the dielectric properties of the materials, however, it is necessary to control the impedance of the signal lines. Details on design and control of impedance characteristics can be found in Part 2, Chaps. 10–12. An excellent review of the electrical considerations in the design of a high-speed computer hardware system can be found in Ref. 33.

As signal speeds increase the interconnections become a significant contributor to system noise and the resultant loss of signal speed capability. The higher the frequency, the more significant a short electrical discontinuity becomes. An impedance change, even of very short length, will cause a series of signal reflections that increase the system noise. This has led to the development of controlled impedance interconnections for high-speed systems. Each level of packaging also adds electrical delay, which reduces the signal speed capability. Many applications now require that each interconnection level be considered from a signal integrity standpoint. References 27–33 review the important high-speed signal transmission issues associated with interconnections.

13.3.3 Environmental Requirements

J. H. Whitely has said, "As much as we may hate to admit it, and as much as many of us have worked to improve the situation, there is still no generally applicable and technically accepted relationship between contact resistance, its magnitude and variation, and the practical performance, life, and reliability of the associated contact."[25]

Whitely's statement highlights the difficulties associated with relating short-term evaluative tests to long-term field use of connectors. Despite this fact a number of common test types and uses have been developed over the years. In general, these tests use high-temperature and high-humidity exposures and exposure to highly corrosive atmospheres to establish short-term failure criteria.

13.3.3.1 Temperature and Humidity. Obviously, the environmental requirements for connectors vary considerably depending on the application. One of the worst common environments for electronic components is in automotive applications, under the hood as well as inside the passenger compartment. The lowest severity environment is likely to be a typical clean room used for chip packaging and hybrid or multichip module manufacturing.

In general, accelerated tests fall under three categories: elevated temperature aging, temperature cycling with high humidity, and thermal shock tests. These tests are used to estimate the long-term life characteristics of the connector system. The materials used to produce a connector (e.g., housing, contacts, contact-force-generating mechanism) must be designed to withstand elevated temperatures and humidities. This is true regardless of the real application temperature. Additionally, the system design must withstand thermal shock testing, which can loosen components such as sockets and pins molded into a plastic housing.

13.3.3.2 Corrosion.[34] While the corrosive nature of environments for electronic components varies widely, the sensitivity of electronic materials to extremely low levels of contaminants is well established. Fortunately, both system and component housings provide significant protection for the critical contact regions. This requires, however, that consideration be given to proper housing design to shield the contacts and to the protection of the contacts themselves by the use of contact platings.

There are five main types of accelerative tests used to evaluate the resistance of connectors to corrosion.

1. A 24-h exposure to the spray of a salt solution is frequently used. This has been a standard military test for many years.

2. Gas tightness, a short duration test in an extremely corrosive environment, evaluates how well the contacts are shielded and protected by the connector housing and any contact platings. The most common version of this test is a 1-h exposure to aqua regia, a 1:3 mixture of concentrated nitric and hydrochloric acids. This combination generates chlorine gas and will dissolve gold.

3. The third type of test used is a longer-term exposure to a sulfur atmosphere at elevated humidity. There are a number of variations of this test, which range from 24-h to 10-day exposures and ambient to 65°C exposure temperatures.

4. The fourth type is a flowing mixed-gas test,[34] which has been developed at Battelle Laboratories. This technique involves a chamber with a controlled gas-flow rate and humidity into which is metered small concentrations of corrosive gases, notably H_2S, Cl_2, and NO_2. Flowing mixed-gas tests more closely simulate the kinetics of actual corrosion mechanisms than the first three test types discussed above. An important factor is the synergism of sulfide and chloride exposure. Note that the previous tests involve either sulfide or chloride separately as the primary corrosive component. Flowing mixed-gas testing is relatively new and involves fairly expensive equipment. See Ref. 34 for an excellent review of environments for electronic equipment and the development of the flowing mixed-gas test.

5. The last type of test is used to evaluate fretting corrosion. Fretting is caused by micromotion between contacts and may require special contact spring and housing designs, depending on the application and/or contact materials. The most common tests for fretting corrosion involve long-term vibration exposure or dry thermal cycling.

The important, and most difficult, factor in all of the above tests is the analysis and interpretation of results. Experience has taught the connector industry to use severe tests interpreted conservatively in order to avoid unanticipated long-term failures.

Similar or identical tests to those described above for connector assemblies are used to evaluate open contacts. In this case the subject of evaluation is the quality and consistency of the environmentally protective platings on the contact surfaces. These types of evaluations are important to check for creep of corrosion over the top surfaces of gold, for example, and the tendency of corrosion to attack the boundaries between different metals, causing a separation between metal layers. Solder connections and wire bonds are susceptible to this type of attack at a mixed-metal interface. They are also susceptible to deterioration of the interfacial contact due to interdiffusion of the different metals (e.g., solder embrittlement caused by the formation of a tin-gold alloy).

The concept of protective contact platings requires complete coverage of the base metals. For this reason plating-specific porosity tests are used to evaluate the coverage, or porosity, of top coat platings. Unfortunately, the relationship between these results and field performance of associated connectors is tenuous.

13.3.3.3 Dust Exposure.[35] It is difficult, if not impossible, to prevent the ingress of dust particles into the contact region of a connector, especially in the unmated condition. This factor and the nonconductive oxides that form on contact surfaces have been the primary cause for the use of wiping between contacts during mating. The importance of this requirement has led to the development of complex corrosive dust mixtures for use in testing.[35] Simple classified dust, consisting primarily of silica, is more extensively used. While dust exposure tests exist in many connector specifications, they are often not utilized because it is difficult to relate them properly to actual field requirements.

13.3.4 Density Requirements

Increasing contact density has been, and will continue to be, one of the primary driving forces behind the development of new interconnection techniques. In addition to the decrease in system speed as the packaging level increases, the interconnection density also decreases. As previously discussed, connectors are used to provide the transition between high-density and low-density components. In general, the lower the packaging level, the more valuable space is on that package level. Thus, direct chip attachment techniques have extremely high interconnection density, as many as 10,000 contacts per square inch of IC chip, while system-to-system interconnects are typically three orders of magnitude lower in interconnect density.

When considering the contact density capability of a particular design it is recommended that the number of contacts (I/Os) per square inch of surface area occupied by the connector be calculated. This calculation should include grounding requirements since this can greatly affect the contact density. The importance of this calculation will be evident when considering product literature. For example, the term *pitch* is used to describe the distance between the centers of two adjacent contacts. A connector with contact spacings within a row, and between rows, of 100 mils may be quoted as having 50-mil pitch if alternating rows are offset by 50 mils. This connector will clearly only provide the contact density of a 100-mil pitch system, not that of a true 50-mil pitch connector.

13.4 TEST METHODS AND SPECIFICATIONS[36–40]

There are numerous good sources for test methods and specifications including, of course, military specifications. Most major buyers of connection products have their own specifications and test procedures, which are frequently available and generally follow the same guidelines as discussed in each category below. Overall, the best single source of connector specifications is probably the Department of Defense Standard Mil-C-55302C,[36] which uses Mil Std 1344[37] to define test procedures.

13.4.1 Contact Resistance[25,41–43]

Contact resistance is the most important and the most frequently measured characteristic of connectors. It is used as the primary measure of the effect of environmental testing, plating effectiveness, and aging, among others. Typical contact resistance measurement techniques are described in Refs. 38, 39, and 41. All of these tests utilize the four-wire technique shown schematically in Fig. 13.2. This technique eliminates the resistance of the test probes and traces from the measurement. A known current is generated across the connection using two wires, and the voltage drop is measured across the other two wires using a micro- or nanovoltmeter. Dividing the voltage drop by the current gives the resistance. As long as the joining of the two wires or traces on each side of the interconnection are very close to the contact interface, the result will be the contact resistance only.

As discussed in Sec. 13.2 the contact resistance consists of constriction resistance and film resistance components. The test voltages applied during contact resistance testing are limited to what is called a *dry circuit.*[42,43] A circuit is dry if the voltage is too low to electrically puncture the thin film that causes the film resistance. The minimum voltage level for thin-film breakdown has been shown to be about 100 mV.[25] The voltage limit for contact resistance testing is normally 20 mV.

Specifications for contact resistance vary widely depending on the application. Most requirements for initial contact resistance are in the range of 1 to 25 mΩ. Additional limits are placed on acceptable increases in contact resistance after

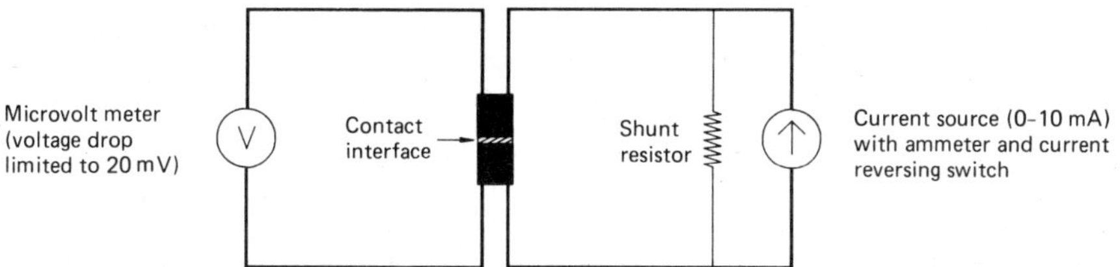

FIGURE 13.2 Four-wire contact resistance measurement technique—eliminates any lead or trace resistance from the measurement.

environmental exposure tests. The highest typical contact resistance specification is no more than 100 mΩ.

13.4.2 Current-Carrying Capacity[26,44]

This test measures the temperature rise caused by the current flowing through the contact interface. A series of current levels are applied and a graph of temperature rise versus current is produced. An in-use temperature limitation can be established for a connector using this data if the temperature capability of the connector components are known.

13.4.3 Dielectric Withstanding Voltage

This test is used to determine whether a connector can withstand momentary voltage overpotentials due to switching, surges, or the like. The test uses a high-voltage source, either direct or alternating current (dc or ac), a leakage current meter, and a fault monitor. The fault monitor is used, along with examination of the part, to check for failure that can occur due to flashover, sparkover, or breakdown (surface, air, or puncture discharges, respectively). The withstanding test voltage is usually set at 75 percent of the minimum breakdown voltage of the connector and therefore is not a dielectric or insulation breakdown test (see Sec. 13.4.4). The operating voltage is, in the same way, less than the test voltage (usually ⅓).

The test voltage is applied for 60 s between adjacent pairs of conductors and between the shell, or ground, and the nearest conductor. If ac current is used, it is usually specified to be 60 Hz. Because the withstanding voltage is greatly affected by the barometric pressure, this needs to be specified as well.

13.4.4 Insulation Resistance

This test determines the resistance of the connector insulation, seals, and other components to current leakage. A specified potential (usually 500 V) is applied between adjacent contacts and, separately, between the ground or shell and the nearest contact. The resistance is measured (MΩ). The test is usually run before and after some type of humidity aging. In some cases the insulation resistance requirements are lower after temperature and humidity cycling. A good example of this is Mil-C-55302C, which specifies 5000 MΩ before cycling and 1000 MΩ after cycling. Typical temperature and humidity conditions are 40°C and 90 to 95 percent relative humidity (RH) with exposure times varying from 8 h to 56 days.

13.4.5 Mechanical Shock and Vibration

Mechanical shock and vibration tests are used to evaluate the ability of connectors to withstand handling and operational conditions. In both types of tests the failure criteria are physical damage and loss of electrical continuity for a specified duration. Typical discontinuity duration limits are 10, 100, or 1000 ns.

Mechanical shock is applied in each direction in each of three mutually perpendicular axes (6 total). Usually, three shocks of each type are used (18 total). The peak gravities (or g's) of deceleration, duration, and shock pulse waveform of the impacts are specified. All of the connector contacts are wired in series, and a test current is applied in order to measure any discontinuities. Shocks are applied with current flowing (operating) and/or without current flowing (nonoperating) with different discontinuity requirements for each case (shorter limit for nonoperating).

Vibration is performed similarly with a specified number of hours of exposure in each of three axes. The time for each axis is the total time for a series of sweeps covering a range of frequencies at a given amplitude. Again, all of the contacts are wired in series and checked for any discontinuities.

13.4.6 Durability (Mate-Demate Cycling)

Durability testing consists of complete connection and disconnection cycles up to some specified limit. In general this limit ranges from 25 up to as many as 500 cycles with the lower values most common. The connector is then checked for visible wear or damage and for contact resistance changes. The estimated number of field-use connections and disconnections will greatly affect the specification limit.

In some cases durability tests are used prior to other environmental testing such as corrosion exposure. The number of mate-demate cycles in these cases are usually small (e.g., 25 cycles).

13.4.7 Thermal Shock

This test is used to evaluate the ability of the connector to withstand temperature fluctuations in shipping, storage, and use. Typically this involves a small number of transitions (5 to 10) between very low and very high temperatures. The most common temperature limits used are −55 to +65°C and −65 to +125°C. The transfer time between temperatures is less than 5 min. Dwell times vary depending on the test method and the size (mass) of the sample. Dwell times range from ½ to 4 h, with the shorter times being most common. Evaluation is primarily visual inspection for physical damage such as cracking, loosening of parts, and the like.

A second type of thermal shock test is a solder pot exposure for connectors that might be directly exposed to these conditions. Typically this involves a 5-s dip in solder at 450°F (232°C).

13.4.8 Corrosion

These tests are designed to evaluate the resistance of a connector to a corrosive atmosphere. There are five basic types of corrosion tests: salt spray, gas tightness, sulfide atmosphere exposure, flowing mixed gas, and fretting corrosion. The first three of these tests (salt spray, gas tightness, and sulfide exposure) are the most common and, in general, all three should be performed on a given connector.

13.4.8.1 Salt Spray. One of the oldest and most common corrosion tests, salt spray exposure has been the approved military test for connector corrosion resistance. The test involves creating a fog of a sodium chloride solution of either 5 or 20 percent and exposing the connectors for either 48 or 96 h. The military evaluation is inspection of the contacts for signs of pitting, peeling, or blistering of the metal, etc. Frequently, industry evaluation will include contact resistance with a limit on the acceptable increase (less than 10 mΩ increase).

13.4.8.2 Gas Tightness. Gas-tightness testing evaluates the ability of a connector to shield its contacts from penetration of a highly corrosive gas. This is usually accomplished by a 1-h exposure to aqua regia vapors. Aqua regia is a 3:1 mixture of concentrated hydrochloric and nitric acids. This combination generates chlorine gas and will dissolve gold. Aqua regia exposure is a very effective short-term test for corrosion resistance. Evaluation is by contact resistance before and after exposure and may be preceded by mate-demate cycling.

13.4.8.3 Sulfide Atmosphere Exposure. Sulfide atmosphere exposure evaluates the resistance of a connector to sulfide corrosion and uses contact resistance as the evaluative criterion. A good example of this type of test is exposure to flowers of sulfur. A mixture of sulfur, water, and sodium carbonate is used a produce a corrosive atmosphere and maintain 80 percent relative humidity at the test temperature of 65°C. The connectors are exposed for 10 days. It is highly recommended that some type of sulfide atmosphere exposure be included in a test program. This is an excellent test that can also be used to evaluate plating quality over copper by visual inspection for black deposits caused by the reaction of copper and sulfide. There are also shorter-term sulfur dioxide, ammonium sulfide, or hydrogen sulfide exposures, some of which are geared specifically to open-contact plating evaluations rather than full-mated connector tests. Typical of this type of unmated connector test is a 24-h exposure to a humid 1 percent SO_2 atmosphere with contact resistance after mating used as the evaluation method.

13.4.8.4 Flowing Mixed Gas (FMG).[34] Flowing mixed-gas testing has been developed by Battelle Labs in their attempts to measure and duplicate the kinetics of actual connector contact corrosion during field use. The connector is exposed to small concentrations of hydrogen sulfide, chlorine, and nitrogen dioxide in a flowing gas stream. The metering of controlled amounts of the corrosive components into a continuous gas flow has the great advantage of avoiding depletion while allowing the use of very small concentrations of corrosive material. Depletion is avoided in other corrosion tests by the use of high concentrations. However, this has the disadvantage of not matching the kinetics of field-use results as well as FMG tests.

The metering of the corrosive materials is accomplished by the use of diffusion tubes in which the materials are separately stored as liquids. The tube composition and system design control the amount of material exiting into the gas stream.

There are a number of different concentrations of materials and exposure times (test classes) used for FMG testing. While there are now commercial sources for this type of test equipment (Interfact Associates Ltd., Dresher, Penn.), it is relatively expensive compared to the simple exposure evaluations described above. It also has limited sample throughput capability due to the exposure times and test chamber sizes. Therefore, this type of test is not used for general connector testing and may remain a development tool only. Again, contact resistance is the evaluative method for this test with limits placed on the acceptable increase.

13.4.8.5 ***Fretting Corrosion.***[7] Fretting corrosion is caused by relative micromotion of the contact surfaces. This motion continually breaks up the oxide layers, exposing new base metal and adding to the mass of oxide material until it interferes with the quality of the connection. This effect is quite different from general corrosion and is not commonly evaluated for most connectors. Fretting is tested in two different ways. One is by mechanically producing relative motion of the contacts directly or by vibrating the entire connector for a large number of cycles. The other is by dry thermal cycling to produce small relative motions of the contacts. Both types of tests are not easily related to real-use conditions. Because of this, and the fact that many connectors do not show significant susceptibility to fretting, fretting corrosion tests are used more for development than for specification purposes.

13.4.9 Temperature and Humidity Aging

There are wide variations in the types of tests used to evaluate the resistance of a connector to temperature and humidity deterioration. These can be divided into four major types: humidity aging, elevated temperature aging at ambient humidity, temperature cycling, and temperature cycling with humidity. Except for the humidity aging test, contact resistance and visual inspection are used as the evaluative techniques. The tests are accelerative and attempt to mimic long-term real-use effects of stress relaxation of components (especially the contact-force-producing components), condensation, fretting corrosion, oxidation of contact surfaces, and the like. The temperature cycling tests are by far the most commonly used in the industry today.

13.4.9.1 ***Humidity Aging.*** As noted in Sec. 13.4.4 the most common humidity exposure is carried out at 40°C and 90 to 95 percent RH. In general this test is used to evaluate any changes in insulation resistance but is sometimes also used to monitor the effect of high humidity on contact resistance.

13.4.9.2 ***Elevated Temperature Aging.*** Conditions for elevated temperature aging range from +55 to +200°C for anywhere from 96 to 5000 h. The most typical conditions used are 65, 85, or 100°C for 1000 h.

13.4.9.3 ***Temperature Cycling.*** Temperature cycling tests vary considerably in temperature limits, cycle times, total duration, and number of cycles, all at ambient humidity. Compiling the most common aspects into a single representative test might produce something like the following: a low-temperature limit of −55°C and a high-temperature limit of +85°C; a 4-h cycle time of dwells (and temperature ramps if specified) for a total of two days (12 cycles) of exposure.

13.4.9.4 Temperature Cycling with Humidity. Conditions and cycling characteristics vary for this type of test but most methods conform fairly closely to the following descriptions: Temperature limits are +25°C and +65°C (75 or 85°C are also common upper temperature limits). Relative humidity limits are 50 and 95 percent. The cycle time, including ramp and dwell times, is 24 h with a total test duration of 1000 h. A typical cycle might start with 4 h at 25°C and 50 percent RH, go to 4 h at 65°C and 95% RH, then 65°C and 50 percent RH for 16 h and then be repeated.

13.4.10 Dust Testing[35,45,46]

The ability to make reliable electrical contact in spite of the presence of dust particles and nonconductive oxides on the contact surfaces is an important requirement for most connectors. This is the reason most connectors provide some kind of wiping (relative movement between the contacts during mating). By applying dust to the surface of the contacts before mating the ability of a connector design to wipe away and/or break up these particles can be evaluated. Contact resistance with and without the application of dust is used to measure the relative effectiveness of a connector. Dust testing may be combined with durability cycling and corrosion testing as part of a complete test program.

The most extensive reported work on the development of a connector dust test has been done at IBM.[35] See Ref. 45 for a good example of the use of this test in a connector test program. IBM has developed a complicated dust mixture containing 17 different materials including magnesium sulfate, calcium oxide, alumina, silica, and computer card dust. Other tests have been developed[46] that use only, or primarily, silica particles. In all cases the dust is classified into a mixture of certain particle sizes. A good source for such material is classified Arizona Road Dust, which is used in the evaluation of automobile air filters. Arizona Road Dust is available from the AC Spark Plug Division of the General Motors Corporation.

There are a number of difficulties associated with dust testing. These include adequate application techniques, determination of the proper amount of material to apply, and interpretation of results. These complications account for the fact that while many companies have a dust test specification, they are infrequently used in practice.

13.4.11 Signal Characteristics[47–50]

The simplest and most informative test method for determining the quality of the signal transmitted through a connector is time-domain reflectometry (TDR). Test methods for connectors are usually adapted from standard methods developed for evaluating flat cable or circuit-board transmission lines. The criterion for connectors is to minimize any discontinuity in impedance that will cause signal reflections of increasing severity as the frequency increases. The TDR test uses a short rise-time pulse generator (typical rise time of 35 ps) and a coaxial cable with a probe fixture for launching the signal onto the device to be tested. An oscilliscope and/or computer system is used to measure the launched and the reflected signal. By comparing these as a function of time, the effect on impedance, rise time, and crosstalk (with an adjacent line) can be determined.

13.4.12 Other Tests

This section includes tests that are either not full connector tests or are specific to certain categories of interconnections.

13.4.12.1 ***Plating Porosity.***[51–55] The quality and coverage of platings used as undercoats and topcoats over the base metal of connector contacts are critical to a connector's environmental performance (corrosion resistance). This is especially true in recent years as the plating thicknesses have been reduced for cost considerations. Porosity testing is used to evaluate the quality of the coverage. Coverage can be affected by the surface roughness of the base metal and plating, contaminants on the surface to be plated, or in the plating baths and the plating conditions, among others. Porosity testing is, as such, a test of the contact surfaces specifically rather than a connector test per se and does not apply to fused contacts such as wire bonds. See Ref. 51 for a review of porosity testing and test methods.

There are three predominant types of porosity tests: nitric acid vapor exposure, sulfur atmosphere exposure, and electrographic techniques. In order to be effective the test must attack the base metal under the coating and cause corrosion products to fill the pore up to the surface of the coating.

The nitric acid vapor exposure test consists of placing the sample in a desiccator suspended above a nitric acid solution. Exposure time is usually 1 to 2 h. This test is only of general use for evaluating the porosity of gold coatings.

The sulfur atmosphere tests range from exposure to the vapors from a solution of 10 percent sulfur dioxide for 24 h to the 10-day flowers of sulfur exposure test described in Sec. 13.4.8. The most common of the sulfur dioxide tests is called the Clark and Leeds method.[52] All these tests are run at high humidity.

Electrographic tests use either a gel or a treated paper which is brought into contact with the surface of the coating and made either the cathode or the anode (the sample is most often anodic) in creating an electrochemical cell.

All of these tests create visible spots or marks where pores exist. The results are then tabulated in one of three ways: the number of pores per unit area of test surface, the percent of the test surface area covered by the pores, or the area of the largest spot on the significant portions of the test surface.

13.4.12.2 ***Contact-Force Tests.*** There are a number of different test types used to evaluate the mechanical integrity or mechanical contact-force system of a connector. These tests apply depending on the type and design of the connector and include contact insertion and removal force (e.g., a pin contact inserted and removed from the connector housing), connector mating and unmating forces (e.g., insertion force for a pin grid array into and out of a socket), contact engagement and separation force (e.g., insertion and removal of an individual male-female connection rather than an entire connector), and contact-normal-force measurements. Consult the general test method references for details on these tests and their application.

13.4.12.3 ***Wire Bond Pull Test.*** This test uses a small hook and a force gauge to measure the attachment strength of a wire bond by pulling on the wire until failure. In general, specifications for this test are in the 3- to 5-g range and failure can be in the bond region or, for very fine wire, it can be tensile failure of the wire itself.

13.4.12.4 Dielectric Constant and Loss.[56–58] The electrical properties of the insulating materials used to construct connector systems have an important influence on the transmission of electrical signals through the connector. The frequency of interest is important, however, because dielectric properties of materials can change with frequency and because the measurement techniques become significantly more difficult as the frequency of interest increases.

Standard methods are available for measuring the dielectric constant (permittivity) and dissipation factor (dielectric loss) at low frequencies[56] and at microwave frequencies.[57,58]

13.5 CHIP PACKAGE TO BOARD INTERCONNECTIONS[71,73,78]

Integrated-circuit (IC) chips may be mounted in one of hundreds of different package types, on a multichip module, a hybrid, or directly onto a printed-circuit board. Despite the variety of packages and systems to which chips are attached, there are only three common techniques used for making electrical connection to the chip. These are wire bonding, flip-chip soldering, and tape automated bonding (TAB). For information on chip interconnections, chip packages, and their construction consult Refs. 59–92.

13.5.1 Direct Soldering[11]

The majority of components of all types, and IC packages in particular, are through-hole mounted and soldered in place. This means that the package has leads that are inserted into plated through-holes in the printed-circuit board. Insertion may be done by hand or by automatic equipment. In some cases the leads are bent over on the back side of the board to hold the component in place through the soldering operation.

Wave soldering is the primary soldering technique and involves passing the loaded circuit board over a flowing stream (wave) of solder. The solder wicks up into the plated through-holes and fuses the package lead to the wall of the plated through-hole. The solder and the plated through-hole become the interconnection. Thus, the reliability and testing requirements for plated through-holes are important interconnection issues. A typical plated through-hole has a resistance of between 5 and 10 mΩ. Consult Ref. 11 for information on wave soldering and plated-through-hole construction and reliability.

13.5.2 Surface-Mount Soldering[11,93–98]

Surface mounting of IC packages involves applying a 3- to 4-mil coating of a solder paste onto contact pads on the surface of the printed-circuit board, placing the IC packages onto the pads, and reflowing (melting) the solder. This fuses the package in place and makes the electrical connection. Surface-mount soldering has a number of advantages, including its adaptability to automated production techniques. It saves board space by allowing the use of smaller packages with dense interconnection patterns, and it reduces the number of board layers required. Blind vias and smaller plated through-holes can be used to improve routing instead of plated through-holes large enough to accommodate leads or pins. Surface-mount soldering also allows components to be mounted on both sides of a board. These advantages contribute to a lower assembled cost, the primary driving force for the use of surface mount. In addition, if a leadless IC package can be used, the elimination of the large lead (combined with the ability to use small plated through-holes and/or blind vias) can significantly reduce signal reflections and improve signal quality.

The advantages for surface mount have not yet translated into large volume use for a number of reasons. Surface-mount components account for only about 5 percent of the market for chip carriers, primarily due to the cost and availability of these packages in comparison to dual in-line packages (DIPs), and other plentiful, low-cost package types. Nevertheless, the use of surface-mount soldering is increasing rapidly as speed and complexity increase because its board density advantages become more important as I/O counts increase.

Surface mounting requires a significant change in equipment and expertise from standard board manufacturing techniques in order to take advantage of its potential benefits. The largest differences lie in component placement using automatic equipment dedicated to surface mount and changes in soldering techniques and conditions. Consult the listed references for details.

Component placement and board design issues include proper contact pad design, avoiding via holes within the pads or underneath components, interpackage spacing limitations, and component standoff height above the board for proper cleaning, testing, inspection, and repair requirements. Unfortunately, surface-mounted boards are much more difficult to test than boards using standard mounting techniques. This is due to the dense component packing and component mounting on both sides of the board. Standard boards are most frequently tested using bed-of-nails probe systems.

There are a number of different solder reflow techniques that can be used for surface mounting (e.g., laser, hot gas, hot bar) but the most common techniques are vapor-phase reflow and infrared reflow. In general, vapor-phase reflow provides the best control of temperature and the most uniform heating. Typical conditions might be 45 to 60 s at 215°C.

The most significant reliability problems associated with surface mounting occur at the solder joint. Leaded chip carriers have problems due to lead coplanarity variation. If the ends of the leads, whether butt end, J, or gull wing, are not within about 2 mils of each other, then the solder reflow process cannot adjust for the lead ends that are too short. This results in poor or nonexistent solder joints. Unfortunately, lead coplanarity variations as high as 10 mils have been reported.

Leadless chip carrier solder joints have problems due to coefficient of thermal expansion (CTE) differences between the package (primarily ceramic) and the board (primarily epoxy-glass compound). Temperature changes arising from the heat generated by the active circuit components cause the board and the package to expand. Because of differences in the CTE, the dimensional changes in the package and board differ. This causes significant strain on the solder joint between the package and the board. Over time and use the resulting temperature cycles cause the solder joint to fail by cracking. Leaded chip carriers are not as susceptible to failure because the strain is distributed over the length of the lead rather than concentrated on the small solder joint itself. Leaded components are more expensive, however. In addition, gull wing leads take up added board space and are easy to damage, while J lead types are hard to test, inspect, and repair. The fact that surface-mount solder joints need to be visually inspected means that its use is limited to packages with I/Os around the periphery only. Grid array pattern packages cannot yet be reliably surface mounted.

The interest in utilizing surface-mount techniques for board assembly coupled with solder joint reliability problems have led to a number of developments in materials or alterations in the nature of the solder joint itself. One of the primary developments, discussed in Sec. 13.7.3, has been the use of sockets specifically designed for leadless packages, thus avoiding the issue altogether. Material options include the use of plastic or epoxy-glass-based chip carriers that, compared to ceramics, more closely match the CTE of typical board substrates. Changes in board materials can also be made by using metal-core layers, such as Invar, which have very low CTE values. This prevents excessive expansion of the epoxy-glass board and reduces the strain on the solder joint. Alternatively, dielectric materials such as Rogers RO2800 are available that have low modulus and moderate CTE properties. The low modulus reduces the strain on the solder joint.

Other options for improving solder joint reliability create a leaded package from leadless packages by adding edge clips or creating solder columns.[97,98] Edge clips, such as those available from NAS Electronics or Berg, are stamped and formed leads of tin-lead-alloy coated phosphor bronze or similar materials. The edge clips are placed around the periphery of the leadless package and a solder reflow step fuses the clips to the package and to the board. Clips are available in different styles to match various package types and may be provided with preformed solder bumps. They cost about ½¢ per contact.

Soldier columns consist of a helix of copper wire covered with solder. The columns are held in place by a frame. Again, the added lead length reduces the localized strain on the solder joint, improving reliability.

13.5.3 Sockets[99–103]

Sockets overcome some of the difficulties associated with direct and surface-mount soldering while providing a mechanism for simple mate-demate operations on chip packages. Sockets allow the use of fine pitch (e.g., 50-mil) chip carriers on a standard printed-circuit board by providing a fan-out from the fine pitch of the package to the 100-mil pitch capability common to most standard industry circuit boards. Sockets also solve the problems caused by CTE differences between the package and the board. Spring contacts used in the sockets provide the needed compliance. As the number of contacts increases and the value of the chips increases with the use of VHSIC (very high-speed integrated circuits) and ASIC (application-specific integrated circuits), sockets become more valuable because of the difficulties associated with soldering high-I/O-count parts and the risks involved in subjecting the chips to the high temperatures and related strains of soldering. For these reasons almost all nonmilitary memory and microprocessor chips are socketed, most of them for computer manufacturing. Because most of the IC packages sold are of the DIP (dual in-line package) type it is not surprising that about 70 percent of all sockets sold are for DIP packages. See Ref. 99 for an excellent review of socket types including manufacturer listings.

13.5.3.1 Standard Sockets. Sockets for leaded chip carriers, primarily DIPs as discussed above, can have either stamped and formed or screw-machine contacts. Stamped contact types are shown in Fig. 13.3 and can be single beam, single beam with opposing metal wall, or dual beam. The single-beam types are generally precompressed somewhat before loading into the plastic housing so that they will

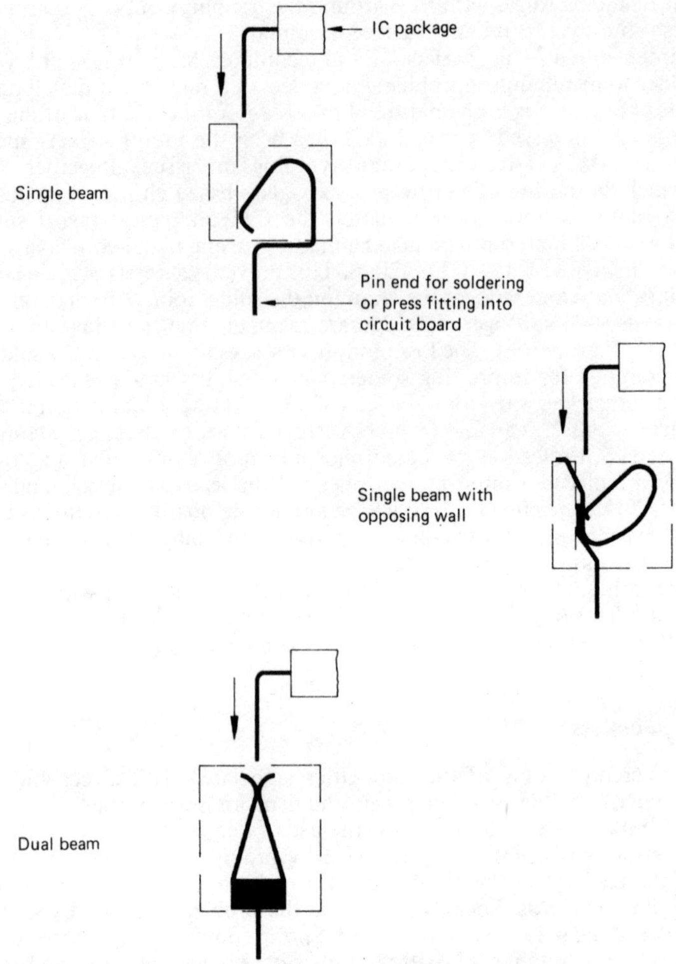

FIGURE 13.3 Stamped and formed socket contact types for DIP packages.

generate the required contact force. Dual-beam types generally provide a lower contact force because the beam deflection is smaller.

Figure 13.4 shows some examples of contact types used for leadless (or J-leaded) chip carriers. Sockets of this type generally require the use of an insertion and extraction tool. Most sockets generate between 1 and 2 oz of insertion or extraction force per contact. At high I/O counts the total force is therefore quite high and tools are required to avoid damage to the chip package. Socket types designed for leadless chip carriers frequently utilize a clamping frame on the top surface of the package. The contact force is generated by compressing the contact springs downward rather than outward. In this case heat sinks can be incorporated into the clamping structures as an added feature.

Most contact springs are made from beryllium copper because of its broad temperature use range (up to +125°C). Phosphor bronze is also used (up to

+105°C) for less critical applications. Tin or tin-lead alloy is the primary coating. Gold is also frequently used, especially for the lower-contact-force socket applications (e.g., dual-beam type and leadless chip carrier type). The socket contact lead ends that are inserted into the circuit board for soldering are frequently of the compliant type. Compliant leads (or pins), as shown in Fig. 13.5, contain a locking barb or spring-type feature, which is designed to provide holding force to ensure that the socket remains in proper position through the handling operations prior to soldering. In many cases compliant pins eliminate the soldering step completely if adequate sealing and contact force is created. See Refs. 102 and 103 for more details.

Many sockets have an anti-overstress feature to prevent damage to the spring contacts by bent or misregistered package leads. This is accomplished by correct size and placement of a molded feature within the socket housing. Some sockets incorporate other features, including solder preforms on each pin lead that eliminate the need for wave soldering, a wafer that fits tightly around the pins to prevent solder from wicking up above the top of the board, and ceramic capacitors mounted on the top surface of the socket under the package. Mounting a capacitor on the socket places the capacitance as close to the IC chip as possible and limits noise problems during signal switching by maximizing the decoupling of the power and ground. Add-on chip capacitors are also available for mounting between the chip package and the board or socket, sharing the same plated through-holes or socket contacts.

A significant disadvantage to the use of a socket is the loss of board surface area and the added height occupied above the board (most sockets are about 0.25 in tall). Sockets also add significant cost, ranging from 3¢ to 5¢ per contact for leaded chip carrier sockets and 6¢ to 8¢ per contact for leadless chip carrier sockets.

13.5.3.2 Press-Fit Sockets. An alternate socket contact, the screw-machined type, is shown in Fig. 13.6. These contacts are more expensive than stamped and formed types (typically 4¢ to 5¢ per contact in strip form) but have lower insertion

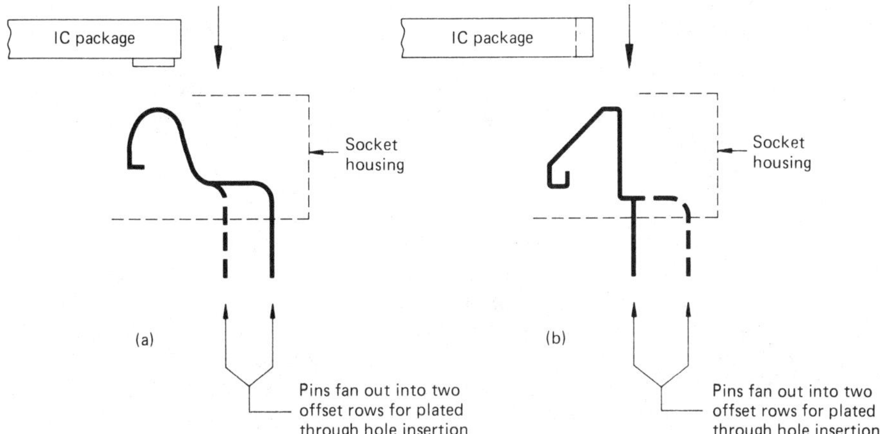

FIGURE 13.4 Socket contact types for leadless packages. (*a*) Contact on the bottom of package. (*b*) Contact on side of package (e.g., castellations).

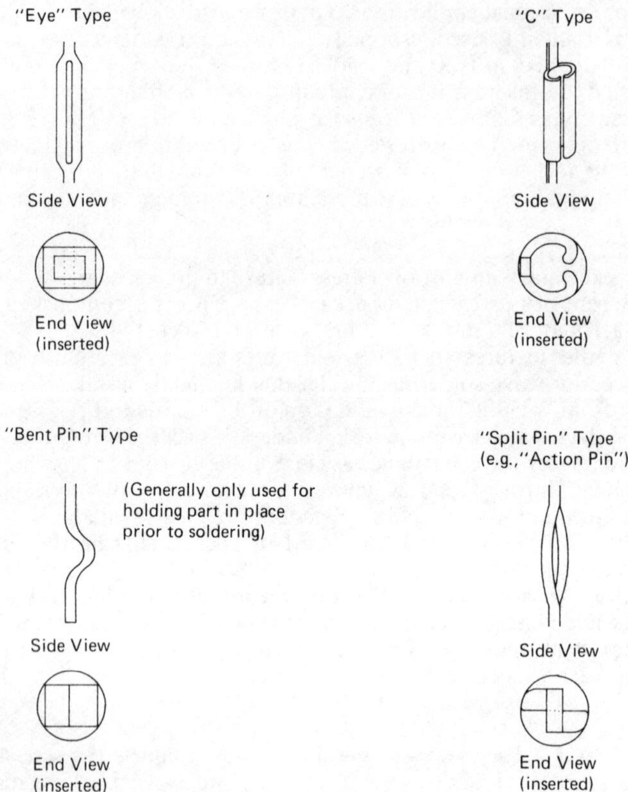

FIGURE 13.5 Compliant pins for board insertion.

force, which is virtually a necessity for socketing high-pin-count parts. Most pin grid arrays (PGAs) are socketed in this way. Screw-machined contacts come in four- and six-finger versions. The six-finger type has lower contact force (lower insertion force) but compensates with larger contact area between the fingers and the IC package lead. The contacts are generally supplied at 100-mil pitch either mounted in a frame (molded epoxy or an epoxy-glass board) or on a carrier strip, which may be removed after the contacts have been inserted and soldered in place on a board. This method produces a housingless socket in which the chip package is simply pressed (press fit) into the board or the frame. This system offers flexibility and a very low profile (height above the board surface).

13.5.3.3 Low Insertion Force and Zero Insertion Force Sockets.[104,105] Typical socket insertion and extraction forces of 1 to 2 oz per contact can be prohibitive for high-I/O-count packages due to part damage. Because of this, sockets have been designed that have reduced or nonexistent insertion force. These are low insertion force (LIF) or zero insertion force (ZIF) sockets. LIF types are less common and usually involve designs similar to standard sockets. An example is an Amp socket for PGAs in which the individual lead sockets are staggered vertically so that less than the total number of contacts are engaging at once. A greatly different approach, however, is the wire sleeve or hyperboloid type (see Sec. 13.6.2). The sleeve is designed so that the center is narrower than the ends and the wires stretch over the inserted pin.

Most ZIF socket designs use a cam mechanism in which a rigid member physically restrains the contact springs from closing. After the package leads are inserted into position a lever arm is thrown, releasing the restraining member and allowing the contact springs to engage. An alternate approach uses a sliding set of ramps in which the ramps are forced against a set of matching contact springs by actuating the socket. One of the most complicated sockets available is a grounded ZIF socket produced by ITT Cannon for a pin grid array with over 1000 I/Os (see Ref. 104).

An unusual ZIF socket design produced by Raychem[105] uses a shape memory alloy (SMA) as the spring force member. A shape memory alloy is a metal that has the unique property of undergoing a reversible crystal phase transformation which allows it to return to a prespecified shape by changing its temperature. The most common shape memory alloy used for electronic connectors is a nickel-titanium alloy called Nitinol (nickel titanium, Naval Ordinance Laboratory). The Raychem system, called Cryocon, uses a slotted tube female socket surrounded by a band of Nitinol. When cooled (using a spray coolant) the band expands to an oval shape, loosening the socket and allowing ZIF insertion of the package pins into the socket. As the Nitinol warms to ambient temperature the band returns to its original round shape, compressing the slotted tube and creating the required contact force.

The primary disadvantages of ZIF (and LIF) sockets are the same, but greater, than those of standard sockets. The extra board space required and the added cost

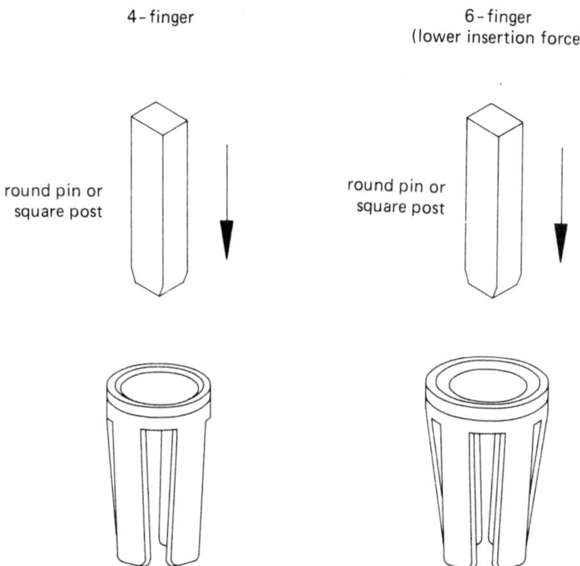

FIGURE 13.6 Screw-machined sockets.

are much larger for ZIF designs (costs up to 18¢ per contact). Nevertheless, these sockets are finding applications. In many cases they are the only commercially developed way to reliably interconnect high-lead-count chip packages.

A special category of sockets exists for high-temperature chip test and burn-in procedures. They are primarily of the LIF or ZIF design type. Because of high-temperature requirements (about 200°C) these socket designs use beryllium nickel or stainless-steel contacts and special polymers for the housings. Sockets for test and burn-in are more robust in design compared to standard sockets because of the large number of mate-demate cycles required.

13.5.3.4 Surface-Mount Soldered Sockets.[106,107] Sockets for IC package interconnection can themselves be surface-mount soldered rather than through-hole mounted. As with surface mounting IC packages, lead compliance is an important issue in solder joint reliability. For this reason most surface-mounted sockets use gull wing leads for the soldered connection to the board. Unfortunately, the stress that can be placed upon sockets during handling and package mate-demate cycles usually requires that there be some kind of mechanical anchoring (e.g., screws, rivets, heat stakes) to ensure reliability. This requirement adds complexity and cost. Generally, surface-mount sockets are not used unless the entire board needs to be surface mounted. Since most boards contain a mix of technologies it is not surprising that most sockets are through-hole mounted.

13.5.4 Z-Axis Connection Techniques[108–111]

The continuing increase in I/O count and contact density for high-speed digital systems has led to increasing use of grid array pattern packages. Such packages can be connected to a board in two ways. First, and most common, is in pin grid array form in which contact pins on the bottom surface of the package are directly soldered or socketed (generally ZIF or LIF types due to the high lead count and insertion force). The main disadvantage of using a pin grid array, whether directly soldered or socketed (with a through-hole mounted socket), is related to the plated through-holes themselves. Plated through-holes large enough to accommodate the pins of the package or socket create routing problems. Limitations in routing require a larger number of board layers and the associated costs. In order to achieve very high density, small-diameter plated through-holes and blind vias (plated holes that do not pass through the entire board but stop at a specific layer) need to be used. Smaller plated through-holes and blind vias simplify routing, increasing the density capability and reducing the number of board layers required. This lowers total system cost. Converting to small blind vias also allows components to be mounted on both sides of the board, increasing density.

The factors described above are the main source for the development of surface mount. Unfortunately, because the solder joints of any interior pads cannot be inspected by common techniques, the use of surface-mount soldering is generally limited to contacts at the periphery of packages. Because of the density advantages of using a grid array and the problems with CTE mismatch for surface-mount soldering in general, a number of grid array connection alternatives have been developed. These techniques are called *Z*-axis connectors. They interconnect rows, or arrays, of contacts on two opposing parallel surfaces. Thus, they can be used to interconnect a circuit board and a pad grid array (or any leadless package with contact pads on the bottom surface). These techniques also provide easy mate-demate operation by eliminating soldering and desoldering requirements. The disadvantage of *Z*-axis connectors is that all require hardware to compress the package and board together to create the contact force.

There are five basic types of *Z*-axis connectors as shown in Fig. 13.7. The first type is commonly called a Zebra strip connector from Tecknit, Inc. or the STAX connector sold by PCK Elastomerics, Inc. They consist of alternating rows of conductive and nonconductive silicone elastomer. The elastomer itself provides the contact force when compressed. Loading the silicone with either silver or carbon produces the conductivity. The difficulties associated with these connectors are their high contact resistance and high total electrical resistance (about 100 Ω for the carbon loaded and several hundred mΩ for the silver loaded). For this reason they are limited to connecting liquid-crystal displays (LCDs) and the like where such high resistance can be accommodated.

A similar connection method is represented by the metal-on-elastomer (MOE)

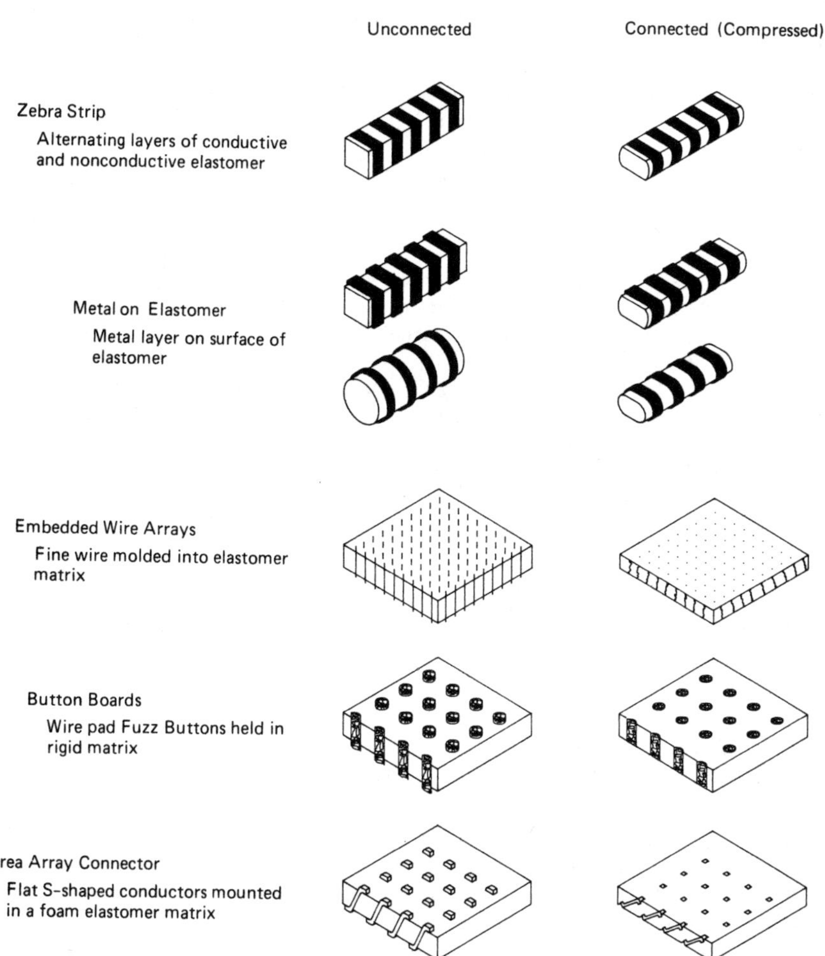

FIGURE 13.7 *Z*-axis connection techniques.

technique of PCK and Cambiflex from Midland-Ross Corporation. These systems use a series of conductive traces produced directly on a silicone elastomer core or on a thin, flexible dielectric layer, which is subsequently wrapped around the core. This provides lower contact resistance as required for IC package applications. A significant disadvantage of both the Zebra strip and metal-on-elastomer techniques is the board space they occupy. Because of this they limit the row-to-row spacing that can be interconnected. Thus, these techniques are primarily useful only for contact pads on the periphery of a package and cannot be easily used for pad grid arrays unless the row spacing is large.

Arrays of wires embedded in solid silicone elastomer sheets such as that supplied by Shin-Etsu can be used to connect pad grid arrays or peripheral pad arrays. These types are primarily designed for electromagnetic frequency interference (EMI) or radio-frequency interference (RFI) gasketing, however, and have not been shown to be reliable for signal interconnections.

Two systems specifically designed for interconnecting pad grid arrays are available:[109–111] Button Boards and the area array connector. Button Boards, as shown in Fig. 13.7, are an array of Fuzz Buttons mounted in a rigid matrix support that aligns the buttons and holds them in place. Fuzz Buttons consist of very fine wire, typically 2 mils in diameter, which is gold plated and randomly formed into a cylindrically shaped pad. Typical overall button size for pad grid array use is between 30 and 50 mils in height and in diameter. The system is designed such that the buttons protrude about 10 mils from each surface of the rigid matrix which is clamped in place between the pad grid array and the circuit board. Fuzz Buttons rely on the random orientation of the fine wire to provide sufficient spring contact force and contact area on each surface. Fuzz Buttons are available from Tecknit and their use in a Button Board is available for license from TRW, Incorporated. Fuzz Buttons of the size described here can be used to connect pad grid arrays at 50-mil pitch.

The second technique specifically designed for connecting pad grid arrays is the area array connector from Rogers Corporation. This system uses rigid conductors approximately 10×20 mils in cross section. The conductors are die formed into a flat-S shape, nickel and gold plated, and inserted into apertures in a silicone foam elastomer matrix. The apertures and the shank of the conductors are at an angle to the surface of the foam matrix. In this way the conductors rotate on their axes when the matrix is compressed between the pad grid array and the circuit board. Thus, the conductors are not deformed in use and the contact force is generated and controlled by the elastomer only. This design provides wiping during interconnection, but is limited in contact density to between 40- and 50-mil pitch.

13.6 BOARD-TO-BOARD INTERCONNECTIONS[1,112]

This section describes board-to-board jumper interconnections, which can be differentiated from board-to-backplane connections (Sec. 13.7) in that the connector is mated and demated from the board as opposed to the board being inserted and removed. This requires the use of a wiring system in which the connector is the interface between the wiring and a board. Systems of this type are used to connect certain signal lines as a supplement to a backplane or, if sufficient I/O can be accommodated, as a replacement for a backplane.

Jumper wiring provides the point-to-point electrical interconnection between the connector interfaces. Electrical requirements such as loss (attenuation), impedance control, and shielding can be extremely important since the path length may be quite long. The most important jumper wiring types are discrete wiring, collated (or ribbon) cable, flexible circuits, and coaxial cable. See Refs. 112–116 for more information.

13.6.1 Jumper Wiring to Connector Hardware Interface

The medium for signal transmission (e.g., cable, flexible circuit) is rarely attached directly to the board(s) that it interconnects. With some important exceptions, discussed in Sec. 13.6.2, the cable or wiring is permanently or semipermanently joined to a connector hardware part that is the direct interface with the board. This adds an interconnection at each end of the jumper but is more convenient for mate-demate operation. There are three basic methods used to make electrical connection between connector hardware and the insulated conductors of the signal transmission medium: insulation displacement, crimping, and soldering. There are a large number of automatic machines available for feeding, cutting, and terminating the various cable types with connector hardware.

13.6.1.1 Insulating Displacement (IDC) Connectors.[117] This type of connector is used primarily for ribbon cable, twisted pair ribbon cable, and collated cable. Insulation displacement involves forcing the insulated conductor into a slotted tab as shown in Fig. 13.8. The slot is designed to cut through the insulation and bite into the conductor wire. This provides a large area of contact with high contact force producing a gas-tight connection. In most cases the slotted tab is one end of a stamped and formed contact which has a socket for pin interaction at the other. Reference 117 describes the basic technique as applied to a 25-mil pitch cable.

13.6.1.2 Crimping. Crimping requires stripping the insulation from the conductor(s) before connecting. In its conventional form crimping is accomplished by inserting the conductor into a formed metal feature that is then permanently deformed. This traps the conductor within the feature and creates the required contact force. This method is used most often with single or bundled discrete wires to connect to eyelets, banana plugs, flag fastons, and the like. Other methods that can be considered crimp types are spring clip types and wire wrapping. Spring clips (a nonpermanent connection) generate the required contact force by a spring contact member. Wire wrapping uses the wire itself to provide the contact retention force. These methods are used primarily for single-discrete-wire interconnections and do not generally have a connector housing. Coax cables are frequently attached to a connector with crimping techniques. There are also coax connectors that thread onto the stripped end of the cable. These operate like a reverse wire wrap where the contact has internal threads that dig into the bare conductor wire.

13.6.1.3 Soldering.[118] Soldering is very common for discrete wires and bundled discrete wires when connecting to eyelets, pins for spring type sockets, banana plugs, and the like. Soldering is also used for ribbon cable and collated cable. This technique is especially common for controlled impedance collated cable. A section of the insulation is stripped, leaving a small portion of insulation on the end of the cable to hold the conductors in alignment while the ground and signal con-

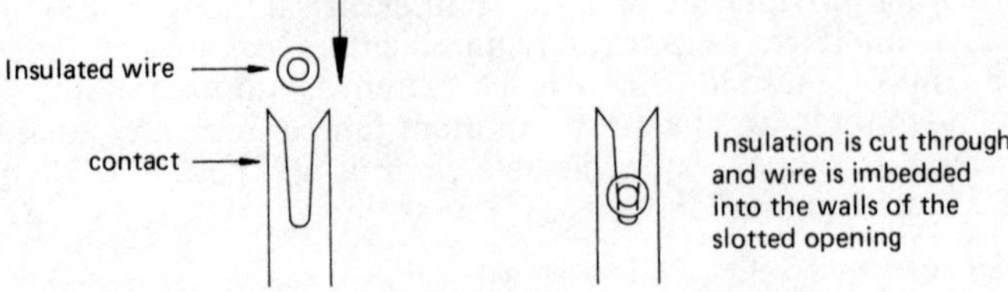

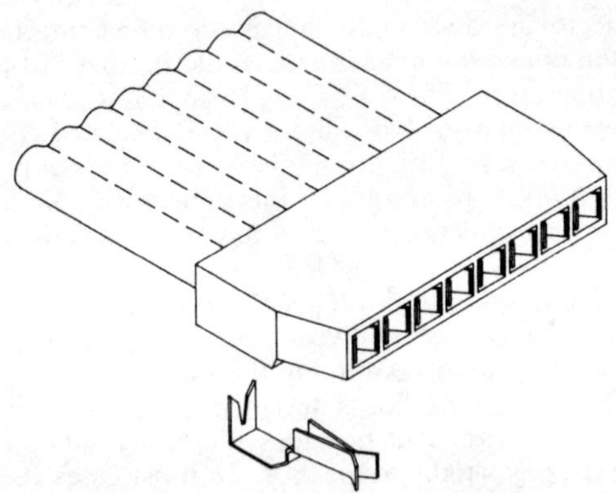

FIGURE 13.8 Insulation displacement connector (IDC) contact for insulated wire.

ductors are separated (see Ref. 118). The ground conductors are soldered to a bus and the signal conductors are soldered to individual socket contacts. The entire collection of wire ends, insulation, and stamped and formed socket contacts are then molded into a single connector housing.

Soldering is a common interface technique between flexible circuits and connectors of all types. In this case the connector pins are wave soldered to contact pads or into plated through-holes in the flexible circuit. Soldering is also common for interconnecting coaxial cable and coaxial connectors.

13.6.2 Board-to-Board Connector Types[119,120]

13.6.2.1 Edge-Card Connections. One of the most common board-to-board connector types is the edge card. This type of connector slides over the circuit board to which it attaches, trapping the board between stamped and formed contacts within the housing of the connector. There are provisions within the housing and features on the board to ensure proper alignment. The board has one row of contacts along the edge of each surface that mate with the spring contacts within the housing. The contact spacing on each surface is typically 100-mil pitch although there are connectors now available at 50-mil pitch. Four contact spring configurations are in common use: cantilever, folded cantilever, looped cantilever, and bellows, as shown in Fig. 13.9.

The advantages of edge-card connectors are relatively low cost and ease of use. It is one of the oldest board connection techniques and is very well developed and understood in the industry. The primary difficulties associated with this technique are contact-force variations caused by board thickness variations and warping of the board. In addition, there are significant contact density limitations with edge-card connections because they are limited to one row on each surface and limited in contact pitch.

13.6.2.2 Pin-and-Socket (Post-and-Box) Connections. A number of different socket configurations are used with square, rectangular (flat), and round pins. The term *pin and socket* refers to round pin connectors and *post and box* refers to square or rectangular pin connectors. For simplicity the term pin and socket will be used here inclusively. There are many different types and styles of pin-and-socket interconnections as shown in Fig. 13.10. The socket (female) or the pinned

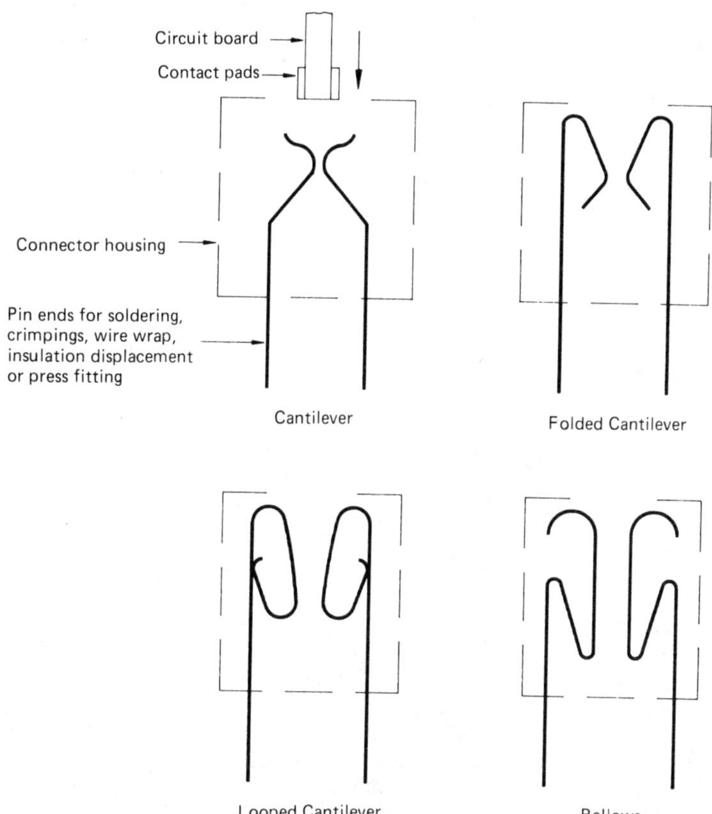

FIGURE 13.9 Edge-card connector contact configurations.

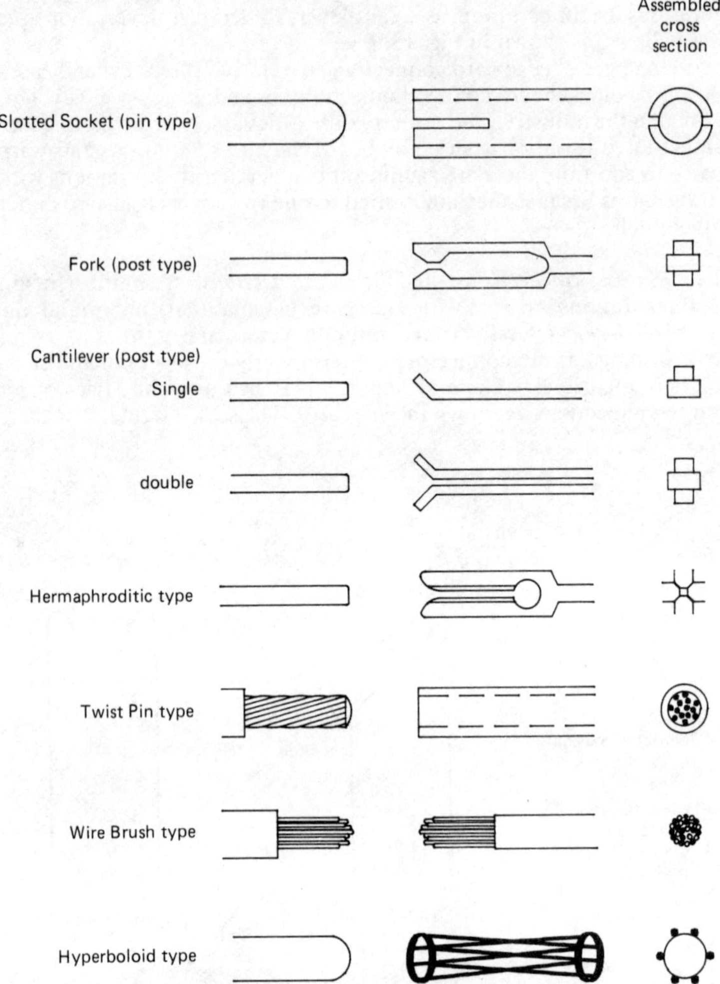

FIGURE 13.10 Pin-and-socket and post-and-box contact types.

portion (male) may be the removable half, the other portion being fixed to the board. Hermaphroditic connections, which have identical mating portions, are also available. Pin-and-socket techniques are two-piece connectors as opposed to edge-card connectors, which are one piece.

The most common contact pitch is 100 mils between contacts within a row and 100-mil pitch between rows. The board half of the connector housing is mounted to the board by soldering pins, or press-fitting compliant pins, into plated through-holes. Simple compliant pin versions are sometimes used simply to hold the part in place up to the soldering operation (see Fig. 13.5).

The biggest advantage of the pin-and-socket technique is its versatility. Pin-and-socket connectors can handle larger numbers of contacts than an edge-card system because multiple contact rows can be used. It lends itself quite well to plated-through-hole board manufacturing techniques and does not require the contacts on the board to be gold plated like many edge-card connectors.

Despite an advantage in the number of contacts and contact density that can be accommodated relative to edge-card connectors, this technique has its own contact density limitations. This limitation is now being encountered as system capability requirements increase. It is being addressed by the development of finer contact pitch pin-and-socket systems (<100 mils). Pin-and-socket connectors also have some problems, such as high crosstalk and large electrical reflections, as signal frequencies increase. This is due to the lack of impedance control and the relatively large feature sizes (e.g., the pins, sockets, and plated through-holes) when compared to the feature size of typical circuit-board traces.

13.6.2.3 Pressure-mated Pad Connections.[105,121–124] This type of board-to-board interconnection separates the electrical contact component from the contact-force-generating mechanism. Pressure-mated pad connections are usually made using flexible circuits. The flexible circuit has a contact pad array that matches the pad array on the circuit board as shown in Fig. 13.11. The contact pad arrays

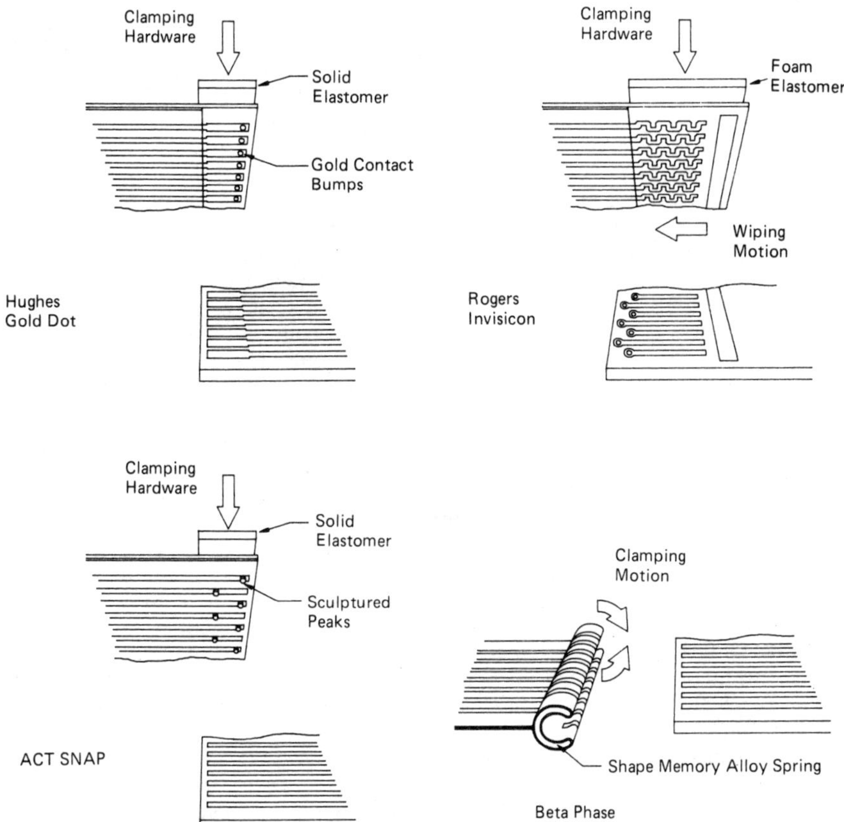

FIGURE 13.11 Pressure-mated pad connection techniques.

are then clamped together by hardware that contains some mechanism for applying contact force. Typical contact-generating mechanisms include metal springs and elastomers. Flexible circuits are preferred for this technique because of their conformability. The contacts on both surfaces are almost always gold plated, frequently with a nickel undercoating, for environmental reliability. The advantages of this technique include the ability to achieve high contact densities (contact pitch as small as 10 mils) and the elimination of the contact interface between the jumper cable wiring and the board.

An example of a pressure-mated pad interconnection is the Hughes Gold Dot system.[121,122] This technique uses 5- to 10-mil diameter, ½-mil thick, solid gold bumps that are plated on the copper contact pads of the flexible circuit. Then the entire contact pad with bump is plated over with gold for environmental protection. The basic concept is to use high contact force with a small area of contact. The contact force is generated by backing the flexible circuit with a solid elastomer sheet and compressing the contact pads together by clamping hardware. Because there is only a small region of contact between the bump and the contact pad on the circuit board, very high contact forces are generated (up to 49,000 lb/in^2). This is designed to break through surface oxide films without the use of wiping (relative movement between contacts during mating). This system is expensive, however, and has been used primarily in military applications.

A second technique is the Invisicon system[123] from Rogers Corporation. This method uses a large area of contact with a much smaller contact force but includes wiping in order to remove dust particles and to break through oxide layers. This system uses a complex contact pad design shown in Fig. 13.11. Combined with wiping, it assists in scraping away foreign material, and it improves the high-frequency electrical performance of the system. The contact region is backed by a silicone foam elastomer to control the contact force and is aligned by hardware which, depending on the application, may or may not provide wiping. Invisicon provides controlled impedance by using microstrip or strip-line circuit constructions. Improved electrical performance is obtained by use of a low dielectric constant, low dissipation factor (loss) fluoropolymer flexible-circuit material (RO2500). These factors combine to create an interconnection with excellent electrical performance even at very high frequencies (pulse rise times less than 1 ns). The technique is capable of high contact densities, especially since all of the I/Os can be used for signals because a separate strip connection is used for ground. This is an advantage when compared to pin-and-socket connectors, where many of the pins need to be dedicated to ground. The disadvantage of this type of system is that it is relatively expensive.

There are two other flexible-circuit interconnection techniques that utilize alternative contact-force-generating mechanisms. One is the SNAP (sustained necessary applied pressure) connector from Advanced Circuit Technology. SNAP uses a single wire spring that grabs the circuit board and forces the circuit into contact when the hardware mechanism is engaged. The second method, available from Beta Phase, Inc. as described in Ref. 124, uses a shape memory alloy. The alloy is in a C-shape configuration that opens for attachment when heated by a resistance heater built into the flexible circuit. When the alloy cools it closes, forcing the contacts of the flexible circuit and the circuit board together. This is basically a flexible-circuit edge-card connector.

13.6.2.4 Coaxial Cable Connections.[116,125–127] A coaxial cable connector usually has a solid metal center pin that is inserted into a slotted cylinder during connector mating. This forces the cylinder to expand creating the contact force. The shielding sections are butt-end mated or overlapped. In many cases the shielding portions are threaded and constitute the connector housing itself (see Fig. 13.12).

There are many different coaxial connector types available, varying in size, bayonet or threaded mating, compatible cable type, and electrical performance. Most of these variations have a letter designation (e.g., BNC, SMA, N) that can be very confusing. Consult the references for more information. Reference 125 contains a listing of coaxial connector suppliers by connector type.

Coaxial interconnection systems are used where signal shielding is important and because of their low signal loss and small signal degradation (minimal reflections) even at high frequencies. Coaxial systems are expensive to use because they join only one I/O per connector. They have very low contact density when compared to almost any other connection technique. Nevertheless, because of their electrical advantages, they are the interconnection of choice for many high-frequency and/or interference-sensitive electronic systems. This is especially true for microwave systems where the important packaging characteristics can be quite different from most electronic systems. See Ref. 126 for a review of some of these differences.

The interconnection between a coaxial connector and a circuit board is handled in one of two ways. The first method is used when the circuit board is mounted in a housing (e.g., hybrid or microwave circuits mounted in a metal case). In this case the coax connector is usually part of, or mounted within, the circuit-board housing. The coax cable connector half is plugged into the housing as in a panel or rack connection. The connector housing and the circuit board housing (case) are usually grounded together. The signal line connection between the circuit board and the housing connector portion is most often a wire bond (see Fig. 13.12).

The second technique uses a connector body that is directly mated to the surface of the circuit board by soldering and/or screw mounting the connector onto the board (see Fig. 13.12). In this case the signal connection is made by a flat contact pad in the center, and the shielding is connected by mating the connector body to a contact region on the board or through hold down screws.

13.7 BOARD-TO-BACKPLANE INTERCONNECTIONS[128–132]

A backplane (or motherboard) is used to electrically interconnect a group of circuit boards (daughter boards) while providing mechanical support for those boards. Most backplanes are constructed using a multilayer printed-circuit board, perhaps with a metal support layer. In some cases the backplane is an aluminum panel for use with wire wrapping. Thus, the electrical interconnection between the daughter boards is made using circuit traces within the motherboard or by discrete wiring between wire wrap connections. Many backplane systems use both techniques simultaneously. Regardless of which backplane system is used, a wide range of connector types are available for connecting the daughter boards to the backplane as shown in Fig. 13.13. Reference 128 contains a listing of major motherboard–daughter-board connector suppliers. The important characteristics of backplane interconnections are the contact pitch, the number of contact rows that can be accommodated, the spacing that is possible between daughter boards, the backplane (or motherboard) routing requirements, and the electrical properties.

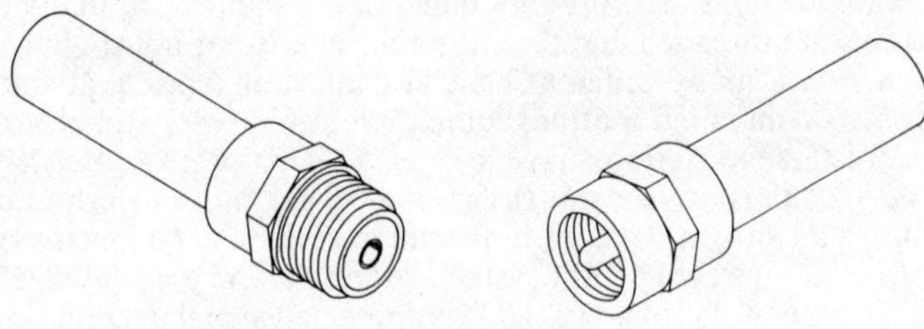

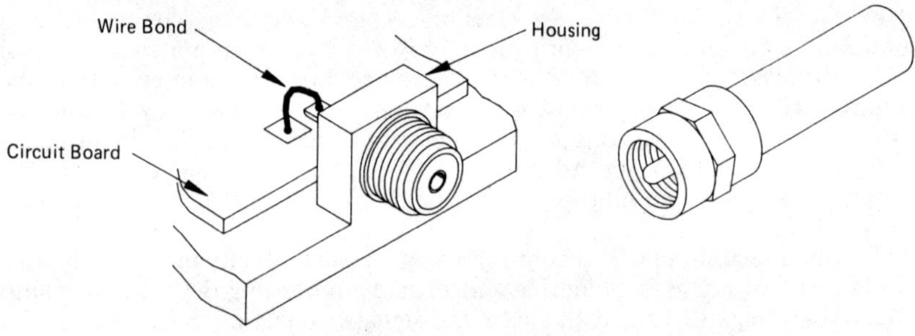

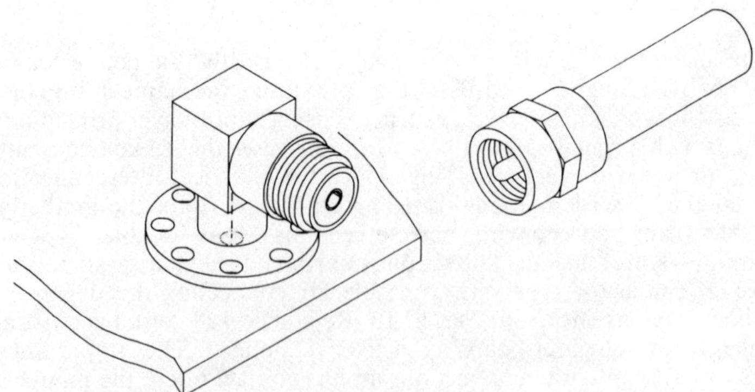

FIGURE 13.12 Coaxial connection techniques.

Perpendicular Mounting:

Two-Piece
(pin and socket
or post and box)

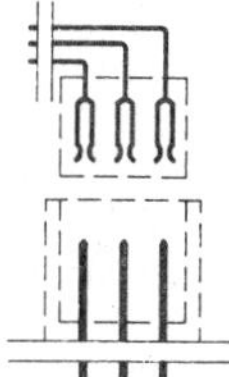

Edge Card
(one-piece)

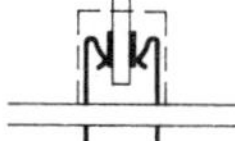

Burndy Surfmate

Flexible Circuit
with Metal Springs
or Elastomer

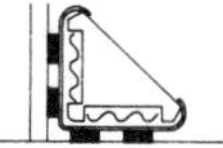

Viking Controlled Impedance
(signal row shown alternates
with dielectric and ground
rows not shown)

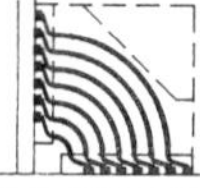

Parallel Mounting

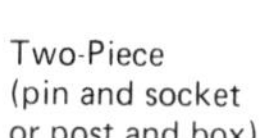

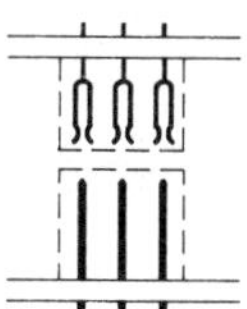

Deformable
Metal Contacts

FIGURE 13.13 Backplane connectors.

13.7.1 Perpendicular Board Mounting

In most applications the daughter boards are mounted perpendicularly to the backplane or motherboard (see Fig. 13.13). The daughter boards are inserted into a rack, or cage, and plugged into the motherboard. This method is widely used because it is very flexible and has many standard bus configurations.

Split backplanes, in which the daughter boards are mounted between two motherboards to increase the number of possible interconnections, are sometimes used. This technique has the disadvantage of requiring complete disassembly unless special ZIF connectors are used.

13.7.1.1 Edge-Card (One-Piece) Connectors. This type of backplane interconnection has been in use for many years and accounts for nearly half of the total backplane connector market. The connection techniques used with edge-card backplane systems are basically the same as those used for edge-card board-to-board interconnections as described in Sec. 13.6.2. Most edge-card backplane connectors are 100-mil pitch. The primary disadvantage of this type is the limited contact density because it uses only a single row of contacts on each side of the daughter board. In addition, high insertion forces are needed to ensure good contact despite warping and thickness variations in the daughter boards. The problem with high insertion forces has led to the development of LIF and ZIF backplane connector types. LIF and ZIF designs include mechanically actuated and shape memory alloy versions.

13.7.1.2 ***Post-and-Box (Two-Piece) Connectors.*** This type of interconnection also accounts for nearly half of the total backplane connector market. Post-and-box types usually use a 25-mil square pin with socket designs similar to those used for board-to-board interconnections. Either the socket housing or the pin (post) housing can be mounted on the motherboard. The advantages of this technique for backplane systems are lower insertion force and multiple-contact-row capability, which allows a greater contact density compared to edge-card types. Backplane connectors with up to four signal rows of contacts at 100-mil pitch are available. Teradyne has developed a five-row connector, called High Density Plus, in which the fifth row is dedicated to ground and/or power interconnection. LIF and ZIF versions of two-piece backplane connectors are also available.

13.7.1.3 ***Other Connectors.*** Two alternate motherboard–daughter-board interconnection techniques have been developed. The first technique uses deforming contacts of specific geometry in order to obtain the needed insertion and contact forces. An example of this is the Burndy Surfmate connector shown in Fig. 13.13. Another example is a controlled impedance backplane interconnection available from Viking. The Viking system uses alternating layers of ground, dielectric, signal contacts, dielectric, etc., arranged in a row, which is then clamped to the motherboard. The daughter board is inserted and pressure-mated to the contact region by a hardware system.

The second technique uses flexible circuits that are held in place by a hardware system which generates the contact force. A metal spring mechanism can be used as in a Berg Electronics backplane connector, where the springs are actuated by rotation of a cam system. Compression of an elastomer backer can also be used, as in the Rogers Invisicon system. The advantages of using a flexible-circuit system are contact density and control of electrical properties. The flexible circuit can be soldered to the motherboard or to the daughter board, if desired, because in most cases only one easily mateable-demateable interconnection is needed.

13.7.2 Parallel Board Mounting (Stacking Bus)

Mounting the daughter boards perpendicularly to the motherboard limits the number of boards that can be accommodated because of the limited size of the motherboard. It also constrains the number of connectors that will fit on the motherboard and the total number of I/Os that can be connected. In addition, the signal paths can be very long, which creates electrical problems as signal speeds increase. For these reasons many system designers are utilizing stacking connectors in which the daughter boards are connected in series. Stacking connectors can be adapted for many applications and eliminate a separate backplane.

They avoid the major difficulties discussed above and readily allow for adding boards. Unfortunately, they require disassembly of the entire system to replace a board.

The primary connector type used for these applications are post-and-box types, similar to those used for perpendicular mounting. These require the use of plated through-holes in each board, which may limit routing and add complexity to the boards. Avoiding this disadvantage are deformable metal contact types such as ITT-Cannon's Parallel Interconnect, Teledyne Kinetics Surface Stack connectors, or similar designs available from Viking. These connectors typically use sideways-mounted V-shaped conductors. The conductors are mounted in a housing and the boards are clamped together onto the housing. The housing controls the amount of contact compression. *Z*-axis connector types (described in Sec. 13.5.4) such as Zebra strip, metal-on-elastomer, the area array connector, or Fuzz Buttons can also be used in a similar fashion.

ACKNOWLEDGMENT

I would like to thank Sharon Fitts for her excellent work in executing the figures included in this chapter.

LIST OF TRADEMARKS

Button Board is a trademark of TRW, Incorporated.

Cambiflex is a trademark of Midland-Ross Corporation.

Cryocon is a trademark of Raychem Corporation.

Fuzz Button is a trademark of Tecknit, Incorporated.

Gold Dot is a trademark of Hughes Aircraft Company.

GTH is a trademark of Burndy Corporation.

High Density Plus is a trademark of Teradyne, Incorporated.

HPT is a trademark of Molex, Incorporated.

Invisicon is a trademark of Rogers Corporation.

Parallel Interconnect is a trademark of ITT-Cannon.

RO2500 is a trademark of Rogers Corporation.

RO2800 is a trademark of Rogers Corporation.

Sculptured Circuits is a trademark of Advanced Circuit Technology, Incorporated.

SNAP is a trademark of Advanced Circuit Technology, Incorporated.

STAX is a trademark of PCK Elastomerics, Incorporated.

Surface Stack is a trademark of Teledyne Kinetics.

Surfmate is a trademark of Burndy Corporation.

Zebra Strip is a trademark of Tecknit, Incorporated.

REFERENCES

1. G. L. Ginsberg (ed.), *Connectors and Interconnections Handbook,* Electronic Connector Study Group, Inc., Fort Washington, Penn., 1978.
2. R. Holm, *Electric Contacts,* 4th ed., Springer-Verlag, Berlin, 1981.
3. J. P. B. Williamson, "The Microworld of the Contact Spot," *Electrical Contacts/1981—Proceedings of the Holm Conference on Electrical Contacts,* Illinois Institute of Technology, Chicago, September 1981.
4. K. E. Pitney, *Ney Contact Manual,* J.M. Ney Company, Bloomfield, Conn., 1973.
5. L. Jedynak, "Where the (Switch) Action Is," *IEEE Spectrum,* October 1973, pp. 56–62.
6. J. P. Bare, "Preventing Contact Degradation," *Connection Technology,* September 1986, pp. 51–56, reprinted from *Proceedings of the Thirty-First Meeting of the IEEE Holm Conference on Electrical Contact Phenomena,* Chicago, IEEE, New York, 1985.
7. M. Antler, "Survey of Contact Fretting in Electrical Connectors," *Electrical Contacts—1984—Proceedings of the 12th International Conference on Contact Phenomena and the Thirtieth Annual Holm Conference on Electrical Contacts.* Illinois Institute of Technology, Chicago, 1984, pp. 3–22.
8. P. A. Clayton, *Handbook of Electronic Connectors,* Electrochemical Publications Limited, Ayr, Scotland, 1982.
9. R. Sard and R. G. Baker, "Significance of Contact Finish Requirements," *Plating and Surface Finishing,* April 1980.
10. R. G. Baker and T. A. Palumbo, "Contact Materials—A Science in Transition," *Plating and Surface Finishing,* December, 1983, pp. 63–66.
11. C. F. Coombs, Jr., *Printed Circuits Handbook,* 3d ed., McGraw-Hill, New York, 1988.
12. American Society for Metals, *Metals Handbook Ninth Edition,* Vol. 6: *Welding, Brazing, and Soldering,* American Society for Metals, Metals Park, Ohio, 1983.
13. F. A. Lowenheim, *Electroplating—Fundamentals of Surface Finishing,* McGraw-Hill, New York, 1978.
14. T. Gray, "Thin Film Deposition Technology for Hybrid Circuits," *Hybrid Circuit Technology,* September 1987, pp. 45–47.
15. A. Rose, "Composition and Manufacturing of Thick Film Inks," *Hybrid Circuit Technology,* September 1986, pp. 29–34.
16. The Institute for Interconnecting and Packaging Electronic Circuits, *Gold Handbook,* IPC, Evanston, Ill., 1981.
17. H. G. Tompkins and M. R. Pinnel, "On the Rate Controlling Step of Copper Diffusion/Oxidation Through Gold," *J. Appl. Phys.,* **50** (11), 7243–7244. (1979).
18. M. R. Pinnel, "Diffusion-Related Behaviour of Gold in Thin Film Systems," *Gold Bulletin,* **12** (2): 62–71 (1979).
19. M. Antler and M. H. Drozdowicz, "Gold-Plated Contacts: The Relationship Between Porosity and Contact Resistance on Elevated Temperature Aging," *Plating and Surface Finishing,* September 1976, pp. 19–21.
20. H. C. Angus, "Properties and Behaviour of Precious-Metal Electrodeposits for Electrical Contacts," *Transactions of the Institute of Metal Finishing,* **39** (1): 20–28 (1962).
21. M. Antler, M. H. Drozdowicz, and C. A. Haque, "Connector Contact Materials: Effect of Environment on Clad Palladium, Palladium-Silver Alloys and Gold Electrodeposits," *IEEE Transactions on Components, Hybrids, and Manufacturing Technology,* **CHMT-4** (4): 482–492 (1981).
22. M. R. Pinnel, H. G. Tompkins, and J. A. Augis, "The Effect of Gold Film Grain Size on Copper Diffusion and Surface Accumulation by Oxidation," *Microstructural Science,* vol. 8, Elsevier North-Holland, Amsterdam, 1980, pp. 14–27.

23. M. E. Peel, "Evaluation of tin-lead as a contact finish," *Electronic Packaging and Production,* December 1980, pp. 172–184.

24. D. W. Rice, K. Bredfeld, and J. Kral, "Corrosion Inhibiting Lubricants for Separable Connectors," *Proceedings of the 35th Electronic Components Conference,* Washington, D.C., IEEE, New York, 1985, pp. 127–131.

25. J. H. Whitely, "Reflections on Contacts and Connector Engineering," *Proceedings of the 33rd IEEE Holm Conference on Electrical Contacts,* Chicago, IEEE, New York, September 1987.

26. R. A. Pope and D. J. Schoenbauer, "Temperature Rise and Its Importance to Connector Uses," *Proceedings of the 37th Electronic Components Conference,* Boston, IEEE, New York, May 1987, pp. 24–31.

27. O. A. Horna, "Connectors in Very-High-Speed Digital Circuits," *IEEE Transactions on Parts, Hybrids, and Packaging,* **PHP-9** (4): 256–261 (1973).

28. R. K. Southard, "High-Speed Signal Pathways from Board to Board," *Proceedings of the IEEE Wescon Conference,* IEEE, New York, 1981, pp. 1–8.

29. W. S. Fujitsubo, "Controlled Impedance Interconnections: Theories, Problems, Applications—Parts 1 and 2," *Electrionics,* November 1986, pp. 56–58, and December 1986, pp. 55–56.

30. M. Gailus, "Making High Speed Connections—Parts 1 and 2," *Connection Technology,* November 1986, pp. 38–42, and January 1987, pp. 35–39.

31. J. E. Johnston, "Good Interconnect Design Optimizes IC Performance," *Computer Design,* October 1986.

32. M. W. Gailus and J. A. Siemon, "Characterization of Connector Performance for High-Speed Signal Applications," *VLSI Design,* March 1985, pp. 66–70.

33. E. E. Davidson, "Electrical Design of a High Speed Computer Package," *IBM Journal of Research and Development,* **26** (3): 349–361 (1982).

34. W. H. Abbott, "The Development and Performance Characteristics of Mixed Flowing Gas Test Environments," *Electrical Contacts—1987, Proceedings of the Thirty-Third IEEE Holm Conference on Electrical Contacts,* Chicago, IEEE, New York, September 1987, pp. 63–78.

35. L. White, "Development of a New Connector Dust Test," *Electrical Contacts—1987, Proceedings of the Thirty-Third IEEE Holm Conference on Electrical Contacts,* Chicago, IEEE, New York, September 1987, pp. 87–92.

36. Mil-C-55302C, *Military Specification—Connectors, Printed Circuit Subassembly and Accessories,* Department of Defense, Washington, D.C., January 1980.

37. Mil-Std-1344, *Military Standard—Test Methods for Electrical Connectors,* Department of Defense, Washington, D.C., September 1977.

38. EIA Standard RS-364, *Standard Test Procedures for Low Frequency (Below 3 MHz) Electrical Connectors,* Electronic Industries Association, Washington, D.C., December 1969.

39. *Test Methods Manual,* The Institute for Interconnecting and Packaging Electronic Circuits, Evanston, Ill., 1984.

40. Mil-Std-202F, *Military Standard—Test Methods for Electronic and Electrical Component Parts,* Department of Defense, Washington, D.C., April 1980.

41. B 539-70, *Standard Methods for Measuring Contact Resistance of Electrical Connections (Static Contacts),* American Society for Testing and Materials, Philadelphia, Penn., 1975.

42. T. Thomas, "The Reality Behind the Theory of Four-Terminal LRC Measurements," *Evaluation Engineering,* September 1987, pp. 94–102.

43. M. Peel, "Constriction Resistance—The Key to Dry Circuit-Contact Performance," *Electronic Packaging and Production Magazine,* January 1972, pp. 90–100.

44. *Electromechanical Components for Electronic Equipment; Basic Testing Procedures and Measuring Methods,* pt. 3, Current Carrying Capacity Tests—IEC Standard Publication 512-3, International Electrotechnical Commission, Geneva, Switzerland, 1976.

45. W. L. Brodsky, "Testing of Design Parameters for Zero Insertion Force Connector," *Proceedings of the 37th Electronics Components Conference,* Electronics Industry Association, Boston, Mass., May 1987, pp. 32–40.

46. Standard RS-364-50, *Sand and Dust Test Procedure for Electrical Connectors,* Test Procedure 50, Electronic Industries Associates, Washington, D.C., October 1983.

47. IPC-FC-201, *Guidelines and Test Methods for Use of Flat Cables as Digital Signal Transmission Lines,* Institute for Interconnecting and Packaging Electronic Circuits, Evanston, Ill., August 1973.

48. IPC 2.5.18, *Characteristic Impedance Flat Cables (Unbalanced),* Institute for Interconnecting and Packaging Electronic Circuits, Evanston, Ill., July 1984.

49. IPC 2.5.21, *Digital Unbalanced Crosstalk, Flat Cable,* Institute for Interconnecting and Packaging Electronic Circuits, Evanston, Ill., March 1984.

50. C. Theorin and H. Van Deusen, "Differential TDR Testing Techniques," *Connection Technology,* March 1988, pp. 35–41, reprinted from *Twentieth Annual Connectors and Interconnection Technology Symposium,* Electronic Connector Study Group, Fort Washington, Penn., 1987.

51. S. J. Krumbein, "Porosity Testing of Contact Platings: Parts 1 and 2," *Connection Technology,* January 1988, pp. 21–26 and February 1988, pp. 27–29, reprinted from *Twentieth Annual Connectors and Interconnection Technology Symposium,* Electronic Connector Study Group, Fort Washington, Penn., 1987.

52. M. Clark and J. M. Leeds, "A Sulphur Dioxide Porosity Test for Coatings of Gold and the Platinum Metals on Substrates of Copper and its Alloys, Nickel, and Silver," *Transactions of the Institute of Metal Finishing,* 1968, pp. 81–86.

53. B 583-83, *Porosity in Gold Coatings on Metal Substrates,* American Society for Testing and Materials, Philadelphia, Penn., 1983.

54. F. I. Nobel, B. D. Ostrow, and D. W. Thomson, "Porosity Testing of Gold Deposits," *Plating,* October 1965.

55. Standard 364-53, *Nitric Acid Vapor Test, Gold Finish Test Procedure for Electrical Connectors,* Test Procedure 53, Electronic Industries Association, Washington, D.C., April 1986.

56. D 150-81, *Standard Test Methods for A-C Loss Characteristics and Permittivity (Dielectric Constant) of Solid Electrical Insulating Materials,* Sec. 10, Vol. 10.02, American Society for Testing and Materials, Philadelphia, Penn., 1981.

57. D 3380-82, *Standard Test Method for Permittivity (Dielectric Constant) and Dissipation Factor of Plastic-Based Microwave Circuit Substrates,* Sec. 10, Vol. 10.02, American Society for Testing and Materials, Philadelphia, Penn., 1982.

58. D 2520-81, *Standard Test Methods for Complex Permittivity (Dielectric Constant) of Solid Electrical Insulating Materials at Microwave Frequencies and Temperatures to 1650°C,* Sec. 10, Vol. 10.02, American Society for Testing and Materials, Philadelphia, Penn., 1981.

59. S. T. Riches and G. L. White, "Wire Bonding to GaAs Electronic Devices," *Hybrid Circuits,* No. 14, September 1987, pp. 75–79, reprinted from *European Microelectronics Conference,* Bournemouth, England, June 1987.

60. *Device Attachment to RT/duroid Laminates,* Rogers Corporation, Rogers., Conn., January 1985.

61. T. Goida, "IC Assembly/Packaging," *Proceedings of the Advanced VLSI Packaging Course,* University of California Berkeley, January 1988.

62. D. L. Brownell, "Flip Chips—The Real World," *Proceedings of 1973 ISHM Conference,* 3B-2-1, International Society for Hybrid Microelectronics, Montgomery, Alabama, 1973.

63. D. L. Brownell and G. C. Waite, "Solder Bump Flip Chip Fabrication Using Standard Chip and Wire Integrated Circuit Layout, Part A, Semiconductor Chip Attachment with Small Bump Flip Chips," *Proceedings of the 1974 ISHM Conference,* International Society for Hybrid Microelectronics, Montgomery, Alabama, 1974.

64. M. Schnieder, "Flip Chip Bonding Offers Packaging Alternative," *Hybrid Circuit Technology,* March 1988, pp. 29–31.

65. N. Matsui, S. Sasaki, and T. Ohsaki, "VLSI Chip Interconnection Technology Using Stacked Solder Bumps," *Proceedings of the 37th Electronic Components Conference,* IEEE, New York, 1973, pp. 573–578.

66. P. W. Rima, "The Basics of Tape Automated Bonding," *Hybrid Circuit Technology,* November 1984, pp. 15–21.

67. T. Dixon, "TAB Technology Tackles High Density Interconnections," *Electronic Packaging and Production,* December 1984, pp. 34–39.

68. M. Eleccion, "Tape-Automated Bonding Pushes in New Directions," *Electronics,* September 1987, pp. 90–92.

69. P. W. Rima, "TAB Gains Momentum," *Connection Technology,* August 1987, pp. 28–32.

70. M. Mahalingham and J. Andrews, "TAB vs. Wire Bond—Relative Thermal Performance," *Proceedings of the 37th Electronic Components Conference,* IEEE, New York, 1987, pp. 164–170.

71. S. Chin, "The Chip Carrier's Checkered Progress," *Electronic Products,* July 1986, pp. 43–48.

72. R. B. McPhillips (ed.), *Surface Mounting Directory,* D. Brown Associates, Warrington, Penn., 1984.

73. N. Janota, "Chip Packaging and Board Assembly Trends," *Connection Technology,* May 1985.

74. R. Hannemann, "Physical Technology for VLSI Systems," *ICCD 1986—Proceedings of the IEEE International Conference on Computer Design: VLSI in Computers,* Port Chester, N.Y., IEEE, New York, October 1986.

75. E. M. Foster, "The Electrical Effect of Single-Chip CMOS Packages," *Proceedings of the 37th Electronic Components Conference,* Boston, Mass., IEEE, New York, May 1987, pp. 342–353.

76. L. T. Olson and R. R. Sloma, "Chip Carrier Enhancements for Improving Electrical Performance," *Proceedings of the 35th Electronic Components Conference,* Washington, D.C., IEEE, New York, May 1985, pp. 372–378.

77. C. J. Stanghan and B. M. Macdonald, "Electrical Characterisation of Packages for High Speed Integrated Circuits," *Proceedings of the 35th Electronic Components Conference,* Washington, D.C., IEEE, New York, May 1985, pp. 356–364.

78. S. Chin, "Surface-mounted Components Are Not All Alike," *Electronic Products,* October 1985, pp. 50–57.

79. M. F. Blackshaw and F. J. Dance, "The Design, Manufacture, and Assembly of High Pin Count Plastic Pin Grid Array Packages," *Proceedings of the 35th Electronic Components Conference,* Washington, D.C., IEEE, New York, May 1985, pp. 199–205.

80. J. N. Snook, "Substrates for the Hybrid Industry," *Hybrid Circuit Technology,* February 1987, pp. 15–16.

81. R. D. Jones, *Hybrid Circuit Design and Manufacture,* Marcel Dekker, New York, 1982.

82. G. S. Szekely, "Glossary of Hybrid Terms—Parts 1, 2, and 3," *Hybrid Circuit Technology,* January 1985, pp. 35–40, February 1985, pp. 27–31, and March 1985, pp. 49–53.

83. G. Clatterbaugh and H. K. Charles, Jr., "Electrical Characterisation and Design of Multilayer Thick Film Circuit Boards for High Speed Digital Applications," *Hybrid Circuits,* No. 13, May 1987, pp. 77–82.

84. F. J. Belcourt and T. A. Lane, "Electrical CAD Analysis for Multilayer Package Design," *Hybrid Circuits,* No. 14, September 1987, pp. 38–41.

85. M. Terasawa, S. Minami, and J. Rubin, "A Comparison of Thin Film, Thick Film, and Co-fired High Density Ceramic Multilayer with the Combined Technology: T&T HDCM (Thin Film and Thick Film High Density Ceramic Module)," *Proceedings of the 3rd Annual Electronics Packaging Conference,* Itasca, Ill., International Electronics Packaging Society, Glen Ellyn, Ill., 1983.

86. F. C. Rydwansky, L. M. Higgins III, and J. L. Thomas, "Multilayer Ceramic Modules and Motherboards," *Proceedings of the 3rd Annual Electronics Packaging Conference,* Itasca, Ill., International Electronics Packaging Society, Glen Ellyn, Ill., 1983, pp. 399–406.

87. A. V. Hall and F. B. Zykoff, "Multilayer Ceramic Via Formation Technology," *Proceedings of the Fourth Annual Electronics Packaging Conference,* Baltimore, Md., International Electronics Packaging Society, Glen Ellyn, Ill., October 1984, pp. 518–524.

88. D. Balderes and M. L. White, "Package Effects on CPU Performance of Large Commercial Processors," *Proceedings of the 35th Electronic Components Conference,* Washington, D.C., IEEE, New York, May 1985, pp. 351–355.

89. R. C. Landis, "High-Speed Packaging for GaAs Interconnection," *Proceedings of the 35th Electronic Components Conference,* Washington, D.C., IEEE, New York, May 1985, pp. 384–388.

90. A. J. Blodgett, Jr., "Microelectronic Packaging," *Scientific American,* July 1983, pp. 86–96.

91. M. A. Schmitt and B. K. Bhattacharyya, "Electrical Characterization of a Multilayer Ceramic Pin Grid Array Package," *Proceedings of the 37th Electronic Components Conference,* Boston, Mass., IEEE, New York, May 1987, pp. 370–376.

92. J. Lyman, "The Door is Opening for Chip-On-Board Assembly," *Electronics,* December 18, 1986, pp. 101–102.

93. S. Chin, "Navigating the Surface-mounted Path," *Electronic Products,* October 15, 1985, pp. 57–58.

94. R. P. Prasad, "Designing Surface Mount for Manufacturability," *Printed Circuit Design,* May 1987, pp. 8–11.

95. T. Hilvers, "Surface Mount Standards, Specifications and Guidelines," *Printed Circuit Assembly,* March 1988, pp. 16–18.

96. C. Mangin and S. McClelland, "Characterization of Surface Mount Assembly Equipment," *Printed Circuit Assembly,* March 1988, pp. 10–15.

97. W. Engelmaier, "Surface Mount Attachment Reliability of Clip-Leaded Ceramic Chip Carriers on FR-4 Circuit Boards," International Electronics Packaging Society, Wheaton, Ill., *IEPS Journal* **9** (4): 3–11 1988).

98. G. Cherian, "Use of Discrete Solder Columns to Mount LCCC's on Glass/Epoxy Printed Circuit Boards," *Proceedings of the Fourth Annual International Electronics Packaging Conference,* Baltimore, Md., International Electronics Packaging Society, Wheaton, Ill., October 1984, pp. 702–710.

99. S. H. Leibson, "IC-Socket Innovations Keep Pace With Improvements In Packaging Technologies," *EDN,* September 19, 1985, pp. 61–76.

100. J. Bussert, "Socketing Military VLSI Chips," *Connection Technology,* October 1987, pp. 22–25.

101. C. T. Carter, "Packaging Trends for Burn-In Testing," *Connection Technology,* October 1986, pp. 16–20.

102. E. H. Key, "Development of a New Drawn-Wire Compliant Pin," *Connection Technology,* May 1988, pp. 38–41, reprinted from the *Twentieth Annual Connectors and Interconnections Technology Symposium,* Electronic Connector Study Group, Inc., Fort Washington, Penn., 1987.

103. F. J. Dance, "Compliant Press-Fit Pins for Solderless Backplane Assembly," *Connection Technology,* May 1988, pp. 26–30.

104. D. S. Goodman and J. W. Anhalt, "Design Notes for a ZIF Pin Array System," *Connection Technology,* March 1985, pp. 24–27.

105. R. Flot, J. McCullough, and T. McGaffigan, "Shape-Memory Effect Alloys as an Interconnection Technology for High Density IC Packages," *Proceedings of the Fourth Annual Electronics Packaging Conference,* Baltimore, Md., International Electronics Packaging Society, Wheaton, Ill., October 1984, pp. 717–730.

106. S. L. Spitz, "Surface-Mount Connectors: More Than Through-Hole Devices," *Electronic Packaging and Production,* April 1987, pp. 22–25.

107. J. Rose, "Surface Mount Connectors: Where the Industry Stands Today," *Connection Technology,* November 1986, pp. 35–39.

108. R. T. Bjornsen, Jr., "Application Guidelines for Elastomeric Connectors," *Connection Technology,* March 1988, pp. 21–22.

109. R. Smolley, "Button Board—A New Technology Interconnect," *Proceedings of the Fourth Annual International Electronics Packaging Conference,* Baltimore, Md., International Electronics Packaging Society, Wheaton, Ill., October 1984, pp. 75–91.

110. R. G. Dawson, "Button Board: The Short-Cut Connector," *Connection Technology,* November 1986, pp. 15–16.

111. S. S. Simpson and M. S. Zifcak, "Pinless Grid Array Connector," *Proceedings of the Sixth Annual International Electronics Packaging Conference,* San Diego, Calif., International Electronics Packaging Society, Wheaton, Ill., November 1986, pp. 453–464.

112. C. H. Harper (ed.), *Handbook of Wiring, Cabling, and Interconnecting for Electronics,* McGraw-Hill, New York, 1972.

113. D. Karmann and R. Poklemba, "Planar Cable Shielding," *Connection Technology,* May 1987, pp. 27–30.

114. C. Shmatovich, "Connector, Cable Crosstalk in Controlled Impedance Cable Assemblies," *Electronics,* August 1984, pp. 51–54.

115. C. Shmatovich, "Digital Signals Demand High Cable Performance," *Electronic Products,* October 1, 1984.

116. E. Trompeter, "Electronic Systems Wiring and Cable," *T-15C Catalog,* Trompeter Electronics, Inc., Westlake Village, Calif.

117. S. V. Worth and G. F. Zisk, "The 0.025″ Micro Mini Connector System: Miniaturization Without Electrical Degradation," *Connection Technology,* December 1986, pp. 21–23.

118. C. Shmatovich, "Constructing Reliable Vehicles for Digital Signal Transmission," *Electronics,* August 1984.

119. "Planar Cable Connector Suppliers," *Connection Technology,* May 1987, pp. 28–29.

120. D. Weiss, "Flat Cable Connector Applications," *Connection Technology,* June 1986, pp. 26–29.

121. R. J. Pommer, "Gold Dot—A Nonconnector Approach for Flat Cable Interconnections," Technical Paper IPC-TP-160, presented at Institute of Printed Circuits 20th

Annual Meeting, Orlando, Fla., Institute of Printed Circuits, Evanston, Ill., April 1977.

122. M. J. Howett, "A High Density Interconnect System for Military Applications," *Connection Technology,* January 1988, pp. 13–15.

123. J. M. Mersereau, S. S. Simpson, and H. B. Gordon,"Rogers Solderless System," *Proceedings of the Fourth Annual International Electronics Packaging Conference,* Baltimore, Md., International Electronics Packaging Society, Wheaton, Ill., October 1984, pp. 43–53.

124. J. F. Krumme, "Electrically Actuated ZIF Connectors Use Shape Memory Alloys," *Connection Technology,* April 1987, pp. 41–44.

125. P. Wagner, "Designing Coaxial Transmission Systems," *Connection Technology,* March 1987, pp. 18–23.

126. H. W. Markstein, "Miniaturized Microwave Packaging—A Different Game," *Electronic Packaging and Production,* August 1982, pp. 46–50.

127. J. Morelli, "Coaxial Connector Trends," *Connection Technology,* March 1986, pp. 16–19.

128. J. Rose, "PCB Connector Designers Guide," *Connection Technology,* April 1987, pp. 35–40.

129. C. M. Hayward, "Backplane Design Considerations," *Connection Technology,* October 1986, pp. 35–40.

130. G. Lawrence, "Connectors Boost System," *Electronics Week,* January 21, 1985, pp. 51–54.

131. C. Van Veen, "The Evolution of Backplane Interconnection Systems," *VLSI Design,* March 1985, p. 69.

132. R. W. Rollings, "Interconnecting Digital Circuits: Surface-Mounted Double Density Backplane Connector," *Proceedings of the Technical Program of the National Electronic Packaging and Production Conference,* Anaheim, Calif., Cahners Exposition Group, Des Plains, Ill., February 1985.

CHAPTER 14
TRANSCEIVER TECHNOLOGY AND DESIGN

R. V. Balakrishnan
National Semiconductor Corporation
Santa Clara, California

14.1 INTRODUCTION

Until the mid-1980s, the backplane transceiver had received little or no attention as a critical component of the bus system. However, rapid increases in bus bandwidth requirements have created significant interest and focus in this area. The system designers have come to realize that the bus transceiver design plays a dominant role in solving some fundamental problems that limit bus transfer rates and data integrity. A better understanding of the backplane physics in combination with the latest IC (integrated-circuit) technology has led to transceiver designs that overcome these limitations, extending the bus bandwidth by an order of magnitude. And, at the same time, these new designs reduce power requirements and improve data integrity (better noise and crosstalk immunity).

Selecting the transceiver has been an afterthought in most bus designs in the past. When the design runs into speed, noise, or power problems, it has been addressed and fixed in an ad hoc fashion, resulting in reduced speed, increased power requirement, intermittent or unreliable operation, and related field-service problems. In part, this is due to the lack of understanding of the backplane physics by the system design engineers who are not comfortable with the subject. As will be evident throughout this chapter, a thorough understanding of the backplane physics is a must for designing or selecting the transceiver. Although the backplane physics is not covered in detail as an independent subject within this chapter, it is addressed in other parts of this book and in the reference materials indicated. However, a brief, intuitive explanation of the physical phenomenon that is sufficient for understanding the problem is provided. In addition, formulas, both derived and empirical, are included as tools for designing bus systems. The emphasis throughout this chapter is on providing practical design information for the design engineer and not on the theoretical analysis or proof.

14.2 THE TECHNOLOGY EVOLUTION

Since the 1960s, transistor transistor logic (TTL) has been the most popular logic signaling standard for interconnection between digital ICs and functional blocks. It was based on bipolar technology with saturated logic levels. Figure 14.1 shows a typical circuit diagram of a TTL gate with totem-pole output, along with the equivalent circuit of idealized switches in two logical states. When the input voltage is higher than the required minimum input high level V_{IH} (2 V) the lower output transistor is turned ON and the upper output transistor is turned OFF. This forces the output down to a voltage that is less than or equal to the guaranteed output low level V_{OL} of 0.4 to 0.6 V. If a voltage less than the required input low level V_{IL} (0.8 V) is applied to the input, the lower output transistor turns OFF and the upper output transistor turns ON. The output level gets pulled up to about two diode levels below the +5 V supply rail (approximately 3.5 V), which is guaranteed to be higher than the minimum output level V_{OH} of 2.4 V.

As a side note, it is important to avoid both switches being ON at the same time, as this will create a low impedance path between the supply voltage V_{CC} and ground. However, practical designs do have some amount of overlap that varies from design to design. In special high-current TTL drivers used for driving buses,

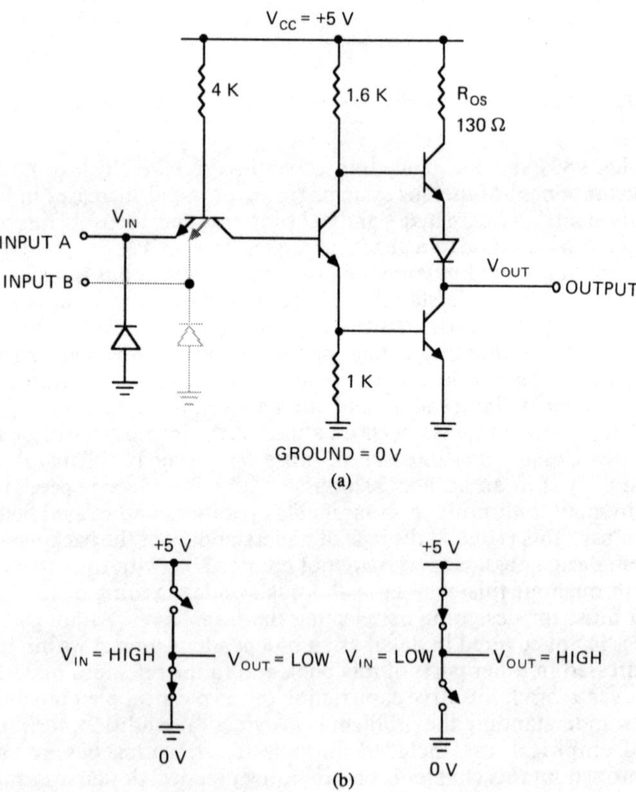

FIGURE 14.1 (*a*) A typical TTL gate circuit; (*b*) simplified switch diagram.

the overlap could cause severe noise spikes on V_{CC} and ground lines, especially when multiple drives switch simultaneously. This is a drawback of the totem-pole TTL output. Although it is possible to practically eliminate the overlap by special circuitry, there is usually a penalty in terms of increased delay and an undesirable step in the output waveform.

Some of the TTL input characteristics that are important to note are the following: a reasonable amount of sink current (usually 1 mA) is needed to pull the input down, but there is high input impedance when a high level is applied; the input threshold is basically two diode drops and therefore can vary widely (0.8 V to 2 V) with temperature.

Because totem-pole outputs have active pull-up and pull-down devices with low impedance, they provide fast switching times and good noise immunity. They are very good for transferring data in one direction, from one output to one or more inputs. But they cannot be used in shared-bus operations with multiple drivers since the driver always forces the line to 0 or 1.

14.2.1 The Open-Collector Driver

One way to address this problem is by replacing the active pull-up device with a passive one as shown in Fig. 14.2. Such an output is called an open-collector (OC)

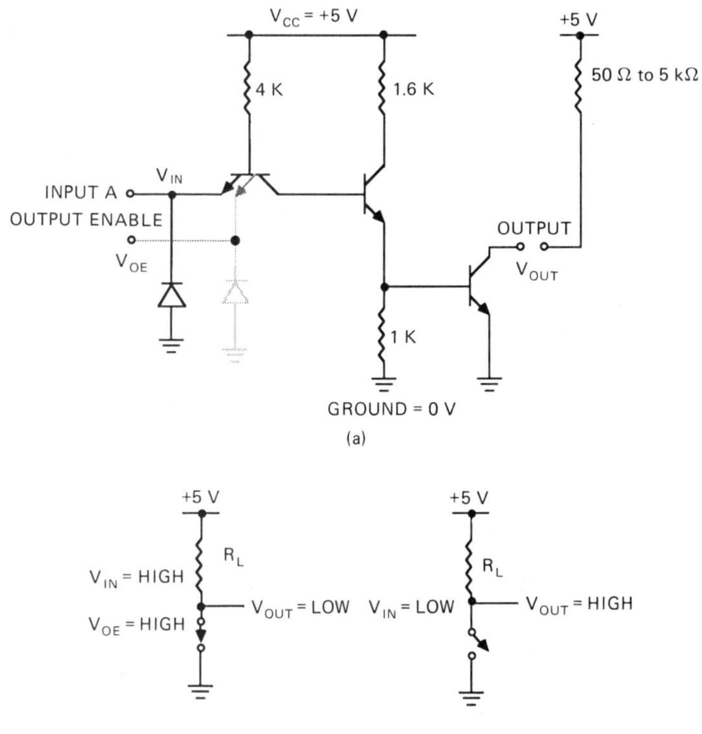

FIGURE 14.2 (*a*) A typical open-collector TTL gate circuit; (*b*) simplified switch diagram.

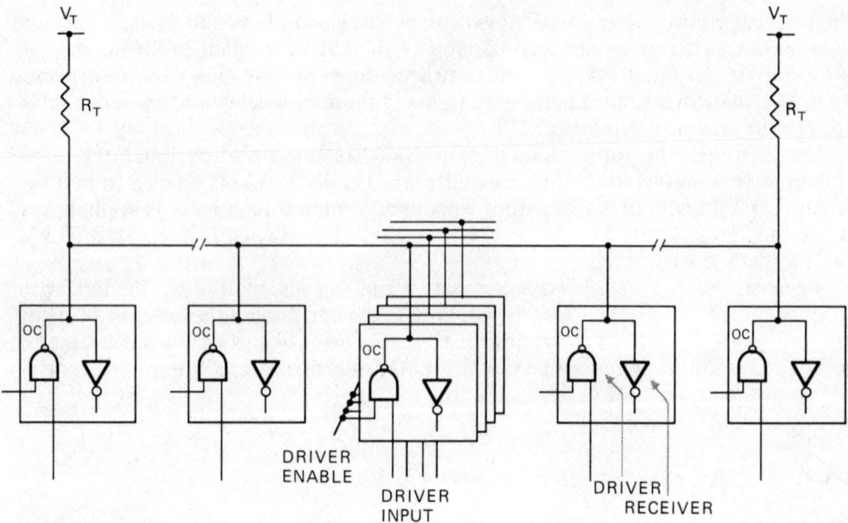

FIGURE 14.3 A bidirectional open-collector bus.

output because the pull-up resistor is usually external to the device shared among many drivers. The open-collector device has an active low state and a high-impedance state that also corresponds to the high state. This allows multiple drivers to share the same line as long as only one of the drivers is active at any given time, with the others being in the high-impedance state. Figure 14.3 shows an open-collector bus with pull-up resistors that also act as terminators. By using a two-input NAND function for the driver both data and control inputs can be provided. On a parallel bus the control inputs of multiple drivers on the same board can be connected together to provide a common control line.

When multiple open-colllector driver outputs are connected and then activated at the same time, the resulting output is an OR of all signals (Fig. 14.4).

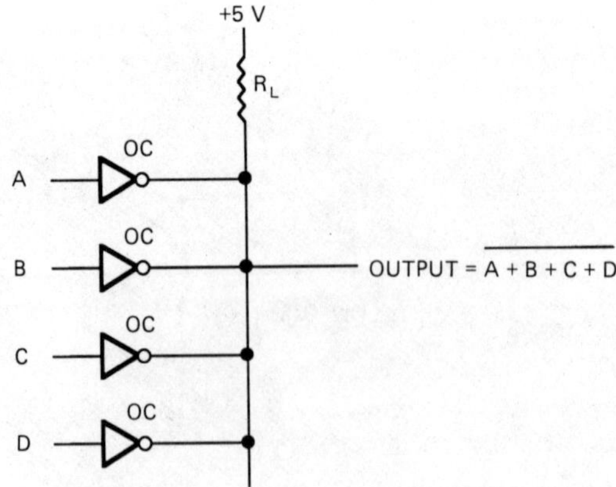

FIGURE 14.4 Wire-ORing using open-collector devices.

This is called wire-ORing and is a very useful feature of the open-collector drivers. The wire-OR feature is needed on some control lines on most buses.

When wire-ORing on a transmission line such as a backplane bus, it is important to realize that there is a fundamental phenomenon called wire-OR glitch that can occur during active to high-impedance transition. The glitch can be up to one round-trip delay in width (twice the one-way propagation delay of the line t_p) and the receivers connected to the wire-OR lines should have the capability to reject them. A detailed explanation of this phenomenon is given by Theus and Gustavson.[1]

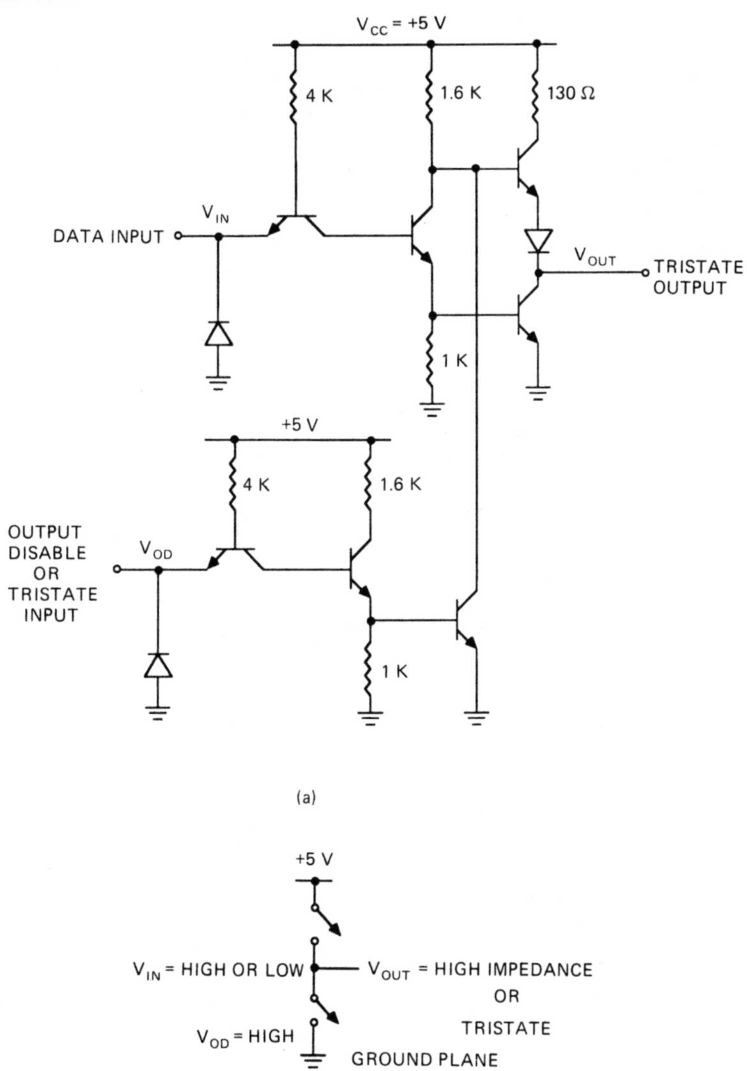

FIGURE 14.5 (*a*) A TTL Tristate output circuit; (*b*) simplified switch diagram.

There are some drawbacks, however, to open-collector drivers. Passive pull-up devices are slow, especially when driving large capacitive loads. Using smaller resistors to overcome this problem increases dc power dissipation. Also, there is always dc power dissipated when the output is low, whereas the totem-pole devices do not have any load current except while switching.

14.2.2 The Tristate Driver

A more elegant solution was provided through the invention of Tristate logic. By turning both the lower and upper transistors of the totem-pole output OFF using a separate control path that overrides the input (Fig. 14.5), the output can be put in a third high-impedance state, called the Tristate. In this way, multiple Tristate drivers can share a bus line as long as all but one are forced into Tristate. This provides the best of both worlds, the high-speed and no-dc-current advantages of totem-pole devices and the busing capability of open-collector devices. For this reason, Tristate drivers have been the most popular devices for driving buses to this day.

TTL technology has advanced rapidly since the early 1970s through several generations of product families, such as Schottky TTL (STTL), low-power Schottky TTL (LS), advanced Schottky TTL (AS), advanced LS (ALS), etc. The addition of Schottky clamps to avoid saturation of transistors and continuous improvements in bipolar IC and hence technology has given way to ever-increasing speeds. The latest TTL family, Fairchild's advanced Schottky TTL, known as FAST, has propagation delays of 3–4 ns per gate and rise and fall times of 1 to 4 ns.[2] With the increase in speed, the limitations of TTL transceivers for bus applications have become apparent. In order to understand the issues involved, it is necessary to review the transmission line theory as it applies to buses.

14.3 THE PHYSICS OF THE HIGH-SPEED BUS

When the rise and fall times of a signal become small enough to be of the same order of magnitude as the propagation delay (t_p) of the line being driven, the distributed nature of the transmission line become visible in the form of reflections. The lumped-circuit approximation of a single capacitive load, which is very convenient to use at slower speeds, is no longer accurate. A useful rule of thumb is that the transmission line theory should be used when $t_r \leq 3t_p$, where t_r is the rise or fall time of the signal measured between 10 and 90 percent.[3] The resistive components of a bus line are usually very small when compared to reactive components, and therefore they can be approximated by a lossless transmission line that has an impedance Z_0 and a propagation delay t_0 given by

$$Z_0 = (L/C)^{1/2} \tag{14.1}$$

$$t_0 = l(LC)^{1/2} \tag{14.2}$$

where l = length of the bus
L = distributed inductance per unit length
C = distributed capacitance per unit length

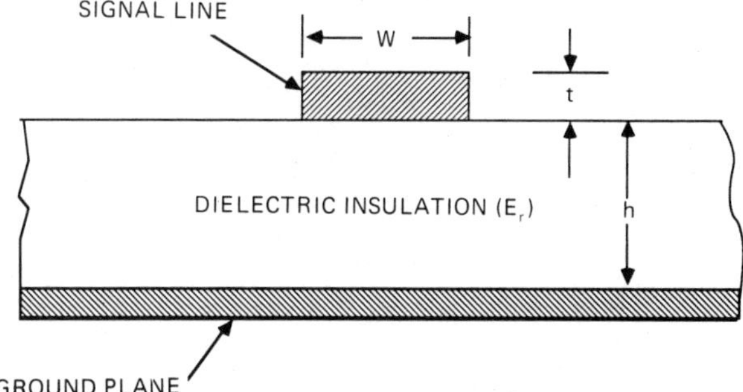

FIGURE 14.6 Cross section of microstrip bus line.

A typical bus line is a PC board trace of microstrip construction as shown in Fig. 14.6. Its Z_0 and t_0 can be calculated using the following empirical equations:

$$Z_0 = [87/(E_r + 1.41)^{1/2}]\{\ln[5.98h/(0.8\mathrm{W} + t)]\}\ \Omega \tag{14.3}$$

$$t_0 = 1.017(0.475E_r + 0.67)^{1/2}\ \mathrm{ns/ft} \tag{14.4}$$

where E_r = relative dielectric constant of the PC board material (E_r = 4.7 for fiberglass boards)

w, h, t = dimensions indicated in Fig. 14.6

Using the following nominal values for the dimensions

$$t = 1.4 \text{ mils}$$

$$w = 25 \text{ mils}$$

$$h = 1/16 \text{ in}$$

we get

$$Z_0 \cong 100\ \Omega$$

$$t_0 = 1.7 \text{ ns/ft}$$

These values are based on a setup with no transceiver loads attached to the line. In a practical backplane bus, however, there are capacitive loads corresponding to daughter cards attached at regular and frequent intervals as shown in Fig. 14.7. The loaded impedance Z_L and propagation delay t_L of a uniformly loaded line is simply calculated by adding the load capacitance per unit length C_L to C in Eqs. (14.1) and (14.2).

$$Z_L = [L/(C + C_L)]^{1/2} = [(\mathrm{L/C})/(1 + \mathrm{C_L/C})]^{1/2}$$
$$Z_L = Z_0/(1 + \mathrm{C_L/C})^{1/2} \tag{14.5}$$

$$t_L = l[\mathrm{L(C + C_L)}]^{1/2} = l[\mathrm{L_C(1 + C/C_L)}]^{1/2}$$

$$t_L = t_0(1 + \mathrm{C_L/C})^{1/2} \tag{14.6}$$

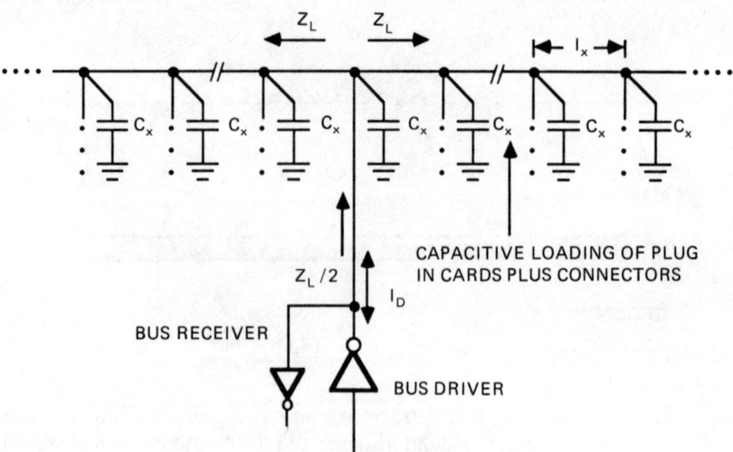

FIGURE 14.7 An uniformly loaded line.

For the microstrip example, the distributed capacitance is about 20 pF/ft (this can be easily measured in the laboratory or calculated). This does not include, however, the capacitance of the connectors mounted on the backplane bus and the associated plated-through-holes, which can amount to 5 pF per card slot. The loading capacitance of the plug-in card is dominated by the capacitance of the transceiver, which can be 12–20 pF for a TTL device. Most of this capacitance is due to large transistors in the output of the driver. Allowing another 3–5 pF for printed-circuit-board traces and the connector, the total loading per card slot C_x can add up to 30 pF. For a typical backplane with 15 card slots per foot (l_x = 0.8 in), C_L = 450 pF/ft.

Therefore,

$$Z_L = 100/(1 + 450/20)^{1/2} \approx 20\ \Omega$$

$$t_L = 1.7(1 + 450/20)^{1/2} = 8.25 \text{ ns/ft}$$

14.3.1 Effects of Capacitive Loading on the Bus

Several startling observations can be made from the above calculations:

1. Using the rule of thumb discussed earlier, for a rise time of say 3 ns, which is slower than many FAST drivers, the maximum bus length that can be approximated by a lumped capacitive load corresponds to the condition

$$t_r = 3t_p$$

$$t_p = 3 \text{ ns}/3 = 1 \text{ ns}$$

For the bus discussed earlier, t_L = 8.25 ns/ft. Therefore the maximum bus length (1 ns)/(8.25 ns/ft) = 1.5 in. This corresponds to barely three slots in our example. Reducing the spacing between the slots will make this length even smaller due to increased propagation delay t_L. Considering that spacings less than

0.8 in and rise and fall times less than 3 ns are quite common in high-performance bus systems, it is safe to conclude that most backplane buses should be treated as transmission lines.

2. The impedance of both the Z_0 and Z_L are purely resistive as shown in Eqs. (14.1) and (14.5). This means that the bus driver sees a purely resistive load, not a large capacitive load as the lumped-circuit approximation would indicate. For example, by lumped-circuit approximation, the driver load for a 2-ft bus in the above calculation would be $(C_L + C)2 = (450 + 20) \times 2 = 940$ pF. Furthermore, the impedance of the bus is independent of the length of the bus, whereas the lumped equivalent capacitance increases linearly with length.

3. The capacitive loading drastically alters both the impedance and propagation delay of the bus. In this example, $1 + C_L/C \cong 5$, and therefore the impedance reduces by a factor of 5, from 100 to 20 Ω, and the propagation increases by a factor of 5, from 1.7 to 8.25 ns. The increased propagation delay due to loading reduces bus throughput.

4. The actual load impedance seen by the driver is lower than the bus impedance by a factor of 2. This is because, at any arbitrary point on the bus, the driver is actually driving two transmission lines of impedance Z_L, in parallel, in opposite directions as shown in Fig. 14.7. This equates to a driver load impedance of 10 Ω in our example above.

5. To avoid reflections, the transmission line needs to be terminated at its impedance (Z_L). Since a bus carries data in both directions it is necessary to terminate the TTL bus in both directions at 20 Ω. This requires the driver to drive a dc load of 10 Ω, which is also the ac load impedance.

TTL drivers are not designed for driving a 10-Ω load, ac or dc. In order to drive 20-Ω terminations (R_T) connected to V_{cc} at each end, the TTL driver would be required to sink a nominal output low current (I_{OL}) of 450 mA:

$$(V_{cc} - V_{OL})/(R_T/2) = (5\text{ V} - 0.5\text{ V})/(10\ \Omega) = 450\text{ mA}$$

This current could be reduced to about 300 mA by using a termination voltage of 3.5 V instead of 5 V. But it is still too high when compared to a TTL bus driver, even a high-current one that is capable of sinking an I_{OL} of 48 to 64 mA. In practice, the lines are terminated at the lowest value allowed by the dc sink capability of the driver. This value of termination is invariably much higher than the loaded impedance of the bus of 20 Ω. Consequently, reflections are always present and take several round-trip bus delays to settle down before the data can be reliably sampled. This settling time limits the bus transfer rates on a TTL bus and is commonly referred to as the *bus-driving problem.*

14.3.2 Bus Termination

In order to analyze the settling time, it is necessary to understand how buses are terminated. In a TTL bus it is common to use a two-resistor termination, one to V_{CC} (R_1) and the other to ground (R_2), as shown in Fig. 14.8. The Thevinin equivalent circuit shows that this is the same as a termination resistor R_T, which is the parallel combination of resistors R_1 and R_2, connected to a voltage source V_T, which is the open-circuit voltage of the resistor divider formed by R_1 and R_2.

Any passive termination network can be reduced to the Thevinin equivalent

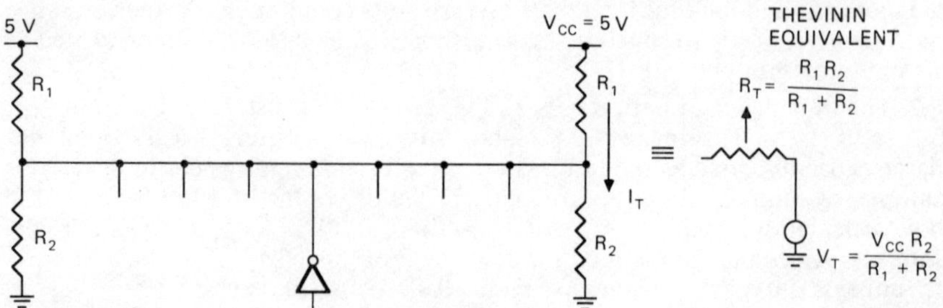

FIGURE 14.8 Termination.

above. Therefore, all the discussions in this chapter will refer to the termination resistor R_T and termination voltage V_T, independent of their implementation in practice. It should be noted, however, that the power dissipated in the terminations can be different between the two cases discussed above. For example, when using two-resistor termination, there is always a current flow from V_{CC} to ground, even when the line is not being driven, whereas a single resistor with the Thevinin voltage source does not dissipate any power when the line is not being driven. Therefore it is better to use a separate termination voltage supply in wide backplanes to minimize system power.

The typical values of R_1 and R_2 for a TTL bus with 50-mA drivers are 200 and 470 Ω, which correspond to an R_T of 140 Ω. These resistors are derived as follows. When a TTL output is low, the voltage across R_1 with V_{CC} at its maximum is (assuming a 5 V ± 10% supply)

$$V_{CC} - V_{OL} = 5.5 - 0.5 = 5 \text{ V}$$

Since the driver is capable of sinking only 50 mA and there are two R_1's in parallel,

$$R_1 = (5 \text{ V}/50 \text{ mA})2 = 200 \ \Omega$$

R_2 is chosen to further reduce the termination resistor R_T without draining significant current from a TTL totem-pole driver output when it is high. This is because most TTL totem-pole outputs, when high, cannot supply significant amounts of dc current. Even if they could, the on-chip power dissipation would be higher for the current sourced from the upper state (I_{OH}) due to a larger drop across the chip in the high state. There is a 1.5-V drop between V_{CC} and the output in the high state versus a 0.5-V or less drop across the lower output transistor when the output is low. The on-chip dc power dissipation is crucial to the number of transceivers that can be integrated into an IC package. Making the I_{OH} higher also increases the overlap current discussed earlier, increasing the V_{CC} and ground bounce during switching. For these reasons, V_T is usually chosen to be 3.5 V, which keeps the driver current near zero when high. This also has the added benefit of a guaranteed high state during bus idle, that is, when all drivers are OFF. On open-collector lines, V_T of 3.5 V sets the output high level with a good noise margin.

The value of R_2 for V_T = 3.5 V can be calculated as follows:

$$(V_{CC}R_2)/(R_1 + R_2) = V_T$$

$$R_2(V_{CC} - V_T) = V_T R_1$$

$$R_2 = (V_T R_1)/(V_{CC} - V_T) = (3.5 \times 200)/(5 - 3.5) = 467\ \Omega$$

The nearest standard value resistor is 470 Ω.

In general, most commercially available TTL buses terminate the bidirectional lines with an R_T of 130 to 200 Ω, depending on the current capacity of drivers specified and also on the power the user is willing to dissipate. The V_t is usually set between 3 to 3.5 V.

14.3.3 Settling Time

To understand the effect of using a 50-mA driver on a 20-Ω bus, let us look at an open-collector driver at the center of a 2-ft bus going from a low to high state (Fig. 14.9). Let us assume that the bus is terminated at the minimum R_T allowed by the driver, that is, the driver sinks the maximum current of 50 mA when low. This corresponds to an R_T of 130 Ω and V_T of 3.4 V for a typical V_{OL} of 0.4 V.

$$I_{OL} = 2\,(V_T - V_{OL})/R_T = 2(3.5 - 0.4)/130 = 50\text{ mA}$$

For simplicity, the rise and fall times are assumed to be fast compared to the round-trip delay. When the transistor turns off, releasing the bus at time $t = 0$,

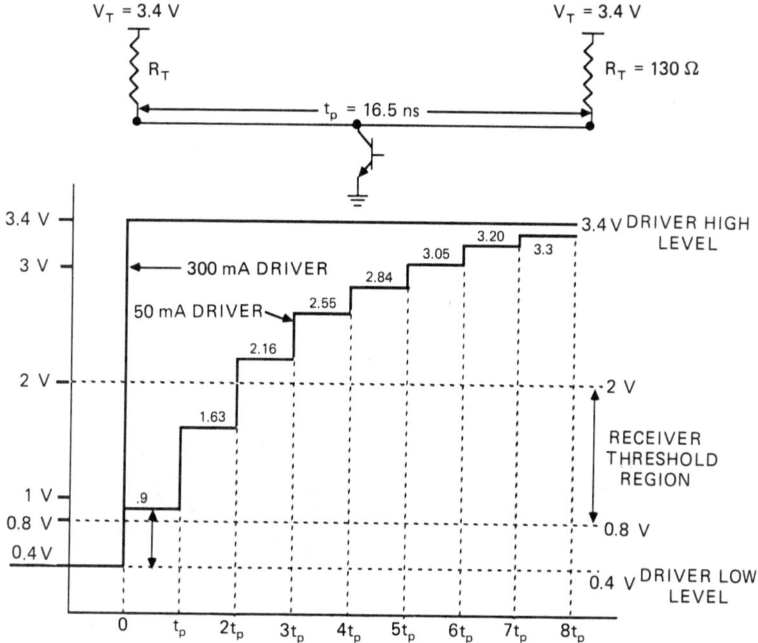

FIGURE 14.9 Open-collector TTL bus waveforms; 50-mA vs 300-mA driver.

the standing current in the transmission line of 50 mA raises the bus voltage by 0.5 V (50 mA × 10 Ω = 0.5 V) to 0.9 V. This voltage step travels to the termination at both ends and gets reflected back. The reflection coefficient

$$\rho_T = (R_T - Z_L)/(R_T + Z_L) = (130 - 20)/(130 + 30) = 0.73$$

Therefore, the reflected step amplitude[3]

$$V_R = 0.73 \times 0.5 \text{ V} = 0.37 \text{ V}$$

By neglecting the attenuation (which is small), the two reflected signals, one from each end, increase the voltage at the driver by another 2 × 0.37 V to 1.63 V after one round-trip delay, which equals 16.5 ns ($0.5\, t_p \times 2 = t_p$). It takes two reflections or 33 ns for the waveform to cross the 2-V upper limit on the receiver threshold region. This delay is called the settling time. After every transition one has to wait for the duration of the settling time before the data can be reliably sampled.

When using totem-pole drivers the situation is significantly better. This is because the upper output transistor, although not rated for much dc load current, is capable of providing 10–100 mA of ac current during the low-to-high transition. For example, a 50-mA pull-up current, in addition to the 50-mA termination current, would result in a 1-V first step, which would put the driver output at 1.4 V. The first reflection brings this up to 2.86 V, which is higher than the maximum receiver threshold level of 2 V. On the high-to-low transition most 50 mA (I_{OL}) TTL drivers, open collector or totem-pole, are capable of sinking 80 to 150 mA dynamic current. However, they also have to swing further (3.4 V − 0.8 V = 2.6 V) on the negative transition to get below the 0.8 V lower threshold limit of the receiver. But because of the higher available current they can usually do this in two steps (one reflection). Figure 14.10 shows a typical totem-pole TTL bus waveform as measured on a real-world bus. The settling time in the case discussed above is only 16.5 ns. But, since the driver can be placed anywhere along the line, the worst-case settling time of $2t_p$ = 33 ns should be used. As a point of reference Multibus II and VME bus allow for a settling time of 35 ns.

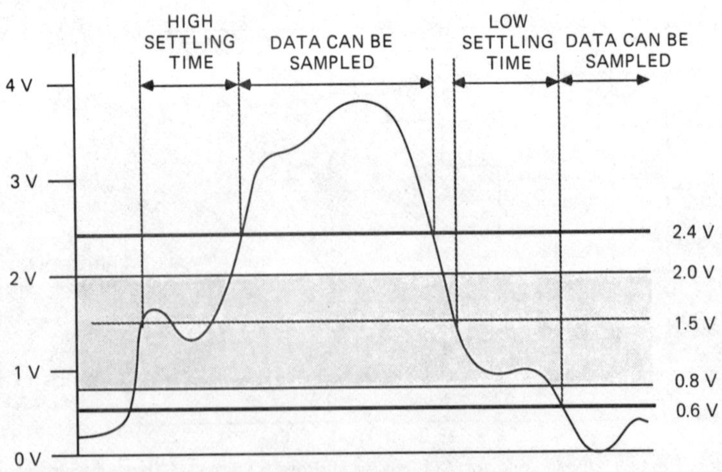

FIGURE 14.10 Typical totem-pole Tristate bus signal waveform.

Obviously, the settling time puts a limit on how fast data transfer can take place and it is dependent on the bus length. Trying to reduce the bus length by placing cards closer will not solve the issue. This is because closer spacing of capacitive loads increases bus propagation delay and reduces the impedance even further. Consequently most high-end TTL buses today are limited by settling time in terms of their performance.

Another problem, that is not so obvious, is the voltage steps in the threshold region that can cause multiple triggering in case of strobe and clock signals. Ad hoc solutions are used to solve this problem on these critical lines on a case-by-case basis.

Clock lines are unique in the sense that they are unidirectional and, therefore, need only one termination at the far end. This allows the termination value to be reduced by half when compared to the bidirectional case. Also, the loads on the clock line consist of only receivers and, therefore, of lower capacitance. Since there are only few (usually one) clock lines on a bus, V_T for these can be lower at the expense of added transceiver power when the line is high. Special high-current (HC) transceivers with an I_{OH} of 40 mA and I_{OL} of 64 mA are usually specified. Combining these factors together, an R_T of 30 to 50 Ω and a V_T of 2.5 to 3.5 V, as shown in Fig. 14.11, usually takes care of the problem.[4]

For bidirectional lines one approach that is used frequently is to reduce the receiver threshold region to a narrow range (e.g., ±200 mV) and to increase the driver current to 100 mA or higher until the first transition is able to cross over the threshold region. Once again this is an ad hoc solution and used only on those lines affected by the significant increase in power involved.

Power is an important factor in modern buses because of the large number of active lines involved. For example, 32-bit buses usually have over 70 lines being driven. Therefore switching to a 300-mA driver would increase the system power requirements drastically. But even if we assume that power is not an issue for the sake of argument, this brute-force solution will only provide a marginal improvement. This is because higher-current drivers have correspondingly higher output capacitances that increase the bus loading and thus reduce the bus impedance further. This in turn requires an even higher drive current for proper operation. In addition, higher capacitive loading increases bus propagation delay and therefore reduces bus throughput. Large drive currents also cause excessive ground noise and increase crosstalk.

14.3.4 Tristate versus Open-Collector Drivers

TTL was really not meant to drive low-impedance transmission lines. It is ideal for transferring digital signals over short distances on unterminated, lightly

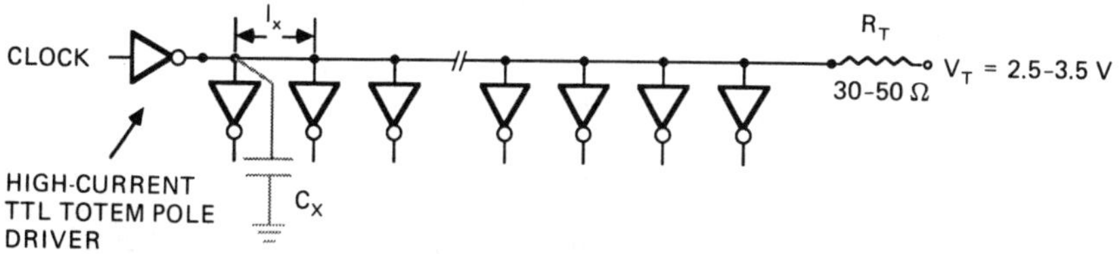

FIGURE 14.11 Termination scheme for TTL clock lines. l_X = 0.8 in.; C_X = 20 pF (no driver load); C_L = (20 × 12)/0.8 = 300 pF/ft; C_C = 20 pF/ft; Z_0 = 100 Ω; $Z_L = Z_0/\sqrt{1 + (C_L/C)}$ = 25 Ω.

loaded (i.e., loading does not alter Z_0 or t_0 appreciably) lines. We can convert the rule of thumb of $t_r \geq 3t_p$ for lightly loaded lines by substituting $t_p = t_0 = 1.7$ ns/ft for a typical PC board trace. The translated rule of thumb is that TTL can drive up to a foot of unterminated line for every 5 ns of rise and fall time. Therefore, a FAST Tristate driver, with 2.5 ns rise time, can only drive 6 in of unterminated line. Any loading along the line reduces this distance even further.

Another point, worth noting here, is that the Tristate device is excellent for the applications mentioned above. That is, they provide very fast rise and fall times and do not consume dc power at the output except while switching. However, when they are used to drive transmission lines ($t_r \leq 3t_p$) that have to be terminated, they no longer are more advantageous than an open-collector driver. The terminating resistor dissipated dc power in both cases and serves also as a pull-up resistor for the open-collector driver. With respect to rise and fall times, since the load is purely resistive, there is no significant difference between resistive pull-up and active pull-up devices because the effective impedance of an active pull-up device in a Tristate driver is usually larger than the load being driven ($Z_L/2$). In fact, due to the reflections caused by insufficient termination the Tristate devices have a much longer effective rise time than specified in the data sheet. On the other hand, open-collector devices have several advantages in this application. First, they allow for wire-ORing, which is needed on some bus lines. Second, when multiple drivers are activated at the same time on the same line, accidentally (bus contention) or intentionally (wire-ORing), there is no damage incurred to the drivers. In contrast, with Tristate drivers, bus contention can cause excessive currents and consequently damage the drivers permanently. The ability to overlap drivers can be utilized in bus protocols to reduce delays and thus increase bus transfer rates. The third advantage is the fact that there is no overlap current that causes severe ground and V_{CC} noise spikes with Tristate drivers, particularly the fast, high-current (low-impedance) drivers. In fact, the maximum ground-switching current for an open-collector driver is no more than the load current except for a small current due to parasitic capacitances, and there is no V_{CC} bounce caused by the output stage because the load current does not pass through V_{CC}. The output impedance of an open-collector driver can be made as small as necessary to drive the low-impedance bus line, and it can be switched as fast as necessary without having to worry about the overlap current. It should be noted, however, that the resulting di/dt will still cause inductive drops in the ground and output leads that cannot be ignored.

14.4 BACKPLANE TRANSCEIVER LOGIC

There is yet another advantage to the open-collector driver, which is exploited in a new signaling scheme called *backplane transceiver logic* (BTL). Developed by National Semiconductor in 1983 in cooperation with the IEEE 896.1 Futurebus Committee, BTL solves the bus-driving problem in a very elegant fashion.[5,6]

The root of the problem is the large output capacitance of the bus driver. By simply adding a Schottky diode in series with an open-collector driver output, the capacitance of the drive transistor is isolated by the small reverse-biased capacitance of the diode in the nontransmitting state (Fig. 14.12). The Schottky-diode capacitance is typically less than 2 pF and is relatively independent of the drive current. Allowing another 3 pF or the receiver input capacitance and the package capacitance of the transceiver IC, the total loading of the BTL transceiver can be

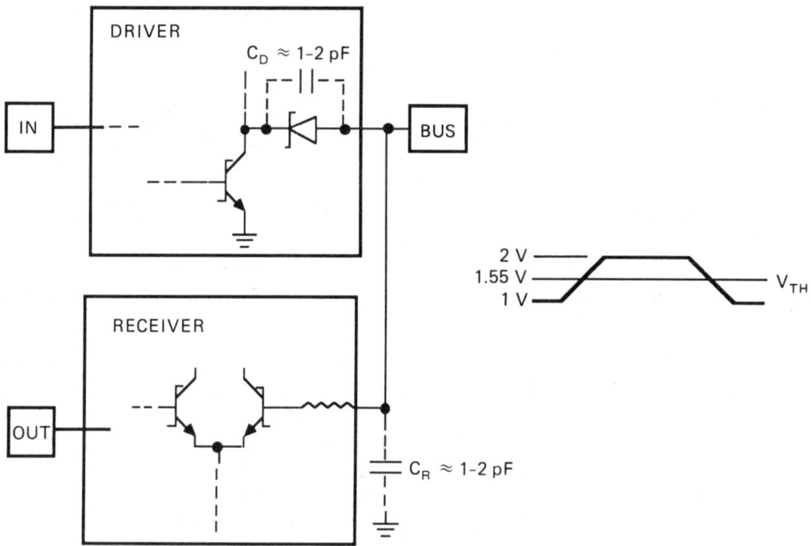

FIGURE 14.12 The BTL transceiver and bus signal waveform.

kept under 5 pF. This is a factor of 3 to 4 times better than a 50-mA I_{OL} Tristate transceiver.

In addition to the low output capacitance, BTL has two other attributes, namely, a lower signal amplitude and a precision receiver threshold, that reduce power and increase noise immunity. Obviously, lower loading capacitance increases bus impedance and consequently reduces the power required to drive it. However, a larger part of power savings comes from a reduced voltage swing of 1 V on the bus, which is about one-third of the TTL swing.

An immediate concern stemming from the reduced signal swing is the reduced noise margin. The largest noise component in a backplane bus is crosstalk from adjacent lines, which is a function of the signal amplitude. As long as all lines on the bus use the lower swing, the crosstalk amplitude is scaled down proportionately. Therefore lower swing does not reduce crosstalk immunity as long as the relative noise margin, that is, the noise margin expressed as a percentage of the signal swing, is maintained. However, the absolute value of the noise margin is critical for noise induced from sources external to the bus. Fortunately, the low impedance and relatively short length of the bus lines make this externally generated noise component insignificant. Even if strong external noise is a problem in some severe applications, the bus can be easily shielded either by using a multilayer board with ground or V_{CC} planes on the outer layers or by using an external shield.

Interestingly enough, the use of precision thresholds on the BTL receiver keeps even the absolute noise margins around the same level as the TTL counterpart. This is illustrated in Fig. 14.13, which shows the noise margins on the high-current TTL transceiver specified in the VMEbus standard and the BTL bus transceiver.

The BTL low-level voltage (V_{OL}) is specified at 1 V as a typical value, with a maximum of 1.2 V. This is higher than the typical TTL V_{OL} of 0.5 V in order to

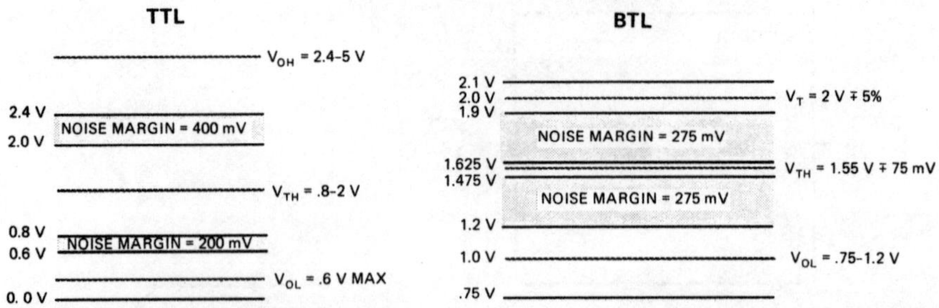

FIGURE 14.13 Noise margins, TTL vs BTL.

accommodate the 0.5-V drop across a forward-biased Schottky diode. The high level (V_{OH}) is set by the termination voltage V_T at 2 V to provide a nominal swing of 1 V. In order to maximize the noise margin and make it equal in both states, the receiver threshold V_{TH} is specified as 1.55 V with a narrow tolerance of ± 75 mV. If we assume a $\pm 5\%$ tolerance on the V_T, these specifications correspond to a symmetrical noise margin of 275 mV under worst-case conditions. In comparison, the TTL transceiver has a nonsymmetrical noise margin of 200 mV in the low state and 400 mV in the high state. Thus, even with a much smaller swing, the BTL transceiver provides comparable (or better) absolute noise margins. Consequently, the noise immunity to external sources is basically unchanged, but the crosstalk noise margin has improved by a factor of 3 over the TTL transceiver due to the scaling-down effect of the crosstalk signal amplitude.[4]

The overall power saving of BTL over TTL can be calculated for the bus example discussed earlier. With the lower transceiver capacitance of 5 pF it is important to keep the parasitic capacitance low to get the maximum benefit. By using reasonable care, it is easy to keep the capacitance of the combination of trace, connectors, and the plated-through-holes, both on the daughter card and the backplane, under 8 pF per card. This translates to a loaded impedance of

$$100/\{1 + [(5 + 8)15/20]\}^{1/2} = 30\ \Omega$$

The drive current required for a 1-V swing under the worst-case loading is

$$I_D = 1/(30/2)$$

However, with precision receiver thresholds specified in BTL, it is possible for the driver to swing past the threshold region with a comfortable margin even if the first step climbs to only 75 percent of the final amplitude under worst-case loading. Therefore, the drive current can be reduced by 25 percent to save power without affecting performance:

$$I_D = (2/30)0.75 = 50\text{ mA}$$

At this current level the power dissipated is

$$V_T \times I_D = (2\text{ V} \times 50\text{ mA}) = 100\text{ mW per bus line}$$

For a properly driven TTL drive the power dissipated is

$$3.4\text{ V} \times 300\text{ mA} = 1020\text{ mW}$$

This is an order of magnitude reduction in power.

The greatest benefit of BTL is that it eliminates the settling time caused by reflections as shown in Fig. 14.14. It is important to remember that the data sheet values of propagation delays for TTL are measured with lumped capacitive loads and therefore do not include the settling time, which is a function of the loaded round-trip propagation delay of the bus and the number of reflections it takes to cross the threshold region. In contrast, the propagation delays for the BTL devices are specified with the actual resistive loads that they are designed to drive, usually in the range of 10 to 20 Ω. Therefore, the specifications are realistic when used on a properly terminated bus and the settling time is zero. This saves between 30 and 50 ns per transition on a typical bus, allowing for much higher transfer rates.

There is yet another benefit of BTL that is not so obvious. It arises from the lower bus propagation delay, which is a result of lower capacitive loading.

Recalculating the loaded bus propagation delay of our example for BTL yields

$$t_L = 1.7\{1 + [(5 + 8)15/20]\}^{1/2}$$

$$= 5.57 \text{ ns/ft}$$

This is more than a 30 percent improvement over TTL, which allows for further improvements in bus speed.

In summary, BTL has the following attributes:

1. Low output capacitance
2. 1-V nominal swing
3. Precision receiver thresholds

They translate to the following advantages:

1. Settling time delays are eliminated.
2. Power required for proper drive is reduced by an order of magnitude.

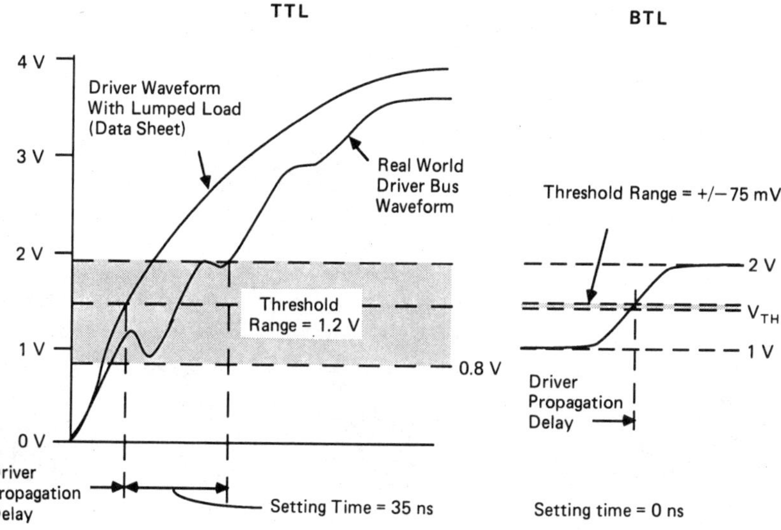

FIGURE 14.14 Settling time, TTL vs BTL.

3. Crosstalk immunity is increased by approximately a factor of 3.

4. The load current is reduced by a factor of 6 for proper drive. This reduces both dc and inductive ac drops across ground and output lines correspondingly.

5. Use of open-collector drivers eliminates switching transients on V_{CC} and ground caused by overlap in totem-pole TTL outputs.

6. The bus propagation delay is reduced by more than 30 percent over TTL.

Figure 14.15 shows a comparison of BTL and TTL signals as measured on a fully loaded bus with 28 slots, spaced 0.6 in apart. It is interesting to observe that the small noise disturbances seen on the BTL signal are caused by the transitions on the TTL signal.

A typical BTL bus based on our example is as shown in Fig. 14.16. The termination resistor, which is based on the 50-mA drive current calculated earlier, is determined as follows:

$$R_T/2 = 1\text{ V}/50\text{ mA}$$

Therefore $R_T = 40\ \Omega$.

The nearest standard value resistor is 39 Ω. This configuration is identical to that in the IEEE P896.1 Futurebus, which specifies BTL transceivers. As calculated earlier, its fully loaded bus impedance is 30 Ω under worst-case conditions, that is, when all components that contribute to bus loading are at the maximum limit of their capacitance. Typically, the bus impedance is around 40 Ω when all cards are plugged in. When there are no cards plugged in the bus impedance is around 50 Ω. This is because the backplane half of the connector and the associated plated-through-holes are still loading the bus with about 4 pF per slot.

Therefore

$$Z_L = 100/[1 + 4 \times 15/20]^{1/2} = 50\ \Omega$$

The selected termination value of 40 Ω is between the two worst-case limits of 30 and 50 Ω and offers a good compromise.

At the time of this writing nearly a dozen BTL devices from four different semiconductor companies are available. They range in output currents of 50 and 100 mA and come in several different configurations. Some of the common con-

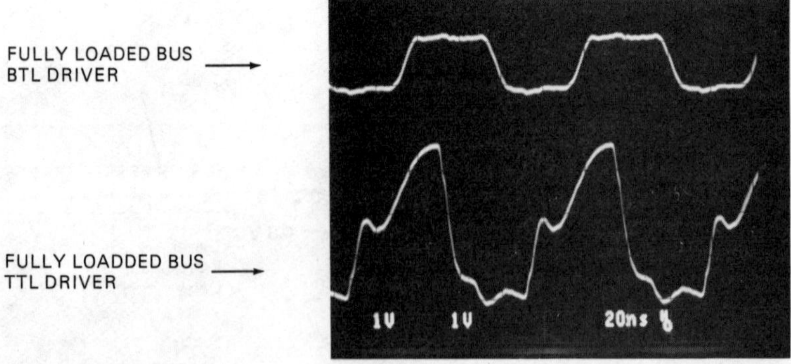

FIGURE 14.15 Actual bus signal waveforms, TTL vs BTL. Slot spacing = 0.6 in.; number of slots = 28.

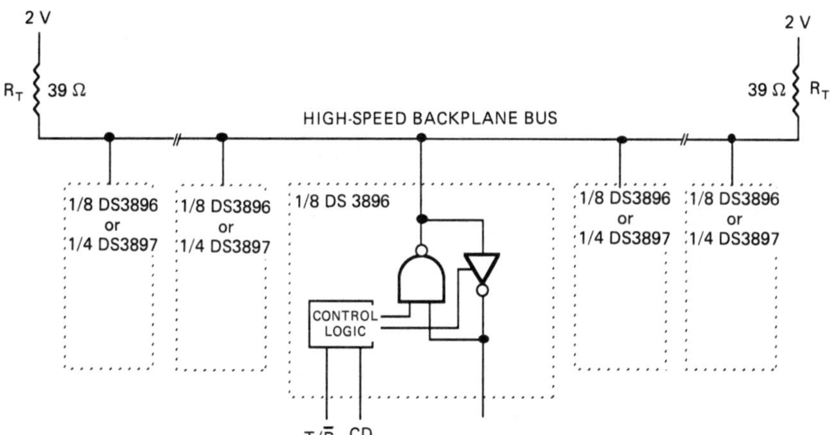

FIGURE 14.16 A typical BTL bus configuration. T/$\overline{\text{R}}$ = transmit/$\overline{\text{receive}}$: controls direction. CD = chip disable: tristates both the receiver and transmitter.

figurations are shown in Fig. 14.17 *a–c*. With 100-mA drive capability it is possible to drive loads down to 10 Ω or a bus impedance of 20 Ω. Therefore, tighter board-to-board spacing and use of strip lines that usually have lower impedance are made possible.

With BTL, it is no longer necessary to have different types of transceivers and terminations for different types of lines on the bus. All lines can be exactly the same, independent of whether or not they are data/address, wire-OR control lines, strobe lines, or clock lines. The electrical environment is close to an ideal terminated transmission line in all cases. This provides for high electrical integrity, resulting in predictable performance and reliable operation.

14.5 OTHER TECHNOLOGIES

14.5.1 Complimentary Metal-Oxide Semiconductor (CMOS)

Like TTL, CMOS transceivers provide both totem-pole with Tristate and open-drain (equivalent of open-collector) options (Figs. 14.18 and 14.19) and can operate on a 0 to +5 V supply. However, there are many differences worth noting. The CMOS transistors act much more like ideal switches and therefore the outputs swing from rail to rail, particularly when there is no dc load. Since CMOS inputs do not draw any dc current (other than leakages) there is no dc load except when driving terminated transmission lines or TTL inputs.

Another difference is that the CMOS input threshold is usually set at the midpoint between the supply voltage rails for maximum noise margins in both high and low states. Furthermore, because of the low gain of MOS devices, the outputs do not switch completely until the input voltage is close to the supply voltage rails. For the same reason there is considerable overlap between lower and upper output transistors, causing a large overlap current between V_{CC} and ground during switching, particularly in high-current drivers. Thresholds are usually made

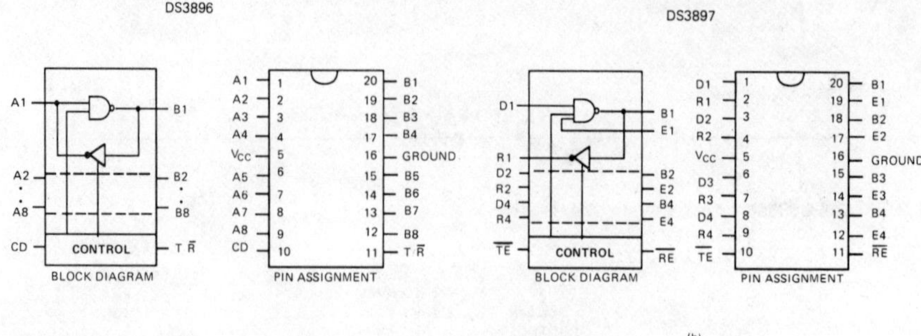

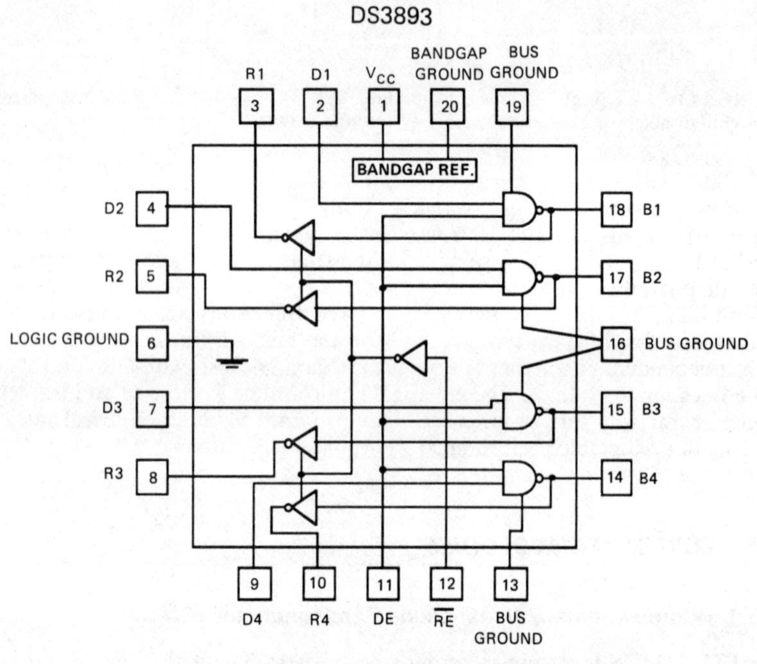

FIGURE 14.17 Some common BTL transceiver configurations and pin layouts: (*a*) 8-bit, 50-mA Trapezoidal transceiver with common control inputs; (*b*) 4-bit, 50-mA Trapezoidal transceiver with independent as well as common control inputs; (*c*) 4-bit, 100-mA transceiver common control inputs for all drivers and receivers.

sharper by adding more stages in series to increase gain, but at the expense of longer propagation delays, which affect bus transfer rates.

One of the biggest advantages of CMOS, of course, is the absence of dc power dissipation. However, when driving heavy dc loads such as a terminated line, there is no significant advantage in terms of power dissipated in the output stage

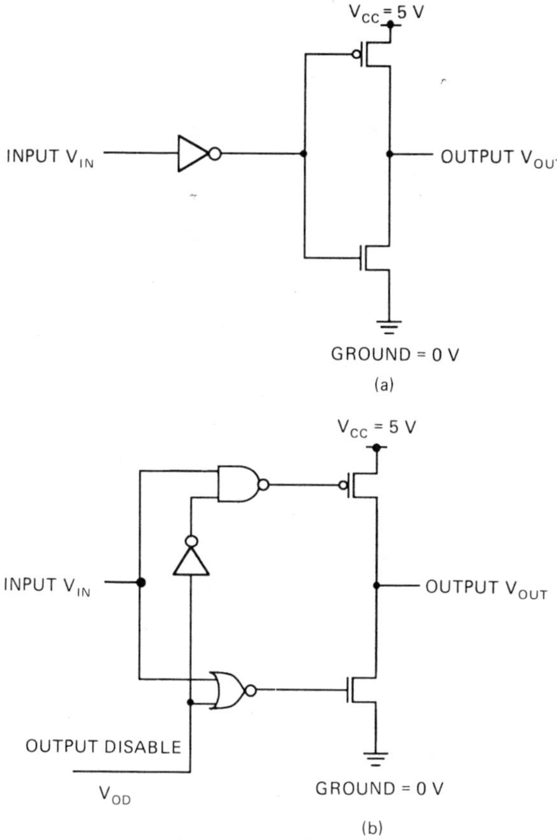

FIGURE 14.18 CMOS driver circuit (noninverting): (*a*) totem-pole output; (*b*) Tristate output.

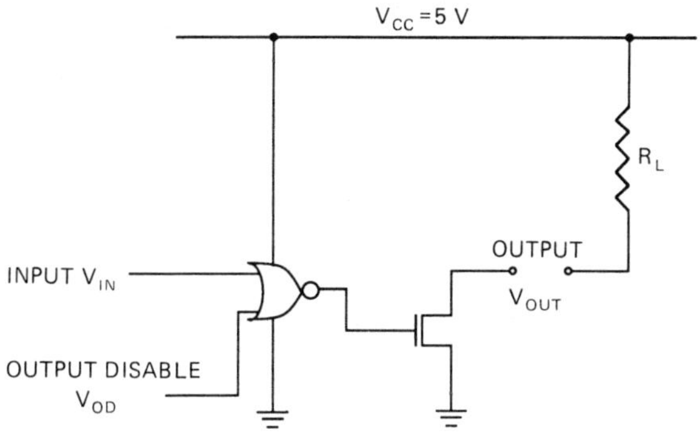

FIGURE 14.19 CMOS open-drain driver circuit (noninverting).

and the termination, compared to TTL. Nevertheless, the power savings in the rest of the chip, particularly in the Tristate mode, is significant.

Because of the nature of MOS transistors, CMOS outputs can handle high dynamic currents. However, to sink or source large dc currents requires extremely large transistors, compared to bipolar technology, which increases output capacitance and the overlap current. Schottky diodes (or any isolated diodes for that matter) are generally not available in CMOS processes to implement BTL. For these reasons CMOS drivers are not very suitable for driving fully terminated lines.

On the other hand, CMOS Tristate devices are ideal for driving unterminated buses. Their high-dynamic-current capability provides fast rise and fall times, and their large symmetrical swing in relation to the receiver thresholds provide good noise margins. Also, due to zero dc current of inputs, the capacitive bus line can be used as a storage element. For example, drivers can be turned off (put in a Tristate mode) soon after they drive the bus to high or low level and the bus will stay at this state until driven to the opposite state by the same or a different driver on the same line. This reduces the delay to switch from one driver to another, speeding up bus transactions.

CMOS transceivers can be integrated with other logic functions into a custom or semicustom VLSI chip, which is a significant advantage. For this reason alone, CMOS transceivers are frequently used to drive unterminated or lightly terminated buses despite the reduction in performance caused by long settling time delays.

14.5.2 Emitter Coupled Logic (ECL)

Figure 14.20 shows a typical ECL gate circuit with complementary outputs. When the input is greater than V_{BB}, the OUTPUT is high and $\overline{\text{OUTPUT}}$ is low. When

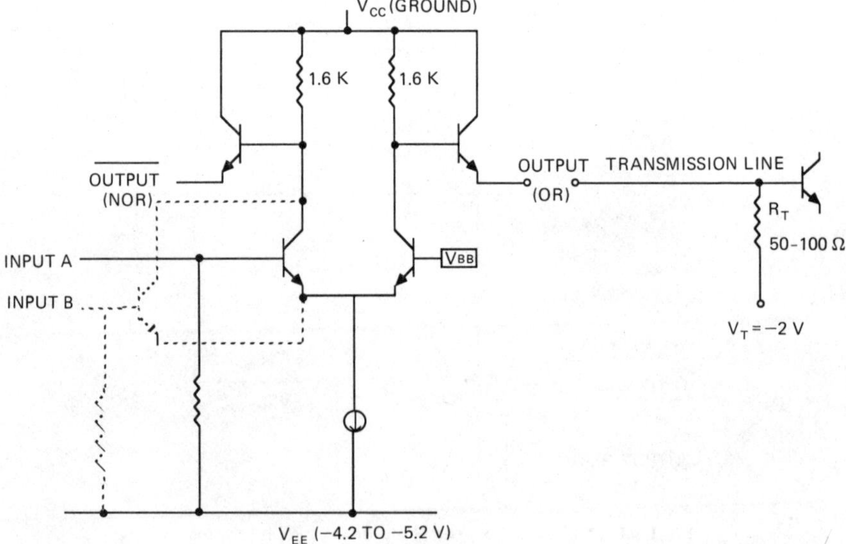

FIGURE 14.20 An ECL gate circuit.

the input is lower than V_{BB}, the OUTPUT is low and $\overline{\text{OUTPUT}}$ is high. This circuit can be made into an OR or NOR gate by adding another input, as shown in dotted lines.

ECL uses nonsaturating bipolar technology to achieve very high speeds. Consequently, ECL outputs are designed for driving terminated transmission lines. For example, 100K family devices have rise and fall times that are as low as 0.5 ns. Using our rule of thumb ($t_r \geq 3t_p$) any PC trace greater than 1.2 in in length behaves like a transmission line requiring a termination.[7]

Because of the open-emitter output stage, the output impedance is very low (under 10 Ω), which makes it easy to drive loads down to 50 or 25 Ω. Also, outputs can be connected in parallel to obtain more drive.

Open-emitter outputs allow wire-ORing just like open-collector TTL or BTL devices. In fact, it is rather interesting to consider ECL outputs as an inverted version of BTL outputs (Fig. 14.21). That is, ECL outputs pull up to positive rail (usually ground), whereas BTL devices pull down to negative rail (also ground). The alternate state is higher impedance for both devices. What is even more inter-

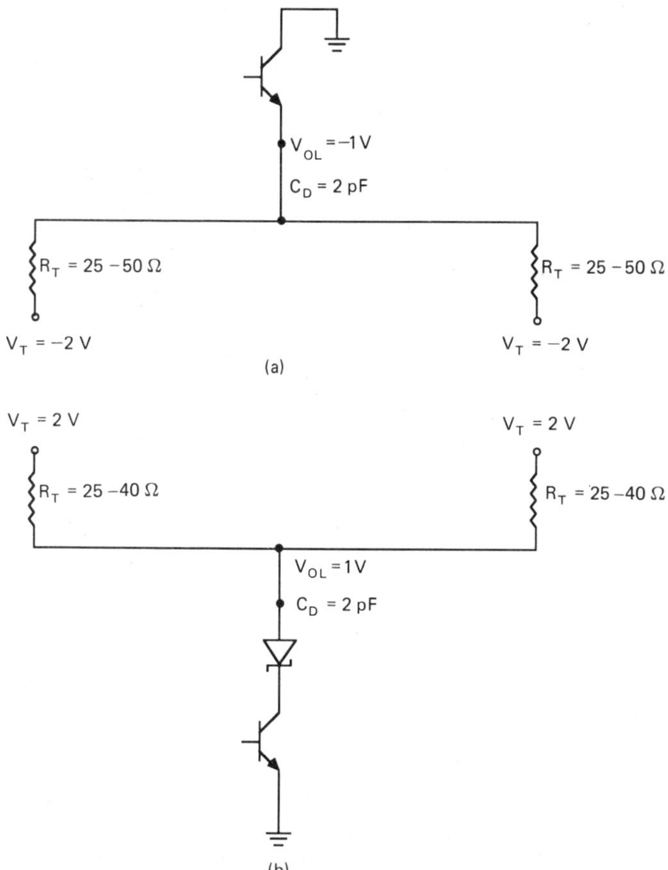

FIGURE 14.21 Driving low-impedance buses, ECL vs BTL: (*a*) 100K ECL; (*b*) BTL.

esting is that the ECL outputs are usually pulled down to −2 V by the 25- to 50-Ω terminations at the far end of the transmission lines, which is exactly the complement of BTL (+2 V). Furthermore, when 100K ECL output is asserted (high), it is typically 1 V from ground, just like BTL. Finally, the output capacitance of the ECL output is about the same as BTL, which is around 2 pF.

It is therefore clear that ECL output is comparable to BTL in its ability to drive a low-impedance transmission line. However, there are some disadvantages to ECL in a backplane bus application.

ECL receivers have a wide threshold region compared to the signal amplitude, which leaves only a small noise margin. All ECL families before 100K also have large temperature and supply voltage variations on the signal amplitude and thresholds. Since, in a backplane bus application, the driver and receiver are on different boards, they could be at different temperature and supply voltage extremes. This squeezes the worst-case noise margins even further in backplane bus applications.

The 100K ECL devices use temperature compensation to reduce signal and threshold levels in order to provide maximum noise margins. But even for these devices, the noise margins are around 140 mV in the worst case as shown in Fig. 14.22. It could be argued that ECL devices need lower margins because they generate less noise due to their complementary nature, which results in no supply current change between two states of a gate. However, this is true only if the whole system is based on ECL and the unused bus-driver output is pulled down with a resistor that is half the termination resistor at each end of the bus. The power required for driving the bus is now doubled.

An obvious question that then arises is, why not use differential signals on the bus? The problem is that there is no simple way to wire-OR the differential driver or set it in Tristate mode. One way this could be accomplished is by making both outputs, which are usually in opposite states, go to the low state. But, when no device is driving the bus, the bus voltage would be at the middle of the receiver threshold, causing noise that would trigger receivers randomly.

Another item to keep in mind is that ECL in general uses more power due to the nonsaturating nature of the logic, even in the nontransmitting state. In contrast, by using a CMOS bipolar process, BTL could be made to have near-zero dc power in transmitting and nontransmitting states if the output power is excluded.

To summarize the discussion on ECL, it is probably convenient to use ECL on the backplane if the entire system is ECL based. Even in this situation BTL

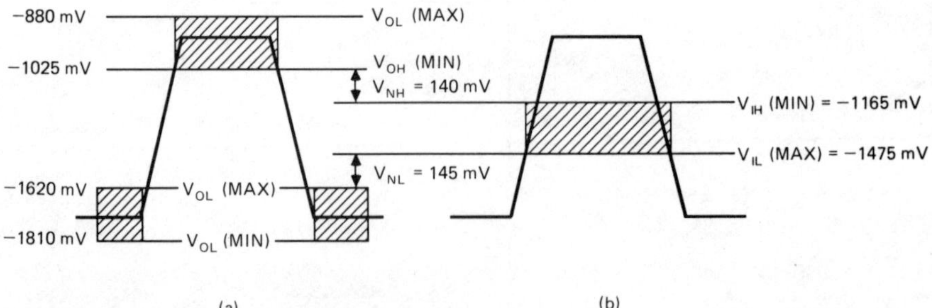

FIGURE 14.22 100K ECL signal voltage and threshold tolerances: (*a*) output voltage tolerances; (*b*) input threshold tolerances.

has some advantages over ECL, and it could be used on the backplane if transceivers were to be developed with an ECL interface on the daughter-card side and a BTL interface on the bus side.

14.6 POWER

With high-performance computers moving to the desk top, power consumption has become a major issue. There are several components of the power dissipated in the backplane bus system. Although the total power is of concern to the system designer, the way this power is distributed among the components has a major impact on cooling costs and the level of integration possible in transceivers.

14.6.1 Power Components

14.6.1.1 Termination Power (P_T). This is the worst-case power dissipated in the termination. If termination dissipates more power in one state than the other, the higher of the two should be used. This is because in a general case all lines on the bus could be in the state that dissipates most power. Termination power is the easiest component to handle from a cooling point of view.

14.6.1.2 Driver Output Power (P_O). This is the power dissipated in the output stage of the driver when it is active. There are two components to this power, ac and dc. For backplane applications the ac or switching power is usually negligible compared to the dc power dissipation due to the low value of dc termination that is being driven. The only exception is when using Tristate drivers on an unterminated bus. Here the dc dissipation is small because there is no load current except while switching, which leads to some ac power. In case of totem-pole TTL outputs on a terminated bus the power dissipation is usually higher when the output is low than when it is high. This is because the terminations are usually designed to sink the maximum load current (I_{OL}) into a low output (to provide the lowest possible termination resistance) with an equivalent Thevinin source voltage of 3 to 5 V, so as to not draw appreciable current (I_{OH}) when the output is high. It is important to keep the high-level load current small because the larger voltage drop across the TTL upper output transistors will increase on-chip power dissipation. In any case, the worse of the two power dissipations should be used for power calculations because all drivers within a chip could be low or high at the same time.

Single-ended ECL drivers dissipate more output power when they are high (less negative) than when they are low. Of course, when both of the complementary outputs are loaded, the power does not vary between the two states.

14.6.1.3 Termination Supply Power (P_{VT}). This is basically the power supplied by the termination supply under worst-case conditions, that is, when all lines on the bus are drawing maximum current. This is usually the sum of P_T and P_O.

14.6.1.4 Transceiver Active Power (P_A). This is the power dissipated by the receiver and/or the driver circuitry when there is no external load current. When the receiver output of a transceiver is connected to the driver input, only the receiver or the driver can be active at any given time. In this configuration the driver active power is usually of concern because it occurs in combination with the driver output power. Since the receiver usually drives an unterminated internal bus on a PC board, its output dissipation is very small, except in ECL technology.

In transceivers that provide a separate receiver output, the receiver may be ON all the time, and therefore the logic power will include both that of the receiver and driver.

Once again there are ac and dc components of the logic power. In bipolar technology the ac power is negligible compared to the dc power, whereas in CMOS technology ac power, even though very small, is the dominating component, as the dc power is near zero.

The dc logic power can be calculated by multiplying the supply current (from the data sheet) under the driver active condition with the supply voltage.

14.6.1.5 Transceiver Standby Power (P_{SB}). It is important to realize that the majority of the transceivers spend most of their time with drivers in the nontransmitting state (in standby conditions). Therefore, from the point of view of total system power consumption and cooling requirements, the standby power is the most crucial factor. Most TTL and ECL devices dissipate equal or more power in the nontransmitting state than in the active state due to the type of circuitry used. Using CMOS for the logic portion of the TTL device (bipolar-CMOS or BI-CMOS process) can cut down the standby power to near zero. The standby power can be calculated by multiplying the standby supply current (provided in most data sheets) with the supply voltage.

14.6.1.6 Total Backplane System Power (P_{BS}). In order to compare the various bus transceiver technologies in terms of power requirements we can define P_{BS} as the total worst-case power needed for all the transceivers and termination on a backplane bus system.

To do this comparison, a typical 32-bit backplane with 70 active bus lines (N_l) and 20 slots (N_s) is assumed. Since only one driver can be active on any given line, the others being in the standby mode, the power P_{BS} is given by the equation

$$P_{BS} = N_l (N_s - 1)P_{SB} + N_l (P_A + P_{VT})$$

14.6.2 Power Comparison

Table 14.1 shows the equations and typical calculation for various power components for the different technologies under all possible termination schemes. The following assumptions are made:

1. ac power is ignored in all cases.
2. In case of ECL, single-ended drive is assumed with no loading on the complimentary output.
3. Calculations are based on data sheet values for standard components that are available in the market.

As can be seen, the standby power P_{SB} dominates the total backplane system power in all technologies except CMOS. It is, however, possible to reduce P_{SB} (and P_A) to zero in Tristate TTL and BTL technologies by using CMOS for all but the output stage (BI-CMOS process).

Zero standby power or not, it is obvious from Table 14.1 that BTL has the

TABLE 14.1 Backplane System Power Calculations and Comparison

Type of termination	Unterminated		Under terminated		Fully terminated	
Type of transceiver	Tristate TTL	Tristate CMOS	Tristate TTL		BTL	ECL
Settling time	$>2t_p$	$>2t_p$	$2t_p$	0	0	0
Reference transceiver	74F245	74AC245	74F245	Imaginary	DS3896	DP8482/83 (ECL PART ONLY)
P_T	**0 mW**	**0 mW**	$(V_T - V_{OL})I_{OL}$ $(3.5 - 0.5)50 =$ **150 mW**	$(V_T - V_{OL})I_{OL}$ $(3.5 - 0.5)\ 300$ **= 900 mW**	$(V_T - V_{OL})I_{OL}$ $(2 - 1)\ 50 =$ **50 mW**	$(V_T - V_{OL})I_{OL}$ $(2 - 1)\ 50 =$ **50 mW**
P_O	$N_S \times V_{IL} \times V_{OL}$ $20 \times 1 \times 0.4 =$ **8 mW**	**0 mW**	$V_{OL} \times I_{OL}$ $0.5 \times 0.5 =$ **25 mW**	$V_{OL} \times I_{OL}$ $0.5 \times 300 =$ **150 mW**	$V_{OL} \times I_{OL}$ $1 \times 50 =$ **50 mW**	$V_{OH} \times I_D$ $1 \times 50 =$ **50 mW**
P_{VT} (= $V_T \times I_D$)	**0 mW**	**0 mW**	$3.5 \times 50 =$ **175 mW**	$3.5 \times 300 =$ **1050 mW**	$2 \times 50 =$ **100 mW**	$2 \times 50 =$ **100 mW**
P_A (= $I_{CCmax} \times V_{CCmax}$)	$120/8 \times 5.25 =$ **79 mW**	**0 mW**	$120/8 \times 5.25 =$ **79 mW**	$120/8 \times 5.25 =$ **79 mW**	$135/8 \times 5.25 =$ **89 mW**	$140/5 \times 4.8 =$ **134 mW**
P_{SB} (= $I_{CCz} \times V_{CCmax}$)	$110/8 \times 5.25 =$ **72 mW**	**0 mW**	$110/8 \times 5.25 =$ **72 mW**	$110/8 \times 5.25 =$ **72 mW**	$135/8 \times 5.25 =$ **89 mW**	$140/5 \times 4.8 =$ **134 mW**
P_{BS}	**101 W**	**0 W**	**113 W**	**175 W**	**132 W**	**194 W**
BI-CMOS P_{SB} = O	**5.5 W**	**0 W**	**12 W**	**74 W**	**7W**	**194 W**

lowest power requirement for zero settling time. However, having zero standby and active power reduces the power requirement from 132 to 7 W for a 50-mA drive (or 14 W for 100-mA drive), which is very significant.

The transceiver output power P_O and the active power P_A determine the number of transceivers that can be integrated into a single IC package. Since the use of BI-CMOS process can reduce P_A to zero, P_O ultimately determines the level of integration for transceivers.

Tristate CMOS devices provide the lowest power solution as long as the performance loss due to settling time is acceptable.

14.6.3 Low-Power Applications

It does take significant amounts of power to drive low-impedance lines with zero settling time. Even though BTL (especially when implemented in BI-CMOS) reduces the power requirement drastically, the power may still be too high for some applications. The only alternative then is to use Tristate CMOS drivers with no termination and accept a loss in performance. This loss can be minimized by using as short a bus as possible. Also, the performance level can be increased by using wider buses to increase overall bandwidth.

When using unterminated buses, as in the case above, it is sometimes advantageous to bypass the reflection problem by slowing down the rise and fall times on the transceivers to the point at which the signal line on the bus can be approximated by a lumped circuit. This would increase the propagation delay of the driver by at least half the rise or fall time. Based on the rule of thumb, the rise time needs to be at least 3 times the bus delay (t_p) for the lumped-circuit approximation. Hence, this would add an additional delay of $1.5t_p$ plus any tolerance associated with the rise-time control circuitry to the driver propagation delay. Adding a bus signal delay of t_p to this brings the total to $2.5t_p$ minimum. This is higher than the settling time of $2t_p$ for one reflection (which includes the bus propagation delay), but less than $4t_p$ required for two reflections. However, using slow rise and fall times has many other advantages, such as reduced crosstalk, ground, and V_{CC} noise and no steps in the waveform that could cause multiple triggering. This is covered in more detail in the next section of this chapter.

14.7 DATA INTEGRITY

As the backplane bus bandwidth is extended to handle ever-increasing clock rates, the noise susceptibility of a bus poses a serious threat to overall system integrity. There are several sources of noise that need to be taken into account in the design and layout of the transceiver, the PC board backplane, and the bus terminations to avoid intermittent or total failure of the system. They are

1. Reflections
2. Crosstalk
3. Ground and V_{CC} noise
4. Other (external noise, packaging, layout)

In any practical implementation these noises are inevitable. For example, even on a fully terminated bus there are always some reflections due to nonuniform loading arising from some unused slots. However, it is important to estimate and minimize the noise components of the bus system mentioned above. The combined contribution of the noise under worst-case conditions should be within the noise margin for reliable operaton.

The design of the transceiver (including packaging, pin layout, and layout) plays a key role in protecting the data integrity of the system against all of the noise sources listed above. We have already seen how the reflections can be minimized by either using a transceiver that is capable of driving a fully terminated bus or by using a transceiver that has controlled rise and fall times that are greater than $3t_p$, so that the bus appears like a lumped circuit. The second option is a better alternative to having fast transitions that take a long time to settle anyway. This is because slower edges also cut down crosstalk, V_{CC}, and ground noise especially when multiple drivers are simultaneously switched and ringing caused by package inductances and by reflections on the stub connecting the transceiver to the backplane. It is important to note that the $t_r = 3t_p$ relation is an approximate rule of thumb and even at this limit there will still be some amount of ringing due to reflection on an unterminated line. However, the amplitude of this ringing is less than 15 percent of the signal, as measured on the bench.

14.7.1 Crosstalk

Crosstalk is caused by distributed coupling—both capacitive (C_c) and inductive (L_c)—among the bus lines. When crosstalk is observed on an undriven sense line that lies next to the driven line with both lines terminated at their characteristic impedances ($Z = R_T$), near-end and far-end (also referred to as backward and forward crosstalk, respectively) crosstalk have quite different features, as shown in Fig. 14.23. The respective peak amplitudes for the near-end (V_{NE}) and far-end (V_{FE}) crosstalk components are[8–10]

$$V_{NE} = K_{NE} 2t_p V_I / t_r \qquad \text{for } t_r > 2t_p \tag{14.8}$$

$$V_{NE} = K_{NE} V_I \qquad \text{for } t_r < 2t_p \tag{14.9}$$

$$V_{FE} = K_{FE} l V_I / t_r \tag{14.10}$$

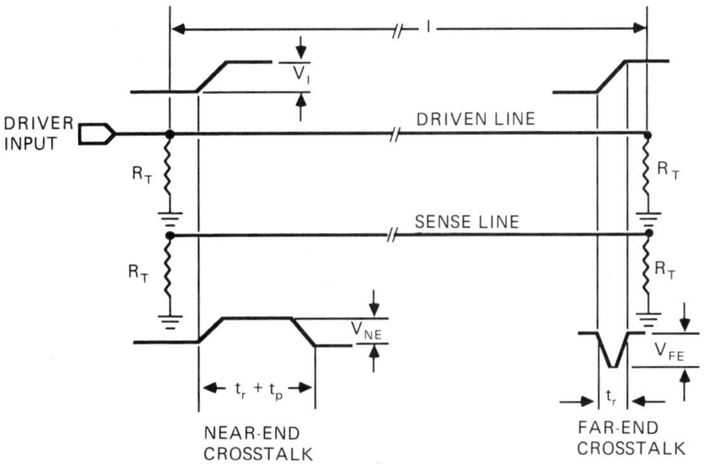

FIGURE 14.23 Crosstalk under ideal conditions.

where V_I is the amplitude and t_r the rise time of the signal on the driven line and l is the length of the bus. The coupling constants K_{NE} and K_{FE} are given by the expressions

$$K_{\text{NE}} = (1/4t_p)(C_cZ + L_c/Z) \tag{14.11}$$

$$K_{\text{FE}} = (1/2)(C_cZ - L_c/Z) \text{ ns/ft} \tag{14.12}$$

In addition, the pulsewidth of the near-end crosstalk pulse is $t_r + 2t_p$, whereas that of the far-end crosstalk pulse is t_r, as shown in Fig. 14.23.

The amplitude of the near-end crosstalk component reduces to zero at the far end and vice versa. At any point in between, the crosstalk is a sum of fractions of the near-end and far-end waveforms. As the last two formulas indicate, far-end crosstalk can have either polarity, whereas near-end crosstalk always has the same polarity as the signal from which it arises. In microstrip backplanes, the far-end crosstalk pulse is usually opposite in polarity from the source pulse.

Even though the situation depicted in Fig. 14.23 is idealistic, it makes it easier to analyze mathematically and provides insights into the crosstalk phenomena that have direct implications on transceiver design. Several key observations can be made from the above experiment. To start with, it is obvious from Eqs. (14.8)–(14.10) that the amplitude of both near-end and far-end crosstalk pulses scale with that of the signal. Therefore, from the point of view of crosstalk immunity on a bus that has the same signals on all lines, the noise margin expressed as a percentage of the signal amplitude is the critical parameter, not the absolute value of the noise margin.

Therefore, in order to improve the crosstalk immunity, the percentage noise margin has to be maximized. This can be achieved by reducing the receiver threshold range and by centering the threshold between the high and low levels. Interestingly enough, these are the very same features that also help solve the bus-driving problem in BTL transceivers, as discussed earlier.

In the limit, when the receiver threshold range is infinitely small and at the center of the swing, the percentage noise margin is 50 percent in both high and low states. However, the percentage noise margin could be further improved by using hysteresis at the receiver input.

It is clear from the discussion above that reducing the signal amplitude on the bus does not affect crosstalk immunity as long as noise margin expressed as a percentage of the signal amplitude is maintained. On the other hand, lower signal amplitude significantly reduces power consumption. With use of a design based on these principles, the BTL transceivers are able to provide 3 times the crosstalk immunity with one-third the swing over TTL and at the same time reduce power consumption by an order of magnitude.

Second, when $t_r \leq 2t_p$, which is the case for most high-speed buses, the near-end crosstalk amplitude V_{NE} expressed as a percentage of signal amplitude V_I is independent of the rise time t_r. In fact, it is a function only of the physical layout. Thus the near-end crosstalk immunity for a given percentage noise margin has to be built into the backplane PC layout. Because $V_{\text{NE}}/V_I = K_{\text{NE}}$ for this case, K_{NE} should be kept lower than the available worst-case noise margin. K_{NE} may be reduced by either increasing the spacing between lines or by introducing a ground line in between. The ground line, in addition to increasing the spacing between the signal lines, forces the electric field lines to converge on it, significantly reducing crosstalk. Fortunately, even without the ground lines, the near-end crosstalk, in most practical buses, is quite small and therefore much less of a problem than the far-end crosstalk. It is interesting to note, however, that the near-end crosstalk pulse width is $t_r + 2t_p$, which increases with the length of the bus and could be much wider than the far-end crosstalk pulse.

The amplitude of the far-end crosstalk pulse, on the other hand, is always an inverse function of the rise time, independent of whether $t_r > 2t_p$ or $t_r < 2t_p$. That is, the faster the rise time of the signal (smaller t_r), the larger the far-end crosstalk pulse. Furthermore, the amplitude increases as the length of the bus l is increased. However, the pulse width is much smaller compared to near-end crosstalk in typical implementations because it is always less than or equal to the rise time t_r, independent of the bus length.

It is quite easy to exceed noise margins with far-end crosstalk in practical high-speed bus designs when using microstrip bus lines. Therefore it is important to make sure that this does not happen. One solution is to increase the rise and fall times to reduce the far-end crosstalk amplitude to an acceptable level. However, it is difficult to find transceivers that have externally adjustable rise and fall times. Moreover, this solution is ad hoc, in the sense that it needs to be fine-tuned to each and every situation based on the length of the bus, available noise margin, etc.

A much more general solution is provided by the Trapezoidal transceivers such as DS3662 from National Semiconductor. It uses controlled rise and fall times on the driver of 15 ± 5 ns on the driver, which reduces crosstalk. In addition, the receiver input incorporates a filter that selectively rejects noise pulses up to 20 ns.[11] Since the far-end crosstalk pulse width never exceeds the rise times, the far-end crosstalk problem is eliminated, independent of the length of the bus.[12–14]

14.7.1.1 ***Crosstalk Measurement.*** Actual measurement is the best way to determine the amount of crosstalk quantitatively in a real-world bus, which is a much more complicated situation than the setup discussed earlier. For example, when multiple lines on either side of the sense lines switch simultaneously, the crosstalk is considerably larger, typically 3.5 times the single line switching case for microstrip backplanes. Also, the location of the drivers on the driven lines and the receiver on the sense line for worst-case crosstalk differs for the near-end and far-end cases, as shown in Figs. 14.24 and 14.25 for a uniformly loaded bus. But if the far-end crosstalk is not of the opposite polarity, the crosstalk could have a larger amplitude and pulse width at a point near the middle of the sense line in Fig. 14.24. So in a general case, or in the case of a nonuniformly loaded bus, it is advisable to check the sense line at several locations along the length of the bus

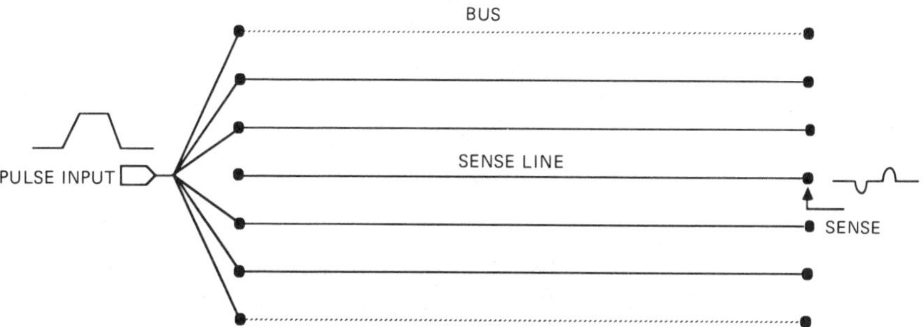

FIGURE 14.24 Worst-case far-end crosstalk measurement. All lines terminated at both ends (not shown).

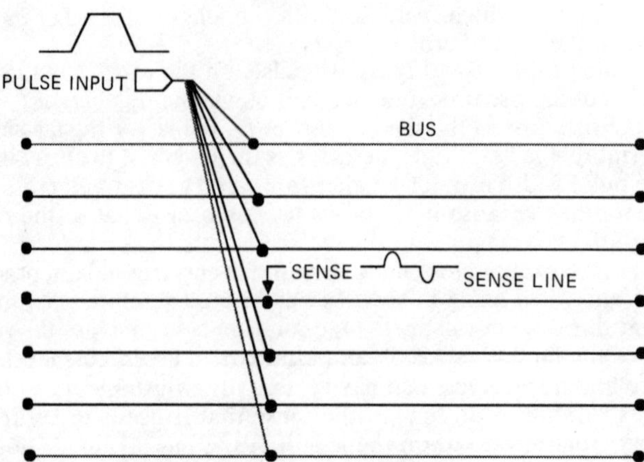

FIGURE 14.25 Worst-case near-end crosstalk measurement. All lines terminated at both ends (not shown).

to determine the worst-case crosstalk. The measurement should be made for both the positive and the negative transition of the drive signal.[8]

14.7.2 Rise and Fall Time Control

One common theme that seems to emerge through these discussions is that there are many benefits to increasing the rise and fall times to as high a value as possible that is consistent with the speed requirements by controlling the output waveform. Slower edge rates not only reduce noise problems in the bus system, such as reflections, crosstalk, ground and V_{CC} noise, ringing, etc., but also reduce electromagnetic radiation, making it easier for the end product to meet Federal Communications Commission (FCC) regulations. Many system designers use Trapezoidal transceivers in buses for the last reason alone.

Many Trapezoidal transceivers both in TTL and BTL technologies are now available. Their popularity is growing slowly but steadily as designers realize that it is not always advantageous to switch as fast as possible, particularly on a bus or a transmission line. Also, noise filtering in the receiver not only eliminates far-end crosstalk but also reduces susceptibility to external noise. This is especially useful in buses that extend out of an enclosure through cables.

BTL Trapezoidal transceivers combine all the advantages of BTL such as zero settling time, low power, etc., with Trapezoidal noise rejection features described above to provide both speed and data integrity.

Trapezoidal features do increase the delay of drivers and receivers to some extent. This is because it takes a $t_r/2$ delay before the driver output reaches the receiver threshold after having switched. Also, due to higher complexity of the circuitry, both driver and receiver tend to have larger propagation delays compared to conventional devices. However, the delay penalty in Trapezoidal BTL transceivers is small compared to the settling time penalty paid by non-Trapezoidal TTL transceivers. Therefore even though the delays on the data sheet for the Trapezoidal BTL devices look larger than the conventional TTL devices, they are faster overall in terms of the data transfer rate they can achieve on the bus.[15,16]

14.7.3 Pushing the Speed Limit

Nevertheless, when speed is of utmost importance and every nanosecond counts, it is possible to solve the noise problems in other, more difficult ways. By giving up Trapezoidal features, devices such as the DP3893-BTL Turbo transceiver provide significantly higher speeds but impose restrictions on layout and construction of the PC board traces on both the plug-in board and the backplane.

Without rise and fall time control the transitions are quite fast (1 to 2 ns) and far-end crosstalk could become a problem on microstrip backplanes. Therefore, the use of strip lines for bus lines is mandated.

The strip line, by the nature of its construction (Fig. 14.26), encloses the field generated by the signals passing through it. Unlike microstrip, the signal line in the strip line is surrounded by the PC board material, which has a uniform dielectric constant and thus creates a relatively uniform field. For the case of a uniform field, the far-end crosstalk reduces to zero in theory because the inductive and capacitive components in Eq. (14.12) become equal in value but opposite in polarity.[10] In practice the far-end crosstalk is small on the backplane and noise filtering is not necessary in the receiver. However, care should be taken to minimize crosstalk in the connector and in the boards (or modules) that plug into the backplane. This leads us to the next subject below.

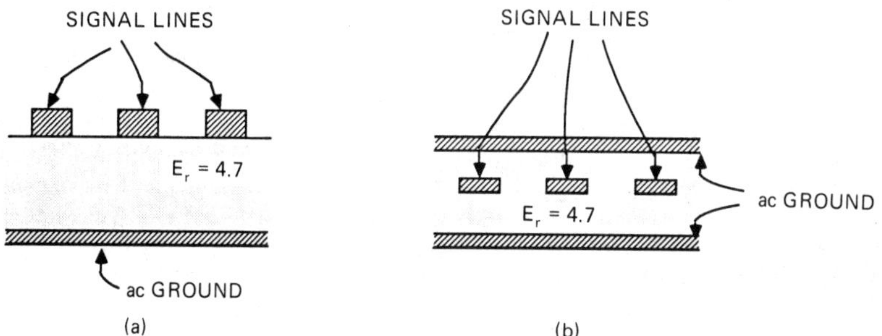

FIGURE 14.26 Cross section of (*a*) microstrip backplane bus; (*b*) strip-line backplane bus.

14.7.4 Packaging and Layout Considerations

Transceiver packaging and its layout on the plug-in board are very critical in controlling ground and V_{CC} noise, load capacitance on the bus, and ringing. Many noise problems on existing buses can be traced to poor packaging and careless layout. For example, TTL transceivers usually use the pins at extremes of the dual-in-line package (DIP) for V_{CC} and ground for historic reasons. Unfortunately, these pins have the longest lead lengths inside the package and therefore the highest inductance. This leads to large ground and V_{CC} bounce, particularly, when all the transceivers in a package (usually eight) are switched at the same time. In some instances this can cause unwanted glitches on the bus or if the device has a latch built in, the data could be changed. Another problem with the standard TTL pin layout is that the V_{CC} and ground pins are usually at the opposite ends of the package, making it difficult to bypass the chip effectively at high frequencies (due to long, inductive trace or lead lengths in series with the bypass capacitor).

With the arrival of transceivers especially designed for backplane application, such as the Trapezoidal TTL and BTL transceivers, this has changed. Figure 14.17*a* and 2.14.17*b* show DS3896 and DS3897 BTL Trapezoidal transceivers in DIP packages. Notice that the power pins are in the middle of the package on opposite sides. These pins have the shortest lead length and bonding wire lengths inside the package, providing a very-low-inductance path for ground and V_{CC}. To reduce the inductance further, multiple bonding wires in parallel are used on these lines. Moreover, controlled rise and fall times on the trapezoidal waveform reduce peak ground currents when all the drivers switch simultaneously.

When rise and fall times get below 2 or 3 ns, the packaging becomes even more critical. Figure 14.17*c* shows how this situation is handled in the DS3893 Turbo BTL transceiver. First, the device is available only in a surface-mount plastic leaded chip carrier (PLCC) package, which has short leads of the same length on all pins. Second, each output ground (emitter of the output open-collector transistor) is brought out separately without connecting to the internal on-chip ground. The package is required to be mounted as close to the bus connector as physically possible, with the driver side of the package facing the connector and all driver grounds returned to the nearest ground pin on the connector (Fig. 14.27). This arrangement returns the ground current to the backplane ground, reducing ground noise inside the chip.[14] Also, the ground noise does not worsen when all drivers switch simultaneously. It is imperative that the connector have ac ground pins connecting to the backplane ground, spread uniformly, at frequent intervals, along the length of the connector, to provide a low-inductance return path for the driver current. Some readers might wonder why the two drivers in the center of the package in Fig. 14.17*c* share a single pin for ground return. Inside the package, the driver grounds are connected to this pin through separate bond wires. The inductance of the pin is very small compared to that of the bonding wire that connects the chip to the pin. This is because the pin lead frame has a very large cross-sectional area compared to the bond wire, and it is very short in length on this package. Thus sharing a pin between two driver grounds in this way does not appreciably change the lead inductance.

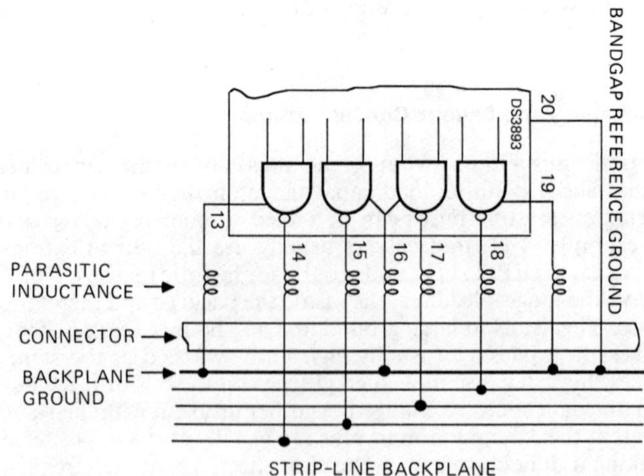

FIGURE 14.27 Recommended layout for bus transceivers on the plug-in card.

Another packaging feature is the separate bandgap ground provided for sensing the backplane ground voltage (BG, GND, pin 20). This pin is required to be connected to the backplane ground through a sense pin on the connector that is not connected to any ground on the plug-in card (to avoid any voltage drops along the sense line). The BTL receiver thresholds are set by the bandgap circuit relative to the backplane ground voltage sensed through this pin. In this way, the ground noise inside or outside the package does not alter the receiver threshold. Since the sense line does not carry any current, it could be shared between multiple transceiver packages on the same plug-in card. Figure 14.27 shows the suggested layout for this transceiver.[14]

14.8 A LOOK AT THE FUTURE

As rise times decrease the length of the stub from the backplane transmission line to the driver begins to act like a transmission in itself. If the rise is less than the round-trip delay of the stub, there will be severe ringing due to reflections. These reflections occur because the impedance of the stub is usually much larger (70–100 Ω) than the backplane load ($Z_L/2$ = 10 to 20 Ω). With a 100-Ω stub attached to a 10-Ω load driven by a fast BTL driver ($t_r \ll 2t_p$), the initial overshoot can reach 10 times that of the signal as shown in Fig. 14.28. The reflected signal crosses well below the receiver threshold several times, which could cause false triggering of the high-speed receiver. Although the case shown is for a theoretical

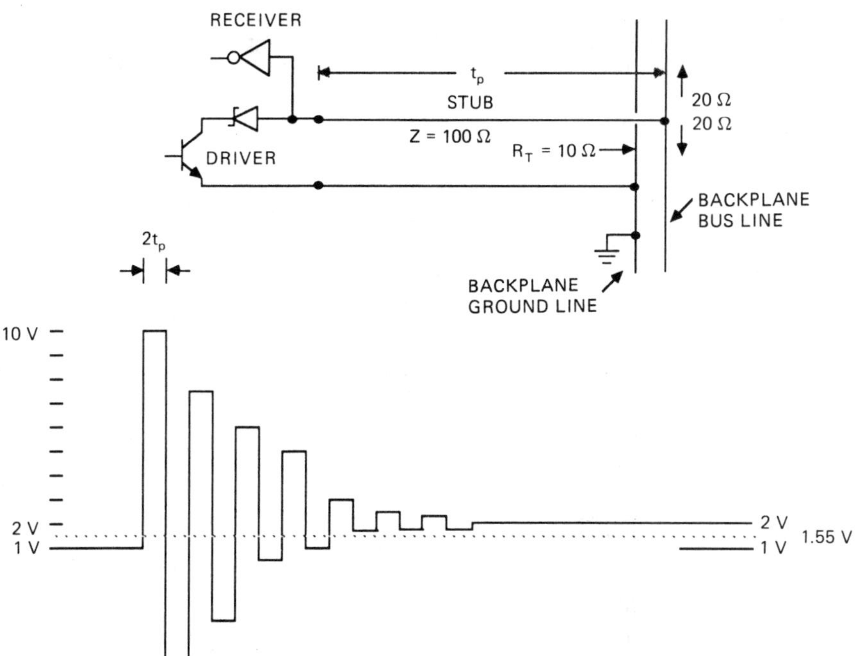

FIGURE 14.28 Ringing at the driver output due to stub reflections.

worst-case condition, it is not uncommon to get similar levels of ringing when rise times are less than 1 ns and the stub is 4 to 5 in long. Other than reducing the stub length or increasing the rise and fall times, there is very little that can be done. Providing a voltage clamp in combination with increased rise time can bring the ringing on the bus under control. Decreasing stub impedance is not an alternative because it increases the loading on the bus.

14.8.1 The Active Backplane Concept

In Figs. 14.27 and 14.28 the driver draws current from the backplane bus line through the connector and PC trace (stub) only to return it back to the backplane bus ground through the PC board and the connector once again. The obvious question that comes to mind is, why not the move the transceiver to the backplane and bring the driver input/receiver output to the plug-in card through the connector (Fig. 14.29)? In this arrangement the transceiver isolates the low-impedance backplane from the plug-in card and connector, and thus the lead length between the plug-in card and the backplane is no longer a problem. With careful layout of the transceiver on the backplane, the stub length between the transceiver and backplane becomes negligible, and ringing is practically eliminated for rise and fall times down to 100 ps or so. The concept described above is called an *active bus backplane.*[17]

There are many other advantages to the active bus backplane.

1. It is easier to dissipate heat on the backplane because it is easier to heat sink and cool the transceivers on the back of the bus away from the plug-in cards. Remember that the transceivers tend to dissipate the most power on a plug-in card on a modern system that implements most of the logic in CMOS. Unfortunately, in most cases transceivers are physically located in the most difficult place

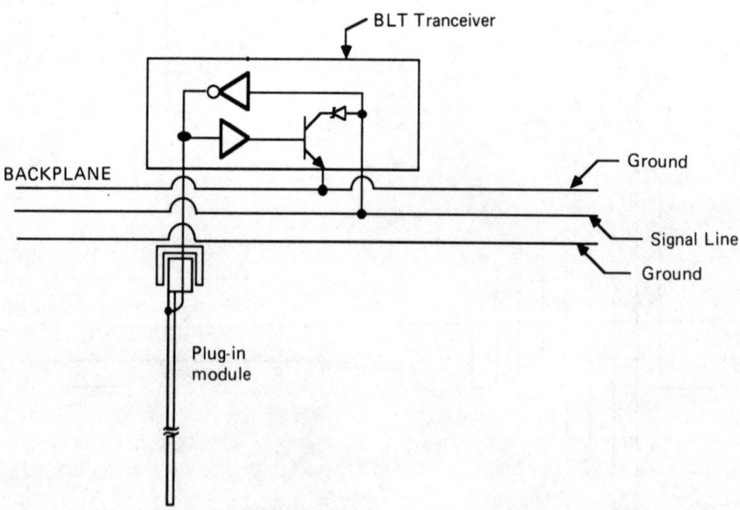

FIGURE 14.29 Active backplane.

for heat removal: close to the backplane between cards. Tight spacings between cards virtually eliminate heat sinks and forced air cooling is the only alternative. In the active bus backplane, on the other hand, all the high-power devices are on the backplane and the plug-in cards can be entirely CMOS. With heat sinking on the backplane, noisy fans for air cooling can be eliminated.

2. The capacitive loading of the bus is now reduced to a minimum, 5–7 pF instead of 10–15 pF for a BTL transceiver. This increases the bus impedance, reducing the drive current needed. Accordingly, the total system power requirement is reduced.

3. Lower capacitive loading, as we have seen earlier, reduces bus propagation delays, which allows for higher data transfer rates.

4. Furthermore, the bus is always uniformly loaded independent of how the bus is populated with plug-in cards. The impedance stays constant, allowing for perfect termination of the bus under all loading conditions.

5. The data integrity of the bus can be measured and guaranteed independent of the plug-in cards, allowing for greater level of electrical compatibility of boards from different manufacturers. The layout of plug-in board is no longer critical to the electrical performance of the bus.

6. Since all high-current switching is isolated to the backplane the plug-in cards have less problems with ground and V_{CC} noise. Short lead lengths on the backplane keep the noise down even at very high switching speeds.

7. All transceivers associated with a plug-in card can be powered through a jumper in the card so that they are powered ON only when the card is plugged in. This saves power on transceivers connected to empty slots. However, this scheme can only be implemented if the transceivers stays in high impedance on the bus line when powered down. Many transceivers now have this capability as a part of glitch-free power-on and -off feature that guarantees that the bus line will be held in a high-impedance state during the power-up sequence until the supply voltage is high enough for proper operation.

Putting transceivers on the backplane does raise some manufacturing and maintenance issues. The bus is no longer a simple passive component but a relatively complex board full of active components, making it expensive and difficult to troubleshoot. However, the increase in performance may well justify the cost and the manufacturing difficulties.

14.8.2 Device Skews—The Next Hurdle

The peak data transfer rate on a modern bus such as VMEbus, Multibus II, or NuBus is limited by the several delay components: driver and receiver delays; setup and hold times of receive latches; clock to output delay of the transmitting latch; bus propagation delay; skew between drivers, receivers, and latches in the data path versus those in the control strobe path; settling time of the bus reflections; and spatial skew of a centrally generated clock (if there is one).[16]

The peak data rate on these buses is limited to one transfer per 100 ns or 10 megatransfers per second (MT/s). Of this delay, 30 to 35 percent is due to the settling time, which is the largest delay component. Using BTL will eliminate this delay, but that would only improve the transfer rate to around 15 MT/s.

The second major component is the skew in the delay between chips such as transceivers and latches that may carry different slices of data and control lines in a parallel bus. For instance, if the parallel data and control signals such as the clock on strobe signal pass through different transceivers to and from the bus, it is possible that they may arrive at different times at the destination. To ensure that the control signal always arrives after the data is stable, it is necessary to add an intentional delay in the control path to compensate for chip-to-chip skews. For example, a top-of-the-line bus transceiver has driver and receiver propagation delays of 1 ns minimum and 7 ns maximum. In a worst-case design it is necessary to assume that the driver and receiver in the control path have the minimum delay and the same elements in the data path have the maximum delay. So, in order to guarantee that a control signal such as a strobe signal always arrives after a data signal, the strobe signal has to be delayed by 2×6 ns. Similiarly, the clock to output delay of the transmit latch and clock setup and hold times at the receiver plug-in cards can have similar skews, adding up to 25 ns of total skew delay needed in the control path. This would limit the peak transfer rates to a theoretical maximum of 40 MT/s. In practice, the transfer rates are limited to even lower values as seen earlier, due to spatial skews on the centrally generated clock. The finite propagation delay of the backplane bus causes the clock edges to arrive at different times at different plug-in modules. This could cause a worst-case skew of t_p. In addition, clock drivers (if more than one) and clock receivers contribute to the skew.

It can be shown that, independent of the location of the central clock on the bus, the theoretical maximum rate of transfer cannot exceed $1/t_p$. The only way to get around this problem is to always have the transmitting module send the clock along with the data (source synchronization) using a noncompelled protocol. In a noncompelled protocol, the transmitter clocks (or strobes) the data at a predetermined rate without waiting for an acknowledgment from the receiver.

Using a noncompelled protocol with source synchronizationa and BTL transceivers with 7-ns propagation delay, it is possible to achieve the 40-MT/s peak transfer rate. Any further speed enhancement would require reduction of chip-to-chip delay skews.

As a side note, the use of "megatransfer per second" for measuring bus speed separates the raw electrical performance of the bus from the bus data width. The bus bandwidth is more commonly expressed as megabytes/second (Mbyte/s), which takes into account the width of the bus. Thus, a 32-bit bus running at 10 MT/s would correspond to 40 Mbyte/s because there are 4 bytes to every transfer.

In order to overcome the skew hurdle, it is necessary to examine the reasons for the large variation in delays on the chip. The range 1 ns minimum to 7 ns maximum corresponds to a $\pm$ 75% variation in delay (4 $\pm$ 3 ns). Approximately $\pm$0.5 ns ($\pm$12.5%) of this variation is due to testing tolerances needed in producing, resulting from the finite accuracy of testers. Of the remaining $\pm$2.5 ns, roughly half is due to process variation and the rest is due to temperature and supply variation over the specified range.

On a plug-in card it is very unlikely that one transceiver is at one extreme of temperature compared to another. Also, the supply voltages are usually within a few millivolts of each other on the same board. Therefore, the transceiver skews can be specified at constant temperature and supply voltage, which would reduce the delay variation by about $\pm$1 ns (from 6 to 4 ns).

The only way to get around the process variation of delay, which is the dominating component ($\pm$1.5 ns), is to put all the transceivers in the data and control paths on the same chip. This technique has an additional advantage: the supply and temperature variations are also eliminated. In fact, the skew is then only limited by how well the delays can be matched on chip. For the same type of transition (positive or negative) the delays on chip can be matched within a fraction of a nanosecond as long as the outputs are loaded the same way. Since the control signal can be a different type of transition compared to one or more of the data signals, the delay matching is usually limited to 1 or 2 ns. This is still much better than the 6-ns delay. As technology advances, all the skews will reduce proportionately.

In modern buses, which are 32 bits or wider, putting all transceivers in one chip creates many problems. For instance, a 32-bit bus would require nearly 40 transceivers on one chip (allowing for command, status, and control lines), dissipating several watts of power. Also, the chip size will be limited by pads, that is, the number of bonding pads required along the edge of the die will make the die area larger than necessary, adding significantly to the cost of the chip. But it may still be worth taking this approach if performance is important. The heat can be dissipated by using a heat sink and/or forced air cooling.

14.8.3 On-chip Skew Compensation

A better, more elegant way to solve the problem is to send a strobe with every slice of data that passes through a chip. As long as a strobe is associated with each slice of data on the same chip, there is no limit to the number of transceivers or latches that are used to accommodate the data width. However, an additional control line for every slice of data is required. The slice is usually a byte but could go up to a 16-bit word or more (plus one for the strobe, of course) as long as the power and pin layouts can be accommodated.

The data transfer of each slice of data from transmitting to receiving boards occurs independent of other slices, and some way for detecting the completion of the transfer needs to be implemented. Also, it is necessary to guarantee that the strobe delays on each chip are slightly longer that data path delays on the same chip.

With this technique skews can be limited to 2 ns or less on each chip, reducing the overall skew to smaller than 10 ns. This would allow transfer rates of up to 100 MT/s; 400 Mbyte/s for a 32-bit bus and 800 Mbyte/s for a 64-bit bus.

14.9 CONCLUSION

As can be seen from the discussions in this chapter, the transceiver technology and design play a major role in determining the speed and data integrity of the backplane bus. As processors and memories become faster compared to the delays involved in the bus transaction, the design of the transceiver becomes more critical.

The data transfer rates on typical TTL buses is limited to 10 MT/s mainly due to the large settling time caused by reflections. BTL overcomes this problem extending the data rate up to 40 MT/s. As this point, skew becomes the major delay component. Using a skew reduction technique along with BTL allows data rates of up to 100 MT/s based on the technology available at the time of this writing. As technology advances, higher transfer rates will become possible.

Data integrity on the backplane is threatened by reflections, crosstalk, and noise. Once again, BTL overcomes reflections by providing adequate drive. Moreover, it also increases crosstalk immunity by maximizing percentage noise margins and reduces ground and V_{CC} noise by using minimum drive current and eliminating noise spikes due to overlap. Further reduction in crosstalk can be obtained by using Trapezoidal noise filtering techniques or by using strip-line backplane construction. Ringing due to reflections on stubs can be minimized by rise time control and careful layout. For higher data rates, the active backplane may be the answer.

Finally, power is a critical issue for most applications. BTL implemented in BI-CMOS technology provides at least an order of magnitude reduction in power over other technologies when driving a terminated bus. If this power is still too high, then the use of CMOS Tristate devices without termination is the only option. The reflections can be treated by allowing for a settling time or by controlling the rise and fall times to make the bus appear like a lumped circuit. In any case, there is a loss in performance associated with this approach that is a function of bus length. This loss can be compensated for by using wider buses at added cost.

ACKNOWLEDGMENTS

I would like to thank the following people who helped in writing this chapter: Joel Martinez and Dave Hawley for reviewing the document; Michaell Ross for typing the manuscript; Sheila Felt for doing the artwork; Paul Borrill for encouraging me to find a solution to the bus driving problem; Des Young and Paul Sweazey for their ideas on enhancing bus transfer rates; Joseph Di Giacomo for being persistant in convincing me to write this chapter; and my wife and son for sacrificing their time with me so that I could finish this project on time.

LIST OF TRADEMARKS

REFERENCES

1. John Theus and David B. Gustavson, "Wire-OR Logic on Transmission Lines," *IEEE Micro,* vol. 3, June 1983, pp. 51–55.
2. *Fairchild Advanced Schottky TTL (FAST) Data Book,* Fairchild/National Semiconductor, 1985.
3. *Linear Interface Data Book, Transmission Line Information,* Fairchild/National Semiconductor, Chap. 19, 1978.
4. R. V. Balakrishnan, "32 Bit System Buses—A Physical Layer Comparison," BUSCON WEST, 1987.

5. ANSI/IEEE Standard 896.1-1987, IEEE Backplane Bus Specification for Multiprocessor Architectures: Futurebus, Institute of Electrical and Electronics Engineers, New York, 1988.
6. R. V. Balakrishnan, "The Proposed IEEE P896 Futurebus-A Solution to the Bus Driving Problem," *IEEE Micro,* August 1984.
7. *F100K ECL Handbook,* Fairchild National Semiconductor, 1985.
8. R. V. Balakrishnan, "Reducing Noise on Microcomputer Buses," IECON/82, Professional Workshop Record on Microcomputer Realities, November 1982.
9. R. V. Balakrishnan, "Cut Bus Reflections, Crosstalk with a Trapezoidal Transceiver," *EDN,* pp. 151–156, August 4, 1983.
10. A. Feller, H. P. Kaupp, and J. J. Di Giacomo, "Crosstalk and Reflections in High Speed Digital Systems," Proceedings of the Fall Joint Computer Conference, 1965, pp. 511–525.
11. R. V. Balakrishnan et al., "Data Bus Transceiver," U.S. Patent 4,320,521, March 16, 1982.
12. R. V. Balakrishnan, "Eliminating Crosstalk Over Long Distance Busing," *Computer Design,* March 1982, pp. 155–162.
13. R. V. Balakrishnan, "Bus Optimizer," National Semiconductor Application Note 259, Interface Databook, April 1981.
14. *Interface Data Book, Bus Transceivers,* National Semiconductor, 1988 ed., Sec. 2.
15. R. V. Balakrishnan, "Advances in Backplane Technology," MIDCON, 1985.
16. D. Hawley and R. V. Balakrishnan, "Timing Analysis of Snychronous and Asynchronous Buses," Buscon West, Conference Management Corporation, Feb. 1988, pp. 237–245.
17. R. V. Balakrishnan, "Active Bus Backplane," U.S. Patent 4,697,858, October 6, 1987.

P · A · R · T · 3

BUS USER ISSUES

CHAPTER 15
BUS STANDARDS

Clyde R. Camp
Texas Instruments, Inc.
Dallas, Texas

Michael Smolin
Smolin & Associates
Palo Alto, California

15.1 INTRODUCTION—THE STANDARDS BUSINESS

Of the nine buses described in Part 1, six were adopted as standards by the Institute of Electrical and Electronics Engineers (IEEE). *Adopted* means that a specification document, developed and agreed upon in an open consensus process, was formally approved by the IEEE Standard Board. The IEEE is an important component in the development of standards because its membership is composed of individual contributors rather than companies. In addition, the members of the Working Groups (WGs) who do the actual work of writing the draft are not required to be members of the IEEE or any of its societies. Most other standards-generating organizations charge a membership fee, which often prohibits individuals or small companies from participating.

Within the IEEE, the Computer Society has been the major contributor of bus standards. Since 1985, twelve bus standards have been developed (see Sec. 15.6) and seven more were in progress as of July 1988. As new technologies emerge to meet the growing need for intercommunication between computational resources, additional requests for bus standards are sure to occur.

It should be noted at this point that the standards being discussed are purely voluntary as opposed to regulatory. Regulatory standards are usually generated by governments and enforced by law; violations can result in civil or criminal legal action being taken. Voluntary standards, on the other hand, are not enforced by any legal methods. Adherence to them is insured by market pressures more than anything else.

One question that immediately arises is, "What good are so many *different* standards—why not just one?" One major reason is that no bus is perfect for all applications. With multiple standards, the parameters of a particular bus may be optimized for speed, loading, cost, physical size, or other factors that are important to the designers and to a certain class of users. New users may pick and choose from a variety of standards for one that fits their particular needs.

Another reason for bus standard proliferation is that a *de facto* standard may have naturally occurred as different vendors attempted to remain compatible with a particular product. In this case a standards body may eliminate inconsistencies and provide more completeness in its act to "formalize" the standard which has evolved.

For whatever reason they are developed and adopted, bus standards serve the same purpose as standards in other areas—they record a specification at some particular stage of evolution. This stabilization promotes a wider range of vendor participation since vendors no longer need worry about investing effort in a product that might change unexpectedly. This in turn permits end-users to shop for the best value while reassuring them of product compatibility among vendors. In addition, government interest is always greater for standardized products, and government contracts are big business to many manufacturers.

Standards in the nonelectronic world are so pervasive that they are thought about only when there are deviations from them or when they disappear. For example, the fact that you can shop for automobile tires from a variety of manufacturers with the assurance that they will all fit is the result of standards for wheels and tires within the automotive industry.

Standards are also a respectable business in their own right. In addition to increased sales of equipment due to standardization, the sales of the standards themselves is a $3.3 million business for the IEEE alone, with the price of a single copy of a standard ranging from $5 to $100.

The remainder of this chapter focuses on the standards practices of the IEEE Computer Society (IEEE/CS) under the Microprocessor Standards Subcommittee of the Technical Committee on Microprocessors and Microcomputers. While this discussion is primarily about buses, it is generally applicable to any other standards development. Section 15.2 discusses the organizational entities involved while Section 15.4 discusses the steps in a conventional standards development cycle.

15.2 ORGANIZATIONAL RELATIONSHIPS

15.2.1 International Organizations

The international standards development arena is extremely complicated with many organizational entities competing for pieces of the standards business. Figure 15.1 depicts the rough hierarchy of organizations that are encountered during the development of an international bus standard. This is a very simplified figure depicting mainly information flow—there is little or no direct authority of one organization over another.

The two primary international standards organizations are the International Standards Organization (ISO) and the International Electrotechnical Commission (IEC). They are completely separate and distinct entities that happen to be housed in the same building. Despite their physical closeness, they have different charters and compete fiercely for standards business in areas that overlap these charters (such as the computer and electronics industries).

To minimize potential conflicts, a new international standards body on information systems (the Joint Technical Committee I or JTC1) was created in 1987

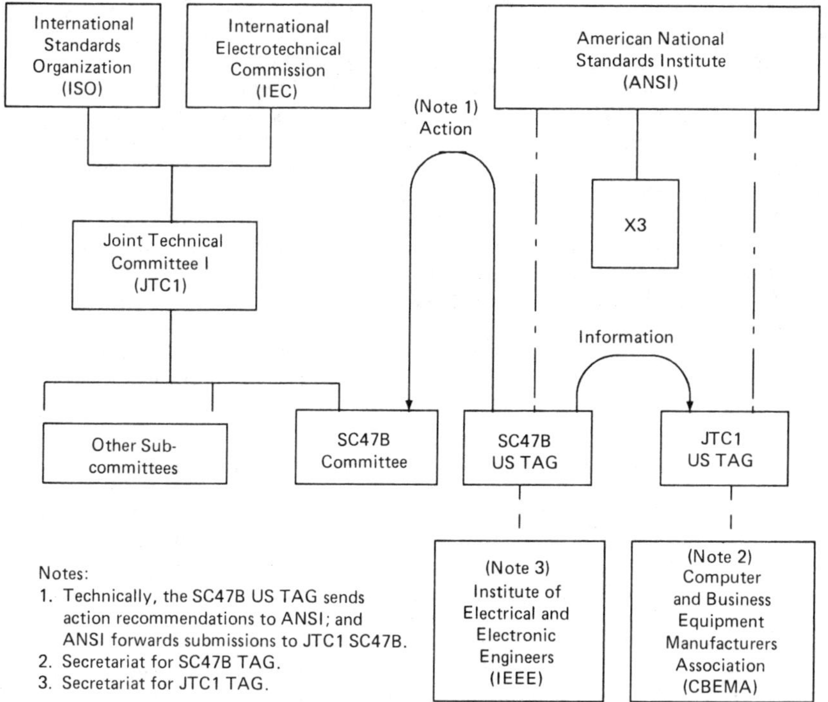

FIGURE 15.1 International standards relationships.

from parts of IEC and ISO. JTC1 is a joint committee of both IEC and ISO and its component parts were formerly

- ISO TC97 Information Systems
- IEC TC83 Information Technology
- IEC SC47B Microprocessor Systems

At this time, these committees retain much of their original identity, although they have each lost their IEC or ISO prefix in becoming subcommittees of JTC1. The JTC1 SC47B Committee (Microprocessor Systems) is the international entry point for bus standards. Its U.S. participant, the SC47B Technical Advisory Group (TAG), meets (at least) yearly and usually in advance of JTC1 SC47B meetings. SC47B meetings are held in a different country each year, and official proceedings are usually distributed in English and French. The secretariat for the U.S. SC47B TAG is the IEEE (see Sec. 15.2.4).

15.2.2 U.S. Standards—ANSI

The American National Standards Insititute (ANSI) is the United States national coordinator for standardization with a congressional charter to create American national standards. The United States is represented in international standards activities by the U.S. National Committee (USNC), which is administered by ANSI and which appoints U.S. delegates to both the IEC and ISO. The IEEE's participation in the IEC and ISO is through the USNC.

ANSI accepts adopted standards from many U.S. standards organizations such as the IEEE or the Society of Automotive Engineers. These are true consensus standards in that they have already been through a consensus process, balloted, and formally adopted by their respective organizations. Standards produced by the IEEE are routinely submitted to ANSI.

ANSI also accepts proposed documents from accredited standards committees such as X3. These documents must go through an additional consensus gathering and balloting process since X3 does not adopt standards itself. X3 also serves as ANSI's Technical Advisory Group (TAG) to the JTC1 TC97 Committee (Information Systems).

The Computer and Business Equipment Manufacturers Association (CBEMA) serves as secretariat for X3 as well as being its funding and administrative entity.

15.2.3 U.S. Standards—Accredited Standards Committees

Accredited standards committees (perhaps the best known of which is X3) are independent committees with organizational representation and possible membership fees. They do not adopt standards on their own, but generate proposed standards that go to ANSI for balloting and adoption. Study groups and Technical Committees within them tend to be more generic in nature than are Working Groups within the IEEE, although this is not always the case.

X3 has more than 75 internal entities and over 3000 volunteers working on over 600 projects dealing with information processing systems technology. It meets three times a year in February, June, and October. The meeting venue is determined two years in advance.

15.2.4 U.S. Standards—Institute of Electrical and Electronics Engineers (IEEE)

The IEEE is recognized and accredited by ANSI as a standard-writing body. This means that IEEE adheres to ANSI rules for the generation of standards, that IEEE standards are eligible for adoption as National Standards, and that they may be presented by the United States National Committee to international standards organizations for adoption abroad.

Traditionally, the primary international organization with which IEEE has been involved has been the IEC. The IEC has adopted many IEEE bus standards in the microprocessor and microcomputer area. The IEEE principally participates in the international activities through the U.S. National Committee. The USNC is the official body that appoints U.S. delegates to ISO and IEC. IEEE members often serve on IEC or ISO Technical Committees, working to create new standards and to maximize compatibility between IEC Standards and IEEE Standards. Even so, it is not uncommon for there to be a European standard and an American standard on the same subject. IEEE standards are frequently adopted as IEC standards, and the reverse sometimes takes place.

Since the IEEE is a transnational organization, it also operates a portion of its standards-making functions outside of ANSI.

All new and revised IEEE standards are submitted to ANSI for adoption as ANSI standards. With the current structure, most of the standards being devel-

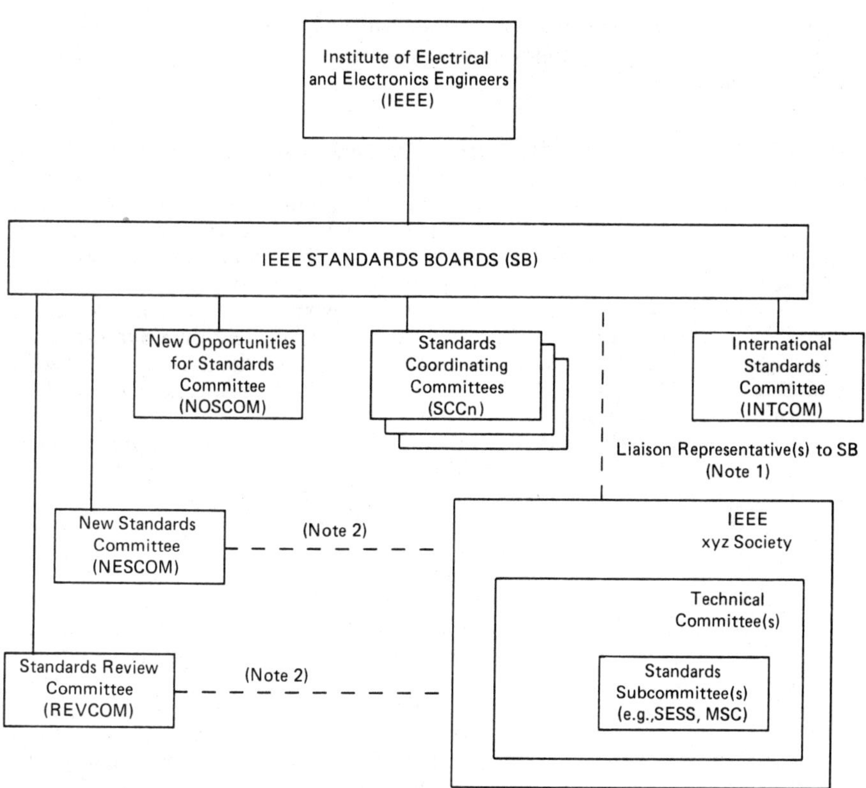

Notes:

1. Appointments of liaison representatives to the Standards Board are at the discretion of the Society.
2. Although a Society may have member representatives on NESCOM or REVCOM or both, it is not guaranteed that any given Society will be represented on either.

FIGURE 15.2 IEEE standards organization.

oped in the IEEE Computer Society will be submitted to JTC1 via the appropriate U.S. TAG (if it is desirable for them to be considered for adoption as international standards.)

The IEEE standards organization is shown in Fig. 15.2. A brief description of its components follows.

15.2.4.1 Standards Board. The IEEE has a formal committee, the IEEE Standards Board, which is chartered by IEEE bylaws with responsbility for standards development across all IEEE societies.

The IEEE Standards Board meets four times a year to consider standards-related matters and has a permanent support staff near IEEE headquarters in New York City. Beneath the IEEE Standards Board are several permanent committees, the most pertinent of which are the New Standards Committee (NESCOM) and the Standards Review Committee (REVCOM).

The Standards Board is one of six boards that report to the IEEE and whose chairs are members of the IEEE Board of Directors. The Standards Board is ultimately responsible for authorizing a standard to be started or adopted and published, although it usually follows the recommendations of NESCOM and REVCOM in these matters.

15.2.4.2 ***New Standards Committee.*** The New Standards Committee (NESCOM) considers applications from sponsoring IEEE organizations for the authorization of new standards projects. Such an application is in the form of a project authorization request (PAR) as shown in Fig. 15.3. NESCOM makes recommendations to the IEEE Standards Board, which takes the actual action of approving the PAR. A particular PAR may either be to revise an existing standard or to create a draft proposal for a new standard in a particular area. The PAR must state the scope and purpose of the project and identify patent or copyright issues (although these do not necessarily cause problems.) Once the PAR is approved, a project number is issued and the Working Group may formally proceed to develop its standards proposal.

When a standards project is contemplated, the sponsoring organization is required to submit a PAR to NESCOM for approval at the earliest opportunity, preferably before work gets started. Without a formally approved PAR, work on a project is not authorized beyond six months. For this reason, informal study groups often do much of the preliminary work to determine feasibility and scope prior to recommending that the sponsor request a PAR. Every PAR submitted for approval is circulated to all members of the IEEE Standards Board, to liaison representatives from IEEE Groups and Societies, and to external organizations for a 30-day review and comment. Comments received are compiled and presented at the NESCOM meeting.

NESCOM is responsible for ensuring that a proposed standards project is within the scope and purpose of the IEEE, that standards projects are assigned to the proper society or other organizational body, and that all interested parties are appropriately represented in the development itself.

NESCOM normally meets on the day preceding the quarterly Standards Board meeting so that the comments can be reviewed and acted on prior to presenting recommendations to the Board. The NESCOM Chair is by definition a member of the Standards Board, as may be other NESCOM members.

15.2.4.3 ***Standards Review Committee.*** The Standards Review Committee (REVCOM) considers the proposed standard that has been developed and recommended for adoption by its sponsor. REVCOM does not usually review the proposed standard for technical accuracy, but it does ensure the following:

- All IEEE requirments have been met.
- Proper procedures have been followed.
- The final ballot was balanced so that all interested and affected parties are represented (usually users, producers, and general interest groups although other categories may be defined).
- A proper response has been made to all negative comments.

REVCOM meets simultaneously with (but separately from) NESCOM and is primarily a procedural review committee of at least 12 members. The Chair is by definition a member of the Standards Board, as may be other REVCOM members. All are individuals who have a strong background of technical administrative experience in their professional fields.

STANDARDS PROJECT AUTHORIZATION (PAR)

When completing this PAR refer to instructions in the PAR Submitter's Guide

1. ______________ Date of Request

Revised Par [ ] Yes [ ] No

12. Standards Board Assigned Project No.______
Approved:______
(For Standards Office Use Only)

2. [ ] Standard [ ] Recommended Practice [ ] Guide
[ ] New [ ] Revision of: ______

3. Project Title:

4. Scope of Proposed Standard (use attachment sheet if necessary):

5. Purpose of Proposed Standard (use attachment sheet if necessary):

6. Sponsor:
Technical Committee:______ Society:______

7. Proposed Coordination: Method of Coordination:

8. Name of Group that will write the Standard

9. Are you aware of any patent issues? [ ] Yes [ ] No (If yes, attach a sheet with complete description)
Are you aware of any standards or projects with a similar scope? [ ] Yes [ ] No (If yes, attach a sheet with complete description)

10. Person Delegated to Receive Communications and Conduct Liaison with Interested Parties:
Name:______
Company:______ Telephone No:______
Street Address:______ Telex No:______
City:______ State:______ Zip Code:______

11. Submitted by:
Name:______
Company:______ Telephone No:______
Street Address:______ Telex No:______
City:______ State:______ Zip Code:______

Note: Copies of PAR Submitter's Guide and the IEEE Standards Manual are available from the IEEE Standards Office

FIGURE 15.3 Project authorization request form.

15.2.4.4 IEEE Standards Coordinating Committees. The IEEE Standards Coordinating Committees (SCC*n* where *n* is the committee number) handle standards issues that do not belong in any of the societies or that span multiple societies. One of the most important of these is SCC10, which is responsible for the *IEEE Standards Dictionary*.

15.2.4.5 XYZ Society. Most of the standards work falls under the auspices of one IEEE society or another (such as the Power Engineering Society or the Computer Society). Each society has its own internal structure, but from a standards development standpoint, most are similar to the Computer Society.

15.2.5 Computer Society

The IEEE consists of member societies, such as the Computer Society, the Instrumentation and Measurements Society, or the Communications Society. Within the IEEE, the single largest developer of standards has historically been the Power Engineering Society. The Computer Society is now the second largest with approximately 91 standards completed or in work. However, 90 of these 91 have been initiated since 1980, making the Computer Society one of the largest contemporary contributors in the world of standards. Since most of the newer computer bus standards have been developed in the IEEE Computer Society, it will be used as an example of how the standards development process works. The Computer Society Standards organization is shown in Fig. 15.4 and its components are described in the following sections.

15.2.5.1 Technical Committees. Within any IEEE society, the technical expertise is assumed to lie in its Technical Committees (TCs.) They are the normal sponsors of standards development activities for the IEEE (although some delegate such responsibility to a Standards Subcommittee.) Each TC has a general area of responsibility or expertise, although there is sometimes quite a bit of overlap between TCs, and projects are occasionally jointly sponsored. The Technical Committee on Microprocessors and Microcomputers (TCMM) is responsible for standards applicable to microprocessors and microcomputers (although the distinction between these and mainframe computers is becoming a little vague). Most of the Computer Society's bus standards have been developed within the TCMM.

It is the function of the sponsor to ensure that the draft is technically sound, that the document meets the goals for which the Working Group and project were sponsored, and that procedural requirements have been met. The sponsor may approve the document, reject it, table it, direct the Working Group to make changes, or take any other appropriate action.

15.2.5.2 Computer Society Standards Subcommittees. Each TC may have one or more Standards Subcommittees (SSCs) under it. Each SSC is responsible for a more specific set of standards. The creation of a Standards Subcommittee is at the discretion of the sponsor TC, and there is frequently only one such committee under a particular TC. If it exists, the SSC is given the responsibility to handle all standards activity for the TC. For bus standards, the Microprocessors Standards

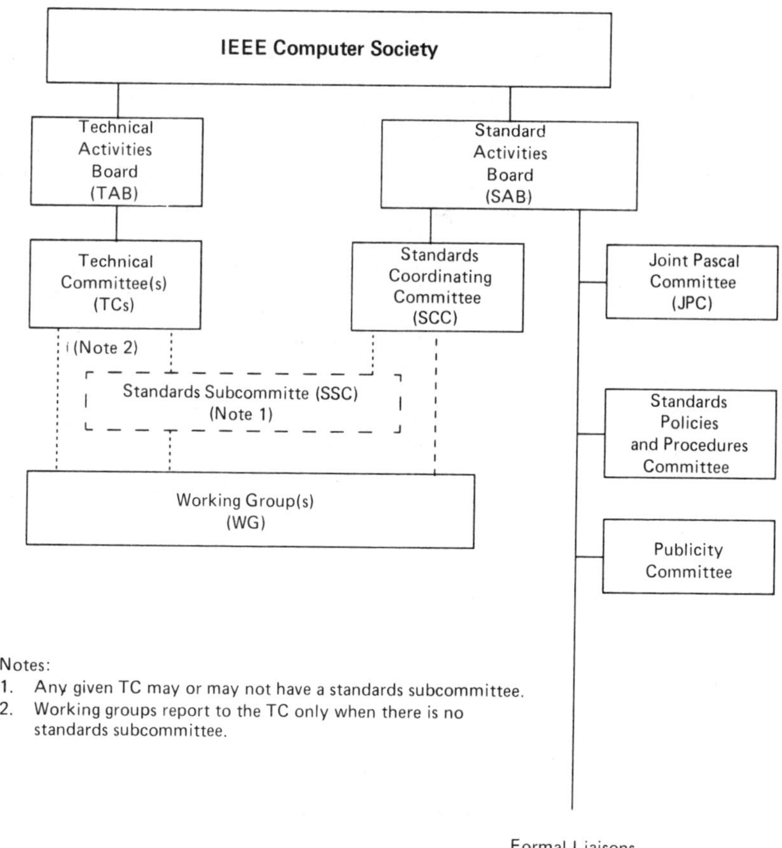

FIGURE 15.4 Computer Society standards organization.

Committee has become the Standards Subcommittee for the TC on Microprocessors and Microcomputers.

15.2.5.3 Technical Activities Board. The Technical Activities Board (TAB) generally oversees and administers the Technical Committee. Technical Committee chairs are appointed by the Vice President for Technical Activities, who is also the Chair of the Technical Activities Board. The board's members are the chairs of the various TCs.

15.2.5.4 Standards Activities Board. In the Computer Society, the Standards Activities Board (SAB) performs four functions:

1. It recommends to the Computer Society Board of Governors all policies and practices with respect to standards.
2. It enforces procedural conformity in standards development across the various TCs within the Computer Society.

3. It handles all standards publicity matters.

4. It acts as a special sponsor for the Joint Pascal Committee (JPC).

All members of the SAB must be members of the Computer Society and its chair is the Computer Society's Vice President of Standards.

15.2.5.5 Standards Coordinating Committee. The Computer Society Standards Coordinating Committee (SCC) should not be confused with one of the IEEE Standard Coordinating Committees (SCC*n*), which will have a number as part of its name (e.g., SCC21.) The Computer Society SCC is responsible for the internal coordination of all of the working groups under the various Computer Society TCs. Each Working Group chair and Standards Subcommittee chair is a member of the SCC. The SCC also acts as the sponsor for working groups that do not fit under one of the Society's existing TCs.

15.2.5.6 Working Group. The Working Group (WG) is the committee that actually does the technical and editing work necesary to generate the draft standard, which will (hopefully) become an IEEE standard.

15.3 DOCUMENT CLASSIFICATION

There are several classes of draft standard documents developed by the Working Groups and eventually submitted for adoption by the IEEE Standards Board. With the exception of the trial-use standard, all classes are updated at five-year intervals (or sooner) and the sponsoring organization may *reaffirm, revise,* or *withdraw* the document. The document classes are as follows:

- *Full-use standards* (usually referred simply to as *standards*) are documents with mandatory requirements.
- *Trial-use standards* also contain mandatory requirements but are treated in special ways as discussed in Sec. 15.3.1. While a full-use standard has a five-year life, a trial-use standard must be *reaffirmed, revised,* or *withdrawn* within two years.
- *Recommended practices* are documents in which preferred procedures and positions are presented.
- *Guidelines* are documents in which alternative approaches to good practice are suggested but no clear-cut recommendations are made.

Standards tell you what you *shall* or *must* do, recommended practices what you *should* do, and guidelines what you *might* do. Although IEEE adopts and publishes standards, it does not engage in product testing or in certification of products to comply with those standards. Manufacturers and vendors may claim compliance of one of their products to an IEEE standard, but it is left to the industry to police itself.

Reaffirmation of any of the standards documents requires approval in a sponsor ballot by at least 50 percent of the interested and affected parties if there are no negative votes. If there are negative ballots, then a 75 percent approval is required. A 75 percent approval is also required in the case of revision.

For withdrawal, a 50 percent approval in a sponsor ballot is required. If the sponsor fails to take timely action to reaffirm, revise, or withdraw a standard, the IEEE Standards Board can withdraw a standard with approval from 50 percent of the Standards Board members.

15.3.1 Trial-Use Standards

The IEEE has a special standards category of trial use. A document may be given this designation for any of several reasons, some of which are listed below.

1. A trial-use standard may be adopted when it is felt that a generally acceptable draft (from a technical and procedural standpoint) requires additional input from a broader base of the interested and affected community. The IEEE prefers the use of trial-use standards to the widespread distribution of unapproved drafts.

2. A sponsoring organization may submit a draft for adoption as a trial-use standard when adequate consensus cannot be achieved in the sponsor ballot. This usually occurs when the sponsor cannot adequately resolve negative ballots or when aspects of the document are uncertain. This has been used by sponsors to distribute incomplete documents when there is great demand for the partial results.

3. A submitted draft may be adopted by the IEEE Standards Board as a trial-use standard when the Standards Board cannot reach approval for its adoption as a full IEEE standard. This may occur when there are questions about proper response to sponsor ballot negatives or other procedural questions.

A trial-use standard, unlike other standards documents of the IEEE, has an effective life of two years. If no comments are received during the trial period, the sponsor may recommend adoption of the document as a full IEEE standard. Received comments may become the basis for revision of the document, which then must go through another sponsor ballot to approve its recommendation to the IEEE Standards Board for adoption as an IEEE standard.

An IEEE trial-use standard may be adopted by ANSI as a Draft American National Standard (DANS), although there is an important distinction between the two. A DANS is published mainly to solicit criticism and comment. A trial-use standard, while also published for the solicitation of comments, specifically allows for claims of conformance and so, for example, may be part of a purchase-order specification.

15.4 THE BUS STANDARD DEVELOPMENT CYCLE

The TCMM is the official sponsoring organization for most new bus activities within the IEEE. It has, however, relegated its standards responsibilities to its Standards Subcommittee, the Microprocessor Standards Committee (MSC).

Figure 15.5 depicts the specific organization of the Computer Society that produces most of the bus standards within the IEEE. A typical development cycle is shown in Fig. 15.6.

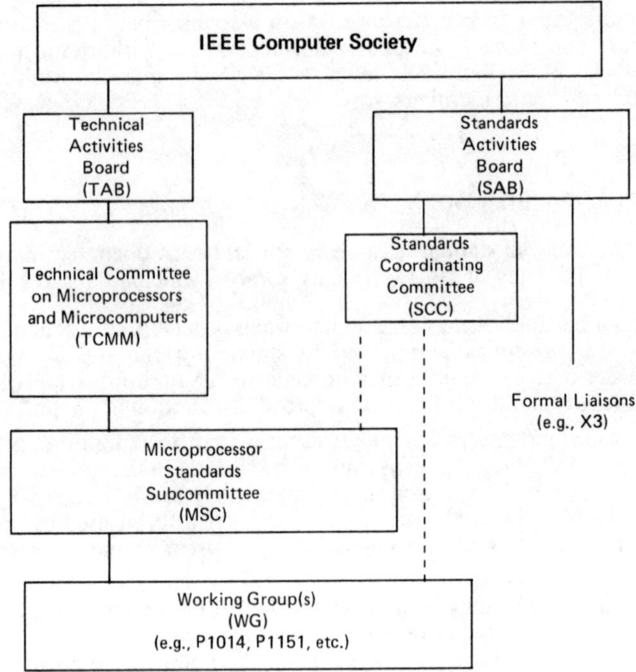

FIGURE 15.5 Computer Society bus standards organization.

15.4.1 Project Identification

Potential bus projects are identified by individuals or groups that feel that there is a need for a new (or revised) standard, and they undertake to find a sponsor for that activity. The initial contact may be through the IEEE Standards Office, a Society officer or volunteer member involved with standards, or a committee involved with standards or other projects in that area. The contact is eventually passed to the MSC. Sometimes the TCMM or MSC itself recognizes a need for a standards project and actively solicits interested parties to participate.

When an interested group or individual is identified, they are encouraged to make a short presentation defining the proposed activity, explaining why it is important, and in general why a standard is necessary. The presenter may be anyone, although it is preferred that it be someone who is willing to chair the proposed activity. This presentation takes place at one of the regular meetings of the MSC and is usually followed by a motion to proceed with the standardization process by requesting that a PAR be filed with the Standards Board by the sponsor.

At that point, the sponsor may

- Agree to sponsor the project as proposed
- Agree to sponsor the project but change some aspects of the proposal to either broaden or narrow its purpose
- Decide to investigate the issue further via a study group

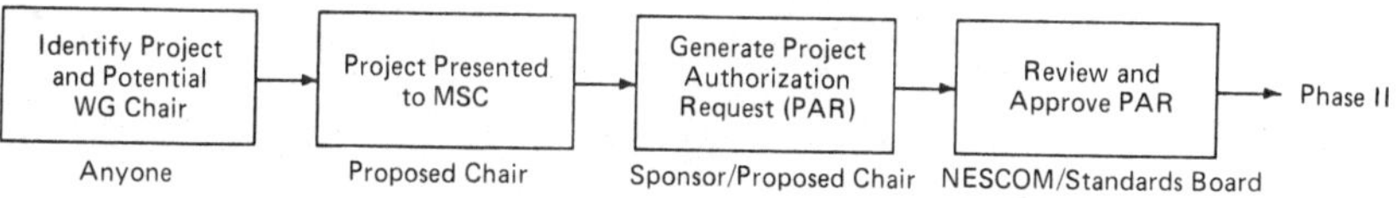

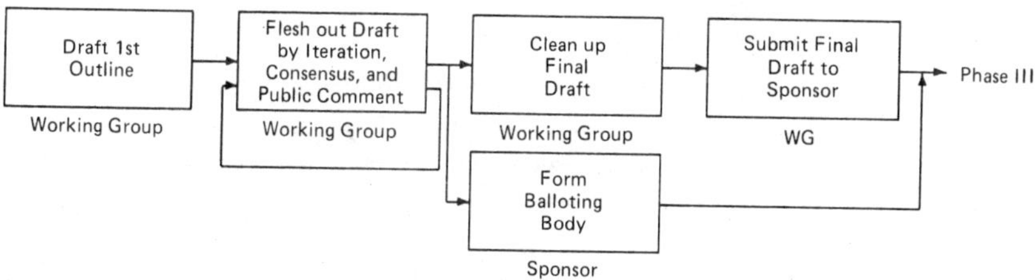

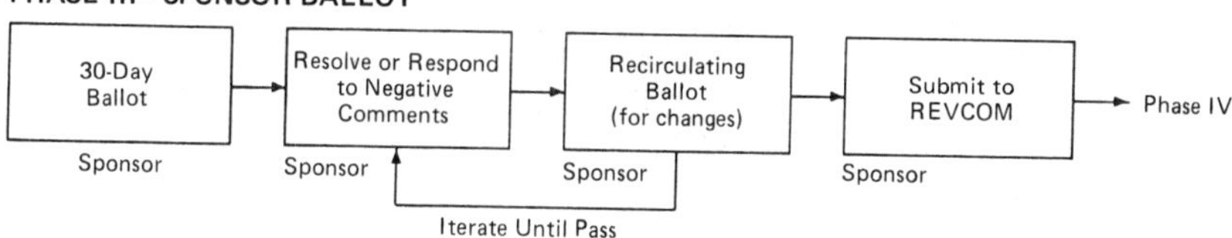

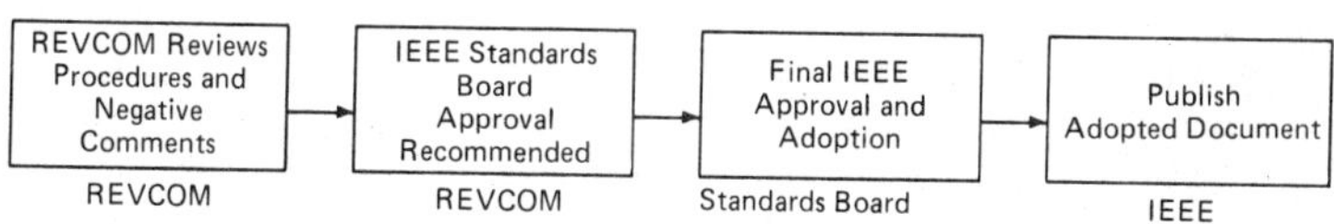

FIGURE 15.6 Bus standard development cycle.

- Table the issue for future action
- Reject the proposal and decline to sponsor the project

In the latter case, another TC or organization may be recommended as a more suitable project sponsor.

When the MSC (acting for the TCMM) agrees to sponsor a project, a PAR is submitted to NESCOM. Often, a Study Group is formed in advance of the PAR submittal so that it can recommend the wording of the *scope* and *purpose* portions of the PAR to the sponsor. The PAR identifies the project by title, scope, purpose, and sponsor. The group that will write the draft as well as other standards bodies with whom formal coordination will be undertaken during the project is also specified. In some cases, the Working Group may be formed immediately and start working while awaiting a response to the PAR.

NESCOM reviews the PAR request, ensures that the correct liaisons are specified, assigns a number to it and, by its approval, recommends it to the Standards Board. The IEEE Standards Board usually approves all NESCOM recommendations as a single item on a consent agenda.

15.4.2 Draft Development

After the sponsor appoints the Working Group Chair, the chair forms and organizes the Working Group. In some cases a chair and co-chair may be assigned, in other cases a chair and vice-chair. Co-chairs have equal authority and responsibility as chairs in all matters while vice-chairs act in place of the chair when the chair is unavailable. The chair (and co-chair) must be members or affiliates of the Computer Society. The MSC is responsible for the proper running of its Working Groups and may replace the chair if it becomes necessary.

Working Groups have only a few actual requirements placed on them:

- They must have open meetings and publicly announce them sufficiently ahead of time for people to make travel arrangements.
- They must record and publish minutes in a timely fashion.
- They must act in a fair, open, and reputable manner.

The principal task of the Working Group is to develop and write the drafts for the standard project authorized by its PAR. This draft will then be balloted by its sponsor as an IEEE standard.

The members of the Working Group are expected to work as individuals promoting the good of the profession. The Working Group is required to coordinate its activity with other standards-generating bodies that have interests in the subject being standardized. These bodies may include domestic groups such as X3, other Societies of the IEEE, the Department of Defense, or international organizations such as ISO and IEC. Part of this coordination is formally specified in the PAR.

In the process of developing a draft standard, members of a Working Group are encouraged to author articles and papers about their project for publication in Society publications (e.g., *Computer, MICRO*). However, the publication of the actual unapproved draft (i.e., not an adopted standard) is *not* permitted since it creates the possibility that archival copies could reside in libraries and perhaps be interpreted as conforming to the final version of the standard.

The Working Group is required to be responsive to comments from outside the Working Group and to actively solicit such comments from the interested and concerned professional public at large. Articles and presentations encourage comments, some of which may result in improvements to the draft. All must be considered by the Working Group and should be responded to in writing.

As work nears completion, the sponsor should be notified so that it can begin assembling a balanced balloting body in parallel with the Working Group's effort to finalize the draft. This parallelism is important as it helps minimize delays. When the Working Group determines (by a consensus process) that it has completed its task, it votes the draft standard out of the Working Group to its sponsor. Once the draft is ready for sponsor ballot and reported out of (the Working Group) committee the Working Group can make no further changes to it.

At this point, the draft is presented to the MSC and a motion made to pass it on to the sponsor for formal balloting. Once the draft standard has been accepted by the sponsor for balloting, the Working Group is formally finished with it. As a practical matter, the sponsor may use the Working Group experts during the balloting process to assist in resolving negative comments and during the publication phase to proof the final document.

For a full-use standard, the Working Group is dissolved when its project is adopted by the IEEE. In the case of a trial-use standard, the Working Group is usually retained to address comments received during the trial-use period. At the end of the trial-use period, a new draft document should be available and a PAR initiated to upgrade the trial-use standard to a full-use standard.

15.4.3 Sponsor Ballot

It is the responsibility of the sponsor to ensure that the draft standard is technically correct and meets by consensus the requirements of the general audience to whom the standard is addressed. It accomplishes this by means of a formal mail ballot. The balloting may be delegated to a subcommittee of the TC membership plus others who represent concerned interests not otherwise represented. The balloting body must be made up of IEEE or Computer Society members. Nonmembers may be allowed by the Standards Board on an exception basis in special cases where specific expertise is needed. Working Group members who are also IEEE or Computer Society members often form part of the balloting body.

The sponsor itself does not normally make changes in the draft. However, in its oversight responsibility the sponsor may add a cover letter commenting on the draft, recommending certain action (approval or disapproval) to its balloting body.

Voters in the balloting body have 30 days to respond officially to the ballot (i.e., send in their vote), but this is often extended to allow for delay of the various mail services around the world. For the ballot to be valid, 75 percent of the ballots must be returned with legitimate votes. The rules of the IEEE require that a vote be one of the following:

- Approval.
- Approval, but with attached comments (often used to point out small or editorial errors).
- Rejection, with reason. The reason must be worded such that if it were agreed to, the negative vote would be changed to positive. This does not imply that such a resolution will occur.
- Abstention, with reason (such as lack of time or lack of expertise).

Given that the ballot is made valid by at least a 75 percent return, 75 percent of the nonabstaining returns must be favorable for the proposal to pass.

All negative comments received during the sponsor ballot must be considered by the sponsor and responded to in writing. (Although only IEEE or Society members may actually vote, the mailing is often to a wider audience and negative comments from nonmembers are addressed in the same manner as for members.) The received comments may result in the sponsor making changes to the document. If significant comments or changes are made, the members of the sponsor balloting body must be given a chance to consider the changes and an opportunity to change their votes. This is usually done by a shorter recirculation ballot under the same rules, except that no response is taken to be a nonchange in each voter's previous position. This is an iterative process that continues until the 75 percent approval is reached and all of the negative responses are satisfactorily answered.

After all requirements are met and the vote is favorable, the sponsor submits the proposed standard to REVCOM. REVCOM verifies that the proper procedures were followed and that the number of negative comments from those ineligible to formally vote is not excessive. If REVCOM determines that the consensus of the balloting body is positive, then it recommends to the Standards Board that the proposed standard be adopted. When the Standards Board approves the proposal (usually just a formality), it becomes an official IEEE Standard. Because of typesetting and printing backlogs it may be some time before a new standard is formally published, but copies of the final, adopted draft may be obtained from the IEEE or from the CS sponsor.

15.5 GOVERNING DOCUMENTS

The total documentation governing the standards development activity would comprise a stack of paper about two feet high. This can be somewhat intimidating to those newly involved in a standard.

Fortunately, the true "rules" are relatively few and the bulk of the documentation is intended to handle events and circumstances that the average Working Group is unlikely to encounter.

The basic documents are the latest versions of the following:

- IEEE Standards Manual
- IEEE Standards Style Manual
- Computer Society Constitution, Bylaws, Policy and Procedures (Sec. 12)
- IEEE Bylaws
- IEEE Policy and Procedures Manual

15.6 MSC BUS STANDARDS

15.6.1 Adopted Bus Standards as of July 1988

Standards projects sponsored by the Technical Committee on Microprocessors and Microcomputers have culminated in the adoption of the following IEEE Standards. Those in print may be ordered from the IEEE Service Center.

- IEEE Std. 696-1983, Interface for Microsystem Components (S-100 Bus)
- IEEE Std. 796-1983, Microcomputer System Bus (Multibus I)
- IEEE Std. 896.1-1987, Futurebus
- IEEE Std. 959-1988, I/O Extension Bus (SBX Bus)
- IEEE Std. 961-1987, Eight-Bit Microcomputer System Bus (STD Bus)
- IEEE Std. 970-1988, Advanced Backplane Bus (Versabus)
- IEEE Std. 1000-1987, STE Bus
- IEEE Std. 1014-1987, Versatile Backplane Bus (VMEbus)
- IEEE Std. 1096-1988, Multiplexed High-Performance Bus Structure (VSB)
- IEEE Std. 1101-1987, Mechanical Core Specifications for Microcomputer Backplanes

- IEEE Std. 1196-1987, NuBus
- IEEE Std. 1296-1987, Multibus II

Credit card orders of IEEE Standards may be made by phoning the IEEE Service Center at (201)562-3800. They may also be available through Computer Society Publications at (714)821-8380.

15.6.2 Bus Standards in Progress as of July 1988

As of July 1988, the following additional bus projects were underway in the MSC. The chairs of the various projects are subject to change as are their addresses, but current information is available from the IEEE Standards Office.

- P896.1 Futurebus Revision

  Paul Borrill, (408)721-7443
  National Semiconductor—MS 16-181
  2900 Semiconductor Drive
  Santa Clara, CA 95052-8090

- P896.2 Futurebus Firmware

  Paul Borrill, (408)721-7443
  National Semiconductor—MS 16-181
  2900 Semiconductor Drive
  Santa Clara, CA 95052-8090

- P1132 Versatile Serial Bus (VMS Bus)

  Ad Willemse
  Nederlandse Phillips Bedrijven B.V.
  Building TQ III-1-59
  5600 MD Eindhoven
  The Netherlands

- P1155 A High Speed Backplane Instrumentation Bus (I-Bus)

  Co-chaired by:

  Bill Maciejewski, (314)553-4628
  Emerson Electric—MS4628
  8100 West Florissant
  St. Louis, MO 63136

  Marlyn Huckeby, (619)292-1287
  Tektronix
  5770 Ruffin Rd.
  San Diego, CA 92123

- P1156/P1496 Rugged-Bus

  Paul Cook, (312)519-7643
  Ameritech Services, Inc.
  1900 East Golf Road, Suite 750
  Schaumburg, IL 60173-5032

- P1394 A High Performance Serial Backplane Bus

  Michael Teener, (408)973-3521
  Apple Computer, Inc.—MS 5F
  10475 Bandley Dr.
  Cupertino, CA 95014

- P1395/1396 COM Bus

  Gary Nelson, (312)519-7620
  Ameritech Services, Inc.
  1900 East Golf Road, Suite 750
  Schaumburg, IL 60173-5032

- Scalable Coherent Interface (previously Superbus)

  Dr. David B. Gustavson, (415)926-2863
  Stanford Linear Accelerator Center
  P. O. Box 4349, Bin 88
  Stanford, CA 94309

ACKNOWLEDGMENTS

Standards development in the IEEE succeeds due to the efforts of a large number of dedicated volunteers and staff, a number of whom provided support and information for the writing of this chapter. The authors would especially like to thank Bob Davis, Louise Germani, Sava Sherr, Helen Wood, Paul Borrill, and Andrew Salem for their participation; *IEEE Micro* and *The Standards Bearer* for the use of previously published material; and Dex Cook, Paul Kristoff, and Kathi Camp for proofreading. Lastly, thanks to the Texas Instruments Computer Science Center for the use of its facilities and time to generate the manuscript.

LIST OF TRADEMARKS

Multibus I and Multibus II are trademarks of Intel Corporation.

Versabus is a trademark of Motorola, Inc.

VMEbus is a trademark of Motorola, Inc.

NuBus is a trademark of Texas Instruments, Inc.

CHAPTER 16
BUS GUIDELINES AND TRENDS

David B. Gustavson
Computation Research Group
Stanford Linear Accelerator Center
Stanford, California

16.1 EVOLUTION OF BUSES—WHAT IS COMING NEXT?

Early computer buses were introduced to provide for incremental expansion of memory and I/O. As the level of integration increased, the amount of memory that would fit on a board increased from 1K through 4K, 16K, 64K—suddenly the entire address space of a microprocessor could be filled by the memory of one board! Special techniques had to be introduced to make holes in the memory address space so that small EPROMs could temporarily appear in place of part of the RAM to provide the bootstrap program for start-up procedures. Soon 64-Kbit chips appeared, making it easy to put an entire microprocessor and its memory system on the same board. I/O devices became more compact, too. A serial port that once occupied a board by itself soon became a few chips and then one, allowing many ports on one I/O board, or one or two ports right on the processor board. Disk controllers shrank. The next step was to expand processor address space through bank switching, segmentation, or other memory management schemes so that larger memories could be used. Memory density continued to increase, so that soon after each processor enhancement it again became possible to put all the memory the processor could address on the same board with the processor.

Today the norm is 32-bit microprocessors (68030, 80386), and 1-Mbit memory chips. At this time, address space is not limiting the memory size; however, it is easy to fit memories that are appropriately matched to present processor power on the same board with the processor. As processor power increases, memory sizes should increase too. Chips with 4-Mbit capacity are nearing production, 16-Mbit chips are being demonstrated, and 64-Mbit chips are under development (estimated arrival quoted as 1994). For a 32-bit-wide memory, this would provide 256 Mbytes of on-board memory, which is a satisfactory match for a 100 million instruction per second processor.

However, as processor power increases, memory speeds must increase as well as sizes. This generally implies one or more levels of cache memory, relatively small but very fast memory that is matched to the processor speed requirements. The top-level cache is probably located on the processor chip. It tries to keep the processor busy by prefetching a few instructions and by holding recently used instructions that might be part of a short loop. The second level of cache is much larger and tries to keep whole pages of instructions and perhaps even whole arrays of data close at hand. To keep the processor running efficiently, this cache should contain the desired item almost all the time, and only rarely should the processor wait for an access to main (slow) memory. Even more rarely should the processor need to wait for an off-board access that uses the system bus, because bus access potentially has a long delay associated with it: there may be conflicting traffic on the bus, and perhaps there are even other processors of higher priority waiting to use it first. In some systems all the memory on the processor board is treated like a large cache with a central shared main memory accessed via the bus, or a virtual memory system may simulate a large main memory by swapping blocks to and from disk storage as needed.

As the need for processing power increases, it becomes increasingly attractive to provide it by adding processors. Because of the delays associated with using the system bus, these processors will have their own on-board memory and cache. The system bus will be used for loading the memories initially from disk storage, for interprocessor communication, and for some kinds of I/O. Most traffic will be block transfers, but a significant number of accesses will be short transfers for process synchronization.

With multiple processors and caches, it becomes important to avoid inconsistency. Suppose an item is entered into two caches, and then one processor changes its copy. The other would continue to see the original value, unless a cache coherence mechanism is used to force all copies to be updated whenever one of them changes. With a coherence mechanism in place, process synchronization activity (looping while testing a lock variable) does not cause bus traffic until the lock variable changes, a significant gain in efficiency.

The buses described in this handbook range in performance from tens to hundreds of megabytes per second. Why can't they go faster?

Synchronous buses, such as NuBus or Multibus II, are limited for all time by their standard clock frequency. This frequency is chosen as high as practical at the beginning of the bus's life and cannot be changed compatibly even though technological advances might make it easy to increase it later. In practice, there is not as much room for growth as one might have thought, because of the time it takes for signals to travel from one end of the bus to the other. Typical propagation speeds are a fraction of the speed of light because of capacitive loading of the bus transmission lines, and the imperfections of the transmission system require extra time for signal reflections to settle out.

It is impossible for buses based on TTL or CMOS signaling to be driven and terminated as proper transmission lines: The loaded bus impedance is so low, because of distributed capacitance (typically under 40 Ω), and the signal voltage swing is so large (3 V or more) that the currents needed are unrealistic (150 mA or more per signal in the given example—note that the driver "sees" two transmission lines in parallel, so the current is 2 × 3/40 A). To reduce the current to tolerable levels, the termination resistance is typically increased to something over 120 Ω, but this causes the signals to be too small at first, because the current change is too small, and then to reflect back when they reach the ends of the bus. Only after several reflections do the signals reach their desired 3-V height, and thus the system must provide some delay before using the signals so that they have time to reach near full size before they are used.[1]

Older asynchronous buses, such as VMEbus, are limited by the propagation delay for signals from transmitter to receiver, and again for the acknowledging signal back to the transmitter, and these delays are further increased because of the imperfections of the transmission system in the same way as for the synchronous buses described above.

Modern asynchronous buses, such as Futurebus+ or FASTBUS, gain much of their speed advantage by careful attention to the physics of signal transmission. Low-capacitance transmitters and receivers, combined with small signal voltages, allow better termination of the bus, which speeds the transmission system and generally eliminates the need to wait for reflections to settle. Nevertheless, the round-trip propagation delay is still a fundamental limitation.

Pipelined transfer modes can be used in order to solve this problem. Once the connection between sender and receiver has been established, the sender can clock out a block of data at any mutually agreed rate, without waiting for the receiver to return its acknowledging handshakes. This is a kind of source-synchronous transmission, the clock flowing with the data instead of centrally generated, and is thus well suited to long transmission paths such as cable buses. Throughput is independent of distance (approximately).

Even pipelined transfers have limits, however. The obvious limits are the transceiver maximum frequency of operation and the high-frequency attenuation of the bus transmission lines, but in practice a less obvious limit, skew, is more important.

Skew is the difference in propagation delay from one bit to another across the transmitted word. Slight differences in the transmission lines or loading may change propagation velocities, differences in transceivers may change delays, or differences in switching thresholds may change apparent delays due to the finite rise and fall times of signal waveform edges.

In some manner, when a sequence of words is transmitted along the bus, it must be possible to tell which bits belong to which word when they arrive; if the skew is too large compared to the signaling rate, some bits from one word may arrive after the first bits of the next word, confusing the receiving logic and mixing the data. With sufficient effort skews can be made very small, but in practical worst-case designs the skew allowances must be amazingly large and significantly limit the throughput of pipelined transfers.

Throughput can be increased by widening the bus, and although this usually results in some increase in skew, it is certainly a net gain. System considerations such as power dissipation, number of pins available on reasonably priced connectors, and transient-current magnitude (consider switching 256 signals each >50 mA at the same time, e.g.) tend to set practical limits.

Note that even the high-performance buses multiplex the address and data on the same set of lines. Although it would be slightly faster to have separate lines for the address, the gain is so small compared to the cost that separate lines are impractical. This is especially true in systems that use block transfers (one address cycle followed by many data cycles), such as systems containing high-performance cache memories near the processor. In fact, it is easy to see that given the extra lines for addresses, you gain by widening the bus correspondingly and multiplexing the new wider path.

In short, it is hard to imagine improving bus systems even a factor of 4 beyond the present FASTBUS or Futurebus+. Buses are not going to improve at the same rate as processor performance or system demands.

So what can be done?

The first step is to abandon cycle-by-cycle handshakes, carrying the pipeline idea a step further: transmit a packet, containing address, data, and command information. Expect a packet in return containing an acknowledgment and perhaps requested data.

The next step is to abandon the bus structure, using a collection of unidirectional differential signaling links instead. Differential signaling eliminates transient ground current, especially if unidirectional and continuously operating. (Turning off one set of drivers and turning on another, which happens on a bus while changing from an address or write cycle to a read cycle, or while changing from one master to another, does cause a major redistribution of current, i.e., transients, even when using differential signaling.)

To increase multiprocessor systems communication throughput, connect the links through a switch network.

To reduce wasted intercommunication for synchronization, etc., use caches and provide a mechanism for keeping all the caches consistent.

A new IEEE Computer Society Microprocessor Standards Committee project P1596, Scalable Coherent Interface (SCI), was started in October 1988 to pursue this approach. Its goal is to support up to 64K processors with 1 Gbyte/s per processor, using distributed cache directories to maintain coherence. It also has a "small and cheap" mode, which connects multiple boards as a ring (output link of one connected to the input link of the next) rather than through a switch, dividing the 1 Gbyte/s among them.

The 1-Gbyte/s speed was chosen as a barely practical number for current technology, balancing the difficulty of transmitting signals and the difficulty of making fast integrated circuits large enough to handle the interface. There is no fundamental limit to future versions' throughput, though of course the speed of light always limits the latency, the time between a request for information and the corresponding response.

16.2 CHOOSING A BUS

After seeing the variety and complexity of the available buses as described in this handbook, you may wonder how to select the right one.

Of course, the vast majority of computer users need not concern themselves with choosing a bus at all and should simply buy the available system that best meets their needs. The fact that you are reading this handbook, however, suggests that you may have more complicated requirements.

Perhaps you are a system architect, planning for your company's successful future. You want to choose the optimum bus, considering breadth of market, competition, reliability, performance, convenience, economics, and smooth growth path.

Perhaps you are designing your own interface board. You want to choose a bus with the functionality your board demands, but which also has good software and bus monitoring hardware available to support debugging. If you plan to manufacture the board for sale, you care about the market associated with your bus. If you need to run your business with the same machine or want to standardize on one machine for all your needs to gain reliability through redundancy (often a good idea), you may need to consider the availability of software and tools in fields far different from that of your own board design and use.

Sometimes the best solution is to use multiple buses, with interfaces between them. For example, you might use VMEbus, STD bus, or STE bus for an expandable simple I/O system, and interface to Futurebus+, which you use to build your multiprocessor. For very large I/O requirements (multiple crates) or for large "farms" of processors (which are independent enough not to need a cache coherence mechanism) you might use FASTBUS, with an interface to Futurebus+ for tape or disk I/O or for smaller coherent multiprocessor subsystems (even Futurebus+ cannot easily maintain cache coherence beyond crate boundaries).

Bus interfaces are simple if the I/O side never has any masters and has a small address space compared to the processor side. If both sides have masters (even DMA controllers) things become much more difficult, because there is then the possibility that traffic may try to go through the interface in both directions at once. Unless at least one of the buses supports a back-off mechanism, this can result in deadlocks. FASTBUS and Futurebus+ were designed to work with bus interfaces, but VMEbus and many of the simpler buses have fundamental problems. If the I/O side has too large an address space, some kind of address translation mechanism will be needed to map part of the processor address space onto part of the I/O space. It will be inconvenient to manage this translation during system operation.

Another problem area for bus interfaces is the handling of a multiprocessor synchronization semaphore or lock variable. There must be some way to prevent any interference from other processors while a lock variable is being tested and set. On a single bus, this may be accomplished with a read-modify-write operation, but if any of the boards are multiply ported (e.g., a two-port memory with another processor or bus on the other side), the other ports must be locked out also during the critical sequence. At first, this seems beyond the domain of the bus specification, but if this kind of appropriate lock behavior is not provided, it may be impossible to operate multiprocessor systems reliably.

Some buses provide a much better growth path than others. Unless expandability was considered in the design at the start, it is likely that you will meet significant barriers when you overflow a single crate. Address space is the most difficult resource to expand, though we *have* had a lot of experience with that problem. A bus that does not support bus interfaces will cause great expansion trouble (which usually does not show up until the end of the development cycle, when bus activity gets high and the multiprocessor operating system starts running). Some buses claim to offer multiprocessor support but begin to fail when bus loading and the number of processors is high.

Some features that receive prominent treatment in the promotional literature may not be very important to you in practice. For example, you probably do not need special hardware support for a message-passing facility as long as you have some shared memory and a directed interrupt mechanism that permits one processor to signal another. On the other hand, message-passing hardware may provide an inexpensive protection mechanism that limits one processor's access to another to reduce the system's vulnerability to program errors.

Significant features that may help you select a particular bus are noted below. I/O in the following means simple parallel registers, analog-digital-analog converters, etc. High-performance I/O such as disk controllers probably need DMA and bus mastership capabilities, and thus should be treated like a processor and included on the processor bus.

FASTBUS (ANSI/IEEE 960 and IEC 935 Standards). Support for many crates allows for large systems with lots of parallel noninterfering activity. A cable version operates reliably over many-meter distances. Excellent heat handling, power distribution, and ground distribution including a "clean earth" quiet analog ground. Very high performance. Large boards. Very economical for large systems (about half the price of VMEbus per unit of usable board area, powered and cooled, according to the CERN laboratory, which is a large user of both). Supports bus interfaces and some lock mechanisms. Expandable protocol and addressing. Transfers full words; byte addressing and partial-word transfers must be handled by the processor-bus interface. An associated software interface standard provides application portability.

Futurebus+ (P896.1 Project). Cache coherence mechanism (for a single crate—coherence across a few crates can be achieved with complex interfaces, or perhaps more easily by interfacing each crate to SCI, converting to SCI's directory-based coherence mechanisms). Medium-size boards. Supports bus interfaces and lock mechanisms. Performance in practice about the same as FASTBUS; 64- and 128-bit-wide versions can outrun FASTBUS in a single-crate system.

Futurebus+ probably will have wider commercial support than Fastbus—the U.S. Navy has endorsed Futurebus+ as its next generation architecture; VITA (the VMEbus manufacturers organization) has declared it to be their next step after VMEbus; the Multibus II Manufacturers Group (MMG) has also declared its intention to support Futurebus+, at least for cache coherent subsystems.

A standard bus-independent control and status register (CSR) and I/O architecture is being developed (IEEE Computer Society Microprocessor Standards Committee project P1212) to make migration easier. This was begun as part of the SCI project and then made independent so it would be equally applicable to Futurebus+ and the P1394 serial bus, and also to the older buses as new products are developed for them.

The recommended strategy is for users of the older buses to move gradually toward Futurebus+ (via bus interfaces or converters and via CSR and I/O architecture) and then on toward SCI, providing a smooth growth path that provides practically unlimited expansion and power.

Multibus II (ANSI/IEEE 1296 Standard). Moderate performance for a few processors. No cache coherence mechanism, so expansion into a highly parallel coherent shared-memory implementation is constrained. A rich and complex architecture, including hardware support for message passing.

NuBus (ANSI/IEEE 1196 Standard). Moderate performance for a few processors. No cache coherence mechanism. A very simple and elegant system, efficient to implement. Used in the Apple Macintosh II family at the standard 10-MHz speed. The protocols are used in the NeXT machine in a 4-slot 25-MHz CMOS version (not compatible with standard NuBus boards).

VMEbus (ANSI/IEEE 1014 Standard). Major commercial support, many I/O cards available. Suitable for single or few-processor systems, or for an I/O system used with another bus.

STD (ANSI/IEEE 961 Standard) or STE (ANSI/IEEE 1000 Standard). Many I/O cards, small format, many vendors; good simple I/O buses for use with another bus.

SCI (P1596 Project). Under development as IEEE Computer Society Microprocessor Standards Committee project P1596, Scalable Coherent Interface,* it may be worth considering by the time you read this. It is designed to support bus interfaces, lock primitives, and cache coherence over a distributed system containing large numbers of processors, providing 1 Gbyte/s per processor. For small

*SCI should become a finished IEEE standard sometime in 1990. As of this writing (June 1989), however, the best introduction in print is "Scalable Coherent Interface" by Ernst H. Kristiansen, Knut Alnæs, Bjorn O. Bakka, and Marit Jenssen, Eurobus Conference Proceedings, Munich, 9–10 May 1989. Because SCI is still actively evolving, only the principles are likely to remain constant—details have already changed slightly.

systems, several processors can be connected in a ring to divide 1 Gbyte/s among them, at low cost. Large systems require a more costly switch system for interconnecting the processors. The architecture is based on 64 bits, but the physical hardware uses a narrower path (typically 16 bits). A serial fiber-optic (1-bit-wide) version is also planned, running at lower speed but over longer distances.

LIST OF TRADEMARKS

NuBus is a trademark of Texas Instruments, Inc.

Multibus II is a trademark of Intel Corporation.

VMEbus is a trademark of Motorola, Inc.

Macintosh II is a trademark of Apple Computer, Inc.

REFERENCE

1. D. Gustavson, "Computer Buses—A Tutorial," *IEEE Micro,* 4 (4): 7–22, 1984.

CHAPTER 17
BUS CACHING

Gurbir Singh
BiiN
Hillsboro, Oregon

17.1 INTRODUCTION

Today's high performance processors place a great demand upon the bandwidth of memory systems. The advent of RISC architectures and high-speed VLSI implementations have greatly reduced the cycle times of processors. Although computer memories have improved in performance, the ratio of memory speed to processor cycle time has continued to increase. Shared-memory multiple-processor architectures have also become more common and have increased the bandwidth requirements of system memories and the buses that connect them. This has lead to the increasing use of cache memories.

Caches are high-speed buffer memories that store the most frequently used instructions and data for quick access by the processor. Caches exploit the spatial and temporal locality of memory references. Spatial locality is the property of computer programs to naturally tend to execute instructions stored in close proximity to each other. Programs also exhibit temporal locality in that over a small period of time they tend to access a small subset of the entire data a number of times. Cache hardware keeps track of the data accessed by the processor and saves it with the high likelihood that it will be requested again. Typically a cache memory is 20 to 1000 times smaller in size than the system memory but is 5 to 20 times faster.

Cache memories have been in use for a long time. The first cache memory was implemented in an International Business Machine (IBM) System 360 Model 85 in 1968.[1] Caches in high-performance minicomputers such as the Digital Equipment Corporation (DEC) PDP-11/70 followed.[2] VLSI processors such as the Intel 80960 processor[3] and the Motorola 68030 processor incorporate on-chip caches.

17.2 CACHE BASICS

Logically, cache memories are composed of a number of lines or blocks that can hold the contents or correspondingly sized elements of system memory. Whenever the processor issues a memory reference it is checked against the contents of the cache. If the data is already in the cache due to a previous access to system memory, it is returned to the processor immediately and is termed a cache hit. A cache miss, however, requires that data be fetched from system memory and sent to both the processor and the cache.

Figure 17.1 shows the block diagram of a simple cache. Physically the cache is composed of two high-speed memory arrays of equal length. One array is for the cached data and each element of the array is a cache line or block. The other array is for the cache directory. The memory addresses from the processor are composed of three fields: the tag, the index, and the byte number. The index is used to access both the directory and data arrays. The contents of the directory, a previously stored tag, are compared with the tag field of the address. A match indicates a hit and the appropriate bytes of data, selected by the byte field, are returned to the processor. A tag mismatch indicates a miss and the address is forwarded to system memory. The data returned from memory overwrites that in the cache. The tag in the directory is also updated.

17.2.1 Associativity of a Cache

The simple cache described forces a one-to-one correspondence between the blocks of system memory and the lines in the cache. This relationship is called the associativity of the cache and for the cache described it is one, or we have a

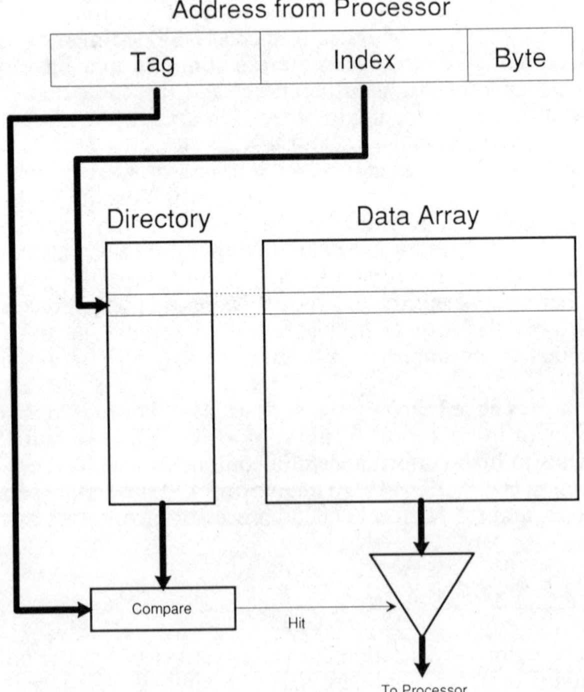

FIGURE 17.1 A direct mapped cache.

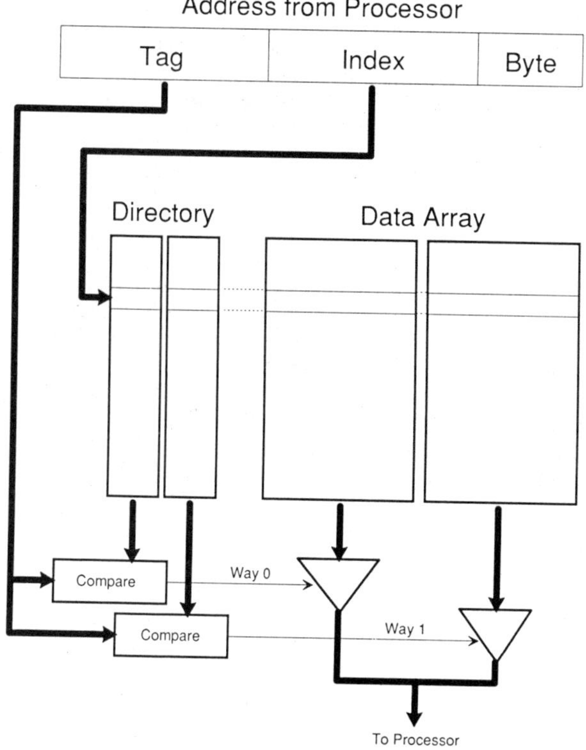

FIGURE 17.2 A two-way set-associative cache.

one-way set-associative cache. It is also called a direct mapped cache. The associativity of a cache can range from one through two-way and four-way on to a fully associative cache. The associativity of the cache determines the number of lines that can be referred through a single index. As the associativity of the cache increases so does the number of possible lines where the cached data could be stored. Every processor address must be compared with the tags of all these locations simultaneously in order to determine a hit. In a fully associative cache no restrictions exist upon the mapping of memory blocks to cache lines and the entire directory must be searched for a cache hit. Figure 17.2 shows the block diagram of a two-way set-associative cache.

17.2.2 Replacement Policies

For caches with an associativity greater than one, the cache hardware must determine which of the possible lines in the set must be replaced upon a cache miss. One of three possible replacement algorithms can be used. The least recently used (LRU) policy replaces the line in the set which was accessed furthest back in time. This increases the likelihood of that line being no longer actively used by the processor. The LRU policy is the best choice among the three policies, but it is the hardest to implement in hardware for caches with a high degree of associativity. The second policy randomly selects among the lines in the set for replacement. The random policy is not as optimal as LRU but represents a good compromise between implementation complexity and performance. The third policy treats the lines in the set as a FIFO replacing the next one in sequence. FIFO replacement is even simpler to implement that random replacement but can result in poor performance for certain types of programs.

17.2.3 Handling Writes

The cache hardware can handle the write traffic as either write through or write back. In the first case all writes update the cache and are also written through to system memory. The time penalty of the write can be reduced by issuing the write to memory simultaneously with the update to the cache and allowing the processor to proceed. The subsequent access would then be held up waiting for the write to complete only if it was another write or a read miss. The second case of a write-back cache updates the data in the cache for a write but does not send the data to memory. The cache directory must, however, keep track of all lines in the cache that have been modified by the processor by a dirty bit. When a line is selected for replacement it is written back to memory if it has been marked as dirty.

The cache memory must also be capable of dealing with updates to memory by I/O processors or direct memory access channels. For this purpose the cache hardware must monitor the system bus traffic and invalidate any lines in the cache that have been updated by the I/O devices. This is called bus watching.

17.3 DESIGNING A BUS CACHE

The two primary functions of a cache are to reduce the effective memory latency for the processor and to reduce the system bus traffic. Both of these parameters are dependent upon the miss ratio of the cache. The miss ratio of a cache is defined as the ratio of the number of memory accesses that miss the cache to the total number of accesses generated. The effective memory latency is related to the miss ratio as follows:

$$L_{\text{eff}} = L_{\text{cache}} + ML_{\text{memory}}$$

where L_{cache}, L_{memory}, and M are the latency of the cache, the latency of the system memory, and the miss ratio, respectively. The system memory traffic generated by the processor is

$$T_{\text{system bus}} = MT_{\text{processor}}$$

where $T_{\text{processor}}$ and M are the total traffic generated by the processor and the miss ratio of the cache, respectively. Both these parameters are very dependent upon the miss ratio of the cache, and minimizing it should be the first objective of any cache design. The miss rate of a cache is dependent upon a very large number of parameters, of which the key ones are discussed below. The tradeoffs in the selection of these parameters is also discussed. Further information can be found in Refs. 4 and 5.

The miss ratio of the cache is inversely related to its size. This is particularly true for small (1- to 16-kbyte) caches. As the cache size grows to be comparable to the *working set* of the typical programs run on the processor, the benefits of the increase in size decrease significantly. The working set of a program is the entire set of memory references generated by it during the course of execution. Larger caches tend to be slower in operation due to the longer time required to look up the larger directory and data arrays.

The cache line size most strongly affects the miss ratio of the cache after the size of the cache itself. The longer line sizes exploit the spatial locality of the memory references by effectively fetching instructions ahead of the processor. For a cache of fixed size there exists an optimal line size that offers the lowest miss ratio. Increasing the line size beyond it increases the miss rate as the total number of lines available in the cache are reduced. Reducing the line size increases the miss ratio as the cache is not taking full advantage of the spatial locality of the memory references. However, the choice of line size is very heavily influenced by the system bus used. Buses that support multiple-word transfers are better suited for caches with large line sizes, as the entire line can be fetched from memory on a miss. If the cache were to fetch a word at a time from memory, the penalty for a miss would negate the advantage of the larger line size. The larger lines also result in increased traffic over the bus and could adversely impact the performance of a multiple-processor system. For further discussion on cache line sizes, see Ref. 6.

The associativity of the cache affects the miss ratio significantly. Over a short period of time the memory references of a processor tend to center around the instructions being executed and the data being referenced. It is quite possible that the instructions and data map into the same set in the cache. For a direct mapped cache this would result in a very high miss ratio as every instruction access would displace the data required by the instruction. This phenomenon, called *thrashing*, is minimized by increasing the asociativity of the cache. Typically a two-way set-associative cache has a lower miss ratio than a similarly sized direct mapped cache. This is particularly true of small caches. Increasing the size of the cache reduces the possibility of thrashing, and the benefits of the two-way cache are not as large. Increasing the associativity beyond two pays significantly reduced dividends, although caches with an associativity as high as 16 have been built. The nature of the programs that are run on the processor also influence the choice of cache associativity. Processors that tend to switch rapidly between applications are better served by caches with high associativity, as there is a smaller likelihood that a dormant task's data or code will be overwritten in the cache. For further information regarding the associativity of caches, see Refs. 7 and 8.

The effective memory latency is dependent upon the latency of both the cache and the system memory. The latency of the cache is determined by its size and associativity. A large cache may be slow as it is forced to take advantage of technology that offers denser storage given the constraints of board area and cost. The speed of a cache is also dependent upon the organization. A direct mapped cache offers a major speed advantage in that the data and the tag are fetched in parallel. The result of the hit comparison determines whether the processor accepts the data or waits for the memory to deliver it. A set-associative cache must first access the directory to determine which line in the set ought to be fetched, serializing the access to the tag and data.

The latency of the cache as seen by the processor can also be reduced by virtual-address caches that do not suffer the delay of the address translation. Address translation is only required during a cache miss. However, I/O devices normally refer to memory in the physical address space and any updates to system memory must also be reflected in the cache. This requires a reverse translation buffer to be built as part of the cache, adding to its complexity.

The latency of the system memory, determined by the bus speed and the speed of the memory subsystem, influences the target miss ratio of the cache. A relatively slow system memory will require a cache with a very low miss ratio to compensate for the memory latency. The cost of the system may be reduced by selecting a faster bus and system memory and an inexpensive cache. Further information on the tradeoffs in cache design are discussed in Refs. 9 and 10.

17.4 MULTIPLE-PROCESSOR CACHES

Caches play an important role in shared-memory multiple-processor systems in reducing system bus traffic.[11] However, when a number of processors share the data from a common memory they must ensure that all copies of data in their caches are consistent. This is called the *cache coherence problem.* Cache coherence can be treated in software by ensuring that no more than one copy of the data exists in the caches at a time and no tasks are allowed to migrate between processors.[4] Another approach is to have the cache logic implement a *cache coherence protocol* to ensure that all copies of data in the caches are maintained in a consistent state.

The simplest hardware-based solution to the coherence problem is to implement write-through caches and have all the caches monitor the system bus for write traffic. If a write on the system bus affects a line in a cache, it can either choose to invalidate the line or update the data in it. However, the write-through traffic can still be sufficiently large to limit the number of processors that can be supported by a system bus.

The bus traffic can be reduced significantly if the caches implement a write-back strategy where modified lines in the cache are written to memory upon replacement. The cache coherency protocol ensures that the data between the various caches is kept consistent. A number of cache coherency protocols have been suggested for write-back caches.[5,11-14] The Illinois[13] cache coherency protocol is presented below to illustrate the additional requirements placed upon a bus by such a protocol.

17.4.1 A Cache Coherency Protocol

The Illinois protocol requires that the caches on the bus have specific read and write characteristics. A cache issuing a read request should be able to determine if the data it received came from another cache or system memory. The caches should be able to inhibit a reply from system memory and interject a reply instead. If multiple caches attempt to interject, then their priority on the bus must be used to resolve the contention.

The protocol requires that the cache maintain information regarding the consistency of each line in the cache. The protocol permits a line in the cache to exist in one of four possible states.

1. *Invalid:* This state indicates that there is no valid data in the line and an access to it would be considered a cache miss.

2. *Exclusive:* This state indicates that the line contains the only cached copy of the data. However, the data is consistent with that in the system memory.

3. *Shared:* This state indicates that the line contains data that also exists in one or more other caches. This data is consistent with memory.

4. *Dirty:* This state indicates that the line contains the only copy of the data. The data is not consistent with system memory.

Figure 17.3 shows the state transition diagram of the coherency protocol. A read request from the processor hits the cache if the line is in any state other than invalid. The cache returns the data to the processor without the line changing state. If the read request misses, then the request is placed upon the system bus where all other caches check the address for a coherency hit. If any of the other caches has the data and it is in a shared or exclusive state, then the one with the highest priority returns the data and the system memory is inhibited. If the data is in one of the caches and in the dirty state, that cache will provide the data and also write it to memory. In either case all caches with the data will go to the shared state. If no other cache has the data, then it will be read from system memory and the receiving cache will load the line in the exclusive state.

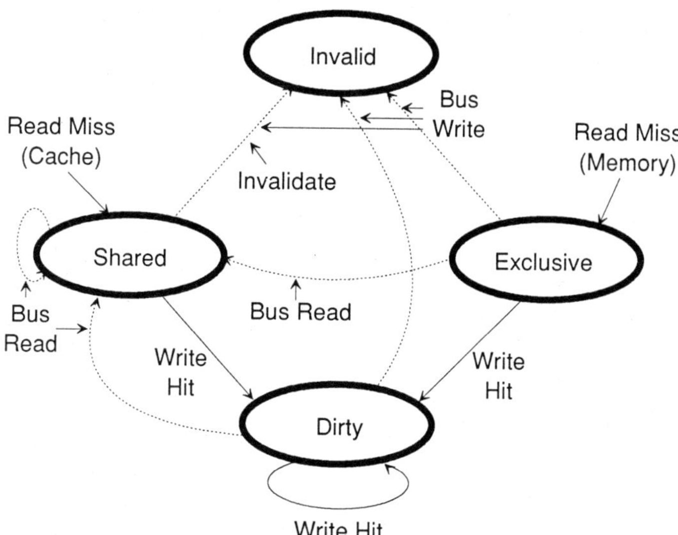

FIGURE 17.3 State diagram of the cache coherence protocol.

A write request that hits an exclusive or dirty line can update the data immediately and the line will go to the dirty state. If the line is shared then the write address is broadcast on the bus and all other caches that have copies of the data will go to the invalid state. The data in the line is then updated and the states set to dirty.

A write request that misses the cache causes a read request to be issued on the bus, and the data is returned by a cache or system memory. However, the request is marked as one generated by a write miss so that all caches with data go to the invalid state. This could be considered an ownership read request. The requesting cache updates the data and sets the state to dirty.

The processor requests can miss the cache either because the line is invalid or the address tags do not match. In the latter case the data in the cache will have to be written out to memory only if it is the dirty state.

17.4.2 Bus Requirements

It is clear from the discussion of the write-back protocol that the caches in a multiple-processing system need to communicate among themselves and system memory with a layer of protocol that is beyond the simple read and write requests. Typically caches need to be able to signal when they have the requested data and inhibit the system memory. Also signal(s) must exist to indicate the source of the data for a reply. The standard buses with the exception of the Futurebus (Ref. 15) do not provide any support for multiple caches as part of their protocol. It is possible, however, to generate a superset of the bus of choice and route the additional signals between modules.

17.5 CONCLUSION

The choice of a bus influences the characteristics of a system to a very large extent. Bus caches provide the ability to support increasingly faster processors without trading away the performance advantage they provide. Multiple-processor caches, however, place the additional burden of maintaining coherency, and this may affect the choice of bus or cache protocol.

REFERENCES

1. J. S. Liptay, "Structural Aspects of the System/360 Model 85, Part II: The Cache," *IBM Systems Journal,* 7 (1): 15–21 (1968).
2. W. D. Strecker, "Cache Memories for PDP-11 Family Computers," *Proceedings of the Third International Symposium on Computer Architecture,* January 1976, pp. 155–158.
3. *80960KB Programmer's Reference Manual,* Intel, 1988, p. 2-2.
4. D. R. Cheriton, G. Slavenburg, and P. D. Boyle, "Software Controlled Caches in the VMP Multiprocessor," *The 13th International Conference on Computer Architecture,* ACM SIGARCH, IEEE Computer Society, New York, 1986.
5. R. Katz, S. Eggers, D. A. Woods, and R. G. Sheldon, "Implementing a Cache Consistency Protocol," *Proceedings of the 12th International Symposium on Computer Architecture,* IEEE, New York, 1985, pp. 276–283.
6. A. J. Smith, "Line (Block) Size Choice for CPU Cache Memories," *IEEE Trans. on Computers,* C-36 (9): 1063–1075 (1987).
7. A. J. Smith, "A Comparative Study of Set Associative Memory Mapping Algorithms and Their Use for Cache and Main Memory," *IEEE Trans. on Software Engineering,* SE-4 (2): 121–130 (1978).
8. M. D. Hill, "A Case for Direct-Mapped Caches," *IEEE Computer,* 21 (12): 25–40 (1988).
9. S. Przybylski, M. Horowitz, and J. Henesey, "Performance Tradeoffs in Cache Design," *The 15th Annual International Symposium on Computer Architecture,* ACM SIGARCH, May 1988, pp. 290–298.
10. A. J. Smith, "Design of CPU Cache Memories," Computer Science Division Report 87-357, University of California, Berkeley, June 1987.
11. J. R. Goodman, "Using Cache Memory to Reduce Processor-Memory Traffic," *Proceedings of the 10th International Symposium on Computer Architecture,* IEEE, New York, 1983, pp. 124–131.

12. E. McCreight, "The Dragon Computer System: An Early Overview," Tech. Rep., Xerox Corporation Technical Report, 1984.

13. M. Papamarcos and J. Patel, "A Low Overhead Coherence Solution for Multiprocessors with Private Memory Caches," *Proceedings of the 11th International Symposium on Computer Architecture,* IEEE, New York, 1985, pp. 348–354.

14. C. Thacker, L. Stewart, and E. Satterthwaite, Jr., "Firefly: A Multiprocessor Workstation," *IEEE Trans. on Computers,* 37 (8): 909–920.

15. P. Sweazey and A. J. Smith, "A Class of Compatible Cache Consistency Protocols and their Support by the IEEE Futurebus," *Proceedings of the 13th International Symposium on Computer Architecture,* IEEE, New York, 1986, pp. 414–423.

CHAPTER 18
LIMITS OF PERFORMANCE OF BACKPLANE BUSES

Paul Sweazey
Apple Computer, Inc.
Cupertino, California

18.1 INTRODUCTION

If computing and instrumentation systems are destined to increase in speed, then the future of backplane buses within those systems depends on increased speed also.

A backplane bus is an example of an interconnection topology where modules are connected in parallel, and where each module must take turns transmitting information. Other topologies include switching networks, where one of multiple potential connection paths is dynamically chosen, and rings, where a single path passes through each module and information is selectively intercepted or forwarded to the next module in the ring. Switching networks and rings both allow multiple simultaneous transmissions in exchange for greater complexity. A bus is conceptually much simpler because a module does not need to store and forward packets not destined for itself.

The measures of goodness of a bus are configurability, cost, scalability, reliability, and speed. Bus-based systems are highly configurable because each backplane slot preserves the same connectivity with all other backplane positions. A bus tends to have lower cost than active interconnections because the passive nature of a backplane connection—just a connector—reduces the cost of unused slots. A bus has limited scalability due to the physical and electrical constraints of connecting multiple transceivers to the same conductors and the restriction of allowing only one bus master at a time; it is not reasonable to connect thousands of processing elements via a bus topology. In principle, the reliability of a bus can be very high with a well-defined electrical environment and logical protocol; in practice many buses have had poor reliability because they were poorly designed or specified. Regarding speed, many systems have reached the limits of backplane bus speed using traditional, simple bus design techniques and circuit technologies. However, these speed limits are not fundamental to the nature of backplane buses.

18.2 HIGH-SPEED MEMORY-ACCESS BUS

The assumptions and constraints of a backplane bus are that (1) all slots are essentially equivalent, both logically and physically, (2) one bus master at a time may transmit information, and (3) any number of slaves may receive information. Additionally, in most buses the current master is able to perceive some status information (e.g., error status) from any or all slaves simultaneously. Since we wish to explore the limits of bus performance, we also assume that the electrical interconnection consists of terminated transmission lines, and that a signal emitted from one module is perceived as passing through the receiver threshold of every other module on the first propagation of the wavefront from the transmitter to the terminations at each end of the backplane.

No bus can be considered high speed unless its basic mechanism for transmitting a packet of information is fast. We will examine various synchronization mechanisms for transmitting information packets on a bus, but first we must present a physical phenomenon that ultimately limits bus performance. Often we think of the absolute value of signal delay from one module to another as the limiter of bus speed, yet this need not be the case.

18.2.1 Skew

An agent receives information on a bus by evaluating the data pattern appearing on a group of bus lines. The data pattern is evaluated during a time period designated by a synchronizer signal. Because the data pattern on the bus changes with time, a synchronization signal is required to identify when the information is valid.

The rate of information transfer on a bus is limited by the difference between the propagation speed of the information and the speed of the synchronizer. This timing uncertainty is inherent in traditional backplane buses because the synchronizer and every bit of information all travel via uniquely different physical paths, along separate electrical conductors, and through separate drivers, receivers, and latches. At each stage—from the transmitters, through the backplane, and into the receivers—a degree of uncertainty is introduced that reduces the effective sampling window during which the receiver is assured that the data is valid. The difference in progapation delay introduced by two parallel paths is called *skew.* The period of time when information is known to be valid on a group of lines in a bus is called a *sampling window,* or a window of validity. Every set of distinct parallel paths introduces skew and decreases the effective sampling window.

Figure 18.1 illustrates the way in which skew affects the sampling window. Suppose that all of the data lines become valid at the same time at the input to a group of bus drivers on a module in a backplane. The lines are known to remain valid for a period of time, and a synchronizer signal is switched at the middle of the input sampling window. What can we say about the relative timing of the data and the synchronizer on the bus, at the outputs of the bus drivers? Each bus driver is specified with a maximum and minimum propagation delay. Each signal arrives at the output with a delay that is within these limits. In Fig. 18.1 the synchronizer arrives at the bus somewhere between the signals Fast Sync Out and Slow Sync Out. In addition, a portion of the data path may propagate as slowly as shown by Slow Data Out, while other data path signals may propagate as fast as the field marked Fast Data Out. The worst-case skew could result in either very little setup time or very little hold time, depending on if the synchronizer path is

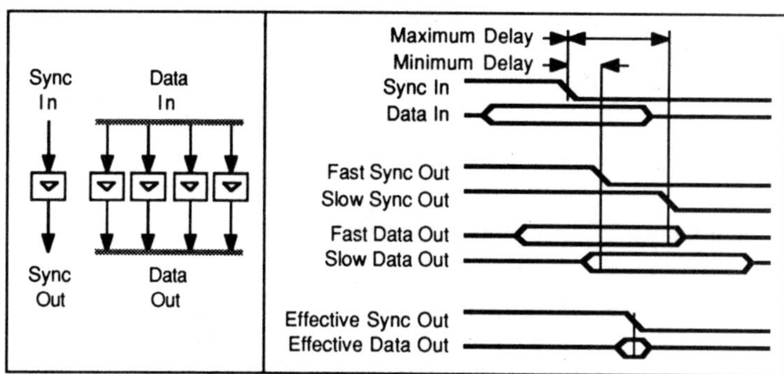

FIGURE 18.1 Skew reduces the effective sampling window of valid data.

very fast or very slow. Although it is always true that the entire data field is guaranteed to be stable and valid for a much longer period of time than that shown by Effective Data Out, it is impossible to predict if the stable period is setup time or hold time, because of the uncertainty in the delay of the synchronizer itself. If we define the skew to be the difference between the maximum delay and the minimum delay of our bus buffers, then the effective data sampling window is reduced by twice the skew of the buffers for each buffering stage in the data path.

The above description refers to tolerance-induced skew, or skew that is a function of the tolerance with which distinct parallel paths can be guaranteed to exhibit matching delays. *Intermodule skew* is the delay variance that can be guaranteed over supply voltage, temperature, and time. If a warm running system is shut down for a moment and a cold module is inserted in an empty slot of the backplane, the system should work as soon as it is turned on again. Such interoperability is ensured by assuming that the same component type between two different modules may exhibit the absolute extremes of their timing specification. Intermodule skew is the specified maximum delay minus the specified minimum delay.

Interdevice skew is the timing difference between two components on the same module and therefore at "similar" temperature and voltage. *Intradevice skew* is the timing difference between two components in the same package and on the same die, and therefore assumed to be operating at a very similar voltage and temperature and to have well-matched manufacturing-process-dependent characteristics.

Obviously, intradevice skew is smaller than interdevice skew, which in turn is smaller than intermodule skew. The skew-dependent performance of a system can be improved by removing sources of the most dominant types of skew. Unfortunately, inter- and intradevice skews are not commonly specified by device manufacturers, so intermodule skew must usually be assumed for a worst-case-reliable design.

18.3 SYNCHRONIZATION MECHANISMS

The most common and simplest synchronization mechanism is a *centralized-synchronous* protocol, using a central clock source to transmit data. To improve performance, *source-synchronous* protocols can be used that emit the synchronizer from the same source as the data. A source-synchronous technique called a *compelled* protocol allows the transfer speed to dynamically adapt to the capabilities of the participating agents, eliminating the need for a central clocking resource. A faster but less flexible source-synchronous scheme is called an *uncompelled* protocol.

18.3.1 Centralized-Synchronous Protocol

A centralized-synchronous protocol is simplest to implement. A central clocking source is provided, perhaps from circuitry on the backplane or by a module that is capable of providing "central services" and that is installed in a specially designated slot. Every module in the backplane perceives the central clock almost simultaneously. The perception of the clock is not truly simultaneous because of what is called *spatial skew.* Spatial skew is introduced due to the physical separation of the modules and the finite propagation speed of the clock, as well as the interdevice skew between clock receivers that are within physically distinct devices on different modules. The arrival of the active clock edge causes the transmitter to switch the data path from the old data word to the next word. The same edge causes the receiver to store the old data word before it disappears and is replaced by the new word.

The transmitter places the data on the bus as soon as possible before the clock edge that validates it. Figure 18.2 shows the timing of the data field as issued by the transmitter and shows a different, shorter period when data is assumed to be valid by the receiver. The difference between the sampling window as issued by the transmitter and the window assumed by the receiver is due to skew from variations in propagation delay of different signals in the backplane. The backplane itself may be thought of as a device in the data path that introduces skew.

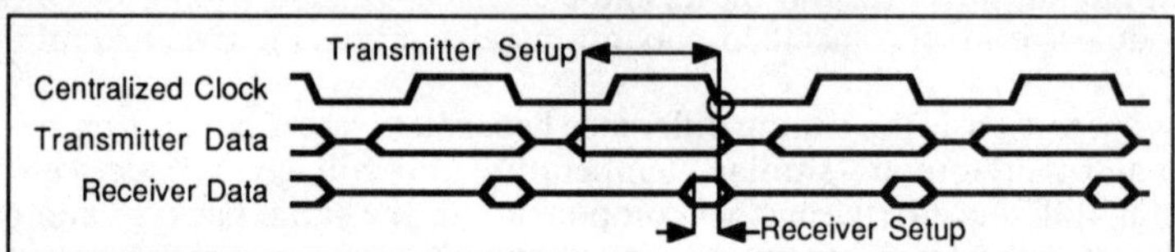

FIGURE 18.2 Centralized-synchronous protocol timing, using the falling edge of the clock.

18.3.1.1 Spatial Skew. Spatial skew occurs when the source of the information is spatially displaced from the source of the synchronizer. Imagine, for example, a clock source in the center of the backplane and a module at one end of the backplane that is receiving data. If the data is being transmitted from a module adjacent to the receiver, then both modules perceive the clock at the same time, and the data incurs almost no delay between the transmitter and the receiver. If the transmitter is in the center of the backplane, then the transmitter perceives the clock sooner than the receiver does and sends the data earlier. The data is transmitted one-half backplane delay earlier but it takes one-half backplane delay to arrive at the receiver, so the effect is the same as if the transmitter were adjacent to the receiver.

What if the transmitter were at the opposite end of the backplane? The clock propagates in both directions from the center, so both the transmitter and the

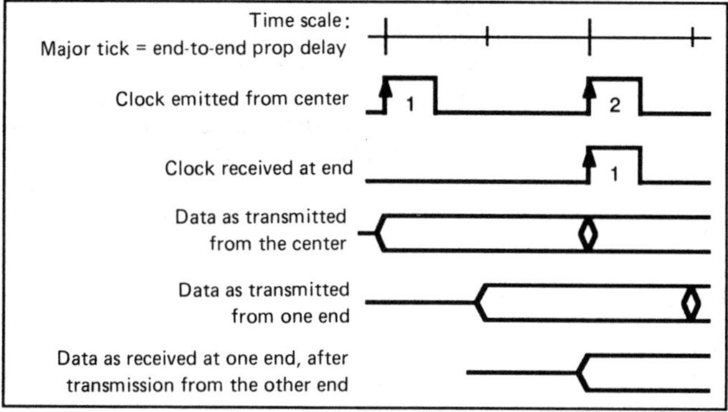

FIGURE 18.3 Timing diagram illustrates the effect of spatial skew.

receiver see the clock at the same time. Unfortunately, the data takes one full backplane delay to propagate to the receiver. Figure 18.3 illustrates how the data is perceived relative to the clock at different points in the backplane. The maximum operating frequency of the clock is limited by that difference.

Spatial skew is the uncertainty in the timing relationship between the information and the data that is caused by spatial separation of the two sources. For a centralized-synchronous backplane, the minimum spatial skew is one end-to-end backplane delay.

18.3.2 Compelled Protocol

The idea behind a compelled protocol is that no module is required to have any explicit knowledge about the timing requirements of other modules in the backplane, but that the speed of data transfer dynamically adapts to the speed of the communicating modules. There is no system clock. Rather, the participating modules form a single asynchronous state machine. The state of one bus interface is compelled to enter its next state only when it receives permission from the other interface and vice versa.

The timing diagram of Fig. 18.4 illustrates the operation of the compelled data transfer mechanism as it appears on the bus. The arrows indicate the cause-and-effect relationships of events in the protocol. The transmitter must guarantee that data is valid on the bus before it induces a transition on its synchronizer signal. The transmitter does so by delaying transmission of the synchronizer until it is sure that the data field is stable and valid. The receiver is guaranteed a zero setup time of data before the synchronizer and must delay receipt of the synchronizer to allow for any setup time required by its data-receiving circuitry. Data hold time

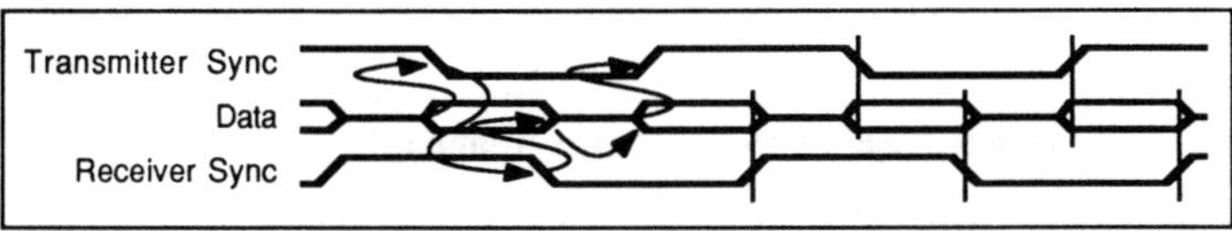

FIGURE 18.4 Source-synchronous, compelled protocol timing.

is controlled by the receiver, because the transmitter cannot change the data until the receiver emits a transition on its synchronizer.

Both the transmitting module and the receiving module have complete control over the speed at which the data transfer may progress. This is the great strength of a compelled protocol—dynamically adaptive timing—and it is also a fundamental limiter of the maximum realizable transfer speed. The speed of any transaction is bounded by the round-trip propagation delay of the handshake, which varies with the physical distance that separates the transmitter and the receiver.

18.3.3 Uncompelled Protocol

The source-synchronous nature of compelled protocol avoids spatial skew, but introduces its own round-trip handshake delay. This delay can be avoided if the receiver forfeits its power to dynamically control the transfer rate. An uncompelled protocol is quite similar to the centralized-synchronous protocol, except that the source of the "clock" changes with time. The transmitter of data issues both the synchronizer and the data, which propagate to the ends of the backplane with negligible skew. The transmitter agrees not to switch the synchronizer faster than some fixed, maximum rate, just as all modules in a centralized-synchronous bus assume a maximum clock rate. An uncompelled synchronization scheme, however, is not necessarily constrained to a single, periodic data rate, but can dynamically slow down. An uncompelled protocol must establish a performance ceiling, but no performance floor is required or implied.

Figure 18.5 illustrates an uncompelled data transmission that assumes a sampling window that is symmetrical about the synchronizer transition. Note that the receiver must assume a smaller sampling window, based on the sources of skew (in the backplane, bus drivers and receivers, etc.) between the data source and destination.

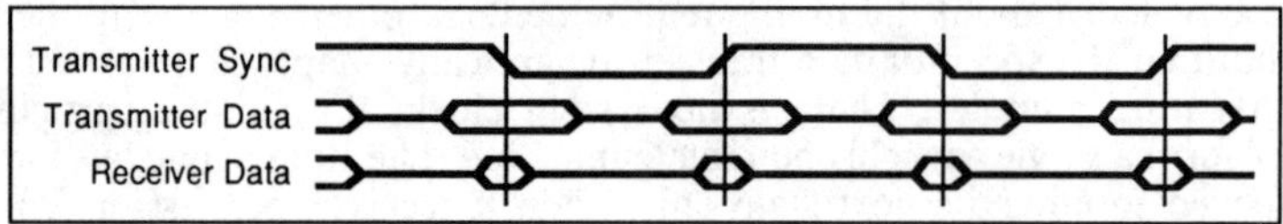

FIGURE 18.5 Source-synchronous, uncompelled protocol timing.

18.4 TECHNOLOGY SNAPSHOT OF TRANSFER SPEED

It is of value to carry out a quantitative analysis of various synchronization mechanisms to better understand the parameters that limit maximum throughput. Using small- and medium-scale integrated circuits, we can apply a similar level of aggressiveness and complexity to each synchronization method, compare the results, and understand the strengths and weaknesses of each.

18.4.1 Centralized-Synchronous Timing Analysis

Two modules are installed in a backplane together with a centralized-service module that supplies a clock signal, issued from the center of the backplane. See

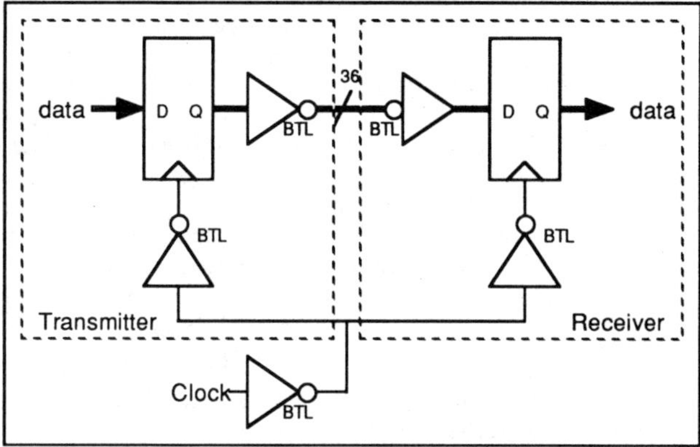

FIGURE 18.6 Centralized synchronous handshake logic.

Fig. 18.6. Synchronized with this clock, one module transmits a continuous stream of data to the other module. How fast can this transfer operate? A reliable data transfer requires that the setup and hold times of the receiving data storage device not be violated. For a worst-case analysis, let us assume that the transmitter is at one end of the backplane, and that the receiver is as close as possible to the clock source at the center of the backplane. (This causes each module to perceive the clock at different times—a worst-case scenario.) The clock is emitted to the backplane at time T_0.

The maximum possible delay for the data to arrive at the receiving register plus the minimum data setup time must exceed the minimum possible time for the clock to arrive.

$$T_c \leq T_d(\text{max}) + T_s(\text{min}) \tag{18.1}$$

To know the maximum transfer rate we must find the minimum allowed clock period of the central clock. This changes our inequality to the following equality:

$$T_c(\text{min}) = T_d(\text{max}) + T_s(\text{min}) \tag{18.2}$$

(The elapsed time after T_0 when the clock arrives at the receiving data register is T_c. The time after T_0 when the data arrives at the register inputs is T_d. The setup time of the register is T_s.)

The clock arrives at the transmitter ($T_{\text{bp}}/2$), passes through the clock receiver (T_r), and arrives at the clock input of the data transmit register, causing the next data word to appear at the output of the register (T_{cko}). The new word is propagated through BTL drivers to the backplane (T_t), from the transmitter at the end of the backplane to the receiver at the center of the backplane ($T_{\text{bp}}/2$), through the BTL receivers (T_r), and arrives at the input pins of the receiving data register. The sum of these delays is the data path delay, T_d.

$$T_d(\text{max}) = T_{\text{bp}}(\text{max})/2 + T_r(\text{max}) + T_{\text{cko}}(\text{max}) + T_t(\text{max}) + T_{\text{bp}}(\text{max})/2 + T_r(\text{max}) \tag{18.3}$$

$$T_d(\text{max}) = T_{\text{bp}}(\text{max}) + 2T_r(\text{max}) + T_t(\text{max}) + T_{\text{cko}}(\text{max})$$

(The electrical length of the backplane—the propagation delay of a signal from one end to the other—is T_{bp}. The propagation delay of a signal through a bus receiver is T_r, and through a bus transmitter is T_t. The delay from receipt of a clock edge until the output data from a register becomes valid is T_{cko}.)

The new data word is stored in the receiving data register on the next clock edge. The path of the clock to the receiving register is simply the propagation delay of the clock receiver, as the receiving module is not spatially separated from the clock source in the center of the backplane. The delay after T_0 when the clock arrives at the receiver is the clock period (T_{ck}) plus the clock receiver delay (T_r).

$$T_c(\text{min}) = T_{ck}(\text{min}) + T_r(\text{min}) \tag{18.4}$$

(The backplane clock period is T_{ck}.)

In order to guarantee that the data is correctly stored, the clock edge must not arrive at the receiving register before the new data word has been stably present for the minimum data setup time of the register. By combining Eqs. (18.2) and (18.4) and solving for $T_{ck}(\text{min})$, we obtain the minimum clock period of a centralized-synchronous data transfer.

$$T_{ck}(\text{min}) = T_d(\text{max}) + T_s(\text{min}) - T_r(\text{min}) \tag{18.5}$$

Substituting the results of Eq. (18.3) for $T_d(\text{max})$ yields:

$$\begin{aligned} T_{ck}(\text{min}) = {} & T_{bp}(\text{max}) + 2T_r(\text{max}) + T_t(\text{max}) \\ & + T_{cko}(\text{max}) + T_s(\text{min}) - T_r(\text{min}) \end{aligned} \tag{18.6}$$

18.4.2 Compelled Source-Synchronous Timing Analysis

Figure 18.7 is a circuit diagram for a pair of compelled, source-synchronous modules in a backplane. There is no clock source from elsewhere in the backplane. Instead, the synchronizer is emitted from the transmitting module together with a stream of data. Each module is designed to be as fast as it possibly can be without making any assumptions about the speed of any other module. Data transfers between fully compelled modules are highly reliable and flexible because the data transfer speed dynamically adjusts to the maximum speed possible between the two modules involved, but the speed is constrained never to operate beyond the capacity of either module. The timing diagram illustrating the signal sequences is found in Fig. 18.4.

Correct operation is guaranteed because of signal delay elements that are inserted into the handshake logic of each module. These delay elements account for any skews that may be introduced by the flow of information and synchronization through different paths, and they account for the maximum rate of data transfer that the remainder of each module is capable of sourcing or sinking. Since the backplane is also a source of skew, it too is designed so that the synchronizer paths are electrically longer than the data paths, ensuring that the data is always valid before the synchronizer switches.

Assume that the transmitting module is waiting to begin transmitting the next word to the receiving module. When the receiving module asserts a data synchronizer called DS*, that signal is received and causes a data word (say "odd data") to be selected and transmitted across the backplane to a pair of data registers on the receiver. The receipt of DS* also causes the transmitting module to assert a data acknowledge signal called DK*, but this event is delayed by a delay element

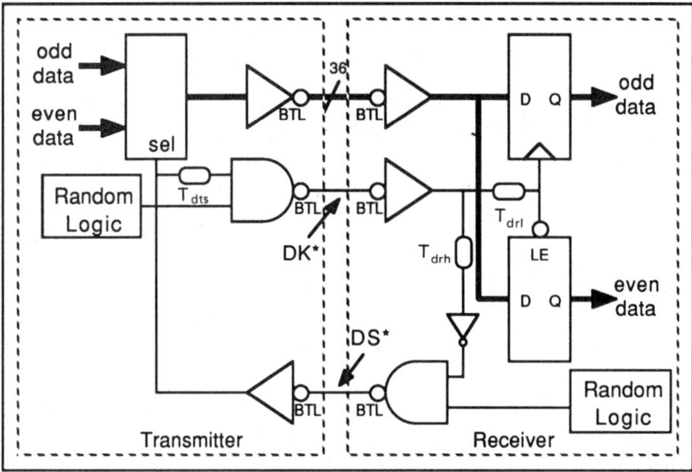

FIGURE 18.7 Compelled handshake logic.

(T_{dts}, delay for transmitter setup) that guarantees that the data arrives at the backplane before the change in DK* does. The receiving module uses the receipt of DK* to store the incoming data field ("odd data") in the upper edge-triggered register, but it also delays the register clock with a delay element (T_{drl}, delay for receiver latch) to account for its own skews, ensuring sufficient register setup time. The receiving module also uses the receipt of DK* to induce the release of DS*, and this also involves a delay element (T_{drh}, delay for receiver hold) to ensure that the transmitter cannot possibly remove the incoming data before the register hold time is satisfied. (From a purist's design perspective, the transmitter could be infinitely fast!) The release of DS* causes the transmitting module to select and transmit its "even data" word, and to release the data acknowledge signal DK*, after which the receiving module latches the new data in the lower, negative-edge-latching register. This process repeats for the length of the data transfer packet, with the speed of data transfer determined by the actual typical propagation delays of the bus transmitters and receivers and by the values of the involved delay elements.

The key, of course, is to choose the minimum values for the delay elements that are still guaranteed to result in correct operation by accounting for the skews inherent in each module. In the following analysis it is assumed that the remainder of each module is capable of sustaining whatever data transfer rate the specified bus interfaces may be capable of transferring. Thus we fix the values of the delay elements only based on the worst-case design requirements of the bus interface circuits. In order to guarantee that the setup time of the receiving data storage device is observed, the receiver latch delay T_{drl} must be greater than or equal to the sum of the skew between the backplane data and synchronizer buffers [$(T_r(\max) - T_r(\min)$] plus the specified setup time of the registers themselves [$(T_s(\min)$].

$$T_{drl}(\min) = T_s(\min) + T_r(\max) - T_r(\min) \qquad (18.7)$$

The tolerance of the delay elements, ∂T_d, is finite, fixed, and specified. The maximum receiver latch delay is therefore

$$\begin{aligned} T_{\text{drl}}(\max) &= T_{\text{drl}}(\min) + \partial T_d \\ &= T_s(\min) + T_r(\max) - T_r(\min) + \partial T_d \end{aligned} \tag{18.8}$$

Another delay element, T_{drh}, is placed in the path of the receiver response synchronizer. This delay is needed to guarantee that the receiver hold time is not violated. In order for the modules to be free of all explicit assumptions about the timing characteristics of other modules, the receiver must assume that the data on the bus may change as soon as its response synchronizer transition reaches the backplane. The receiver hold delay must be greater than or equal to the sum of the maximum receiver latch delay $[(T_{\text{drl}}(\min) + \partial T_d)]$, plus the actual register hold time (T_h), minus the minimum delay through an inverter (T_{inv}), backplane synchronizer transmitter (T_t), and the receiving data path backplane buffers (T_r).

$$T_{\text{drh}}(\min) = T_{\text{drl}}(\min) + \partial T_d + T_h(\min) - T_{\text{inv}}(\min) - T_t(\min) - T_r(\min) \tag{18.9}$$

The transmitter module also has a delay element that guarantees that its emitted synchronizer will not switch until the next data word has become valid on the backplane. The transmitter setup delay T_{dts} must be greater than or equal to the maximum delay of the transmitting data selector (T_{sel}), plus the maximum delay through the backplane data path transmitters minus the minimum transmitter synchronizer delay through a backplane transmitter $[T_t(\max) - T_t(\min)]$.

$$T_{\text{dts}}(\min) = T_{\text{sel}}(\max) + T_t(\max) - T_t(\min) \tag{18.10}$$

The data transfer period T_{ck} is determined by adding all of the delays in the handshake loop. This also includes the propagation delay through the backplane (sT_{bp}) which is a function of the fraction (s) of the total backplane length separating the two communicating modules.

$$T_{\text{ck}} = 2T_t + 2T_r + T_{\text{inv}} + T_{\text{drh}} + T_{\text{dts}} + sT_{\text{bp}} \tag{18.11}$$

To find the minimum data transfer period, we substitute for T_{drh} and T_{dts} from Eqs. (18.9) and (18.10) into (18.11), using minimum values for each term. To find the minimum, we assume that the modules are physically adjacent, so $s \approx 0$ and there is not added delay.

$$\begin{aligned} T_{\text{ck}}(\min) = {} & 2T_t(\min) + 2T_r(\min) + T_{\text{inv}}(\min) + T_{\text{drl}}(\min) + \partial T_d + T_h(\min) \\ & - T_{\text{inv}}(\min) - T_t(\min) - T_r(\min) + T_{\text{sel}}(\max) + T_t(\max) - T_t(\min) \end{aligned}$$

$$T_{\text{ck}}(\min) = T_r(\min) + T_{\text{drl}}(\min) + \partial T_d + T_h(\min) + T_{\text{sel}}(\max) + T_t(\max) \tag{18.12}$$

Next, we substitute for T_{drl} from Eq. (18.7):

$$\begin{aligned} T_{\text{ck}}(\min) = {} & T_r(\min) + T_s(\min) + T_r(\max) - T_r(\min) \\ & + \partial T_d + T_h(\min) + T_{\text{sel}}(\max) + T_t(\max) \end{aligned}$$

Simplification yields

$$T_{\text{ck}}(\min) = T_s(\min) + T_h(\min) + T_{\text{sel}}(\max) + T_r(\max) + T_t(\max) + \partial T_d(\min) \tag{18.13}$$

A similar process yields equations for the maximum and typical data transfer period. The typical separation of modules is one-third of the backplane length.

$$T_{ck}(\text{typ}) = 2T_t(\text{typ}) + 2T_r(\text{typ}) + T_{inv}(\text{typ}) + T_{drh}(\text{min}) + T_{dts}(\text{min}) + \partial T_d(\text{typ}) + 2T_{bp}(\text{typ})/3 \quad (18.14)$$

After substitutions and simplification,

$$T_{ck}(\text{typ}) = 2T_t(\text{typ}) + 2T_r(\text{typ}) + T_{inv}(\text{typ}) + T_s(\text{min}) + T_h(\text{min}) - 2T_t(\text{min}) - 2T_r(\text{min}) - T_{inv}(\text{min}) + T_{sel}(\text{max}) + T_t(\text{max}) + T_r(\text{max}) + 2\partial T_d(\text{typ}) + 2T_{bp}(\text{typ})/3 \quad (18.15)$$

The maximum transfer period for this design is

$$T_{ck}(\text{max}) = 2T_t(\text{max}) + 2T_r(\text{max}) + T_{inv}(\text{max}) + T_{drh}(\text{min}) + T_{dts}(\text{min}) + 2\partial T_d(\text{max}) + 2T_{bp}(\text{max}) \quad (18.16)$$

After substitutions and simplification,

$$T_{ck}(\text{max}) = 3T_t(\text{max}) + 3T_r(\text{max}) + T_{inv}(\text{max}) + T_{sel}(\text{max}) + T_s(\text{min}) + T_h(\text{min}) - 2T_t(\text{min}) - 2T_r(\text{min}) - 2T_r(\text{min}) - T_{inv}(\text{min}) + 3\partial T_d(\text{max}) + 2T_{bp}(\text{max}) \quad (18.17)$$

18.4.3 Uncompelled Source-Synchronous Timing Analysis

Figure 18.8 is a circuit diagram for modules that communicate in a backplane using an uncompelled, source-synchronous protocol whose timing diagram is found in Fig. 18.5. Unlike compelled modules, the data transfer rate is predefined to not exceed a fixed maximum, much like centralized-synchronous modules that

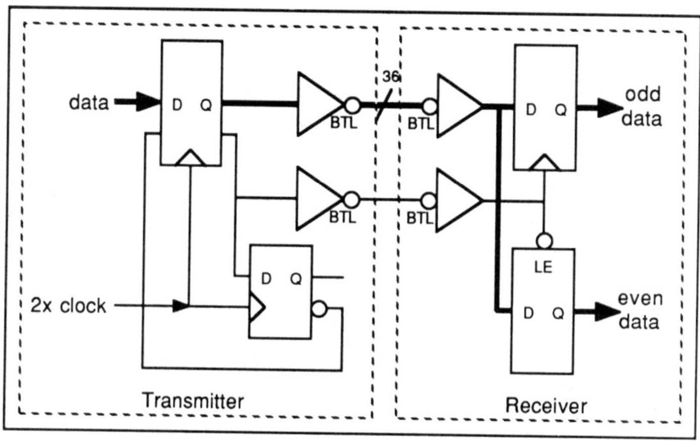

FIGURE 18.8 Uncompelled handshake logic.

are designed to operate at the same clock rate. But here the emitter of the synchronizer is the same module that emits the data, just as compelled modules function. Uncompelled synchronization adopts the speed-enhancing attributes of the other synchronization mechanisms.

The transmitting module in Fig. 18.8 operates from its own internally generated clock source at twice the frequency of the transfer rate. Each alternating positive clock edge either causes the switching of the data path to the next word or induces the next transition of the data synchronizer signal DS*. Within the limits imposed by skews of the transmitter's logic, the synchronizer transition occurs at the center of the sampling window of data on the backplane.

The receiver uses a scheme similar to the receiver for the compelled protocol. Two data registers are employed, one that latches incoming data on the rising edge of the synchronizer, and another that latches data on the falling edge. Unlike the compelled example, there is no return handshake to dynamically throttle the progress of the data packet, and the remainder of the module must be capable of dealing with the output data from the receiver registers at full speed.

The speed advantage comes from the absence of spatial skew (information and synchronizer from the same source) and from the absence of a data acknowledge (and its round-trip handshake delays).

The formulas presented below establish the maximum data transfer rate of the illustrated uncompelled protocol subsystem.

From the time that the 2× clock ($T_{2\times}$) rises on the transmitting module, the elapsed time until data arrives at the receiver module's register inputs (T_{data}) is the clock-to-output delay (T_{cko}) of the transmit data register plus the bus driver delay (T_t) plus the bus receiver delay (T_r).

$$T_{data} = T_{cko} + T_t + T_r \tag{18.18}$$

$$T_{data}(\max) = T_{cko}(\max) + T_t(\max) + T_r(\max) + T_{bp}(\max) \tag{18.18a}$$

$$T_{data}(\min) = T_{cko}(\min) + T_t(\min) + T_r(\min) + T_{bp}(\min) \tag{18.18b}$$

A similar formula for propagation delay of the synchronizer can be written.

$$T_{sync} = T_{cko} + T_t + T_r \tag{18.19}$$

$$T_{sync}(\max) = T_{cko}(\max) + T_t(\max) + T_r(\max) + T_{bp}(\max) \tag{18.19a}$$

$$T_{sync}(\min) = T_{cko}(\min) + T_t(\min) + T_r(\min) + T_{bp}(\min) \tag{18.19b}$$

The nature of the transmitting circuit is that on alternating cycles of the 2× clock either the data changes or the synchronizer switches. At their origin these events are separated in time by the 2× clock period ($T_{2\times}$). We can write a formula for the actual setup time of the data at the receiving module's data registers using this fact.

$$T_s = T_{2\times} - T_{data}(\max) - T_{sync}(\min) \tag{18.20}$$

Likewise, the following formula quantifies the actual hold time (T_h) at the latching registers on the receiving module:

$$T_h = T_{2\times} - T_{sync}(\max) - T_{data}(\min) \tag{18.21}$$

The faster the transmitter clock, the faster the data is transferred. The minimum transmitter 2× clock period corresponds to the minimum receiver setup time (and, symetrically, hold time).

$$T_{2\times}(\text{min}) = T_s(\text{min}) + T_{\text{data}}(\text{max}) - T_{\text{sync}}(\text{min}) \tag{18.22}$$

Obviously, the word transfer period (T_{ck}) across the bus is twice the transmitter clock period.

$$T_{\text{ck}} = 2T_{2\times} \tag{18.23}$$

To determine the maximum uncompelled transfer rate, we must write an equation for which the setup (or hold) time of the receiving registers is preserved while accounting for the worst-case difference in propagation speeds of the data versus the synchronizer.

$$T_{\text{ck}}(\text{min}) = 2[T_s + T_{\text{data}}(\text{max}) - T_{\text{sync}}(\text{min})] \tag{18.24}$$

We can substitute values from Eqs. (18.18*a*) and (18.19*a*) to expand Eq. (18.24).

$$T_{\text{ck}}(\text{min}) = 2T_s + 2[T_{\text{cko}}(\text{max}) - T_{\text{cko}}(\text{min})] + 2[T_t(\text{max}) - T_t(\text{min})] + 2[T_r(\text{max}) - T_r(\text{min})] + 2[T_{\text{bp}}(\text{max}) - T_{\text{bp}}(\text{min})] \tag{18.25}$$

The same logic yields an answer of the same form when analyzing the receiver hold time. The circuit symmetrically preserves the same values for setup and hold time.

This clearly shows us that the performance of uncompelled protocols is completely limited by the receiver sampling window and the skew—that is, not the absolute value of the propagation delay, but the relative difference between the fastest path and the slowest path.

$$T_{\text{ck}}(\text{min}) = 2T_s + 2[T_{\text{cko}}(\text{skew}) + T_t(\text{skew}) + T_r(\text{skew}) + T_{bp}(\text{skew})] \tag{18.26}$$

18.4.4 Quantitative Comparison of Transfer Speed

The transfer rate formulas alone are insufficient to get a feeling for the relative performance potential of the three synchronization mechanisms. We can quantify the comparison by applying some real-world parameters to the components that make up each example circuit, and we can compare the results. Table 18.1 gives hypothetical but realistic propagation delay specifications for TTL-compatible logic devices.

18.4.5 Worst-Case Design

By applying the values from Table 18.1 to the performance formulas for the different synchronization mechanisms, we obtain the data shown in Table 18.2.

The compelled protocol is capable of outperforming either of the other methods of transmitting data, although it is typically slower. The strength of the compelled protocol is that it takes advantage of actual (rather than worst-case) device operating speeds and dynamically adjusts its transmission rate to the situation.

TABLE 18.1 AC Timing Parameters of SSI/MSI, TTL-Compatible Components

Parameter	Minimum	Typical	Maximum
T_s	3		
T_h	3		
T_{cko}	3		6.5
T_{sel}	3		7.5
T_t	1	3	7
T_r	2	3.5	8
T_{inv}	1	2	3.5
∂T_d	0	1	2
T_{bp}	4	5	6

On the other hand, both the centralized-synchronous and uncompelled protocols must fix their maximum operating speed for all transactions. (Actually the uncompelled protocol is also capable of dynamically slowing down, but only based on the requirements of the transmitter.)

18.4.6 Synchronizer per Chip

So far we have used intermodule skew values for our performance estimates. Intermodule skew is the only specification that is deducible from most device data sheets. What if we could control skews with greater precision than is assumed by simply subtracting a device's minimum propagation delay from its maximum? What would be the comparative effect on performance?

We can operate faster if only intradevice skew (delay path divergence within the same chip) is involved. This requires that the entire data path plus associated synchronizers connect to the same physical device. For a wide bus this either implies a high pin count, high-power chip, or the bus must be divided into "slices," with separate synchronizers for each slice entering each bus interface chip. Table 18-3 is an expanded version of Table 18.1. It includes skew specifications for inter- and intradevice skew. These values represent the assumptions of the author about what ought to be reasonable with current technology, but do not represent the position of any device manufacturer.

The result of reduction in skew (Table 18.4) is a minimal improvement in centralized-synchronous data transfer, a greater improvement in compelled transfer rates, and a doubling of performance in uncompelled data transmission.

TABLE 18.2 Comparison of Performance Potential with SSI/MSI Components

Synchronization mechanism	Timing, ns			Typical transfer rate, Mbyte/s (32-bit-wide data path)
	Minimum	Typical	Maximum	
Centralized synchronous	36.5			110
Compelled	28.5	41.8	76.0	96
Uncompelled	41.0			85

TABLE 18.3 Parameter Values Accounting for Controlled Skew Specifications

Parameter	Minimum	Typical	Maximum	Interdevice skew	Intradevice skew
T_s	3				
T_h	3				
T_{cko}	3		6.5	3	2
T_{sel}	3		7.5	4	2
T_t	1	3	7	4	2
T_r	2	3.5	8	4	2
T_{inv}	1	2	3.5	2	1.5
∂T_d	2	2	2		
T_{bp}	4	5	6		

Centralized synchronization is almost entirely independent of skews, being limited mostly by specified worst-case delays. Its simplicity means that although these are worst-case delays, there are few of them, so the total is low and the speed is high. In contrast, the uncompelled method is limited entirely by skews.

18.4.7 Latching Transceivers

Another important step toward enhanced performance is to incorporate data storage into the bus interface chips. This eliminates the absolute delay of a separate driver and receiver chip from the synchronous interface, and removes two skew-inducing stages from the uncompelled interface. Table 18.5 shows the effect of using on-chip data latches and registers with a single-chip or synchronizer-per-chip bus interface. Again, the centralized-synchronous and uncompelled protocols nearly double their performance potential over the compelled protocol, and uncompelled data transfer is fastest.

Further improvements in data transfer speed require improvements in the specifications of Table 18.3. If it is easier to control the relative speed differences between two paths on the same chip than it is to increase the absolute delay, then uncompelled data transmission becomes the obvious winner.

18.4.8 Theoretical Transfer Speed Limit

We are now just a few small steps away from the theoretical speed limit of parallel data transfers in a backplane bus. Effects of the asymmetry between rising and

TABLE 18.4 Performance Potential with One-Chip Interface

Synchronization mechanism	Timing, ns			Typical transfer rate, Mbyte/s (32-bit-wide data path)
	Minimum	Typical	Maximum	
Centralized synchronous	32.5			123
Compelled	13.5	33.8	60.0	118
Uncompelled	20.0			200

TABLE 18.5 Performance Using a Single-Chip, Latching-Transceiver Circuit

Synchronization mechanism	Timing, ns			Typical transfer rate, Mbyte/s
	Minimum	Typical	Maximum	(32-bit-wide data path)
Centralized synchronous	16.5			242
Compelled	13.5	25.5	52.0	157
Uncompelled	12.0			333

falling signal edges are removed by use of differential signal pairs, so that every signal transition has both a rising and a falling component. To completely eliminate skews each data bit stream must embed or imply within it its own synchronizer. Thus, each individual line in the data path may be thought of as its own independent serial channel where, by definition, the synchronizer and the data incur no skew, as they share exactly the same propagation path. The last step is to "purify" the backplane electrical environment by using only point-to-point electrical interconnections instead of bussed lines. Of course, at this point we no longer have a bus!

Since there are not yet any backplane buses that operate at 12 ns per transfer (source-synchronous, compelled, synchronizer-per-chip, registered transceivers, single-ended bussed signals), it is reasonable to assert that the backplane bus is not yet obsolete.

18.5 SUSTAINED SYSTEM THROUGHPUT

The raw data transfer rate is only one parameter in the formula for increasing system throughput on a backplane bus. The three components are (1) control, (2) data, and (3) exchange of mastership. Control includes address, master command, and slave status transmission; data is that which we desire to transmit from one module to the other; and exchange of mastership is the the time required for one master to release the bus and for the next master to begin a new transaction. It is quite possible to design a poorly balanced bus where the speed of the data transfer has almost no impact on the total system throughput, simply because the time required for non-data-transfer activity dominates each transaction. To take advantage of the high raw data transfer rates possible in a backplane bus, the time required for control and exchange of mastership should be less (hopefully, much less) than the data transfer time.

The *sustained system throughput* is the mean quantity of data transferred per unit time. The limit of sustained throughput is called the *saturated bandwidth* of the bus. This is the asymptote of performance that the actual sustained throughput of a particular system cannot exceed.

Table 18.6 assumes a total of 200 ns of address, control, exchange of mastership, and memory access latency for read transactions, 100 ns for write transactions, and a 2-to-1 ratio of read versus write transactions.

This information is shown graphically in Fig. 18.9. There is more to increasing bus throughput than just having a fast data handshake. Control and exchange of mastership can consume significant portions of time. As data transfer accelerates, this overhead can completely dominate the bus throughput. To gain the maximum benefit, all three elements must be accelerated.

The curves of Fig. 18.9 correspond to a 32-bit backplane bus for which control and exchange of mastership are fixed but ambitious values, if one assumes access to dynamic memory modules by processing bus masters. One-third of the transactions are writes that do not incur the penalty of read latency. Two-thirds of the transactions are reads. A write is assumed to consume 50 ns to transmit address and control, a read consumes 150 ns, and 50 ns are consumed when the last master released the bus and the next master acquires control.

Two curves are shown. The lower curve corresponds to transmission of a 16-byte burst in four transfers for each transaction. Note how major improvements in data transfer rate provide little comparable gain above 100 Mbyte/s. At this point less than 50% of any increase is seen in actual throughput. If the size of the data transfer is increased to 64 bytes per transaction (16 data transfers), then the point at which saturated bandwidth is one-half of the data transfer rate is about 200 Mbyte/s.

To maximize throughput, we can increase the size of the transferred data packet, or we can reduce the fixed control overhead.

18.5.1 Mastership Arbitration

Exchange of bus mastership is managed by a control acquisition or arbitration system. To minimize the load of arbitration on system throughput, separate bus lines are usually dedicated to arbitration. Those lines are used by all modules in

TABLE 18.6 Burst Rate versus Saturated Bandwidth

ns/transfer	Mbyte/s	16-byte line	64-byte line
100	40	28.2	36.2
80	50	32.9	44.2
66.7	60	36.9	51.9
57.1	70	40.5	59.2
50	80	43.6	66.2
44.4	90	46.5	72.9
40	100	49	79.3
33.3	120	53.3	91.4
28.6	140	56.9	102.6
25	160	60	113
22.2	180	62.6	122.6
21.1	190	63.8	127.1
20	200	64.9	131.5
16.7	240	68.6	147.7
14.8	280	71.5	161.9
12.5	320	73.8	174.5
11.1	360	75.8	185.8
10	400	77.4	195.9
8	500	80.5	217.2
6.67	600	82.8	234.1
5.33	750	85.1	254
4	1000	87.6	277.5
0	∞	96	384

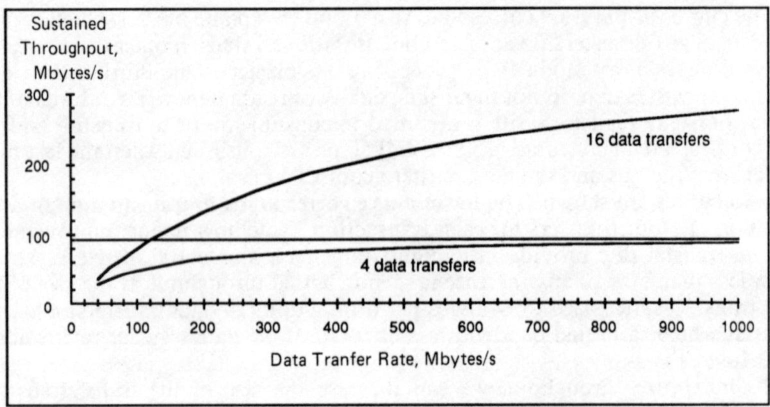

FIGURE 18.9 Saturated bandwidth versus data transfer rate. Assumptions: 32-bit data path width; control + memory latency + exchange of mastership = 200 ns (for reads), 100 ns (for writes); ⅔ reads, ⅓ writes.

the backplane that wish to compete for mastership, without disturbing the ongoing transaction of the current bus master.

There is a difference between bus arbitration and exchange of mastership. These ought to be clearly distinguished. When a module is driving a group of bus lines, a finite time is required for that module to release those lines, then for another module to drive those lines stably. This period of time is the *exchange of mastership*—the unusable, idle time between back-to-back transactions by different masters. In a backplane bus, the theoretical lower limit of this period is the round-trip propagation delay of the backplane. The mechanism by which the next master is identified is called arbitration. This must obviously occur before the exchange of mastership may complete, so there is a sequential coupling of arbitration and exchange of mastership. System performance can be hampered if sufficient care is not taken to cleanly couple those two, to minimize the effect of the arbitration handover on the actual length of the exchange of mastership.

18.5.1.1 Distributed Parallel Contention. Two common approaches to arbitration are *parallel contention* and *radial contention.* In parallel contention, any number of competing potential masters place a binary-coded vector on the same set of bus lines. The arbitration vector lines employ open-collector or equivalent wired-OR logic, so that the resulting state of the vector field is the logical OR of all the asserted vectors. Each module compares the vector that it has issued with the wired-OR result, removing its vector if it deduces that another module has issued a higher-priority vector number.

Identical arbitration state machines reside on each potential master module (see Fig. 18.10). Together, they form a single distributed arbitration state machine. Each machine synchronizes itself with the other arbiters by means of arbitration synchronizer signals in the backplane. Some systems use a centralized clock for this purpose. An alternative is to use multiple-bussed, open-collector signals that are driven and received by all modules, keeping them in lock step with each other.

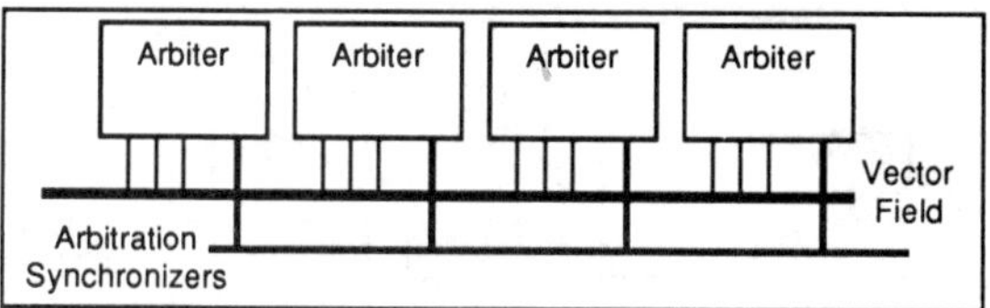

FIGURE 18.10 Distributed parallel contention.

18.5.1.2 Centralized Radial Contention. An approach that is especially popular in proprietary buses is centralized radial arbitration (see Fig. 18.11). It is especially attractive when the bus already uses a central clock, and when all modules, including the arbiter, operate from that clock source. Arbitration logic on each module is very simple, few connector pins are consumed, and the arbitration is usually resolvable within one clock cycle.

18.5.1.3 Centralized versus Distributed Resources. The primary drawback in nonproprietary systems is the centralized nature of the arbiter. Some have argued that centralized arbitration—or any centralized resources—are a reliability problem because they constitute a "single point of failure" that can stop the entire system. This is not a valid argument, however, since a failure in any one element of a distributed resource can also cause the entire distributed resource to fail.

There is a major advantage to the use of distributed resources, however. If, for instance, an arbiter on one module of Figure 18.11 fails, it causes the entire system to fail. However, as soon as the module with the faulty arbiter is removed, the system will again operate correctly. In contrast, a failing system employing centralized resources cannot be restored to operability just by removing the failing module but requires that a spare central service module be available.

18.5.1.4 Distributed Radial Contention. It is possible to apply the speed advantages of radial arbitration to a distributed arbitration system. Figure 18.12 shows a distributed radial arbitration system.

If the reliability or servicing advantages of distributed resources and of aggressive arbitration speed are both important, then the price to be paid is an increased number of bussed backplane lines and connector pins. A request line is needed for each slot in the backplane, and the minimum number of connector pins required is equal to the number of slot positions plus one more pin. Each module

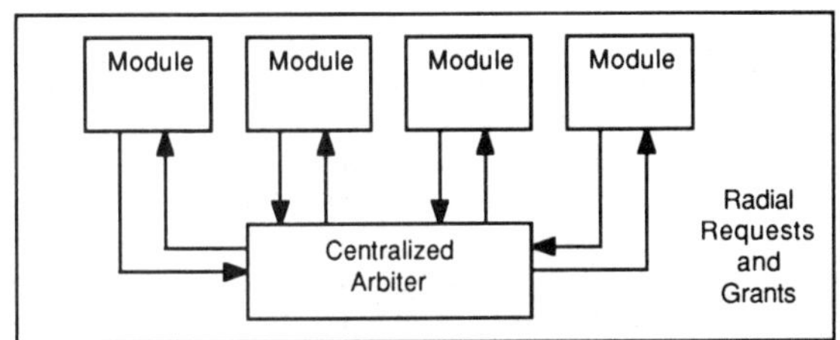

FIGURE 18.11 Centralized radial arbitration.

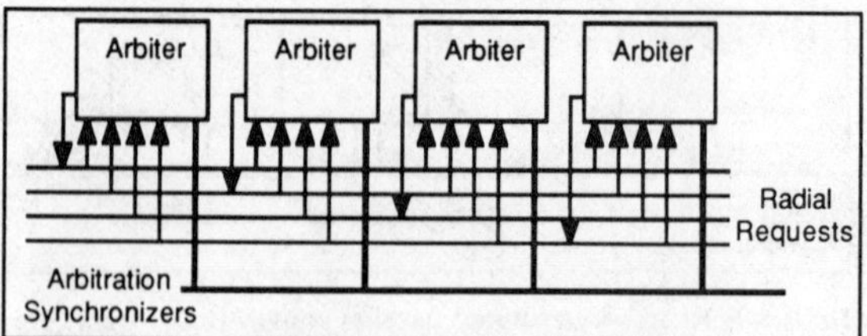

FIGURE 18.12 Distributed radial arbitration.

drives its mastership request signal through the additional pin, which is connected within the backplane to the bussed request line corresponding to the geographic position of the module. All modules receive all bussed request lines, and based on the arbitration synchronizer signals, all arbitration circuits implement the same state machine and simultaneously pass through the same sequence of arbitration states. No grant line is needed in the backplane. Rather, each arbitration circuit drives a module-internal grant signal when it (as well as all other arbiters) determines that its host is to be the next bus master.

18.5.2 Throughput and Latency

To guarantee that the maximum throughput is obtained from a backplane bus, transactions should be as efficient as possible (maximum ratio of time spent moving data versus time to move control), and the unused time between transactions should be minimized. This does not necessarily require very fast arbitration, but only requires that the capacity of the arbitration system be greater than the peak potential transaction rate of the data transfer bus.

Idle-bus arbitration is the operation of the arbitration system when only one module is contending for bus mastership and when no transaction is in progress by the current bus master. An arbitration system that is completely adequate for a nearly saturated bus may unnecessarily slow system througput when the bus is not near saturation.

Suppose that a cache-based, shared-memory multiprocessor system is built using a shared bus. The system is composed of a number of processor modules and a number of memory modules. The processor modules access the bus through an on-board cache memory, and the cache memories read and write packets (lines) of data across the bus. The memory modules may respond to these reads and writes, or other cache interfaces may respond. Since each processor usually find the data it needs within its cache, most of the time it does not need the bus. Whenever a processing module incurs a cache miss, the cache that tries to access shared memory will quite possibly find that the bus is idle and available. The speed of the particular task on that processor—the *single-stream* performance—is directly affected by the latency of gaining mastership of the idle bus, as well as the latency of the cache-filling memory access that follows. While the *multiple-stream* (multiple-process) performance of a system with a saturated bus may be unaffected by idle-bus arbitration, the single-stream throughput of any individual process is directly affected by the speed of idle-bus arbitration. Simply stated, if nobody else needs the bus, then arbitration should be very fast.

18.5.3 Circuit-Switched versus Packet-Switched Transactions

A *circuit-switched* bus performs transactions as single, inseparable set of events in which control and data are kept together. A *packet-switched* bus breaks transactions into parts (usually a request and a response) so that multiple transactions can be in progress at the same time.

When a processor module reads data from a memory module, the module issues a read request and the memory module responds with the requested data. On a circuit-switched bus, the bus master is the processor module, the memory is the slave module, and the read transaction is completed during a time period for which the data transfer bus is exclusively dedicated to the task. On a packet-switched bus, the processor becomes bus master to issue the read request and then releases the bus. Some time later the memory becomes bus master to write the requested data back to the requesting processor, and in the interim the bus is available for the use of other modules. On a circuit-switched bus, masters read data and write data, forming a virtual circuit with the selected slave, and memories do not become bus masters. On a packet-switched bus, masters either write a request or write data, but do not read data, and both processors and memories can be bus masters.

Circuit-switched (or read-write) buses are simple because only one transaction (request plus response) is active at a time. They yield the maximum single-stream throughput in a lightly loaded system because only one bus master is involved and only one arbitration victory is needed, and also because the bus is guaranteed to be available when the memory becomes ready to begin transmission of the requested data.

Figure 18.13 shows a time line for a circuit-switched bus. The control and the data are never separated, and a transaction consists of one temporally continuous event. Between transactions is an exchange of mastership, during which time no transaction may progress. In parallel, the arbitration system chooses the next bus master. Of course, the arbitration must be completed before the exchange of mastership may complete.

Packet-switched (also called split-transaction, write-only, split-cycle, and pended) buses have a higher saturated bandwidth potential because the bus is available for use during memory access latency. They are appropriate for multiple-backplane systems where backplanes are connected by bus repeaters, since packet-switched access of a resource through multiple repeaters does not tie up all of the intervening buses during the entire transaction. A packet-switched bus allows multiple transactions to overlap in time. This improves throughput, but it also creates the potential for deadlock that must be explicitly recognized and avoided.

Figure 18.14 shows a time line for a packet-switched bus. The transactions

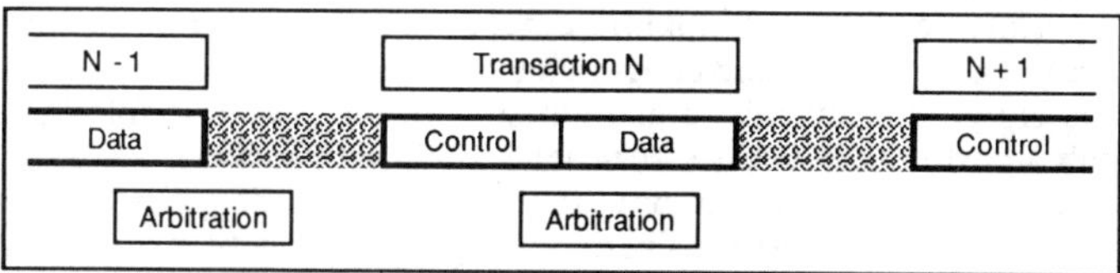

FIGURE 18.13 Transaction structure of a circuit-switched bus.

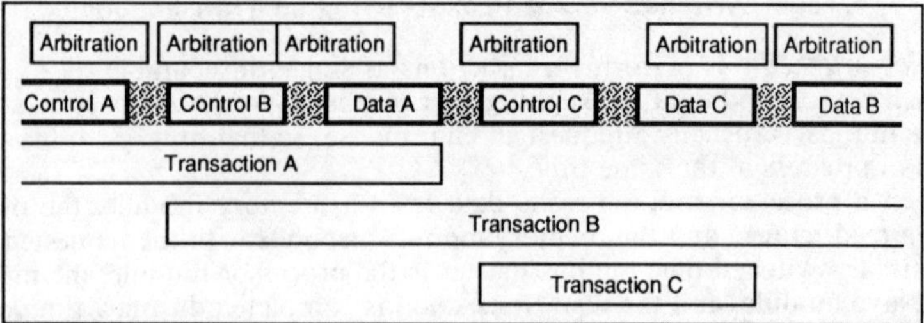

FIGURE 18.14 Transaction structure of a packet-switched bus.

overlap in time, although the data transfer bus can only operate on one transaction at a time. Transaction A is logically still in progress when transaction B begins. Transaction C begins and ends while transaction B is still in progress. The value of a packet-switched transaction protocol is that individual modules may be very slow, yet they do not slow the throughput of other faster modules. Transaction B may be a read access to a large, slow memory module. Transaction C may be a write access or a read to a very fast memory or other device. The memory module of transaction B only needs to have a small, fast data buffer in the bus interface, and the progress of transaction C is unaffected by the slow memory module. In a circuit-switched bus, transaction C could not begin until the slow memory module were to complete and transmit the read data.

The arbitration system becomes more critical in terms of performance in a packet-switched bus, and its throughput must increase. Each read transaction, for example, requires two successful arbitration competitions. Also, some mechanism (usually arbitration priority or transaction queue control) must be provided to ensure that response throughput is always greater than or equal to request throughput.

18.5.4 Module Response-Time Constraints

A circuit-switched bus may be thought of as having "fully compelled" transactions, analogous to the compelled data transfer handshake discussed previously. The transaction is not completed until the slave is ready to respond, either with fulfillment of the request or with some error response. Every module that responds to a circuit-switched transaction is required to respond very quickly in order to avoid extending the transaction. Guaranteed response time becomes critical to fully utilize the bus.

This is especially problematic in shared-memory multiprocessors, using coherent, eavesdropping, copy-back cache memories. Such caches on a circuit-switched bus must perform a directory lookup on every address that appears on the bus, responding to each address during its bus transaction with sharing or ownership status. It is extremely difficult to guarantee fast response time for cache eavesdropping in a cost-effective processor-cache module. If just one cache module is unable to respond quickly, the transaction must be extended, during which time the bus performs no useful work. There is a high likelihood that at least one module will be unable to respond quickly.

The great advantage of circuit-switched transactions is that the speed of the response portion of a transaction has a negligible impact on the forward progress of the remainder of the system. As the bus speeds up, requests and responses become faster and faster, making circuit-switched status response less and less practical. It is obvious that the ultimate performance demands packet-switched transactions, yet the complete elimination of circuit-switched responses is very difficult, and probably unnecessary. Circuit-switched slave status signals should be minimized and limited primarily to retry and hardware error indications.

18.6 SUMMARY

Depending on the chosen data transfer synchronization mechanism, the limit of speed may be the sum of worst-case delays, only a function of signal skew, or a combination of the two. Speed is only one reason to choose a particular synchronization mechanism; other factors include ease of design or simulation, importance of compatibility with slower or faster modules, etc.

Centralized-synchronous data transfer is fairly insensitive to skew but is highly sensitive to absolute delay. Uncompelled data transfer is independent of absolute delay but is highly dependent on minimizing the skew for its speed. Compelled data transfer is somewhat dependent on both skew and absolute delay, trading some speed for robust interoperability between fast and slow modules.

Product marketeers want high data burst rates; system designers and users want high system throughput. Maximizing throughput depends on a balanced acceleration of data transfer, control transfer, and exchange of mastership.

INDEX

ABOUT THE EDITOR IN CHIEF

Joseph Di Giacomo is a senior member of the IEEE. In addition, he is an Assistant Professor of Electrical Engineering at Villanova University, where he also serves as the chairman of the Research Committee, working in conjunction with corporations on advanced technology issues. He is the editor of McGraw-Hill's *VLSI Handbook* (1989).